DEVELOPING DIFFERENCE

Developing Difference

Wendy Johnson
Department of Psychology,
University of Edinburgh, UK

First published 2014 by
PALGRAVE MACMILLAN

Palgrave Macmillan in the UK is an imprint of Macmillan Publishers Limited, registered in England, company number 785998, of Houndmills, Basingstoke, Hampshire RG21 6XS.

Palgrave Macmillan in the US is a division of St Martin's Press LLC, 175 Fifth Avenue, New York, NY 10010.

Palgrave Macmillan is the global academic imprint of the above companies and has companies and representatives throughout the world.

Palgrave® and Macmillan® are registered trademarks in the United States, the United Kingdom, Europe and other countries

ISBN 978–0–230–30344–7

This book is printed on paper suitable for recycling and made from fully managed and sustained forest sources. Logging, pulping and manufacturing processes are expected to conform to the environmental regulations of the country of origin.

A catalogue record for this book is available from the British Library.

A catalog record for this book is available from the Library of Congress.

Contents

v

List of Figures

Preface

When my daughter was born 23 years ago, I hadn't been around babies since my sisters were born when I was not quite 2 and not quite 4. Needless to say, I didn't remember this in any way likely to be relevant to my new situation. But I had been reading during my pregnancy. I had heard the oft-repeated observation that parents tend to believe the environment is everything until they have second children, and I had read the Gessell Institute's nice series of books on one-year-olds, two-year-olds, and so on. I had the strong impression that this (screaming) bundle in my arms was some unique mixture of individuality and 'newbornness' and was dying to know which was which. Just who would my daughter become and how and why? What had we, her parents, passed to her from our genomes, and what would we pass to her through the experiences we would take her through? What experiences would she create for herself?

I sent her to daycare at the age of 2 months, and I went there too. I would go down to feed her during the day when I could from my job as a consulting actuary, and watch the other infants while I nursed. As they ranged in age from 2 to 12 months, I could observe for myself over time what was '2-month-oldness', what '6-month-oldness', and what the individuality of each of them, helping me to understand my daughter as an individual. I continued with this when her brother was born almost two years later because I found the glimpses I could get of the patterns fascinating. Enough so that a few years later I left my consulting actuary career behind and entered the PhD programme in Individual Differences and Behaviour Genetics at the University of Minnesota.

I loved my studies there and the Differential Psychology Research group I entered at the University of Edinburgh after I received my degree. But I was frustrated too. Researchers studying individual differences didn't seem to think about development, and researchers studying development seemed to treat the topic as if everyone develops in lockstep. Similarly, everyone at least implicitly assumed that genetic and environmental influences operate independently, even when they were discussing the fact that they do not. I could find very little material that grappled seriously with how our biology transacts with the world we have created in the course of our development as the individuals we are, and that's what I wanted to understand. This book is the outgrowth of that frustration. I had two purposes in writing it.

The first was overtly selfish: I wanted to review the literature from a perspective on development of individual differences myself, to help shape my own research in the most productive direction. But the second was for the rest of the interested world: I knew there was nothing like this book already out there, and, frankly, the field needed one. So that's what this book is: a compilation of where the field is in thinking about the development of individual differences in psychological characteristics and behaviour, as seen in the context of how human biology, genetics, and evolution are playing out in today's world. The book is intended for use in upper-level undergraduate and post-graduate courses in Psychology, Epidemiology, Sociology and related fields, but it's also the kind of book I think many generally well-educated and curious and interested people outside of academia might enjoy as well.

As the reader will see, I think we've learned much about the basic principles that form the foundation of human development and the sources of individual differences. But we really don't so much about how these principles come together to result in the unique individuals we all are. Moreover, some of what we think we know is based on very imprecise and even possibly misleading methods of measurement and overgeneralizations, making it likely wrong. I hope this book can be helpful in encouraging future researchers to think critically about the assumptions they make in applying the measurement tools they develop and use, and in pointing out productive directions for future research. Writing it has done that for me.

WENDY JOHNSON

Acknowledgements

The publishers and author would like to thank the organizations listed below for permission to reproduce material from their publications:

Figure 7.1, reprinted with permission from the American Psychological Association, from Abraham H. Maslow, 'A Theory of Human Motivation', *Psychological Review*, 1943, vol. 50, pp. 374–96, published by APA.

Figure 11.1, reprinted by permission from Macmillan Publishers Ltd, on behalf of Cancer Research UK: *Nature Reviews Genetics, 5*, 826–837 doi:10.1038nrg1471.

Part I
Key Themes

The Importance of Individual Differences in Development

Always remember you're unique, just like everybody else.
(popular expression)

The two streams of scientific psychology

Look at almost any group of people gathered for almost any purpose. What do you see? Bear with me for a paragraph or so and let me tell you. Whatever the purpose of their gathering, you see differences in behaviour. Some move much more than others; some appear intent, in others the eyes appear glazed over; some add their voices frequently to the ambient noise, others remain quiet; some smile or laugh readily and rarely seem negative, others frown or curse just as easily and rarely seem positive; some are centres of attention and action within the group while others remain on the sidelines of activity even if they are centrally located, and still others use their attention, body language, and voices to give the central figures their central positions. Of course the people differ in physical ways as well: some are tall, others short; some are fat, others thin; some are blonde, others dark; some are male, others female; some seem physically fit and healthy, others frail or even ill, some old, others young. And they differ in ways related to earlier behaviour: some are fashionably dressed, others not; some seem dressed to attract attention, others to blend into the woodwork; some seem scantily clad for the weather, others bundled up. But differences related to earlier behaviour are not limited to appearance: some are central figures because there is prior agreement among many that they are dominant, while others are completely new to the gathering and display behaviours indicating they are exploring an unfamiliar situation.

Despite all these and many other behavioural differences, presuming the gathering is peaceful and public, there are common human behaviours you are unlikely to see: anyone striking another with a weapon; overt sexual behaviour or defecation; depending on the nature of the gathering, even behaviours such as eating or singing or sleeping may be restricted. Thus, though there are many ways in which individuals display different behaviours in the same general social circumstance and those differences in behaviour have roots in the individuals' prior experiences and behavioural tendencies, the situation exerts general constraints on behaviour as well. More subtly, the situation exerts its behavioural constraints on individuals in different ways and to different degrees. Some may be more likely to speak their minds in large groups of people than in intimate settings, while others may respond to such situations in the opposite way. Taking this further, despite such general behavioural tendencies, depending on pre-existing goals and motivations, some may see an opportunity to carve new social roles for themselves by consciously striving to behave in new ways, while others may have no preconceived thoughts about their behaviour at all.

Experimental psychology

These individual differences in behaviour in any one situation may have little importance. In fact, the consistency of behaviour across individuals may be more important than whatever differences they show. We are all human, and it is obvious that we share many psychological processes and mental capacities. A large portion of research activity in the science of psychology has been undertaken from this perspective: that identification of the regularities or laws of human behaviour is the goal. To accomplish this, the psychological researcher has followed the kinds of experimental practices traditionally carried out in the physical sciences: placing participants in situations with strict control of environmental conditions and task requirements, examining performance of the 'average' individual in one set of circumstances, and observing the 'average' response to some change in that set of circumstances. Usually this is accompanied by a theoretical rationale for the specific set of circumstances and tasks used and the specific manipulations of those circumstances made. The researcher draws conclusions about the accuracy of the theoretical rationale from the overall response rates. As in the physical sciences, psychologists have learned much from this approach. For example, most of our understanding of learning and memory processes, the basic biology of emotional response, and early childhood motor and cognitive development has come from this approach.

This approach always relies on some form of sampling due to the presence of measurement error and random processes, poorly understood processes that pass for random, or extraneous processes that are involved but have not been controlled. One trial is never sufficient to establish a general principle. The Law of Large Numbers tells us that the more trials we make, the closer the average result will come to the true underlying value. But presentations of this law tend to overlook the fact that convergence to this true underlying value will be much slower when the data are 'noisier' than when they are not. This creates a much bigger problem for psychologists than it does for physical scientists. For example, we can measure even relatively ephemeral or remote physical properties such as the opacity of glass to be used in bathroom windows or atmospheric density on Mars with greater accuracy than we can the strength of an individual's motivation to perform well on a high-stakes cognitive test to be used in application to university. That is, our callipers are better in the physical sciences than they are in psychology. We can be more sure there that we got close to the true value on any one measurement attempt.

Correlational psychology

It is not just a matter of having good callipers though. In the physical sciences, for example, atoms of one material are interchangeable: they will act identically in the same environmental circumstances. This is simply not the case with human behaviour. Each person brings to any situation his or her own ways of perceiving that situation, based on some highly individualized soup of experiential and genetic background. These perceptual differences affect even the most standardized situations. In fact, if we test the same individuals in the same situation repeatedly over time, the most common result is that the variation among individuals is every bit as great as, if not greater than, the variation within individuals. This means that, in addition to measurement and other apparently random sources of error, behavioural researchers are presented with variation that is independent of the circumstances under examination, yet systematic. This increases the sample sizes necessary to obtain reliable indications of the overall effects of the circumstances in any one investigation, and makes it likely that, even with large samples, the specific overall effects may vary with small differences in circumstances. It also means that the average effect can sometimes be relatively irrelevant to many of the individuals within the sample and the broader population from which it was drawn. That is, whatever systematic processes create the individual differences may sometimes be of greater importance to the outcome of interest than the particular situational circumstances under investigation.

These facts of the magnitude and importance of individual differences have also generated a large portion of research activity in the science of psychology. The approach taken differs considerably, however, from that taken in experimental psychology. As Chronbach (1957) noted over fifty years ago, from this perspective the psychological researcher is interested not in the variation in average effects created by experimental manipulations but in the properties of the naturally occurring variation in those effects among individuals or groups of individuals that share some characteristic. The basic question under investigation tends to be one of association: how are individual differences in one set of circumstances associated with or related to individual differences in another? The resulting investigation tends to be observational rather than manipulative, with the statistical evaluation of the observations made in the form of correlations, broadly construed, rather than mean differences, equally broadly construed, as in experimental psychology.

Causation and control

Scientific investigations generally have two, often related, goals, and psychology is no exception. The first goal is to understand the causes underlying the phenomena we observe, and, close on its heels, the second goal is generally to use that understanding of underlying cause to manipulate the phenomena to serve our purposes. Experimental psychology brings the situational variables under tight control and makes it possible to conclude that the experimenter's manipulations have caused whatever differences in average outcome are observed. But the extent to which this is valuable is limited to our ability to make meaningful manipulations in circumstances. Moreover, its value is limited by the extent to which there is actual consistency of response among individuals. When there is more variation in response than there is consistency, it is clear that the experimenter does not have sufficient control over the circumstances of the situation to be sure that all relevant causes of the phenomenon have been identified. This is where correlational psychology comes in: this approach can identify patterns of association that occur naturally. It is much more difficult to make causal attributions using this approach, but the broader perspective on patterns of association can suggest general theories of causal mechanisms that link otherwise isolated islands of experimental observation.

In the physical sciences, theories may be developed using this correlational approach to evaluating broad patterns of phenomena, and then subjected to test using experimental approaches, limited only by technical and financial resources. Psychology, however, faces additional difficulties in this regard. Experimental psychologists manipulate the situational circumstances experienced by living participants, both human and non-human, and basic morality requires that those experiences not be harmful or overly traumatic. However lofty may be the ultimate goal of situational control, the experimental manipulations necessary to be sure we have nailed the causal pathways may involve actions we are not willing to take for moral reasons. For example, we may hypothesize that maltreatment in childhood is a cause of antisocial behaviour in adolescence and adulthood, particularly perhaps in individuals with certain characteristics (Kim-Cohen, et al., 2006), but we will not carry out the experiment that would establish the causal association conclusively because it would entail deliberately subjecting some children to maltreatment.

Psychology's 'two realms'

Together with the large and consistent individual differences in response, this practical limitation on psychologists' ability to investigate their phenomena of interest has tended to balkanize the field. Some psychologists perform experiments, while others conduct studies observing associations among people's characteristics as they tend to occur in nature. (By 'nature', I mean of course the conditions in which people actually live their lives – our societies as we have constructed them.) But this basic difference in investigative approach is not the only symptom of balkanization. The different approaches suggest different statistical methodologies. In experimental psychology, the complications arise in the design of the experiment, in establishing the controlling conditions and the manipulation that will distinguish clearly between alternative hypotheses. Because causal attribution is clearer once these have been established, the experimental data generated can usually be analysed appropriately using relatively straightforward statistical techniques. In contrast, in observational studies of associations, focus is directly on the properties of the measurement instruments used to record the individual differences in response. Moreover, because the researcher exerts no control over the situations of the participants, any potential causal attribution given to observed associations must rely on statistical control of extraneous variables. The net result is that experimental psychologists have tended to receive extensive training in the qualitative aspects of experimental design and less training in the quantitative, statistical aspects, while training for correlational psychologists has tended to have the opposite emphases.

Though there is no inherent reason that it should be so, the two approaches have also been applied to rather different areas of interest within psychology. For example, learning and memory, perception, emotion, and motivational drive states have all tended to be studied experimentally, ignoring individual differences in how much individuals learn, perceive, respond emotionally and are motivated in any given situation. This is apparent even in the most technologically modern studies using brain imaging. Brain imaging techniques average the data from all individuals to reach conclusions that particular brain areas are involved in particular kinds of responses, resulting in conclusions that gloss over the individual differences in response and leave the impression that brain function is much more regionalized than is probably actually the case. In contrast, occupational selection (both by job candidates and employers) and the manifestation of psychopathology have tended to be studied correlationally, based on the assumption that individual differences in one situation bear systematic relations with individual differences in another, thus ignoring the many deviations from this pattern. This outlook has been apparent particularly in modern studies of genetic influences on behaviour, where correlational psychologists have tended to assume that genes have direct, deterministic causal influences on behaviour, independent of environmental circumstances.

The process of development

Human behaviour changes dramatically across the lifespan. Newborn infants are very dependent on parental care. They can also initiate only the most limited agentic behaviours, though new mothers exhausted from constantly responding to their infants' expressions of need may disagree. Though newborn infants are rather limited in some perceptual abilities such as vision, which is blurry, they have accentuated perceptual abilities in other areas such as the ability to perceive phonemic differences in language. Ability to make learned associations emerges before birth and only continues and accelerates afterwards, but, because of the status of perceptual and agentic abilities, they use this associative ability somewhat differently than they will later. Given typical environmental stimulation and care, they also rapidly grow physically, and this growth carries with it rapid changes in awareness of their surroundings, motor abilities such as reaching and grasping, supporting their own weight, and locomotion.

Of course this is just the beginning, as infants become toddlers, then children, adolescents, and young, middle-aged, and finally older adults. We use these broad labels, and sometimes subdivisions of them such as 'pre-adolescents', to refer to people of similar age because most people do seem to manifest similar patterns of extensive changes in behaviour in similar sequences and at relatively similar ages. We would be as surprised to see a middle-aged adult running and jumping around in a yard as we would that middle-aged adult throwing a temper tantrum because it is bedtime. Developmental psychology has tended to focus on describing the characteristics and timing of these patterns for several reasons.

First, the developmental changes in childhood are particularly dramatic. Psychology has emerged as a science during the last 150 years or so, during a period in which communication and transportation facilities improved dramatically. Our society became increasingly physically mobile, with people travelling long distances to attend school or to seek and accept employment. This meant that families became increasingly dispersed, so that many young people have not had much experience with infants and young children when they become parents. Many of these young parents are hungry for information about their offspring. When do babies start to show that they recognize their parents? At what age should discipline start? Should the parent worry if the child does not talk by age 3? Will my child be more intelligent if I read to her? By focusing on normative patterns, developmental psychologists can help to answer these questions.

Second, societies take many actions intended to increase general social welfare. They provide educational programmes aimed at basic social literacy and citizenship, medical intervention programmes intended to improve health, and legal systems to manage transgressions. All of these activities require information about the quality and timing of developmental processes. Are young children generally ready to learn to read at age 5, or would it be better to delay instruction until age 6? Are there ways to prevent mental disorders such as autism or schizophrenia, and, if so, how should we identify those at risk for such disorders and at what age should intervention begin? How do children's perceptual and cognitive capacities differ from those of adults, and do these differences impact their abilities to testify as witnesses in legal cases, or to be responsible for their own criminal actions. Again, developmental psychology can often be most helpful in dealing with such questions by focusing on normative developmental patterns.

And third, people are blessed, or cursed, with curiosity about their own human nature. We want to understand our motivations, emotional responses, how our memories work, how we learn, and what we need in order to be satisfied with our lives. Because many of our most profound experiences involve awareness that we are all in this, whatever it is, together, we have throughout history had some intuition that we share much. By focusing on generally applicable observations about behaviour and the timing of its emergence, developmental psychologists can help to satisfy that curiosity. From this perspective, one early developmental psychologist in particular, Jean Piaget, can be considered in many ways the inspiration for much of the way in which developmental psychology has emerged as a scientific discipline.

Box 1.1   Jean Piaget and his scientific legacy to developmental psychology

Jean Piaget (1896–1980) was a Swiss developmental psychologist and philosopher. From a young age, he was interested in biology and the natural world, and received his doctorate in natural history and philosophy in 1918 from the University of Neuchatel, Switzerland. He had become interested in psychology and psychoanalysis, however, and moved to Paris in 1919 to teach at the Grange-Aux-Belles Street School for Boys and help its director, Alfred Binet, in marking his newly developed intelligence tests. In the process of doing this, Piaget noticed that young children consistently gave the same kinds of incorrect answers to certain questions. He was intrigued by this consistency. It suggested to him that young children's cognitive processes are qualitatively different from those of older children and adults, and formed the basis of a lifetime of observation and experimentation and the development of his global theory of cognitive development from infancy to adulthood.

To pursue this intuition, Piaget returned to Geneva, Switzerland, in 1922 as director of research at the Rousseau Institute, a private school dedicated to the idea of placing the child, rather than the teacher, at the centre of the educational process. In this position, Piaget developed many of the observational and experimental techniques he used to formulate his theory of cognitive development. He continued his research after becoming Professor of Psychology, Sociology, and Philosophy of Science at the University of Neuchatel in 1925. This position was followed by a series of posts at the University of Geneva and other universities in Switzerland and France beginning in 1929. He officially retired from the University of Geneva in 1971, but retained his posts as emeritus professor there and Director of the International Centre for Genetic Epistemology in Geneva until his death in 1980. He was the recipient of many awards and honorary degrees. His many books and papers have been some of the most influential in psychology, with two of them receiving more than 5,000 citations and another five receiving more than 2,500 citations.

Among the many things for which Piaget is well known are his detailed observations of the spontaneous behaviour of his own three children during their infancy and childhood. He used these observations to develop ideas about the cognitive processes in which they engaged as they behaved, developed tasks that could be used to distinguish among various possibilities, and brought these ideas and tasks to his work with students at the schools at which he taught and to his experimental laboratories. He also developed structured interviews to assess children's thought processes in carrying out his experimental tasks and used standard psychometric techniques to transcribe their answers and his observations of their behaviour into robust quantitative data. But he extended his structured clinical interviews by beginning with standard questions and, depending on the answers he received, asking additional non-standard exploratory questions.

This approach helped him to formulate a very comprehensive theory to explain the differences he observed between the performances of younger and older children on the cognitive tasks he devised. The theory is firmly grounded in the experimental psychological tradition because he proposes a series of invariant developmental stages through which, he contends, all children progress in sequence, with transitions normally occurring within a narrow range of ages. Thus, the theory focuses on what is common in children's cognitive development rather than on the individual differences among them. It is probably the single most influential theory of children's cognitive development because it is in many ways an example of the ideal in science: his very specific observations of children's behaviour in very specific situations were matched by equally specific proposals of the kinds of cognitive processes in which children engaged in order to produce those behaviours, and then generalized to articulate the developmental processes that caused children's behaviour to change as they grew.

For example, Piaget noted that, before the age of eight months, he could offer his son Laurent a small toy and Laurent would reach for it as long as he could see it. But if Piaget blocked Laurent's view of the toy, Laurent would drop his arm and abandon his attempts to get it. By the age of twelve months, however, Laurent would continue to pursue the toy even when he could not see it. Piaget proposed that this was because, at eight months of age, Laurent (and infants of that age more generally) did not understand that objects continue to exist even when they are not visible; infants of that age lack the ability to maintain mental images of objects when they cannot see them. In the terms that have become customary descriptions, these young infants lack the concept of object permanence. With an additional four months' development and experience, however, Piaget suggested that the ability to form this concept emerged, but remained rather weak. That is, between eight and twelve months of age, he observed that infants continued to work to obtain objects even when they could not see them, but the images they maintained of the objects appeared to be fragile: if the infants had observed objects hidden in one location and retrieved them from there several times, they would continue to search in that location again, even when they watched the objects hidden in a different location. To Piaget, it was as if the infants had grasped the concept that objects continue to exist when not visible, but not the concept that they could exist out of view in varying places.

This has become known as the 'A-not-B error', and it is another way in which Piaget's theory is an example of the ideal in science. That is, his theory involves very specific observations of behaviour that can be subjected to replication, it offers very specific explanations for the observations, and it goes on to offer comprehensive explanations for the whole series of observations. These characteristics both give the theory great potential explanatory power should it be correct, and make its correctness very testable. They also make the theory an excellent target for subsequent work by other scientists, and Piaget's theory has in many ways defined work in developmental psychology since the 1950s.

In this example, one observation is that eight-month-old infants do not retain interest in pursuing objects if the objects are removed from the infants' fields of vision. A second observation is that eight-month-old infants cannot maintain mental images of objects they cannot see, so that it is to them as though the objects have ceased to exist. A second observation is that, by the age of twelve months, infants will repeatedly uncover objects that they have watched being hidden from view in one location, but if they then watch the objects being hidden in different locations, they will continue to try to uncover them in the first locations. Piaget's explanation for the first observations is that the infants do not understand that objects that are no longer visible continue to exist. His explanation for the second observations is that by 12 months of age infants have a rudimentary understanding that objects no longer in view continue to exist, but they cannot use their experience of watching an object being hidden in a new location to overcome their experiences of having recovered the hidden object in its original location. Piaget's comprehensive explanation for this and many other behaviours in infants and young children that strike adults as puzzling is that development consists of organizational and adaptive processes through which infants, and organisms in general, adjust their physical and cognitive structures to environmental demands, through assimilation of new information and environmental demands into the existing structures, and accommodation, or qualitative changes in those existing structures, when the incoming information and environmental demands cannot be assimilated by the existing structures.

The specificity of Piaget's observations and his explanations for them has defined much of the work in developmental psychology for such a long period of time because it has given developmental psychologists following him clear experimental targets for their own work. Challenging and refining theories is one of the major occupations in any science, and its first step is to replicate the initial observations that generated the theory. Piaget's observations about infant behaviour have survived this challenge well: they have been replicated consistently. They are arguably among the most robust observations in psychology. His explanations for his observations, however, have met more mixed fates. Continuing with the example of the A-not-B-error, Piaget's tasks require what turn out to be rather complex motor responses from infants: they must reach for and remove barriers hiding the objects in order to uncover them when their visibility has been obscured. Yet Piaget's explanations are about infants' understanding of the objects in the world. If his cognitive explanations are accurate, they should hold up to modifications of the tasks that require less sophisticated motor responses. Many developmental psychologists have introduced such task modifications. For example, Aguiar and Baillargon (2000) used two toys and left both uncovered. One was set on the far edge of a towel, and the other was set behind and not on another towel. Nine-month-old infants were able to retrieve one toy by pulling on the towel on which it was set, and could do so repeatedly. If the positions of the toys were reversed, however, so that, for example, the toy on the left was placed on the towel and the toy on the right was placed behind the towel, the infants continued to try to retrieve a toy by pulling on the towel on the right. It was not until 11 months of age that they could pull on the correct towel to retrieve a toy, despite the whole situation being in plain view. This suggests that ability to hold mental images of invisible objects in mind has little to do with the phenomenon Piaget observed. It does nothing, however, to refute Piaget's overall explanation for these and other phenomena, which remains quite plausible.

The fate of Piaget's explanation for the A-not-B error is typical of many of his explanations for the performance of infants and children on the tasks he devised. That is, his observations are readily replicable, but clever modifications of the tasks intended to test his explanations have shown in general that his explanations do not appear to be correct, or at least are oversimplified. Articulating alternative explanations that fit performance data, testing them by devising new variations on tasks that distinguish among the possibilities, formulating new theories that can account for the new performance data in many ways has kept at least developmental psychologists who focus on infants and children busy ever since. It has also kept their focus squarely on experimental psychology, and their emphasis on normative patterns of behaviour. The typical study in the area compares the average performance of, say, 3-year-olds to that of, say 4-year-olds, notes the inability of the 3-year-olds to perform successfully, however that is defined, and the successful performance of the

4-year-olds, and draws conclusions about what kinds of function develop during that year of growth. The same patterns are typical in the recently burgeoning study of later-lifespan development: studies that compare the average perform-ance of young adults, often university students, to the average performance of older adults and draw conclusions about the ageing process. Even when studies are conducted longitudinally, making conclusions about developmental proc-esses much stronger, the focus tends to remain on the average performance in the developing group. It is a tribute to the richness of Piaget's observations and theory (as well as no doubt an oversimplification) that his legacy of experi-mental design and method of approach is so strong.

The legacy of the trait as the core concept in individual differences research

A trait is a feature or characteristic of an object or person that distinguishes it from otherwise similar others. This denotation of the word carries with it the connotation that the feature or characteristic has the power to make this distinction over some reasonably extended period of time: the trait shows some stability. Long before psychology existed as a science, philosophers and other commentators observed that there is considerable consistency in people's behaviour over time. With the advent of a scientific approach to the measure-ment of behaviour, it also became clear that the variation among individuals is comparable with or greater in magnitude than the variation within individuals. This led early psychological theorists such as Allport (1937) to think of the consistencies in people's behaviour as manifestations of traits. This concep-tualization carries with it the assumption that the trait has some causal influ-ence on behaviour, and the causal role of traits in behaviour was certainly an intended part of Allport's theory. He proposed that traits originate in the functioning of the nervous system and that they guide behaviour and render it consistent by making otherwise diverse stimuli functionally equivalent in terms of the responses they generate in the individual.

Allport clearly recognized that traits develop through reciprocal transactions between internally inspired disposition and acquired habits of environmental adaptation. He (1937) used the example of a child growing into a gregarious adult to illustrate the process: the child begins with pleasant social interac-tions with her mother. These rewarding experiences encourage the pursuit of other social contacts as the child grows and meets new people, and the child finds these experiences rewarding too. With further growth, she comes to miss social contact when not available, and actively seeks it through a variety of social outlets such as going to church, to the theatre, to family gatherings, to social clubs, etc. She also expresses the trait of gregariousness through behav-iour in those situations, such as making others feel comfortable, inviting others to share experiences, expressing herself in conversation, listening to others and expressing concern for them, and so on. The situations have become equivalent in eliciting these behaviours from her, and she does not display these behaviours when she spends an evening at home alone. In Allport's example, the trait develops through an amalgamation of a predisposition to behave in certain ways, positive reinforcement in the form of pleasant experiences of doing so, and the formation over time of the habit of behaving in those ways, and the trait comes to be characterized by the habitual nature of the behaviour.

Correlational psychologists focusing on individual differences have long tended to run with this conception of the trait as developed habitual behaviour rooted originally in some aspect of inherent biology. The assumption of inherent biological origin for traits is an important aspect of the perspective they have taken: it has fostered an interest in genes as the source of the inherent biology. Early writers on individual differences such as Galton (1869) assumed that individual differences in psychological traits were largely genetically determined, but this view largely fell from favour in most areas of psychology after World War II. The perception that genetic influences were involved persisted among psychologists interested in individual differences, however, and the increasing availability of computer technology made estimating the extent of such influences increasingly tractable. Studies estimating genetic influences on intelligence date back at least to the 1920s (Burks, 1928), but some of the earliest studies of individual differences in personality and other characteristics date back only to the late 1970s and were carried out by Tom Bouchard in the Minnesota Study of Twins Reared Apart (Bouchard, Lykken, McGue, Segal, & Tellegen, 1990; see also Segal, 2000). Like many at the time, as he began these studies he expected that some psychological traits would show little or no genetic influence while others would show substantial influence. Instead, to the surprise of many (including him), by now results from more than a thousand studies in perhaps the order of 100 different samples consisting of tens of thousands of individuals have consistently shown that essentially all psychological traits show moderate levels of genetic influence, accounting for, in general, some 30-60 per cent of population variance in the traits. The results have been so consistent that the field of psychology in general has come to acknowledge them; Turkheimer (2000) has called the presence of substantial genetic influences on psychological traits the 'First Law of Behaviour Genetics,' and the consistency of genetic influence has reinforced the conceptualization of individual differences as traits.

Because overall behaviour changes so much from infancy to childhood to adulthood yet stabilizes considerably in adulthood, it is clear that, whatever psychological traits are, they are not manifested in the same rather fixed manner throughout the lifespan as is, for example, eye colour. It is equally clear that both what changes systematically across individuals during development and what differentiates among individuals have some basis in biology, if only for the superficially trivial reason that humans are biological organisms. Understanding these biological processes and differences has become a primary research focus in psychology, during the past 30 years or so, fed in part no doubt by the rapid development of powerful new tools that make possible the measurement of biological properties such as hormonal levels, genetic variants, blood flow within the brain, etc. In this book, I thus feature what has been learned and what remains to be understood about the biological bases and consequences of behaviour.

Even when they can be measured using the same measuring instrument, most traits tend to show substantial mean changes when measured longitudinally at various points in the lifespan, as well as differences among people born at different times but measured at the same age. And many measuring instruments are not suitable for people of different ages. This can be the case to relatively small degrees, as when the measuring items are useful in measuring traits of people at different ages but tend to be interpreted differently at different ages or to bear different relations to each other at different ages. For example, questions about one's level and enjoyment of social activity, often used to measure the personality trait of extraversion, may be interpreted quite differently by young single adults, older married adults with young children, and still older retired adults. Such questions may also bear different kinds of associations with other questions also used to measure extraversion such as those involving assertiveness or excitement seeking. These differences can often be important, though some clear correspondence across ages remains. But measuring instruments can also be completely unsuitable for people of different ages. For example, there would be little point in asking infants to complete most standard tests of intelligence, yet, with age-appropriate measures that are superficially quite different, there is evidence for considerable trait-like stability of intelligence (Fagan, Holland, & Wheeler, 2007).

Individual differences psychologists have thus made most of the case for psychological traits by providing data on the degree of rank-order stability they display over time. The rationale is that, even though there are normative overall changes in behaviour with age, those 'lower' on a trait than their contemporaries at one point in the lifespan tend to be 'lower' to about the same degree on that trait than those same contemporaries at later points in the lifespan, and similarly for those 'higher' on the trait. Just getting to the point of making this kind of comparison of trait levels among individuals, however, requires considerable elaboration on the concept of trait. It is here that much of the efforts of individual differences psychologists have been placed.

One major issue that must be addressed in conceptualizing behavioural traits is how the essentially infinite range of human behaviour can be categorized into traits. What behavioural patterns that show individual differences are consistent enough to be important, and what are the relations among them? This is a massively multivariate problem. Attempts in the early 1900s to address it objectively led to the development of important statistical analytical tools such as factor analysis. Factor analysis is essentially a technique to evaluate the patterns of correlation among a large group of variables to identify objectively which variables are more closely related to each other than they are to the other variables. The idea is that those variables most closely related together constitute some higher-order dimension or category that either causes or is the emergent result of the links among the lower-order variables. Thus, combining these lower-order variables in some way expresses the essential nature of the underlying trait more accurately than any one of the individual variables does alone. Not coincidentally, it also acts to reduce the numbers of variables to some more tractable number.

With substantial enhancements made possible by the development of computer technology, the ideas behind factor analysis and related techniques such as multidimensional scaling remain those in use today. The statistical analytical process, however, is only one aspect of the problem of defining traits. The other is how to define the universe of variables that might form the basis for the traits. This problem is so large that it inevitably involves some kind of ultimately subjective approach. This has meant that individual investigators have come up with varying solutions even when they have taken similar approaches, and trying to understand the implications of the differences in trait definitions that have resulted has consumed much energy in this area of research. Perhaps fortunately, no matter how they are specifically defined, constructs labelled as traits generally do display the kind of rank-order consistency that individual differences psychologists have posited they should (e.g., Deary, Whiteman, Starr, Whalley, & Fox, 2004; Moffitt, Caspi, Harkness, & Silva, 1993; Roberts & DelVecchio, 2000).

The substantial work involved in establishing reasonable definitions of trait contents, statistical methodologies for reducing the large number of possible variables to manageable levels, and the presence and magnitude of genetic influences on the traits has led to a primary focus on studying individual differences among adults in individual differences research. Typical studies in this area rely tacitly on the assumption individual differences simply pre-date the timing of the studies and have been essentially stable over some time period preceding them, without considering how the differences actually might have emerged.

Integrating developmental and individual differences psychology

I noted above that traits exhibit the kind of rank-order consistency over time that individual differences psychologists have posited that they should if they are rooted in some inherent biological nature. This is true when the traits are measured in a general way such as by asking people how they typically behave or what kinds of activities they typically prefer. The consistency of responses is not just a matter of conceit, as asking people to make ratings of others they know well in the same general or typical manner results in similar levels of stability over time. Despite this, when people's actual behaviour is rated for the manifestation of traits in specific situations, no matter who makes the ratings, the rank-order consistency tends to be dramatically lower. That is, for example, the student who is the life of the party on a Friday night may be very slow to speak up in class during the week, while another may volunteer interesting comments and questions regularly in class but not even attend the weekly parties. Or one person may be very willing to experiment with trying new foods from other cultures, but reluctant actually to travel to the countries that display those cultures, while another may welcome travel itself but stick as closely as possible to his/her usual diet while travelling. This is by way of saying that the specific environment in which a trait is being evaluated often has a big effect on the extent to which the trait is displayed.

There are at least two major reasons that this might occur. The first is that we may not have gotten the definition of the trait right. To refer to the first example above, we may think of talkativeness as one of the primary manifestations of some kind of sociability (or extraversion) and of sociability as one of the primary traits on which humans show individual differences. We may point to the heritability of sociability and to the parts of the brain that show responses to social stimuli in fMRI scanners as evidence of the biological basis of the trait of sociability. Thinking this way makes the reversal of rank ordering of the degree to which the two individuals display talkativeness in the classroom and party situations appear to contradict the underlying trait concept. But what if the relevant trait with the biological basis is really self-confidence, and one student is very confident of her intellectual skills but not of her social skills and the other feels the opposite about his skills? As I will discuss later in this book, both heritability estimates and fMRI scans are blunt enough indicators of biological relevance that they would still produce the results we observe for sociability.

The other major reason such reversals might occur is that people (and other animals) have multiple and varied goals and objectives. Not only that, but they bring psychological content to their appraisal of situations, in the form of learned associations between particular aspects of situations and prior experiences, expectations of cause and effect, and capacities to regulate responses to stimuli, of which they may or may not be aware. Because people (and other animals) differ in all these factors, even individuals with identical trait levels can be expected to appraise the same situation in different ways, and for reasons associated with their inherent biological make-up as well as their experiences in the environments in which they have lived so far. This means that any situation will provide stimuli that have different levels of relevance to different individuals, and that some individuals will be responding primarily to some aspects of the situation while others are responding primarily to completely different aspects of the same situation.

Response to situations is the basis for successful adaptation to the environment. Successful adaptation to the environment takes place moment-by-moment, but it also takes place over much longer time periods. For example, the presence of an unexpected oncoming car has only one really adaptive response, and it had better be immediate. But one may respond in many different ways to the presence on the calendar of a final exam in three weeks: by studying a little at a time each day, waiting until the last minute to study at all, or even ignoring the whole thing and not showing up to take it. On the day of the exam itself (once the hours of administration have passed), these different tactics may manifest no difference at all in extent of environmental adaptation. Even several weeks later when marks are posted, differences in extent of environmental adaption may be few. It may be only when course degrees are awarded and job prospects evaluated that differences in extent of environmental adaptation become apparent. This is where individual differences in goals, motivations to achieve them, learning experiences, expectations, and capacity to regulate behaviour come in.

For example, two students may find studying for exams similarly unpleasant in comparison with other ways of spending their time. The students may share the stated goal of achieving a first degree, but one student may have had the experience of exam success with frequent, brief study sessions over the weeks prior to the exam, while the other may have, so far, gotten through exams relatively well with very little formal study. Their prior experiences may make the first student much more willing than the second to tolerate the work involved in studying regularly, and create quite different habitual responses to the situation of upcoming exams, despite similar emotional responses. Two things are important here. First, over time, through the habit of regular studying and the reward of exam success it presumably makes possible, the first student may come, inherently and biologically, to find such study sessions more pleasant, thus effecting true change in some trait-like aspects of personality and even ability. That is, consciously chosen behavioural patterns may affect underlying biological function through development of adaptive capacities. And second, the first student is regularly making a conscious decision to remain at least in the short term in a situation that is not optimal, for the purpose of eventually reaching a more optimal longer-term situation.

The importance of individual choice in development of individual differences

The emphasis here is on the fact that individuals always have some amount of choice of environmental circumstances. For humans in our societies, movement from situation to situation is never completely free, of course, but neither is it ever completely restricted, even in the most closely managed societies and disadvantaged social groups. People (and other animals too) consciously and unconsciously constantly size up their environmental circumstances and the other environmental opportunities around them and respond to them by moving towards some and away from others. They make their choices about movement in two ways.

First, people (and other animals) differ in the extent to which they find any particular set of environmental circumstances pleasant or adversive. All else being equal, which of course it almost never is, those who are most adversely sensitive to any particular set of circumstances are most likely to make efforts to move away from it, and those most sensitive to any particular set of circumstances in a pleasant way are most likely to move towards it. And second, again all else being equal, those most capable of moving are going to be most likely to move away from adverse circumstances and towards pleasant circumstances. Both environmental sensitivity and capability of movement are rooted in behavioural traits, and thus in some inherent aspect of biological function. Over time, through repeated movements towards circumstances individually perceived to be pleasant and away from those individually perceived to be adverse, individuals tend to sort into environmental niches they individually find biologically compatible. In the process, adaptation to those aspects of the general circumstances that may not immediately be optimal tends to strengthen and reinforce the underlying biological differences that inspired the movement patterns in the first place.

But because movement is never completely free, many are often stuck in circumstances that are not optimal and which they have not chosen. This tends to produce stress, which when endured over time causes deterioration of biological function. This may in turn both increase biological sensitivity to the adverse circumstances and impair ability to move away from them, thus creating further adaptive difficulties. My point is that the presence of individual differences is completely enmeshed in developmental processes, and we cannot properly understand either without understanding the other. Developmental and individual differences psychologists are, from their separate camps, just beginning to realize this and to put together methodological approaches that can reveal the mechanisms involved. It is thus an exciting time to be in the field.

Why this book?

The separate research traditions in individual differences and developmental psychology have deep historical and philosophical roots. They have focused on different problems for sure: individual differences psychologists on the presence of variation in the population, the causes of this variation, and how it can be quantified, and developmental psychologists on characterizing typical development, its causal mechanisms, and the processes involved. But these are not their only differences. Psychology in general ultimately seeks to make the human situation better somehow, to help people cope with problems, to make life more satisfying, to improve task performance, or to prevent or treat mental illness. This ultimately means the development of interventions that can accomplish those goals. For individual differences psychologists, the goal of intervention is to increase average well-being, performance, whatever, by helping each individual reach his/her own optimal situation, through an infinite range of different treatments, different activities, different rewards and punishments. In direct contrast, for developmental psychologists, the goal of intervention is to find the one way of treating everyone that will bring about the highest overall level of well-being, performance, whatever, so that differentiation of handling is unnecessary. Every success in one area acts to put the other out of business.

There is a fascinating psychological study to be written of the emergence of problem focus among scientists. One feature of this study will no doubt be how Darwin's theory of evolution shaped political, social, and scientific thought in the years following its publication. Political thought has always been separated along the lines of those who were relatively satisfied with the status quo and sought to preserve it (conservatives), and those who were dissatisfied and sought to change it (liberals), but the theory of evolution provided a crystallizing framework for that distinction. Though Darwin focused on the process of speciation, from the beginning many have interpreted the theory as applying to individuals within species, and especially to humans within social structures. That the fittest tend to survive best has meant to conservatives that our environmental institutions foster the process of natural selection of the fittest, and the psychologist's ultimate job is to identify those who will fit best within the environment as it exists. This has tended to be the focus of individual differences psychologists, and it emphasizes the competition among individuals for positions within static institutions presumably already optimized. Liberals, on the other hand, have tended to see the struggle for survival that Darwin portrayed as everyone against the environment. This has tended to be the focus of developmental psychologists. From this perspective, the psychologist's ultimate job is to shape an environment, our institutions, so that everyone can survive, and even thrive, within them.

Both views are oversimplifications of evolutionary theory. We miss the boat when we think generally of overall adaptation to the environment broadly construed and single definitions of the survival of the fittest. Instead, every feature we have contributes in some way to our adaptation to each and every situation we encounter, and our environmental adaptation is a continuing, ongoing, dynamic process that can take many different forms depending on the specific circumstances we encounter and our responses to them. Moreover, the nature of the contributions of our pre-existing characteristics to our adaptation to any give situation can only be understood within the context of that situation. From this perspective, which requires integration of the individual differences and developmental perspectives, the psychologist's ultimate jobs are to develop a manageable range of environmental options and to help individuals make good decisions in finding places for themselves within them. Importantly, the needed integration requires a new understanding of the roles that biology, and in particular, genes play in our development, and that of all species. To reach this understanding, we need to take a stroll through the way in which scientists synthesized the ideas of Mendelian genetics and evolutionary theory. Traditionally, based on classical Mendelian genetics, the dominant understanding has tended to be that there is a direct match between gene and trait: genes are 'for' specific traits. A single gene may make only a very tiny contribution to a quantitative trait, but that tiny contribution is its 'job'. According to this understanding, genes and environment exert independent effects, and genetic variation is the basis of natural selection within the environment. Genes are expressed in ways that can be specified with respect to timing, type, and amount of gene product, and mutation, which is to say genetic variation itself, is the primary source of novelty on which natural selection and thus evolutions act. Moreover, the proportion of variance in the population for which genes account gives us a good indication of the extent to which these genetic variants control the characteristics displayed.

Embryologists and evolutionary biologists have, however, long taken a somewhat different view, and it is becoming increasingly clear that psychologists need to become more familiar with this view. According to it, evolution acts on the traits actually displayed, rather than on the genetic variation that might contribute to the traits. When examined closely, the idea that evolution could act on the genetic variation contributing to traits rather than on the traits themselves quickly seems a little absurd: natural selection is about adaptation to environmental circumstances, and adaptation takes place through the manifestation of characteristic behaviours, not the possession of particular combinations of genes. Selection will take place as long as there is variation in the traits displayed, regardless of the source of that variation.

Yet the dominant understanding has not been completely misplaced with respect to the role of gene variants in evolution. If whatever selection takes place is to be transmitted from one generation to the next, that is, to reflect evolution, genetic variants have to be involved somehow. And we know that they are, in virtually every psychological trait. So, indirectly rather than directly, genetic variation is the source of natural selection and thus evolution after all. But the fact that it is the source indirectly rather than directly is critical. Genes may confer a kind of developmental blueprint, but organisms develop over time: none of their characteristics springs forth in mature form from conception. Just as the blueprint of a house may require changes once the workers start actually digging the foundation and find that there is quicksand around the place in which they planned to place one of the pillars of the foundation, so patterns of gene expression may differ in different environmental circumstances. That is, geneticists have traditionally looked to mutation, or changes in DNA sequence, as the driving force in evolution among species. But novel characteristics may result at least as often from alterations in development brought on by changes in expression of already existing genes. Among other things, this can help to explain high conservation of genetic material across species despite major morphological differences. For example, humans share some 98 per cent of our DNA with chimpanzees, our closest living interspecies relatives, but we also share some 50 per cent with worms and insects.

This is important because it can also help to explain the maintenance of individual differences within species, in particular among humans. Our populations vary genetically, but even within relatively genetically similar subgroups they also live in varying environmental circumstances. Because we are developmentally plastic, we are differentially responsive to the varying environmental inputs, which may include the actions of genes, both genes that vary among humans and those that do not. That is, genes can act as environments to other genes by modifying their internal environments, creating new characteristics at the cellular level. In turn, these new cellular characteristics may provide input to higher organizational levels, altering the developmental programme so that very different surface-levels traits emerge. It is through this process that we can understand how individual differences develop. And ultimately, we need to understand this process of evolution writ small, at the level of the individual in society as we know it, in order to develop policies and institutions, preventives and interventions to maximize life outcomes for all. The purpose of this book is to provide the background information necessary to appreciate this idea, and, more importantly, to show how this idea reverberates throughout human lifespan development.

Organization of the book

The first section, Chapters 2–4 of the book, provides background information on three major paradigms that are crucial to this idea. Chapter 2 covers evolution. Evolution is not something long past but continues today, though its manifestations have changed, sometimes substantially, because of the development of safe and effective birth control, medical treatments that dramatically reduce infant and maternal mortality, and routine use of antibiotics to control infectious disease. The chapter shows why, despite evolution and natural selection, genetic variance, and thus genetically influenced individual differences, remains in populations by reviewing the basic ideas of natural selection, sexual selection, mutation as driver of selection, environmental change (including migration) as driver of evolution, balancing selection, antagonistic selection, etc., giving examples of each from both non-human animal and human evolution. It briefly recounts the anthropological record of human emergence from Africa, and introduces and describes the importance of the principle of coevolution, or the process by which biological and cultural inheritance factors transact to result in transmission of culturally influenced behaviours and attitudes from one generation to the next through modification of natural selection pressures. These processes are the basic stuff of development too, both as normative processes applicable in general and as sources of individual differences.

Chapter 3 focuses on two intertwined subjects: human brain neuroanatomy and genetics. I outline overall brain organization in terms of both structure and function, with emphasis on the existence of variation in structure and function among individuals. I explain not just what we know but how we know it and the extent to which there is uncertainty in what we know. I describe how brain function is integrated with somatic function, and what this means for both intra- and inter-individual differences: differences in state within individuals due to fatigue, food and drug consumption, motivational state, etc., and systematic differences across individuals that remain reasonably stable over time. I outline basic genetic principles, beginning with the genome as a whole and how DNA is translated into phenotypic expression of traits that do not vary among humans, working into phenotypic expression of Mendelian traits that do show inter-individual differences, and then into how our understanding of genetic action has changed in the last 10 years or so with the mapping of the human genome and the realization of the importance of regulatory genes beyond those that synthesize proteins.

Chapter 4 explores individual differences in reactivities to environmental stimuli and their roles in the generation of stress responses, coping capacity, and resilience. I discuss inflammation, immune and allergic response, emotional and cognitive responsiveness, tendencies to experience negative and positive emotions, tendencies for emotions to persist, responsiveness to ingested substances including food and medications, blanket measures of these kinds of responses such as allostatic load and cognitive reserve, and the ways in which psychological and physiological responses are interconnected. I discuss the U-shaped nature of stress reactivity: some stress is constructive because it spurs us to action, but too much is destructive because it overwhelms our abilities to cope. Yet, in addition to individual differences in reactivities to environmental stimuli, there are also individual differences in tolerances for any given level of reaction, and individual differences in capacities to mount constructive responses. Each of these levels of individual difference magnifies the individual differences in coping capacity. Having established this, I explore the development of coping resources, both psychological and physiological, and describe the factors involved in resilience. With this background in place, I will show how the actions of individuals in response to their developmental environments form the building blocks of processes which, in aggregate, lead to evolution of species. This sets the stage for more specific discussion of these processes at the various age periods of the lifespan, and concludes the first section of the book.

The second section of the book focuses on the application of these concepts to developmental processes in the various phases of the lifespan, beginning with formation of what might be considered the developmental foundation in gestation. Because genetic background is covered in Chapter 2, Chapter 5 focuses on foetal environment during gestation and how individual differences in maternal condition and behaviour influence foetal development. I discuss maternal physiology, infection load, immune response, nutrition, inflammation, and seasonal effects, as well as maternal psychological condition and maternal behaviours such as smoking and alcohol and drug consumption, including both illicit recreational substances and medications. I address the impact that timing of exposure may have on the effects of exposure, stressing the fact that individual differences in foetal response may result from differences in timing of exposure as well as from differences in exposure itself and from genetic differences in sensitivity to exposure. I describe what we have learned from the studies of the offspring of women who were pregnant during major periods of famine during the 19th century and World War II, as well as from studies of women who sought but could not obtain abortions. Though the focus will be on maternal individual differences and therefore uterine conditions, I will stress that the foetus is not completely passive during this period: it responds to maternal conditions and to external stimuli. Thus, its own individual differences are in play from conception.

Chapter 6 opens with a description of the state of the infant brain at birth in terms of perceptual abilities (sight, hearing, touch, taste, smell), motor capacities, emotional responsiveness, information processing and attentional capacities, diurnal rhythms, sleeping and feeding patterns, rates of habituation to sensory stimuli, activity levels, and emergence of attachment-related behaviours. In each of these areas, I detail the kinds of ranges that are considered normal, including sex differences, as well as individual differences that are considered indicative of disability or disorder. With this background, the real focus of the chapter is on showing how the basic perceptual, information processing and attentional capacities, along with emotional and social responsiveness, diurnal patterns, and activity level, transact with each other and with caregiver responsiveness and physical experiences to begin to put together a brain with recognizably human functions, yet with both individual characteristics and characteristics that reflect the culture of origin. Emphasis is on the integration of language and emotional development with caregiver attachment and the integration of physical and perceptual experiences such as reaching and grabbing, sensory experiences, and the emergence of the ability to move voluntarily through space by creeping and crawling with the development of cognitive abilities, using the frameworks of experience-expectant and experience-dependent processes or capacities.

Chapter 7 does the most to articulate the principles linking evolution and development, which are important because they become increasingly relevant as the child gains increasing ability to move through space and to make decisions about which activities to pursue. The ideas presented here, however, will reverberate throughout the rest of the book. In particular, I develop Experience Producing Drive Theory. This is the idea that the individual child, with his/her particular conglomeration of individual and general human characteristics, is an active participant in the development of his/her own patterns of behaviour through genetically as well as environmentally influenced tendencies to seek particular kinds of environmental experiences: cognitively, emotionally, and socially. These experiences occur actively through the child's individual exploratory behaviours and evocatively through behaviours that elicit systematic patterns of response from the child's social environment. They also occur passively when parents and other caregivers act in ways that reinforce the child's own proclivities. I touch on cultural variation in the treatment of infants and young children, but also stress how the individual child's own patterns of emotional responsiveness and exploratory behaviour drive the development of cognitive and personality traits and habits of behaviour within that culture. At the same time, though there are environments that create risks for development of psychopathology and physical disorder, it is unlikely that there are genetic variants that are similarly unilaterally associated with risk. That is, many genes and the experience-producing drives they influence may create vulnerabilities to dysfunction in some environments but potentials for particularly good function in other environments.

Chapter 8 covers adolescence and the transition to physical adulthood. In industrialized cultures, the transition to physical adulthood takes place as it always has, during adolescence, but the transition to social, emotional, and cognitive adulthood takes place later. I describe the physical, emotional, and cognitive changes that take place during adolescence, while individuals now typically remain in residence with parents and under their financial support in industrialized countries. I also describe normal variations in timing and extent of these changes and their associations with other characteristics showing individual differences such as antisocial behaviour and early parenthood, as well as abnormal variation and how it can help us understand normal variation. I devote attention to sexual awakening, both heterosexual and homosexual, and discuss the role of culture both in constraining and encouraging, even sometimes demanding, sexual behaviour.

The primary task of young adulthood in much of the world today is finding a place in which one's skills and abilities can be of constructive use, that provides the opportunity to become financially self-supporting, and that provides appropriate social stimulation and support, thus completing the transition to social, cognitive, and emotional adulthood. Chapter 9 describes how individual differences that exist at adolescence, while most are still generally supported by parents, influence the possibilities of success in this endeavour, and how the actual experience of identifying one's 'place in the world' shapes subsequent adult development. I focus on the intertwined cognitive and emotional challenges involved in pursuing the goals of identifying a congenial prospective mate and a satisfactory occupation, and show why the transitions involved leave the individual particularly vulnerable to psychopathology at this time, especially when the individual encounters substantial difficulties in meeting these challenges.

In middle age, focus shifts from finding a place in the world to maintaining and extending it. Increasingly, for many this also involves making changes in one's place in the world, whether physically through relocation, cognitively through retraining and new careers, or socially through parenting or divorce. Chapter 10 describes how individual differences in places in the world and individual differences in adjustments to those places and goals for maintaining and extending them tend to reverberate over time and across physiological and psychological lines in ways that reflect evolutionary processes. This will include responses to parenting, relationship and career stress, the need to care for ageing parents, and, increasingly in our modern world, technological change.

Chapter 11 focuses on the changes in social, emotional, and cognitive perspectives that tend to take place in later life. In addition to ideas about the effects of compression of time horizon, I make use of data from master's athletes (those that compete formally with others of their age groups in sports like swimming and running) to argue that many if not most of these psychological changes are primarily related to reduced perceptual and physical abilities, often due to deteriorating physical capacities including health. Individual differences in ageing also take place because of individual differences in the timing and severity of onset as well as course of disease. I show how psychological changes with age may be primarily responses to the physical and physiological changes associated with ageing, and how these physical and physiological changes may aggravate the psychological changes taking place anyway. At the same time, maintenance of general well-being with increasing age may help to slow the physical and physiological ageing processes. I discuss the concept of terminal drop, or the idea that cognitive decline accelerates shortly before death, with individual differences in age of onset that are tied to longevity, as well as the reasons for sex differences in longevity and the extent to which there are genetic influences on longevity.

Chapter 12 concludes the book by discussing the role of timing of birth in life outcomes and psychological responses. I review long-term trends in longevity, height, and intelligence test performance and the possible evolutionary, sociological, and historical reasons for these trends. I cover the epidemiological and psychological effects of major historical events such as World War II and the Great Depression, and present and explain the idea that there are major historical cycles that have systematically different effects on the various generational cohorts in different phases on the lifespan. These cycles consist of cataclysmic historical events followed by relatively quiescent periods that then lead to social unrest and reawakening, followed by social readjustment. I discuss how the psychological effects of such cycles could be expected to reverberate across observed individual differences that vary with age.

Further reading

Bouchard, T. J., Lykken, D. T., McGue, M., Segal, N. L., & Tellegen, A. (1990). Sources of human psychological differences: the Minnesota study of twins reared apart. *Science, 250*, 223–228.

Cronbach, L. J. (1957). The two disciplines of scientific psychology. *American Psychologist, 12*, 671–684.

Deary, I. J., Whiteman, M. C., Starr, J. M., Whalley, L. J., & Fox, H. C. (2004). The impact of childhood intelligence on later life: Following up the Scottish Mental Surveys of 1932 and 1947. *Journal of Personality and Social Psychology, 86*, 130–147.

Roberts, B. W., & DelVecchio, W. F. (2000). The rank-order consistency of personality traits from childhood to old age: A quantitative review of longitudinal studies. *Psychological Bulletin, 126*, 3–25.

Segal, N. L. (2000). *Entwined Lives: Twins and What They Tell US About Human Behavior.* New York: Plume.

Evolution

The origins and development of the theory of evolution

Like most great ideas or inventions, the theory of evolution can itself be seen as the object of an evolutionary process. Though today it is often attributed somewhat singlehandedly to Charles Darwin (1859), with Alfred Russel Wallace (1892) sometimes acknowledged as a co-developer, naturalists had for some time been aware that fossil records indicated that the earth had once been populated by many species that no longer exist. They had noted that the bones found in older geological strata were not the same as those found in more recent strata, and that those found in older strata differed more from those in the animals around them than did the ones in more recent strata. They also were aware that, among the great variety of extant species, there were often striking structural similarities. Not only do humans, chimpanzees, and orang-utans all have five digits on each hand and foot, but cats and dogs have five claws on their front paws, including one that takes a position on the paw that might be considered analogous to the position of the thumb on the hand. Perhaps even more strikingly, the wings of birds and the flippers of seals show very similar structure, and the basic body plan of a head resting on a central body core with four appendages is nearly universal throughout the mammalian, bird, and reptile kingdoms. There was even knowledge that embryos of very different species pass through very similar developmental stages before birth. All of these observations had suggested to many that life forms were not static, that they underwent some kind of change process over time.

Early naturalists had also made another important kind of observation. They had noted that many species possess characteristics that seem to have purpose. Molluscs and snails have shells that protect extremely delicate bodies from the hostile forces in the surrounding environment. Most mammals have ears that protrude from their bodies, making them more efficient in picking up sound waves. Many plants have thorns that deter animals from eating them. Given that life forms are clearly not static, it was easy to begin to wonder how these special features that appeared to make life easier for their bearers had come to be. Though naturalists interested in these features had come by the turn of the 19th century or so to call themselves 'evolutionists', their use of the term reflected only their observations. They lacked a compelling conception of a causal mechanism or process that might explain them.

Some ideas had been suggested, however, and scientists associated with two of them deserve mention. Jean Lamarck became known for synthesizing several ideas in the air at the time to formulate two sources of potential change in organisms. The first was a tendency for natural and differential movements of fluids (derived from the traditional alchemical view of chemical processes) within the body to create organs of different function within tissue, thus leading to greater complexity. The second, and related, source of change was that organisms might use or not use the features created in the first process in adapting to their environments, thus creating, through the first process, features that are ever more specialized to the environment. The crucial aspect of this source of change was that, as long as the environmental modifications are common to both sexes that produce offspring, they are transmitted to those offspring. The early formulation of this idea is important because, though the concept of 'soft inheritance' was rejected as inaccurate with the introduction of Mendelian genetics and Darwinian evolution, geneticists are now realizing that epigenetic mechanisms can have exactly these kinds of effects.

The other scientist to mention here is Georges Cuvier. He was a palaeontologist and anatomist interested in explaining the newly discovered patterns of extinction of species and both gaps and clear lines of species succession in the fossil records. He suggested that, in the geologic past, the earth may have been affected by sudden, short-lived catastrophic events that involved large areas and could even have been worldwide in scope. Examples might include major earthquakes, floods. Cuvier saw these events as recurring, natural phenomena, interspersed with long periods of relative stability. This led him to believe that the earth was at least several million years old. Though his writings were devoid of metaphysical and religious speculation, his idea that Europe may have been inundated for a long period by the sea was picked up by a group of geologists interested in proving that the flood through which Noah's Ark survived actually took place. This contributed to Cuvier's ideas being largely supplanted in mainstream geology by views that change in the earth's appearance takes place more gradually through processes such as erosion. Cuvier vigorously attacked the idea that existing species could be modified over time by environmental conditions, seeing the catastrophic events as requiring the emergence of completely new species after the event. Still, his idea that species evolution has been impacted by natural geological catastrophes remains important because modern geologists now tend to think in both catastrophic and gradualist terms. With respect to the fossil record, for example, the extinction of the dinosaurs is now generally thought to be related to a collision between the earth and an asteroid, though the details of this remain hotly debated.

The theory of evolution itself

Publication of Darwin's (1859) *Origin of Species* provided the beginning of the kind of explanatory mechanism for evolutionary change that had been lacking. His explanation was especially important because it was actually two-fold. That is, it offered accounts of both *why* life forms change over time, and *how* these changes take place. The spur for his account was his five-year voyage to the Galapagos Islands in the Pacific from 1831 to 1836, aboard the *Beagle*. During this voyage, he collected many bird and other animal samples, over which he pored when he returned home. In particular, he had presumed that the Galapagos finches that resided on many of the islands were all the same species, but careful study back home convinced him that each island's finches actually constituted a species distinct from the others. He began to think in terms of the finches all having had a common ancestor but each species adapting to the specific conditions of its home island.

This idea was strengthened, with some inspiration from Alfred Russel Wallace who was thinking along very similar lines, by reference to the ideas of Thomas Malthus, who had written on population dynamics during the late 1700s. Malthus suggested that organisms typically reproduce in far greater numbers than can survive to live to reproductive age themselves. The result, he wrote, had to be a 'struggle for existence'. It was Wallace's and Darwin's insight that the implication of this was that the strongest would survive and the weakest would die out; over time this would lead to the formation of new species increasingly well-adapted to their environmental circumstances, as long as the adaptations could be passed reliably from one generation to the next.

According to the theory as Darwin formulated it, evolution takes place when there is variation in the inherited traits within a population of organisms. This evolution takes place precisely *because* the variation among organisms means that some can reproduce more successfully in the prevailing environmental conditions than others. Effective reproduction can arise through either greater ability to survive to reproductive age, greater numbers of reproductive cycles, or greater fertility within reproductive cycles. Because the reason for the variation is *heritable*, or transmissible from one generation to the next, the characteristics of those that reproduce more successfully over time become more common in the population while the characteristics of those that reproduce less successfully become less common and may eventually die out. Darwin saw this differential reproductive success as resulting from an overtly competitive process among the individuals in an ecosystem in which natural selection acts rather directly on those best fitted to environmental conditions. In Wallace's (1892) writings on the subject, however, the natural selection process took a softer form, acting more like a set of checks and balances on adaptive deficiencies within the species. That is, while Darwin tended to think of only the most suited surviving to reproduce, Wallace tended to think of only the least suited dying out. Our perspective today would recognize that the capacity of the environment to provide support probably tips the balance in one direction or the other. But the two perspectives foreshadow the divergence of perspective between developmental and individual differences psychology discussed in Chapter 1, and the political overtones that accompanied it.

Despite many popular interpretations that do, the theory of evolution itself involves no concept of 'progress' or intent. Eagles did not evolve long wingspans through extending the wings they had in order to cover more surface area. Instead, those that happened by chance to have inherited longer variants of wingspan were able to fly longer using less energy and therefore became better predators and lived to sire more offspring. The process through which this takes place, according to the theory, is very gradual, with particular species features emerging over many, even thousands and perhaps millions of generations. When the environment is stable, little or no change may take place at all, but when circumstances change suddenly and dramatically, change can be much more rapid. The theory is extremely powerful in accounting for the why and how of species change in one package, and at the same time offering an explanation for the quality of the adaptive features of organisms that humans seem to see so easily as purposive and uniting the organic heritage of all species.

Evolution and genetics: the modern synthesis

Many biologists at the time were initially sceptical of Darwin's theory of evolution. One of their most strongly voiced objections was that the theory lacked a clear mechanism for inheritance. Darwin wrote as if inheritance were a blending process, through which offspring ended up with characteristics midway between those of their parents, much like mixing white and black paint produces grey. For many traits such as height or limb length, this idea seems very reasonable, but it lacks clarity: Exactly *how* does this blending take place? *What* is blended? Darwin did not say. Around the time of publication of Darwin's *Origin of Species* (1859), an answer became available in the form of Gregor Mendel's (1901) work on pea plants. He sent his papers on the subject, actually read in 1866 at a conference, to Darwin, but the conference reading attracted little attention and Darwin either did not read Mendel's papers or did not realize their significance. The result was that Mendel's discovery was essentially overlooked by the scientific community until the turn of the next century, when it was re-discovered and quickly replicated. By then, Darwin's theory of evolution had become quite generally accepted among scientists.

Mendel's discovery, however, introduced a complication to Darwin's theory. This was because what Mendel had discovered through careful cross-breeding of pea plants with different visible characteristics was that the mode of inheritance was 'particulate' rather than blended. That is, parents pass along to offspring particles which he called genes that control the characteristics the offspring display. The parents do not acquire these genes during their lifetimes but rather inherit them intact from their parents. Mendel correctly surmised that offspring inherit one set of these genes from each parent, so that each generation carries two copies of each gene. He also correctly surmised that offspring do not inherit these sets of genes originating in each set of grand-parents intact, but that they are randomly mixed within each parent before transmission to the offspring.

This presented biologists, many of whom had struggled to assimilate Darwin's theory of evolution but had finally accepted it, with a new problem. Mendel's particulate world of white or purple flowers and wrinkled or smooth peas was incompatible with empirical observations that most traits actually vary continuously and with the theoretical implication of evolution that such continuous variation should be the case. The fact that Mendel's observations were readily replicable, however, made reconciliation of the two perspectives essential. This reconciliation was accomplished in large measure by Fisher (1918; 1930). He showed mathematically that continuous variation could arise from the independent actions of many discrete genetic loci, thus rendering Mendelian genetics consistent with evolution by natural selection.

Fisher's mathematical demonstration of consistency was so welcome and so conclusive from a mathematical perspective that it still underlies the most generally accepted conceptualization of genetics within evolution today. Known as the Modern Evolutionary Synthesis, this conceptualization relies on two assumptions that have come to be taken basically for granted. These two assumptions are that gene actions are independent of (1) each other and (2) environmental circumstances. With these two assumptions in place, continuous variation can be explained as multiple genes of small effect. It was first formulated in the 1940s and then updated to incorporate the discovery of DNA. The present version can be summarized as follows:

(1) Heredity takes place through the transmission between generations of dis-
     crete units of DNA called genes.
(2) Transmission of variation across generations is indicative of variation in
     DNA base sequence.
(3) Variation in DNA base sequence is maintained by random re-combinations
     of existing alleles during sexual reproduction and by new DNA variants
     that occur spontaneously and accidentally through mutation.
(4) Natural selection occurs at the level of the trait manifested in individual
     organisms, which may also be affected by transactions with symbionts and
     parasites.
(5) Heritable variations typically have small effects, making evolution grad-
     ual. Nevertheless, it is sufficient to create the large changes in the earth's
     paleontological record.

Genetics, behaviour and ethology

Darwin considered that natural selection applied not only to morphological features but also to individual and social behavioural characteristics. Many people, both within and outside science, however, have had trouble with this idea. The fossil records and even a brief trip to the zoo will show the clear similarities and patterns of change in morphological features, but behavioral characteristics leave no fossils, and the idea of evolutionary and/or genetic control of behavior undermines at least naïve ideas of our cherished sense that we have free will. Still, several lines of evidence support Darwin's view. Probably the most important is that behavior takes place within the context of morphological structure. For example, walking upright is a behavior, and it requires a whole system of structural characteristics of bone and muscle through the back and legs to make it possible. Similarly, talking requires not just understanding of the symbolic nature of words but also some very specific structural formations of the mouth, tongue, larynx, airways, and throat. In addition, just as species can be bred, which uses artificial selection in a way analogous to the operation of strong natural selection, for physical characteristics, they can also be bred for behavioral characteristics. For example, dogs can be bred for coat colour or size or snout length, but they can also be bred for aggressiveness or even traits as specific as shepherding ability.

The field of ethology, or the study of non-human animal behavior, has been devoted to developing a third line of evidence that natural selection contributes to behavioral traits. Non-human animal behaviour is important because, despite the apparent removal of modern human life from what evolutionary psychologists have called the Environment of Evolutionary Adaptation, evolution remains governed by the same principles in humans as it does in all other organisms. We have much to learn about those principles through studying other animals as they generally have much shorter lifespans than we do and we maintain fewer ethical restrictions in manipulating them. One of the first and most famous ethological phenomena to be documented was imprinting in ducklings. Newly hatched ducklings appear to be evolutionarily primed to form an image of and to follow the first moving object with which they come into contact. Usually, this object is their mother, and their learned association serves them immediately and well in offering access to food and protection from danger. Lorenz (1965) famously demonstrated that, if the first moving object the ducklings see is a human leg (his own), the ducklings would follow it for days as if it were their mother.

Ethologists have typically been interested in what have become known as the four 'whys' of behavior, as articulated by Tinbergen (1951), one of the founders of ethology. These issues are (1) the immediate causes of the behavior, or its eliciting factors (for the ducklings, the movement of the mother); (2) the ways in which the behavior changes with age (for the ducklings, the fact that, after a while, they stop simply following their mother); (3) the function of the behavior, or how it helps the organism to survive and reproduce (for the duck-lings, following their mother keeps them close to her, which affords protection and access to food during infancy when they are especially vulnerable); and (4) the evolutionary or phylogenetic origins of the behavior, how it might have arisen in one species and/or be related to analogous behaviors in related species (for the ducklings, do other waterfowl display similar imprinting behaviours?). Each of these levels of explanation is important and contributes to under-standing the behaviour.

Natural selection, in its most basic form, operates to bring about uniformity of species features. For example, not only is having two legs and two arms and two eyes in a single head the norm for humans, but this four-limbs-and-a-head-with-two-eyes body plan is very common throughout the animal realm. There are evolutionary mechanisms involved in individual differences and I will discuss them below, but ethologists have focused on behaviours mani-fested uniformly within species. Using the principles of stimulus–response, they have developed several concepts to explain uniform behaviour patterns in animals that they believe to be innate and to have resulted from natural selec-tion. Most of these can be considered variants of what is known as the *fixed action pattern*. This is a routinized behavioural sequence in which an animal engages automatically in response to a specific stimulus. Once the stimulus appears, the animal automatically executes the whole behavioural sequence to completion. The behaviour is thus *instinctive*, or spontaneous and unthinking, to the point that it is automatically carried out whether it serves any purpose at the time or not, even when considerable expenditure of energy is involved. Ethologists have identified many such fixed action patterns, especially though far from exclusively in birds. Birds are generally used in experiments of this kind because it is relatively easy to work with them rather than because they are considered the primary focus of interest in their own right. The idea is that the way fixed action patterns develop and are manifest in birds is typical of the ways in which these patterns develop and are manifested in many species. One such example in birds is that newly hatched chicks of many species move their beaks in particular ways, triggering the mother's regurgitating response to feed them. And, if they see egg-shaped objects near their nests, many adult waterfowl will roll the objects back into their nests, and they will persist with the rolling motions even if the objects they were rolling are removed. They will also respond more vigorously to larger egg-shaped objects than to smaller ones. Thus, they will roll large plastic eggs or eggs of other species that are larger than their own into their nests, in the process ignoring smaller real eggs that are their own.

Most scientists, including geneticists, and others working with these ideas have tended to interpret the Modern Synthesis to mean that there is a direct match between gene and trait. Thus the evidence that natural selection applies to individual behavioral and social characteristics has been interpreted as indi-cating that these traits must be genetically influenced in the same very direct way. Of course genes do not actually code for traits like behaviours, continuously varying physical characteristics like height, or even having two eyes. Genes code for proteins, which are biological building blocks for enzymes, which in turn influence cellular functions, and so on up a long chain of transactions that finally culminate in the manifestation of traits such as patterns of behaviour or height or having two eyes. But the idea of one gene = one protein, and this one protein launches a direct pathway to the trait, has long been considered established. It has been inferred to mean that, even though natural selection operates on the level of the *phenotype* or manifested trait, genetic variation is the basis of natural selection. Thus, without genetic variation, natural selection would have nothing on which to operate. The one gene – one protein idea has also been inferred to mean that gene expression is uniform with respect to timing, type, and amount of gene product. This in turn implies that mutation is the primary source of novelty on which natural selection acts, and that *heritability*, or the proportion of population variance in a trait that can be attributed to genetic influences, gives us a good indication of the extent to which genetic processes determine traits. Implicitly, this interpretation again relies on Fisher's assumptions that gene actions are independent both of each other and of the environment.

At the time the Modern Evolutionary Synthesis was developed, many considered human psychological and behavioural traits to develop completely under environmental influence, so the Modern Evolutionary Synthesis and its interpretations were considered largely irrelevant. As will be discussed in more detail in Chapter 3, however, fifty years of twin, adoption, and family studies have convinced the field of the involvement of genetic influences on human psychological function and behaviour. This has taken place within the prevailing interpretation of the Modern Evolutionary Synthesis, without drawing attention to this interpretation's reliance on the assumptions about the independence of individual gene actions. In fact, the assumption that this interpretation is correct continues to underlie the new methods developed in the last ten years to search for the specific genes involved in human psychological and behavioural traits and medical and psychiatric disorders.

Some lessons on natural selection from modern ethology

In science, things are rarely as simple as we might hope, or as our first theories propose. With respect to natural selection and evolution, some indications of the complexity of the processes have come from recent ethological studies. Though fixed action patterns on which early ethologists focused appear to be common and did provide important evidence that natural selection does operate on behaviour, the lack of adaptive function of the more extreme kinds of responses such as birds preferring to retrieve large plastic eggs to their nests over their own real eggs makes clear that most adaptive behaviour must occur with more flexibility. Among other observations supporting this, studies have shown that patterns of behaviour that had been thought to be fixed can be manipulated by changing the environmental circumstances in which the animals develop, suggesting apparently fixed action patterns may actually be much more flexible and thus operate through some more complex mechanism than strict genetic determination through natural selection of the specific pattern itself. One way this has been demonstrated has been by revealing the extreme artificiality of some of the experimental conditions in which the apparent fixation of the action patterns has been documented. This is important because it is generally thought that humans display few of these rather rigid fixed action patterns. And if even these patterns are more flexible than strict genetic determination would indicate, so must be the genetic influences on human behaviour (see Box 2.1).

Box 2.1   Behavioural flexibility

In a series of studies, David White and colleagues have developed a nice example of behavioural flexibility in cowbirds, a form of songbird that breeds *parasitically* (White, 2010). That is, cowbirds are unusual among bird species in that they do not build nests or raise their young. Instead, they lay their eggs in the nests of other bird species that have fixed action patterns to accept all egg-shaped objects in their nests and to raise all generally bird-shaped young that will accept their form of feeding. Infant cowbirds are thus reared by foster parents of species other than their own, with different songs and mate preferences. This is critically important because song preference in female songbirds in general has long been thought to be a fixed action pattern present at birth or shortly thereafter and triggered by something besides exposure to male song (e.g., King & West, 1983). This interpretation has meant that, in order to produce the next generation, female cowbirds were thought to execute inherently existing fixed action patterns of reproductive behavior, including response to specific male cowbird songs by females, regardless of their environmental exposure. Though males were known to adapt their songs to environmental exposure, males' use of song was thought to be similarly fixed and independent of experience.

Evidence for this had been provided by studies of infant cowbirds raised by humans and isolated from other cowbirds until maturity (King & West, 1983). But this is not the way cowbirds typically behave and is thus an example of an extremely artificial experimental condition. As soon as they leave their foster-parent nests, they typically locate other cowbirds and flock together with them, spending the rest of their lives in these flocks. Experiments with manipulation of social exposure provided a much more nuanced view of the triggers for reproductive behaviors. While male cowbirds do develop mature songs in isolation from other males, when they are presented with the songs of other males, they readily copy those songs. To study why this might be the case, White, King, and West (2002) housed some juvenile cowbirds with both adult males and females, and others only with adult females. Those housed with adult males could thus hear and copy the songs of other males, and those housed only with adult females could not. By the end of the one-year experiment, those raised only with females had developed more attractive songs, in the sense that females solicited copulation with them more frequently upon hearing their songs than they did with others.

But this was not the only effect. Male cowbirds typically engage in singing competitions to establish dominance hierarchies as well as using their songs to elicit female copulation solicitation displays. The male cowbirds housed only with females did not use their songs to compete with other males and they did not regularly use them to attract females. Moreover, instead of pair-bonding with individual females as cowbirds typically do, they mated promiscuously with many different females. In contrast, the young cowbird males housed with both adult males and females carried out all of these activities as cowbirds typically do. The following year, a new generation of juvenile males was housed either with adult females and males who had spent their youth with only females, or adult females and males who had spent their youth with both males and females (White, King, West, Gros-Louis, & Paphakian, 2007; White, King, West, Gros-Louis, & Paphakian, 2007). The new generation of juveniles behaved as did the males with whom they were housed, even before they had seen these adult males display those behaviours. Thus, the transmission of something that might be considered culture appeared to take place not through copying or imitation or learning, but through the environmental triggering of one of several different potential fixed action patterns.

It has long been known that juvenile male cowbirds will copy the songs of older conspecifics if they are available, indicating that male behavior is responsive to social context. The prevailing understanding, however, had been that female response to male songs is fixed. Female cowbirds display a particular posture soliciting copulation in response to male songs. Some songs elicit this display from females more successfully than do others, and researchers have observed female response to recordings of different males' songs to evaluate the attractiveness to them of the songs. As with males, when raised in social isolation, female preferences did not vary with song experience (King & West, 1983). Again as with males, however, things changed when females were reared in more social situations (King, West, & White, 2003; West, King, White, Gros-Louis, & Freed-Brown, 2006; White, et al., 2006). Introducing only females to the juvenile housing environment, broadcasting recordings of male songs before the mating season, and then broadcasting them and other songs again during the mating season demonstrated that the females produced more copulation-solicitation displays to the songs which they had heard previously than to those they had not. This suggested that the juvenile cowbirds might be copying the preferences of the adults with whom they had been raised.

It was possible to test this directly, because in addition to the copulation-solicitation posture during the mating season, in the early spring before mating season females produce a characteristic chatter vocalization in response to male songs they find attractive. Thus juvenile female cowbirds typically get a reliable indication of which males the older females find attractive. Broadcasting recordings of male songs followed by female chatter, and then later broadcasting these and other songs to the juvenile cowbirds produced more copulation-solicitation postures for the songs that had been originally paired with chatter (Freed-Brown & White, 2009). Thus female cowbirds also display variability in mating-related behaviors that depends on environmental, in particular social, circumstances.

This is important for understanding the manifestation of fixed action patterns, but relates to whether or not natural selection has acted upon them and evolution only to the extent that more copulations lead to greater reproductive suc-cess. Female cowbirds display considerable variation in egg production, ranging as much as from 0 to 35 in one six-week breeding season within and between groups (White, Gros-Louis, West, King, & Tuttle, 2010). Two behaviors of males appear to be involved. Across 17 captive flocks, the amount of song directed by males to females contributed to copulation success, but not to egg production, while the amount of song delivered by males in competition with other males contributed to egg production. The attrac-tiveness of the songs did not contribute to copulation success. Recall from above that males raised with exposure only to adult females produced especially attractive songs in the sense that they inspired females to copulate with them when they did sing to them, but that these males did not regularly sing to females. Moreover, they did not sing competitively to other males. Thus, though their songs were especially attractive, these birds with impoverished social experience should not be very reproductively effective. And, importantly, the behaviors that do contribute to reproductive success appear to be dependent on social experience. This suggests that natural selection does act on these behavior patterns, but that it does so in transaction with environmental experience, and that the behavior patterns themselves are far more flexible than had originally been thought. Again, the thought in documenting this in cowbirds is that this kind of dependence of the specific manifestation of behavior patterns on environmen-tal conditions is not unique to them but general throughout the animal realm.

A long co-existing alternative perspective on evolution

More recent ethological observations (such as those described in Box 2.1) are consistent with a perspective on evolution that provides an alternative to the specifics of the Modern Synthesis. This perspective dates back to the time of Darwin and Wallace. Recall that Darwin saw natural selection as focused on competition for survival among individuals, while Wallace saw it as focused on individual adaptation to environmental circumstances. Darwin's views on evolution were presented within the established scientific institutions of the time, while Wallace remained largely outside those institutions. As the theory of evolution became incorporated into the scientific *zeitgeist*, geneticists, who focused on presence and absence of traits, tended to take a Darwinian perspec-tive, emphasizing competition among individuals and survival of the fittest. Embryologists and evolutionary biologists, however, were more focused on developmental change, and interpreted evolution in a way more compatible with Wallace's writings. This perspective focused on evolution as acting on the traits actually expressed, the phenotypes, so that selectable variation is pheno-typic variation, regardless of whether the source of the variation is genetic or environmental (Mayr, 1963; West-Eberhard, 2005). According to this perspec-tive, selection takes place based on differential reproductive success that can also be derived environmentally; these developmental biologists stressed that it is only if the adaptations conferring differential reproductive success are

ocurring through processes involving genotypic variation that genetic inheritance will be the mode of transmission and species will evolve new genetically
influenced features.

This may sound like merely a semantic distinction, but it is not. Organisms
develop over time: none of their phenotypes springs forth in mature form from
conception, and all emerge through some kind of genetically (and environmentally!) influenced developmental programme. If phenotypes rather than
genotypes are the objects of selection, then novel phenotypes may result from
the impact on their development of new environmental conditions, as well
as through new genetic material (mutation), which has been the mechanism
assumed by most geneticists. Among other things, this alternative perspective
does a better job of explaining the high conservation of genetic material across
species with major morphological differences that the fossil records display.

This perspective can also help to explain the maintenance of individual differences within species. Darwin's focus on competition within species and survival
of the fittest tends to suggest that evolution should be constantly driving genes
for 'the fittest' to fixation, yet it is clear that, within all species, substantial
genetic variation remains. If anything, humans tend to be more genetically
similar to each other than are members of other species, even the other primates
most closely related to us. Despite this, human populations clearly vary widely,
and often to greater degrees than do other species. Moreover, most species show
developmental plasticity, and humans are certainly no exception. This suggests
that individuals within any species, including humans, must be differentially
genetically responsive to the varying environmental inputs they receive. With
respect to any one gene, these environmental inputs may include the actions of
other genes, and the gene actions may come from genes that vary within the
species or genes that are shared by all members of the species. That is, environmental and/or genetic expression states may modify the internal environments
of other genes, creating new phenotypic elements within cells. In turn, these
new phenotypic elements may provide input to higher organizational levels of
individual organisms, altering their developmental programmes so that very
different surface-levels traits emerge.

A famous example of genetic adaptation to environment during development

In 1942, the Dutch morphologist Slijper reported a two-legged goat that can
help to illustrate the processes involved. The goat was born with a congenital
defect of the forelegs. The cause of the defect was unknown, but it made the
goat's legs unable to support its weight. The goat adapted by learning to walk
and even to run on its hind legs alone. After its accidental death, Slijper dissected
it. He documented extensive differences from normal goats in the bones of
the hind legs, extensive modifications of the pelvis and thoracic skeleton,

major differences in the arrangement of small tendons in the leg muscles, and a greatly thickened and elongated gluteal tongue. The particular anatomic alterations do not matter here. What does matter is that the alterations were extensive and involved much more than simple anatomy. Slijper concluded that whatever caused the abnormality of the front legs had apparently set in motion a network of adaptive differences from the 'normal' developmental programme involving behavior, muscle, and bone. Other normally quadruped animals trained or forced to walk upright have manifested similar patterns of differences from their typical conspecifics. This has led West-Eberhard (2005) and Slijper (1942) and others to suggest that the emergence of bipedalism in humans might not have been the difficult evolutionary step involving repeated mutations, each of which determines a specific kind of alteration, that has been commonly assumed. The anatomical features allowing bipedal running in humans are very similar to those in the bipedal goat (Bramble & Lieberman, 2004). This suggests that developmental plasticity contributed to the anatomical changes that made human bipedal walking and running normal. We need to keep this in mind in studying both characteristic behavioural differences between humans and other primates and trait-like individual differences in behaviour among humans.

William Hamilton and inclusive fitness

These are not the only ways in which Darwin's original ideas of evolution have undergone expansion and modification since they were originally articulated. One of the most prominent of these modifications has been William Hamilton's idea of *inclusive fitness*.

In his doctoral dissertation, Hamilton (1964) took the position, and demonstrated mathematically, that the classical idea of fitness in the sense of evolution by selection was too narrow. Classically, evolutionary theory has been interpreted as meaning that an organism's fitness depends on the number of its own offspring it produces and supports to reproductive maturity. From this perspective, though inheritance of genetic variation makes possible the transmission of adaptive characteristics, the focus is on individual organisms as wholes. If this is the case, at least superficially there is little reason for organisms to display altruistic or cooperative behaviours. Yet many organisms, and in particular humans, do display such behaviours, ranging from the use of alarm calls to warn conspecifics of the presence of predators to the extremely cooperative activities of social insects such as bees and ants. This seeming contradiction had led to the concept of *group selection*, or the idea that selection can operate on genes in a population because those genes provide benefits to a whole group of organisms rather than specifically to individual members within the group. If so, one member of a group might limit its own reproduction in situations of, for example, restricted food supplies, in order to maximize the number of conspecifics that could survive. The only groups within the species that survive are those whose members possess such characteristics that are beneficial to their groups as wholes, and the genes contributing to these characteristics are gradually selected and eventually go to fixation.

Hamilton theorized that the focus of natural selection was therefore not on the reproductive fitness of the organism but was instead on the reproductive fitness of the individual gene. Thus, natural selection can favour any characteristic that causes the organism's genes to be passed on, whether or not this takes place through the organism's own reproduction. This can work to the benefit of indvidual genes because biological relatives – kin – share many of the genes on which conspecifics can vary, and the closer the kinship, the more genes they share. This suggests that, parental care, or nurturance of an organism's own offspring, is just a special case of fostering the reproduction of more copies of many of the very genes the organism carries itself. And any activity that helps any biological relative, be it brother, sister, niece, nephew, or whatever, to survive and reproduce has similar consequences for reproductive success of the genes involved. It was this broader conception of evolutionary fitness to which Hamilton applied his term *inclusive fitness*.

Hamilton's idea revolutionized the concept of evolution for two reasons. First, it extended the range of characteristics on which natural selection might act to include the effects of organisms' actions on the reproductive success of their biological relatives. But because, with the exception of monozygotic or identical twins or asexual reproduction, even biological relatives do not share all of their genes, the beneficial effects of these actions on behalf of kin to any organism's own genes are less than the beneficial effects of actions on its own behalf. This means that, to assess their relevance to natural selection in the kinds of mathematical models typically used, the effects of actions on behalf of kin must be weighted by the degree of genetic relationship. Thus, for example, actions on behalf of full siblings, with whom an individual shares on average 50 per cent of the genes that vary within a species, need to be weighted by 0.5, and those on behalf of grand-offspring, with whom an individual shares 25 per cent of the genes that vary within a species, have to be weighted by 0.25.

The second reason that Hamilton's theory revolutionized the concept of evolution was that it introduced the idea of focusing evolution at the level of the gene. Though recognizing that genes do not think or take any kind of deliberate action, biologists conceptualized this by thinking of what a gene would 'do' to maintain the maximum number of copies of itself in the environment. The classical understanding of reproductive fitness implies the existence of genes that generate activities in the individual organism that create the maximum number of viable offspring, meaning survival to reproductive age and beyond and creation of many mating opportunities. Inclusive fitness, however, required the addition of activities that help the survival and reproduction of other already existing individuals that carry more copies of the gene. In models, because of the weighting by degree of genetic relationship, primary focus of evolutionary fitness remains on survival and direct reproduction, but the activities on behalf of others are also important.

The idea of inclusive fitness was important in helping biologists to explain the apparent evolution of altruistic behaviours, or those in which an organism incurs costs to itself in order to benefit conspecifics. For example, even a warning call about the presence of a predator is a potentially costly act to the caller because it may draw the predator's attention, thus increasing the risk that the caller becomes the predator's next meal. If those hearing the call, however, are close kin to the caller, this could be a good strategy from the gene's perspective of maintaining as many copies of itself as possible. The idea of the gene's perspective, however, has a limitation that is more apparent now than it was when Hamilton theorized about inclusive fitness, due to our vastly increased knowledge of the genome since the 1960s.

Most species share most of their genes with many other species. For example, humans share something on the order of 98 per cent of their genes (figures vary) with chimpanzees, our nearest living relatives, and on the order of 50 per cent of their genes with species as distant as worms and bacteria. The genes on which humans vary are some 0.1 per cent of the total that humans carry. Given this, and retaining the inaccurate but nonetheless helpful metaphor of genes taking deliberate actions to maintain the maximum possible number of copies of themselves, genetic relatedness can only really matter if some genes take this assignment much more seriously than do others because when, for example, a cat eats a mouse, the cat eliminates many copies of genes it carries itself, in particular the vast majority it shares with the mouse. Moreover, if this action really takes place at the level of the gene, there is no need to focus on any one particular species. If, for example, an individual who warns conspecifics of a predator does happen to become the predator's next meal, most of its genes are preserved in the body of the predator anyway. I have not seen this addressed, however, in the literature.

'Outcomes' of evolution

With the general acceptance among biologists of evolutionary theory, attention had turned to examining and testing ideas about its consequences. One way in which these consequences have been discussed is by classifying the products of evolution. For example, Tooby and Cosmides (1990) have described four products of the evolutionary process: *adaptations*, *byproducts*, *exaptations*, and *noise*. These categories are important because many consistent features of human behaviour could fall into one or another. Adaptations are inherited characteristics that develop reliably and normally in all members of a species, that emerged through natural selection and that help to solve a particular problem of survival or reproduction. An adaptation does not have to be present at birth and many develop well after birth. The placenta in mammals is an example of an adaptation, as are breasts in women. Importantly, adaptations are rarely optimal mechanisms for their adaptive purpose. Natural selection does not work by designing adaptations from scratch. Rather, they are pieced together from existing features in ways that are often clumsy at best and can even be downright maladaptive for other purposes (Marcus, 2008). For example, the human spinal column manages to support our weight upright, poised at the top of two legs, with two more limbs that project outward from this column and generate their own important forces of motion, but only at the cost of, for many people, painful back pain and resulting restricted range of motion. From a purely engineering perspective, it would have made more sense for us to have four legs and two arms, to provide greater support for the spinal column and torso from which the arms project, but our bodily structure evolved from the structures of four-legged creatures that did not walk upright. In too many ways, we are like Slijper's (1942) goat. Our retinas, the light-sensitive parts of our eyes, face the backs of our heads rather than the fronts. This causes a blind spot in each eye. And in males, instead of connecting the testis directly to the penis as would make most sense, the tubing that runs from the testis to the urethra loops around and turns 180 degrees to circle back to the penis, creating much greater opportunity for clogging and severance along the way than would be optimal.

Byproducts are characteristics that do not increase survival or reproductive fitness themselves, but are associated with characteristics that do. This is generally because they are the results of characteristics that are adaptive. For example, the human navel is a byproduct of the umbilical cord, which is an adaptation. The belly-button has no function of its own, but results from the vital existence of the umbilical cord in the prenatal period. In contrast, exaptations are characteristics that have existed for long periods of evolutionary time, but are, at some point, co-opted for some other survival or reproductive function. The original characteristic may be an adaptation in its own right, or it may be a byproduct of an adaptive function. The exaptation also may or may not continue to undergo natural selection in its own right. The bird feather is generally considered to be an exaptation of a characteristic that evolved for heat regulation but was co-opted for flight, and underwent further natural selection in the process. The practice by subdominant wolves of licking the mouths of dominant wolves to signal submissiveness is considered to be a direct exaptation of the practice by wolf pups of licking their mothers' faces to stimulate them to regurgitate food for the pups. The classification of characteristics into these categories requires considerable knowledge of their function and evolutionary history and even subjective judgement, especially for exaptations. But the concept of exaptation represents one of the primary ways in which evolution likely proceeds, and exaptations are capable of generating many of the less than optimal characteristics such as our upright posture on a base of two legs and retinas oriented towards the backs rather than fronts of our heads.

Noise is the fourth product of evolution. Noise refers to individual differences among members of a species for which there is no apparent reason. It may arise through changes in the cell genotype due to DNA copying errors during division either in germ or somatic cells. In germ cells, such mutations will end up contributing to all the cells in the body of the resulting new offspring if the germ cells are fertilized. In somatic cells, such mutations will affect only the lineage of the cell in which they occur, though of course there could be consequences of the somatic mutation to the rest of the body. For example, somatic mutation is a common source of cancer. Noise may also arise through accidental damage to existing cells such as may occur through exposure to radiation that may or may not involve DNA. It may also arise through developmental sequelae of the sort that occurred with van Slijper's goat or through environmental exposure, including experience of accidental injury and disease. Some of the random effects of noise are relatively beneficial or harmful to survival and/or reproduction. When this is the case and genes are involved in their emergence, they may be passed to the next generation and subject to natural selection, gradually either increasing in population frequency or dying out, depending on the qualities of their effects. When the random effects are neutral, they may remain in the population for extended periods of time.

Specific aspects of selection that maintain genetic variation

Taken at face value, the process of natural selection suggests that, over time, genetic variation within a species should be reduced, and eventually even eliminated, as genes that confer greater reproductive success become more frequent and those that confer poorer reproductive success are gradually eliminated. This is not, however, what seems to happen. Genetic variation in humans is lower than in many other species, despite our species being generally more recent in emergence. Moreover, it is generally believed that the human species *homo sapiens sapiens* evolved in Africa, and gradually moved from there to inhabit the rest of the earth. Despite being the descendants of the oldest human groups, indigenous Africans display more genetic variation than do indigenous populations in other, more recently inhabited, areas. Even in the face of long-term artificial selection for specific traits, there can remain substantial genetic variation in the selected traits sufficient to re-generate levels of observed variation apparently equivalent to the original (Hill, 2005). Several mechanisms through which this genetic variation remains have been identified, but it is clear that we have not yet identified all of them. Attempts to understand how these mechanisms contribute to individual differences in psychological traits such as personality and intelligence (e.g., Penke, Denissen, & Miller, 2007) and to vulnerability to medical conditions (e.g., Dudley, et al., 2012) comprise an active area of current research.

The first of these mechanisms reflects the straightforward fact that environments do not remain completely static over time. Characteristics that foster reproductive success in one generation may not do so in the next due to environmental changes. As long as the environment changes a little more rapidly than genetic variation can be stripped from the population through natural selection, genetic variation will remain. Relatedly, 'the environment' may never be completely uniform at any point in time in any meaningful way. For example, it may be slightly warmer and drier in one part of a population's ecological niche than in another, and plants may differ in their ability to adapt to that condition. Those seeds that adapt better to that condition and happen to blow into it will be more reproductively successful than their sister seeds that blow into the other area, and vice versa for the seeds that adapt better to the cooler and wetter area. Because the seeds blow around the whole area and the conditions and their adaptations to those conditions vary, their genetic variation in adaptability will remain. This is known as *balancing selection*.

It is not only the environment that can change, of course. Mutations in the genotypes of individual members of species occur regularly. Some, even most, of these have no effect on survival or reproductive fitness and thus may be transmitted from one generation to another and maintained in the population. This is called *selective neutrality*. Other mutations are harmful to survival or reproductive fitness, but only mildly so. Thus, they are selected against, but it takes a long time for them to be eliminated from the population. In the meantime, for every such mutation that drops from the population, another may occur, resulting in a rather stable balance between the force of natural selection on these mutations and the rate of occurrence of new mutations. This is known as *mutation-selection balance*, and results in maintenance in the population of a certain 'load' of mildly deleterious genetic alleles, some of which can even end up coming in handy following later environmental changes.

Genetic variation may also be maintained through *antagonistic selection*. Individual genes may be involved in more than one trait. This is called *pleiotropy*. Selection is antagonistic when the manner in which a particular gene is involved in traits is beneficial to survival and/or reproductive fitness with respect to one trait, or at one point in the lifespan, but harmful with respect to another. Many of the traits for which this kind of selection appears to apply involve increased reproductive fitness during young adulthood that is associated with the development of health problems and increased mortality later in life. For example, high levels of testosterone in males have been associated with enhanced physical development and behavioural vigour, and the attainment of social dominance and mating success in young and middle adulthood, but also with compromised immune function (Folstad & Karter, 1992) that can contribute to increased risk of disease in old age and premature mortality (Adams, Sueta, Gheorghiade, Schwartz, Koch, & Uretsky, 1999). In fact, antagonistic selection is one of the primary theories offered to explain the processes of ageing and senescence (Kirkwood, 2000; 2005). Selection can also be antagonistic when genes contribute to traits that foster survival and/or reproductive fitness in some members of a species but not others, due to other genetically influenced characteristics of those members. For example, genes may contribute to fitness when carried in one sex but harm fitness when carried in the other sex (Foerster, Coulson, Sheldon, Pemberton, Clutton-Brock, & Kruuk, 2007). The fact that fathers pass these genes to their daughters as well as their sons keeps the versions of these genes from becoming dominant in the population.

Another mechanism for maintaining genetic variation is *frequency-dependent selection*. When this takes place, the relative advantage of one genetic variant over another for survival and/or reproductive fitness is dependent on their frequencies in the population. This is usually because the rarer variant confers some appearance novelty that offers an advantage in avoiding predation or attracting mates, or both. Thus, those carrying it are relatively reproductively successful compared to those carrying the more frequent variant. This causes its prevalence to increase. If it eclipses the frequency of the other variant, so that the other variant in turn becomes the rare variant, then the situation is reversed and the reproductive advantage shifts to the other variant. The frequencies may oscillate over time, or they may stabilize after some period of oscillation. Colouration pattern in guppies is an example of this (Olendorf, Rodd, Punzalan, Houde, Hurt, Reznick, et al., 2006).

Sexual selection

The concept of sexual selection dates back to Darwin's earliest (1859) writings on the subject of evolution. It refers to the operation of evolutionary selection forces on physical and behavioural traits and social dynamics associated with mate choice and competition for mates. Despite Darwin's (1871) clear articulation of the reasons for distinguishing sexual from natural selection and of the principles under which it operates, sexual selection did not receive serious attention as an evolutionary pressure until the second half of the 20th century (Cronin, 1991). During that period, however, the importance of its role was established firmly (Andersson, 1994; West-Eberhard, 1983). Sexual selection involves two major components of socially oriented behaviour: *intersexual choice* of mates, or the basis in each sex for choice of mates from the other, and *intrasexual competition* over mates, or competition between members of one sex for a small pool of especially attractive members of the other sex. Together these contribute to the maintenance of sexual reproduction and *sexual dimorphism*, or differences in morphology and behaviour between the sexes. These components, in different ways, both arise from sex differences in *parental investment,* or the degree to which parents invest of themselves in their offspring. The conceptual development of our understanding of this is owed largely to Trivers (1972) and Williams (1966; 1975).

In many, if not most, species of animals, there is some sex difference in parental investment, and in most species the female invests more than the male.

Often, this is because she supports the offspring with her own body until it (or they) is (are) ready to be born. For example, in mammals, the female carries the offspring inside her own body. Female birds, on the other hand, expel the immature offspring from their bodies in the form of eggs encased in shells, but then have the major if not sole responsibility for incubating them until they are ready to be hatched, leaving the females dependent on males for provisioning during that period. In addition to this prenatal support, females in many species often provide primary support to offspring after birth as well: in mammals through lactation and protection against predators. Williams (1966) suggested that this difference in the cost to the individual of reproduction leaves males more ready to engage in reproductive behaviour than females. Trivers (1972) extended this idea to suggest that individuals devote resources to reproduction through a combination of mating efforts (in the form of searching for mates and activities intended to attract them), parental investment, and sometimes *nepotism* (assisting the survival and/or reproductive activities of kin). Trivers proposed that parental investment draws the most individual resources, and the reproductive activity level of the sex that invests the most in offspring places an upper bound on the reproductive activity level of the sex that invests the least. The result is that, in the lower-investing sex, reproductive success is more dependent on the number of mates that can be found than on the survival and well-being of individual offspring. In contrast, the reproductive success of the higher-investing sex is more strongly influenced by investment in offspring than in multiple matings. This leads, in general, to greater competition among males for access to female mating partners, and to greater choosiness for the 'best' mates among females.

There are many exceptions to the generality that there is greater competition among males than among females, and greater mate choosiness among females. These exceptions tend to occur in species in which the biological sex roles described above are reversed: that is, males incubate the fertilized eggs and/or provide the majority of parental care. For example, in many species of pipe-fish and seahorse, females transfer fertilized eggs into pouches on the males' bodies, and the males carry them until gestation. In the red-necked phalarope, a shorebird, males build the nests and incubate the eggs. The fledglings fend for themselves after hatching. In these species, there is greater competition among females than among males (Reynolds, 1987; Wilson, Ahnesjo, Vincent, & Meyer, 2003), and females in such species may show other characteristics that are more commonly associated with males, such as larger size, brighter plumage, higher levels of aggression, and mate guarding. These reversals in the more common pattern provide evidence for the behaviours as consequences of the biological reproductive patterns. This leads to speculation that less sex-differentiated social roles in humans might also be associated with less sex-differentiated mate choice patterns.

In the more common biological pattern and clearly in humans, once an egg is fertilized and the reproductive cycle begins, the mother of that zygote is effectively removed from the reproductively active population until the zygote either dies or has been parented to the point of bodily (if not economic) self-sufficiency. The father, however, is generally biologically (if not also socially) immediately free to re-enter the reproductively active population. This makes it possible in concept for males to monopolize many females, if they can provide whatever resource support is needed by the females during their periods of gestation and postnatal parental care. The requirement for males to provide whatever support is needed by females means that males can only actually monopolize many females if the females require very little support, or if at least some males can accumulate both substantial resources and sexually receptive females within territories they can control. There is substantial evidence from many species that, when resources are concentrated in territories in this way, males compete with each other for strong territorial positions, and *polygyny*, or multiple female mating partners for some males and very few or no mating partners for other males may result. Where resources are more dispersed over wider spaces and territorial control is less possible, biparental care is more common, and there is less male–male competition (Geary, 2010). Competition among males can thus drive evolutionary change because those males of the species that are most successful in competing with their conspecifics end up also being more reproductively successful, and their genetically influenced characteristics that fostered their competitive success become more common in the population.

Male competition as a common feature in nature, whatever its role in evolution, seems intuitively reasonable because it is so visible in the natural world. Thus, once sexual selection was considered seriously by naturalists and evolutionary biologists, male–male competition as one of its mechanisms was accepted relatively readily (Cronin, 1991) and traces of it were seen in human activities ranging from prowess in battle and sports to guitar-playing in rock bands. Darwin's (1871) proposal that female choice was also an important mechanism required more development. The way in which this development proceeded once again hearkens back to the early debates over evolution between Darwin and Wallace. Darwin (1871) emphasized the role of male appearance in female choice (now often termed 'good taste'), while Wallace focused more on male ability to provide resources and/or parental support (now often termed 'good genes'; Wallace, 1892). Because Darwin was the more established scientist, the good taste explanation tended to dominate discussion during at least the first half of the twentieth century.

Sexual selection in action

One of Darwin's (1871) most important insights was that many physical differences between males and females cannot reasonably be attributed to natural selection as he had defined it in 1859. In particular, the bright and often precariously large plumage of males in many species of birds, the extremely large antlers of male deer, the heavy manes of male lions, and prominent male features in many other species likely make life harder for their bearers by increasing the risk of predation, the difficulty of carrying out predatory activities, and/or the metabolic costs of maintenance. Classically, we would expect natural selection to eliminate such expensive traits unless some other process were also operating. Darwin argued that these traits were maintained because females preferred the appearance of males with larger and more flamboyant versions of these traits, thus making their bearers more reproductively successful and leading to the evolution of even greater flamboyance in the traits over time. The preference might originally develop from a female sensory bias for certain colour patterns that made it easier to locate food or males against commonly occurring background features.

When (or if) good taste, or simple female preference for the appearance of a trait, is the source of sexual selection, there may be no advantage to either the females or their offspring from mating with males with more flamboyant versions of the trait. But flamboyant traits that are expensive to maintain because they make survival more precarious may attract females for reasons other than simple appearance. The fact that an individual male is able to maintain a particularly flamboyant version of a trait may signal to females that this male carries genetic variants that are especially robust to environmental stresses such as parasites or infection or is particularly healthy and thus better able to provide paternal support. If this is the source of sexual selection, then both the female herself and her offspring may benefit from mating with such a male. When (if) sexual selection operates in this manner, it should be a more potent evolutionary force than sexual selection that operates only through female preference for appearance. It is also more likely that strength of female preference for the flamboyant trait may become genetically linked to the flamboyance of the trait in males, further increasing the potency of sexual selection. Empirical studies that can isolate the reasons for female preference for male appearance are difficult to design. In general, however, it is relatively easy to develop evidence that the quality of sexually attractive flamboyant traits is a good indicator of male health, and that females and their offspring benefit from matings based on the condition of these traits. For example, Zuk, Johnsen, and Maclarty (1995) infected a group of male wild chickens with a parasitic worm and compared their growth and later reproductive success with that of an uninfected group. The infected males grew more slowly and their combs, a sexually selected characteristic, were smaller and duller, but many other physical characteristics did not differ between the groups. Females preferred the uninfected males as mating partners 2:1, and their choice was related to comb length and not to other physical characteristics. In humans, Miller (2000) has made the case that much of human nature, and intelligence in particular, has been shaped by sexual seletion.

Box 2.2   Sexual selection in the wild

Female preference for appearance, whether as indication of good genes or not, may be linked with physical features in males that are related to male–male competition. Males in many species are not only often well-ornamented, they are also often larger than females and have features such as horns or spines that can be used as weapons in intraspecies competition for territory, social dominance, resources, or access to females. Similarly, males may compete with each other in ways that do not involve actual combat, and females may be responsive to these behavioural displays. A classic example of this occurs in the bowerbird (Gilliard, 1969). Male bowerbirds build elaborate structures in which to court females from twigs and leaves, decorating them with feathers, flowers, shells, bones, almost anything they can find. These structures are not nests; the bowerbirds do not raise their young in them. They are used only to attract females to visit and mate. Numbers of female visitors to the bowers are related to their quality in the form of overall structural symmetry, their stability and density as reflected in the number of sticks used, whether they are decorated with unusual objects such as rare flowers or snail shells, and the quality of their 'painting,' which is accomplished by males chewing on vegetation and using the resulting saliva–vegetation mixture to cover the interior walls of the bowers (Borgia, 1985). Moreover, the males that build the most elaborate bowers sire the vast majority of the offspring, as demonstrated by DNA fingerprinting (Reynolds, Dryer, Bollback, Uly, Patricelli, Robson, et al., 2007).

But males actively compete with each other over resources for bower-building. They develop skill in bower-building and maintenance through both experience and social learning, but also through social dominance (Borgia & Wingfield, 1991). Social dominance is determined by threat displays at communal feeding sites, which in turn contribute to raids on others' bowers to damage them and steal their decorations. These raids are almost always conducted when the builders are away. Borgia (1985) found that, while bowers of socially dominant males were just as likely to be raided as those of less dominant males, the raids were shorter in duration and thus less damaging.

In the bowerbird, sexual selection has apparently resulted in both large sex differences in behaviour (females do not build bowers at all, but rather simply visit them) and very elaborate competitively oriented behaviours in males that are not centred primarily around physical prowess but rather around construction skill and strategic raiding. These birds have larger brains than do other birds that live in similar habitats but do not build bowers (Madden, 2001), and, within the family of bower-building species, brain cerebella size is related to complexity of bowers (Day, Westcott, & Olster, 2005). As the cerebellum appears to be important in the social learning process young bowerbirds use to develop skill in building bowers (Leggio, Molinari, Neri, Graziano, Mandolesi, & Petrosini, 2000), this suggests that sexual selection can affect cognitive and behavioural traits in the same ways as it affects physical traits, when these cognitive traits are associated with reproductive success. Miller (2000) has treated this topic with respect to humans in detail.

In this discussion of sexual selection, I have focused on competition among males for social, material, and reproductive resources, and on female choice of mating partners. This is not meant to imply that females do not compete among themselves for resources as well, nor is it meant to imply that males do not exert choice in their mating relationships.

Speciation

Ultimately, some of the strongest evidence for the evolutionary processes of natural and sexual selection come from observations that *speciation*, or the divergence of one species from another, has taken place. Understanding this process is important to understanding the development of individual differences because at bottom they are one and the same: that is, speciation is the culmination of the development of differences between two or more groups of individuals that are systematic and extensive enough that the two groups must be considered separate species. Discussing this process, or at least what we know about it at this time, requires first a definition of *species*. Developing a rigorous definition has proven to be surprisingly difficult, particularly for organisms that do not reproduce sexually. Many, though definitely not all, biologists, however, accept some version of Mayr's (1942, 1999) definition that species consist of natural populations that can interbreed with each other, and that are reproductively isolated from other natural populations. This definition clearly applies only to sexually reproducing species, but, as humans are the focus of this book, this is not a limitation for purposes of this discussion. Even within such organisms, however, it is often difficult to classify groups as species because biologists often do not know whether morphologically similar species that live in different geographic areas may be capable of interbreeding. Moreover, the degree to which matings are successful can vary with environmental conditions. And sometimes members of groups living geographically adjacent to each other can interbreed, but members of groups not living adjacent to each other cannot, suggesting that both criteria may be continuous rather than discrete. In the extreme, such groups of organisms can form *ring species*. For example, *ensatina* salamanders in California apparently originated in northern California, and expanded their habitat southward along two mountain ranges that are separated by California's Central Valley. The two lineages mate freely within each mountain range and their habitats overlap in southern California, where their members differ in appearance and generally fail to interbreed (Irwin, Irwin, & Price, 2001). Ring species have been instrumental in helping biologists articulate the processes involved in speciation.

The idea that members of species can interbreed with each other implies that they are, at least within sex, alike in some fundamental genetic sense. That is, basically any two members of the opposite sex within that species share enough genes that a random half of the genes on each chromosome of one of them can be combined with a random half of the genes on each chromosome on the other one to form a new member of the same species. Yet natural selection emphasizes the individual differences among the species members and any underlying genetic differences that contribute to them because it is on these individual differences that it acts to optimise adaptation to environmental conditions. Moreover, speciation often takes place when environmental circumstances diverge enough that the characteristics for optimizing adaptation to one set of circumstances differ so much from the characteristics optimizing adaptation to the other set of circumstances that this halving-and-matching process is no longer viable. This implies the direct involvement of environment in triggering genetic diversity. Several kinds of speciation have been identified.

Allopatric speciation takes place when a population splits into two geographically isolated groups due to geological changes such as volcanic eruptions or floods or to social changes such as emigration. The isolated groups then diverge genetically and/or in observable characteristics as natural selection acts on their adaptations to their newly differing circumstances. They also diverge genetically through random differences in gene frequencies at the time the groups diverge that become accentuated over time due to random mating and genetic mutation. This kind of speciation is often the explanation for species unique to islands. In contrast, speciation can be *parapatric* when populations are only partly separated, so that individuals from each group may come into contact occasionally, but the products of cross-group matings show reduced fitness. This is the kind of speciation usually involved in the emergence of ring species. Speciation can also be *sympatric* when a species diverges while inhabiting the same general area. This may take place, for example, when members of insect species become dependent on different plants. It is more difficult, however, to be sure that this is the process through which species have differentiated. Both parapatric and sympatric speciation, in which reproductive isolation is incomplete, are dependent on the existence of *reinforcement*, or the Wallace Effect. The process of speciation is reinforced when initially lower fitness of offspring from cross-group matings causes those matings to be reduced in frequency. It has a direct analogue commonly discussed in humans in the form of assortative mating, or the tendency for people to select their mates systematically with respect to certain traits. For example, spousal correlations for IQ commonly run on the order of 0.4. This has the effect of increasing overall population diversity for genetic variants contributing to IQ.

Whatever the type, speciation often involves some kind of action on the parts of individual organisms within the original single population. A population could be divided into two groups by a sudden event such as a flood that divides a habitat in two in a way that does not involve action by any individual members of that population, but migration into new territory is likely a more common reason for the division. When migration is the reason, some members of the group migrate and some do not. Because the action of migration is undertaken voluntarily at some level, it is possible that the group members who migrate differ in some way from those that do not, and that natural selection can operate on those differences. To the extent that these differences contribute to better adaptation to the new environment, they will accelerate the process of speciation. Importantly, circumstances in the new environment may trigger expression of genetic variance that lay dormant in the old environment, offering new opportunities for both environmental adaptation and the operation of natural selection. This can act to accelerate the process of speciation. This is one of the most important ways in which speciation is closely bound together with developmental processes.

Coevolution

Coevolution is naturally selected change in a biological organism triggered by change in some biologically oriented environmental circumstance. In biology, the term is often used to refer to situations where the environmental circumstance is itself another biological organism. In such situations, each organism in the coevolutionary relationship exerts selective pressure on the other, so that they affect each other's evolution. One common example of this kind of coevolution is hummingbirds and the flowers that they pollinate and from which they feed. The flowers have nectar that provides appropriate nutrition to the hummingbirds, in a shape that fits their bills and a colour suited to their vision. Such a situation is mutualistic: both organisms benefit from it. But sometimes the coevolutionary relationship is antagonistic. Often predator–prey relationships take this form. For example, rough-skinned newts have a powerful neurotoxin in their skin. The neurotoxin reached its present level of potency through an evolutionary arms race in which garter snakes that prey upon them developed resistance to prior levels of the toxin, spurring development of increasingly potent levels of the toxin in the newts. Sometimes the relationship is detrimental for one member but enhancing for the other. This is typical of virus–host relationships. For example, human immune responses have evolved to fight off the effects of viruses such as colds and flu's, and in response the viruses have evolved greater potency to infect us. The extent to which they do so, however, is limited: it is not in their evolutionary 'interest' to become so potent as to kill us. They thrive best when we are just sick enough to keep on going while coughing and sneezing over everyone around us.

Within human genetics, anthropology, and other human social sciences, *coevolution* generally takes on a more specialized meaning that reflects the importance of culture in the human environment. In these areas of science, *coevolution* refers to transactions between genetic and cultural influences that result in transmission of culturally influenced behaviours and attitudes from generation to generation in ways on which natural selection can act (Cavalli-Sforza & Feldman, 1981; Durham, 1979). Culture is a broad term, used in many different ways, but the sense in which it is used for purposes of thinking about coevolution is that it is the body of information about their environment that individuals acquire through social learning processes such as teaching and imitation (Richerson, Boyd, & Henrich, 2010). Much of this information is transmitted from one generation to another with sufficiently high fidelity that culture can be considered to be passed from one generation to the next to an extent generally similar to the genetic transmission of traits (Henrich & Boyd, 2002). That is, cultural information undergoes changes with time, but much of it also remains very similar over long periods of time.

Two characteristics of this form of coevolution are important. First, it involves natural selection of genetic variation contributing to better cultural adaptation. That is, genetic variation contributes to ability to adapt to the cultural environment, and those who adapt better to the culture are more reproductively successful within it. Second, the genetic variants that contribute to better adaptation also influence the individuals who carry them to seek environmental circumstances that will enhance their ability to adapt (Johnson, 2007). This process is facilitated because parents transmit both genetic and cultural influences to their biological children. Though I have focused this definition of coevolution on culture, the underlying idea of individual selection of 'comfortable' environmental niches does not limit this form of coevolution to humans. Coevolution is generally involved in at least the initial stages of all forms of speciation that involve some level of behavioural control on the parts of individuals because most behavioural choices involve genetic influence to some degree.

In humans, lactose tolerance is one of the classic examples of coevolution. Like most mammals, in many humans ability to metabolize the lactose sugars in dairy products drops off rapidly around the age at which weaning typically occurs. After this time, consumption of dairy products causes abdominal discomfort and flatulence. Some humans, however, carry a genetic mutation in chromosome 2 that makes it possible for them to continue to consume dairy products comfortably throughout their lives. This mutation, and the lactose tolerance it makes possible, is particularly common in northern European and East African populations that have historically relied on dairy cattle as a primary source of food. Relevant mutations appear to have arisen independently and recently from an evolutionary perspective in several geographic regions (Enattah, Sahi, Savilahti, Terwilliger, Peltonen, & Jarvela, 2002). At least one mutation is dominant, so that only one copy is needed to confer lactose tolerance. This would have sped up the process of making lactose tolerance common in that population.

Neolithic hunter-gatherer populations were not lactose tolerant (Burger, Kirchner, Bramanti, Haak, & Thomas, 2007), nor do current hunter-gatherer populations appear to be (Malmstrom, et al., 2010). The ability to digest lactose and thus to consume dairy products comfortably into adulthood would have been useful to humans only after the domestication of animals, primarily cattle, sheep, and goats, that could provide consistent sources of milk. The oldest genetic mutations associated with lactose tolerance appear to have reached significant frequencies only in the last 10,000 years or so (Coelho, Luiselli, Bertorelle, Lopes, Seixas, Destro-Bisol, et al., 2002), and to have been subject to strong recent natural selection (Bersaglieri, Sabeti, Patterson, Vanderploeg, Schaffner, Drake, et al., 2004). This suggests that these genetic variants arose and were naturally selected during the period in which domestic relationships with milk-producing animals were established. The several genetic variants conferring lactose tolerance that have been identified apparently spread in frequency at different rates across different geographic regions. In general, lactose tolerance is common in northern but not southern Europe, North and East Africa, and the Mongolian steppes, and is particularly rare in Asia.

Of course humans do not select the cultures in which they are born. But, within any population, culture is not uniform in all respects and generally contains cultural subgroups or niches. Most individuals do have some opportunity to select among these niches. Though lactose tolerance is offered as a classic example of coevolution because it is one of the very few for which we have clear data about the genetic sources of the tolerance and can track their association with cultural occupation and dietary practices, we should not expect that it is in any way unique. Rather, because subcultures are pervasive, most humans do have opportunities to select among them, and most human psychological characteristics show genetic influences, we should expect coevolution to be common. The next chapter turns to the topics of human brain structure and function, and the means through which we understand that human psychological characteristics show genetic influence. We will return to the theme of coevolution many times throughout the book.

Further reading

Geary, D. C. (2010). *Male, Female: The Evolution of Human Sex Differences*, 2nd ed. Washington, DC: American Psychological Association.

Hamilton, W. D. (1964). The genetical evolution of social behaviour I and II. *Journal of Theoretical Biology, 7*, 1–52.

Hill, W. G. (2005). A century of corn selection. *Science, 30*, 683–684.

Johnson, W. (2007). Genetic and environmental influences on behavior: Capturing all the interplay. *Psychological Review, 114*, 423–440.

Marcus, G. (2008). *Kluge*. Boston, MA: Houghton Mifflin.

Mayr, E. (1942, 1999). *Systematics and the Origin of Species, from the Viewpoint of a Zoologist*. Cambridge, MA: First Harvard University Press.

Miller, G. (2000). *The Mating Mind: How Sexual Choice Shaped the Evolution of Human Nature*. London: Heinemann.

Richerson, P. J., Boyd, R., & Henrich, J. (2010). Gene-culture coevolution in the age of genomics. *Proceedings of the National Academy of Sciences of the United States of America, 107*, 8985–8992.

Tinbergen, N. (1951). *The Study of Instinct*. New York: Oxford University Press.

West-Eberhard, M. J. (2005). Developmental plasticity and the origin of individual differences. *Proceedings of the National Academy of Sciences, 102*, Supp. 1, 6543–6549.

Brain Neuroanatomy and Genetics

The adult human brain weighs about 1.5 kg. It has an average volume of around 1,260 cubic centimetres in men and 1,130 cubic centimetres in women. There are large individual differences in both weight and volume, but, adjusted for body size or body surface area, men's brains are still perhaps 7 per cent heavier on average than women's (Cosgrove, Mazure, & Staley, 2007). This sex difference does not correlate in any straightforward way with finer measures of brain tissue nor with measures of cognitive performance. Brain tissue is very soft and cannot support even its own weight; likely as an evolutionary result, it floats in cerebrospinal fluid, which is a colourless bodily fluid that occupies some of the space between the brain itself and the skull, provides both physical and immunological protection to the brain, and helps to support the brain's weight. This fluid support reduces pressure on the brain's base and the shock to the central nervous system that could be produced by sudden head movement. In addition, the skull consists of particularly rigid bone structure, making it one of the least deformable objects found in nature. It requires a force of about 1 ton to reduce the diameter of the skull by 1 cm (Holbourn, 1943).

Brain and body metabolics

At about 1.5 kg., the adult human brain makes up around 2 per cent of body weight, but it consumes as much as 20 per cent of the energy used by the body, more than any other single organ. It is thus a very expensive organ to develop and maintain. Throughout the animal realm, many body features are associated with body weight, including bodily power consumption, metabolic rates, time to sexual maturity, lifespan, and brain weight. The association has a logarithmic form, so that the logarithm of the body feature is equal to some constant times the logarithm of body weight, plus some constant (Allman, 2000). The brains of primates are heavier, relative to body weight, than those of other species, though they scale with body weight in much the same way. The result is that primate brains tend to be about 2.3 times larger than those of other animals of the same body weight. Bodily power consumption increases with body weight in the animal realm at about the same rate as brain weight, primarily because of the large energy demands of the brain.

Among primates, the association between log of body weight and log of brain weight is not completely uniform. That is, among different primate species with similar body weights, there is still considerable variation in brain weight (Allman, 2000). For example, chimpanzees weigh about the same as humans on average, but the human brain is about three times the weight of the chimpanzee brain. This sounds on the surface like a huge deviation from the claimed logarithmic association, but the logarithm of 3 is about 1.1, so, while the deviation is certainly important, it is not actually particularly large. In general, among primates, those that eat mainly fruits tend to have larger brains than those that eat mainly leaves. This is true of other animals as well. For example, parrots, who consume mostly fruits and nuts, have larger brains than do other birds that do not rely on fruits (Allman, 2000). This is thought to be because consumption of fruit requires greater planning than consumption of leaves. Fruit trees are generally widely dispersed and bear at different times, requiring animals that rely on their consumption to remember their location and the timing of their availability. In addition, fruit is particularly easy to digest and highly nutritious, making it attractive to many species and increasing competition for it.

The association between brain size and fruit consumption appears to be no evolutionary accident at a broader level as well. There is an association in most animals between brain and gut, which begins with spatial position. That is, the brain is generally located near the entrance to the gut (Allman, 2000), with the brain being just above the mouth in most vertebrates. In addition, there are several systems of genes that contribute to development of both brain and gut in the model organisms embryologists use to understand the mechanisms of development (including in humans). For example, the gene *BF1* regulates forebrain size and also regulates formation of the gut. Aiello and Wheeler (1995) noted that, in primate species, digestive system size is negatively correlated with brain size, and that digestive system size is highly correlated with reliance on high-quality food that is easy to digest. Because the organs involved in digestion are as metabolically expensive as is the brain and other metabolically expensive organs such as the heart, liver and kidney, they are tightly constrained by body size. Aiello and Wheeler (1995) proposed that the large primate, and especially human, brain evolved at the expense of the sizes of the digestive organs. The idea is that a primate with a smaller brain may rely for food on more readily available leaves that require more energy to digest, while one with a larger brain may expend more energy seeking more nutritious fruit and meat that can be digested using less metabolic energy. The total energy investment may be the same, or even favour the larger, more metabolically expensive brain.

The brain is separated from the rest of the body by what is known as the blood–brain barrier. This is true not just of humans, but of most members of the animal realm. Bacteriologists suspected its existence dating back about 100 years. They observed that bodily injections of chemical dyes, used to make fine internal biological structures of animals more visible, stained most of the organs in their bodies, but not their brains. They also observed that injections of the dyes into the animals' brains did stain the brains, but not organs in the rest of their bodies. The existence of the barrier was not verified, however, until introduction of the scanning electron microscope in the 1960s. The blood–brain barrier separates the blood circulating in the rest of the body from the brain's cerebrospinal fluid using tight junctions around capillaries that restrict the passage of larger molecules and microscopic objects such as bacteria from the rest of the circulatory system into the vessels and arteries of the brain. These junctions do not restrict the passage of smaller molecules such as oxygen, hormones, carbon dioxide, and other metabolic products. The blood–brain barrier is very effective in protecting the brain from many, though not all, bacterial infections, as well as many biochemical poisons with particularly large molecules, including many that contaminate food. When infections of the brain do occur, they are difficult to treat because most antibodies and antibiotics are too large to cross it. Viruses, however, can bypass the barrier by attaching to circulating immune cells that do cross it. When inflamed, the barrier becomes more permeable, which can help with getting antibodies and medication to the brain, but also makes the brain more vulnerable to further invasion.

The brain is heavily dependent on a consistent inflow of oxygen and other metabolic products across the blood–brain barrier. Unlike the muscles, it cannot store its fuel, which is primarily glucose, and it cannot extract energy without oxygen. Thus, the brain receives its blood flow from the heart continuously and steadily, again unlike muscles and even digestive organs that receive varying quantities depending on their current levels of activity. Even a one-second interruption in blood flow spends most of the brain's stored oxygen, and a six-second interruption produces unconsciousness. Permanent damage can occur within a few minutes.

Brain neuroanatomy and development

The process of brain development during gestation highlights features of its structure and its evolutionary history, so I will present brain neuroanatomy within the context of its development. Most of the detailed information we have about this comes from model organisms of course, because scientists cannot experiment with living human foetuses. We can, however, infer from the similarities of structures at various stages of development that human processes are similar. In model organisms, scientists inject pregnant animals with radioactive substances that become incorporated in foetal cells at the time of injection. The radioactive labels are not transferred when the cells divide, however, so it is possible to follow the movements of the labelled cells as development takes place. Classically, movements of the cells were observed by injecting the radioactive labels, waiting some period of time, and sacrificing the foetus (and sometimes the mother) in order to dissect the brain and observe the location of the labelled cells. Opossums and chickens have been commonly used as model organisms in order to avoid sacrificing mothers. Opossums are mammals with a relatively short gestation period, whose infants are born with unusually immature brains. Chickens are useful because it is possible to open small windows in their eggshells without disrupting development of the chicken embryos inside. Recent developments in microscopic photography and magnetic resonance imaging now make it possible to observe some of these movements as they take place, by, for example, photographing the region under investigation every two minutes over some extended period of time.

In humans, the central nervous system begins to develop at about the 18th day after conception. Part of the outer layer at the back of the embryo thickens and forms a surface that begins to curl in upon itself to form a tube running in a line directed both towards what will become the face and what will become the feet. After about three days, the edges of this surface meet and close to become the neural tube from which the brain and spinal cord will develop. Where the edges of the surface of the neural tube have joined, some cells break away to form the *basal ganglia*, which will be involved in control of motor movements. By the 28th day after conception, three interconnected chambers have developed at the end of the neural tube facing the face. These chambers will remain but fill with cerebrospinal fluid. One, called the third, will be located at the brain's midline, and its walls will divide the brain into symmetrical halves. The other two chambers are connected to it and will become the larger, lateral ventricles (the first and second, but they are never called this), each of which extends into one of the two symmetrical halves of the brain.

The tissue that develops around these chambers becomes the three major parts of the brain: the forebrain (consisting of the *telencephalon* and *diencephalon*, and also known as the *proencephalon*), midbrain (*mesencephalon*), and hindbrain (*rhombencephalon*), with the forebrain located towards what will become the face. Figure 3.1 shows these structures at 4 and 6 weeks of gestation. The cells that form this tissue come from divisions of the ventricular cells that line the inside of the neural tube, taking the shapes of neurons that will absorb and transmit information throughout the brain and glia that support and protect them. By 10 weeks of gestation, the brain is about 1.25 cm long, but it is mostly empty (ventricular) space. By 20 weeks of gestation, the brain is about 5 cm long and has the basic shape of the mature brain, with much more tissue than ventricle evident.

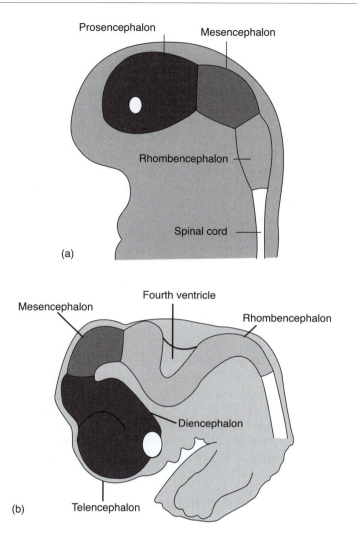

Figure 3.1   Brain structure at (a) 4 and (b) 6 weeks' gestation

The hindbrain develops into the cerebellum, the pons, and the medulla oblongata. These structures are located at the top of the spinal cord and support vital bodily processes that generally function unconsciously, such as breathing, swallowing, blood circulation, and muscle tone. They also receive and process information from visual areas to control eye and body movements and balance and are involved in maintaining patterns of sleep and arousal. The midbrain is located, as its name implies, in about the centre of the brain, below the forebrain and above the hindbrain. It surrounds the central aqueduct, or part of the third ventricle that extends towards what will become the back of the head and the top of the spinal cord. It consists of the substantia nigra involved in motor control, motivation, and habituation to environmental circumstances: four optic lobes and the oculomotor nerve that control eye movements and pupil construction; and the cerebral peduncles involved in communication from one brain region to another. This area of the brain is most conserved across vertebrate species, and dates back furthest in evolutionary history. Development of the hindbrain followed it in evolutionary history, and is also conserved across most vertebrate species.

The forebrain consists of two sections. The diencephalon lies adjacent to the midbrain, surrounds the third ventricle, and is also conserved across most vertebrate species. It develops into the thalamus and the hypothalamus. The thalamus is adjacent to the basal ganglia, and consists of two lobes connected by a bridge of grey matter, at least in most people. Interestingly, this bridge is missing in 20–30 per cent of humans, more commonly in males than in females. It is quite large in non-human mammals, but not in those humans who have it, though it tends to be larger in females than in males. Its function in those who have it is unknown (Olry & Haines, 2005). The thalamus relays sensation, proprioocentric information, and motor signals to the parts of the brain involved in higher processing, and helps to regulate consciousness, sleep, and alertness. It consists largely of projection fibres, or sets of neurons that arise in one region and communicate directly with neurons in another region. The hypothalamus lies underneath the thalamus. It controls the autonomic nervous system and links the nervous system more generally to the endocrine system of hormones that regulate the body through the pituitary gland from which most of the hormones originate. This means that the hypothalamus is intimately involved in organizing behaviours related to survival, often termed the four Fs: fighting, fleeing, feeding, and, well, mating.

The second section of the forebrain is the telencephalon, which develops into the cerebrum. In humans, it is by far the largest part of the brain, and is the part we usually mean when we refer to the brain. It is located above the rest of the brain and includes both of the symmetrical hemispheres. The cerebrum is the newest structure in the brain from an evolutionary perspective, and is largest and most developed in mammals. In more complex mammals, this part of the brain is heavily folded into many furrows and ridges, known as sulci and gyri, which make it possible for its surface area to be extremely large relative to its volume. The cerebrum directs the volitional motor actions of the body and organizes complex behaviours such as learning, memory, judgement, thought, social interactions, and, in humans, speech and language. Most of this activity takes place in its outermost layer called the cerebral cortex. In the most primitive vertebrates, such as amphibians and lobe-finned fish, the cerebrum is primarily involved in olfactory sensation. In mammals, reptiles, and birds, however, its functions

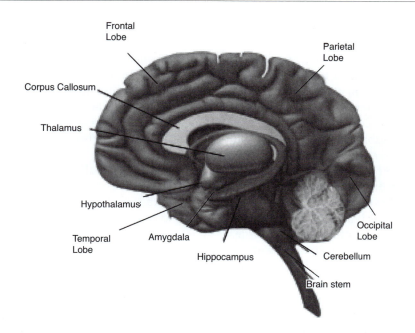

Figure 3.2 A side view of one of two cerebral hemispheres of the brain

are considerably broader. The cerebra of birds and mammals are considerably enlarged relative to those of reptiles, but they take different forms. The corpus callosum, which connects the two symmetric hemispheres of the brain, is observed only in mammals. Figure 3.2 shows the basic structure of the adult brain.

Adult brain structure and function

The outermost part of the cerebrum, which surrounds the cerebral hemispheres in a layer only about 2–4 mm in thickness, is so grooved with sulci and gyri that it has approximately triple the total area of the surface it appears to cover. It consists mostly of glia and neurons and the axons that connect neurons. When preserved, these neuronal cells take on a greyish colour, which is the source of our term 'grey matter'. Chains of axons continue beneath the cerebral cortex, linking it with neurons in other regions of the brain. These axons are *myelinated*. That is, they are covered with an electrically insulating sheath of fatty insulators that grows from the glial cells. This sheath increases the speed with which the electrical impulses that neurons transmit from one to another can move by effectively allowing them to jump from one to another across the gap between them. The presence of myelin sheaths also helps to allow regrowth when a nerve fibre is severed. Myelinated axons are white in colour, which is the source of our term 'white matter' with respect to the brain. Production of myelin begins in humans around the 14th week of gestation, but very little myelin is yet present in the brain at birth. Production accelerates immediately afterwards, however, and continues into adolescence. Myelin is found in the brains of all vertebrates, and it has also evolved independently in some invertebrates.

The cortex is generally described as consisting of sensory, motor, and association areas. The sensory areas receive and process information routed to them through the thalamus from the eyes, ears, and via the sense of touch. The sensory exception to this process is olfactory information, which passes through the olfactory bulb rather than through the thalamus. These sensory areas are located at the back of the head, on the inner folds of each hemisphere. Information from the left side of the body is processed in the right hemisphere's sensory areas, and vice versa. In general, these brain regions are organized in the same format as the sensory organs themselves. That is, information from, for example, adjacent areas of the retina is processed by adjacent areas in the visual cortex. The motor areas control the body's voluntary movements. They too are located in both hemispheres of the cortex, and the left side of the body is controlled by the motor area in the right hemisphere and vice versa. They extend across the middle of the top of the head. Very specific regions control the movements of specific limbs of the body, and adjacent specific regions select the voluntary movements of these limbs. These two sensory and motor areas of the cerebral cortex together occupy only a small part of its total area, and are considered to be located in its *posterior*, or rear, region. The rest of the cerebral cortex is considered the *anterior*, or front, region and accomplishes all of what we generally call thinking: perceiving, learning, remembering, planning, and executing actions. This anterior region is known as the association area. Much of what we know about how these structures' function comes from experiments with model organisms and from examination of humans who have suffered localized brain injuries or strokes.

The association area consists of four areas, called lobes, which were named for the bones of the skull that cover them. These lobes are shown in Figure 3.2. More accurately, there are eight of these areas, as each has a lobe in each brain hemisphere. The frontal lobes are largest, and extend across about half the head just behind the forehead. The parietal lobes lie just behind them. Underneath them lie the temporal lobes, and behind both the parietal and temporal lobes, at the back of the head, lie the occipital lobes. Within the frontal lobes, the parts lying most directly behind the forehead are known as the prefrontal cortex. This area of the brain is most heavily involved in what we think of as thought and planning.

Two structures in the temporal lobes deserve particular mention because their functions are frequent subjects of discussion in psychological studies.

The hippocampus is located in the middle of the temporal lobe. Like the other regions I have discussed, it is actually a pair of structures, with mirror-image parts located in each brain hemisphere. It is evolutionarily conserved among mammals. It is involved in attention, behavioural inhibition, memory in general but particularly spatial memory, and navigation. It also appears to be involved in behavioural control, as rats with hippocampal damage show increased levels of activity. It plays an important role in the formation of new memories for experiences, apparently through the detection of novel stimuli. This takes place, in the hippocampus as in other areas of the brain, through lasting enhancement of the strength of transmission between two neurons that occurs when they are simultaneously stimulated. This is termed *long-term potentiation*. In rats and mice, particular hippocampal neurons fire bursts of electricity when the rodents pass through particular parts of their known environments, giving rise to the idea that the hippocampus may carry some kind of cognitive map of the known environment. This idea is reinforced by observations that accurate performance of some spatial tasks such as finding the way to a hidden goal requires an intact hippocampus (Morris, Garrud, Rawlins, & O'Keefe, 1982), that the hippocampus shows greater activity during correct navigation in humans (Maguire, Burgess, Donnett, Frackowiak, Firth, & O'Keefe, 1998), and that a famous study of London taxi drivers showed larger hippocampi than ordinary citizens, with the sizes of the drivers' hippocampi varying with the length of their taxi-driving experience (Maguire, Gadian, Johnsrude, Good, Ashburner, Frackowiak, et al., 2000).

The other temporal lobe structure of particular interest is the amygdala. Again, this is actually a pair of structures, each located deep within each brain hemisphere, and conserved among most vertebrates and particularly mammals. The amygdala is involved in the formation and storage of associations between emotional responses and experienced events. Involvement with these associations was first observed with respect to fear responses and conditioning, so the amygdala was long thought to be mainly involved in negative emotional responses, avoidance of danger, and stress. More recent studies, however, have made clear that it is also involved in positive emotional responses, processing of reward stimuli, and approach to potentially rewarding situations (Paton, Belova, Morrison, & Salzman, 2006). Moreover, different cells within the amygdala process positive and negative emotional responses. The amygdala is not, however, necessary for the processing of emotion-related stimuli, as people with amygdala damage still show normal reactions to experimental conditions intended to test such responses, such as exposure to photographs of faces expressing fear (Tsuchiya, Moradi, Felsen, Yamazaki, & Adolphs, 2009). Despite this, the amygdala routinely shows activation in response to fearful (and positive) stimuli, even when that exposure is subliminal (Williams, Liddell, Kemp, Bryant, Meares, Peduto, et al., 2006).

Regional communication within the brain

The two hemispheres of the brain, with their parallel components, cooperate with each other, but do not operate in tandem. In addition to the fact that motor functions are contralateral, with the left side of the brain processing information from, and controlling, the right side of the body and vice versa, each hemisphere tends to be more specialized than the other for particular kinds of processing. The media has popularized the idea that the left hemisphere of the brain is rational and logical, and verbal and emotionally positive, and the right side of the brain is creative and intuitive, and spatial and emotionally negative. Reality is far less polarized than this. In general, however, the left hemisphere of the brain is more involved in extracting and identifying the elements of an experience, while the right hemisphere is more involved in synthesis, or putting otherwise isolated elements together to perceive them as a whole. This means that the left hemisphere tends to handle recording the order of events in memory and controlling behaviours that must be executed in sequence, including productive language functions such as talking and writing, and absorptive language functions such as reading and understanding others' speech. We know this because these are the functions that are disrupted when the left hemisphere suffers damage. In contrast, the right hemisphere tends to be involved in making sketches of three-dimensional objects, putting together larger objects composed of smaller pieces, and reading maps. Again, we know this because these are the functions that are disrupted when the right hemisphere suffers damage. In the brains of some 10 per cent of otherwise normal individuals, these functions are reversed.

Of course we have no awareness of these somewhat distinct perspectives and functional roles within our brains because our perceptions and memories are unified. The unification takes place via the *corpus callosum*. This is a wide, flat, bundle of highly myelinized nerve fibres running beneath the cortex and connecting the two hemispheres. It is found only in mammals, though birds, reptiles, amphibians, fish and marsupials do have other structures that manage communication between the hemispheres. In primates, the speed of nerve transmission throughout the brain depends on degree of myelination, which is a function of the diameter of the nerve. That is, nerve diameter tends to increase with body size, so that speed of transmission increases with required travel distance, making coordination of sensory and motor impulses possible and efficient. This has not taken place completely in humans, however; though our brains are considerably larger than those of chimpanzees, our nerves are myelinized to a degree similar to theirs, making time to communicate across the brain hemispheres greater in humans than in chimpanzees (Caminiti, Ghaziri, Galuske, Hof, & Innocenti, 2009).

Dating back 100 years or more, studies have suggested that there are sex differences in the size and function of the corpus callosum. With the development of more sophisticated brain imaging techniques, the claims about differences in size have been increasingly questioned (Bishop & Wahlsten, 1997; Luders, Narr, Zaidel, Thompson, & Toga, 2006). Within the corpus callosum, however, recent studies appear to show sex differences in directionality of communication between cells, rates of metabolism, and microstructure (e.g., Dubb, Gur, Avants, & Gee, 2003). In addition, the corpus callosum appears to be larger and perhaps structured somewhat differently in left-handed than in right-handed people (e.g., Westerhausen, Kreuder, Sequeira, Walter, Woerner, Wittling, et al., 2004). The significance of these differences remains unknown.

There are many other structural and functional units within the brain that can be separately identified. Increasingly, neuroscientists are thinking of these units as networks, or groups of disparate neurons that are interconnected in recognizable circuits. While connections within networks are, by definition, more common within neuron groups, there are also connections between groups, or links from one network to another. Networks of neurons tend to be physically localized. Early brain development consists of both expansion of neural tissue and formation of neuronal connections. Most basic neuronal connections between brain regions are thought to be in place by about nine months of age (Conel, 1963), but the formation of synapses and myelination of those synapses take place over much longer timeframes. Numbers of synaptic contacts in the cortex increase dramatically from about 30 weeks of gestation to the end of the second postnatal year, and, overall, the cortex tends to increase in thickness until sometime in middle childhood. About two years after birth, however, some synaptic connections begin to be pruned, or broken and eliminated, while others continue to be formed. Both new synaptic connections and pruning of connections depend on experience: connections are formed through learning and repeated activity, and they are pruned when activities are ceased or something that was learned is no longer activated.

Until about 10 years ago, it was believed that new synaptic connections were not formed in adulthood. In recent years it has become clear that this is not the case: new synaptic connections can be formed even in old age. The rates of formation, however, slow considerably after physical maturity. By sometime in middle childhood, rates of pruning typically exceed rates of formation of new connections, causing overall thinning of the cortex to begin. Exact timing of the beginning of cortical thinning shows considerable individual differences, and there is some association with both general mental ability and psychiatric disorder in this timing, though understanding of this remains limited. Children with higher IQ scores tend to show delays in the inception of cortical thinning (Shaw, Kabani, Lerch, Eckstrand, Lenroot, Gogtay, et al., 2008), as do children with attention-deficit-hyperactivity disorder (Shaw, Eckstrand, Sharp, Blumenthal, Lerch, Greenstein, et al., 2007). In contrast, children with autism tend to show increased cortical thickness in early childhood (Hazlett, Poe, Gerig, Styner, Chappell, Smith, et al., 2011). Associations between cortical thickness and depression, obsessive-compulsive disorder (Fallucca, MacMaster, Haddad, Easter, Dick, May, et al., 2011), and schizophrenia (Bakalar, Greenstein, Chavez, Miller, Tossell, Clasen, et al., 2010) have also been reported in children. Myelination follows a similar pattern of a high rate in infancy and early childhood, followed by later slowing but not cessation. The overall pattern is delayed, however, relative to that of formation of synapses.

So far, I have provided a basic outline of brain structure, its development, and the extent to which brain structure is conserved across the animal realm. The extent of this conservation is striking, provides insight into human brain structure and function, and suggests the manner in which genes have their influences on them. Recent developments in embryology have started to illuminate some of the processes involved, and I turn now to discussion of these processes.

Developmental genetics: the homeobox

One of the major issues since Darwin and Wallace proposed the theory of evolution has been the difficulty of explaining specificities of form among species. Historically, it has been much easier to see how natural selection can account for the presence of two eyes in many species and more difficult to understand how the eye could have evolved in the first place. William Bateson was one of the first geneticists to address this question directly. He noted that, within individual organisms, many morphological (body structural features) are repeated. The *vertebrae*, the bones or bone segments that make up the spine, are examples of such repeating structures in humans. Normally, the vertebrae spanning the thorax, or the region between the neck and the abdomen, are connected to the ribs, which provide an example of a repeating structure (Allman, 2000). In most humans, the cervical vertebrae of the neck do not have ribs connected to them. Bateson noted, however, that some rare humans have cervical vertebrae that are connected to ribs, and others have thoracic vertebrae that are not connected to ribs, as if the normal matching between vertebrae and ribs were out of synch or because there were too many or too few of one of them. He catalogued thousands of such deviations from normality in specimens from throughout the animal realm (Bateson, 1894), including bees with legs instead of antennae, and humans with extra fingers, ribs, and nipples. He suggested that repeating structures such as these, that appear as finite numbers of units, could be the basis for the emergence of the kinds of discontinuities in structure that characterize the emergence of new species. That is, he believed that, through the development of extra copies of some of these units, organisms could undergo substantial changes in form. This appears to result from the presence of duplicated genes.

Much of the work demonstrating this has been carried out in fruit flies, but the principles involved appear to be much more general. Fruit flies have two important advantages as model organisms in embryology. First, they reproduce very rapidly, so we can observe the effects of our manipulations across many generations quickly. Second, they have giant chromosomes, 150 times the usual size, in their salivary glands, making observation of their genetic structure unusually easy. In 1915, Calvin Bridges, a geneticist at Columbia University, discovered a mutation in fruit flies that transformed the third segment of the fly thorax into the second segment (Allman, 2000). The transformation was similar to that which takes place in human cervical vertebrae when they are attached to ribs. That is, normally flies' wings are attached to the second thoracic segment, and the third has attached to it a pair of sensory structures. In flies with Bridges' mutation, the third thoracic segment did not have the sensory structures and did have wings, so that the flies had two sets of wings, one on the second thoracic segment and one on the third. Bridges went on to note that flies' chromosomes contained bands of apparently repeated sets of genes. He proposed that duplication of genes might be a way in which evolution could create genetic diversity, as, after duplication, the new genes could mutate separately.

The mutation Bridges discovered, which generated flies with four wings, was termed *homeotic*, based on the term *homeosis*, coined by William Bateson (1894). Bateson had used this term to express a process of making two things similar, as when a cervical vertebra of the neck acquired a rib as if it were a thoracic vertebra. Discovery of more homeotic genes followed soon after Bridges' discovery. The geneticist Edward Lewis extended Bridges' idea about the evolutionary power of such duplications to suggest that they all involved genes regulating the development of the body, and that the existence of the duplication allowed the additional copies to escape the effects of natural selection on the original copy. Thus, for example, one of the duplicated genes could mutate and generate a new effect, while the other remained intact and continued to play its, presumably crucial, role in preserving the original characteristics in which it was involved (Allman, 2000). Lewis discovered that, in flies, the homeotic genes that control the development of the different body segments are in the same order on the chromosome as the body segments they control. This proved to be the case for homeotic genes controlling head development as well.

Then, in 1983, two groups of researchers independently discovered the *homeobox*. This is a particular sequence of DNA that is found in all the homeotic genes of the fruit fly. It encodes a sequence of specific proteins, called the *homeodomain*, that regulate where and when the homeotic genes are expressed in the developing embryo. These genes thus act as master genes to control the function of other genes that in turn produce bodily structure. Since their discovery in fruit flies, homeobox genes have been found in genes throughout the animal realm, including hydra, planaria, sea urchins, nematodes, beetles, locusts, fish, frogs, chickens, mice, and humans. The homeobox genes take different specific forms in different species, but they are all derived from gene duplications that took place at different times in evolutionary history, and can be traced back to an original homeobox gene in the common ancestor of the animal realm.

This is important because it can help us understand both the genetics and the evolution of the human brain. As noted earlier, the human brain is about three times as large as the brain of our nearest living evolutionary relative, the chimpanzee. Yet humans and chimpanzees share 98-99 per cent of their genes. The 1-2 per cent of genes that differ between them must account for all the many obvious differences in their appearances, metabolisms, and many of their behaviours, so less than 1 per cent of the genome must be involved in creating the brain difference. The homeobox genes make this possible because the brains of both species develop in sections analogous to the body sections of fruit flies or the vertebrae of the spinal cord. That is, for example, the major components of the brain – the forebrain, midbrain, and hindbrain – begin as sections of the neural tube, and their subsequent development into the more detailed brain regions described above is controlled by series of homeobox genes that function slightly differently in the two species. Some of the differences in function, and thus resulting development, occur not just through differences in the degrees to which homeobox genes allow expression of other genes, but through differences in the ordering of the timing of expression they assign to those other genes.

This makes an important point about mutation. The homeobox genes regulate the expression of genes that are involved in the development of structure and function in many parts of the body in addition to the brain and central nervous system. Geneticists have tended to identify mutations by the specific observable effects they produce, and have inferred from those effects that the single function of the gene in which the mutation is located is to produce the usual, or wild-type, characteristic. But mutations in either the homeobox genes or the genes they regulate may disrupt or alter only very specific aspects of expression during certain developmental periods or in specific organs, leaving all other patterns of expression unaltered. This possibility makes questionable the inference that the result of a mutation signals the general function of the gene in which the mutation is located.

The role of the homeobox in brain development

We understand the roles of the homeobox genes in brain development best in the vertebrate hindbrain because those roles are well conserved among vertebrates, including humans. In vertebrates, the hindbrain consists of a series of ridges that emerge across it during development. These ridges develop into distinct segments, each of which is regulated by a series of homeobox genes that appear in the chromosomes in the same linear order as their hindbrain segments do in the brain. The expression patterns of the homeobox genes determine the boundaries between adjacent hindbrain segments by creating barriers to cell migration from one section to another, so that the segments remain distinct. Each of the segments thus ends up with a distinct structure and function. For example, the eighth cranial nerve, which connects the sense organs for balance and hearing with the rest of the brain, extends from the fourth hindbrain segment (Allman, 2000).

The homeobox genes are important regulators of brain development, but their expression in turn is controlled by other factors, including environmental circumstances. With respect to hindbrain and spinal cord development, one of these factors is the concentration of retinoic acid in the region. Retinoic acid, the biologically active form of vitamin A, diffuses through the developing embryo, binding to specialized receptors that are similar to the receptors for thyroid hormone. Like thyroid hormone receptors, retinoic acid receptors regulate the expression of genes involved in hindbrain development. The homeobox gene that controls the hindbrain segment that is located closest to the forebrain is the most sensitive to retinoic acid, and the further a segment lies from the forebrain (thus the closer it lies to the spinal cord), the less sensitive it is to retinoic acid. This means that expression of the homeobox genes begins with those that control development of the segment nearest the forebrain and progresses across the genes controlling the segments lying further from the forebrain and closer to the spinal cord with increasing levels of retinoic acid. In experiments with model organisms, administering extra retinoic acid to developing embryos accelerates the timing of expression of homeobox genes, causing the segments they control to take on the characteristics normally shown by segments located closer to the spinal cord. Retinoic acid plays similar roles in the development of the eyes, the limbs, and other body structures. In humans, the ingestion of excessive amounts of vitamin A during pregnancy can cause severe birth defects (Allman, 2000).

I discussed the association between development of the brain and development of the gut and digestive system above, but, in mammals, brain development is also related to development of the teeth and jaw structure involved in managing food consumption to facilitate digestion. The teeth develop from cells that emerge from the neural tube during early gestation and migrate away from the developing hindbrain. These cells that develop into the molar teeth are under the control of genes containing the homeobox sequence, which also control the development of parts of the forebrain (Allman, 2000). Moreover, the first region of the neocortex, the outermost and most evolutionarily recent layer of the cortex, to develop during gestation is the part that represents the mouth and tongue. Development of the neocortex then fans outward in concentric rings from this region. This is thought to be related to the need of young mammals to nurse as soon as they are born.

Some basic genetics

Thus far, I have referred to genes and their actions and effects from the perspective of general knowledge, as if everyone knows what genes are, what effects they have, and how they achieve those effects. This is actually far from the case. Arguably, in fact, no one knows what genes are or how they act, even highly trained geneticists, because ideas about this have undergone so many changes in recent years. This is not a particularly useful perspective, however, and there is actually much that we can say about them. Laying out this background knowledge is important, for, once it is accomplished, I will rely on it throughout the rest of this book.

Chromosomes and DNA

Publication of the sequencing of the human genome in 2004 received much public attention. One of the most startling facts that sequencing established was that the human genome contains only 20,000-25,000 genes, somewhat more than the genome of the fruit fly at about 15,000, but fewer than that of the mouse at about 30,000. The human genome consists of the genetic material contained on the 46 chromosomes carried by each genetically normal human. As in all living organisms, each of these chromosomes consists of a single, extremely long molecular formation called DNA, deoxyribonucleic acid. DNA, in turn, as described by Watson and Crick in 1953, consists of two chains of nucleotides, each of which is a more basic molecule containing phosphate, sugar, and one of four other chemicals called *bases*. The chains are twisted around each other somewhat like bedsprings, forming what is called a double helix. The four bases are adenine, guanine, cytosine, and thymine, often abbreviated to A, C, T, and G. A and G are similar in chemical structure, but distinct from C and T, which are similar to each other. On the two strands within one molecule of DNA, each C base on one strand is matched with a G on the other, and each A base on one strand is matched with a T on the other. This pairing, however, is usually not mentioned in discussions of genomic structure, as it is automatic and involves the basic structure of the DNA molecule rather than genetic variation among individuals. Rather, one strand is arbitrarily selected as the reference, and the base at each location, or *genetic locus*, on this strand is considered an *allele*.

Like DNA, the 46 chromosomes come in what are called homologous pairs, with one exception. That is, there are 22 sets of chromosomes (or DNA molecules) called *autosomes* that consist of (almost) matching sets of A, C, T, and G bases, and one set of sex chromosomes that do not match in this way. One of each of the chromosomes in each set, including the set that does not match, comes from each parent. On the autosomes, almost all C–G or A–T pairs on one chromosome have analogous C–G or A–T pairs on the other, homologous, chromosome. These analogous pairs of alleles, or *base pairs of C–G or A–T*, together make some contribution to genetic structure or function in the individual. The human genome consists of some 3.2 billion of these pairs, allocated unevenly across the chromosomes. There are normally two possible sets of sex chromosomes. Males normally have one X chromosome and one Y chromosome, while females normally have two X chromosomes. In males, the Y chromosomes come from their fathers and the X chromosomes from their mothers. In females, one X chromosome comes from each parent. The X chromosome is much larger, containing many more base pairs of alleles, than the Y chromosome. The X and Y chromosomes share analogous base pairs in one small region on each of them. Because the X chromosome is much larger than the Y chromosome, however, females receive two copies of many of the alleles in the non-analogous regions, while males only receive one. This contributes to sex differences in some disorders such as colour blindness, which is much more common in males than in females. The allele involved is recessive, which means that it can only be expressed when it is not in the presence of the other, dominant allele. In males, expression of colour blindness occurs whenever the allele is present. In females, however, two copies are required for expression. For many alleles, the presence of two copies in females but one in males might present what is known as the 'dosage problem'. That is, females might have twice as much gene product as males, and this 'double dosage' could create problems. This does not occur, however, because expression of most of the non-analogous alleles is randomly inactivated during early embryonic development on one X chromosome or the other.

One of the primary functions of DNA is to code for the proteins that build body structure and execute bodily functions. Despite this, less than 2 per cent of the human genome is involved in coding proteins (Birney, 2007), and we are only beginning to understand what the other 98 per cent does. So how do 3.2 billion base pairs translate to some 20,000-25,000 genes? There are two ways. First, each gene that codes for a protein consists of a long segment of DNA base pairs called an *exon*, and, second, there are long DNA segments called *introns* between each exon that do not code for proteins. Until sometime around 2000, geneticists generally believed, and textbooks taught, that the DNA in introns was 'junk' and had no real function, but today we know that this is not true. The DNA in introns has several kinds of regulatory functions but we know little about the specific functions of many intronic regions.

The role of exonic DNA in building proteins is to transcribe, or produce a slightly altered copy of its region of base pairs called *messenger RNA* (mRNA; ribonucleic acid) that in turn goes on to manufacture the protein for which it codes. Nearby introns can sometimes be swept into this transcription process and other times not. There is not currently a clear definition of the boundaries of a gene along a strand of DNA, but the boundaries can generally be considered to be the base pairs at which transcription into mRNA starts and finishes. Because, for many specific transcription processes, certain introns are sometimes included and sometimes not, the boundaries of genes are somewhat flexible. The inclusion or not of introns is generally functional: a single exon may produce different proteins depending on whether or not specific introns are included. This introduces a layer of complexity in gene function and is known as *alternative splicing*. About half of the 'genes' (by which geneticists usually mean exonic regions) in the human genome are coded for related but distinct proteins through alternative splicing (Stetefeld & Ruegg, 2005), which considerably undermines the long-dominant assumption that any one allele has one specific function. Only about 25 per cent of introns, however, are involved in alternative splicing. Much of the rest is transcribed into another form of RNA that has other regulatory functions. One of these is to influence whether or not other introns are swept into RNA transcriptions (Mattick, 2009). This is to say that some DNA acts to regulate how other DNA is regulated.

Each gene also has other regions of DNA associated with it. Transcription proceeds in one direction along the DNA strand, and is triggered in a *promoter* region located 'upstream' (in the direction opposite the direction of transcription) but often near (a few hundred DNA base pairs) to the site at which gene transcription starts. These promoters regulate the rate of transcription, which controls the amount of gene product produced. Though promoters are often located near to the genes they regulate, this is not always the case. Some are very remote from the genes they regulate. There are also regions immediately on either side of the gene's coding regions that are transcribed but not translated into mRNA, known as *untranslated regions*, that can affect the specific characteristics and stability of the mRNA produced.

Box 3.1   Genetic variation in the human genome

Because they are both human, any two otherwise unrelated people share well in excess of 99 per cent of the base pairs of DNA in their genomes (Kruglyak & Nickerson, 2001). There is still plenty of room for genetic variation among humans: with some 3.2 billion base pairs of DNA, the less than 1 per cent on which humans differ could still easily amount to 15 million base pairs. Despite this, humans share the vast majority of their genomes with many other species. By way of comparison, humans share about 98 per cent of their genomes with chimpanzees, our closest living relatives, and some 50 per cent even with insects and worms. Though our knowledge of the functions of most of the base pairs on which humans differ is at best scanty, we do know of many examples (including cystic fibrosis, phenylketonuria, and sickle cell anaemia) in which a single base pair difference in a gene that spans more than a thousand base pairs has devastating effects on the individual carrying it (Rimoin, 2007).

The DNA base pairs on which humans tend to differ most frequently have just two variants, or alleles, though this is not always the case. That is, for example, one variant may be A, the other may be G, and either C or T are never observed. To make the huge numbers involved in working with the entire genome manageable, geneticists have arbitrarily made some conceptual distinctions. When one gene *locus*, or location on the genome is *bi-allelic* (has two variants) and the least commonly occurring (*minor*) allele occurs in the population at least I per cent of the time, the locus is said to be *polymorphic* or a *polymorphism*, meaning normally or regularly taking more than one form. If the frequency of the minor allele (*minor allele frequency; MAF*) is less than I per cent, this allele is designated a mutation. The most commonly studied genetic variants are known as *single nucleotide polymorphisms* or *SNPs*. These are defined as variants with MAFs greater than I per cent that involve the substitution of one DNA base pair by another. More than 10 million of these SNPs have been identified, and they are thought to be the most common variants in the human genome.

This makes the human genome sound very large, but neatly and manageably organized, so that the ways in which it differs from individual to individual could be meaningfully summarized. Unfortunately, it has become clear that this is not the situation. In fact, no two individuals (except possibly some pairs of monozygotic twins, and even they can vary in this regard) have the same number of base pairs, and there are many ways in which the numbers of base pairs can vary from person to person. For example, some polymorphisms are found in some individuals but not at all in others. These polymorphisms are not usually limited to single loci, but consist of some sequence of DNA base pairs, ranging in length up to as many as 1,000 base pairs. Within these sequences, some of the alleles may vary in those carrying them, though the vast majority generally do not. A well-known example of this in the behavioural sciences is a polymorphism in the promoter region of the serotonin transporter that has been associated with response to stress and depression. One allele is known as the 'short' allele. It is 44 DNA base pairs shorter than the 'long' allele (Heils, Teufel, Petri, Stober, Riederer, Bengel, et al., 1996). This means that those carrying the long allele have 44 more base pairs in their genomes, all else being equal, than those carrying the short allele. This is the terminology usually used to describe this genetic variant, but it is rather confusing because the term 'allele' is generally defined as a single DNA base pair.

Specific numbers of base pairs may also differ among individuals because some sequences of DNA are present in some individuals, repeated in some individuals but not in others, or in different numbers of copies in some individuals than in others. As described earlier, duplication of DNA sequences has been a primary way in which evolution has proceeded, so this should not be particularly surprising. Such repeated DNA sequences tend to be known as *variable number tandem repeats (VNTRs)* when the repeated sequence consists of about 20 DNA base pairs or less (though there is no agreed upper limit), and *copy number variants (CNVs)* when the repeated sequence is longer than this. Some of these repeated sequences can be thousands or even millions of base pairs in length. In the behavioural sciences, a well-known VNTR is found in the dopamine D4 receptor gene. There, a sequence of 48 base pairs will be repeated from two to 11 times (at least as so far observed). Another example is the disorder Williams Syndrome, which involves the deletion of about 2 million base pairs of DNA on Chromosome 7. Sequences of DNA base pairs can also be *inverted* (reversed in sequence within the genome) or *translocated*. When translocations occur, sequences of DNA base pairs have been transferred from their usual position on one particular chromosome to another. There is a rare form of schizophrenia that is associated with such a translocation from Chromosome I to Chromosome 11 (Hodgkinson, Goldman, Jaeger, Persaud, Kane, Lipsky, et al., 2004). The removal of the sequence from Chromosome I disrupts the gene in which the sequence normally occurs, and the translocation creates extra genetic material on Chromosome 11. It is unclear which of these two circumstances contributes, or whether perhaps both do, to the development of the schizophrenia. These definitions of different kinds of variations in numbers of DNA base pairs overlap, so the categories they define are not clearly distinct from each other.

Awareness of the variety, frequency, and numbers of DNA base pairs involved in these variants has largely emerged since the project to sequence 'the' human genome, which was based essentially on the genome of a single individual, was planned. This awareness has made clear that no single genome, nor even the genomes of a few individuals, can give us a true picture of the nature and scope of human genetic variation. This has led to the development of several projects. Some of these projects seek to establish publicly available records of all the genetic loci that show variation. Others are intended to establish banks of human genomes from all the world's major population groups. They are huge undertakings, but should greatly expand our understanding of human genetic variation.

Heritability

Understanding that genetic alleles are laid out along the chromosomes in regular sequences (with some variation), and that these sequences make up genes that code for proteins that form the foundations of physiology, has only developed in the last 30 years or so. Paralleling this has been the realization that genetic influences on behavioural and psychological characteristics are substantial and pervasive. This realization has occurred through the estimation of what is known as *heritability* for trait after psychological trait in a broad range of large population-representative samples drawn from most areas of the world. These genetic influences form the foundations of individual differences in responses to all forms of stimuli and also the foundations of individual differences in self-initiated actions. This latter is important: as I have stressed before and will throughout this book, individuals always have some control over their own actions and some choice among available alternative actions. The situation and the individual's environmental history may set the stage and limit the range of choice of action, but the individual's genotype is involved both in the actions taken and in the individual's presence in this situation in the first place. We cannot understand development without taking this into consideration.

Estimation of heritability provides a reliable way of demonstrating the presence of genetic influence in humans, but the concept was actually developed by agriculturalists to measure expected response to controlled breeding selection in plants and animals. Of course we do not practise such controlled breeding selection in humans, so some of the concepts used in defining and estimating heritability are less applicable to human populations. Despite this, the basic principles remain intact; it is the precision of the magnitudes of the estimates that tends to suffer. Heritability is a population statistic involving variance. It is defined as the ratio of genetically influenced variance in the population to total population variance. When heritability is, say, 40 per cent (a common estimate for traits of all kinds, including human behavioural patterns, expressed in continuous terms), agriculturists mean formally that 40 per cent of the variance in the trait will 'breed true' to the next generation. That is, for example, if we breed only those cows that produced milk in excess of 1 standard deviation above the mean in the current herd, we can expect milk production in the next generation to be 0.4 standard deviations higher, assuming that environmental conditions are the same for the two generations. Heritability estimates are never used in this way with respect to human characteristics, however, because we do not breed humans in this manner. What we do mean by them with respect to humans is subtle and requires some explanation, and it is easier to begin with what we do *not* mean.

First, we do not mean anything that applies to the characteristics of any of the individuals in the population. In particular, we do not mean that 40 per cent of any individual's level of the characteristic can be attributed to the individual's genes. The term refers only to population variance, and not to mean levels or to individuals in any way. Second, whether the next generation's mean is actually 0.4 standard deviations higher than the previous one's, when a trait with 40 per cent heritability is selected, depends on whether the relevant environment is constant over the generational time span. Many genetic effects are only elicited by specific environmental conditions. For example, genetic influences on reading ability can only be manifested by appropriate exposure to printed material. Moreover, magnitudes of genetic effects can vary considerably with environmental circumstances, so changes in environmental conditions over time can have major effects on population mean levels of traits. Thus, for example, levels of population literacy rose dramatically in the last 200 years in western countries as access to free education became standard, and there is no reason to suspect that the increases involved genetic changes in the population. Studies have been frustratingly unsuccessful in identifying the specific environmental factors that shape psychological characteristics, but one thing we do know is that, since the emergence of psychology as a formal experimental science, the environmental circumstances in which people live have varied dramatically over both time and place. Thus, heritability does not indicate the extent to which the observed level of a characteristic in the population is genetically influenced in any meaningful way. That is, heritability may be consistent in magnitude across several generations despite large changes in mean levels during that time. Human height is an example of this, as is human intelligence as measured by IQ tests.

In humans, heritability estimates of psychological characteristics have most commonly been based on samples of twin pairs, though this is not their only source. In the human species, in which experimental environmental manipulation and artificial selection cannot ethically be practised, twin pairs present a convenient natural experiment because there are two kinds. Monozygotic (MZ or identical) twins develop when a single fertilized egg divides very early in gestation and two embryos develop. They thus share essentially the same genotype. Dizygotic (DZ or fraternal) twins develop when two eggs are released during ovulation and both are fertilized. They thus are genetically equivalent to full singleton siblings and share on average 50 per cent of the alleles on which humans differ. Most commonly, both kinds of twins grow up together in the same home, sharing many environmental circumstances. Thus, given the accuracy of several important assumptions, if MZ twins are more similar in some characteristic than are DZ twins, it is reasonable to infer that this greater similarity can be attributed to their greater genetic relationship and thus that the characteristic in general is subject to genetic influence. Similarly, if MZ twins are less than twice as similar as DZ twins (because they are twice as genetically related) it is reasonable to infer that some of the similarity in both kinds of twins can be attributed to the environments they share, and thus that the characteristic in general is subject to the kinds of environmental influences that act to make two children similar when they grow up in the same home with the same parents. And finally, because MZ twins are never identical for any psychological characteristic, we can be sure that environmental influences also act to make twins, and by extension people in general, different from each other.

The assumptions underlying heritability estimates and implications of their violation

The assumptions underlying these inferences surround two ideas. The first is that genetic and environmental influences act independently of each other. In agricultural breeding, this idea is probably pretty generally accurate because uniformity of conditions makes for efficiency in feeding and maintenance. Even when some individuals are purposely selected for environmental manipulation, the manipulated plants or animals themselves rarely have any choice about the manipulations they receive. But, as this book stresses, humans do select and manipulate many of their environmental circumstances. Because the characteristics they use to do this are genetically influenced, correlations and interactions between genetic and environmental influences are created, violating the assumption of their independence on which heritability estimates depend. This rarely matters if the basic question is simply whether or not genetic influences are present, but it has substantial implications for the magnitudes of heritability estimates.

Gene–environment correlations exist when there is genetic control of exposure to environmental circumstances, that is, when genetic influences lead people to seek or avoid certain kinds of environmental situations or experiences.

The environment that is correlated with genetic influences is considered shared when it acts to make family members similar to each other, or nonshared when it acts to make them different from each other. Gene–environment correlations are also classified as passive, active, or evocative. When passive, an individual merely inherits both genes and environmental circumstances that reinforce each other, with no action on the individual's part (as when children of bright parents both inherit genes for intelligence and grow up in intellectually enriched homes and attend good schools, or the opposite). When active, genetic influences propel the individual to seek environments that reinforce the genetically influenced characteristics that led the individual to seek those environments (as when socially inclined people seek situations where they can meet and mingle with others and end up with many friends). When evocative, the individual acts in genetically influenced ways that evoke responses from the environment reinforcing the characteristics that contributed to the original actions, as when aggressive behaviour provokes aggressive responses from others that in turn provoke further aggressive behaviour. These latter ways of conceptualizing gene–environment correlation overlap considerably, but it should be clear that, given human ability to select at least some environmental circumstances and genetic influences on essentially all psychological characteristics, they are common.

Gene–environment interactions occur when environmental circumstances trigger different responses in individuals with different genetic backgrounds. Such interactions are probably ubiquitous: some people react badly to pollen and dust while others do not, some people thrive on challenge and adversity while others quail, some people gain weight easily with small increases in food consumption, while others remain skinny no matter what they eat, etc. And because humans have some ability to move towards environments that make them more comfortable and away from environments that they find uncomfortable, gene–environment correlations and interactions will tend to co-exist (Johnson, 2007).

The presence of gene–environment interactions and correlations produces systematic biases in heritability estimates based on samples of twins. The biases occur because the covariance caught up in the correlations and interactions really involves both genetic and environmental influences, but the estimation procedure requires that it be assigned to one source or the other because data from twins do not offer enough detail to make further distinctions. If genetic and shared environmental influences that make family members similar are correlated, heritability estimates are understated. But if genetic and nonshared environmental influences that act to make family members different are correlated, heritability estimates are overstated. This is also the case if genetic and shared environmental influences interact, but if genetic and nonshared environmental influences interact, heritability estimates are understated. Thus, without some understanding of the natures of genetic and environmental correlations and interactions, it is not even possible to guess the direction of bias in any particular heritability estimate.

Heritability estimates also typically rely on the assumption that there is no assortative mating for the characteristic in question. Assortative mating takes place when mating is not random, that is, when spouses are more similar, or more different, for the characteristic in question than are randomly selected pairs of men and women in the population. This may result from social stratification for similar characteristics. If this is the case, at the individual level the assortment may take place simply through propinquity: people tend to select their spouses from the people around them socially. Assortative mating may also result from active selection, as when people of one religious faith specifically select their spouses from among those of that faith. Either way, when the characteristic is genetically influenced, assortative mating for similarity results in increased genetic similarity between spouses even though they are not familially related in any recognizable way. And assortative mating for difference results in greater genetic diversity between spouses. In twin studies, assortative mating for similarity (of the parents of the twins) results in overestimates of shared environmental influences and underestimates of heritability because it increases the similarity of DZ twins without affecting the similarity of MZ twins, and the opposite for assortative mating for difference. Assortative mating tends to be low for many psychological characteristics such as personality, as opposites may be as likely to be attractive to each other as are people who are similar, and social stratification for personality does not appear to be very great, at least as personality is commonly measured. For other characteristics, such as antisocial behaviour and intelligence, it can, however be substantial. For intelligence, for example, spousal correlations often run about 0.4 (Jensen, 1998). Though there is evidence that people may select spouses actively for intelligence, there is also no question that social stratification, particularly in universities, plays some role.

The second major idea involved in the assumptions underlying heritability estimates is that twins are ordinary people. That is, there is nothing about being born as a twin rather than as a singleton that affects the characteristic of interest. One of the specific assumptions underlying heritability estimates from twin studies involves both this idea and the idea that genetic and environmental influences act independently of each other. This is known as the *equal environments assumption*. It is the proposition that environmental circumstances act to the same degree to make MZ and DZ twins similar or different. That is, the greater genetic similarity of MZ than of DZ twins does not create greater environmental pressure on them to become still more similar. The accuracy of the assumption has been questioned because many suspect that, when parents know that their twins are MZ rather than DZ, they tend to treat them more alike than they otherwise would. Of course, more similar treatment would not have to depend on knowledge of twin zygosity; it could arise simply because the twins act more similarly, but then this would be an example of evocative gene–environment correlation. In response to the questioning, the assumption has been tested in many studies. In general, it has appeared that MZ twins do experience more similar environments, but the greater environmental similarity does not contribute to the similarity of the traits of interest. This has most often been tested by examining whether treatments such as sharing bedrooms and classrooms and being dressed alike, circumstances such as sharing extra-curricular activities and friendships, and the greater contact that commonly exists between MZ twins than DZ twins contributes to greater similarity in psychological characteristics. It is possible, however, that these are not the most relevant ways of testing the assumption. For example, what is relevant to similarity of psychological characteristics might not be whether twins are dressed alike but how it is that they are dressed, the style of clothing, whether it is clean and neat, etc. Any greater similarity of MZ than DZ twins could be due to the greater similarity of MZ than DZ response to *how* they are dressed rather than to its sameness, *per se*. This would then be a form of gene–environment interaction.

The prenatal environment is another source of potentially greater similarity in MZ than DZ twins. About two-thirds of MZ twin foetuses share a chorion in the placenta because the chorion had already developed before the single fertilized egg from which they develop divided. All DZ twins have separate chorions. The effect of sharing a chorion is, however, often counterintuitive. For anthropomorphic measures such as height and weight, MZ twins who have shared a chorion generally show less similarity than those who have not. This is because they usually also share the maternal circulatory system that supports both of them, and the blood supply flows first through one twin and then through the other, causing the second twin to be smaller than the first. In the few studies that have addressed this topic, effects of sharing the chorion on psychological characteristics such as cognitive abilities and personality have not been consistent. This may be partly because chorionicity information is rarely available, particularly in older samples, and partly because any information that is available may not be accurate, due to a long-standing misimpression that twins with two chorions are always DZ.

To produce population-accurate estimates of heritability, twins must also be representative of the rest of the population, in the sense that there is nothing about twinning itself that affects development of the characteristic of interest. Twin pregnancies are generally more difficult than those of singletons because of the additional stress on the mother's system involved in carrying two growing foetuses rather than just one. This often results in somewhat shorter gestational periods and lower than average birth weights. Moreover, once labour begins, first one twin must be born and then the other, which means that one twin may spend an unusually long time in the birth canal. As will be discussed in greater detail in the next chapter, these kinds of birth complications can be associated with psychological and health characteristics. Though twins seem to overcome relatively low birthweight and early birth better than singletons (matching for weight and gestational age), this is still an important concern. For many years, for example, studies observed that twins tended to score slightly less well on average than singletons on intelligence tests. More recent studies, especially those that compared twins with their singleton siblings, have shown no differences. One explanation for this is that improvements in medical technology have minimized the risks associated with pre-term birth, low birthweight, and birth complications.

One other way that twins must resemble the rest of the population is that there must be nothing about the social aspects of twin relationship itself that affects development of the characteristic of interest. Because they are the same age, twins often grow up in much closer association with each other than do singleton siblings, sharing school classes, friends, and activities. This could cause them to make extra efforts to seek their own environmental niches, making them more different from each other than they otherwise might have been, or they could welcome the closeness and thereby become more similar to each other. In general, studies of this issue have found evidence for a little of each, and it is likely that some twins react to their twinship in one way, while others react in another, so that overall there is little consistency and thus no overall effect on heritability estimates. Being a twin could also affect the average level of the characteristic. For example, one study of personality in a large group of twins and singletons showed no differences for most aspects of personality (Johnson, Krueger, Bouchard, & McGue, 2002). For Social Closeness, or the tendency to prefer the company of others to being alone, however, twins scored slightly higher than singletons.

It is very likely that the assumptions underlying estimates of heritability are very often violated. This means that their magnitudes should be taken as, at best, approximate. This would be necessary in any event, however, as heritability estimates are specific to the environmental circumstances of the sample and also to the genetic composition of the sample. Despite this, they have provided clear and consistent evidence that genes do influence psychological characteristics. Over the last 40-50 years, this evidence has transformed much of psychological theory from thinking of individuals as interchangeable sponges absorbing the effects of environmental circumstances to incorporate recognition that each individual brings something inherent to his or her own development. This has primarily been accomplished, however, within an often implicit assumption that correspondences between genes and traits are one-to-one.

Human genetic variation and identifying the effects of specific genes

Reliance on this assumption has led to the development of spectacular technologies for isolating and identifying the SNPs in DNA extracted from individuals. These new technologies, which were very expensive when first developed, have increased rapidly in power and precision, and decreased at least as rapidly in cost of use. This has made it possible to collect DNA from large, population-based samples and to develop analytical methods to match the presence of specific SNPs to particular traits.

The methods used to do this have relied heavily on the assumption that the links between SNPs and phenotypes are direct and strong. The first method to be developed, called *linkage analysis*, is based on the fact that alleles that are located close to each other on the genome are likely to be transmitted together from parent to child. This suggested that SNPs could be used as map markers for the genome by identifying, or genotyping, specific SNPs at regular intervals along the genome. In family groups in which a disease or other trait is transmitted according to the basic mendelian laws of inheritance, a marker SNP found to be reliably associated with a disease or other characteristic indicates that there is a genetic locus in the genomic 'neighbourhood' of the marker SNP that is actually involved in the phenotype, though it may not be the marker SNP itself. The underlying theory is that the linkage between the actual genetic locus and the phenotype is strong, but the linkage between the marker SNP and the phenotype is not expected to be particularly strong. This is because during the cell divisions that create sperm and egg cells that have only half the genetic material of functional cells in the body, the chromosomes in the individual that came from his/her mother and father 'cross over' (exchange *homologous*, or corresponding, genetic material with each other), so that the resulting egg or sperm cell contains chromosomes that are some mixture of the original ones in the individual. The probability that two SNPs on one chromosome in the individual will be transmitted together in the formation of an egg or sperm cell is roughly proportionate to the distance between them on the genome. This is called *linkage disequilibrium*. Linkage analyses have often been based on estimates that, in family samples showing both members displaying and not displaying the phenotype of interest, about 400 genetic markers spanning the range of the genome should be sufficient to identify the region in which the actual genetic locus responsible is located and linked to the marker.

Linkage analysis was important in identifying the genes associated with Huntington's Disease, cystic fibrosis, a rare form of breast cancer, as well as more than 2,000 disorders that are transmitted from one generation to the next in direct fashion according to Mendel's laws of genetic transmission. This success has reinforced the tendency among geneticists to think in terms of direct correspondence between genotype and phenotype, but many phenotypes do not show these direct patterns of transmission from generation to generation and clearly involve more than single genetic loci. This has become increasingly clear because many early studies that showed strong linkage with particular SNPs have not proven to be replicable. More recent technologies have been developed to increase the specificity of the genetic location identified as associated with the phenotype, and thus the robustness of the association. This has been done in two ways.

First, allelic association studies make use of educated guesses about specific genes that may be involved in particular phenotypes, based on existing knowledge about the genes' functions. They thus evaluate only one or a very small group of genetic loci for association with the phenotype. Because there is a specific reason for suspecting association, the sample can be any population-based group and does not have to contain groups of families. With rare disorders, however, case-control groups have commonly been used to generate adequate numbers of cases. For example, a single SNP, known as Val/Met for the two allelic forms it takes, in the catechol-O-methyl gene is involved in the catecholamine brain neurotransmitters dopamine, epinephrine, and norepinephrine. The Val allelic form results in less available dopamine in the synapses between neurons following neurotransmitter release. This in turn reduces the stimulation that dopamine provides to the next neuron. Because the drugs used to treat many psychopathological conditions including hyperactivity, Parkinson's Disease, anxiety, and schizophrenia modulate the production of dopamine, and dopamine is also involved in executive brain functions, many studies have examined whether the Val/Met allele is associated with these and other conditions and even with general intelligence. Though some studies have shown the anticipated associations, replication has again presented a problem, specifically in studies of the COMT gene and also in association studies more generally. Still, the technique has produced some widely publicized successes.

The well-publicized discovery of the association between the apolipoprotein (APOE) E4 allele and Alzheimer's Disease (Corder, Saunders, Strittmatter, Schmechel, Gaskell, Small, et al., 1993) is one of these, and its circumstances help to explain why association studies have proven difficult to replicate. The genomic region in which this allele lies was originally identified as associated with Alzheimer's Disease through linkage analysis. The APOE polymorphism was one of the few known to lie in this region, so it became the candidate for association studies for lack of a better choice. The APOE polymorphism was known at that time for its involvement in transporting lipids throughout the body, so an association with Alzheimer's Disease was initially puzzling. It has been confirmed repeatedly, however (Bertram, McQueen, Mullin, Blacker, & Tanzi, 2007), and the confirmation has led to greater understanding of the mechanics of Alzheimer's Disease by revealing how lipid transport is involved in the development of the brain neurofibrillary tangles and amyloid deposits that characterize the disease. Despite the robustness of the association, the risk allele E4 is neither necessary nor sufficient for development of Alzheimer's Disease. Many who carry it do not develop the disease, and a third to half of Alzheimer's patients do not carry it. This is partly because diagnosis of Alzheimer's Disease is categorical while the plaques and tangles and memory impairments that characterize the disease are continuous, so some who carry the risk allele may show impairments that do not reach the threshold for diagnosis. Still, it is plain that many other genes, as well as environmental circumstances and transactions between them, contribute to development of the disease. If a genetic association is not very strong, and/or varies considerably with environmental circumstances, samples that differ in the frequency of the focus polymorphism, other genetic background, and environmental circumstances may show association to very different degrees.

The second technique, developed since 2000, combines the linkage and association approaches. As the cost of genotyping has come down, it has become feasible to think in terms of developing, rather than 400 genetic markers, 400,000 or even 1 million genetic markers and applying the linkage analysis approach to general population samples rather than to family groupings. The idea remains the same as in linkage analysis, but the linkage between any identified marker and the actual locus associated with the trait of interest is expected to be much stronger because the markers are much more densely packed together. These *genome-wide association* studies have become very common, but, again, despite some spectacular successes, they have been plagued with failures to replicate across samples. In addition, even when replication is possible, the genetic loci involved have explained only very small percentages of the genetic variances in the phenotypes (Maher, 2008). This has led to the development of newer technologies to sequence rare as well as common genetic variants, copy number variations, runs of homozygosity, and patterns of gene expression. As costs associated with these techniques fall, they are increasingly being implemented. In general, these techniques are based on the same underlying theoretical conception of a clear map between gene and trait.

This section of the chapter has provided a grounding in some of the genetic principles, conceptual orientations, and techniques that have been and continue to be used to develop the body of knowledge on which the remainder of this book is based. Together, the two sections of the chapter are intended to provide a framework in developmental neurophysiology through which the remainder of the book's focus on psychological development can be understood. Before that, however, the next chapter explores the general topic of how brain and body, together, respond to and cope with stress.

Further reading

Allman, J. (2000). *Evolving Brains*. New York: Scientific American Library.

Bishop, K. M., & Wahlsten, D. (1997). Sex differences in the human corpus callosum: Myth or reality? *Neuroscience Biobehavioral Review, 21*, 581–601.

Cosgrove, K. P., Mazure, C. M., & Staley, J. K. (2007). Evolving knowledge of sex differences in brain structure, function, and chemistry. *Biological Psychiatry, 62*, 847–855.

Johnson, W. (2007). Genetic and environmental influences on behavior: Capturing all the interplay. *Psychological Review, 114*, 423–440.

Rimoin, D. L. (2007). A half century of medical genetics: Where do we go from here? *American Journal of Human Genetics, 81*, 670–672.

Stress Response, Coping Capacity and Resilience

Just what is stress?

Before we can discuss stress response, we need to define stress. This is more difficult than it might appear, as the term is often used in different ways. First, it is often used to refer to situations or events, particularly ones that portend danger, threat, or material or personal loss. This is not always the case, however; sometimes the term 'stress' is used to refer to some form of challenge that leads to opportunity to better one's situation if the challenge can be met. Second, rather than the triggering situation or event itself, the term 'stress' is sometimes used to refer to one's response to that trigger. And third, the term is sometimes used to refer to a chronic state of imbalance between external stimuli and internal coping resources. In this book, I use the term to describe situations or events external to the individual that elicit physiological and behavioural responses within the individual that go beyond those necessary to maintain resting physiological and neurological function.

Response to stress involves many physiological systems, from the circulatory system to the immune system to specific hormonal levels to memory and learning functions. Responses in each of these areas are closely interrelated and involve mutual feedback loops. So far, however, research methods are not adequate to address all of these mechanisms simultaneously. Instead, research has been balkanized to focus on individual systems almost as if they acted independently, despite clear awareness that they do not. This means that understanding of stress response is a little like the legend of the blind men and the elephant: one blind man thought the elephant was rather like a snake because he felt the trunk, while another, who felt a leg, thought the elephant was rather like a tree. Clearly, this situation will have to change in order to understand stress response fully, but, at present, the reader must simply keep it in mind.

Though many responses to stress are physiological, interpretation of a situation or event as threatening or challenging or not takes place in the brain, and it is this interpretation that determines the organism's (be it human or some other animal) response. The hypothalamus, parasympathetic nervous system, and brain stem are essential for autonomic and neuroendocrine responses, but higher, more cognitive areas of the brain are also involved through the interpretive processes. Like the rest of the body, these areas are also targets of stress hormones and the brain responds to other physiological responses such as increased heart rate as well. Thus the brain plays a central role in stress response, and emotional/psychological responses to stress are intimately linked with physiological responses. The brain may in some sense lead the way through its interpretive role, but this leading role is far from the only role it plays in stress response.

Stress is a double-edged sword. Too much and all organisms, including humans, become physiologically and/or psychologically disordered in some way. That is, they become physically and/or mentally ill. Not enough, and physiological processes begin to atrophy, and people also tend to become physically and/or mentally ill, though the kinds of illnesses they display tend to differ from those associated with too much stress. Just enough stress, and people rise to the occasion, performing splendidly and generating a blossoming of physical health and psychological well-being. What constitutes the 'right' amount of stress to stimulate this oh-so-positive response instead of the unfortunate and debilitating illness response varies considerably from individual to individual. It varies in several other ways as well. Stress can vary in some measure of absolute intensity of the stress itself (voltage associated with electric shock, for example), it can vary in absolute intensity of the recipient's response (increase or decrease in heart rate, for example), and it can differ in the individual's psychological experience of that response (the context of the experience for the individual and the individual's interpretation of that context). In addition to these sources of differences in the stress experience itself, there can be individual differences in vulnerability to disorder resulting from stress response. That is, under whatever constitutes excessive stress for an individual, some may develop depression, while others develop cardiovascular disease and still others cancer. Taken together, the existence of four different sources of large differences in stress response guarantees that individual differences in response to any particular kind of stimulus intended to be stressful should be expected to be large. These individual differences in stress response, however, must be placed within the general patterns of response to stress before they can be properly understood. I therefore begin with these general patterns.

Functional and non-functional patterns of response to stress involving the HPA axis

Behaviourally, responses to stress have classically been thought of in terms of 'fight or flight': in the presence of stressful stimuli animals, including humans, either flee the situation or stand to defend themselves. This is of course too simplistic, particularly for humans who often resort to diversionary responses to stress such as overeating, smoking, alcohol consumption, and drug abuse, as well as to anxiety and worrying. These responses might be characterized as relatively passive combinations of fight and flight: the diversionary activities help to combat the immediately felt stress, which might be considered a way of fighting the situation by enduring its presence, but they are indirect, which might be considered a way of escaping the effects of the stress at least temporarily. Similarly, anxiety and worrying might be considered ways of fighting the situation by facing its possible negative consequences, but they too are indirect, so the actual fight is at least postponed.

These more passive, indirect responses to stress tend to occur more frequently in response to some kinds of stimuli than to others. This is important in understanding the processes involved in stress response. Many stress responses evolved under conditions in which there was little prior warning of challenge that might generate anticipatory stress response. For example, prey animals commonly find themselves suddenly attacked by predators, and must respond quickly if they are to respond at all. We infer, and have substantial evidence to believe, that human responses to such situations parallel those of most mammals, and particularly those of primates, very closely. It is not uncommon for such encounters to be extremely brief, lasting as little as 45 seconds (Sapolsky, Romero, & Munck, 2000). During this time, the prey animal either escapes or does not, and the response includes cognitive awareness of the threat and a skeletomuscular activation both of which can be extreme. The skeletomuscular activity is regulated by the central nervous system, but our understanding of how this physical response is integrated with the neuroendocrine responses that take place in the brain is limited because of the narrow focus of most investigations in this area. Because the subject of this book is psychological development, I concentrate my description on the neuroendocrine responses.

An initial wave of neuroendocrine responses is generated by the *sympathetic nervous system*. This is the part of the autonomic nervous system that prepares the body to react physically to emergencies. It consists primarily of adrenal gland fibres that reduce digestive secretions, increase heart and breathing rate and blood pressure, contract blood vessels, dilate pupils, and decrease the tone and contractility of smooth muscle, all of which mobilize the body for physical action. In addition, the first wave of brain response, which takes place within the first few seconds (importantly, after the initial skeletomuscular responses have been initiated if the animal hopes to survive the encounter), involves increased secretion of the catecholamine neurotransmitters norepinephrine and epinephrine. This triggers the hypothalamus to increase secretion of corticotropin-releasing hormone (CRH), and, about 10 seconds later, to decrease secretion of gonadotropic-releasing hormone (GnRH). About the same time, the pituitary releases adrenocorticorticotropic hormone (ACTH), and then responds to the decreased secretion of GnRH by decreasing secretion of gonadotropins. The pituitary also secretes prolactin and growth hormone, and the pancreas secretes glucagon. A second, slower, wave of hormonal responses takes place on the order of 10 minutes after the initial triggering event, well after many threatening events have taken place, presuming the event has been survived. These responses involve increased secretion of glucocorticoids (GC, often also commonly known as stress hormones) by the adrenal gland, and decreased secretion of gonadal steroid hormones.

The transactions among the organs that generate these responses, the hypothalamus and the pituitary and adrenal glands, are, together, known as the *hypothalamic-pituitary-adrenal (HPA) axis* (see Figure 4.1). In addition to its involvement in response to stress, this axis regulates digestion, the immune system, sexuality, moods and emotions, and energy storage and expenditure. This fact alone should make clear that physical and psychological responses are intimately connected. Within the first minute after a sudden unforeseen stressor, the hormones released by the HPA axis divert energy to the muscles

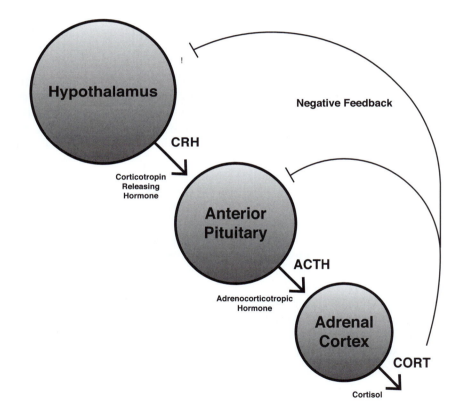

Figure 4.1 The HPA axis

Note: Under stress, the hypothalamus releases corticotrophin-releasing hormone to the anterior pituitary. This in turn releases adrenocorticotropic hormone to the vascular system, which carries it to the adrenal cortex. This signals the adrenal cortex to release cortisol, the body's major stress-response hormone. Once it is released into the bloodstream, the presence of cortisol acts to indicate to the hypothalamus and anterior to modulate production.

by mobilizing stored energy, inhibiting further storage of energy, and stimulating gluconeogenesis, or the conversion of non-carbohydrates such as lactate, glycerol, and many amino acids to glucose in order to maintain blood sugar levels. To make delivery of increased energy to the muscles possible, the HPA axis hormones also enhance cardiovascular tone, stimulate immune function, inhibit reproductive physiology and behaviour, decrease feeding and appetite, and sharpen cognition through increased cerebral utilization of glucose and blood flow to the brain. The 'sharpening' of cognition takes specific forms that may have relevance for long-term cognitive function when stress responses are prolonged. Under stress, individuals become hypervigilant. This means that attention to the surrounding environment is intense and focused, reducing attentional resources available for effortful concentration on tasks not involved in the immediate stress. Because of both this change in attentional focus and the effects of the GCs released in response to stress on brain structures such as the hippocampus and amygdala, episodic memory (which would tend to involve material not directly related to the stress) is impaired while learning and memory for emotionally salient events (which would tend to be those immediately related to the stress) are enhanced (Meaney, 2001).

The first wave of responses generates a second, much slower, wave of stress-induced effects in the targeted tissues. Many of these effects involve GCs and do not materialize for about an hour after the initial triggering event. The others involve gonadal steroids and do not materialize for several hours.

In addition to their activities in direct response to stress itself, HPA axis activities have several purposes, as summarized by Sapolsky, Romero, and Munck (2000). *Permissive* levels of HPA axis hormones are present before the stress. They prime the HPA axis responses to the stress and make possible the initial physiological and neurological responses that take place before the HPA axis responses to the event can have their downstream effects on further responses. *Suppressive* actions of the HPA axis are initiated approximately an hour after the stress and act to rein in the hormones released by the axis in direct response to the stress, contributing to recovery. *Stimulating* actions are also initiated at least an hour after the stress. They act in ways opposite to the suppressive actions and enhance the effects of the direct responses to the event. Whether suppressive or stimulating actions predominate during this time period clearly involves some level of cognitive appraisal of the necessity of further action. Finally, *preparative* actions act over a longer timeframe to adjust permissive levels of HPA axis hormones to modulate ability to respond to future stressful events. They may be either suppressive or stimulating and also involve some level of cognitive appraisal of the necessity of further action. If we think of a stress as analogous to a military attack, the direct HPA axis responses would be the first defensive shots fired. Permissive actions would be the actions taken to put the defensive forces in place and available to take those first shots. Stimulating actions would be additional actions taken after the initial attack to enhance responsiveness, such as calling up reserve forces. Suppressive actions might include restraining activities of one unit to avoid friendly fire, and preparative actions might include imposition of rationing to maximize the time that available resources will last.

The four longer-term kinds of HPA axis activities form the bridge between the physiological and behavioural responses to unpredictable stressful events and the physiology and behaviour involved in the routine activities of life. These routine activities include obtaining appropriate nutritional inputs to maintain normal movements, breeding activities, migration, acclimation to cold and heat, etc., and involve homeostatic mechanisms that function to maintain physiological and behavioural stability despite basically predictable environmental fluctuations. The level of homeostasis achieved, and therefore preparedness for unpredictable stressful events, however, depends on the burdens imposed by the surrounding basically predictable environmental conditions. These burdens include external environmental conditions such as parasite and infection load, chronic disease, permanent injury, social status, and pollution. But they also include internal psychological conditions related to cognitive appraisal of the likely necessity of further action. Attentional vigilance is involved here. In the relatively straightforward example of a lone prey animal, at least by adulthood, members of any species have some representation of their predators and the kinds of conditions in which they are more likely to experience assault that it is probably fair to term knowledge or understanding, and they can often take some actions that will help them to be alert to and to avoid those conditions. Thus, though any particular predatory assault may be of very brief duration, general awareness of being prey and whatever stress response this awareness generates is a permanent condition of life. Greater attentional vigilance is the primary response to this awareness and it may inspire greater avoidance actions, but greater attentional vigilance is maintained through higher HPA axis activation. Both HPA axis activation and any resulting physical movements have energy and metabolic costs that must be balanced against any reduced risks of predation. The same principles are involved in the more complex human (and many other animal) environments where stress-generating situations can extend over long periods of time.

Allostasis

Incorporation into models of mammalian stress response of the often long-term nature of stressful events and the psychological and physiological responses to them has led to development of the concept of *allostasis* (McEwen & Wingfield, 2003; Sterling & Eyer, 1988). Allostasis is the process through which the body seeks stability in its physiological systems that maintain life, in the face of changing external conditions. The term is generally used in a way that implies a very long-term view of the search for stability, as it is often used to encompass recognition that the various physiological set-points that define stability at any one point in time may also change throughout the lifespan, due both to changes in external conditions and to internal genetically influenced developmental processes. At any point in time, the body has some *allostatic state*, which may be balanced with respect to metabolic resources and environmental demands, or unbalanced so that some metabolic resources are present in excess of environmental demands, while others are insufficient to meet them. Examples of imbalance might be hypertension, perturbed diurnal rhythms of GC production, or elevation of inflammatory cytokines in combination with low GCs. Such imbalances are metabolically costly, but they can be maintained for limited periods of time, and may even be normal in some situations. For example, bears consume much more food than immediately necessary in the period before entering hibernation.

As the concept of allostasis has been developed, a fundamental aspect of the process of allostasis itself is the restoration of balance to an unbalanced allostatic state, but this is more metabolically costly than maintenance of a balanced allostatic state. When the body is called upon to restore balance to unbalanced allostatic states, the additional costs accumulate in damage to the physiological systems involved. This damage is termed *allostatic load*. Allostatic load develops through high frequency of stress responses to novel stressors, failure to adapt to a repeated stressor, failure to modulate the stress response when the stressor has past, and/or inadequate response from one stress mediator that leads to hyperactivity of other mediators. Increases in allostatic load contribute to development of chronic disease states that can be considered results of *allostatic overload*.

Allostatic overload is considered to take two forms (McEwen & Wingfield, 2003). In the first, some emergency event generates demands for energy that exceed energy income and the energy that the body can mobilize from stored sources of energy such as body fat. To survive, the body alters normal metabolic patterns, adopting ones that temporally require less energy. For example, reproductive activities might cease and/or body mass might be lost, with a new homeostatic balance between energy demands and resources maintained for the duration of the emergency. Once the emergency situation is past, the body can restore original metabolic levels. This form of allostatic overload is adaptive, and the responses described above to a predatory assault would be considered allostatic overload of this type. In the second type of allostatic overload, as a response to stress the body takes in and accumulates greater energy stores than it needs. If this state of imbalance persists, it causes changes in the stress response systems due to long-term exposure to nonoptimal levels of stress-response hormones, including remodelling or loss of neuronal pathways in the hippocampus, enlargement of the cells of the left ventricle of the heart due to elevated blood pressure, development of athersleotic plaques that thicken artery walls and reduce blood flow, increased blood sugar levels, and immune system imbalance. These conditions bring on fatigue and chronic pain and contribute to the development of chronic illnesses commonly seen among humans and captive animals, including heart disease, diabetes, depression, and cancer.

Other physiological responses to stress

Besides the HPA axis responses to stress, other metabolic systems also mount responses. Like HPA axis responses, when the stressful event is of brief duration and responses are adequate to meet demands, they are adaptive, and recovery from the stressful event can be complete. When responses are not adequate to meet demands, some form of metabolic accommodation to the situation must take place, and this accommodation usually has long-term debilitating consequences for health and well-being.

Inflammation is one of the major responses of the vascular tissues to harmful stimuli such as infectious agents like bacteria and viruses, damaged cells, and chemical irritants. It is a protective attempt by the body to remove the harmful stimuli and repair the damage it has caused. Inflammation is typically classed as acute or chronic. As with HPA axis responses, it is easiest to begin to understand inflammation by considering some of its most common acute manifestations, those brought on by injuries and intrusions into the body of foreign bodies including infectious agents and toxins. Acute inflammatory responses include pain, redness of tissue (hence the name inflammation), immobility or loss of function at the site of injury or intrusion, swelling, and heat. The redness and heat are caused by increased blood flow to the site. Swelling is caused by accumulation of fluid in the area, and pain results from response-induced stimulation of nerve endings. Loss of function can have many causes. The cells that initiate these processes are normally present but not active in all tissues, including white blood cells and other specialized cells of the immune system. Their responses to the intrusion are *reflexive,* which means that they take place automatically and without conscious intervention.

Initial responses all involve vascular changes, particularly dilation of blood arteries and vessels, increases in cell permeability, and slowing of blood flow. The purpose of these changes is to bring increased plasma, which is contained in blood and in turn carries the proteins that neutralize the invading agents, directly into the tissue so that the neutralizing proteins can act. All this requires the mobilization of energy resources, especially those in the liver, which secretes both the inflammatory proteins that neutralize the invading agents and many of the compounds that generate the necessary energy. These processes are initiated within about an hour of invasion or injury, and are generally maintained over a period of several days. After that, additional aspects of the immune system become involved. Many of these immune responses also involve the HPA axis responses discussed above. The acute-phase responses cause immediate expenditures of energy that typically exceed available intake, thus inducing sickness behaviours including reduced appetite and lethargy. If the invasion or injury cannot be cleared, the inflammatory systems and their attendant downstream immune responses remain overactivated, generating another source of allostatic load.

Importantly, in jawed vertebrates, including of course humans, the immune system is adaptive. That is, the many types of proteins, cells, organs, and tissues that participate in the immune system operate in a dynamic network that can tailor its operations to recognize and respond to specific pathogens more efficiently through the development of immunological memory. Still, the immune system can malfunction in two ways. When the immune system is less active than normal, this immunodeficiency results in recurring infections that can become life-threatening. This can occur through genetic defect, or it can be induced by drugs or infection, such as by the virus that causes acquired immune deficiency syndrome (AIDS). Sometimes, instead, the immune system becomes hyperactive, fails to distinguish the body's own tissue from foreign invaders, and turns its defence mechanisms on its own systems. Many chronic illnesses have such *auto-immune* features. Perhaps surprisingly, recurrent infections can co-exist with auto-immune conditions.

Many of the molecules involved in the body's stress response systems survive and act in the body over long periods of time. Inevitably, this means that they can accumulate changes in structure from exposure to invading pathogens, and these changes can affect their ability to perform their normal functions. The immune system includes both processes for molecular repair by specific enzymes and regeneration of function through synthesis of new molecules and turnover of old ones, but these can be inadequate to meet needs. *Bystander damage* takes place when the rate of damage exceeds the rate of repair. It is termed 'bystander' because it occurs passively during otherwise normal immune system activities. It is important because it can impair future immune function either through suppression of immune function leading to immuno-deficiency or through reduction of ability to distinguish the body's own tissue from pathogens, leading to autoimmune disorders. There are four basic ways in which bystander damage takes place.

First, un-neutralized *free radicals* can cause bystander damage to body tissue directly. Free radicals are atoms or molecules that have single, unpaired elec-trons in their outer shells. These single, unpaired electrons make the atoms or molecules highly unstable and reactive. Free radicals of many elements and compounds are formed when they come into contact with oxygen, which is common as the body's stress response and inflammatory systems carry out their functions. When free radicals are created through the loss of one or more electrons, the process is known as *oxidation*. When free radicals are created through acquisition of one or more electrons, the process is known as *reduc-tion*. The formation of rust on iron exposed to water is a familiar example of the process of oxidation, and another is the way that fruit exposed to air turns brown on the surface. Analogous effects of oxidation and reduction in the body are involved in the means used by the body's inflammatory responses to destroy invading pathogens, as well as in the body's repair mechanisms following activation of stress responses of all kinds. When stress responses remain either hypo- or hyperactive, however, the resulting free radicals cause damage analogous to rust in the body's own tissues. The lungs are particularly susceptible to such damage, through exposure to cigarette smoke, air pollution, and allergens, and damage to the lungs has downstream consequences on heart function, which in turn affects transmission of oxygen to the brain, and thus brain function.

Second, oxidative damage to cell DNA, lipids, and proteins can result from ongoing exposure to blood glucose (Finch, 2007). Glucose is a compound normally found in blood and essential to normal bodily function, but, as for all such compounds, there is a level of blood glucose that is functionally optimal, yet the body can maintain basic functionality within some range of blood glucose levels. Bystander damage occurs when levels of blood glucose are greater or less than optimal over extended periods of time. Similarly, hyper- or prolonged responses of the immune system generate elevated levels of immune response cells that have memory for specific forms of pathogen relative to naïve immune response cells. Such increased differentiation of immune response cells appears to affect the DNA in the thin layer of cells that lines the interior surface of blood vessels throughout the circulatory system from the heart to the smallest capillaries. These cells cause blood to be pumped through the vessels more smoothly by reducing its turbulence. Increased differentiation of immune response cells appears to cause bystander damage through erosion or shortening of *telomere length* in the DNA of these cells. A telomere is a region of repetitive DNA sequences at the end of each chromosome. It protects the end of the chromosome from deterioration, from loss of important genetic information during cell division, and demarks the end of the chromosome so that it cannot become fused with the end of a neighbouring chromosome. Reduction in telomere length is associated with ageing and many disease processes. Finally, bystander damage can be purely mechanical, as when changes in blood flow associated with the accumulation of the chemical debris of the stress response system create stress forces that cause fissures or breaks in blood vessels.

Attachment theory

Humans, along with many other mammals, are social organisms. This is apparent from early infancy. Because it is also clear that many of the sources of stress in human environments involve social interactions, general patterns of development of social development are also important in understanding individual differences in stress response, coping mechanisms, and resilience. The best established theoretical explanation of these patterns was developed by the psychiatrist and psychoanalyst John Bowlby, who published his exposition of his *attachment theory* in a three-volume collection (Bowlby, 1969, 1973, 1980). No doubt importantly for its comprehensive perspective and its extended and important influence on our understanding of social development, stress response, and resilience, the theory was strongly grounded in evolutionary biology, ethology, theories surrounding the operation of dynamic systems, and theories of cognitive development. The theory is currently quite generally accepted.

Attachment theory posits that each infant needs a relationship with at least one person who can serve as primary caregiver in order for normal social, emotional, and cognitive development to occur. This need is based on the infant's inability to provide its own nutritional sustenance and safety. From an evolutionary perspective, because of this need, the theory also posits that infants are genetically predisposed to seek this relationship instinctively, and they form attachment bonds with any individual who is at least somewhat consistently sensitive and responsive to their physical needs and interacts with them socially in any way. Most often, the primary attachment figure is the mother, but infants can and readily will form attachment bonds with anyone who interacts with them with some consistency. According to the theory, the sensitivity of the social interaction to an infant's needs and emotional state is more important than the time spent. Infant behaviours involved in attachment serve to maintain both the attention of and proximity to the attachment figure. Formally, attachment bonds are not considered to emerge until well into the second half of the first postnatal year, but preliminary attachment-related behaviours occur well before this age. From birth, infants cry to attract the attention of caregivers. They also smile, though without apparent connection to any positive emotion. During the first eight postnatal weeks, the 'social smile' that is linked with positive emotion and caregiver recognition emerges, and infants begin to babble, both of which typically generate responses from caregivers. In these first few weeks, these behaviours appear to be, and are inferred to be, directed at others indiscriminately. Between the ages of two and six months, infant behaviour increasingly discriminates among familiar and unfamiliar others, and infants make increasingly successful efforts to maintain proximity to familiar others.

By one year of age, a range of these proximity-maintaining behaviours is typically in evidence. Infants will protest caregiver departure (often vehemently), display greeting and welcoming behaviour upon caregiver return, cling to caregivers when frightened, and both follow to the extent they are able and use the caregiver as a secure base from which to move in order to explore the immediate environment. The caregiver's presence makes exploration more appealing to the infant because potential sources of stress response or activation of the infant's HPA axis are removed or muted. If the caregiver is temporarily unavailable or unresponsive, the infant will protest or attempt to follow. With increasing cognitive development, toddlers begin to see their caregivers as independent people with their own goals and patterns of activity. This does not diminish the importance of the attachment bond, but it lessens the intensity of protest to and reduces expressions of anxiety during temporary separations or periods of little response. This process of increasing tolerance for separation, increased understanding of caregivers' independent goals and objectives, and increased ability to negotiate terms of interaction with caregivers continues throughout early and middle childhood, leading ultimately to adult autonomy.

Infant attachment-seeking behaviours consistent with this theory can be readily observed and there is a clear and straightforward rationale for their adaptive function and survival value during human evolution. Analogous behaviours can also be observed throughout the animal realm, further strengthening the evidence for their evolutionary significance. Perhaps the strongest evidence for the evolutionary significance of these behaviours comes, however, from the observation that the presence and strength of attachment in humans appears to be independent of the quality of caregiver responsiveness. That is, infants form attachments to those around them even when those around them mistreat them. Ironically, but also perhaps typical of developmental psychology, this is also where much of the empirical evidence for attachment theory becomes messy.

Measuring attachment and testing the theory

Testing any theory of course requires measurement of the relevant constructs. Most of the methods used to assess attachment relations were developed originally by Mary Ainsworth in the 1970s. With colleagues at the Tavistock Clinic in London, she devised a procedure, known as the *Strange Situation*, to observe the quality of attachment relations between a parent and young child, generally a toddler. The procedure involves observation of the child's activities during a 20-minute period in an experimental room that is unfamiliar to the child. The parent and child are first alone in the room. The parent is instructed to sit quietly and the child is allowed to explore the toys in the room at will. A person strange to the child then enters the room, engages the parent in conversation, and then approaches the child, distracting the child so that the parent can leave inconspicuously. After a short period alone with the stranger, who accommodates behaviour to that of the child, the parent returns and greets the child. Both parent and stranger then leave the room and the child is alone. The stranger then re-enters, and again accommodates behaviour to that of the child. The parent then returns and greets and picks up the child. The child's behaviour during these events is tabulated in four ways: (1) amount of exploration (for example, playing with the toys in the room) throughout, (2) reactions to the departures of the parent, (3) expressions of anxiety while alone with the stranger and, (4) behaviour on reunion with the parent. The Strange Situation is intended for use with children between the ages of about eight months to about three years, but it is sometimes used with older children as well.

Based on the behavioural ratings in these areas, Ainsworth placed attachment patterns in three categories: Secure, Avoidant, and Ambivalent/Resistant. The subsequent researcher Mary Main added a fourth Disorganized category to the list, and this four-category list is generally used today. The categories have been important in developing our understanding of stress response because they have been the primary means of describing and differentiating how young children adapt to the care provided to them. A child categorized as Secure uses the parent as a base for exploration, setting off on his/her own and returning to share some object or looking back to share reactions to discoveries. The child protests the parent's departure, but can accept some comfort from the stranger. When the parent returns, the child seeks proximity, but is readily comforted and resumes exploration. The child shows a clear preference for comfort from the parent but is reasonably open to others too, and the parent's actions are in tune with the child's expressions of need. In contrast, the Avoidant child evinces little sharing of affect during exploration, expresses no particular distress at the parent's departure, no particular response to the parent's return, and will even ignore the parent or turn away if the parent moves to pick the child up. The child behaves similarly with the stranger. The parent offers little or no response to any expression of distress from the child, encourages independence, and discourages crying. The Ambivalent/Resistant child evidences continual anxiety about whether and how the parent will respond, hesitates to leave the proximity of the parent to explore, and expresses distress at separation. Despite this, the child expresses ambivalence and even anger upon the parent's return, and refuses to accept parental comfort. The child does not accept comfort from the stranger. The parent's responses to the child are inconsistent, sometimes being neglectful and other times hyper-responsive. To generalize, the parent may tend only to respond after escalated attachment-seeking behaviour from the child and then do so overbearingly. Finally, the Disorganized child shows truly troubled behaviours such as rocking, freezing, or approaching the parent while looking in the opposite direction, and appears to have no coherent strategy for establishing parental contact. The parent may behave abusively and/or appear to be frightened, and may misinterpret the child, be consistently negative in response, and/or appear to look to the child for attachment reassurance.

In western countries, about 65 per cent of children are typically classified as Secure, with the remainder allocated to the other categories reasonably evenly, though inability to make a definitive categorization is not uncommon (Prior & Glaser, 2006). Theory suggests that attachment should be established in infancy and remain stable through childhood and even adulthood, contributing to self-esteem and ability to respond constructively both to negative stress and to challenges that may contain positive opportunities if met. In the short term, such stability is generally present, but stability declines substantially with greater time between testings. This has led to substantial criticism of the Strange Situation, both as an appropriate measure of attachment within the theory and as providing evidence supporting attachment theory. Some of the criticism surrounds perception that the theory describes attachment as a characteristic that likely varies continuously in both quality (however operationalized for measurement) and strength, and questions the idea that any taxonomy of categories, such as those arising from the Strange Situation as typically applied, can adequately describe attachment and thus test the theory. At least based on the Strange Situation, Fraley and Spieker (2003) showed in a sample of 1,139 15-month-old children that variation in attachment patterns tended to be continuous rather than categorical. This could contribute to the difficulty in reaching definitive categorizations for some children. Other criticisms surround the artificiality and brevity of the Strange Situation, its roots in developed western cultures, and the fact that children may differ considerably in the extent to which they have experienced similar situations prior to the test. None of these criticisms actually questions the accuracy of the theory itself, however, as it does not specify that patterns of attachment are supposed to fall into discrete categories of any kind.

More substantive criticism involving the lack of stability in attachment status based on the Strange Situation surrounds the idea, very important to the theory, that attachment status in infancy and young childhood sets a child up for better life adjustment and greater social competence in later childhood, adolescence, and adulthood. Within the Strange Situation framework, Secure attachment is clearly the desirable category that should foretell positive outcomes, and the other categories describe various ways of adapting on the part of the child to less than optimal caregiving. In general, empirical data support this premise (Pearce & Pezzot-Pearce, 2007), but there are exceptions, and associations have not been particularly strong or uniform. In general, securely attached infants are more likely to grow into socially competent children and adults, but insecurely attached infants by no means all show adjustment problems, and influences such as peer relationships and relationships with adults formed well after infancy also have been shown to affect later adjustment. Perhaps even more importantly, instability in attachment status in infants and young children has often been associated with changes in caregiver conditions and responsiveness. Experience of stressful negative life events on the parts of parents, such as illness, abuse, divorce, or job loss, have also been commonly associated with instability in attachment status, and particularly with changes from Secure to insecure (Belsky, Fish, & Isabella, 1991; Del Giudice, 2009). But parents can also change their response patterns in positive ways that improve child attachment status, for example by taking parenting classes. Even older children's behavioural problems may vary considerably with improvements and deteriorations in parenting associated with parentally experienced stress.

Still, the overall pattern suggested by attachment theory and measured by the categories used in the Strange Situation does generally prevail empirically. That is, Secure attachment in infancy tends to be associated with positive life adjustment and good mental health, and all the other attachment patterns in infancy are at greater than average risk for adjustment problems and psychopathology. The risk is non-specific with respect to type of psychopathology. There are, however, a few general patterns. Disorganized attachment appears to confer the greatest risks, and it is associated with experience of maltreatment. Very generally, in samples of maltreated infants, some 80 per cent will be classified as Disorganized, compared with perhaps 12 per cent in community samples, and only perhaps 15 per cent of maltreated infants will be classified as Secure. Moreover, children with Disorganized attachment patterns in infancy often manifest rather disturbed patterns of relationships with peers, characterized by 'fight or flight' alternations between aggression and withdrawal. Overall, children with Ambivalent/Resistant attachment in infancy are more likely to experience internalizing problems such as depression and anxiety, while children with Avoidant or Disorganized attachment in infancy are more likely to experience externalizing problems such as conduct disorder, attention-deficit-hyperactivity disorder, and, later perhaps, substance abuse.

The roles of stress and stress response in development

Just why infant attachment status is associated with later psychopathology gets directly into the roles of stress and stress response in development. I have characterized patterns of attachment as adaptive responses on the parts of infants to the manner in which parents and other caregivers to whom infants look for both the development of their own social abilities and satisfaction of their emotional and physical needs. When an infant experiences stressful stimuli, from normal hunger and discomfort to extremes of pain or fright, and caretakers respond with sensitivity to resolve the source of stress and provide comfort, the infant's stress response system is activated but then calmed. Beyond that, negative emotions are aroused by the stress, but the responsive caretaking also arouses positive emotions. Even when caregiver response cannot remove all the negative emotions, the arousal of positive emotions helps to stabilize the stress response system. Over time, repeated experiences of this pattern help to train the stress response system to produce the appropriate levels of hormones so that it can regulate efficiently and effectively. In addition, the infant learns, in cognitive terms both implicitly and explicitly, from these experiences both what to expect from caretakers and how to manage his/her own behaviour to generate these satisfying responses. In the process, she/he forms an impression of his/her own importance in the surrounding world. Responsive caretaking, even when negative emotions and sources of stress cannot be completely removed, tends to lead to the development of positive self-esteem, trust in others, and constructive behaviour, which then extends to the broader world as the infant's experience expands.

In contrast, nonresponsive, neglectful, and/or abusive treatment from caregivers generates different stress response and emotional patterns and teaches different lessons about what to expect from others and the infant's importance in the world. When needs are not met and/or an infant suffers abuse, the stress response system remains aroused, with all the physiological consequences that have been discussed above. Importantly, if this happens often, the stress response system is not trained to regulate itself efficiently and effectively, potentially beginning a problematic combination of excessive stimulation of escalating stress responses and increasingly poorly developed modulating responses to counteract them. At the same time, the infant begins to accumulate negative emotional experiences without balancing positive emotional experiences, and to learn more about how she/he must behave either to meet his/her own needs without caretaker intervention and/or to avoid negative responses from caretakers. Either way, the lesson is that his/her needs are either unimportant or silly, which tends to lead to the development of negative self-esteem, and may contribute to mistrust of others and patterns of behaviour that attract negative attention from others, especially when the infant has experienced very inconsistent caregiver responses, as thought to be evidenced by Disorganized attachment.

Temperament

Despite the basic general truth of the above, attachment is clearly about more than simply caregiver responsiveness to infant expression of needs and quality of social interaction. That is, infants display considerable individual differences in the magnitudes of their responses to any given level of stress, their abilities to be soothed from any given intensity of expression of distress, the natures of the experiences that generate stress responses, their tolerance for disruption in routine, and the readiness with which they engage in social interaction. Most of these individual differences have their roots in individual differences in temperament and in physiological responses to stress, and many of these individual differences have underlying genetic influences. Exploring this is relatively new within the community of researchers studying attachment in humans, but has a longer history among those studying social development in other primates.

Temperament refers to the aspects of an individual's personality that reflect innate, biological responses to stimuli. The concept dates back to ancient Greece, where physicians believed that health and psychological well-being depended on balance among four 'humours', or aspects of biological function. Historically, discussion and theorizing surrounding the concept has tended to be dominated by the idea that adults differ in temperamental 'types', and many different temperamental typologies have been suggested. As psychology has become more rigorously scientific over the past 150 years or so, however, psychologists have recognized that the kinds of behavioural patterns that become the personality traits discussed in Chapter 1 develop through adaptive transactions between innate biological responses comprising temperament and the environmental stimuli actually experienced. Because the role of experience is strong and cumulative, during the past fifty years or so, psychologists interested in identifying the behavioural characteristics and biological markers that comprise temperament have tended to focus on infants, for whom relatively little experience has yet accumulated.

Many different infant temperament typologies have been suggested, but none has so far found complete empirical support. As with the Strange Situation, the difficulty in obtaining empirical support probably reflects several factors, including lack of stability in the behaviour of young infants, need for the behaviour to be evaluated by others who inevitably bring perceiver biases to their observations, and, perhaps most importantly, likelihood that any categorization of behaviour patterns into types is arbitrary because the underlying dimensions on which the categorizations are based are continuous and do not have naturally occurring boundaries. Still, brief examination of two of these typologies is helpful in understanding both the major dimensions that have been considered and some of the difficulties that have been encountered in working with them.

Box 4.1   Classifying temperament

Perhaps the classic 20th-century temperament classification scheme was developed by Thomas, Chess, and Birch (1968). Based on the New York Longitudinal Study begun in the 1950s, they identified nine dimensions of infant behaviour that they theorized would affect how well these infants would adapt to their childhood family, school, and peer environments. They recognized that these behavioural dimensions were continuous, and theorized that both unusually low and unusually high positions on these dimensions were likely of concern. The nine dimensions they assessed were: (1) activity level or physical energy; (2) regularity of biological functions such as waking, becoming tired, hunger, and bowel movements; (3) initial reaction (approach v. withdrawal) to new people or situations; (4) adaptability to changes in routine or in the environment; (5) intensity of responses, both positive and negative; (6) general mood, positive or negative; (7) distractibility by environmental circumstances and activities; (8) ability to persist in the face of frustration, and (9) threshold of responsiveness to environmental conditions such as noise levels, textures in clothing and food, light levels, etc. From these dimensions, Thomas and Chess (1977) observed that about 65 per cent of infants could be categorized into one of three groups they called Easy, Difficult, and Slow-to-Warm-Up. Of the 65 per cent, 40 per cent were Easy, 10 per cent were Difficult, and 15 per cent were Slow-to-Warm-Up. The Easy babies generally displayed positive moods, were regular in biological function, and adapted quite readily to new situations. The Difficult babies were essentially the opposite: they cried a lot, were often irritable and fussy, and had irregular sleeping and eating patterns. Slow-to-Warm-Up babies had low activity levels, withdrew from new situations and people, and were slow to adapt to them, though they generally eventually succeeded.

Some of the difficulties of measuring temperament are highlighted in this classification scheme. The nine dimensions articulated by Chess and Thomas clearly overlap to some degree, but they also seem to refer to distinct aspects of infant behaviour. Yet they reduced, in Chess and Thomas' scheme, to three categories of temperament, and these categories do not clearly apply to all infants. This is again reminiscent of the Strange Situation, and probably for many of the same reasons. Chess and Thomas' three-class measure of temperament formed the basis for one of the temperament measures still most commonly used, the Emotionality, Activity, and Sociability Survey (Buss & Plomin, 1984).

Goldsmith and Campos (Goldsmith, 1993; Goldsmith & Campos (1982) have conceptualized temperament differently. Instead of focusing on behaviours, they have defined temperament as individual differences in tendencies to experience and express emotions. They are clear in their focus on emotions that they mean all emotions, not just negative emotions. With Mary Rothbart, Goldsmith has developed several inventories to measure temperament (Goldsmith, 2000; Goldsmith & Rothbart, 1996). Unlike Chess and Thomas, however, more recent versions of the inventories include more dimensions than earlier versions (Goldsmith, 2000; Goldsmith & Rothbart,, 1996). All their inventories have included a component that goes beyond both emotion *per se* and the dimensions identified by Chess and Thomas. This is emotion regulation, sometimes also called 'effortful control'. It can be thought of as processes that monitor and evaluate emotional reactions in order to moderate them and the behaviours they stimulate to make it more possible to accomplish one's goals. A complex construct, the processes involved are generally considered to take place after some event that triggers an emotion, but some have argued that emotion and its regulation cannot be distinguished. Buss and Plomin (1984) originally considered emotion regulation in their temperamental system as well, but concluded that the ability to regulate emotions does not develop until well after infancy and thus should not be considered as an aspect of temperament.

Current conceptions of temperament dimensions and their biological markers

With the development of more precise measures of biological function, recent efforts to integrate the various conceptions of temperament have focused on components that have clear biological referents and that also can be observed in nonhuman animals. As will become clear in reviewing the dimensions most commonly studied currently, like attachment the biological markers involved in temperament are also those involved in response to stress. They are also closely related to each other and reflect not just infant behaviour itself, but the effects of infant behaviour on caregivers and others around them. The basic fact that infant behaviour does have effects on caregivers, and vice versa, implies that both typical responses of caregivers to infant behaviour and individual differences in caregiver responses to infant behaviour will have important influences on the ways in which temperamental characteristics contribute to personality and cognitive development in childhood and beyond.

Perhaps the most prominent of these temperamental dimensions is *behavioural inhibition*. As usually conceived, behavioural inhibition focuses on social situations: the behaviourally inhibited child hesitates to join social groups of same-age peers and to respond to or even look at unfamiliar adults, finds any sort of performance in front of others difficult, and has trouble carrying on activities when separated from attachment figures or in unfamiliar circumstances. Many researchers also include avoidance of physical risks within behavioural inhibition. Especially when avoidance of physical risks is included, it is easy to think of fear as the emotion underlying behavioural inhibition, but Jerome Kagan, who has spent most of his long career studying the construct, has argued that this is a mistake (Kagan & Snidman, 2004). Instead of fear, he and his colleagues have argued that the core feature underlying behavioural inhibition is difficulty tolerating uncertainty. Evidence for this view is provided by the amygdala, which has consistently shown associations between response and degree of behavioural inhibition in children (Henderson & Wachs, 2007; Schwartz, Wright, Shin, Kagan, & Rauch, 2003). As described in Chapter 3, this region of the brain was long considered to be involved mainly in negative emotional responses, avoidance of danger, and especially fear. More recent evidence, however, suggests that it is more accurate to think of it as involved in processing of novel, unfamiliar, or ambiguous stimuli more generally than in processing specifically stimuli triggering fear. Several other psychophysiological variables involved in processing novel stimuli also show associations with behavioural inhibition, including differences in electroencephalogram response between the two hemispheres of the brain, brainstem response to auditory stimuli (thought to reflect amygdalar activity), the event-related potentials N400 and P300 (brain waveforms evoked by unexpected or unfamiliar visual events), and heart rate variability, which tends to be lower in those with greater responses to novelty (Kagan, Snidman, Kahn, & Towsley, 2007). All are also involved in the body's autonomic responses to stress, suggesting that behavioural inhibition reflects differences in the degree to which individuals find processing novel stimuli and situations stressful.

The commonly identified temperamental dimension that most clearly reflects caregiver response to infant behaviour is *irritability*, which often also is considered to encompass susceptibility to frustration. Irritability usually refers to readiness to become upset by minor discomforts or impediments to attaining goals, and to express this discomfort in an aversive way that demands immediate relief. High scores on measures of this dimension are generally the primary contributors to classifications of infant temperaments as difficult, to be translated directly as difficult for caregivers to handle. The dimension is associated with greater activation of the HPA axis, and with differences in electroencephalogram response between the two hemispheres of the brain that reflect greater experience of negative emotion (Panksepp, 1998), with relatively greater activation on the right side of the brain indicating greater irritability. It is probably appropriate to consider this dimension linked to propensity to experience negative emotions.

Another commonly identified dimension that clearly reflects caregiver response to infant behaviour is *activity level*. This refers to total energy output as reflected in total amount of movement, its briskness, tempo, and vigour. It is generally assessed by walking speed, talking speed, tendency to hurry, time spent in high-energy activities, continuation of activity after other children have stopped, reactions to enforced idleness, and restlessness. Unlike most of the other dimensions discussed here, activity level probably reflects basic metabolic functions rather than responsiveness to external stimuli. Where high activity is welcomed by caregivers, it tends to become associated with positive emotionality in the active child, but when caregivers find it inconvenient or difficult to manage, it tends to become associated with negative emotionality. Similarly, when low levels of activity are more easily tolerated by caregivers, they tend to become associated with positive emotionality in the relatively inactive child, but when higher activity would be preferred, low levels of activity tend to become associated with negative emotionality.

Another characteristic that continues to be featured in temperament research is ability to maintain attention. This goes by many labels, including attention span, persistence, and effortful control, and is the complex construct mentioned above that does not really emerge until at least the end of the first year after birth. Some split it into two components, one of which is the capacity to maintain attention on a single task and to shift attention as desired, and the other of which is the capacity to plan and to suppress impulses that will thwart attainment of longer-term goals. Caregiver priorities enter into classifications of children along this dimension as well. When a child fails to maintain attention to tasks set by caregivers, it is not uncommon for the caregivers (and other observers) to attribute this to inability on the part of the child to maintain attention. Closer examination of the situation, however, often reveals that the child can maintain attention well when internally motivated to complete the task, but does so far less 'well' when not internally motivated to complete it. Caregiver response to such 'failures' of attention can have implications for the development and maintenance of attachment relationships and also for the way in which underlying temperament is manifested in personality development and environmental adaptation.

Individual differences in attention capacity or effortful control have been associated with three biological networks. The first to develop has been characterized as the *alerting attentional system* (Posner & Rothbart, 2007). As its name suggests, it is involved in achieving and maintaining a state of alertness. This is the system that makes the initial perceptions that a response to external stimuli or stress of some kind is necessary, and thus is expressed primarily through orientation to the external stimuli. Within the brain, it is supported by the locus coeruleus in the brainstem. Along with the adrenal gland, this area produces the neurotransmitter norepinephrine (one of those involved in HPA-axis response), and projects into many other brain regions, including particularly the hypothalamus and the amygdala. Next to develop is the *orienting attention system* (Posner & Rothbart, 2007), which is involved in sorting through the available sensory input to select the information most relevant to organizing a behavioural response. These activities take place in the parietal brain areas and are primarily regulated by the neurotransmitter acetylcholine, which also activates muscles and regulates the autonomic nervous system that controls heart rate, respiration, digestion, etc. The final system, which, formally at least, is considered to emerge towards the end of the first year after birth, is the *executive attention system* (Posner & Rothbart, 2007). This system maintains continuity of behaviour in pursuit of goals despite possible distractions and allows self-directed focus of attention. In the brain, it is supported by the anterior cingulated cortex, the basal ganglia, and the lateral prefrontal cortex. Though it is considered formally to emerge only later in infancy, there is some evidence that much younger infants may use it in rudimentary fashion to control the degree of distress they experience by selecting the stimuli to which they pay attention (Harman, Rothbart, & Posner, 2007).

Though the concept of effortful control involves maintaining attention consciously over time in a manner intended to achieve goals that cannot be attained immediately, the psychophysiological systems that have been associated with maintenance of effortful control are those involved in immediately experienced stress, to which immediate response is warranted, such as the example with which I opened this chapter, of a prey animal encountering a predator. These are also the psychophysiological systems that become, if you will, stuck in 'on' mode when stress is overwhelming and allostatic load develops. Yet effortful control is generally considered to be the ability used to engage in the kinds of deliberate practice necessary to build new skills and the kinds of task persistence that result in attainment of the state that has been termed 'flow' (Csikszentmihalyi, 1996). A person in this state experiences completely focused motivation to pursue the task in which she/he is involved. The emotions are fully immersed in the activity, channelled towards the positive, energized, and oriented towards success. This apparently contradictory situation is no biological accident though. There is probably no clearer way to understand the double-edged nature of stress than to recognize that the same systems that become overloaded when the organism cannot meet the challenges posed by stress are those that deliver the most satisfaction when stressful challenges can be met. These systems also contribute to the experience of both our most negative and our most positive emotions. Moreover, they can contribute to negative emotional experiences both because they fail to maintain the stress responses we need to meet the challenges we face and because these same stress responses fail to shut off, creating additional systemic damage when we face adverse stress from which we cannot escape.

The final temperamental dimension commonly included in current temperament inventories is *positive emotionality*. It is usually conceived as the tendency to process stimuli that may offer potential rewards in the form of overt needs, such as food, as well as stimulation that we find enjoyable and useful, such as social engagement and appreciation of beauty. Behaviours associated with positive emotionality include interest, eagerness and positive anticipation, exploration, smiling and laughing, and sensation and novelty seeking. We probably understand the neurobiological and psychophysiological sources of positive emotionality least well of the temperamental dimensions I have discussed, but they appear to involve dopamine produced in the midbrain, and the endorphins produced by the pituitary glands and the hypothalamus. These are endogenously produced opioids that function as neurotransmitters, and they are produced in vertebrates including humans during exercise, experience of pain, consumption of spicy food, and orgasm. Within the brain, positive emotionality is expressed to a greater degree on the left than on the right side. Tendency to experience positive emotionality is generally considered to be independent of tendency to experience negative emotionality. This is despite the involvement of the same brain regions involved in the stress response. In infancy, the tendency to experience positive emotion is generally quite stable, whether measured in the lab or through parental reports, and it is the characteristic that is most likely to get an infant classified as 'Easy' by caregivers.

Integrating temperament, attachment and stress response

It should be plain from the descriptions of attachment and the commonly studied temperamental dimensions above that they all involve the biological and psychophysiological stress response systems. I described the functions of these response systems at the beginning of this chapter in terms that apply to all, not just humans but even most vertebrates. Yet the foundation of the concept of temperament is that individuals manifest considerable differences in it, and, whatever Bowlby's original theoretical intentions in articulating a universal evolutionarily selected attachment mechanism, the first attempts to describe the associated behaviours with any precision revealed individual differences in their manifestations. This implies that there are also individual differences in biological and psychophysiological responses to given levels of stress, and many studies have demonstrated in many different ways that this is the case. The presence of these individual differences in stress response raises the question of the evolutionary reasons for their preservation. In general, temperament researchers tend to argue that differences in temperament persist because they present different adaptive strengths and weaknesses in different environmental circumstances, and environmental circumstances vary both over time and in space sufficiently to maintain temperamental variation in all human and even most other animal populations. Attachment researchers originally may have considered secure attachment to be optimal, but increasingly they recognize as well that the other attachment types may reflect appropriate adaptations to more difficult environmental conditions. Thus, most would agree that whatever genetic influences are involved in individual differences in stress response are maintained through balancing selection as described in Chapter 2.

This means that understanding how individuals develop the characteristics they do depends on understanding the ways in which environmental circumstances transact with individual differences in temperament that operate within the universally applicable stress response and attachment systems. With respect to any single temperamental dimension, this depends not only on the kinds of external circumstances typically associated with the term 'environment', such things as maternal responsiveness, presence of excessive heat or cold, availability of appropriate levels of stimulation, etc., but it also depends on the individual's levels of the other temperamental dimensions, which in turn depend partly on the same environmental circumstances, but to different degrees and in different ways. Moreover, at some level all the individual-in-environment transactions that take place have to be considered adaptive, in the sense that the individual's responses bring about some kind of person–environment 'fit'. Socially, however, we recognize some forms of person–environment fit as more desirable than others, generally because the individual can be considered healthier, happier, more socially and/or reproductively successful, and/or more clearly financially self-supporting. This causes us to judge some characteristics that are actually adaptive to be pathological.

Researchers are just beginning to consider how one temperamental dimension may moderate the development of another, so empirical observations in this area are still quite limited. One area that has been explored, however, is the link between irritability or propensity to experience negative emotionality and ability to exert effortful control (e.g., Eisenberg, Fabes, Guthrie, & Reiser, 2000; Rothbart & Bates, 2006). The observation is that the ability to exert effortful control is more important to the development of well-regulated, socially valued behaviour in children high in irritability than in children low in irritability. This makes a good deal of intuitive sense: the expression of irritability tends to trigger negative responses in surrounding people, and the child who experiences more irritability is thus likely to generate more of those responses, likely also generating further irritability in the child. But if the child can control the expression of experienced irritability and substitute neutral or positive expressions (no matter what is actually being experienced), this process of escalating negative social interactions can be short-circuited. The child who experiences much less irritability, however, more rarely faces the problem of having triggered negative responses in others and thus has less need to make use of effortful control in order to maintain positive social interactions. Moreover, though the observation itself is limited to these two dimensions of temperament, it highlights both the likely importance of these two dimensions (and the similarity of the biological mechanisms underlying both of them) in adaptation to the external environment in ways that are socially termed positive and the interactive nature of the kinds of interrelations that are likely commonly involved.

Implications for development

Observations of transactions between temperament and environment further emphasize these kinds of moderating associations and the centrality of irritability/negative emotionality and effortful control in the emergence of adaptations that are socially termed positive. Moreover, in these observations, the tenor of parental responses to the child's expressions of temperament figure prominently in characterization of the child's environment. This clearly implicates the attachment system. In general, the observations can be characterized as indicating that children who are especially fearful, behaviourally inhibited, or prone to irritability/negative emotionality are more able to overcome these tendencies when their parents and others surrounding them respond to their expressions of fear and negative emotion with restraint, accepting the children's expressions but not allowing them to restrict the activities going on around them. Similarly, children who show low ability to exert effortful control are helped in developing this ability if their parents exert this control for them by applying gentle but firm discipline when they are very young (see Bates & Pettit, 2007; Rothbart & Bates, 2006, for reviews of this literature).

These observations are consistent with another general observation regarding the development of psychopathology, which can be characterized as adaptations that are socially termed negative. That is, there are two generally recognized major dimensions of psychopathology, generally termed externalizing and internalizing. Habitual excessive or inappropriately expressed aggression and hostility, rule-breaking behaviours, excessive activity, and distractibility during required activities generally contribute to externalizing problems, while internalizing problems are characterized by excessive anxiety and tendency to experience depression. High irritability/negative emotionality is a risk factor for both externalizing and internalizing problems. Low ability to exert effortful control, perhaps in conjunction with high positive emotionality, tends to underlie the development of externalizing problems rather than internalizing problems. Behavioural inhibition tends to underlie internalizing problems rather than externalizing problems. Because the stress response system is involved in both behavioural inhibition and ability to exert effortful control, it would appear that individual differences in levels and combinations of (1) reactivity of the stress response system, (2) toleration of the stress reactions experienced, and (3) ability to maintain conscious control over behaviour during stress underlie and perhaps unify individual differences in the temperamental dimensions most commonly identified.

At some level, our socialization systems are organized so that individual differences in temperamental dimensions are most clearly observable in behaviours labelled problems. That is, the lives of children in industrialized cultures are largely regulated by adults around them. The well-behaved child does what she/he is told to do by the surrounding adults, when she/he is told to do it, and much of parental activity is directed towards encouraging this kind of easily managed behaviour in their children. Even during ostensibly free time, children are often in settings such as play groups, where many kinds of individual behaviour will be considered disruptive to the group and the time allotted to free play is closely scheduled. But children are not always inherently motivated to do what they are told, and, however gently issued, the command to engage in some activity that one is not inherently motivated to carry out is a form of stress. It may be a form of stress that presents a challenge that can be met. If so, the stress system will respond, the required behaviour will be executed, the stress system will return to resting state, and some form of emotional satisfaction will result. But the stress may also present a challenge that cannot be met. If so, the stress system will respond but the child may or may not attempt to execute the required behaviour, depending on how the child evaluates the consequences of an attempt that fails in relation to the consequences of making no attempt at all. Either way, the stress response system is likely to remain activated over an extended period of time, allostatic load is likely to accrue, and some form of negative emotional response is likely to persist. Thus, adult expectations for children's behaviour, the match between those expectations and children's abilities to meet them, and adult responses when children fail to meet them are important factors in the ways in which children with particular temperamental characteristics adapt to the environment and whether or not those adaptations are considered positive or psychopathological by others.

This dependence of children's stress responses on the degree to which they are able to meet the behavioural demands placed on them by adults around them implicates the attachment system in the adaptation of temperament to environment. Though attachment status is usually described as being dependent on caregiver responsiveness to infant needs, one important way in which a sensitive caregiver responds to infant needs is by challenging (stressing) the infant to regulate behaviour in some socially valued direction at just the level the infant is able to meet, a level just a notch above what she/he was able to meet the day before, all else being equal. The Strange Situation was designed to mimic under controlled laboratory conditions the kind of situation that infants (at least in western countries) likely experience very frequently. Thus, for example, within the context of the Strange Situation, the infant and caregiver enter a strange room together and the infant is turned loose to explore it. This is a challenge in itself to many infants, but one most can meet with appropriate caregiver support. During the exploration, the infant may discover something frightening (for example, the stranger) or something she/he does not understand, and return to the caregiver for reassurance. This will arouse the stress response system. Offered in the way generally considered most appropriate, the caregiver will provide a supportive reassuring touch or word cheerfully, but the contact will be brief and it will carry with it the gentle implication that the infant should resume the independent exploration. If the reassurance is successful, the infant's stress response system will return to resting level, and there will be no difficulty with resumption of exploration. When this kind of situation occurs day in and day out in an infant's life, secure attachment develops, but so does a stress response system that is practised both in rising to meet challenges and returning to baseline level.

Recent research has tended to support this conception, though studies have usually been based on simultaneous assessments of temperament, response to stress, and caregiver response activities, preventing inferences about the causal ordering of the associations observed. For example, Hane and Fox (2006) found that, even after accounting for conventional temperament, infants of mothers who provided 'low-quality' care showed greater stress reactivity. Similarly, Jahromi, Putnam and Stifter (2004) observed that maternal responses to infant distress regulated the degree to which infants expressed distress. And Blair, Granger, Willoughby, Kivlighan, and Investigators (2006) found that maternal sensitivity to infant communicative outreaches was associated with more normal cortisol reactivity in response to challenge. In the latter study, less maternal sensitivity was associated with blunted rather than exaggerated cortisol reactivity. This emphasizes the complexity of biological responses to stress. That is, too little response to challenge can present just as much impediment to socially approved adaptation as too much response. Moreover, the stress response system itself appears to adjust and adapt over time to conditions repeatedly encountered.

When the infant's stress response is great, however, it may be very difficult for even a very skilled and sensitive caregiver to find a way to offer a level of support that will help the infant's stress response return to baseline levels. Within the Strange Situation, where the level of stress is, for ethical reasons, very low, this is unlikely, but it is not unlikely that it occurs at least occasionally in the outside world. This highlights that an important source of potential variability in attachment status outcomes besides caregiver responsiveness is individual differences in infant stress reaction to any given level of stress. Most of the focus of attachment research has been on caregiver responsiveness, and individual differences in infant stress reaction as the source of individual differences in attachment status has only relatively recently received attention. Moreover, conventional temperamental dimensions rather than stress reactivity have typically been used. Results have been at best inconsistent and at worst contradictory, as when attachment status was associated with high scores on some temperamental dimension in one study, but low scores on the same temperamental dimension in another (Vaughn, Bost, & van Ijzendoorn, 2008). One, rather small, association between temperament and attachment status that does appear with some consistency is between expressions of negative emotionality and less secure attachment. Perhaps importantly, these associations have been more commonly found with continuous questionnaire measures of attachment security rather than the attachment category assignments associated with the Strange Situation.

For example, van Bakel and Riksen-Walraven (2004) found a modest association between continuously measured security of attachment as measured by observers and social fearfulness measured from a laboratory task. And Szewczyk-Sokolowski, Bost and Wainwright (2005) found a similarly modest association between this measure of attachment security and mother-rated temperamental difficulty in preschool-aged children. Other studies using parental-rated continuously measured attachment security have yielded substantial associations of this nature, but the fact that parents rated both temperament and attachment security calls their results into question. Moreover, contemporaneous measurement of association does not address the question of causal direction. That is, it could be more difficult for more stress-reactive infants to develop secure attachments, or it could be that less secure attachment contributes to greater stress reactivity, or both. Developmentally, we wish to understand how individual differences in temperament present at birth contribute to development of attachment relations in later infancy, and, in turn, how attachment relations contribute to further development of temperament into characteristics we tend to recognize as personality or cognitive traits in later childhood, adolescence, and adulthood. From a theoretical perspective, we should expect that, if it is more difficult for more stress-reactive infants to achieve secure attachment, individual differences in security of attachment, and thus later personality and cognitive outcomes, should be greater in such infants than in those less stress reactive. If less secure attachment contributes to greater stress reactivity and thus to later trait outcomes, we should expect that individual differences in stress reactivity should be greater in those with less secure attachment. This means that, rather than main effects *per se*, we should expect interactive effects involving temperament and attachment in later personality and cognitive outcomes. This is perhaps emphasized by the general observation that while temperamental dimensions tend to show strong genetic influences (50-60 per cent of variation), measures of attachment security, even in adults, tend to show primarily shared environmental influences (Vaughn, Bost, & van Ijzendoorn, 2008), suggesting that, for attachment security, it is primarily parental treatment that matters.

Testing stress reactivity, maternal responsiveness and attachment associations in rats

Interactive associations between stress reactivity and maternal responsiveness have been explored most thoroughly in nonhuman animal models, with work in rodents and rhesus monkeys being perhaps clearest. Early rodent studies in this area demonstrated that environmental circumstances could regulate the development of stress responses by exploring the effects of human handling of neonatal rat pups (Meaney, 2001). In these studies, rat pups were separated from their mothers for brief periods (3-15 minutes) daily for the first several weeks of life and held in the hands of experimenters, or stroked either manually or with paintbrushes. As adults, the rats that had experienced such handling showed reduced fearfulness and smaller HPA-axis responses to many forms of stress, even in old age, apparently because of smaller effects of ageing on the hippocampus (Meaney, Aitken, & Sapolsky, 1991). Importantly, this does not mean that the handled rats were hardier in some absolute sense than rats that had not been handled. For example, Laban, Dimitrijevic, van Hoersten, Markovic, and Jancovic (1995) observed that rats that had not been handled were more resistant to experimental induction of a virus than were handled rats, suggesting that the greater responsiveness of their HPA axes conferred some advantage. Thus, the point is that the rats that had been handled differed in stress response from those that had not, and this difference appeared to have its roots in the difference in their early experience.

The level of stress induced by the handling experience is apparently also relevant to the effects on stress reactivity in rat pups. In normal conditions, mother rats normally leave their nests, and their pups, for periods of 20-30 minutes to search for food, defecate, and so forth. Thus the handling procedure described above, which involves separation of the pup from the mother for, at most, 15 minutes, does not involve longer separation from the mother than the pup would normally experience. Calhoun (1962) noted that in some laboratory conditions that approximated wild settings but included specific feeding sites, subordinate females often ended up with nest locations far from the feeding sites, making it necessary for them to spend periods as long as three hours away from their pups. Based on this observation Plotsky and Meaney (1993) separated rat pups from their mothers for three hours per day from days 2-14 after birth. As adults, these rats showed *greater* stress responses than rats that had not been separated, both physiologically and behaviourally.

As is typical in experiments of this kind, the conclusions were drawn by comparing mean levels of physiological or behavioural response in the rats that had been handled or separated as pups with those that had not. Within each group, however, there were individual differences in response, and, inevitably, some of the individual response levels within the two groups overlapped. These individual differences could of course simply be random noise, but they could also be systematic, and identifying the features involved in them would thus be important in understanding rat stress response. One likely source of these individual differences in stress response would be individual differences in maternal caretaking behaviour. Careful observation of maternal behaviour in normal rearing conditions showed substantial variation in two pup-related behaviours (Sten, 1997): some mother rats lick, or 'groom,' the bodies and especially the anogenital areas of their pups much more than others. These same mothers also tend to nurse their pups with their backs arched and their legs splayed outward, affording the pups very ready access to their nipples, while those that lick/groom their pups less tend to lie on their sides or almost on top of their pups while nursing, leaving their nipples far less accessible. Importantly, these differences in maternal behaviour do not involve differences in amount of maternal time spent with the pups, nor do they involve differences in litter size, sex composition of the litters, pup weights at weaning, or proportion of births reaching weaning age (Meaney, 2001), so they do not appear to indicate differences in adequacy or normality of maternal care. They are also quite stable from generation to generation. Moreover, as adults, rat pups that had experienced greater than average levels of licking/grooming and arched-back nursing (LG-ABN) showed lower physiological and behavioural responses to stress (Meaney, 2001), as did their mothers.

One explanation for the observation that both rat mothers who do more LG-ABN and their pups show lower response to stress would be that stress responsiveness is simply genetically transmitted from one generation to the next, and LG-ABN is correlated with it but has no causative effect on it. The actual situation, however, appears to be much more interesting. That is, transmission of stress responsiveness in rats from one generation to another appears to take place through experience-induced gene expression. This has been demonstrated through carefully constructed cross-fostering studies (e.g., Francis, Diorio, Liu, & Meaney, 1999). In these studies, rat pups of mothers with high LG-ABN were fostered into litters of mothers with low LG-ABN and vice versa. Because fostering entire litters alters maternal behaviour (Maccari, Piazza, Kabbaj, Barbazanges, Simon, & Le Moal, 1995), only two pups of the typical twelve pups in any one litter were cross-fostered. The biological offspring of low LB-ABN mothers reared by high LB-ABN mothers showed significantly less stress reactivity than the pups reared by low LG-ABN mothers, regardless of whether they were the biological offspring of low or high LG-ABN mothers. Moreover, these effects appear to extend into maternal behaviour of the female pups in adulthood. That is, though LG-ABN levels are usually similar in mother–daughter pairs when the mothers have reared the daughters, suggesting straightforward genetic transmission, this was not the case in the cross-fostered rats. Biological offspring of low LG-ABN mothers reared by high LG-ABN mothers did not differ in frequency of LG-ABN of their own offspring from biological offspring of high LG-ABN mothers reared by those mothers, and vice versa for biological offspring of high LG-ABN mothers. Thus individual differences in both stress responsiveness and maternal behaviour resembled those of the rearing mothers rather than those of the biological mothers. Subsequent studies have demonstrated that the mechanisms involved are differences in expression of several specific genes of the rat stress response system activated by the LG-ABN the pups experience in infancy, that these expression patterns tend to remain stable throughout the lifespan (though other kinds of experiences can alter this), and that these patterns can be transmitted beyond the offspring generation to subsequent generations (Meaney, 2010).

These studies have been very informative about the interrelations among stress response, the experience of maternal caretaking in infancy, and adult behaviours in rats, and it is easy to see how parallels to human stress response, attachment relationships, and social adjustment in adulthood could be drawn. This is not necessarily appropriate or accurate, however, as the stress response system in rats is similar to that in humans but not identical, and maternal caretaking patterns differ in rats and humans – how many human mothers carry out anogenetical licking of their babies? Still, the existence of such fundamental patterns of differences in gene expression and transmission of these differences from generation to generation in an animal as ordinary as the rat suggests that these patterns are common, and likely exist in some form in humans. And additional evidence for the general relevance of the rat patterns to humans comes from studies in a phylogenetically closer relative, the rhesus monkey.

These studies are particularly interesting for two reasons. Rhesus monkeys show patterns of attachment very similar to those of humans, and, unlike some other primates more closely related to humans, rhesus monkeys carry a variation of a gene involved in production of the neurotransmitter serotonin that is identical to one carried by humans.

Testing stress reactivity, maternal responsiveness and attachment associations in monkeys

The first experiments in this area were inspired by Bowlby's attachment theory and carried out by Harry Harlow between 1957 and 1963 (Harlow, Harlow, & Hansen, 1963). They became very famous. The emphasis in Bowlby's theory on the importance to infants of attachment over feeding in maternal care was controversial at the time, and Harlow's experiments were designed to address this controversy. In these experiments, two groups of baby rhesus monkeys were removed from their mothers. Those in one group were placed in cages containing monkey mother-sized figures, one of which was covered with soft terrycloth, and the other of which was made just of wire but had an attached baby bottle containing milk. For those in the other group, the terrycloth mother had the milk bottle, and the wire mother did not. The baby monkeys clung to the terrycloth mothers regardless of whether they provided food, and visited the wire mothers only for food. They ran to the terrycloth mothers when frightening stimuli were brought into their cages, regardless of which mother had food. When placed in an unfamiliar room with their terrycloth mothers, they clung to them for some time before exploring the room, again regardless of which mother provided food. But if they were placed in the unfamiliar room alone, they cried, froze in fear, sucked their thumbs, or ran screaming around the room. Those placed in the room with their wire mothers acted in the same way. When they had reached an age when they could eat solid foods, Harlow separated them from their terrycloth mothers for three days. When reunited, they all clung to them and would not explore. Harlow concluded that the need for comforting contact was stronger than the drive to explore. In some experiments, some monkeys were raised with terrycloth mothers only, and some with only wire mothers. The two groups gained weight at the same rate, but those with only wire mothers suffered from digestive problems and diarrhoea more frequently. Harlow inferred from this that lack of comforting contact was stressful to them. This conclusion is still generally accepted, to the point that Harlow's experiments would probably not be allowed today under most guidelines for ethical treatment of experimental animals because the maternal care deprivation would be considered too cruel.

Bowlby posited five behaviours of human infants to be instinctive means of seeking attachment: sucking, clinging, crying, following, and smiling. Baby rhesus monkeys clearly and consistently display all of these except smiling

(Suomi, 2008), and typically spend the first several weeks after birth clinging to the fronts of their mothers' bodies as the mothers move through their activities. Like human infants, the baby monkeys are also able to imitate facial expressions of their mothers shortly after birth (Ferrari, Visalberghi, Pauknet, Fogassi, Ruggiero, & Suomi, 2006). Rhesus monkey mothers fill the same kinds of functions as human mothers as well, providing nourishment, physical and psychological warmth, and protection from predators, the elements, and even other relatives such as older siblings. Mothers and babies develop strong and enduring relationships that are unique in strength and depth, extending throughout the mother's life for females and to puberty (when they typically leave the social group) for males. The mother–infant relationship further resembles that in humans in that, as soon as they can move freely, baby rhesus monkeys use their mothers as secure bases from which to explore their social and physical environments, returning to them when something frightens them. Their mothers also act very similarly to human mothers, monitoring their explorations and retrieving them or restraining them if they try to stray 'too far'. Infant exploratory behaviour is typically disrupted when the attachment relationship with the mother is less than optimal, and the patterns of less-than-optimal attachment relationships resemble those seen in humans. These specific attachment-related behaviours decrease in frequency as the infant grows, and the young monkey increasingly establishes contact with other members of the social group.

As with rat pups, individual differences in attachment status appear to be related both to stress response in the baby monkeys and to maternal caretaking activities. For example, Rosenblum and his colleagues (e.g., Rosenblum & Pauley, 1984) carried out a series of studies manipulating the amount of time and effort mother monkeys had to spend foraging for food. In one condition, food was freely available, while in another the mothers had to spend several hours a day foraging, though plenty of food was available. There were no differences between either mothers or babies in these two steady-state conditions, but there were large effects when they shifted the foraging demands for some mothers from low to high and back again in two-week intervals. The net result was to reduce attachment security in the babies, because the mothers' behaviour towards them changed as a result of changes in the mothers' relationships with the other mothers in the group (Andrews & Rosenblum, 1991). The babies, in turn, manifested behavioural differences that persisted into youth and adolescence, including less social affiliation, greater affective withdrawal, and more subordinate behaviour towards their peers. These behavioural differences appeared to have their roots in the stress response system, as these young monkeys showed both higher concentrations of corticotrophin-releasing factor and lower concentrations of cortisol in cerebrospinal fluid that persisted into adulthood. Persistent differences also involved serotonin levels, growth hormone levels, and immune responses. Mothers who experienced the variable foraging condition showed similar differences from those that did not, but differences in both mothers and offspring were smaller when mothers were more socially dominant (Coplan, Smith, Trost, Scharf, Altemus, & Bjornson, 2000). Together, these studies show that for monkeys, as in rats, environmental circumstances that would be difficult to characterize as truly traumatic can disrupt attachment relationships, and can also have consequences for stress responses that persist through much of the lifespan. Differences in offspring stress response have also been shown to result from differences in maternal care associated with temperamental differences in the mothers rather than with manipulations of environmental circumstances (e.g., McCormack, Sanchez, Bardi, & Maestripieri, 2006).

Moreover, like human infants, baby monkeys display early and stable temperamental differences in behavioural responses to novelty and challenge, and these are associated with elevations of stress responses similar to those in humans (e.g., Suomi, 1991). They also show temperamental differences in impulsivity, especially in social situations with peers, that are associated with chronically low rates of metabolism of serotonin (e.g., Higley & Suomi, 1996). These temperamental differences appear to cause differences in the attachment relationships these young monkeys develop with their mothers, with those that are highly reactive showing greater dependency on their mothers that can go so far as to delay subsequent maternal pregnancies and those that are highly impulsive having difficult, conflicted relationships with their mothers.

Such differences are accentuated when baby monkeys are reared only with peers, as has been demonstrated in many studies (Soumi, 2008). Not only are such monkeys generally more highly reactive than those reared by their biological mothers, but they tend to be more impulsive and prone to aggression, particularly the males. Peer-reared females tend to groom and be groomed less often and for shorter durations than their mother-reared peers, and both sexes tend to remain low in the social hierarchies of their groups, differences that remain stable through adolescence. They also show lower concentrations of serotonin in cerebrospinal fluid. Related to this, they tend to consume more alcohol and to develop greater tolerance to it when it is made available to them in laboratory conditions. Studies comparing peer-reared and mother-reared monkeys of course primarily evaluate means in the two groups, but there are always large individual differences in response within groups as well. The associations with rearing condition strongly implicate environmental experience as important to the development of behaviour patterns involving stress, as with rats and humans, but the presence of individual differences within each group of otherwise very similar environmental circumstances strongly suggests genetic influences as well. This is where the similarity in the genetics of serotonin production and response between rhesus monkeys and humans is important to our developing understanding of the transactions between the genetic and environmental sources of influence.

In Chapter 3, I mentioned a genetic variant in the promoter region of the serotonin transporter gene that varies in length in humans and is associated with variation in production of serotonin. Rhesus monkeys show this same genetic variation, as well as the same associations between genetic variation and serotonin production, and serotonin production and behaviour. The two genetic variants are generally characterized as 'short' and 'long', with the short allele being associated with lower efficiency of gene transcription and thus decreased serotonergic function. Because we can experimentally manipulate the lives of rhesus monkeys more than we can those of humans, we have learned much about the gene–environment transactions involving this allele from them. In particular, studies have shown consistently that peer rearing has different effects on monkeys carrying and not carrying the short allele (Suomi, 2008). In general, these studies can be summarized as showing that most of the negative behavioural effects associated with peer rearing described above are observed in the monkeys carrying the short allele. Those not carrying the short allele show either no behavioural effects or much reduced behavioural effects. This strongly suggests that this serotonin transporter allele and, more generally, serotonin expression levels confer vulnerability to adverse behavioural outcomes. Similar results have been observed in humans, beginning with a study examining the association of stressful life events and depression in those carrying and not carrying the short allele (Caspi, Sugden, Moffitt, Taylor, Craig, et al., 2003) that indicated that those carrying the short allele were more vulnerable to depression in the presence of stressful life events than those not carrying it.

The differential susceptibility hypothesis and resilience

Since then, many studies have attempted to replicate this result, with very mixed results (Munafo, Durrant, Lewis, & Flint, 2009; Risch, Herrell, Lehner, Liang, Eaves, Hoh, et al., 2009). There are many possible reasons for this, ranging from limitations of the studies to differences in the strengths of the effects in different population groups to a chance observation in the original study (Rutter, Thapar, & Pickles, 2009; Uher & McGuffin, 2009), but one that has broad conceptual implications and is beginning to generate substantial research attention is the differential susceptibility hypothesis, which is also often known as the plasticity hypothesis, or the orchid hypothesis (Boyce, Chesney, Alkon, Tschann, Adams, Chesterman, et al., 1995; Ellis, Boyce, Belsky, Bakermans-Kranenburg, & van Ijzendoorn, 2011). This is the idea that differences and changes in environmental circumstances across regions and over time have led to the evolution not just of individual differences in characteristics related to adaptation to the environment but to individual differences in degree of developmental sensitivity to environmental circumstances. That is, individuals differ in the degree to which they are sensitive to both environmental adversity *and* environmental support, with those most sensitive showing the worst outcomes under adverse developmental conditions but the best outcomes under favourable developmental conditions, analogous to the fragile hothouse beauty of the orchid in comparison with the sturdy but not-even-pretty dandelion.

The sensitivity involved is posited to be both genetically and environmentally influenced neurobiological receptivity to cues that suggest different developmental trajectories. Thus, the more sensitive individual is posited to have larger norms of reaction than the less sensitive individual, with larger ranges of potential outcomes along any of many different dimensions. The short allele of the serotonin transporter has figured largely in attempts to articulate mechanisms that might make these greater norms of reaction possible (Belsky, Jonassaint, Pluess, Stanton, Brummert, & Williams, 2009). In fact, Suomi (2006) has gone so far as to note that only two species of primates carry this allele, and they are also the only two that fill diverse ecological niches throughout the world, suggesting that maybe this allele is instrumental in their adaptive success. If so, it seems unlikely that this might take place through presence of a genetic variant that is associated only with increased vulnerability. In the proposed accounts of how the serotonin transporter allele might function to confer differential susceptibility, the trait involved is often conceived to be reactivity of the stress response system. As I have described, however, the temperamental construct of impulsivity or lack of ability to maintain effortful control is neurophysiologically very closely related. The possibility that this serotonin transporter allele is thus involved even more broadly in the development of behaviour patterns is being increasingly recognized (e.g., Carver, Johnson, Joormann, Kim, & Nam, 2011). This is consistent with the well-established involvement of serotonin in a wide variety of brain processes and psychopathologies.

Though a general difference in environmental sensitivity associated with both positive and negative developmental potentials is certainly possible, it seems likely that developmental sensitivity differs along many dimensions *within* individuals as well, with some individuals robust to some kinds of environmental circumstances but not others. The sensitivity proposed is also posited to be potentially manifested at any point in the lifespan, so that more sensitive individuals might display less stable levels of function throughout their lives (Ellis, Boyce, Belsky, Bakermans-Kranenburg, & van Ijzendoorn, 2011), though sometimes actual treatment of the idea better reflects an implicit assumption that sensitivity at one particular point in development has launched the individual on one relatively stable developmental trajectory rather than another. Though proponents of the idea are clear that characterization of outcomes as better or worse is a social construction and all outcomes should be considered evolutionarily adaptive, more specific treatments recognize that this may not always be the case: that is, when the more environmentally sensitive individual dies as a result of the sensitivity and some environmental exposure to which others would not have succumbed, the outcome cannot be considered adaptive.

Despite these vagaries in conceptualization, evidence supporting the differential susceptibility hypothesis has begun to accumulate. The hypothesis inherently involves interactions and variance effects rather than main effects on mean levels, making for more challenging research designs, and this is the nature of the evidence that has been observed. Much of it involves attachment and temperament as well, thus helping to illuminate how these two important developmental constructs are actually related. For example, Bakermans-Kranenburg and van IJzendoorn (2008) found that maternal sensitivity to toddlers predicted the toddlers' externalizing problems two years later, but only for children carrying one particular dopamine receptor allele; with this allele, those who had more sensitive mothers had the lowest levels of externalizing problems while those who had less sensitive mothers had the highest levels of externalizing problems, with those not carrying this allele in between. Lengua (2008) observed that children who were easily frustrated showed increasing externalizing problems when their mothers were rejecting, but decreasing externalizing problems when their mothers were supportive; their peers who were not easily frustrated did not show this sensitivity to maternal behaviour. And Aron, Aron, and Davies (2005) found that, for undergraduate students high in sensitivity to sensory processing, poor childhood parental relationships and difficult childrearing circumstances were associated with higher than average levels of shyness, while good childhood relationships and good childrearing circumstances were associated with lower than average levels of shyness. Students low in sensitivity to sensory processing did not show these associations. In general, the evidence can be summarized as suggesting that it is more difficult to establish a secure attachment relationship with the temperamentally sensitive or difficult child, and the child may thus be at risk due to both temperamental vulnerabilities and vulnerabilities associated with poor attachment relationships. If secure attachment with such a child is accomplished, however, outcomes may be unusually good.

If this is the case, it would be one mechanism through which *resilience* might be achieved. Resilience is another concept that is generating increasing research attention in a variety of disciplines, from psychology, sociology, and psychiatry to biology, genetics, endocrinology, and neuroscience. Despite the interest, as with many of the concepts discussed in this chapter, lack of consensus on both its definition and measurement remain. Essentially, however, the term refers to the ability to maintain or regain mental health following some experience of adversity (Herrmann, Stewart, Diaz-Granados, Berger, Jackson, & Yuen, 2011), and is used to describe the robust observation that, considering almost any kind of adverse experience, some individuals survive the experience well and appear to suffer no long-term consequences from it while others manifest dysfunction in many different ways. That said, some definitions conceptualize resilience as a personal trait, with all the implications of stable, genetically based individual differences that the term 'trait' carries. From this perspective, traits like intelligence, positive emotionality, good self-esteem, spirituality, cognitive flexibility, ability to exert effortful control, and secure attachment have been linked with resiliency. Other definitions focus on resilience as a state, a response to a specific trauma, while still others consider resilience to be the result of a dynamic social support process that helps individuals cope with adversity, and emphasize the mechanisms involved in this support process. From these perspectives, access to social support resources, quality of those relationships, and knowledge of coping techniques are considered crucial to resilience. The idea of resilience is clearly important, but the reader who begins to perceive that this research area is running in conceptual circles and addressing the problem by layering on yet another conceptual buzzword is probably not mistaken. Despite this tendency, there have been dramatic changes in our understanding of the nature and complexity of the processes involved over the past twenty years or so. These changes should certainly generally be considered progress, and we should only anticipate further such changes during the next twenty years.

Further reading

Andrews, M. W., & Rosenblum, L. A. (1991). Security of attachment in infants raised in variable- or low-demand environments. *Child Development, 62,* 686–693.

Belsky, J., Jonassaint, C., Pluess, M., Stanton, M., Brummert, B., & Williams, R. (2009). Vulnerability genes or plasticity genes? *Molecular Psychiatry, 14,* 746–754.

Ellis, B. J., Boyce, W. T., Belsky, J., Bakermans-Kranenburg, M. J., & van Ijzendoorn, M. H. (2011). Differential susceptibility to the environment: An evolutionary-neurodevelopmental theory. *Development and Psychopathology, 23,* 7–28.

Harlow, H. F., Harlow, M. K., & Hansen, E. W. (1963). The maternal affectional system of rhesus monkeys. In H. R. Rheingold, *Maternal Behavior in Mammals* (pp. 254–281). New York: Wiley.

Henderson, H. H., & Wachs, T. D. (2007). Temperament theory and the study of cognition-emotion interactions across development. *Developmental Review, 27,* 396–407.

Higley, J. D., & Suomi, S. J. (1996). Reactivity and social competence affect individual differences in reaction to severe stress in children: Investigations using nonhuman primates. In C. R. Pfeffer, *Intense Stress and Mental Disturbance in Children* (pp. 3–58). Washington, DC: American Psychiatric Press.

Jahromi, L. B., Putnam, S. P., & Stifter, C. A. (2004). Maternal regulation of infant reactivity from 2 to 6 months. *Developmental Psychology, 40,* 477–487.

Kagan, J., & Snidman, N. (2004). *The Long Shadow of Temperament.* Cambridge, MA: Harvard University Press.

McEwen, B. S., & Wingfield, J. C. (2003). The concept of allostasis in biology and biomedicine. *Hormones and Behavior, 43,* 2–15.

Meaney, M. J. (2010). Epigenetics and the biological definition of gene x environment interactions. *Child Development, 81,* 41–79.

Panksepp, J. (1998). *Affective Neuroscience: The Foundations of Human and Animal Emotions.* New York: Oxford University Press.

Posner, M. I., & Rothbart, M. K. (2007). *Educating the Human Brain.* Washington, DC: American Psychological Association.

Sapolsky, R. M., Romero, L. M., & Munck, A. U. (2000). How do corticosteroids influence stress responses? Integrating permissive, suppressive, stimulatory, and preparatory actions. *Endocrine Reviews, 21,* 55–89.

Suomi, S. J. (2006). Risk, resilience, and gene x environment interactions in rhesus monkeys. *Annals of the New York Academy of Sciences, 1094,* 52–62.

Uher, R., & McGuffin, P. (2009). The moderation by the serotonin transporter gene of environmental adversity in the aetiology of mental illness. *Molecular Psychiatry, 15,* 18–22.

Part II
Lifespan Development

Gestation: The Developmental Foundation

5

Foetal development

Gestation refers to the time period from conception to birth, and to the developmental processes that take place during this period. Gestation begins with conception, but exactly when conception occurs is subject to controversy. Spermatozoa deposited via semen into the vagina travel through the cervix and uterus to the Fallopian tubes. If they encounter an ovum there, they are drawn to penetrate it. As its outer, shell-like protective barrier is quite thick, many sperm are necessary to break through it, though only the first one to do so actually fertilizes it by donating its genetic material. Once this occurs, the ovum polarizes, repelling additional sperm. Some embryologists refer to the moment of fertilization as conception, but others restrict the term 'conception' to implantation of the resulting zygote into the uterus, which does not occur for about another five days.

Prior to fertilization, each ovum contains one complete copy of a human genome, including a single X chromosome, and each sperm contains another, different, complete copy of a human genome, including either a single X chromosome or a single Y chromosome. The X chromosome is much bigger than the Y chromosome, and contains many more genes. The Y chromosome, however, contains one gene of major importance, known as SRY. Without this gene, the zygote will develop as a female; with this gene, the zygote will develop as a male. Unlike the sperm, the ovum contains cellular *mitochondria*. These are cellular subunits enclosed in their own membranes that generate *adenine triphosphate*, which is a source of cellular energy. Mitochondria also contain their own genetic material; because mitochondria are found only in the ovum and not in the sperm in any normal XY male, this mitochondrial DNA comes only from the mother.

Upon fertilization, the newly formed single-cell zygote begins to travel down the Fallopian tube towards the uterus, a journey that will take about five days. As it goes, it begins to divide, forming a *blastocyst*. The blastocyst is no larger than the original zygote; the cell division takes place through the formation of smaller cells more tightly packed together. When it enters the uterus, the blastocyst attaches to and then embeds itself in the soft tissue of the endometrium wall of the uterus. This implantation takes place eight to ten days after fertilization. Upon implantation, rapid cell division takes place, and the blastocyst, now considered an *embryo*, begins to grow. At the same time, the cells begin to differentiate as they divide, so that they can take different functions, with some becoming blood cells, others nerve cells or bone cells, etc. Spontaneous abortions are not uncommon at this stage, and they often take place due to genetic anomalies. The embryo is also very sensitive during this period to environmental toxins, including infection, radiation, alcohol and other drugs, and nutritional deficiencies. Generally, if the blastocyst will become monozygotic twins, the division takes place before the blastocyst reaches the uterus, but sometimes it does occur later. When it does, it is much more likely that the twins will be conjoined. This is, of course, very rare.

Cellular differentiation and development take place roughly in evolutionary order. That is, structures such as the backbone, which is evolutionarily old and common to fish and reptiles as well as all mammals, tend to develop very early in gestation, while those that evolved later, such as the human cerebrum, tend to develop last. This is not an absolute rule, but there is a definite tendency for it to take place. For arbitrary reasons, gestational age is calculated from the mother's last menstrual period, usually about two weeks prior to fertilization. By the end of the sixth week of gestation using this calculation, the embryo is about 4 mm in length and has begun to curve into a C-like shape. The heart has begun to beat regularly, and most of the internal organs of the thorax have begun to develop. The neural tube has closed. Arm buds and a tail, an evolutionary holdover that does not continue to develop, are visible. By the end of the period considered embryonic, completion of the tenth week of gestation, the embryo is about 18 mm long and all major organs have begun to function. Spontaneous movements can be detected and the locations of what will become elbows, toes, even nipples and hair follicles, are visible.

Because the major organs have all begun to form, once the embryo enters the subsequent *foetal* period it is less sensitive to environmental insults. By the end of the twelfth week, individual differences in length have begun to appear, so that foetuses of this age range from 30 mm to 80 mm in length. The face is well formed, the genitals are differentiated, the foetus can make a fist, the eyes have closed and will not reopen until after birth, and tooth buds that will become the baby teeth have appeared. By the end of the twentieth week, the foetus has a mean length of about 20 cm. It can make sucking motions with its mouth and moves regularly. Its whole body is covered with a fine hair called *lanugo*, another evolutionary holdover. Eyebrows and eyelashes have begun to appear, along with finger- and toenails. By the end of the 23rd week, the foetus displays hand and startle reflexes, indicating some ability to interact with the environment outside the womb. At this point the foetus can be viable if birth occurs, but a long period of intensive hospital care is required as the nervous system will not be mature enough to control bodily functions for another several weeks. Birth this early is often accompanied by developmental complications such as cerebral palsy. Even births before the end of the 36th week often require medical intervention. The foetus is considered full-term at the end of the 37th week, though birth on average does not typically occur until the end of the 40th week. Some pregnancies extend as much as two weeks beyond that.

Brain tissue develops primarily during the first two trimesters of pregnancy. That is, the number of cells in, for example, the cerebral cortex, is thought not to increase after the 27th week. Despite this, the brain is far from fully developed at that time, and it is much smaller than it will be even at birth. This is because the connections among nerve cells have not yet developed. As brain function relies completely on connections among nerve cells, this also means that the brain is not yet functional. For example, though the eyes have formed fully by about the 23rd week, the brain connections involving the thalamus, which mediates sensory input, do not form until about the 31st week. Thus the eyes are present, but could not function even if they were exposed to light because the images they might pick up could not be interpreted by the brain. The growth in brain volume that takes place after the 27th week results from genesis of synapses between nerve cells to some degree, but most of the growth occurs due to myelination. Myelination begins after the 27th week, but much of it takes place well after birth.

Foetal behaviour becomes increasingly organized throughout gestation. Around the end of the first trimester, the foetus has developed enough to have body parts that can move, but movement is basically random and continuous. By about 34 weeks, it has distinct patterns of rest and activity. While at rest, foetal movement is low and the heartbeat and breathing movements are relatively slow and steady. In the active state, heart rate and breathing movements are more rapid and irregular, and may be responsive to external stimuli such as sounds and pressure on the womb. This is also when the foetus will tend to move around or kick in response to such stimulation. Though there are general trends in alternation of these patterns, the patterns also show considerable individual differences. Peak activity tends to take place when the mother is asleep, and there is often a resting period in the early morning, but there are wide variations around both the lengths of these periods and their specific timing.

Between 23 and 25 weeks, the auditory system becomes mature enough to detect sounds, though the connections to the rest of the brain that turn sound detection into hearing require further development, so that what we think of as hearing remains limited. Moreover, because the foetus is floating in amniotic fluid inside the mother's body, most higher-frequency sounds are blocked, so that the foetus hears mostly low-frequency sounds, including the mother's heartbeat, digestive sounds and, especially, only the low-frequency aspects of her voice. Foetal responses to sounds, in the form of motor movements and increases in heart rate, can be picked up as early as 26 weeks of gestation, and are reliably detected beginning around 30 weeks (Lacanuet, Granier-Deferre, & Busnel, 1995). Sounds are thought to stimulate development of the auditory system, and some of these may be required for normal brain development. These developments appear also to affect perceptual capacities and sound preferences after birth, suggesting the involvement of prenatal learning and memory. This developmental stimulation and experience may extend beyond the auditory system. For example, when the mother speaks, her diaphragm moves, exerting pressure on the uterus that can stimulate movement in the foetus. This suggests that sounds can be associated with stimulation of the sensory pathways involved in detecting pressure, touch, and balance as well.

Sexual differentiation during gestation

One of the most fundamental ways in which individuals differ is their sex. A quick glance is usually sufficient to tell whether a person is male or female, even when clothing is not distinctive. At the same time, individual differences within each sex are massive, and, for most characteristics, there is large overlap in the distributions in the two sexes. The basic fact of sex is genetically determined at conception, but exactly how sexual differentiation proceeds depends on many subsequent developmental events and circumstances. Because sex is such an important aspect of life, its development has been extensively studied, and it involves mechanisms that likely have analogues in the development of other characteristics, I review foetal sexual differentiation in some detail.

As noted, males have one X chromosome and one Y chromosome, while females have two X chromosomes. This establishes the basic fact of sex. In the embryo, the male and female gonads develop from the same group of cells, and, until the ninth week of gestation, any embryo is capable of developing into either sex. Prior to that time, the primitive reproductive tract consists of both the beginnings of the male and the female duct systems and a single opening to the outside for the genital ducts and the urinary system. In the normal male, the beginnings of the *Mullerian duct system* that marks the normal female recede. In the normal female, the opposite occurs, and the *Wolffian ducts* that characterize the normal male recede. The SRY gene on the Y chromosome, known as the *testes determining factor*, codes for a single protein that triggers the initiation of the development of the Wolffian ducts that support the testes during the ninth week of gestation. The primitive testes almost immediately also begin to secrete testosterone and a protein called the *Mullerian inhibiting hormone*. Testosterone causes the Wolffian ducts to begin to differentiate into the structures that will eventually control production of semen and ejaculatory function, and the Mullerian inhibiting hormone does its job of causing the Mullerian ducts to recede. In the absence of the SRY gene, testosterone, and Mullerian inhibiting hormone, ovaries and the uterine system automatically begin to develop around the thirteenth week of gestation from the Mullerian duct system. The female organs develop regardless of whether the ovaries are present, and, unlike the testes, they secrete very little hormone prenatally. The external genitalia in both sexes develop later from different body systems, with development of the male organs dependent on hormonal secretions. The presence or absence of testes is thus determined genetically. After this, however, sexual differentiation is primarily controlled by hormones and not directly genetically, though there may be some direct genetic effects on the brain (Davies & Wilkinson, 2006). The importance of hormonal control is clear because of the existence of several conditions in which normal sex differentiation does not occur.

Box 5.1   Hormonal conditions limiting normal sex differentiation

In the condition known as *androgen insensitivity syndrome*, the person has normal X and Y chromosomes and testes, but mutations in a gene on the X chromosome cause the absence of androgen receptors. The foetal testes thus develop and secrete testosterone and Mullerian inhibiting hormone normally, causing the Mullerian ducts to recede. But the Wolffian ducts cannot respond to testosterone because of the genetic defect, however, so they recede as well. The person thus ends up with testes, testosterone production typical of a male, but female external genitalia, a vagina, and no internal duct system at all. People with this condition look and act like females and think of themselves that way, though they are sterile. At puberty, they develop normal female breasts, because the extent of breast development depends not on absolute levels of oestrogen (theirs are low, and typical of males), but on the ratio of usable oestrogens to usable androgens. Because the adrenals and testes of males normally produce small amounts of oestrogens and people with this condition lack androgen receptors, their functional ratios of oestrogens to androgens are high. In some cases, androgen insensitivity may be incomplete, resulting in a sexual phenotype intermediate between male and female and obvious at birth.

Sexual differentiation in genetically normal females can also be disrupted by foetal exposure to androgens. In the condition *congenital adrenal hyperplasia*, mutations in a gene on another chromosome result in the absence of an enzyme that converts the hormone *androstenedione* to cortisol in the adrenal gland. In the HPA axis (Chapter 4), the hypothalamus and pituitary normally regulate production of corticotropic-releasing hormone and adrenocorticotropic hormone through the presence of cortisol. Because cortisol is not present, they produce excessive amounts of these hormones, which in turn cause the adrenal gland to grow too large and to release even more androstenedione. Some of this androstenedione is converted to androgens, both pre- and postnatally. When this condition occurs in females, the excessive androgens partially masculinize their bodies, enlarging the clitoris to the point that it can in some cases resemble a penis, and making the labia resemble a scrotum. Because the absence of cortisol causes considerable dysfunction of the HPA axis, with consequent health complications, the condition can usually be identified at or soon after birth and treatment with externally administered cortisol is necessary. Under such treatment, further masculinization stops.

A third genetic condition causes even more complex deviations from normal sexual differentiation through hormonal irregularities. Again, mutations in a gene on another chromosome cause insufficient production of *5α-reductase*, which is required to make use of testosterone to form the external genitalia in an XY foetus. The infant is born with ambiguous genitals that resemble the female but are slightly enlarged, with the testes inside what appear to be labia. An individual with this condition is usually raised and identifies as female during childhood, but at puberty the rise in testicular androgen causes the penis and scrotum to grow, and the body develops as a male. This condition is relatively common in the Dominican Republic in the Caribbean, so much so that there is a popular name for individuals who have it. They are known as 'guevedoces', which literally means 'testes at age 12'. In this culture where the condition is not so unusual, most individuals who have the condition transit reasonably smoothly from being considered and acting as girls to wearing male clothes, taking on male tasks, and having girlfriends. Some have interpreted this as clear evidence that sexual biology is destiny and socialization has little to do with it. The frequency of this condition and the popular name for it in this culture, however, suggest that people may treat individuals with this condition somewhat differently from normal girls during childhood, subtly preparing them to take on their culture's more powerful and advantaged male social role after puberty.

Organizational and activating effects of hormones in the brain

The pervasive differences in behaviour between males and females have long generated speculation that something innately biological is involved. The fact that genes are involved primarily only indirectly in prenatal sexual differentiation, though not conclusive in this regard, should make clear that the most likely explanation for sex differences in behaviour is *not* that they are directly genetically determined. Like the physical sex differences, however, it is very possible that some sex differences in behaviour are driven by hormonally influenced sex differences in the brain and central nervous system. This has been extensively explored in nonhuman animals, and, even for primates, the evidence for such effects is strong. Pfeiffer (1934) carried out the first demonstration of permanent masculinization of the central nervous system by hormones produced early in life. Previous work had shown that pituitary function is necessary for ovulation in the rat because ovulation ceased when the pituitary was removed, yet ovulation continued when bits of ovary were implanted in female rats normally exposed to female hormones but not when such bits were implanted in male rats not normally exposed to female hormones. Pfeiffer showed that the difference depended on testicular secretions in the first few days after birth by castrating male rats shortly after birth and giving newborn female rats subcutaneous grafts of testicular tissue. If given surgically implanted ovaries as adults, the castrated male rats ovulated, but the treated female rats did not, either from their own ovaries or from surgically implanted ovaries. Later experiments showed that a single injection of testosterone during the first week of life had the same effect on the female rats. Pfeiffer concluded that early-life exposure to androgen masculinized the pituitary, causing failure of ovulation. Though later work (Harris & Naftolin, 1970) clarified that it was actually masculinization of the hypothalamus that caused the failure of ovulation, the conclusion that early sex hormone exposure can modify the brain and central nervous system remained intact. This particular ovulatory effect involving the hypothalamus does not occur in primates, however (Harris & Naftolin, 1970).

Experiments involving the specific behaviours of rodents during copulation were important in developing key hypotheses about how hormones have their effects on the brain. Phoenix, Goy, Gerall, and Young (1959) studied the sexual receptivity behaviours of female guinea pigs. In this species (and many other rodents including rats), for copulation to take place the female must arch her back to elevate her rump and head, to a position known as *lordosis*. Female guinea pigs normally assume this position in response to mounting by males only during one part of their ovulatory cycle, and removal of the ovaries results in failure to do so at all. The response can be reinstated, however, by injections of oestrogen for 1-2 days, followed by a single injection of progesterone, which simulates the hormonal sequence normally accompanying ovulation. Male guinea pigs will mount others they encounter, regardless of sex, especially if the other is smaller. They simply stop if the other does not assume lordosis. When castrated males are administered the same hormonal regimen that reactivates lordosis in ovariectomized females, they do not display lordosis. This indicates that males and females must be different somehow. Because the lordosis response is behavioural, and behaviour is mediated in the central nervous system, it seemed likely to Phoenix and his colleagues that the difference lies in the central nervous system.

To test this, they prenatally administered testosterone to foetal guinea pigs. The females that had been so treated showed little or no lordosis response as adults even when administered oestrogen followed by progesterone. This inspired Phoenix and colleagues to develop the hypothesis that, in addition to their well-known activational effects, prenatal androgens have organizational effects on the brain. That is, they masculinize the brain in a way that affects behaviour even in adulthood, directly analogously to the organizational effects that they have on sexual differentiation of the body. Because it was plain that administration of testosterone even as early as 12 days after birth did not have these effects, they suggested that the greatest sensitivity to testosterone exposure took place early in gestation, with effects that decreased over time. We know little about why such sensitive periods exist nor how they are regulated, but they are common in development.

The organizational hypothesis made a strong impact on research in behavioural endocrinology during the 1960s. Most work was of course carried out using experimental nonhuman animals, but results were consistent in demonstrating that young animals exposed to androgens tended to display more masculine behaviours in later juvenile periods and in adulthood, while young animals whose normal exposure to androgens was restricted tended to display more feminine behaviours. Particular behaviours could be altered only during specific developmental periods, and these varied from species to species and by type of behaviour. Though there were some exceptions, which were often interesting in their own rights, the range of behaviours involved was large, including aggression, rough-and-tumble play, and even taste preferences in addition to behaviours directly related to copulation. At first the evidence for structural reorganization of the brain was indirect, based on the inference that the behavioural differences observed had structural analogues in the brain. But with increasing technological abilities to observe the brain *in vitro*, the evidence rapidly became direct. The existence of many structural sexual dimorphisms, both large and very subtle, in the brains of many species is now well established, and the timing of their emergence and extents of their sensitivities to hormonal exposure has been documented.

How does all this apply to humans? The basic premise of much work using nonhuman animals is that they can serve as models for humans, and, in general, we would be crazy to think that observations that are consistent across mammals and especially our nearest relatives the primates have no relevance to us. Thus, we should assume that early hormone exposures have some level of organizational effects on brain structure and behaviour in humans. Because there must be individual differences both in timing and level of exposure and in sensitivity to exposure as indicated by the major developmental disorders such as androgen insensitivity syndrome, one implication is that people are rarely either completely male or completely female, because their brains may be relatively masculinized in one area and feminized in another, regardless of chromosomal and physical sex, in much the way that Slijper's goat (Chapter 2) developed a hind leg anatomy more like ours than like his conspecifics'. At a scientific level, this means being very specific about the sexual differentiation process involved in the development of any particular characteristic. At a social level, this means relaxing stereotypes about what constitutes normal and appropriate behaviour for the two sexes.

Physical sexual dimorphism v. prenatal differences in exposure to sex hormones

But to what extent are the human brain and central nervous system physically sexually dimorphic and to what degree can any differences be attributed to prenatal hormone exposure? These questions have proved very difficult to answer because individual differences within the sexes are large, there are so many ethical restrictions on our ability to manipulate humans experimentally, and biological and social sources of sex differences are generally badly confounded. The place to start is with the first question, that of physical sexual dimorphisms in the brain in adulthood, but even this is far from straightforward. Most of the discussions of sex differences in brain structure have centred around four subjects.

First, dating back to the 1800s, it has been known that men tend to have larger and heavier brains than women. But men also have larger bodies than women, and if you adjust measures of brain weight for body weight or height, the sex difference almost completely disappears. Moreover, the brain needs a constant supply of freshly oxygenated blood to function, and rates of regional cerebral blood flow per unit of brain weight are higher in women than men when they are performing cognitive tasks (Gur, et al., 1995). This has been interpreted as indicating performance compensation for the slightly smaller brain volume in women, though rates of regional cerebral blood flow have also been interpreted as indicative of greater mental effort (Larson, Haier, LaCasse, & Hazen, 1995). The ability to remove the sex differences through such adjustments for overall body size has allowed most researchers to dismiss the importance of overall brain size, as it seems to be at least socially possible to take physical sexual dimorphisms for granted in a way not acceptable for dimorphisms involving mental and behavioural characteristics. The distinction is arbitrary, however, and how a link between brain and overall body size arises may impact the appropriateness of such adjustments. For example, the distinction is appropriate if some third factor controls and calibrates brain size to body size for completely structural rather than functional reasons, but may be much less so if brain development controls body development or vice versa, and/or functional mechanisms are involved.

Second, research has focused on dimorphisms of specific brain regions, especially those known to be involved in both specific cognitive tasks and control of hormones. One of these is the hippocampus, which may be more important for visual memory performance in women than in men (Trenerry, Jack, Cascino, Sharbrough, & Ivnik, 1996). Another is the hypothalamus, which, among other things, regulates the female menstrual cycle, so it clearly differs in function between men and women. Because it has neurons that extend into the frontal cortex, it is also likely involved in cognitive tasks and emotion regulation, and there is one area within it that is involved in masculine behaviour. A brain region that differs in size (larger in men than women) is the pre-optic nerve, but the functional significance of this difference is not known. This is a very active area of current research, but conclusions about the robustness of differences and their significance are still premature.

The third subject of investigation is the corpus callosum. As described in Chapter 3, this brain region provides the primary mechanism for transmitting information from one brain hemisphere to the other. Sex differences in this particular region are potentially important because of the fourth subject of investigation, which is sex differences in the extent and nature of specialization of the two hemispheres of the brain. The corpus callosum consists of 200-800 million (some individual differences there!) nerve fibres grouped in a rather irregularly shaped bundle. In rats, its size is responsive to exposure to prenatal hormones (Fitch & Denenberg, 1998), and it tends to be larger in males than in females. In humans, however, evidence primarily centres around larger size and more bulbous shape in females (Steinmetz, Staiger, Schlaug, Huang, & Jancke, 1995), at least in relation to overall cranial capacity, though this has not been found in all studies. The underlying idea is that larger size and greater numbers of nerve fibres are associated with greater transmission of information between the two brain hemispheres in females than in males, thus creating sex differences in how information is processed that impact emotional expression and perception and cognitive performance. The notion that these organizational differences, if they in fact exist, have origins in prenatal exposure to hormones rests on the observation that size varies with prenatal exposure to hormones in rats.

Theories of effects of hormones on cerebral organization

As noted, the fourth subject of investigation of prenatal organizational effects of hormones is sex differences in cerebral lateralization, or the extent to which the two hemispheres of the brain support different activities. Several theories about how and why this might occur have been proposed, with varying degrees of support. For example, J. Levy (1976) suggested that performances on spatial and verbal tasks are optimized when the tasks are carried out primarily in one hemisphere of the brain. Thus, when lateralization is incomplete or weak, presumably due to greater communication between the hemispheres, the two hemispheres compete with each other, reducing efficiency and ultimately accuracy in task performance. Levy posited that this occurred because of hormone-derived differences in rates and patterns of brain development that originated prenatally but extended into puberty. Despite very mixed evidence, most researchers seem to have accepted the idea that women have more bilateral cognitive representations than men (Halpern, 2000), along with the idea that this matters for performance somehow.

A more elaborate theory, more firmly grounded in the premise of organizational effects of prenatal hormone exposure, was proposed by Geschwind and his colleagues (Geschwind & Galaburda, 1987). The right hemisphere of the brain develops more rapidly than the left in humans during gestation. This means that the left hemisphere is at risk for prenatal exposure to toxins and other sources of damage for a longer period of time. Geschwind and his colleagues proposed that high levels of testosterone slow neuron growth, and that timing of testosterone exposure in males is such that the left hemisphere is more subject to this than the right. This, they asserted, results in a tendency for the right hemisphere to be more dominant in males than in females. One indication of hemispheric dominance is handedness: because the left hemisphere controls the right side of the body and vice versa, people who are right-handed are usually left-hemisphere-dominant for language (among other things), and people who are left-handed are often right-hemisphere-dominant, sometimes even for language. If high levels of testosterone slow neuronal growth as proposed, we should expect a higher proportion of males than females to be left-handed. This has been found consistently (Coren, 1990; Stellman, Wynder, DeRose, & Muscat, 1997). Moreover, females with congenital adrenal hyperplasia, who have been exposed to higher-than-normal rates of adrenal androgens, have shown higher rates of left-handedness than other females (Resnick, Berenbaum, Gottesman, & Bouchard, 1986).

If this theory is correct, then other regions of the brain that are sensitive to testosterone should also be affected. One of these is the thymus gland, which is involved in immune function. Its slower development in the right hemisphere should result in greater susceptibility to immune disorders in people who are left-handed than in people who are right-handed. There is reasonably substantial evidence that intestinal autoimmune diseases and diseases such as eczema, allergies, and asthma occur on the order of 2.5 times more often in left-handers than in right-handers (Bryden, McManus, & Bulman-Fleming, 1994; Geschwind & Behan, 1982) but we should also see higher rates in males than in females, and, if anything, the opposite is often the case. Still, males do tend to show advantages in abilities associated with right-brain-hemisphere activity such as spatial ability, and males tend to show higher rates of generally left-hemisphere-based verbal and reading disabilities.

There are other ways of examining this proposed association. One chromosomal anomaly involving the sex chromosomes and thus hormonal levels is Turner's Syndrome. People with this condition have only a single X chromosome; the other is missing or damaged. Because they have no Y chromosome, they have normal female appearance at birth, but because they are short of one X chromosome, they tend to produce very low levels of oestrogens and progesterone, and to require treatment with them at puberty in order to exhibit normal female secondary sex characteristics. They also are usually sterile and have very underdeveloped ovaries. In general, these females tend to show relatively normal verbal abilities, but depressed spatial and mathematical abilities, and abilities associated with face-recognition and processing of emotional content. This is consistent with the ideas that under-exposure to hormones may have effects analogous to those of over-exposure and that these effects may involve brain lateralization, but the directions of the effects are difficult to interpret within the context of the theory. Girls with congenital adrenal hyperplasia also tend to show higher levels of spatial ability than their sisters, to engage in more 'aggressive' play, to have more male sex-typed interests, and to be more likely than their sisters to play with boys' toys – trucks, building toys, etc. (Berenbaum, 1999; Berenbaum & Hines, 1992; Helleday, Bartifai, Ritzen, & Forsman, 1994; Resnick, Berenbaum, Gottesman, & Bouchard, 1986). It is difficult, however, to rule out the possibility that these girls experience slightly different patterns of socialization than their sisters because of their condition.

One other way of examining the effects of prenatal exposure to hormones on brain organization has taken advantage of an experiment no longer performed. During the period from the 1950s until about 1980, treatment of pregnant women with synthetic sex hormones was common in order to prevent miscarriage. Many different specific hormones were used and dosages varied widely, but most had masculinizing effects. One common masculinizing effect of prenatal hormone exposure in nonhuman mammals is increased aggression. Reinisch (1981) tested for such effects of prenatal hormone administration in humans. Her sample of exposed offspring, tested at age 11, was small, only 25, but well constructed; her control group consisted of same-sex siblings who had not been exposed to the synthetic hormones *in utero*. The participants completed a measure of self-reports of fantasies about aggression. Those who had been exposed to the synthetic hormones *in utero* reported higher levels of aggressive fantasies than their same-sex siblings who had not been exposed. Other studies, less well executed, showed effects on mathematical and other cognitive abilities often observed to be higher in males, but these results were not consistently replicable. The hormone treatments were also implicated in development of cervical and other cancers in offspring of the women who had received them so they are no longer routinely administered.

Theories of genetic influences on sexual differentiation

The evidence is strong that genetic control of sexual differentiation, both of brain and body, is primarily exerted by setting in motion the development of the testes in males that then secrete the male hormones. This does not mean, however, that there are no direct genetic influences on sexual dimorphism at all. Though the organizational hypothesis had its origins in behavioural endocrinology and has focused on sex differences in prenatal hormone exposure, there is also no reason that some organizational effects could not be genetic as well as hormonal. As our knowledge of the genome has exploded during the last decade, evidence for direct genetic influences on sexual differentiation of both kinds has grown. The evidence is for direct genetic influences in the aggregate rather than for any direct genetic influences of specific genes, and much of it comes from nonhuman mammals. For example, in adult mice, about 14 per cent of all genes expressed in the brain are differentially expressed in males and females (Yang, Schadt, Wang, Wang, Arnold, Ingram-Drake, et al., 2006). About half of these are expressed more highly in males; the other half are expressed more highly in females. Those expressed more highly in females appear to be overrepresented on the X chromosome, while those expressed more highly in males appear to be overrepresented on the Y chromosome. Similar patterns have been found in foetal tissue in birds (Scholz, Kultima, Mattsson, Axelsson, Brunstrom, Halldin, et al., 2006) and in mice (Dewing, Shi, Horvath, & Vilain, 2003). Evidence of gene expression differences is far from conclusive as evidence of direct genetic control, as expression may be triggered by environmental circumstances including hormonal levels. But the SRY gene itself is also expressed directly in the rodent brain (Dewing,

Chiang, Sinchak, Sim, et al., 2006) and in the adult human hypothalamus and frontal and temporal cortices (Mayer, Lahr, Swab, Pilgrim, & Reisert, 1998). Moreover, on average about 20 per cent of the genes on the X chromosome appear to escape inactivation (Carrel & Willard, 2005). Many of these have homologs on the Y chromosome, but there is evidence that this does not equalize expression levels (Xu, Burgoyne, & Arnold, 2002). Analogous to this, expression of some genes on the X chromosome appears to be up-regulated, so that males receive levels of the proteins involved more comparable with those of females with two X chromosomes (Davies & Wilkinson, 2006). Complicating the picture still further, the gene encoding the androgen receptor is located on the X chromosome and may be expressed differently in the two sexes, and we know that this receptor must process much greater quantities of androgens in males, though we do not know whether or to what degree this has consequences. Finally, some genes are epigenetically marked, or *imprinted*, so that they are expressed only when inherited from one parent and not when they are inherited from the other. Any paternally imprinted genes located on the X chromosome are expressed only in females.

Prenatal programming, foetal origins theory and the Barker hypothesis

Sexual differentiation is not the only dimension for which the influence of prenatal experience has been considered. Epidemiologists have long been aware that adult health appears to be sensitive to prenatal environmental conditions. Kermack, McKendrick, and McKinlay (2001; reprinted from 1934) provided some of the first robust evidence for this. They observed that, during the 19th century in Britain and, in Sweden, the latter part of the 18th and the 19th centuries, death rates appeared to be tied to both age and year of birth, with lower death rates in more recent years of birth. They suggested that improving early life health conditions were conferring stronger physical constitutions in childhood that made better health possible throughout the lifespan. Because improvements in infant mortality lagged those in death rates beyond early childhood, they attributed the improvement in longevity to better health in pregnant mothers, particularly that due to reduction of virulent infections. The starvation periods in Europe during World War II made clear that prenatal nutrition was also important, at least to growth and timing of puberty (Widdowson, Mavor, & McCance, 1964; Widdowson & McCance, 1959); there appeared to be no effects on health as reflected in longevity, as long as recovery of nutritional status was possible. This inspired a major effort to improve prenatal care through nutritional supplements in impoverished regions. Follow-up of these programmes revealed that more than nutritional supplementation was necessary to improve child health (Scrimshaw & Guzman, 1995), but the idea that prenatal nutrition is important has taken firm hold.

During the 1980s, Barker proposed that growth retardation from maternal malnutrition leads to low infant birthweight, which in turn has a primary influence on vascular health in adulthood (Barker & Osmond, 1986). This was supported by correlations on the order of 0.7 between birthweight and mortality due to adult cardiovascular disease, though there was also evidence for effects of birthweight on mortality from respiratory infections. Subsequent studies linked low birthweight to high blood pressure, Type 2 diabetes, and impaired kidney function. These studies have not always replicated well, but meta-analysis has generally upheld the existence of some effects (Huxley, Shiell, & Law, 2000), albeit at smaller levels than indicated in the original studies. The effects appear to be mediated by more rapid than normal growth in the initial period after birth, enabling catch-up to typical size, but apparently slowing metabolic rate so that low-birthweight individuals 'make do' metabolically with less food to support the accelerated growth. Maternal infection during pregnancy apparently has similar effects (Finch, 2007).

Prenatal effects of maternal emotion

It has also long been thought that maternal emotional condition during pregnancy may have long-term effects on the developing foetus, both physiological and behavioural. Sometimes this has taken the form of superstition and ritual, as in folk customs where casting the 'evil eye' on a pregnant woman is thought to bode poorly for the infant's well-being. References to belief in such prenatal influences date to the Old Testament of the Bible, as when, for example, in Genesis, Jacob influenced the colour of lambs born to his ewes. As other examples, in the 1600s, Sir Kenelm Digby attributed King James' fear of naked swords to prenatal influences, and, in 1889, Dabney concluded that 21 of 90 cases showed a credible relation between the timing of some impression made upon the pregnant woman and the nature of the abnormality in her newborn child (Ferreira, 1965). Cases have been made for involvement of emotional factors in conception as evidenced by successful treatment of infertility by psychotherapy, and repeated anecdotal observation that conception often occurs in supposedly infertile couples after they decide to adopt. In general, maternal stress of various forms has been linked to everything from premature birth and/or miscarriage to psychopathology in the adult offspring, with varying degrees of scientific rigour. In recent years, however, much more substantial evidence for such effects has accumulated, and some of the mechanisms involved are starting to be suggested. In all cases, the effects involved are considered organizational. That is, the foetus is thought to be sensitive to a prenatal environment that includes maternal emotional condition, with several windows for foetal metabolic and/or organizational 'set points' that depend on the environmental circumstances encountered, and once set in early development persist into adulthood.

As with research involving brain physiology more generally, much of the evidence for prenatal maternal emotional effects comes from studies of nonhuman animals. In these studies pregnant females are subjected to experimental stressors that lead to observable changes in maternal physiology that presumably also affect the foetal environment. Many of these studies involve physical stressors for which it is hard to imagine likely human analogues, especially in our current environment, including bodily suspension, social isolation, repeated electrical shocks to the tail, saline injection, physical immobilization, and re-housing with unfamiliar others (Huizink, 2008). The lack of likely analogues makes generalization to human pregnancy difficult, but the effects observed do indicate possible biological mechanisms involved, and genetic variance can be both systematically manipulated and controlled through the use of interbred species in order to understand these mechanisms better. Studies that have applied social stresses such as changes in housing conditions and exposure to social hassles to pregnant rodents and primates are especially likely to be relevant (e.g., Gutman & Nemeroff, 2002; Sachser & Kaiser, 1997).

They are limited in experimental lab work, however, to only one aspect of such stress exposure, that which is completely beyond the control of the pregnant mother experiencing it. In humans, some stressors are of this type, such as those associated with war, sudden catastrophic events such as earthquakes, or the sudden deaths of important others. But other stressors, such as the experience of daily hassles, interpersonal conflict, work productivity or school achievement difficulties, or even accidents, all may be at least partly attributable to personal characteristics or lifestyle factors. This complicates assessment of the prenatal stress as a direct cause of any observed offspring associations in humans because the characteristics contributing to maternal experience of stress may be linked genetically or epigenetically to the associations observed in the offspring, so that genetic transmission of traits contributing to tendency to experience certain kinds of stress possibly forms the actual causal mechanism, rather than the actual experience of the stress itself. Moreover, human mothers experience emotional responses to the fact of pregnancy itself, for which we have no evidence of analogues in nonhuman animals. For example, women may experience pregnancy-related anxieties, such as guilt or displeasure at being pregnant at all, worries about their own or foetal health, or fear of giving birth. Any offspring associations with these feelings may also have roots in common genetic influences. Current knowledge of the biological mechanisms through which maternally experienced stress may be transmitted to the foetus is limited. It is clear, however, that enhanced maternal production of stress hormones enters foetal circulation and can affect regulation of the foetal HPA axis (McEwen, 1991; Sapolsky, Uno, Rebert, & Finch, 1990).

There are three known pathways through which maternal stress hormones may affect the foetus. First, maternal levels of stress hormones run 2-10 times higher than those in their foetuses, and the foetuses are normally protected from most exposure to these levels by the presence of the placental enzyme *11β-hydroxisteroid dehydrogenase* (11β-HSD), which converts cortisol into a form not biologically active. Still, some maternal cortisol gets past this enzyme and passes through the placenta to the foetus, especially when maternal levels are particularly high. As little as 10-20 per cent of the maternal level passing through the placenta can double foetal concentration, given that foetal concentrations are generally so much lower. The placenta itself is a second pathway through which maternal stress hormones can be transmitted to the foetus. These hormones are present in the placenta and biologically active to the same degree as those in the hypothalamus, but they are not subject to the negative feedback regulation that takes place within the HPA axis itself, so, once produced, their levels remain high. The third pathway is indirect: maternal stress may reduce blood flow from the placenta to the uterus because the hormones produced constrict blood vessels. Effects on the foetus may result from reduced blood flow from the placenta rather than from the hormones themselves.

Evidence of prenatal effects of maternal stress in nonhuman animals

Despite these complications for extrapolation to humans, nonhuman animal studies have produced fairly consistent evidence that prenatal exposure to maternal stress is associated with greater reactivity, decreased exploratory behaviour, and reduced attention in offspring (Schneider & Coe, 1993; Weinstock, Matlina, Maor, Rosen, & McEwen, 1992). This has typically been measured by subjecting the offspring to stress in the form of a novel, open environment, some kind of raised maze, forced swimming, or awkward social circumstances. In these situations, smaller amounts of locomotor activity, greater defecation, and less vocalization are generally interpreted as indicative of greater reactivity. Some studies, however, have produced contradictory results. For example, Deminiere, Piazza, Guegan, Abrous, Maccari, and Le Moal (1992) found that prenatally stressed rodents showed shorter latencies to explore and were more active in a novel environment than those not prenatally stressed. Conflicting results of this kind may be the result of using different genetically inbred strains. For example, Stohr, et al. (Stohr, Schulte Wermeling, Szuran, Pliska, Domeney, & Welzl, 1998) compared response to prenatal stress in high- and low-activity strains of mice. They observed that prenatally stressed male offspring from the low-activity strain were more active than control offspring that had not been prenatally stressed, but prenatally stressed male offspring from the high-activity strain were less active. Prenatally stressed female offspring were less active in both strains. In this case, both sex and genetic differences appeared to contribute to behaviour that could be clearly categorized as different, but in most studies, interpretation of results as indicating particular dimensions along which differences lie rely on subjective human interpretations, such as the reasons a mouse may show reluctance to swim in a pool of cold water.

Human studies have also shown prenatal effects on behaviour that appear to be analogous to those from the nonhuman animal studies. Children of mothers experiencing stress during pregnancy have been most consistently observed to be at greater risk than average for anxiety (e.g., O'Connor, Heron, Golding, & Glover, 2003), attention-deficit-hyperactivity (e.g., Huizink, Dick, Sihvola, Pulkkinen, Rose, & Kaprio, 2007), and conduct (e.g., Barker & Maughan, 2009) disorders. In addition to these effects, however, some studies have also reported associations between prenatal stress and poorer cognitive function (e.g., Bergman, Sarkar, O'Connor, Modi, & Glover, 2007), increased levels of mixed-handedness (e.g., Obel, Hedegaard, Henriksen, Secher, & Olson, 2003), greater fingerprint asymmetry (e.g., King, Mancini-Marie, Brunet, Walker, Meaney, & Laplante, 2009), and lower male-to-female ratio at birth (Obel, Henriksen, Secher, Eskanazi, & Hedegaard, 2007). The behavioural effects appear to be mediated by altered function of the HPA axis, consistent again with the results of nonhuman animal studies (Glover, O'Connor, & O'Donnell, 2009). Smaller densities of grey matter in particular brain regions, especially the hippocampus, have also been noted in offspring of prenatally stressed mothers (e.g., Buss, Davis, Muftuler, Head, & Sandman, 2009).

The effects reported in these studies tend to be very small, and there are many questions regarding control for external variables such as maternal prenatal education, smoking and alcohol and drug consumption, gestational age, birthweight, and postnatal depression, the extent to and consistency with which this has been done in these studies, and even the appropriateness and effectiveness of applying such statistical controls. Moreover, most studies have not assessed the full hypothesized causal pathway. That is, theoretically, prenatal exposure to stress contributes to establishing some basic organizational parameters and levels of responsivity in the HPA axis that persist into adulthood, and which in turn have consequences for behavioural responses. Most studies attempting to evaluate this theoretical chain, however, have either examined only links between prenatal stress and some physiological measure of early childhood HPA axis function, or prenatal stress and some behavioural outcome, or some measure of physiological measure of early childhood HPA axis function and some behavioural outcome. Confusingly, the latter studies have generally provided the weakest evidence for associations (Glover, O'Connor, & O'Donnell, 2009).

Perhaps even more importantly, few studies have been designed to address the possibility of genetic transmission from mother to offspring of vulnerability to psychopathology or differences in HPA axis function. Nonhuman animal studies strongly suggest that prenatal effects vary with timing of stress exposure during gestation, and, if nothing else, human experience with the drug thalidomide, which caused severe birth defects when administered during the first trimester of pregnancy but not when administered later, indicates that timing can be important in humans as well. Some studies have had sufficient power to examine such differences, but most have not. Where effects appear to differ with timing of exposure during gestation, evidence for prenatal stress being directly causal is greater, as the foetus' genome is established at conception and does not vary during gestation. Still, such evidence does not rule out the possibility that genetic vulnerability involves genetic differences in responses to specific kinds of environments (such as prenatal exposure to maternal stress) at specific times during gestation. Another way of narrowing the range of possible alternative explanations for effects is to provide evidence for particular biological links between prenatal experiences and offspring outcomes. For example, maternal consumption of licorice during pregnancy has been associated with both HPA axis function and adverse cognitive and psychiatric offspring outcomes (Raikkonen, Pesonen, Heinonen, Lahti, Komsi, Eriksson, et al., 2009; Raikkonen, Seckl, Heinonen, Pyhala, Feldt, Jones, et al., 2010). Licorice naturally contains glycyrrhiza, which inhibits placental 11β-HSD, the enzyme that renders maternally produced glucocorticoids inactive and so normally protects the foetus from exposure to them. The question of transmissible genetic differences between those who tend to consume licorice during pregnancy and those who do not remains, but the possibility that this is the explanation is more remote.

Evolutionary explanations for prenatal programming effects

The vast majority of observed associations between prenatal stresses and offspring behavioural outcomes have been negative. As discussed in the previous chapter, the experience of stress can have positive as well as negative effects, and a complete absence of stress undoubtedly has negative consequences. This suggests that there should be positive as well as negative associations involving prenatal stress, and such evidence has occasionally been picked up. For example, DiPietro, Novak, Costigan, Atella, and Reusing (2006) observed that 2-year-olds who had been exposed to prenatal stress tended to show faster cognitive and motor development than controls. One reason that studies have picked up very few positive associations between prenatal stress and offspring behaviour is very likely that, as discussed in the previous chapter with respect to the differential susceptibility hypothesis, measurement of stress has tended to be focused on the kinds of stresses perceived likely to have damaging effects. Another reason, however, is related to the evolutionary explanation generally offered for prenatal effects. This explanation has been characterized as 'predictive adaptive response' (Gluckman, Hanson, & Spencer, 2005). The idea is that foetal development is sensitive to environmental circumstances in order to prepare the foetus to adapt to the environment in which it will live after birth. Within this theoretical perspective, greater HPA axis responsivity that, in today's environment in many places, confers greater vulnerability to particular kinds of psychopathology may, in the environment in which humans evolved, have helped the child adapt better to unsettled or unusually dangerous environmental circumstances. That is, what is dysfunctional in much of today's society in which physical danger is rather low and the physical environment is quite predictable (in terms of access to food, shelter, warmth, safety from predators, etc.) may have been especially functional in many periods during human evolution. Another possibility is that some of the dysfunctional effects observed may reflect extremes of some dimensional distribution that improves function at lower levels.

As discussed in Chapter 2, natural selection takes place based on phenotypic variation, and there are advantages to the population as a whole if, when environmental circumstances vary over time and place, there is considerable population variation. Some of the phenotypic variation has roots in genetic variation that is transmitted consistently and directly to phenotype. But some of it may reflect direct effects of the environment and/or environmentally triggered gene expression such as those posited by prenatal programming, which can include epigenetic changes that can be transmitted from one generation to another. Thus, even if prenatal programming contributes to adaptive flexibility, there may be some lag between changes in environmental circumstances and the prevalence of adaptive responses. Moreover, as discussed with respect to temperament, what appears to be dysfunctional adaptation from one perspective may be quite adaptive from some other perspective. At the same time, the presence of lags between changes in the environment and organism response introduce the possibility that the environment will change again during the lags, rendering the programming effects no longer adaptive. This suggests that programming effects, to be truly adaptive, should not generally be irreversible, and, in particular, implies that perception and sensitivity to ongoing environmental cues even after birth should be important (Frankenhuis & Panchanathan, 2011). There is some evidence that foetal programming effects are, in fact, at least sometimes or partly reversible, as, for example, when prenatally stressed female rat pups receive high levels of licking and grooming after birth, apparently restoring their propensity to lick and groom their own offspring, though not the lower levels of glucocorticoid response seen in their nonstressed peers (Glover, O'Connor, & O'Donnell, 2009).

One of the most robust associations between prenatally experienced stress and psychopathology is that with excessive anxiety. Most operationalizations of anxiety involve hyper-vigilance, or excessive fear. In more dangerous or stressful environments, greater sensitivity to the external environment may offer early warning of impending danger and greater opportunity to plan defence or escape. Another quite robust association is that with attention-deficit-hyperactivity disorder (ADHD). This may seem paradoxical, as ADHD usually involves greater risk-taking, physical activity, attention seeking, and impulsivity, in many ways behaviours that could be considered opposite to those manifested when anxiety is high. Still, a case could be made that these externally oriented behaviours could also be especially adaptive in uncertain or dangerous environments. In such environments, the easily distractible behaviours that disrupt school classrooms and impede academic progress and thus seem dysfunctional today may have contributed to greater alertness to new dangers and/or willingness to seek better, more stable environments in our evolutionary past. Both associations could be true, moreover, if, for example, different genetic backgrounds were sensitive to prenatal stress in different ways. Nevertheless, both rationales are completely speculative, and the contrast between them highlights the fact that it is often possible to come up with reasonable-sounding evolutionary rationales for just about any outcome or association. Still the evidence that prenatal experience of stress has consequences for health and behaviour that extend well beyond birth and infancy remains substantial (though far from conclusive), and the arguments that this sensitivity may be adaptive have merit.

Prenatal learning

Do foetuses learn as their brains develop, and is this learning retained after birth? It was long assumed that they did not, but increasing ability to track foetal behaviour has challenged that assumption. In newborns, one of the primary methods of assessing learning or knowledge is to measure *habituation*, or the decrease in response to an originally novel stimulus that takes place as the stimulus becomes no longer novel. Habituation of this type is universal throughout the animal realm. It must be distinguished from overall decreased responsiveness due to fatigue, however, which is usually accomplished by comparing concurrent responsiveness to repeated and novel stimuli, so that the repeated stimuli should show habituated response levels and the novel stimuli should show *dishabituated*, or increased, responses. The most common way to track foetal responses is by monitoring heart rate, which tends to increase in response to novel stimuli, and return to original, slower levels as the foetus becomes habituated. Things are not this simple, however, as orienting responses involve decreases in heart rate. Thus responsiveness itself rather than direction of response is probably what is critical. Learning over time can be demonstrated when the period required to reach habituation, however defined, is significantly shorter in a second exposure to the same stimulus at some later time point than it was originally.

Most tests of foetal learning have involved vibroacoustic or auditory stimulation. Such studies have observed that the period required to reach habituation by foetuses at 32-37 weeks is considerably shorter than that required by younger foetuses (Morokuma, Fukushima, Kawai, Tumonaga, Satoh, & Nakano, 2004), suggesting that ability to learn is increasing with foetal development. Learning also apparently becomes better coordinated. For example, Morokuma, et al. (Morokuma, Doria, Ierrullo, Kinukawa, Fukishima, & Arulkumaran, 2008) observed that most foetuses at 35–37 weeks' gestation showed both habituation and dishabituation responses, but foetuses at 32–34 weeks' gestation showed only habituation and not dishabituation responses to the same auditory stimuli. At term, shortly before birth, retention of response has been demonstrated over periods of 10 minutes and 24 hours (van Heteren, Boekkooi, Jongsma, & Nijhuis, 2000).

Given evidence that foetuses learn before birth, it becomes natural to ask whether some of this learning is retained after birth. Early studies in this area focused on whether newborns responded differently to sounds to which they had commonly been exposed *in utero*, such as heartbeat, than to other sounds. For example, Salk (1962) observed that infants in a neonatal nursery who heard recordings of a heartbeat sound showed greater weight gains and cried less, and Rosner and Doherty (1979) reported that intrauterine sounds had calming effects on infants, though such effects have not been found consistently (e.g., Detterman, 1978). As with many other kinds of stimulation and response combinations, infant responses to prenatally experienced sounds may depend on level of arousal and the specific manner in which the sound is presented, as well as conditions more specific to research with neonates, such as the experimenter's method of evaluating evidence for recognition of the stimulus (Detterman, 1978).

More recent studies have focused on the mother's voice and language exposure. To a foetus in the womb, the mother's voice is a prominent sound, but it does not come across to the foetus the way it does after birth, largely because most of its higher-frequency sound waves do not travel through the mother's body to reach the foetus. This renders the language content of the voice essentially unintelligible, as well as distorting its quality. Several studies have indicated that, after birth, infants prefer distorted recordings of the mother's voice that mimic the way it sounded to them *in utero* (e.g., Spence & Freeman, 1996), which strongly suggests that the neonate can make use of pre-birth experience in the post-birth environment. Infant responses to normal recordings of the mother's voice and that of a strange female have also been compared. For example, within two hours after birth, infants showed greater movement of their bodies in response to their mothers' voices than to that of a stranger (Moon & Fifer, 2000). This is suggestive of some level of recognition of mother's voice, but does not provide particularly strong evidence for learning, as it is not clear that infants *should* move more if they recognize their mothers' voice, especially if recognition of other familiar sounds such as heartbeat is associated with calming effects. Stronger evidence is provided by studies that have created situations in which the neonate's behaviour has some effect on the environment. For example, Fifer and colleagues (DeCasper & Fifer, 1980; Fifer & Moon, 1989) gave neonates pacifiers that could activate recordings of either their mothers' voices or that of a stranger by sucking. The neonates sucked more to activate the recordings of their mothers' voices than that of the stranger. There is evidence that this difference can be tied to neurophysiological differences in brain response (de Regnier, Nelson, Thomas, Wawerka, & Georgieff, 2000), and that the response patterns are less clearly differentiated in pre-term infants (de Regnier, Wawerka, Georgieff, Mattia, & Nelson, 2002). Neonates have also shown recognition of melodic passages to which they were exposed repeatedly prior to birth (Granier-Defferre, Bassereau, Ribeiro, Jacquet, & DeCasper, 2011).

There is evidence not only for auditory recognition but that infants begin to process aspects of language *in utero* as well. Within the first few days after birth, infants have shown that they can discriminate the language their mothers speak from other languages (Mehler, Jusczyk, Lambertz, Halsted, Bertoncini, & Amiel-Tison, 1988), and that they prefer this language (Moon, Panneton, Cooper, & Fifer, 1993). More than this, however, neonates can recognize specific patterns of speech that they have heard before. The first study demonstrating this dates back to 1986, when DeCasper & Spence (1986) had women in the last six weeks of pregnancy read aloud a single three-minute passage twice daily. After birth, their infants more often activated recordings of this passage than of a novel passage read by their mothers, and also more often activated recordings of this passage over a novel one read by an unfamiliar voice. Since then, many studies have provided corroboration of this result, extending it to emotional content and to recognition memory prior to birth (Kisilevsky, Hains, Brown, Lee, Cowperthwaite, Stutzman, et al., 2009). Infants also appear to key their own early vocalizations to the language around them. Mampe, Friederici, Christophe, and Wermke (2009) observed that the prosodic qualities of the cries of German and French infants differed from each other, and that the differences paralleled the differences in prosodic qualities found in adult speech in the French and German languages.

As is typical of much of the literature on infant development, these studies all focused on evidence of prenatal learning common to all foetuses and neonates. A few studies, however, have suggested that individual differences that characterize infants after birth can be observed prior to birth as well, at least in more rudimentary forms. For example, Gaultney and Gingras (2005) found that infants that had required more trials to demonstrate habituated responses to prenatal stimuli also scored lower after birth on a test of infant response to novelty that indicates risk of low cognitive ability in childhood and adulthood. This suggests that individual differences in some basic biological factor involved in cognitive ability are present very early in development and contribute to the stability of cognitive ability relative to age and cultural peers that persists throughout life. Individual differences in emotions associated with learned material may also be formed prenatally. Harvison, Molfese, Woodruff-Borden, and Wiegel (2009) observed that neonates of mothers who experienced little anxiety during pregnancy displayed more negative frontal slow-wave auditory-evoked responses to their mothers' voices relative to the voice of a stranger. In contrast, the frontal slow-wave auditory-evoked responses of neonates of mothers who had experienced considerable anxiety during pregnancy were more positive in response to their mother's voice relative to the voice of a stranger. This could reflect individual differences transmitted genetically from mother to infant, but it also could reflect prenatal programming effects due directly to the *in utero* exposure to maternal stress hormones.

Taken together, these studies might appear to suggest that human infants are uniquely sensitive to exposure to human speech. This would be consistent with the idea of a uniquely human evolved adaptation in the form of a genetically determined language acquisition device as proposed by Noam Chomsky (1965). It is likely, however, that such a conclusion would be premature. Both the majority of the studies that have been carried out and the experiences of most foetuses and neonates are limited to exposure to human as opposed to nonhuman animal sounds. Voubumanos, Hauser, Werker, and Martin (2010) went beyond this, however, and presented neonates and three-month-old infants with nonsense human speech, rhesus monkey vocalizations, and synthetic sounds. The neonates showed no preference for the nonsense human speech over the rhesus monkey vocalizations, though they preferred both to the synthetic sounds. The three-month-olds, however, preferred the nonsense human speech to the rhesus monkey vocalizations, as well as to the synthetic sounds. This suggests that, even if foetuses and neonates can recognize aspects of human speech with which they have prior experience, it is the presence of this prior experience rather than some biologically wired ability to process it that governs this recognition ability.

Despite this, it is clear that, from birth, speech is an important cue for the development of face processing and social cognition, and learning resulting from prenatal exposure to speech probably plays some role in this process. Many studies have shown that newborn infants follow the eye gaze of others as well as their speech, and that eye gaze is also an important cue for the development of face processing and social cognition. Two recent studies, however, suggest that they are directly linked. Guellai and Streri (2011) familiarized newborn infants with photos of the face of a stranger talking either with gaze directed towards the infants or with gaze averted. The infants were then presented with photos of the previously seen face and of a new one. Indicating that it had more significance for them, the infants looked longer at the face they had previously seen speaking, but only if the speaker's gaze had been directed towards them. This suggested that, after birth, the extent to which auditory experience captures infant attention, and thus is likely to be retained in memory, is dependent on its coordination with speaker eye gaze that includes the infant. But the extent to which visual experience captures attention and is thus likely to be retained in memory may be similarly dependent on its coordination with auditory experience of speech. Coulon, Guellai, and Streri (2011) exposed newborn infants to videos of the faces of strangers either talking to the infants or remaining silent. The infants later looked longer at the face that they had seen talking to them than at the one that had been silent. There is large variability in the extent to which parents and other caregivers interact with and talk to infants, as well as in infant habituation rates to experiences. Both of these may contribute substantially to individual differences in the development of language, social, intellectual, and emotional processing abilities.

Risks to foetal development

Conditions considered to be congenital defects occur in some 3-5 per cent of all live births, and are among the leading causes of infant mortality in countries with well-developed health care systems, accounting for more than 20 per cent of infant deaths. These conditions can have many sources. Some 10-15 per cent are thought to result from chromosomal abnormalities of various kinds. The most serious ones involve extra or missing whole chromosomes, caused by errors in separation of the chromosomes during formation of the sex cells. Such abnormalities that involve the sex chromosomes were discussed earlier in this chapter, but there are others involving the autosomes as well. Most are not compatible with life, so they result in miscarriage of the foetus. Probably the best known autosomal abnormality that is associated with life is Down's Syndrome, which results from all or part of an extra 21st chromosome. The condition is associated with intellectual disability, particular facial features, early-onset dementia, heart problems, and growth abnormalities. The severity of the condition is usually associated with the amount of extra chromosomal material carried. The risk of major chromosomal abnormalities of this kind increases with maternal age, though the reasons for this are not presently known. For Down's Syndrome, risk is about 1/2,000 when the mother is 20. It doubles by maternal age 30, and reaches about 1/200 by maternal age 37. Paternal age may also be associated with greater risk of chromosomal abnormality, though the evidence for this is less clear, and the specific risks are less well defined. Another autosomal abnormality is Williams Syndrome, which is caused by deletion of about 26 genes from the long arm of chromosome 7. Like Down's Syndrome, it is characterized by intellectual disability, particular facial features, and heart problems, though the specifics manifested are different. It is also characterized by cheerful demeanour, excessive friendliness with strangers, fluency in language relative to other cognitive abilities, and low muscle tone. It occurs in 1 in 7,500-20,000 live births. These two conditions illustrate the fact that genetic defects can involve both extra chromosomal material and missing chromosomal material.

Genetic defects can also involve mutations at single specific genetic loci. Some common (at least among such conditions) genetic disorders caused by mutations at single specific autosomal loci are sickle-cell anaemia, Huntington's Disease, cystic fibrosis, Tay-Sachs disease, phenylketonuria, and Marfan Syndrome. They are generally transmitted from one generation to the next in straightforward Mendelian fashion. Some, such as sickle-cell anaemia are recessive and require transmission of the deleterious mutation from both parents for manifestation. Others, such as Huntington's Disease, are dominant and are manifested upon transmission of the deleterious mutation from only one parent. Many differ in frequency across ethnic and racial groups, and sometimes this provides clues to their evolutionary function and prehistoric human migration patterns and activities. For example, sickle-cell anaemia is more common among blacks. Because it is a recessive condition, two copies of the deleterious mutation are required for manifestation of the disorder. Individuals carrying only one copy, however, show greater resistance to mosquito-borne malaria, which has long been and remains a major health problem in Africa. Many of these conditions involve many different forms of mutation at a particular genetic locus, and the severity of the symptoms of the condition may vary with the particular deleterious mutation carried. Most of these conditions also involve many more than single mutations, though each individual case may involve only a single mutation. That is, most genes cover some span of base pairs of DNA, and the disorders may results from mutations in any one of several to many of these individual base pairs. Moreover, many different base-pair substitutions may cause the same condition. This is because function can be disrupted by substituting a functional component with anything that is not capable of carrying out the function, but the component necessary to carry out the function may be very specific. For example, some 400 different mutations that cause phenylketonuria have been identified. All interrupt the conversion of phenylalanine to other compounds essential to normal metabolic function, but they do so in different ways and at different stages of the conversion process. This results in different degrees of severity of the disorder, so that it is best thought of as a spectrum of disorders rather than a single condition.

Congenital defects can also result from exposure to *teratogens*. The term is tautologous, as it refers to environmental agents that can cause birth defects, so the point in its usage is the emphasis on the source of the damage in the environment. Some 10 per cent of congenital defects are attributed to teratogens. Despite the term's definition locating the source of the damage in the environment, it is apparent that sensitivity to teratogen exposure can vary genetically. In fact, this is the first of six principles of *teratology*, or the study of the abnormalities associated with teratogens, that were articulated by Wilson (1973). Understanding of how teratogens exert their effects still rests on these principles. The second principle is that vulnerability to damage from teratogen exposure varies with developmental stage. Many teratogens cause noticeable damage only when organs are under active formation. The third idea is that teratogens exert their effects by initiating sequences of abnormal events. The basic idea is that they alter expression of particular genes that in turn alter expression of downstream genes, starting an abnormal developmental cascade. The fourth principle is that many factors can affect the extent to which any given level of teratogen exposure damages development. These include the particular form in which the teratogen is presented, the route through which the mother is exposed, the mother's genetically influenced sensitivity to the teratogen, and the rate of transfer across the placenta. According to the fifth principle, there are four ways in which teratogen damage can be manifested, which are death, malformation, retardation of development, and functional defect. Finally, manifestations of deviant development are dose-dependent. That is, all else being equal, damage is greater with larger exposure.

Many commonly available drugs and medications have teratogenic effects, including tobacco, caffeine, alcohol, as well as illicit recreational drugs and a host of prescription medications. Environmental and industrial chemicals such as polynuclear aromatic hydrocarbons, polychlorinated biphenyls (PCBs), dioxin, and organic mercury are also teratogens, as is ionizing radiation in the form of fallout from atomic weapons, background radiation, medical x-rays, and radiation therapies. Maternal infections are another common source of teratogenic effects, with herpes virus, syphilis, rubella virus (German measles), and toxoplasmosis being among the most common. Finally, maternal metabolic imbalance can have teratorgenic effects on foetuses. Sources of dangerous metabolic imbalances include maternal alcoholism, diabetes, folic acid deficiency, iodine deficiency, hyperthermia, phenylketonuria, and congenital heart defects. The list of chemicals with known teratogenic effects grows continually as assessment and testing get more thorough. Unfortunately, many of the chemicals involved are medications, and their teratogenic effects have only been identified after they have already been approved for medical usage. Teratogen exposure can result in a wide range of abnormalities, and specific congenital defects are not usually characteristic of any specific teratogen.

Two common teratogens illustrate the kinds of effects involved. Heavy maternal alcohol consumption increases risk of spontaneous abortion, stillbirth, premature placental separation, development and function of the placenta, and restriction of intrauterine growth, all involving the mother's capacity to maintain the pregnancy in ways that can affect the foetus. Foetuses that survive to birth suffer increased risk of Sudden Infant Death Syndrome, a variety of physical abnormalities ranging from mild to severe, and cognitive and behavioural problems. The extent of damage is heavily dose-dependent, and safe levels of alcohol consumption during pregnancy remain a subject of debate. Smoking also increases risk of adverse outcomes of pregnancy. Babies born to women who smoke during pregnancy average 100-200 grams less in birthweight (Walsh, 1994), which tends to have its own developmental consequences, and other sequelae are similar to those associated with heavy drinking. Maternal exposure to second-hand smoke is suspected to have similar, though smaller, effects.

Birth and perinatal complications

The final hurdle of gestation, of course, is birth itself. The timing of birth in humans is a grand natural compromise between the minimum gestation necessary for infant survival, and the maximum the mother can tolerate. The primary reason for the upper limit of maternal tolerance is *cephalopelvic disproportion*, or, essentially a human infant head that is too large to pass easily through its human mother's pelvis. In apes, birth is short and easy because, relatively speaking, mothers have wider pelvises and infants have smaller heads. In humans, however, birth is long, difficult, and dangerous. Our upright posture, which made the narrower pelvis both possible and necessary, is one major reason for the cephalopelvic disproportion, but it is not the only one. Data from australopithecines, who shared our upright posture but not our large brains, make this clear (Berge, 1998). It means that considerable enlargement of the human head evolved after the narrower pelvic area was already in place, creating pressure for birth to occur at less mature levels of brain development in order to maintain manageable head size. It has been estimated that, based on brain growth rates both in absolute terms and relative to size in other species, human gestation should be as long as 21 months (Konner, 2010), but this would be impossible given the current body plan of the adult human female. Other calculations involving lifespan suggest a 12-month human gestation, but even this would severely increase birth difficulties. The primary reason that shorter gestation limits infant survival is the energy cost associated with maintaining the brain by an immature body outside the uterus. In the newborn human infant, this is 74 per cent of available total energy (Cunnane & Crawford, 2003). The brain would require an even greater proportion of available energy if birth normally occurred earlier. As incubation is generally necessary for pre-term infants, it is estimated that this would not be sustainable.

Birth is stressful for the infant, who must leave the protected uterine environment, breathe and regulate its own body temperature in the external world, and process a wide range of new sensory stimuli. More than that, however, because of the cephalopelvic disproportion, the birth process is complex and there are many opportunities for things to go wrong. During it, the foetus' head first becomes 'engaged' in the pelvic area, facing one of the mother's hips. The head then begins to descend down further into the vaginal area. As it does so, the bones of the skull, which are connected only very loosely at this point, are pressed by the mother's pelvis and their shape is contorted to make the head temporarily thinner and thus longer. During this time, the foetal head ideally rotates 90 degrees so that the infant faces the mother's rectum. The head then tilts backwards, so that its forehead comes through the vagina first. Once it is outside, the head rotates towards the normal position with respect to the shoulders, which are still at an angle, but the shoulders complete restoration of normal position once they too have merged. The entire process typically takes about eight hours in first pregnancies, and about four hours in later ones, though much longer labours occur with some regularity and can pose significant risks to the foetus. In countries with modern medical facilities, the mortality rate for foetuses of at least 28 weeks' gestation and infants within the first 28 days of birth is about 1 per cent, but historical rates were far higher.

The process of expulsion from the uterus can become delayed for several reasons, presenting risks of foetal injury or damage. Sometimes the foetus' buttocks or feet rather than head become engaged in the pelvic area, or the head descends properly but the shoulders become caught. Sometimes the mother's body does not produce strong enough uterine contractions to force the foetus to move down the birth canal. The umbilical cord can also become wrapped around the foetus' neck. These are common reasons for obstetrical interventions including cesarian section and the use of forceps to extract the foetus. Perhaps obviously, the risks of all birth complications are greater when the foetus is particularly large and/or the mother is particularly small. There are two primary dangers to the foetus associated with birth complications. One is neonatal infection, which can be caused by prolonged labour or premature rupture of the amniotic membranes, and the other is maternal infection with sexually transmitted diseases. Such infections have more severe effects on infants born prematurely. The other primary danger is *intrapartum asphyxia*, or restriction of delivery of oxygen to the foetus' brain and vital tissues during labour. This can cause long-term impairment, especially when it involves damage to brain tissue.

Individual differences and development during gestation

This chapter has outlined many potential sources of individual differences that affect infant development during gestation, from genetic differences present at conception to differences in responses to individually experienced environmental circumstances and events. These sources ensure that neonates are born with different levels of readiness to learn, different proclivities to experience emotions, different degrees of responsiveness to stress, and different levels of physical resources to manage their own metabolisms (for example, to regulate body temperature). But of course infants also emerge into very different kinds of physical circumstances and emotional climates that are often correlated with the kinds of environmental circumstances they experienced *in utero*. Despite this, it is generally quite easy for obstetrical personnel to judge whether a neonate is 'normal', based on quick examination of relatively few key features. This indicates that these features tend to fall within very narrow ranges. At one level, this testifies to the uniformity of the developmental process that takes place during gestation. At another, however, it is clear that the process is not so much uniform as *robust*, or able to persist in recognizable, viable, form despite perturbations and conditions of uncertainty. This robustness is emphasized by the evidence for differential foetal programming effects that can influence physical and mental health extending into adulthood and even old age. At the same time, to the extent prenatal programming effects themselves represent real phenomena, there is evidence that many of them are reversible over time after birth as well. Birth, or the end of gestation, thus produces a population of infants who differ from each other considerably, yet are poised on the edge of life to develop ever greater differences as they grow. Perhaps the real wonder, however, is that the differences that will emerge as they grow are not even greater than they are.

Box 5.2   Dynamic systems theory

The developmental processes that take place have been modelled using *dynamic systems theory*, which addresses the long-term behaviour of complex systems that show considerable changes in form over time. The theory is also known as complexity or chaos theory. It posits that changes over time in complex systems such as the human brain, the local insect population each spring, and the flow of a river depend on fixed rules which describe the state of the system in terms of time since attainment of some notable state that can be considered a marker of some kind, and that models that describe these processes can be constructed, usually using nonlinear differential equations. Unlike most mathematical models, however, the point in developing dynamic systems models is not to find equations that have specific solutions that describe the system, but to specify equations that describe the processes involved in such a way that observers can address questions such as whether the system will reach a steady state, what ranges of steady states are possible, and whether the long-term behaviour of the system depends on some initial condition. The ideas involved have their origins in Newtonian mechanics, but their implementation was very limited until the advent of fast computing machines. Even with today's computing capabilities, the models are generally great simplifications of the actual processes. Nevertheless, they have been valuable in revealing unexpected properties of many biological systems and developmental processes.

The models that have been used in embryology (e.g., Kauffman, 1993; Goodwin, 1993) have typically begun with models of chemical systems that produce regular patterns after a lot of chaotic activity. They tend to show that, regardless of the particular forms of random activity in the early stages, or the particular mixes of chemicals in which the random activity is simulated, certain patterns of development are much more likely than other patterns. This suggests that, despite both genetic variation and variation in experiential forces, embryonic development is a rather robust process that does not depend in any direct way on either the expression of particular genes or any specific environmental experiences. This could be the case, for example, if some ensemble of mutually regulatory genes emerges from some reasonably straightforward (though not presently known) set of laws of self-organization, consistent with the kinds of general-level actions known to be controlled by the homeotic genes described in Chapter 3. Each of these ensembles might function as an attractor in initially chaotic transactions among genes (Kauffman, 1993), gradually imposing stability on the system. If so, it is likely that natural selection stabilizes the ensembles as attractors through elimination of variations from the most stable pattern, with strong selection or genetic or environmental drift occasionally dislodging one attractor-centred ensemble and replacing it with another. To the extent this account is accurate, development should be considered a process through which the individual characteristics of organisms emerge over time, rather than a process through which the latent, pre-ordained specific characteristics of individuals are revealed. I will return to this topic in later chapters.

Further reading

Barker, D. J., & Osmond, C. (1986). Infant mortality, childhood nutrition, and ischaemic heart disease in England and Wales. *Lancet, 1*, 1077–1081.

Berenbaum, S. A. (1999). Effects of early androgens on sex-typed activities and interests in adolescents with congenical adrenal hyperplasia. *Hormones and Behavior, 35*, 102–110.

Bergman, K., Sarkar, P., O'Connor, T. G., Modi, N., & Glover, V. (2007). Maternal stress during pregnancy predicts cognitive ability and fearfulness in infancy. *Journal of the American Academy of Child and Adolescent Psychiatry, 46*, 1454–1463.

DeCasper, A. J., & Fifer, W. P. (1980). Of human bonding: Newborns prefer their mothers' voices. *Science, 208*, 11741–11776.

Frankenhuis, W. E., & Panchanathan, K. (2011). Individual dfifferences in developmental plasticity may result from stochastic sampling. *Perspectives on Psychological Science, 6*, 336–347.

Glover, V., O'Connor, T. G., & O'Donnell, K. (2009). Prenatal stress and the programming of the HPA axis. *Neuroscience and Biobehavioural Reviews, 35*, 17–22.

Huizink, A. C. (2008). Prenatal exposure and temperament: A review. *European Journal of Developmental Science, 2*, 77–99.

Moon, C., & Fifer, W. P. (2000). Evidence of transnatal auditory learning. *Journal of Perinatology, 20*, S37–S44.

Voubumanos, A., Hauser, M. D., Werker, J. F., & Martin, A. (2010). The tuning of neonates' preference for speech. *Child Development, 81*, 517–527.

Infancy: Building a Brain

In the first year after birth, the human brain more than doubles in volume, reaching about 60 per cent of its adult volume, and the growth rate does not slow much in the second year. This rapid growth of the brain is unique to the human species and testifies to its immaturity at birth. It is likely a direct evolutionary adaptation to the problem of cephalopelvic disproportion described in the previous chapter. The immaturity is especially noticeable with respect to social responsiveness, to the point that some paediatricians refer to the first three months after birth as 'the fourth trimester' of pregnancy. The neonate has a propensity to be comforted by physical contact, feeding, and rocking, and a modest ability to orient to and learn preferential responses to the human face and voice, but not much more. Many new parents find this disappointing and frustrating. The behavioural repertoire of neonates is considered consistent with full development of the peripheral nervous system, extensive development of the spinal cord and medulla, substantial development of the midbrain, and only partial development of the forebrain, primarily below the cortex. This unevenness in development is reflected in the presence of several *primitive neonatal reflexes*.

The primitive neonatal reflexes

Reflexes are involuntary and almost instantaneous responses to particular kinds of stimuli. The responses originate in the central nervous system. Normal neonates exhibit 10 or more reflexes that normal adults and children do not. The reflexive responses disappear or are inhibited by the frontal lobes during infant and early childhood development. Children and adults with neurological conditions such as cerebral palsy may continue to display these reflexes either in general or under certain circumstances. Some of the neonatal reflexes likely have survival value, as they involve behaviours that enable feeding or encourage positive interaction with parents and caregivers before the infant is able to organize these behaviours spontaneously.

The *Moro reflex*, sometimes termed the startle reaction, is present at birth, increases in strength through the first month after birth and then gradually disappears over the course of the next two months, though it can extend as long as six months. In response to some abrupt environmental change such as shift in position of the head (which newborns cannot control well at all), temperature change (as when going outside from a heated house), or sudden noise, the legs and head extend, and the arms jerk up and out with palms up and thumbs flexed. Almost immediately, the arms are then brought together, then hands clench into fists, and the neonate cries loudly. During human evolution, the Moro reflex may have helped infants retain physical contact with their mothers when they or their mothers lost balance. This explanation seemed counterintuitive to many researchers at first, as the sudden extension of the head, legs, and arms would dislodge the infant from the mother. Preschtl (1965), however, showed that the fact that researchers have tended to observe the reflex in infants lying on their backs is the problem. When the infant is already grasping something and there is traction in its arms and hands, the head, legs, and arms do not extend, and the reflex does indeed help to maintain grasping contact. The Moro reflex acts in coordination with the *Palmar grip reflex*, which appears at birth, and lasts until five to six months of age. When the palm of the infant's hand comes in contact with an object, the fingers will close around it and grasp it strongly enough to support its own weight for several seconds.

Several reflexes reflect the unevenness of the states of development of different aspects of the neonatal nervous system. For example, the *walking/stepping reflex* is present at birth. If the infant is suspended above a flat surface so that the soles of its feet brush the surface, it will make walking motions by placing one foot in front of the other in turn. This reflex disappears at about six weeks of age due to increasing leg weight relative to strength. Of course the motion reappears in voluntary form in late infancy. The reflex has direct analogues in animals that have had the cortex or cerebrum removed and in human infants reflects the relative maturity of the spinal cord and medulla in the absence of functional pathways descending from the cortex. The *Babinski reflex* is also present at birth and lasts through about the first year. When the sole of the foot comes in contact with some surface, adults with normal neuronal function will curl the toes down, moving them away from the shin. Infants, and adults with clinical lesions of the corticospinal tracts, will splay the toes outward and upward in the same situation. The reflex disappears with myelination of the appropriate tracts during infancy, and its disappearance is associated with the ability to walk upright (Konner, 2010).

The *rooting reflex* assists in breastfeeding and is also present at birth. The infant will turn its head towards anything that strokes its cheek or mouth, moving its head in arcs and opening its mouth to surround anything it encounters in the process. The rooting reflex is linked to the *sucking reflex*, which generates sucking actions at anything that touches the roof of the mouth. Together, these two reflexes have the effect of allowing the infant to find and latch onto the mother's breast. They last for about three weeks after birth, or until the infant learns to latch onto the breast voluntarily to feed.

In addition to displaying these and several other reflexes, the neonate maintains the skills it had while still in the womb, including ability to get its fingers in its mouth and suck its thumb, stop itself from crying, withdraw body parts from irritations, lift its face from obstacles to breathing, maintain eye focus on the visual scene, coo, and stop crying in response to the sound of a human voice. Its visual capacity is high relative to that of many other mammals. Sharp boundaries between light and dark, such as large checkerboards and bulls' eyes attract infant attention and focus, and have for that reason become popular decorations of infant toys. The infant appears to follow a few almost programmed basic visual action patterns: if alert and the light is not too bright, the eyes are open; if the eyes are open, follow any available light; if the light reveals no edges, keep searching further; if there are edges, stop there and focus (Haith, 1973). There is a clear social bias to these actions: within minutes of birth, infants follow the motion of a black-and-white sketch of a face with their eyes more closely than they do a similar sketch with scrambled features (Als, 1977), or a face shape with no features (Slater, 2000).

Infant crying

Crying is a prominent feature of newborn behaviour. In humans, it is a feature shared with most other mammals, and clearly has a survival function. Though this changes with age, crying in the newborn primarily indicates physical rather than emotional distress (Golub & Gorwin, 1985). It is a strong indicator of some kind of need for care, and appears to be highly effective in that regard. For example, Konner (2010) noted that the German anthropologist Schiefenhovel observed that, among the Eipo of New Guinea, newborn crying was apparently a strong enough signal to reverse even intentional maternal abandonment. Hunger may be its most common trigger, and hunger cries can generally be quite readily distinguished from pain cries by caregivers, whose responses differ accordingly.

There are substantial individual differences in the amounts of crying newborns display in the first few months. These individual differences appear to be predictable from earlier patterns of foetal movement. In one study (St James-Roberts & Menon-Johansson, 1999), pregnant mothers recorded foetal movements over a three-day period around 37 weeks' gestation, categorizing them as weak, medium, or strong. Fussing and crying one week after birth was substantially correlated with foetal movements, particularly those occurring in the mornings, and the weak movements. By 6 to 12 weeks after birth, the strong foetal movements were no longer correlated with infant fussing and crying, but the weak movements remained correlated. The foetal movements did not predict newborn sleeping, other waking, or feeding behaviour at all, nor were they associated with type of delivery, sex, birthweight, birth order, feeding method, or maternal age or education. This suggests that some aspect of temperament may be involved in newborn crying. Particularly because it was weak foetal movements that more consistently predicted newborn crying, however, it is possible that these lower-grade foetal movements reflect some form of mild gastrointestinal or other discomfort *in utero* that is reflected after birth in crying.

Intense crying is, at one level, an indication of infant vigour and health, as only a healthy infant with strong lungs can maintain it. Nonetheless, it can also be maladaptive when it is difficult to soothe, as it easily becomes very frustrating for parents and caregivers. It thus has been associated with infant abuse (Brewster & Nelson, 1998) and can lead to later difficulties in the parent–child relationship (Papousek & von Hofacker, 1998). Moreover, in circumstances where silence is important, persistent and uncontrollable infant crying can endanger the whole group surrounding the infant. For example, in prehistoric times, such crying may have signalled location to predators or enemies, and, much more recently, people fleeing or hiding from the Nazis occasionally smothered crying infants to save the rest of their family members.

Patterns of development across cultures show substantial uniformity, but also important differences, in keeping with the observation within cultures that individual infant crying varies with caregiver responsiveness. In general, crying follows an inverted U-shaped pattern, with the peak at 2-3 months of age. This coincides with the idea of the first three months after birth as the 'fourth trimester of pregnancy' if the increase in crying is associated with increased lung function, physical strength, and ability to direct energy. Consistent with this, the crying of infants born prematurely tends to peak according to their gestational ages rather than according to their birth ages (Barr & Chen, 1996). The decline in crying likely results from increasing ability to express needs in other ways.

Infant smiling

Foetuses routinely produce well-formed smiles beginning around 30 weeks of gestation, both during sleep and when awake. These smiles, however, are reflexive and not connected to any recognizable social or emotional content. This kind of non-social smiling continues into the second month after birth. The emergence of the social smile in an infant tends to produce a marked improvement in infant–parent relationships. It is not uncommon for parents to report that they felt little relationship with their infants prior to the emergence of the social smile, and that its emergence changed everything. Though all of these timeframes show individual differences, by two months of age, infants may smile differently to strangers than to their mothers, and may even smile 'coyly', with averted gaze. By six months of age, infants may smile differently in response to different facial expressions and intensities of smiling on the parts of others (Konner, 2010). Infants missing the upper brain cortex still smile reflexively, so the motor components of the smile do not extend beyond the midbrain level. Development of the social smile does not depend heavily on vision, as blind infants show social smiles within a month or two of normal emergence ages in sighted infants. Like crying, social smile emergence in premature infants tends to take place on a timetable locked to gestational rather than birth age. The timing of social smiling also shows genetic influence, as it is more similar in monozygotic than in dizygotic twins. Reflexive smiling appears to depend only on maturation of cranial nerves that develop prior to birth, while social smiling appears to depend on the coordinated development and myelination of sensory perception that takes place at the top of the brain stem and on ability to control motor actions that takes place in the cerebellum, striatum, and globus pallidus.

By the age of about three months, or the end of the 'fourth trimester of pregnancy', infants have survived the most dangerous period of their lives and developed social smiling, They have also developed the abilities to entertain mutual gazes with others, to recognize familiar objects and others, and to focus on contingently responsive stimuli. The emotional quality associated with their experiences of making use of these abilities appears to be generally positive, but it is largely impersonal, despite ability to recognize the familiar. That is, basically anyone can elicit the infant's social smile and the infant does not yet appear to have strong emotional bonds with any particular individuals. This changes dramatically over the next 6-8 months with the development of infant attachment, the importance of which was discussed at length in Chapter 4.

Measuring infant competencies

With this basic assessment of neonatal and early infant abilities in place, I turn to discussion of how researchers measure infant competencies and their development. Because infant competencies are rather limited, and in particular because infants cannot talk, the methods used must be indirect. Because of this, they rely heavily on adult inferences, and the kinds of inferences that researchers have tended to draw contain some inherent contradictions and preconceptions that may or may not be correct. These inferences have contributed to both important insights into developmental processes and misconceptions that may be hindering further progress in the field. The literature has been dominated by two methods that rely primarily on vision. It is worth discussing these methods and how they have been used and misused in some detail because it helps to place several problems in understanding individual differences in development in context.

The first method in common usage is the *visual preference method*. This simply involves presenting infants with two different stimuli and seeing whether they look consistently longer at one than the other. The difference in looking times is termed a visual preference, and researchers infer first that the existence of the preference indicates that the infants can discriminate between the two stimuli. Position of the two stimuli is usually counterbalanced in such experiments in order to rule out general tendencies to place the head in one position or to look in one direction. The second method in common usage is *habituation*, which was discussed in Chapter 5. There, I discussed it with respect to experiments in which it was assessed by measuring changes in heart rate *in utero*. With newborns, however, it is much more commonly measured using looking time. Sometimes the shorter looking times that define habituation are considered to be early examples of boredom. This is one form of subjective inference, but there is another, more subtle one that is often made. This is that habituation reflects commitment of the features of the stimulus to memory, and thus the existence of the necessary memory capacity. Beyond the inferences of discrimination ability and memory capacity, researchers often also infer from looking preferences and increased looking times after violation of a habituated expectancy that the infants find the stimuli at which they gaze longer more interesting somehow, with many attributions on the parts of the researchers as to what features may be stimulating the infants' interest and what this interest indicates that infants understand.

For example, within the three-dimensional world we inhabit, the positions and orientations of objects with respect to observers change. These changes cause the retinal images subtended by the objects to change in both shape and size. To process information recognizing the constancy of objects, the visual system must accommodate these changes. Piaget (discussed in Chapter 1) had suggested that infants are not able to manage this and thus to perceive objects as constant when they change position until the end of the first year. Slater and Morison (1985) challenged this idea in two experiments making use of preferential looking time. They developed three four-sided shapes, white in the centres, with heavy black edges. The shapes were flat, but suspended in front of the newborns so that they could be rotated through three-dimensional space. One shape was square and the other two were trapezoids, one larger than the square and one smaller. When rotated to specific angles and positioned at specific distances, the square could produce retinal images identical to those produced by the trapezoids when positioned face on (without rotation) at slightly different distances. In the first experiment, Slater and Morison presented the objects to 70 newborns (average age two days), manipulating the angles and distances of presentation, systematically pairing the square with one of the two trapezoids each time, and matching or not matching the retinal images by rotating the square but not the trapezoids. They observed that the infants showed the greatest disparity in looking times when the square was presented face-on, with longer looking times for the square than either trapezoid, but especially the smaller one. This apparent preference for the square decreased as the angle at which the square was rotated increased.

Slater and Morison (1985) interpreted these results as indicating that the infants had overall preferences both for the square over the other two shapes and for the face-on orientation, and that they could perceive and respond to small differences in orientation of the same shape. They did not attempt to account for the infants' apparent preferences for the square shape and the face-on orientation. Their second experiment was designed to see if newborn infants could perceive that a shape was the same no matter the angle of presentation. To do this, however, they needed to work around the infants' preference for the square shape. This is because Slater, Earle, Morison, and Rose (1985) noted that infant preferences for one stimulus over another that appear to have little external rationale, such as that expressed for the square in this experiment, could not be changed by habituating them either to the preferred or to the non-preferred stimulus in the pair.

For the second experiment, therefore, Slater and Morison habituated each of a new set of infants to one of two shapes from the first experiment that presented retinal images other than the square. During the habituation phase the shapes were rotated slightly each time they were presented. Slater and Morison compared the infants' looking times for these stimuli with those for another, novel to these infants, stimulus from the first experiment that also did not present square retinal images. They found that the infants looked longer at the novel stimulus no matter to which stimulus they had been habituated, and concluded that the infants were able to recognize the shape on which the habituation trials had been run no matter how it was oriented to them. This is of course possible, but, without some understanding of the infants' looking preference in the first experiment, some verification that the second group of infants shared this preference and not some other, also unexplained, preference, it is not possible to conclude that this is the most likely explanation. There have been many demonstrations of infant and even adult looking preferences for particular physical features of stimuli that function independently of the context of interest to the experimenter, in which the stimulus is placed. Motion, colour contrast, luminance, and degree of angularity of features have all been involved in expression of such looking preferences, confounding experimental results and thus the appropriateness of inferences about them (Ross & Dannemiller, 1999).

More problematic are experiments that have purported to demonstrate using looking times and preferences that newborn infants have the concepts of abstract ideas such as number or addition, object permanence, object unity, or physical impossibility. For example, Wynn (1992) observed that, after being presented with a sequence in which they first saw one doll and then another was added and the scene curtained, infants looked longer when the curtain was removed to reveal just one doll than when it was removed to reveal two dolls. She claimed that this demonstrated that the infants could add numbers. The infants, however, saw only either one doll or two dolls. Cohen and Marks

(2002) showed that, had the infants also seen no dolls at all when the curtain was removed, they would have paid the scene barely a glance, despite this being an even more unexpected event. Many other experiments call into question the idea that infants can add, including demonstrations that even 3-year-olds do not understand that the number of objects in an array can remain the same despite spatial rearrangement.

There are several reasons that looking time may not be a good indication of understanding, perception, interest, or attention. Perhaps most importantly, there is considerable evidence that in newborn infants, nonhuman animals, and humans of any age, the relation between attention and/or interest and novelty is often not linear. That is, when stimuli are too discrepant from our expectations, newborns and many others may tend to pay them little attention, just as they do when stimuli are completely as expected. Possible reasons for this are that the highly discrepant stimuli appear to be irrelevant and/or that they appear to be beyond comprehension and so not worth the effort. In such circumstances, the greatest attention or interest is instead expressed for stimuli that have the most meaning for the observer, and this can vary with level of understanding, or development of pre-existing conceptual schema. For example, Kagan (2002) reported showing 4-month-olds pairs of photos of their mothers and women who were strange to them. The infants looked longer at the more familiar faces of their mothers. They also looked longer at pictures of facial features as they are normally arranged than at pictures of scrambled facial features. One-year-olds, however, looked longer at the pictures of the scrambled features. A likely interpretation of this difference is that, at the age of 4 months, infants are still 'figuring out' that faces have both common features and individual differences, and that common features such as eyes are generally positioned in particular spatial arrangements. If this is correct, the picture of a face in its normal arrangement might draw more interest from them because it helps them to build and reinforce their emerging concept of the normal face, but they don't even recognize the shapes in the scrambled face as facial features. By the age of one year, however, the concept of the normal face is usually firmly in place for most, and the idea of a scrambled face may now be more interesting because they can identify the shapes in it as facial features and focus on 'figuring out' exactly how those features have been rearranged from the normal.

Looking time may not be a good indication of understanding, perception, interest, or attention for other reasons as well. Infants, and humans more generally, often pay increased attention to familiar stimuli after having just been exposed to a series of novel stimuli, as a way of returning to baseline to process exactly what was importantly different about the other stimuli. But infant attention and interest are also channelled by the immaturity of their capacities to hold events and stimuli in memory and to retrieve them even seconds later for the processing of new events. This ability grows substantially during the first year after birth (Fox, Kagan, & Weiskopf, 1979). Under the age of 7 months, even a 7-10-second delay between seeing the location of an object and being offered an opportunity to reach for it results in failure to reach correctly. And infants under 8 months of age required more than 60 seconds of exposure to pairs of photos consisting of one unchanging and one continuously new and different face before they consistently looked longer at the novel face (Rose, Feldman, & Jankowski, 2001). This means that young infants may look longer at the stimulus that is most salient from the perspective of what they can hold in their memories rather than whatever characteristics the experimenter has designed to reflect their abilities to perceive similarities and differences.

Moreover, looking time is only one way in which attention and/or interest can be manifested nonverbally. Operant responses; changes in heart rate, skin conductance, and vagal tone; and waveforms of event-related brain potentials have all been observed to reflect ability to make distinctions among stimuli, and the inferences they suggest are not always consistent with those of looking time. For example, 7-month-old infants looked longer at faces displaying fearful expressions than happy expressions, but there was no association between these differences and differences in event-related brain potential responses to the two sets of faces (Leppanen, Molson, Vogel-Farley, & Nelson, 2007). Perhaps more importantly, though, psychological states such as surprise, boredom, or interest can be reflected by vocalization, smiling, and changes in facial expression, and these do not always suggest inferences consistent with looking time either. For example, infants presented with tape recordings of babbling by themselves or unfamiliar infants looked longer at the speaker from which the babbling was projected, but vocalized more to the sound of their own babbling (Montague & Walker-Andrews, 2001). And three-month-olds studied pictures of a normal face and a face with only one eye in the middle for equivalent lengths of time, but only smiled in response to the normal face (Lewis, 1967). One explanation of this may be that infants, and humans and other animals more generally, pay prolonged attention to stimuli that suggest stimuli that are generally familiar, but not clearly enough so for immediate assimilation, so that study is required to make sense of them. In contrast, babbling or smiling may reflect more instant recognition. Which is more relevant to expression of infant knowledge varies considerably with context, and lack of attention can indicate complete inability to process as well as automatic recognition.

Developmental stages or continuous development

The looking-time and habituation paradigms are important because they have been used extensively to challenge one of the fundamental tenets of Piaget's influential theory of child development, and their results have been instrumental in changing dominant ideas about the nature of development. In Chapter 1, I discussed how the motivation to make these challenges has acted to maintain the focus of developmental researchers on the use of experimental methods and characterization of development as following relatively uniform, normative processes. Now, however, I resume the topic in order to discuss the tension in understanding development between qualitative and quantitative change over time. Piaget's theories, which dominated developmental psychology during the mid-20th century and still exert considerable influence today, posited that development consists of universally experienced periodic structural reorganizations that cause qualitative changes in functional capacity that transcend major functional domains. Piaget called the timespans between these periodic reorganizations 'stages'. For Piaget and other stage theorists, stages can be thought of as landing platforms in the process of moving from immature to species-typical adult form. According to stage theories, the developmental process follows a single preordained sequence of these stages or organizational structures, and the final mature organizational structure has a clearly defined uniform endpoint. Each stage, in turn, must be a structural whole, applicable to the whole person, while it persists, and all later stages must incorporate the characteristics of preceding stages. Transition from one stage to the next involves a qualitative change in competencies or general cast of mind or level of understanding that applies to all domains of function. The idea is a conceptual analogue of the transition undergone by the caterpillar as it develops into a butterfly; the entire structural morphology is replaced in a way that impacts all aspects of function and applies in the same way to all members of the species. Thus, for example, the 4-year-old has trouble grasping that the same volume of water will have very different heights in jugs of different widths, and also that rows of beads can have different lengths but the same numbers of beads if the beads are simply spaced differently within their rows. The 8-year-old, however, having passed through one conceptual stage and into the next, finds both of these obvious.

Taken to their extreme, stage theories draw a sharp distinction between learning and development. Learning may take place in any area and at any stage of development, but skills in any area attained before the appropriate development has occurred (the necessary stage has been reached) will resemble circus tricks: actions carried out by rote for immediate reward, without true understanding. Within this extreme theoretical framework, individual differences in skills and thus performance can exist across domains, but they can reflect only differences in experiences or contexts, not differences in structure, which applies uniformly to all. In sharp contrast, other theorists have conceived of development as a multifaceted continuous process that is caused by experiences, takes place through learning, and is shaped uniquely in each domain by the learning experiences specifically relevant to it. From this perspective, again taken to extreme, development is as regular and normalized as it is because specific independent variables have regular and lawful effects on dependent variables, and many of the experiences involved in these independent variables are extremely common, at least within cultural groups. That is, there is no structural endpoint towards which development strains, and thus no intrinsic way to characterize any particular level of performance as more mature than another. Individual differences are of primary importance because they are the direct consequences of differences in experience, and there are no inherent organismic structural constraints. In their extreme forms, theorists such as Chomsky (1965) and Gelman (1978) have suggested that newborns have all the logical structures in place necessary to be competent in all areas of human cognition; that is, they posit that newborns possess intrinsic understandings of the grammatical structures of all human languages, properties of number and objects, laws of physics, aesthetic preferences, sequences of events, species differences, etc. To them, development is thus no more than the actualization of these capacities in the context of environment.

As is usually the case with diametrically opposed scientific ideas, there is important but incomplete evidence for each theoretical perspective. Empirical evidence for stages includes evidence of clear sequences of development, consistency in developmental steps across different domains of function, and restriction of sequences and consistencies in developmental steps to those dictated by the characteristics of the developmental stage. One way that evidence of clear sequences of development has commonly been produced is through observations of relations between performance on tasks intended to distinguish theoretically meaningful levels of perception or understanding and age. This might be considered a necessary condition for the existence of stages, but it is hardly a sufficient one. A primary reason for this is that environmental exposure may typically be correlated with age. That is, newborns are not usually given exposure to situations in which, for example, they are asked to compare different quantities of objects directly. Moreover, as it has most commonly been applied, this method of associating age with performance tends to produce quite strong evidence for stages in infancy, but not for later-life stages, including childhood. There, differences in average age of attainment of skill, testing conditions, and individual child responses tend to predominate. This may be because most of the tasks traditionally used to measure the characteristic behaviours and skills associated with stages were originally devised for western European infants and children, but then later applied to children from other cultures as well. When studies of children from non-western cultures have used tasks adapted to the local cultures, evidence for stages has been much stronger (Fischer & Silvern, 1985). This suggests that there are inherent structural constraints on development, but that their specific manifestations are highly dependent on environmental circumstances. It also suggests that dependency on environmental circumstances increases with age, consistent with increasing abilities of infants and children to manipulate and interact with their environments.

If there are stages, what changes from one to the next?

Though evidence of associations between age and emergence of performance competencies may be necessary for establishing the existence of stages,
it provides no means of specifying what newly emerged cognitive quality the
skill taps, nor when the transition between stages takes place or what marks
its passage. Several theories outlining possible processes have been articulated,
but translating these to measurable phenomena has not proved tractable.
Observations of discontinuities in rates of change would provide evidence for
stages as well, as transitions between stages should be characterized by large
and rapid changes in behaviour across many domains of function. This has,
however, rarely been explored. Similarly, the existence of stages implies upper
limits on what can be learned during particular interim stages of development.
Several studies have demonstrated learning capacities specific to stages as
well as failures to learn within stages, though this topic and in particular the
boundaries surrounding the specificity of learning capacity have not been well
explored, especially in infancy. As an example of the kind of study that has
been carried out, O'Brien and Overton (1982) built on the observation that
both children and adults struggle with tasks that require deductive reasoning,
but that performance on such tasks improves in young adults exposed to
information contradicting specific prior faulty inferences, and the improvement generalizes to other reasoning situations. This was not the case with
younger children, whose performance did not improve with similar training.
O'Brien and Overton even suggested that the successful generalization to other
reasoning situations indicated that the information exposure served merely to
remind the younger adults of reasoning capacities they already possessed, and
that the few younger children who managed to arrive at correct inferences did
so effectively by chance rather than true expression of reasoning capacity. This
is a long way from the kinds of tasks and skills on which infants are assessed,
but it demonstrates the way testing the concept has been approached and the
nature of the inferences that have been drawn.

In the end, the strongest evidence for developmental stages may be the existence of 'regressive functions' (Campos, Witherington, Anderson, Frankel,
Uchiyama, & Barbu-Roth, 2008). Regressive functions are behaviours present
at one age that disappear, only to reappear at a later age and at a higher
level of function. The most familiar examples of such regressive functions are
the neonatal reflexes discussed above, but there are a number of others that
cannot be classified as reflexes, including neonatal imitation, reaching and
grasping, localization of sound, and adjustment of posture to enable visual
flow. The fact that these behaviours regress, or disappear, but then later reappear suggests that their morphological similarity is superficial, and that they
may be controlled by different neurophysiological processes at earlier and
later ages. The purposes served by the behaviours at earlier and later ages may
differ as well.

Box 6.1   Reaching and grasping: an example of regression and reappearance of behaviour

The specific behaviours and mechanisms involved in reaching and grasping are illustrative of the kind of developmental process involved in regression and reappearance (Campos, Witherington, Anderson, Frankel, Uchiyama, & Barbu-Roth, 2008). If the heads and trunks of neonates are sufficiently well supported, they will spontaneously extend their arms forward towards objects that catch their eyes. The phrase 'catch their eyes' is relevant here: the arm extension is a rather inflexible reaction to the visual stimulus, and the neonate lacks the capacity to guide the arm visually towards the object. The arm extension usually involves opening of the hand and extension of the fingers, but the reach is not at all reliable in encountering the object, and there is no attempt actually to grasp it; the muscular action involved in opening the hand and extending the fingers is linked to that involved in the arm extension. This is evidenced because the hand opens during forward extension of the arm when the infant extends its arm forward even when not visually fixated on an object (von Hofsten, 1984). These spontaneous neonatal reaches with the open hand and extended fingers become less frequent over the first seven weeks or so after birth, but, beginning in the third month after birth, the hand is increasingly fisted during forward extensions of the arm, and makes what might be called a 'swiping' motion at the object. By 4-5 months of age, however, infants again begin to open their hands when extending their arms forward, but by this time they appear to do so in attempt to grab the object and their arm and hand motions are guided by directed visual gaze rather than gaze that has been captured by the object. One explanation for this shift may be that the neonate's reaching behaviour may help it fix its visual attention on the object that has caught its eye (von Hofsten, 1984). If this is correct, as voluntary control of visual attention is mastered, the need for this primitive neonatal reach falls away, making room for later development of visually guided reaching directed towards a manipulatory goal.

   Early infant reaching provides an example of what might be considered a rather small qualitative difference in the functional purposes of similar behaviours at different 'stages' of development: the purpose of the more primitive infant reach is to assist the needed next step in the development of goal-directed reaching and grabbing, which is fixing visual attention on what is to be grabbed, as this must precede any successful grab. More generally, many early infant semi-reflexive abilities may exist to support and provide the behavioural platforms across which the experiences of the appropriate environmental stimuli can take place to foster the development of more complex abilities. But the functional purposes involved in regressive behaviours could also actually be so different as to be contradictory. For example, neonates will cry at the sound of another neonate's cry, but not to the cry of an older child, a white noise, or the cry of a chimpanzee (Campos et al., 2008). This has been termed 'empathic crying' and no longer occurs by about 5 months of age. Other, more complex, empathic behaviours emerge beginning around 14 months of age, when infants attempt to comfort adults crying. It is possible, however, that the neonate's cry is competitive rather than empathic, linked to the fact that any infant's cry, not just her own, elicits the mother's 'let down' reflex that enables nursing. If so, the neonate's cry may be a reflexive attempt by the infant to ensure that it, rather than some other, receives the now-available milk.

Brain development in infancy supporting the existence of stages

The brain undergoes substantial changes in structure, physiology, and chemistry during the first year after birth. For example, beginning around 6 months of age and continuing for about 6 more months, the neurons of the prefrontal cortex and hippocampus differentiate widely, and undergo considerable myelination. Connections between the amygdale in the temporal lobes and the prefrontal cortex are strengthened, largely through myelinization, and there is increased uptake of glucose (which reflects brain activity) throughout the prefrontal cortex. There are also changes in electroencephalogram and event-related potential activation patterns during task performance. In general, younger infants tend to show activations across the entire cortex while performing many different tasks, while older infants and young children show much more localized patterns of activity that tend to be limited to medial frontal areas and to involve improved coherence of connections between frontal and temporal-occipital areas. The waveforms of the event-related potentials also undergo substantial change. These changes are coincident with infant changes in cognitive capacity, in the form of increases in working memory that make it possible for one-year-olds to hold mental representations of experiences or perceptions in mind for longer periods of time, and to begin to be able to retrieve representations of events that occurred over periods of up to 30 seconds earlier (Kagan, 2008). This may not seem like much, especially since much younger infants show evidence of recognition memory over longer periods, but it reflects substantial improvement in capacity to retrieve memory images directly. These would all be the kinds of structural and functional changes that would support the reorganizations of cognitive schema posited by stage theories.

Imitation and mimicry

Imitation is considered formally to be a complex behaviour in which an individual is consciously aware of observing the behaviour of another and attempting to duplicate it, with intent to reproduce not only the behaviour but its outcome. Imitation can be contrasted with *mimicry*, in which an individual duplicates the behaviour of another without necessarily being aware of the duplication or intending it, either with respect to the behaviour itself, or its outcome. Imitation can also be contrasted with *emulation*, in which an individual behaves in ways consciously intended to bring about the same outcome as another, without duplicating the other's specific behaviours. The distinctions among these three forms of replicating behaviour have been important in conceiving of ways of understanding the cognitive capacities and schema of infants, and those of nonhuman animals as well.

Following the formal definition of imitation, Piaget (1936/1954) theorized that neonates could not imitate because they lacked the requisite concepts of self, other, and goal direction, which he believed emerged only late in infancy. There has been little challenge to the basic observation that the formal concept of the self does not emerge until about this time. Neonates are, however, capable of mimicry, and execute it with some regularity. It is somewhat tricky to demonstrate this because of the limitations in the behaviours that neonates can exhibit, and their tendency to produce these behaviours spontaneously with some frequency. Meltzoff and Moore (1977) carried out the first experimental demonstration of infant mimicry of facial expressions that has come to be considered real evidence for the phenomenon, though it is often termed 'imitation' in the field. To surmount the problem of spontaneous production of the expressions by the infants, they had raters, who had not seen the expressions produced by the adults, match photos of the infant expressions to photos of the adult expressions. This does not, of course, completely surmount this problem, and their paper has received considerable criticism over time. The result, however, has been replicated by many different labs using various approaches to surmounting spontaneous production problem, and the presence of infant mimicry capability is now reasonably consistently considered established. This is important not only because it indicates that neonates have social awareness, but also because it indicates that neonates are able both to perceive facial expressions in others with some clarity and to translate those perceptions into the bodily actions required to produce some semblance of the same expressions on their own faces. This is especially important as infants cannot generally see their own faces.

This could indicate that the neonatal premotor cortex has a high level of function, but as this area of the brain in general is rather poorly developed at birth, it is much more likely that better-developed subcortical areas are involved in the production of mimicked responses. It also suggests that mimicry is actually qualitatively different from imitation. The ability to mimic may subserve the ability to imitate in some way that regresses in importance during development, while supporting the emerging more complex ability to imitate. The sophistication of infant displays of mimicry develops rapidly: by about 6 weeks of age, infants can reproduce the facial expression they saw someone produce 24 hours previously when they are presented with the same person with a passive facial expression Meltzoff and Moore (1994). Infants also consistently respond negatively when presented with still, passive faces when they expected those faces to carry expressions, which corroborates the inference that they are socially aware of others around them.

Mechanisms of imitation and mimicry: mirror neurons?

All of this could take place in the brain through the recently discovered *mirror neuron* system (Iocoboni, 2005). Mirror neurons are neurons that fire both when an individual acts and when the individual watches the same action produced by someone else. They were first documented in a laboratory at the University of Parma, Italy in macaques. Neurophysiologists had placed electrodes in the monkeys' ventral premotor cortices to study how neurons are specialized for hand and mouth activities such as taking hold of and manipulating objects and placing bits of food in their mouths. The researchers were specifically interested in the neuronal activity when a monkey carried out these actions, but they coincidentally observed that the same neurons fired in the same ways when the monkeys observed the humans carrying out the same actions. Since then, mirror neurons have been observed in some birds as well. They are located not only in the premotor cortex, but also in somatosensory cortex and inferior frontal and parietal regions of the brain. Indirect evidence for their existence in humans has also been provided, though brain-imaging resolution has not been sufficiently specific to observe single neurons directly. Thus, evidence of mirror neurons in humans is based on the observation that the same brain regions are active both when humans carry out motor actions and when they see others carrying out the same action. Based on this kind of evidence, human mirror neurons respond to facial gestures and to sounds as well as to hand and mouth actions, a broader range of displays of mirror neuron involvement than is observed in macaques.

The specific function of mirror neurons is not understood, but speculation surrounds their involvement in the coupling of perception and action, mimicry and imitation, ability to simulate observed actions and take the perspective of another, and even language ability. Importantly, however, macaques and other primates appear to learn from others primarily through emulation rather than imitation. Neonatal macaques apparently can mimic human facial movements, but this ability seems to disappear shortly after birth (Ferrari, Visalberghi, Paukner, Fogassi, Ruggiero, & Suomi, 2006). This would be consistent with the idea that early mimicry in humans is qualitatively similar to that in macaques but different from later human imitation, but serves, again in humans, to generate behaviours that foster the acquisition of experiences that support the further development of the emotional and cognitive abilities involved in actual imitation. Presumably, macaque cognitive development proceeds along different lines.

Heyes (2001; 2010) has articulated this idea more thoroughly. Resisting the idea that mirror neurons are evolved adaptations for understanding actions, she proposed that mirror neurons are formed through *associative learning*. Associative learning takes place when two events are repeatedly associated with each other, so that the occurrence of one event reliably predicts the later occurrence of the other. It is an evolutionarily old learning process that can be routinely observed in many different kinds of tasks across both vertebrate and invertebrate species, from humans to sea slugs. In general, it has been demonstrated through changes with learning in the behaviour of the entire organism, but Heyes applied the idea to the formation of the mirror neurons themselves. According to Heyes' hypothesis, neurons develop mirror capacities through the correlated experience of observing and performing the same action. This hypothesis can be used to explain the earlier described developmental pattern of reaching and grasping in infants as follows. Neonates do not have mirror neurons, but they do have a reflexive outreach response to anything that captures their visual attention. This reflexive outreach response to visual stimulation sets the infant up to experience correlation of motor neuron with visual neuron response, and the links between the two responses become tighter with repeated exposure to this experience, until some of the neurons involved fire not only when reaching and grasping are executed, but also when they are observed in another. Because human infants receive much more correlated experience of observing and executing similar actions, human infants develop more extensive mirror neuron systems than do macaque infants. The broader display of mirror neuron involvement in humans could thus be attributed to their human enculturation. This is consistent with evidence of tool-using mirror neurons in monkeys who had received many opportunities to observe humans using these tools (Ferrari, Rozzi, & Fogassi, 2005), and greater mirror activation in pianists than in non-pianists when observing hands engaged in piano playing (Haslinger, 2005).

Additional evidence for the roles of learning and flexibility in apparent mirror function comes from differential mirror responses to different forms of motor training. For example, Catmur, et al. (Catmur, Gillmeister, Bird, Liepelt, Brass, Heyes, 2008) trained one group of participants to respond to images of raised feet or hands by raising their own corresponding feet or hands in similar positions, and another to raise their hands in imitation of images of a raised foot and their feet in imitation of images of raised hands. The images observed were the same in the groups. Brain areas showing evidence of mirror neuron function were identified by comparison of blood oxygen level response to a version of the task in which participants carried it out using written instructions with a version in which participants merely observed the images to which they had been trained to respond, without making any response. The mirror responses of the two groups were reversed: for example, the areas that showed evidence of mirror response to hand images in the group that had been trained to respond to these images with their hands showed evidence of mirror response to foot images in the other group, suggesting that the neurons had no specific intrinsic function but instead responded according to experience. There is clearly much to be learned about mirror neurons, including verification of their actual existence in humans through direct observation. If Heyes' associative learning hypothesis is correct, however, it has far-reaching consequences for understanding developmental processes more generally because it suggests that individual neurons are very flexible in both function and ability to form and maintain synaptic connections with other neurons. It also suggests that this flexibility is distributed widely throughout the human brain, specifically implying that sensorimotor experience and ability to think abstractly are tightly intertwined, and, in humans at least, sociality both supports and is supported by this link.

Box 6.2   Do neurons have specific functions?

Other evidence for the kind of neuronal flexibility in function exhibited by mirror neurons exists, and its recent discovery has unravelled a central premise of neurophysiology that had dominated discussion and experimental design since the nineteenth century, when (Muller, 1826) termed it the law of specific nerve energies. This is the idea that the firing of each neuronal cell has one specific function, and it is the neurophysiologist's job to uncover this function. Ability to record single neuron activity in the prefrontal cortex was not developed until the 1970s. In the initial experiments in this area, Fuster and Alexander (1971) had monkey subjects mounted with microelectrodes in their prefrontal cortices watch as food was hidden in one of two containers. After a delay, the monkeys were allowed to reach into the containers, and, naturally, reached into the one in which the food had been hidden. As Fuster and Alexander had expected, no matter how they varied this basic experiment, they observed neurons that began to fire when the food was hidden, sustained firing during the delay, and then stopped firing when the monkeys were allowed to reach for the food. Moreover, the rates of firing varied with location of the container in which the food was placed, indicating that firing contained information about not just presence but also location of the food. Subsequent experiments became more complex, presenting monkeys with a much bigger array of possible reward locations. This made it possible to observe that the firing of specific neurons corresponded to specific locations, and that there was usually both primary neuronal activity corresponding to the precise location, and some secondary or weaker activity in the neurons corresponding to the immediately surrounding locations. This strongly indicated the presence of a neural short-term memory code that defined a clear mental map of the relative positions of the objects in the task, thus solidifying the idea of a one-to-one mapping between neurons and function.

Subsequent similar work further reinforced this idea, suggesting that, in the occipital and parietal lobes at least, neurons located in the ventral (or bottom) areas are dedicated primarily to recognizing what objects are within vision, while neurons located in the dorsal (or top) areas are primarily dedicated to recognition of where objects are located, and to linking with the motor control necessary for reaching and grasping those objects. This dorsal–ventral allocation of function appeared to extend to short-term memory in the prefrontal cortex (Duncan, 2010), at least until a critical experiment (Rao, Rainer, & Miller, 1997). The experiment was designed so that the activity of individual neurons could be recorded when both recognition memory and location memory were required. In each trial, a monkey was presented first with single pictures on a screen, and then, after a short delay, with two pictures in particular locations on the screen, one of which was the original picture. After another delay, the monkey was cued to respond to the next presentation, which consisted of four dots, two of which were in the locations of the previously displayed two pictures. The monkey was rewarded if he moved his eyes to the location of the dot in which he had seen the originally presented picture when it was paired with the other. From original presentation to response, therefore, the monkey had to remember, first, the identity of the first picture and then, second, its location the second time it was presented. During the first delays, various neurons were activated, coding the identities of the first pictures. As had been the case in prior experiments, these neurons were located in the ventral prefrontal cortex, and the specific neurons that were activated differed according to the different pictures displayed. But, unlike in prior experiments, these same neurons were activated for location during the second delay. There did not appear to be two separate sets of neurons for recording object identity and location at all. Instead, it appeared that, whether located in the ventral or dorsal prefrontal regions, neurons were activated to meet task demands in general, not merely to meet specific task demands.

This strongly indicated that there was no 'specific nerve energy' for prefrontal neurons and that neuronal firing has no specific meaning, but only meaning in the context of the task at hand. If the context changes, so too does the neuron's firing pattern. Many subsequent increasingly diverse and complex experiments confirmed this observation throughout a large region of the prefrontal cortex, involving many different kinds of task performance. In many ways other than just mirror capacity therefore, individual neurons appear to have the flexibility to carry out many different aspects of the same task as well as the flexibility to carry out many different tasks. This makes mirror neurons looks far less 'special' in their capacities, but the particularly social way in which their very ordinary (for neurons) level of flexible capacity is manifested reinforces the importance of social interaction to human cognitive development and function.

Object permanence and the 'A-not-B error'

Recent work involving infant understanding of object permanence and performance on a simple reaching task also highlights the strong links between physical and mental modalities of behaviour that are often considered separate. This is not completely new, as Piaget's (1936/1954) conception also stressed the linkages between them. He theorized that neonates had no actual knowledge of the world, but gradually constructed an understanding of it through perception and experience, with the ability to retain or create mental representations of that understanding following. One aspect of the world on which he focused was infant understanding of the existence of objects as distinct from its own body. He believed that, because understanding has to emerge through perception, neonates could have no inherent understanding that objects that are not within their fields of perception, which essentially means vision for objects not touching or parts of their bodies, nevertheless continue to exist, and that this understanding is not typically firmly in place until about two years of age. He developed this belief through observation of his own children: prior to 9 months of age, they made no response when even objects in which they had expressed great interest were hidden. Even if they had been actively trying to obtain the object, they ceased when it was removed from their view. Though the observation was developed based on Piaget's own children, it has been replicated by many others in many different samples. From this, Piaget inferred that infants have no way to represent an object in their minds when it is out of sight.

Beginning around the age of 9 months, however, Piaget observed that infants would manually search for and locate a desired object when it disappeared from view. To Piaget, this meant that infants were beginning to be able to represent objects mentally even when they were not in view. One of the hallmarks of Piaget's research that has made his work so enduring was that, with each observation that a concept that he believed to be important appeared to have been mastered, he made the task more complicated in a way that would provide evidence of infant understanding of a more difficult concept. With respect to mental representation of objects, the way that Piaget made the object hide-and-seek task more difficult was first to hide the object in one location and let the infant manually seek for and find it, repeating this several times, and then to let the infant watch him hide it in a second, different, location. What he repeatedly observed was that the infant did manually seek again for the object, but in the original location in which it had been hidden several times before, not the new location in which the infant had subsequently watched it being hidden. This observation too has been replicated many times in many variations, and infant persistence in searching in the original location has come to be known as the *A-not-B reaching error*. Infants do not search accurately in the new location until the age of about 12 months. From this and analogous, still more complex observations, Piaget inferred that infant ability to represent objects mentally as they actually exist does not fully mature until about age two.

For many years even psychologists who questioned Piaget's inference about infant understanding of object focused on cognitive explanations such as limited memory capacity or inability to coordinate information about time and space. Hints that this is too simple, that the problem is more than just cognitive, came later from experiments in which the object was placed in the second location but not hidden and thus left within the infant's view (Butterworth, 1977), and when the object was never hidden at all but simply placed several times in one location in plain view and then placed in plain view in the second location (e.g., Munakata, 1997). Infants *still* manually searched in the first rather than the second location. This suggested that the error involved failure of motor coordination in reaching in addition to or rather than failure of mental representation. Eight- to 10-month-old infants are also less likely to make the error when there are fewer A trials before the crucial B trial (Smith, Thelen, Titzer, & McLin, 1999), but 5-month-old infants tend to reach correctly (Clearfield, Diedrich, Smith, & Thelen, 2006)! This makes the A-not-B error another example of regression, and suggests that the error should be generally understood as a stage involving lack of sufficient behavioural flexibility in the process of developing the ability to select appropriately between stable and flexible reaching behaviour.

Dynamic systems theory, as discussed in Chapter 5, has offered an important contribution to this understanding (Smith, 2009). This account begins with analysis of the tasks the infant must carry out to make, or not make, the A-not-B error. First, the infant must focus visually on the object as it is placed in a location and covered with a hiding cloth. Then the infant must formulate a motor plan to reach for the object and maintain the plan over the delay until reaching is allowed. The motor plan is abstract; it does not articulate the specific muscle movements that must be carried out; rather it specifies the relations among the location of the overall body (perhaps the brain that experiences the awareness of wanting the object), the limbs (arms) that can effect attainment of the object, and the object's location. Within this motor plan, the dynamic systems model posits three dimensions: the spatial direction of the reach, its activation strength, and time. A reach is posited not to take place unless the activation strength exceeds some threshold, and three sources of input regulate this strength. The first, which is usually not strong enough on its own to reach the activation threshold, is the sensory presence of the two possible reaching locations (A and B) in vision. The second is the experience of watching the object being hidden in location B. This is the activation that both must be strong enough to push total activation over the threshold and must be maintained over the delay. The third source competes with the second in B trials: it is the relatively long-term motor memory of all the previous reaches to location A. At any infant age, the actual execution of this dynamic motor plan to reach to the location in which the toy is hidden is a function of the relative strengths of these three sources of activation.

For example, correct reaching at 5 months of age can be understood as lack of ability to retain the prior actions in relatively long-term memory about prior reaches, and thus, potentially, a lack of ability to benefit from motor practice. Within this perspective, this longer-term memory and an associated ability to benefit from motor practice has developed by the age of 8 months, but the activation caused by the new experience of watching the object hidden in location B is not yet strong enough to counteract this 'practised' activation pattern towards location A. By the age of 12 months, however, this latter activation has increased in strength, and correct reaching to location B is again observed. According to this model, the processes that take the infant's hand from its first position to one of the two possible object locations are motor plans, but, consistent with the associative learning conceptualization of mirror neurons, so are the memories for previous reaches that create the perseverative error of reaching to the prior rather than the current location. What develops is a series of sensorimotor representations, first the ability to link hand action with gaze direction on a 'one-off' basis, then an ability to use prior experience and the memory of it to make motor actions more automatic (and presumably more efficient somehow, freeing mental and physical resources for other tasks), and finally (at least with respect to the A-not-B reaching task) the ability to evaluate new perceptual data to overrule pre-existing very similar motor plans and create new ones. To the extent the model is correct, it indicates very strong links between motor and abstract conceptions, consistent with the observation of neurons that have mirror properties.

This model of the reaching task as a motor plan receives empirical support in experiments. If this is the correct conceptualization, the motor plan should reflect the hand's position at the inception of the reaching action, not alone, but in relation to the rest of the infant's body as well as in relation to the object to be grasped. Thus shifting the body's posture should act to dislodge the motor plan to reach to the first location, freeing the infant to reach to the second, correct, location. This is in fact what happens: for example, when infants were seated for the A reaches, but lifted to a standing position for B trials, even those in the age range most likely in the usual situation to make the A-not-B error were able to reach correctly (Lew, Hopkins, Owen, & Green, 2007).

Generalizing the guided reaching model to abilities considered cognitive

This model of visually guided reaching has been extended to suggest a way of understanding how older infants, in the last half of the second year, learn words for objects in the usual environment in which names and their referents are paired within streams of events containing potentially many such pairings, often with no reason to focus attention on any particular pairings and with variable time lengths between reoccurrences of specific pairings. This has been accomplished through a series of experiments developed by Baldwin (1993). In the most basic version of these experiments, the child is seated at a table facing the experimenter. The experimenter presents the child with an unnamed object, angling the presentation to one side. Then the experimenter presents the child with another unnamed object, angling the presentation to the other side, and repeating both actions. Next, out of sight of the child, the experimenter places each object into a container, and the two containers side-by-side on the table in front of the child. Finally, the experimenter looks into one container and says 'I see a *modi* (or some other nonsense word) in here.' After a delay, the experimenter retrieves the objects from their containers and asks the child which is a modi. For the child, the object and name were never directly paired, yet most children of this age will identify the object that had been presented on the same side of the table as the container into which the experimenter looked as the modi.

Correct performance on this task bears some conceptual resemblance to the A-not-B *error* in the reaching task, particularly when considered within the context of the motor plan explanation for the error. In the reaching task, if the motor plan explanation is correct, the infant makes the error because the motor memory of the link to one location is stronger than the impetus for formation of a new motor plan created by observation of placement of the object in the new location. Development of some kind of ability to assess the appropriate weight to give new perception relative to motor habit in generating new action is important, but the error could not take place without prior development of the ability to hold in memory some representation of the placement of the object and to coordinate the original motor plan that guides the correct reaches to the first location. Development of this memory ability is thus also important, perhaps even more so. Smith (2009) has suggested that the same kind of memory binding of content of observation with the motor action of looking in a particular direction is involved in linking the strange word to the strange object in Baldwin's (1993) task, thus making emergence of this ability of critical importance for language development. Several recent experiments have supported this conception. For example, when children were presented with the two objects twice each, once angling to each side of the table, they later identified one of the two objects as 'modi' randomly. To the extent that this accounting is correct, it suggests that direction of attention is effectively equivalent to development of a motor plan, thus tightly linking abstract thought with action, again consistent with the observation of motor neurons.

Emotional expression and the emergence of attachment

Neonates produce a range of facial expressions that adults reliably distinguish as indications of distress, pleasure, and interest. Beyond this basic level of detail, however, reliability of classification is much lower, despite the fact that the range of neonatal facial expressions is much wider than three. This suggests, for example, that adults have great difficulty distinguishing an infant's facial expression of pain from one of anger. This could be because infants do not express their emotions consistently through their faces, but it also could be that they do not experience much in the way of emotional subtlety, being limited mostly to positive, negative, and interest emotional experiences at this age. As discussed above, the facial smile expression is present from birth and can even be observed prenatally, but the intentional socially oriented smile does not generally emerge until about two months after birth, suggesting that neonates do not use facial expression consistently to express their emotions, whatever they may be experiencing. It is possible that the emotionally empty early smile is basically reflexive. This would be consistent with several examples I have described of neonatal reflexive or almost-reflexive behaviours that increase the likelihood that the neonate will be exposed to environmental experiences that will stimulate the development of skills that will, in turn, enable the development of abilities to act upon the environment.

Box 6.3   Why do some babies have colic?

From the perspective of reflexes as instinctive means to produce behaviours that spur development of adaptive volition, infantile *colic* may present a paradox. This is a condition in which a healthy infant often displays symptoms of acute distress, usually intense crying well beyond that usually manifested at this age, for extended periods of time, though sometimes also moaning and belching. The condition usually emerges shortly after birth, generally peaks around 6 weeks of age, and generally disappears by 3–4 months of age, sometimes quite suddenly. The crying often begins in the evening, and can last well into the night. Traditionally, colic has been attributed to gastrointestinal distress of some kind, but there is substantial evidence questioning this as at least the sole explanation. For example, premature infants with immature gastrointestinal tracts appear to have no greater incidence of colic than full-term infants, and when they do display it, it begins not when they are born but around their original due dates (Barr, Chen, Hopkins, & Westra, 1996), and remedies such as car rides and vacuum cleaner noises often reduce colic-related crying but would not affect gastrointestinal distress. One possibility is that colic is a reflexive reaction to overstimulation or exhaustion, which has the purpose of eliciting greater parental care because it mimics the expression of distress but is actually as emotionally empty as the early smile. Consistent with this, early colic appears to show little association with later-life temperament, whether in later infancy or childhood and adulthood. If colic is such a reflexive reaction, however, it often appears to back-fire, as colicky infants experience higher rates of abuse, including shaken baby syndrome (Barr, Trent, & Cross, 2006), and it is easy to understand how that might come about, as I can testify from experience.

As noted, by the end of the second month after birth, the infant has typically developed abilities to smile socially, follow and share the direction of gaze of another, and recognize previously observed positive and negative social stimuli as such. Though clearly oriented towards other people in a social way, these abilities are at first undiscriminating; the infant will make use of them with anyone. Beginning around 5 months of age, however, this changes, and most infants begin to express distress at being separated from parents and other familiar caregivers. A little later they also begin to express distress at confrontation with strangers. Intensity of distress expression at separation typically rises over the next several months, peaking at 8-9 months of age and often again at around 12 months before gradually subsiding thereafter (e.g., Tennes & Lampl, 1964). In slight contrast, expression of distress at the appearance of strangers appears to peak once, sometime after 12 months of age. The growing ability of the infant to form emotional attachment, as discussed in Chapter 4, is clearly one explanation for this behaviour, but there is evidence for explanations involving the integration of memory, concept formation, and coordination of motor plans as well. McCall, Eichom, and Hogarty (1977) have suggested that the earlier attachment-related expressions of distress to separation from the parent may occur because at 57 months of age, the infant's memory capacity is becoming sufficiently developed to form the concept that the parent continues to exist when not present, but the infant has no ability to form any kind of motor action plan for either how to prevent the departure or how to act while the separation lasts. Distress at the appearance of a stranger takes place, they suggest, a little bit later because it is dependent on the slightly later conceptual development that action of some sort on the part of the infant may be necessary when a new person appears in the environment, but again, the infant has no ability to form a responsive motor plan for this generally less frequent and more complex occurrence. In other words, both expressions of distress take place because the infant does not know how to integrate motor action with the demands of perception and memory. Thus the crying that parents and caregivers tend to characterize as distress may be more of a reflexive reaction, in this case to uncertainty, than an actual expression of distress.

Emerging theories of emotional development in infants

Characterization of infant emotional experience as relatively lacking in distinctiveness currently enjoys some consensus. If accurate, distinctions among emotions must develop over time, and has meant some re-thinking for traditional theories of emotion that posited the existence of specific innate emotion programmes that presumably have specific locations in the brain and some clear basis in physiology (Ekman, 1972; Izard, 1971) and that presumably organize and motivate actions and organism–environment transactions (Barrett & Campos, 1987). Newer theorists have taken a broader perspective in two ways. First, they have seen emotions as experienced and developing within the context of other aspects of psychological development. Thus, for example, cognitive theories of emotion (e.g., Lazarus, 1991) propose that the neonate is basically capable only of reflexive responses, and that what we know as emotions can only emerge with experiences that foster the development of the ability to make cognitive appraisals of both the surrounding environment and internal physiological responses. Social theorists (e.g., Rogoff, 1990; Vygotsky, 1978) take a similar perspective, but focus on the role of social experiences in developing the necessary appraisals. Though both cognitive and social theories of emotional development recognize the importance of culture in the development of emotion, culture is especially relevant to social theories. The integration of emotion with some aspect of conscious experience, whether termed cognitive or social, and physical status of some kind is consistent with the evidence described above that links cognitive and motor development through progress from reflexive response to conscious directed action.

The second way in which newer theorists of emotion have taken a broader perspective is by incorporating the ideas of dynamic systems theory. Consistent with Heyes' (2001; 2010) ideas about mirror neurons and neural function during cognitive tasks as described above, according to these theories, the brain does not have particular regions innately dedicated to the experience of particular emotions. Instead, the patterns of neural action involved in emotional experience develop through self-organizing processes that emerge with experience. That is, the specific organizational framework of the brain is not specified in advance, but takes a particular shape over time and experience, and would have taken a different shape with different experiences. The manner in which these theories propose that this takes place can be seen by analogy with physical movement, such as walking over uneven terrain, for which a detailed model of the processes involved has been worked out (Thelen, 1985). This walking model was designed to address the question of how the brain can regulate the myriad possible muscle movements to respond to the specific conditions of the physical environment in order to tailor behaviour precisely to those conditions, and to surmount the problems encountered in trying to develop models that relied on coordination by some kind of central control source. This was necessary because any known ways of conceptualizing the central control source became overburdened when presented with any realistic model of the muscle movements possible. The practical reason for developing this model was for application to robot construction.

The solution was to group the possible individual muscle movements into larger groups that can function as ensembles, or motor structures that can coordinate operations. Under the model, the individual muscle movements are thus not directly controlled, but limited in activity because each muscle is linked to the others in its group. The particular linkages arise over time in response to the functional demands placed on the system over time by experience. At the same time, activation of one muscle within a group by any source can bring along with it activation of the other muscles in the group. The result is that the action of the motor system is self-organized, with control over the whole muscular system distributed between both higher- (or central) and lower-level activation sources. In some, more complex, versions of the model, there may not even be a central control source (Camras & Witherington, 2005). With this model, it became possible to explain behaviours that had been difficult to accommodate in previous theories, such as intra-individual variations in behaviour. This was accomplished by positing control mechanisms that might reach threshold for activation in some situations but not others.

Fogel, et al. (Fogel, Nwokah, Dedo, Messinger, Dickson, Matusov, et al., 1992) related this approach specifically to emotional development. They proposed that emotions are self-organized systems of a type analogous to the motor-movement model, that emotions themselves emerge within the context of sequences of social interactions and cognitive appraisals of those interactions, and that, within infancy while emotional capacity, organization, and many cognitive-emotional linkages are developing, variation in intensity of arousal is important in priming the development of what we recognize later as relatively discrete emotional categories. From this perspective, the categories we recognize are arbitrary and driven by cultural practice rather than biologically innate; emotion itself is always present and continuous in content. What we think of as emotional transitions take place when a stable emotional pattern breaks down because of a change in the status of one of its critical components or the addition to the system of a new component. The basic ideas are that the emotional system, and by extension the cognitive, perceptual, motor plan, and social interaction systems, are wholes that cannot be reduced to their component parts, and that it is the relations among the parts rather than the parts themselves that create the features of the overall system as we observe it.

Operationalization for empirical test

These ideas sound plausible, and raise the prospect, in concept at least, of increased ability to understand developmental processes. They require, however, both specific operationalization and the development of data that can provide empirical tests of their accuracy. Thelen and Smith (1994) have proposed at least a start with operationalization. Their first step is identification of an observable variable that reflects the state of the system and serves as an indicator of the varying interrelationships among the groups of lower-order components. Such variables can exist at any level of analysis, from the firing of particular neurons to interactions between a parent and an infant, but their selection fixes the level at which the analysis will be focused. That is, if the selected variable is parent–infant interaction, the lower-level components in the system are very unlikely to reach all the way down to the level of the firing of particular neurons. The selected variables are posited to be capable of assuming a variety of different states, some of which emerge more reliably than others from the interactions of the components. Thus, the second step in operationalizing these ideas is identification of these 'attractor states,' and this is followed by observation of the ways in which the selected variable changes over time. Thus far, however, the applications have been very rudimentary, such as learning to reach and grab, compared with the developmental processes we really want to understand such as the individual differences in personality, intelligence, and interests, or the emergence of psychopathology. We have a long way to go.

Development of individual differences in infancy

Despite sharing obvious immaturity, individual differences in neonates are clear. These differences have their roots in genetic variation as well as differences in gestational characteristics and experiences. Immediately at birth, however, differences in the much wider post-gestational environment and the experiences it generates are layered on top of them, creating additional potential for greater individual differences. The effects of these environmental inputs take place within the constraints imposed by the biological, genetically driven processes that govern growth and development. In turn, however, environmental inputs affect the ways in which genes are expressed and thus the developmental processes themselves. Moreover, from birth, the individual neonate exerts some choice over what stimulation to receive. Despite the limitations I described earlier for habituation and/or looking times as indications of cognitive processes and/or understanding in neonates, these measures are some of the best for revealing these early individual choices. Assessing the effects of these choices on later development, however, is more difficult.

This is, in general, a rather underdeveloped area of research. One area of perennial interest that has made use of the looking-time and habituation measures to observe such choices in process is assessment of sex differences in interests and preferences. The point of discussing these studies is not so much to argue for inherent sex differences, as most of the findings from such studies are actually quite soft. That is, infants of both sexes show interest in all kinds of stimuli as referenced by looking times, and whatever sex differences in mean looking times emerge are generally small in relation to the individual differences within sex. Thus, though it is not usually the primary focus of the studies, these studies are important in demonstrating the presence of early individual differences in behaviour. For example, Connellan, Baron-Cohen, Wheelwright, Batki, and Ahluwalia (2000) presented male and female neonates less than 36 hours old with both a mechanical mobile and a person with hair tied back and a still, neutral facial expression. Neonates of both sexes looked at both stimuli of course, but the females looked longer on average at the face and the males looked longer on average at the mobile. This reflected choices on the parts of all the neonates, and, over time and with increased ability to use choice to interact with the environment, these choices can add up to create differences in cognitive, emotional, and physical experiences and abilities. As many parents have noted, sex-typed toy preferences appear quite early (e.g., Alexander, Wilcox, & Woods, 2009), and are often very persistent despite parental efforts to thwart them.

Two other studies in this area help to illustrate the indicated developmental process of building from passive observation to active environmental engagement. Nagy, Kompagne, Orvos, and Pal (2007) presented neonates 3-96 hours old with a model making specific pointing finger gestures. They noted differences between infant boys and girls in the extent to and manner in which the infants moved their own fingers, both in absolute terms and in relation to a period before presentation of the model. Their results were only marginally statistically significant (which means that variance within sex was nearly enough to drown out any signal from sex and so must have been substantial in its own right) and their sample was small, but they suggested that infant girls made more fine motor movements and movements more closely resembling those of the model than did infant boys. Regardless of whether this suggested sex difference is replicable, there was considerable variance in the extent of finger movement in the infants. It could of course have been completely random, but the data did suggest that some of it was responsive to the actions of the model. Even if it was not, however, the variation opened a window of social response that can affect development. That is, parents and other caregivers show variation in infant treatment, and some of this variation in treatment is directly in response to variation in infant behaviour. Most studies of sex-of-infant differences in caregiver treatment have not taken this into consideration, but those that have done so have generally found reductions or eliminations of the differences in caregiver treatment (e.g., Moss, 1967). Thus, even if it is totally random, individual differences in infant behaviour can contribute to the environments they experience, and thus directly to their developmental trajectories.

But clearly not all individual differences in infant behaviour are random, and non-randomly chosen behaviours may matter even more for developmental pathways. Sticking with the convenient example of sex differences, Benenson, Tennyson, and Wrangham (2011) presented 7-month-olds with a balloon hanging on a string and gave them the opportunity to play with it. They then showed the infants video clips of male and female models either gently cradling balloons or batting them in the air, and gave the infants another opportunity to play with the balloon. The male infants increased their own balloon-batting activities after seeing the video clips, but the females did not. The increases were correlated with the time the male infants spent looking at the male models who were batting, but not with the females who were batting. There were no correlations in the female infants. Thus, in these older infants who had greater motor as well as cognitive skills, individual differences in attention/interest were associated with individual differences in the behaviours they imitated, and thus in the motor experiences they acquired, at least in the boys. Analogous individual differences would likely, over time, be associated with the motor skills they developed. Similar processes are probably involved in the development of cognitive abilities and emotional responses.

Box 6.4   Non-random individual differences beyond genes and environment

Genetic differences in inherent interest and preference may and do contribute to these differences in behavioural decisions, but there is likely non-random developmental variation beyond both this and variation created by variation in environmental circumstances. Vogt, et al. (Vogt, Huber, Thiemann, van den Boogaart, Schmitz, & Schubart, 2008) demonstrated this clearly in clonal marbled crayfish. These crayfish reproduce asexually and are only female, so each clutch, which typically consists of 50-400 eggs, consists of genetically identical individuals, with the exception of genetic mutations. The crayfish were reared in environmental conditions carefully controlled to be identical, and individual differences were assessed only within clutches to minimize any effects of birth season and genetic mutation. The crayfish were fed plentifully, and it was possible to monitor stomach contents of each individual to confirm that all had fed adequately. After each feeding was completed, excess food was removed. Thus, survival stress was minimized. These crayfish go through five life stages, each of which involves several moultings, or shedding of one shell and growth of another. The first two post-birth stages are spent under the mother's abdomen, thus ensuring very consistent environmental conditions. Even after independent feeding begins in the third stage, typical juvenile behaviour is to remain very close to the mother, so environmental conditions are quite easy to control. The same pellet food can be used as the sole food source throughout the crayfish lifespan.

Vogt et al. (2008) observed considerable variation among the clutch-mates in growth, lifespan, colouration, morphological characteristics, *fluctuating asymmetry* (the extent of differences between bilateral body characteristics), reproductive rate, *global DNA methylation* (or differences in gene expression), and behaviour. For example, lifespans of those that died of natural causes ranged from 437-910 days, and there were considerable differences in reproductive success. At the age of 430 days, one female had completed three reproductive cycles and had 219 independently feeding offspring, while four of her siblings had completed two reproductive cycles, with totals of 66, 153, 73, and 92 independently feeding offspring, and another sibling had completed only one reproductive cycle, with 52 offspring. Mass differences between the smallest and largest members of a clutch varied by a factor of 20, and they entered their various life stages at different ages and showed different degrees of DNA methylation. Variations in behaviour, however, are most relevant here. The crayfish evidenced systematic differences in extent of locomotion as soon as they could move. Some moulted regularly in the morning and others in the evening or during the night. Most rested in sitting positions, but some habitually lay on their backs when resting. Some laid their eggs during the night, but some did so during the day. Some removed decaying eggs from their clutches, while others left them there. They even manifested differences in sociability, since some were habitually solitary, while others tended to congregate. The researchers attributed these variations to individual decisions.

The most dramatic behavioural differences were observed when the crayfish were subjected to environmental stress. Five juvenile clutch-mates of matching sizes and pre-stress behaviour patterns were placed together in a rather small and otherwise bare aquarium, with three replications. Over the next 34 days, the crayfish established a clear dominance hierarchy. Those that became dominant displayed increasingly offensive and aggressive behaviours, while those that became subordinates displayed increasing avoidant and defensive behaviours. This did not take place in aquaria furnished with natural formations that provided sheltering areas. Despite continued access to and consumption of plenty of food, the dominants grew much faster than the subordinates. The researchers suggested that slight initial differences in physiological and behavioural characteristics become linked to a broad range of other characteristics through self-reinforcing circuits linking behaviour, sense organs, brain, hormone systems, and metabolism.

These crayfish clearly showed variation that had no direct source in the genome and there was little reason to expect environmental sources either. Moreover, its early manifestations clearly contributed to the emergence of later even greater variation, likely through creation of both environmental niches and the accompanying resulting environmental stimuli and changes in genetic expression. Though this study was specifically designed to feature developmental variation, such variation is commonly observed in many cloned animals, suggesting that it is an important aspect of development in many, if not most or all species, including humans. Labelling such variation 'developmental', however, does nothing to explain it, nor does attributing it to individual behavioural decisions. On what grounds does an individual make any specific behavioural decision? Sometimes, of course, they are very clear, but many behaviours appear to take place either randomly or to have been set in motion by prior sets of behaviours, and something triggering one of these may have been random. Randomness is sometimes misused to characterize events we do not understand, but it is also a real property. An example is radioactive decay. For a large number of identical atoms, it is possible to specify the half-life, or the rate at which the entire collection of atoms will decay. It is not, however, possible to specify when any given atom in that collection will decay because that particular event is random within the overall process.

Randomness in development

Development very likely has a random component analogous to that in evolution. We are used to thinking of evolution as a competitive process for survival in which the genes that contribute most to 'fitness' increase in frequency and those that fail to contribute eventually disappear. But evolution is also massively cooperative: genes act together to develop the organism in which they reside, and the same gene can have very different roles in that process in different organisms or even within cells, organs, or tissues within the same organism. At some level, genes act during development like atoms in a radioactive material: we cannot specify the role of any single atom in the decay process, but we can specify the overall pattern of decay. This pattern is an emergent property of the essentially random individual decays, and it is not necessary to understand the individual decays in order to understand the overall pattern. For development, the emergent properties are both population-level distributions of characteristics such as age of mastery of reaching and grabbing in infancy and individual-level distributions of characteristics such as crying in response to loud, unexpected stimuli. We may be able to specify that 50 per cent of infants master reaching and grabbing by the age of 5 months and 75 per cent by the age of 7 months or that a particular infant David cries 65 per cent of the time after hearing a sudden noise, but not the age at which the infant David will master reaching and grabbing, nor whether he will cry when his father suddenly drops a dish on the tile floor.

The analogy between radioactive decay and development is not, however, complete. Development is cast within sets of both environmental and genetic constraints, many of which are correlated and nonadditive in their individually tiny effects, both with each other, and, especially, with themselves over time, so that emerging patterns take on increasing stability, and infancy, when these patterns are set in motion, is likely of particular developmental importance.

Moreover, and perhaps even more importantly, the individual atoms in radioactive material are interchangeable to us: we do not care which one decays when. The individuals developing within a population are not interchangeable: we care deeply which ones develop which traits, patterns of behaviours, or outcomes, and often wish that some patterns would not emerge at all. Recognizing the power and limits of power of the constraints and the role of randomness are among the major challenges in understanding the development of individual differences.

Further reading

Campos, J. J., Witherington, D., Anderson, D. L., Frankel, C. I., Uchiyama, I., & Barbu-Roth, M. (2008). Rediscovering development in infancy. *Child Development, 79*, 1625–1632.

Camras, L. A., & Witherington, D. C. (2005). Dynamical systems approaches to emotional development. *Developmental Review, 25*, 328–350.

Clearfield, M. W., Diedrich, F. J., Smith, L. B., & Thelen, E. (2006). Young infants reach correctly in A-not-B tasks: On the development of stability and perseveration. *Infant Behavior and Development, 29*, 435–444.

Duncan, J. (2010). *How Intelligence Happens*. London: Yale University Press.

Fischer, K. W., & Silvern, L. (1985). Stages and individual differences in cognitive development. *Annual Review of Psychology, 36*, 613–648.

Heyes, C. (2010). Where do mirror neurons come from? *Neuroscience and Biobehavioral Reviews, 34*, 575–583.

Kagan, J. (2008). In defense of qualitative changes in development. *Child Development, 79*, 1606–1624.

Meltzoff, A. N., & Moore, M. K. (1977). Newborn infants imitate adult facial gestures. *Science, 198*, 75–78.

Papousek, M., & von Hofacker, N. (1998). Persistent crying in early infancy: A nontrivial condition of risk for the developing mother-infant relationship. *Child Care, Health, and Development, 24*, 395–424.

Piaget, J. (1936/1954). *The Construction of Reality in the Child (translated by M. Cook from French)*. New York: Basic Books.

Smith, L. B. (2009). Dynamic systems, sensorimotor processes, and the origins of stability and flexibility. In J. P. Spencer, M. S. Thomas, & J. L. McClelland, *Toward a Unified Theory of Development* (pp. 67–85). Oxford: Oxford University Press.

Vygotsky, L. S. (1978). *Mind in Society*. Cambridge, MA: Harvard University Press.

Wynn, K. (1992). Addition and subtraction by human infants. *Nature, 358*, 749–750.

Childhood: Emerging as a Person

7

Basic toddler skills

The passage from infancy to childhood is marked by many changes. It is often termed *toddlerhood* and ranges generally from the ages of one to three years. Perhaps two of these changes set the rest in motion. Physical mobility increases dramatically and ability to make use of language, both receptively and productively, emerges. The surge in ability to move freely through space opens tremendous opportunities for exploration of the physical environment, and the emergence of language opens at least as wide opportunities to interact with others. Social interaction makes possible direct communication of needs and desires, but perhaps even more importantly, it makes it possible for one individual to learn from the experiences of others beyond simply observing those experiences. Developmental psychologists have done a good job of charting the typical developmental sequences that characterize toddlerhood in these areas. This was strongly motivated in part by the importance of being able to identify when development appears to be going awry, as with the occurrence of medical conditions, so it tends to have a standardized quality that does not reflect the richness of individual differences that exist at any one age, nor does it reflect well that developmental trajectories normally show individual differences too.

At the age of one year, most toddlers are able to use adjacent objects to pull themselves to standing position. Crawling on hands and knees or some variation remains their primary mode of locomotion, but most are beginning to take their first walking steps. There are considerable individual differences, however, in the precise sequences of skills toddlers master in the last months and weeks before they begin to walk. This might be characterized most readily as identification of the last factor that inhibits ability to walk. For some it is leg strength: their legs appear to develop the strength to support the rest of their bodies relatively slowly. As infants, these tend not to have stood much, whether because they were not given the opportunity or because they did not seek it. There also is some tendency for these to be relatively heavy in body. For others, the hindrance to walking is the coordination necessary to put one foot in front of the other and then swing the now-behind foot to a position in front of the original foot put forward, and repeat. As infants, these may have been very avid 'standers' but less physically active and eager to move through space by creeping and crawling, though of course relative restriction of movement could also create this situation. Another large group has been eager to stand as often as possible for months and easily masters the stepping motion, but the final limitation on free walking is balance: if they let go of some piece of furniture or parent's hand, they wobble and fall before they can take a step. These tend to be relatively independent-minded, physically active, and light in body, but the experience of falling so often can undermine their confidence to try to walk alone for quite awhile. Whatever the path to walking freely, mastering it raises the toddler's visual perspective and thus expands his/her view, frees the hands to carry things, and dramatically increases speed and efficiency, and thus physical range, of movement in space.

At one year, most can understand and respond to their own names and a few simple commands, as well as producing often garbled versions of some name for each of their parents and one or two other words, usually nouns, to refer to such things as favourite toys or foods. Researchers studying early language production generally consider a toddler's vocal expression to be a word if the same sound is used consistently to refer to the same thing and with clear intent, regardless of whether the sound made bears any resemblance to the actual word. Often there is little or no resemblance, as toddlers will make use of the sounds they can produce in often rather creative ways if they can succeed in communicating by doing so. For example, at the age of one year, my son said 'tata' to refer to his favourite stuffed elephant. This came from a book he enjoyed that had a page that said 'the elephant says ta-ta'.

By the age of two years, most toddlers can walk stably for quite some distance, run albeit somewhat clumsily, and climb stairs with the help of a handrail, one step at a time on both feet. Productive vocabulary typically ranges 300–400 words, with considerably larger receptive vocabulary, and most can put subjects and verbs together in sensible two-word sentences. By the age of three years, walking, running, and climbing come with ease for most. Most can speak in short but complete sentences, flexibly and often creatively using vocabularies of more than 1,000 words. Overt deviations from these patterns often signal the need for medical attention, but fortunately, such deviations are relatively rare in most stable environments with sufficient food, shelter, and caregiver support.

These dramatic increases in locomotive and communicative abilities are accompanied by cognitive and emotional changes that involve increasing awareness of the self as an active agent, independent of parents and other caregivers. This awareness carries with it excitement in executing even relatively simple physical movements out into the environment as well as in exerting control over the objects and other people encountered in that environment. There are always, however, myriad directions to move physically, many different objects that can be explored and manipulated, and different ways to communicate with other individuals, as well as different ways in which those individuals respond. Place any ten toddlers in turn into the same laboratory environment furnished with the same toys and populated by the same other people positioned in the same ways with the same interaction instructions, and each of those ten toddlers will make different choices about what to explore and how to interact with it, generating 10 very different situational dynamics within a short period of time. The fact of these different choices is one of the primary sources of the development of individual differences. That is, from the earliest ages, the individual plays an active role in his/her own acquisition of experience.

Consider how this takes place, in the context of the example of different toddlers entering the same lab room in turn. Suppose the lab room is furnished with different toys scattered around the floor, in the same arrangement for each toddler, with some over near the window, some near a stuffed chair in the corner, a few on low shelves, etc. Suppose also that a stranger sits quietly in another chair in the corner near the door, so the person is not usually spotted immediately by the toddler on entering the room. Where any toddler looks first is going to be determined partly by standard human visual responses to the lighting in the room and the toddler's size, partly by chance, and partly by the unique combination of interest and experience of that toddler. The eyes of one, for example, may be drawn to the window, and thus to the toys near it. Another may first catch sight of a stuffed tiger because of its brightly contrasting stripes, while still another may be drawn first to a book or a ball or a fire engine or a doll. Some may have a tendency to scan the whole room before taking more than a step into it, while others may immediately rush to that first thing that catches the eye. The stranger may be one more potentially attractive object to some, who thus approach and try to interact with the person, while others may maintain as much distance as possible from that corner of the room, once the person is noticed. And this notice alone may take place after rather different intervals for different toddlers. The role of individual agency, or the individual behavioural choices of each toddler, increases relative to those of chance and such normative human behaviour patterns as visual response to room lighting, object configuration, etc., once a toddler starts to handle any of the toys. Because this concept of individual agency is so important to what follows, I begin by discussing its typical developmental trajectory, some sources of individual differences in that trajectory, and the implications of those differences.

By the age of about one year, toddlers have generally apparently been aware for several months that their behaviour can have effects on the environment around them, both animate and inanimate. This recognition of both the toddler's separateness from the rest of the environment and his/her capacity to affect some of the conditions of that separate environment is the first step in the development of individual agency. The second step has two prongs: development of awareness of what characterizes and occurs within the individual toddler's own self, and development of understanding and acceptance of the extent, limitations, and implications of the toddler's capacity to influence that separate environment. The self-awareness prong involves recognizing the emotional experience of engaging in activities: at its most basic level, does the toddler enjoy the activity and find it interesting, or is engaging in it irritating or boring? The capacity prong is more complex. It involves at least two forms of learning that take place largely during early childhood. The first can be thought of as learning about how everyone, human or other animal, builds skills. It means recognizing that skills in any area are developed through repeated attempts – that is, practice, that practice is most effective when it is not just repetition but repetition that is systematically targeted at increasingly precise executions of the skill, and that greater effort generally brings greater returns. The second can be thought of as learning about the child's own individual experience of learning: his/her emotional experience of the exertion of effort, willingness to tolerate frustration, and perception of reward with success in return for effort expended. Over time, this second form of learning leads to some internal conception of capacity for skill attainment, or ability, which might be thought of as at least tentative identification of some boundary beyond which likely greater task mastery is not worth the effort involved to attain it.

The role of culture in the development of individual agency

Culture is intimately involved in both prongs from birth, and a single dimension, with poles of *collectivism* and *individualism*, is often used to characterize how. Collectivist cultures see individual persons as existing first and foremost in relation to the others around them. In such cultures, people are viewed as interdependent, and their identities tend to be based on their roles in their groups. This means, for the young child, early introduction to the ideas of behaviour appropriate to roles and responsibility to the group, and the fostering of skills that contribute to filling those roles effectively. Obedience to elders and conformity to external expectations are emphasized by caregivers, and choices for specific activities for individual children are made by those caregivers based on overall considerations of group or family welfare, with little room for individual choice on the parts of the individual children. Shame and guilt are triggered when an individual's behaviour brings disgrace to the group. At the same time, external environmental circumstances, rather than internal motivations, are quite readily offered as explanations for particular occurrences considered either good or bad. Social interactions tend to emphasize cooperation rather than competition.

In contrast, individualistic cultures see the individual as a complete unit in his/her own right, with rights and responsibilities independent of those of surrounding individuals. In such cultures, self-identities tend to be based on personal experiences of accomplishments and challenges faced and met. This means, for the young child, early introduction to the ideas of self-determination, self-reliance, self-advocacy, and choice in the areas in which competency and mastery of skills will develop. Individuals are considered to be responsible for making their own decisions about how they will live their lives, and shame and guilt are triggered primarily when internally set goals are not met. Though individuals are left free to set those goals themselves, those surrounding them tend to hold them personally responsible for the consequences of their actions, and to attribute those actions to internal characteristics within individual control. Social interactions tend to emphasize competition over cooperation.

Of course no culture is completely either collectivist or individualist. All cultures lie somewhere along the dimension between collectivism and individualism, and, within cultures, people do not reflect these values and behavioural patterns to the same degrees. Still, western cultures have historically tended to be more individualistic while eastern cultures have tended to be more collectivist, and these traditions persist today. Cultures tend to be more collectivist during times of scarcity and/or threat, when survival may depend on cooperation with others. And cultures tend to be more individualistic when they have access to plenty of material resources and a high standard of living. Within cultures as well, families with more financial resources and/or greater levels of education tend to have more individualistic outlooks, while those with fewer financial resources and/or less education tend to have more collectivist outlooks. This collectivist–individualistic dimension forms a background framework around which understanding what is meant by individual agency within any one culture or group within a culture must be built.

In collectivist cultures, development of self-awareness and agency centre primarily around learning the behaviours considered appropriate and developing the skills needed to meet group expectations for role fulfilment and task performance. In individualistic cultures, development of self-awareness and agency centre primarily around identification of activities a child particularly enjoys and for which the child appears to have appropriate ability to acquire the necessary skills. Either way, though I know of no research that has specifically addressed it, one of the clearest realities to young children must be that, compared with adults and older children, their skills in everything tend to be poor to non-existent. It does not take a research psychologist to be aware that one of the primary ways young children deal with this is by imitating their elders, and that, in general, they have some at least intuitive understanding that they should not expect to be able to do all the things that adults and older children can do. Exactly how these two recognitions balance each other must be crucial in the development of *self-esteem*, as well as agency, though, again, I am aware of no research that has specifically explored how. Self-esteem refers to the value that one places on oneself, as indicated by the ways in which one tends to think and feel about oneself. It can be thought of as the degree to which one 'likes oneself', but it is also generally more than that: most people recognize relative strengths and weaknesses in both character and abilities.

When self-esteem is healthy, there is a stable balance among striving to improve areas of weakness, accepting the existence of weaknesses and minimizing their impact, and capitalizing on areas of strength. Very commonly, however, a feeling of competence in at least some areas is key in maintaining this balance. For young children, such a feeling of competence must come mostly from perception of ability to make progress towards skill mastery rather than from mastery itself.

Children probably use many sources of information to develop perception of ability to make progress towards mastery. One source in both collectivist and individualistic cultures is clearly parents and other caregivers, including older children. Young children get two kinds of information about their progress towards competence from these sources. First, they get impressions about the degree to which their progress meets the expectations of these elders. Children are generally very aware of pleasing or displeasing these important others, and likely keep some kind of running tally in their minds of the relative proportions of the time they accomplish one or the other, in the process forming beliefs about their overall levels of competence. Second, children get specific information from their elders about *how* to do things, *how* to develop skills, as well as information about how to *think about* skill development.

The process of skill development

The Russian developmental psychologist Lev Vygotsky (1896–1934) contributed important ideas about the process of skill development. A contemporary of Piaget, Vygotsky's ideas followed a very different path to prominence, due to the difficulties of conducting scientific research in this area during the Stalinist era in the Soviet Union, and his early death at the age of only 38. Though he was writing during the 1930s, his ideas did not reach the western scientific community until the late 1960s and 1970s, long after his death. He saw interpersonal communication as one of the primary means through which young children acquire skills and abilities in any area. To him (Vygotsky, 1981), knowledge exists *intermentally*, or among individuals, before it can exist *intramentally* within any one individual. Of course, strictly speaking, this is not completely true, or there would be no discovery or development of new information, tools, or procedures; nor, at a more mundane level, would anyone come to understand anything already known on their own. Still, it is a good characterization of the situation facing young children. The child's learning process, to Vygotsky, consists of making externally available information internal to the child. It takes place primarily with the assistance of others, who make use of the child's *zone of proximal development* through *scaffolding*.

The zone of proximal development (ZPD) in any one task or skill area is the range of skill lying between what a child can do when acting completely independently and what the child can do under the guidance of or in collaboration with someone with greater skill and knowledge. It thus encompasses the skills that the child is in process of developing. To the extent such a zone exists, the concept harbours several implicit proposals that deserve consideration in their own rights. First, it proposes that, rather than being an inevitable outgrowth of inherent and independent abilities, skill development depends on opportunities to learn. Second, skill development depends not on having reached some particular inherent developmental milestone, but on the quality of teaching and availability of opportunities to practise. Third, it proposes that the most basic and important opportunities to learn are social in nature; they involve someone who acts as teacher. This embeds all learning squarely in culture, highlighting its power both to restrict and to enhance particular areas of skill development.

'Scaffolding' is a term applied after Vygotsky's death by Wood, Bruner, and Ross (1976) that came into general use in the West in discussing Vygotsky's ideas. It refers to the means by which others more skilled than the child structure the environment to simplify a task so that the child can succeed in completing it, in the same manner that temporarily placed structural supports allow workers to complete construction tasks they otherwise could not reach safely. Examples from Vygotsky's perspective might be actions such as placing a sticker on middle C on a piano so that a child can orient his/her hands correctly on the keys before beginning to play, or offering a number line to use in counting from one number to another in order to complete an addition problem.

Vygotsky's ideas have been very influential in developmental psychology since the 1970s, and there is little question that he was onto much that is important in understanding skill development in childhood. Though Vygotsky's ideas are not generally discussed in these terms, they also present many opportunities for the emergence of individual differences in the skills that children actually manifest. And because skill emergence is often equated with ability by many, not excluding children themselves, Vygotsky's ideas also present many opportunities for the emergence of individual differences in what is seen to be ability. One primary source of such individual differences in children's skill emergence is individual differences in the quality of scaffolding they are offered.

We know more about what constitutes effective scaffolding than we do about how often it is applied. Still, the knowledge we have gives us some clues about how it is applied. For example, Wood (1986) and colleagues carried out a series of experiments to explore what is involved in effective scaffolding. They devised a task that was beyond the abilities of the 4-year-old children whose skill development abilities they intended to test, and taught their mothers how to carry it out. It involved using 21 blocks of different sizes and shapes that could be joined together with pegs to form a pyramid if they were properly oriented. After the mothers had mastered the task, Wood and colleagues asked them to pass their skill along to their children so that the children would be able to carry out the task themselves, and used the results to articulate what constituted effective scaffolding. The first step in this process was to describe and organize what the mothers actually did. The mothers' teaching activities appeared to fall along a dimension of directness of demonstration. That is, some mothers took a very 'hands off' approach and, at least initially, only suggested to their children that they try to build something from the blocks. Others gave general verbal instructions regarding such things as number and size of blocks to start with; still others pointed out specific blocks, and some even helped physically by picking up a block and orienting it properly for placement. The mothers who gave the most direct instructions actually showed the children exactly how to position the blocks. This starting dimension, however, was not what appeared to matter. What appeared to work best was a flexible approach that was closely calibrated to the child's performance. However direct the mother's initial instructions, if the child was not successful in making progress on the task, the child's performance improved most if the mother's next instructions were more direct. On the other hand, if the child was successful with one level of instruction, performance improved most if the mother's next instructions were less direct. As might be expected, most mothers fell short of this scaffolding ideal, but all adopted it to some degree. There were individual differences among them in the degrees to which they displayed this kind of flexibility and how quickly applied it. The fact that it was flexible rather than structured instruction suggests that learning effectiveness depends on maintenance of motivation through intermittent reward in the form of perception of successful learning progress. Some classical principles of learning are relevant here.

Classical learning principles

Two primary forms of learning are generally recognized by psychologists. The first is less relevant to children in learning skills, but I will discuss it here because it will be relevant to later discussions and because it makes sense to discuss the two forms of learning together. This is *classical* or *Pavlovian conditioning*. It was first demonstrated in hungry dogs by Ivan Pavlov (1927). He noted that after some period of time in a lab setting in which they were fed at regular intervals the dogs began to salivate not just when they smelled the food they were about to receive but also when they saw the trainer who usually delivered the food. Pavlov used this observation to 'train' the dogs to salivate to the ringing of a bell. In this form of learning, the learner experiences one stimulus that triggers a reflexive response (here, the smell of the food) in close association with another stimulus that generates no particular response (here, the familiar sight of the trainer who delivered it). After some period of exposure, which can vary from a single to many such pairings, presentation of only the originally neutral stimulus generates the same reflexive response as the original reflexive trigger. Since Pavlov, psychologists have been very creative in designing experimental variations around the general theme of classical conditioning, but the general theme is that development of the learned association takes place outside of the volition or awareness of the learner, and responses are reflexive in nature.

In contrast, during *operant conditioning,* the learner explicitly (though not necessarily consciously) modifies subsequent voluntary (rather than reflexive) behaviour due to the consequences of present and prior behaviour. This form of learning was first studied in detail by Edward Thorndike (1901). He designed 'puzzle boxes' with various levers and pulleys that could open escape doors, and confined cats in them. When first confined, it took a long time for the cats to find behaviours that would make the doors open so they could escape, but, with each new box, the cats performed fewer of the behaviours that had not worked in the past and more of the behaviours that had, so that they escaped more and more quickly with each new box. Work with operant conditioning was continued and extended by B. F. Skinner, who stressed that the conditioned response need not have any psychological content (experience of satisfaction or frustration, for example).

In operant conditioning, the consequences of present and prior behaviour take the form of either *reinforcement* or *punishment.* These two terms have popular, common interpretations, but their technical definitions differ somewhat from these interpretations, so it is important to articulate them clearly. One fundamental difference from common usage is that neither term is applied to the actor who carries out the behaviour; rather, it is the behaviours themselves that are reinforced or punished. Moreover, the consequences that result in reinforcement or punishment need not necessarily be delivered by people or even other living creatures. They may simply be natural occurrences. With those fundamentals established, reinforcement takes place when a behaviour is associated with (not necessarily a cause of) an occurrence that motivates the actor to perform that behaviour more frequently. Punishment takes place when a behaviour is associated with an occurrence that motivates the actor to perform that behaviour less frequently. In addition, once a behaviour has been operantly conditioned, its performance can be *extinguished* when the previously associated occurrence fails to take place anymore. That is, the frequency with which the actor performs the behaviour will decrease when performance is no longer reinforced, and performance will finally cease.

Box 7.1   Subtleties in harnessing operant conditioning

The technical definitions of reward and punishment lead to four kinds of operant conditioning. Again, the definitions of these different kinds of operant conditioning make use of popularly used terms but in ways slightly different from their popular usages. *Positive* refers to stimulus provision rather than to good, rewarding, or positive quality of the stimulus, and *negative* to stimulus removal rather than to bad, aversive, or negative quality of the stimulus. With that in mind, the four kinds of operant conditioning are:

(1) *Positive reinforcement:* This takes place when a behaviour is associated with a rewarding occurrence, and the rewarding experience motivates increasing frequency of the behaviour. Increasingly specific and skilled behaviours can be *shaped* when positive reinforcement is offered selectively to increasingly accurate approximations of the behaviour. Similarly, positive reinforcement can be used to *chain* sequences of behaviour in order to build complex patterns of response.

(2) *Negative reinforcement (escape):* This takes place when a behaviour is associated with removal of a previously occurring aversive stimulus, thus restoring whatever natural motivation to perform the behaviour the actor would have in the absence of the aversive stimulus, or motivating increased frequency of a usually useless behaviour in order to avoid the aversive stimulus. The latter is often called *avoidance learning.*

(3) *Positive punishment:* This takes place when a behaviour is associated with an aversive stimulus, and the aversive experience motivates decreasing frequency of the behaviour.

(4) *Negative punishment:* This takes place when a behaviour is associated with removal of a previously occurring rewarding stimulus, thus restoring whatever natural motivation the actor would have had to avoid performing the behaviour in the absence of the rewarding occurrence.

These different kinds of operant conditioning can be used intentionally to structure learning programmes that lead optimally to the performance of complex combinations of behaviour, and thus also to the development of high levels of skill. More importantly, any context that recurs over time will condition behaviours that follow these patterns. Moreover, it is the organism experiencing it who finds the stimuli rewarding or aversive, and even which stimuli are perceived at all, and this generally shows substantial individual differences within any defined group. This means that programmes of reinforcement and punishment intended to shape behaviours in children according to operant conditioning principles often have unintended consequences. One common example of this is when parents and teachers take actions in response to children's behaviour that are intended to be positively punitive but instead become negatively reinforcing. In such cases, the child often perceives the (negatively expressed) attention received from the admired adult in response to the behaviour as less aversive than the alternative of being ignored, and increases rather than decreases frequency of the generating behaviour. In the process, the child may be especially likely to incorporate into his/her own self-concept whatever form of negative expression the adult's attention takes. A common example is the child who easily becomes bored when adults are engaged in other activities and seeks stimulation through physical activity that disrupts and annoys the adults.

It is very common that children do not decide for themselves which tasks to master; instead adults around them request that children learn to perform tasks the adults think they will need in order to function in the societies in which they live. This means that it matters to the adults that the children master these tasks. Perhaps especially with respect to academically oriented tasks, it also often means that adults have expectations about how quickly children should master these tasks and the extent to which they 'should' manifest interest in mastering them. Clearly, there are cultural differences in the natures of the tasks for which adults hold these expectations, and even within commonly recognized cultural groupings there are large between-family and even within-family differences. Still, the experience of some task-mastery expectations by adults is virtually universal to children in all cultures. Their relative success in meeting these expectations is another source development of children's senses of self-esteem and agency. Here, ideas about *mindset* with respect to ability developed by Carol Dweck (2006) may be especially important.

Mindsets about ability

A mindset is a set of assumptions about how the world works. Assumptions are premises that are accepted as true without the necessity of testing. The assumptions involved in mindsets are held strongly enough that they exert powerful incentives to maintain prior patterns of behaviour and beliefs about behaviour. Dweck proposes, and has backed up with a substantial body of empirical research, that people differ in the extent to which they believe, or assume, that abilities, their own and others', are fixed entities that can only be revealed, or properties that can be developed and cultivated through effort, practice, and persistence. She has demonstrated that these mindsets matter. People who hold *entity* mindsets tend to see any task as a revelation of their own fixed levels of task-related ability. They thus tend to adopt performance goals for themselves that, if achieved, validate that their levels of ability are high, or at least sufficient. If not achieved, however, the failures are indicative to them that their fixed abilities are not high enough. From this perspective, every new task presents a risk of failure, and thus of revealing the inadequacy of their fixed ability. This creates little motivation to invest greater effort in task practice, nor to pursue learning opportunities, and there is reassurance that ability is adequate in sticking to well-practised tasks on which skill levels are high. This entity mindset has been repeatedly associated with relatively low school and sports achievement. In contrast, people who have the mindset that abilities are *incremental*, that abilities can be developed and cultivated through effort, practice, and persistence, tend to see task performance as a reflection of learning effort. They thus tend to adopt mastery goals for them-selves: it makes sense to them to persist in practicing a task until it has been mastered, as greater effort in learning and practice always helps. From this perspective, failure only represents insufficient effort. This attitude creates substantial motivation to invest greater effort next time and to pursue new learning opportunities. Sticking only to well-practised tasks on which skill levels are already high tends to be seen as dull. This incremental mindset has been repeatedly associated with relatively high school and sports achievement (Carr & Dweck, 2011).

Children develop these mindsets through their experiences in learning tasks, and this process begins in toddlerhood or even earlier. In any interactive situation between two people, both are perceivers of the consequences of their behaviour on the other, and this applies to situations of scaffolding by parents and teachers in helping children to learn new skills. This means that the mindsets about abilities held by parents and teachers are important in fostering children's mindset development. Children pick up quickly when parents and teachers are disappointed in their learning progress, and find the expressed disappointment and internally experienced frustration positively punitive. Anything that makes it possible to avoid these aversive experiences associated with the task becomes negatively reinforcing. Repeated experiences of task frustration compounded by awareness of having disappointed adults tends to foster a child's entity mindset that his/her ability is simply inadequate and greater effort will not help. Children also quickly pick up hints adults leave about why people fail to perform successfully and how they believe that people achieve successful task performance. Thus when adults attribute their disappointment in a child's slow learning progress to the child's inherent lack of ability, the child tends to hear this in their communications and adopt the same mindset. Even praise for successful performance that takes forms such as 'Oh, what a good artist you are!' in response to a nice drawing tends to foster the entity mindset, as children hear the approved product of their efforts attributed to a characteristic that is presented as inherent. If, instead, children are praised when they persist and show any progress at all, the praise both serves as positive reinforcement and encourages them to think of ability as responsive to effort. And when task mastery comes easily to a child, ongoing application of effort can be reinforced by focusing attention on the return on effort that was applied and the satisfaction at mastery that comes as a result of that application of effort, along with presentation of an even more difficult task. This in turn fosters development of an incremental mindset about ability.

Operant conditioning in teaching

It is not just children who experience this kind of operant conditioning in the learning/teaching situation. Parents and teachers do so as well. When children express interest in and enjoyment of tasks and show success in learning new ones, adults tend to find the experience of teaching them rewarding, and thus positively reinforcing. The word *reinforcing* is important here. It is intended to emphasize that adults often tend to increase the frequency with which they carry out teaching and other skill-building behaviours when they see that children respond well to them. In contrast, when children do not 'catch on' to new tasks readily and/or seem disinterested or resistant or easily distracted, adults are more likely to find the experience of teaching them aversive, particularly in relation to other activities. Even when they feel responsibility for seeing that children learn specific tasks, the aversiveness of the teaching experience may relatively reinforce carrying out activities associated with other responsibilities, thus decreasing frequency of teaching activities and skill-building behaviours. Of course adults can consciously offset these operant conditioning responses, and many often do in the interest of fostering children's development of skills the adults consider important. Still, the point here is that many often do not. Because exposure to opportunity to practise skills at different levels of attainment is essential in building them, the resulting difference in extent and frequency of adult scaffolding acts to increase whatever individual differences there may be in children's inherent capacities to learn those skills. As children are generally aware of how adults feel about their interactions with them, this has implications for development of children's mindsets about ability as well. The net result of all this is that a child's sense of individual agency emerges through the combination of opportunities offered for self-expression and the requests made for mastery of socially expected skills and behaviours. Just as important are the extent of scaffolding offered by others in mastering the skills involved and the messages communicated to the child about the role of effort in achieving skill mastery, the relative success of the child's efforts, the meaning of that success, and, last but definitely not least, the extent to which the child finds an activity itself intrinsically rewarding and thus reinforcing, absent any social input at all or regardless of social input. Sense of individual agency is the fundamental tool children, and people more generally, use to pursue their motivations.

Motivation and interest

Motivation is one of those commonly used words whose meaning tends to be taken for granted but which is actually quite hard to define. It refers to some latent process in the individual that elicits and sustains behaviour. The term can be applied to behaviours ranging from basic physiological drives such as sexual intercourse or eating that apply in some sense to all, but it can also be applied to very specialized behaviours such as playing the cello that might never even occur to the majority of people at all. With respect to activities that involve skill acquisition, development of motivation involves one's experiences with related learning and ongoing cognitions about current circumstances. Much of the learning and cognitions involve the individual's sense of agency: based on prior experience, is the effort expended going to be pleasurable? Is the effort going to pay off in task accomplishment? Can the individual arrange circumstances so that there is 'room' to exert the necessary effort? Is whatever reward is associated with task accomplishment worth the effort that will be required?

All of the principles I have just discussed contribute to the individual's answers to these questions, whether the individual articulates either the questions or the answers consciously or not.

But biological processes are also involved in motivation. Some motivations involve very basic biological processes such as seeking and eating food when hungry or resting when tired, but many involve much more abstract drives such as meeting achievement goals, establishing social contact, figuring out something puzzling, maintaining physical safety, or retaliating for a wrong suffered. A major distinction in the motivation literature is between *intrinsic* and *extrinsic* motivations. Intrinsic motivation refers to motivation that exists completely within the individual and is driven by enjoyment of or interest in the task activity itself. The individual pursues the activity not as a result of some external reinforcement but because of some internal reinforcement. In contrast, extrinsic motivation originates in incentives to meet goals imposed outside the individual. Individuals with strong senses of agency, particularly in individualistic cultures, tend to pursue intrinsically motivated goals and activities, while individuals with weaker senses of agency are more likely to end up pursuing extrinsically motivated goals and activities. Extrinsic motivators tend to be more common in collectivistic cultures as well. Over time, however, individuals in all cultures accommodate to the patterns of behaviour in their cultures and to its externally imposed goals and interests, so, in these cultures, these extrinsic motivators become at least partly intrinsic (Benedict, 1934).

All, even the most basically biological forms of motivation such as hunger, thirst, fatigue, and pursuit of sexual activity, show large individual differences, and substantial proportions of this variance are genetically influenced. As discussed in Chapter 3, though this says nothing about *how*, the presence of this genetic influence suggests that something inherent to the individual is involved in the development and expression of motivations. One theory that explicitly addresses the *how* is Experience Producing Drive Theory (Bouchard, 1997; Hayes, 1962; Johnson, 2010a). This is the idea that one of the ways in which natural selection affects complex organisms such as humans is that they evolve to be agents who actively seek circumstances that are optimal for their survival and reproduction. Because circumstances can be highly variable, the selected genes do not determine particular means of adaptation; rather, they influence the development of the patterns of behaviour that psychologists label as traits through their contributions to motivations, preferences, and emotional responses. Through biological development of increasing capacity for locomotion, physical coordination, sense of agency, and information processing, these motivations, preferences, and emotional responses drive the individual (whether person or other animal) to seek and acquire particular kinds of environmental experiences. In turn, these experiences result in pursuit and practice of skills, habits, patterns of response, and environmental circumstances, and these conditions and ways of coping with them reinforce the original underlying motivations, preferences, and emotional responses.

Experience producing drive theory

Hayes (1962) originally proposed Experience Producing Drive (EPD) Theory to integrate what were then new findings in the independent research areas of motivation, behaviour genetics, and intelligence, and it remains very applicable to thinking about the development of individual differences in abilities of all kinds. But it can also be applied to all areas of individual psychological differences in humans, including personality, values, interests, attitudes, and idiosyncratic traits unique to each individual. One of the tenets of the theory is that all of these other areas of individual differences are related to individual differences in abilities, so study of any one is simply a matter of selection of focal point (Johnson, 2010a). Because Hayes focused on applying the theory to the development of intelligence, he expressed his ideas with reference to it. Though the ideas are more generally applicable, intelligence does serve as an excellent example of their application. Moreover, it is one of the best-measured personal characteristics in psychology, and contributes substantively to many important life outcomes such as educational attainment, occupation, and income, mental and physical health, and even longevity. Thus, for purposes of discussion, I will work within the framework of the development of ability as well.

Within EPD Theory, what is innate about ability consists not only of, or perhaps not even importantly of, ability capacities such as size of working memory store or speed of neural conductance *per se*, but rather of tendencies to engage in activities that foster learning, whether in general or in particular content areas. Thus much of what is innate about ability is some sort of *drive* or motivation to engage in particular kinds of activities. To consider ability in this way requires some manipulation of the concepts of drive and motivation. Traditionally within psychology, *drive* has referred to the innate perception of an unmet need that energizes an organism to carry out behaviours that will eliminate the deficit. For example, after some period without consumption of food, an organism will initiate food-seeking behaviours. At first the search may be quite lackadaisical and the organism may be quite fussy about the kinds of food sought, but if the search is not successful, the organism will devote increasing amounts of energy to the search and will become willing to consume an increasingly wide range of objects as food. From this traditional perspective, behaviour is motivated by need or lack of something important to biological well-being, and, when the need is met, the behaviour ceases. This perspective has some intuitive appeal and can go some ways towards explaining commonly observed behaviour patterns such as the tendency to eat quite quickly at the beginning of a meal when one is very hungry and for the rate of eating to slow and then stop as one becomes satiated. It clearly cannot explain all behaviours, however, whether in humans or other animals. For example, simple drive reduction does not explain how a hungry human can prepare and cook a meal without devouring all the food first – more generally it cannot explain deferral of gratification. It also cannot explain simple exploratory behaviours, such as the tendency for a rat to enter one of the arms of a T-maze at random the first time it is placed there, but the other arm on the second placement.

Box 7.2   Maslow's classic Hierachy of Needs in EPD Theory

One model that addresses some of the deficiencies of the simple drive reduction perspective in ways that help to articulate EPD Theory is Maslow's (1970) Hierarchy of Needs (see Figure 7.1). Under this model, people and other animals are motivated by a wide variety of needs and drives that require satisfaction. Because there are so many of these needs and they often conflict, there is a natural hierarchy that governs the process of sorting among them to activate behaviours. The most basic physiological survival needs must be met first. When these are at least minimally met, the organism becomes motivated to pursue more complex needs. Though there are individual differences in even the most basic needs, in both quantitative and qualitative terms, much of what is considered individuality is associated with expression of efforts to meet the more complex needs, and this is where much of similarity of the hierarchy of needs with EPD Theory comes in. Like all models, the Hierarchy of Needs is far from a completely accurate description of behaviour. There are many empirical examples of exceptions to it, of people who forgo basic needs in the service of goals that are placed higher on the hierarchy. In addition, the levels of the hierarchy are very difficult, if not impossible, to define empirically without overlap, even across levels of the hierarchy

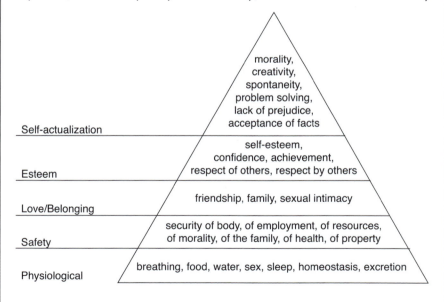

Figure 7.1   Maslow's Hierarchy of Needs

Source: Abraham H. Maslow, 'A Theory of Human Motivation', *Psychological Review*, 1943, vol. 50, pp. 374–96. Reprinted with permission.

that are not supposed to be adjacent, and expectations based on experience with need satisfaction have strong influences on perceptions about need satisfaction (Wahba & Bridwell, 1976). Still, the model also retains some firm grounding in reality that makes explaining it and its relevance to EPD Theory worthwhile.

The most basic level of the hierarchy applies to all organisms, and consists of the physiological needs for sustenance in the form of food, water, oxygen, etc. Different species, of course, consume different kinds of food and respiration in plants in the converse of the process in animals and very different in aquatic than in land animals, but the basic idea of the need for sustenance applies to all. Insufficiencies and imbalances in meeting these needs can disrupt normal function and even survival in all areas, so priority motivation to meet these needs makes evolutionary sense. In modern humans living in developed nations, where most people have plenty of access to food in particular, it is difficult to find evidence for the existence of such priority, or the effects of deprivation on behaviour and psychological state. But strong evidence comes from unusual studies such as the Minnesota Starvation Experiment (Tucker, 2006). This was a clinical study carried out towards the end of World War II to investigate the physiological and psychological effects of the kinds of severe and prolonged dietary restriction that many in the war zones in Europe and Asia were experiencing, and, in particular, to assess the relative effectiveness of different rehabilitation strategies. Participants were conscientious objectors to the war who were thus excused from other military or public service duties. They endured a 24-week semi-starvation period during which they lost 25 per cent of their body weights, kept diaries, and were closely monitored both physiologically and psychologically. Each received one of four alternative 12-week restricted rehabilitation programmes, followed by another 8 weeks of unrestricted rehabilitation but close behavioural monitoring. Most participants experienced severe depression and distress, and were preoccupied with food during both the starvation and rehabilitation periods. They showed dramatic reductions in sexual interest and withdrew socially, becoming increasingly isolated. They complained of declining concentration, comprehension, and judgement, but standardized tests did not show declines in performance, perhaps due to offsets from the effects of practice on the tests.

The second level of Maslow's hierarchy applies to all mobile organisms and consists of basic safety and security including shelter. It might be thought that meeting safety needs takes precedence over meeting physiological needs, as failure to meet such needs can result in death at least as surely as can starvation. But, if this were the case, humans and other animals would not venture out of safe refuges to find food and water, which they clearly do. Again, this makes evolutionary sense, as starvation is certain without food over some period of time, but venturing out of a safe refuge only entails risk of death or injury and may bring large rewards in food acquisition. The third level is expressed in very different ways in different animals. It consists of an appropriate level of belongingness to some social group, including the experience of affection, friendship, and love in humans. In the Minnesota Starvation Experiment, participants did not face deprivation of basic safety (unlike some of the people in war zones the study was intended to gather knowledge to help), so it makes sense that their responses to their situation did not really involve the safety level of the needs hierarchy. Their responses clearly did reflect withdrawal of motivation on the social level, however, as they became increasingly socially withdrawn as food deprivation increased. Within the common realm of experience, when physically ill, people often withdraw socially as well, concentrating their energies on simply maintaining what physical comfort they can. When not under constraints, at the level of behavioural approach rather than withdrawal, people clearly seek companionship with great regularity. Development of a sense of belongingness is a commonly expressed motivation for joining organizations, and people work hard to maintain their positions in existing organizations. They will also set aside activities oriented towards attainment of other goals, particularly those at the next two levels, in order to take up activities to sustain social relationships and social organizations.

The last two levels of the needs hierarchy arguably may apply primarily to humans. Beyond merely social contact and companionship, humans seek first to have reason to think well of themselves. Some of the most readily available reasons to think well of oneself relate to abilities: individuals can perceive themselves to be strong, competent, to have mastered important tasks, to have achieved certain goals, to provide socially useful services, etc. From a slightly different perspective, they may also come to think well of themselves because they perceive that others think well of them, leading to motivation to develop or maintain reputation, prestige, status, fame, attention, glory, recognition in the form of achievement awards, or simply expressions of appreciation from others. In industrialized nations, where the first two levels of the hierarchy are generally quite readily met and adults in much of the dominant society place considerable emphasis for children on academic success, patterns of behaviour among children who are struggling in school for whatever reason can be interpreted within the context of the needs hierarchy. Because they are often socially rejected by their more successful peers, they meet their social needs with each other. And because they have difficulty finding reasons to think well of themselves within the academic setting, they lose motivation in that area and seek other avenues in which to demonstrate competence. In the process, they may come to deny that academic success has any importance at all. The relevance to children of their experiences in scaffolding situations with parents and teachers that I have discussed should be clear.

If the basic need to think well of oneself is met, one more need remains in Maslow's hierarchy. This is self-actualization, and the need that is most relevant to EPD Theory. Children, and people in general, can feel competent at doing the things they are supposed to do according to social expectations, they can feel appreciated by others for this competence, and they can feel that their competencies are generally useful, but they still may feel the need to find their own most creative ways of expressing themselves, or even a need simply for activity. Again, data from nonhuman animals that contradicts both drive reduction theories and straightforward application of the hierarchy of needs may help to articulate the mechanisms involved, though most of the ways in which this need is generally expressed likely apply mostly to humans. After a period of food deprivation, rats show little enhanced interest in it until they have had the experience of eating. They do not respond to food-rewarded learning tasks until they have been deprived of food for an extended period (Ghent, 1957). This suggests that they should starve, as neither basic biological drive nor deprivation of a basic biological need seems to motivate them to seek food. Apparently they do not starve because, left to their own devices, they tend to consume small amounts of food pretty much whenever they find it available, whether they actively need it or not. It is in this sense that drives are conceptualized in EPD Theory, and in which self-actualization may be conceptualized in the hierarchy of needs – left completely to its own devices, this, and not that, is what a person (or other animal) chooses to do.

Bouchard (1997; Bouchard, et al., 1990) extended Hayes' (1962) EPD theory to incorporate the Darwinian idea that evolution operates through the activities in which organisms engage, and that behaviour in even very primitive organisms is quite plastic. This suggests that behaviour is both sensitive to environmental circumstances and internally directed by individual differences in perceptions of particular aspects of environment, or even environment more generally, and tendencies to approach and avoid particular aspects of the environment. The experiences that result from this combination of self-initiated action and response are self-reinforcing – the organism learns quickly to avoid as much as possible the ones that 'felt bad' and to repeat the ones that 'felt good'. Moreover, experience builds: with time, the individual organism becomes more and more adept at avoiding the bad experiences and finding the specific environmental conditions that will maximize the good feelings.

EPDs thus result from coevolution, or the emergence of genetically transmitted biological characteristics triggered by the presence of some biologically oriented environmental circumstance, as discussed in Chapter 2. They are manifested by what ecologists call *extended phenotypes* (Dawkins, 1982). This particular term is usually applied to species-typical behaviours such as the construction by beavers of dams. It refers to the observation that genetic influences are involved not just in the development of characteristics of the body of an organism, but also in the behaviour of that organism, including the ways in which the organism manipulates its environment to increase its own ability to adapt to it. The idea is that the results of these environmental manipulations should be considered every bit as genetically influenced and characteristic of and inherent in the organism as its own bodily characteristics. With recognition that different specific environments manifest very different extended phenotypes as a result of balancing selection (also discussed in Chapter 2), and that balancing selection takes place within as well as across species, it is possible to apply the concept of the extended phenotype within species. Behaviour geneticists have tended to call this *niche-picking* (Scarr, 1996; Scarr & McCartney, 1983), or the tendency to seek environmental circumstances and create situations that complement and reinforce the genetically influenced characteristics that originally led the organism to seek those environmental characteristics. Personality developmental psychologists have voiced similar ideas (Roberts & Caspi, 2003).

In the context of development in childhood, many behaviour patterns common in children can be seen as extended phenotypes resulting from EPDs. For example, my son expressed an interest in building things as soon as he could sit up and stack blocks or cylinders. As he grew, he built things in order to understand them, in order to allay his fears, even just to avoid boredom. At first he used any kind of material he could get his hands on. In preschool he built a violin and bow from cardboard, household string, masking tape, and a stick after a lesson in preschool about musical instruments. It did not actually function because the household string could not be sufficiently tightened to produce a recognizable sound, but he could hold it on his shoulder like a real violin – it even had a chin rest – and the strings could be tightened to some degree with cardboard pegs. At age 5 he built a scale model of the Grand Canyon in the dirt of our campsite after a hike quite a way down the Bright Angel Trail, which he had found scary. And he focused on model airplanes shortly after the September 11 attacks, which took place when he was aged 9. He had always been careful with his building creations, displaying them in his bedroom and throughout the house (to the extent he could get away with that, as the clutter sometimes became overwhelming), but this was when he really started to modify his environment. By the time he left for college (to study astrophysics and aeronautical engineering), a whole room in our house was dedicated to his model airplanes and building equipment. The ones he had completed were carefully labelled and displayed on shelves, his extensive collection of model-building tools was arrayed across his large worktable, his model paints were organized by colour on special shelves, the pieces of models in process were distributed across the table and floor, there was a large stack of boxes, precisely in order of size, of new models awaiting construction, and the book shelves were filled with model magazines and books about the planes themselves. This room could be seen as part of my son's extended phenotype and an outgrowth of his drive to build. The idea is reinforced by the fact that his bedroom was a mess.

Importantly though, not all EPDs may necessarily contribute to what most people would recognize as positive environmental adaptation. Humans generally have many different combinations of EPDs, as well as often-conflicting goals and objectives. At the same time, environments are complex and contain many different kinds of stimuli, and matches among EPDs, social obligations, and environmental stimuli may differ in strength and/or quality. Behaviours that may seem advantageous in the short term may be disadvantageous in the long term, and environmental responses to behaviours may be unexpected, unpleasant, and even harmful. The net result is that people may express EPDs that create extended phenotypes that trap them in cycles of increasingly non-adaptive behaviours. For example, a drive to express anger aggressively can lead to environmental consequences that are at least perceived as unfair, inspiring further anger and aggressive behaviour, ultimately leading to the extended phenotype known as the jail cell.

Testing and applying EPD Theory

Like any good scientific theory, EPD Theory must be both testable and generative of new explanatory mechanisms and research questions that inspire applications. Devising tests that could clearly falsify EPD Theory is difficult, however, because the theory itself directly addresses what may be the messiest problem facing the social sciences: genetically influenced multicollinearity (Johnson, 2010a; Rutter, 2006). It is the subject of endless political debate and policy strategy that the environmental conditions known as poverty, including exposure to toxic pollutants and high crime rates, dilapidated housing, poor-quality schools, and lack of access to medical care and other basic services are all inter-correlated. They are also associated with similarly inter-corre-lated personal characteristics ranging from poor educational attainment to low IQ and income to poor mental and physical health to substance abuse and antisocial behaviour. At the same time, the most coveted environmental conditions, including clean air and water, access to green space, safe neigh-bourhoods, large and comfortable homes full of modern conveniences, access to regular and high-tech health care and services well beyond the basic, and high-quality schools with both state-of-the-art enrichment and special educa-tion programmes are also both inter-correlated among themselves and associ-ated with similarly inter-correlated personal characteristics ranging from high educational attainment to professional occupational status to high income to moderate alcohol consumption, regular exercise, robust health, and feelings of self-efficacy. Moreover, all the personal characteristics, and even the envi-ronmental circumstances, tend to show genetic influences (Turkheimer, 2000), and the genetic influences underlying observably associated variables tend to be linked as well. This makes it extremely difficult, if not impossible, to iden-tify the causal effects of any one variable on any one outcome.

Given the pervasiveness of the patterns of linkages, it is also only too likely that what we might consider to be an outcome at any one moment is nothing more than a fundamental contributor to the next developmental period, however defined. This fits comfortably within EPD Theory, though without doing anything to place it in the danger of falsification necessary to establish it. EPD Theory proposes that development takes place within some geneti-cally influenced range of reactions to environmental stimuli. But the specific environment encountered is always some combination of the circumstances presented to a child and the circumstances within the child's power to seek out on its own. These are always limited in childhood. Without access to the appropriate outlets for the expression of EPDs, the theory proposes that the EPD-relevant characteristics would not continue to develop, would be stunted. The question of what might be relevant stimuli is, however, complex. It begins with what to define and measure as EPDs: should they be characteristics such as curiosity or tendency to seek novel or stimulating experiences in general, or should they be measured in a much more narrowly focused way, such as curiosity about particular topics or tendencies to pursue very specific kinds of activities? If the former, some of the strongest EPDs with the most direct influences on the development of other psychological traits may be missed. If the latter, *which* behaviours/interests should 'count'? How should they be calibrated to typical physical and cognitive development with age, and to the inevitable individual differences in these typical patterns? Moreover, the EPDs themselves are likely quite plastic in expression. For example, I referred above to my son's extended phenotype that included a whole room of our house dedicated to his model airplane building and his university study plans. It's just my intuition, but I suspect that his EPD is to *build*, but *what* he focused on building in his childhood at least – we have yet to see what he does as an adult – was strongly influenced by one dramatic environmental event of pilots flying airplanes directly into buildings, and he might very well have focused on building and knowing about something very different had that not happened about when it did in his development.

Childhood in the context of EPD Theory

EPD Theory is about what captures an individual's attention and interest and what activities that individual tends to pursue in the absence of external demands. At its very heart, it is about correlation between genetic influences and environmental circumstances, or genetic influences that lead people to seek or avoid particular kinds of environmental experiences. For the very young child, freedom to seek all kinds of environmental circumstances is generally very limited, as is self-knowledge of what kinds of circumstances may be experienced positively and negatively. The very young child is thus heavily dependent on the physical circumstances with which she/he is presented, as well as on the social feedback she/he receives from others in response to initiated behaviours, for ongoing expression of EPDs. In addition to genetic influences on individual differences in the particular directions in which EPDs might be expressed, there are likely genetic influences on individual differences in the extent to which children are sensitive to social feedback about their choices of activities and their levels of performance in those activities, as well as genetic influences on willingness to persist with activities in the face of difficulties in carrying out the activity that are rooted in the activity itself, and even differences in the strengths of EPDs themselves. This means that expression of EPDs and development of skills and abilities associated with them depends not just on availability of whatever physical equipment may be helpful or on the presence of others who can teach relevant skills or set relevant examples, but also on the emotional qualities of the relevant experiences, the child's perceptions of those emotional qualities, and the way the child develops to cope with those perceptions. Inevitably, of course, family and more general cultural expectations for behaviour are layered on top of these individual-level person/environment transactions. The result is that cognitive and emotional development are closely intertwined, both with each other and with development of sense of agency and self-esteem.

For example, with respect to academic abilities, EPD Theory would not predict that children who have few EPDs in the areas stressed in school would necessarily achieve poorly in school (Johnson, 2010a). Rather, they would tend to adapt their level of engagement in school, and thus their achievement in school at least within some broad range, to that surrounding them. This adaptation would tend to be inspired by their parents in the early years, and increasingly by their classmates as they grow older. Because many if not most families send all their children to the same school, this would tend to generate primarily gene-shared environmental correlations. In contrast, children who have EPDs for particular academic subjects, or for something about the challenges posed by academic achievement, would create their own intellectual environments and gene-nonshared environmental correlations. They would also tend to have higher achievement in general, regardless of their particular EPDs for two reasons. First, many of the same reading, reasoning, and information processing skills are required in all academic subject areas, as well as in many areas of modern life not directly tied to school. And second, achievement in any school area tends to receive positive feedback from teachers, and often from parents and peers as well, leading to positive reinforcement of the efforts involved to further it.

Adaptation to the school environment is one of the most important childhood tasks, at least in most industrialized countries, both because so many social, occupational, and economic opportunities in these societies depend on academic achievement and educational attainment and because children spend such a large proportion of their waking hours in the school environment. Moreover, parents generally have expectations about their offspring's educational attainment and devote considerable attention to orienting their preschoolers to the coming school entry. Many of these parental expectations for their offspring likely, whether consciously or not, depend now, in a time when several years of school attendance have been essentially compulsory for several generations, on the parents' own experiences in adapting to the school environment during their childhoods (Johnson, McGue, & Iacono, 2007). That is, parents who did not adapt well themselves may tend to downplay the importance of adapting well and educational achievement and attainment more generally, relative to parents who did adapt well themselves, regardless of whether those parents who adapted well were able to attain all the education they might have liked themselves. To the extent this is true, it would serve as one of the primary mechanisms through which children who do not have strong EPDs develop their orientation and adaptation to the school environment. That is, it would be a form of family culture regarding education. In contrast, children with strong academically oriented (or not) EPDs would tend to pursue those EPDs despite their family cultures regarding education. Where their EPDs coincided with those of their families, the behaviours involved would tend to be reinforced and development of related skills and abilities fostered through evocative as well as active gene–environment correlation.

Adaptation to the school environment

Bandura (1986) has theorized extensively about how adaptation to the school environment takes place, and his ideas are relevant to adaptation to life more generally, as well as to actualization of EPDs. According to his *social cognitive theory, self-efficacy beliefs*, which I have above termed individual agency, have powerful influences on behaviour in general and school achievement in particular. This is because they shape the goals people select for themselves, the efforts they make to achieve those goals, the extent to which they persist when they encounter difficulties, and the degree to which the challenges they meet arouse anxiety and fear. Bandura hypothesizes that children make use of information from four sources to develop this sense of individual agency, the most powerful of which is their interpretations of their experiences with task mastery. When they believe themselves to have been successful, their individual agency is bolstered. Their individual agency is shaken when they feel that they have not met expectations, their own or those of important others. No one experience is usually crucial; rather, it is the accumulation of experience over time that matters. Thus individual agency is very plastic in young children and becomes increasingly stable over time, at least when experiences with attempts and success deliver consistent messages. Exploration of new task domains may, however, re-introduce plasticity, especially in individual agency specific to that domain. Importantly with respect to EPDs and scaffolding, Bandura posits that task performance that can only be achieved with help from others does less to build individual agency than successful performance that can be achieved on one's own. Moreover, successful performance on tasks perceived to be particularly difficult or that involve overcoming particular obstacles can be especially important in building individual agency. Clearly, the emerging sense of capacity or ability discussed above is one key aspect of this.

But Bandura's (1986) idea is also that the social environment is very important in building individual agency. That is, as the child's social environment becomes more complex and she/he becomes more aware of surrounding others with age and development, she/he makes increasing use of observations about the performances of these others in evaluating his/her own performances and further developing his/her own individual agency. As discussed above, one source of this social information is teachers and parents, who can be most constructive when they focus comments about the child's performance on the return on performance produced by effort. Likely much more important, however, is comparison with perceived social peers. Here, Festinger's (1954) theory of social comparison and the subsequent modifications to it inspired by empirical tests are important. Festinger posited that people desire to have accurate perceptions of their abilities, and they look to the apparent abilities of similar others to form those perceptions. Festinger emphasized that in many, particularly western, societies, people feel pressure for self-improvement and so compare their abilities with those of people who perform slightly better than they do. Though acknowledging that social comparison often plays this role, researchers such as Goethals and Darley (1977) and Wills (1981) noted that social comparison is also often used to bolster self-esteem through comparison with others who perform more poorly. The dual purposes of social comparison call attention to a major childhood challenge: at some level children clearly recognize that they are growing and developing, that their 'job' in the world *is* to grow and develop, so the orientation towards self-improvement is intrinsic to the state of childhood, and comparison with somewhat better-performing others comes naturally and painlessly with this. At the same time, it is all but impossible for them to avoid noticing the large individual differences in performance of and rates of learning to perform all tasks. Children naturally end up understanding where in the performance hierarchies of their peers they tend to fit, and must come to their own individual senses of self-esteem in light of this understanding. Comparison with others who perform less well than they do on valued tasks is one way to bolster self-esteem. Importantly, self-esteem may also be bolstered or maintained by rejection of the value of mastering a task at all, especially when there are others present who have similarly rejected its value.

Social comparison can thus serve different purposes in different contexts, and most research in this area has focused on identifying the contexts in which different kinds of comparison are used for different purposes (Dijkstra, Kuyper, van der Werf, Buunk, & van der Zee, 2008). I emphasize here, however, the importance to people, and in particular children, of forming accurate perceptions of their abilities, and the importance of social comparison in achieving those perceptions. Even narcissists, whom the rest of the world believes to hold exaggerated conceptions of their own abilities, want to believe that their (own exaggerated) conceptions are accurate, and much of their behaviour that others find obnoxious involves frantic efforts to obtain confirmation of the accuracy of their conceptions. Toddlers and preschool children tend to use social comparison primarily for information about how to perform rather than to evaluate their own performances. With entrance into elementary school, however, children increasingly compare their performances with those of others around them in order to see how they 'measure up'. This tends to coincide with a shift from orientation towards task mastery, or a more incremental theory of ability to orientation towards performance, to more of an entity theory of ability (Seidner, Stipek, & Feshbach, 1988), with all that this implies as discussed earlier. The extent to which this is true, however, reflects its cultural inculcation. For example, Butler and Ruzany (1993) compared the reasons that urban Israeli schoolchildren in first and second grades gave for looking at classmates' work to those given by otherwise similar children attending Kibbutz education. The Kibbutz educational programme is explicitly committed to interpersonal cooperation rather than competition and to learning for mastery. The Kibbutz children all gave task mastery reasons such as 'to see if I was doing it right' for their looking, while 43 per cent of the urban children gave performance-evaluative reasons such as 'to see if mine was better'. This study was important because it also assessed the degree to which the children appeared to have come to understand that there are relatively stable individual differences in performance capacity. The two groups of children expressed equivalent levels of understanding this, suggesting that it is possible to organize educational programmes to retain the performance advantages of holding incremental theories of ability, despite awareness that there is considerable truth to entity theories.

Most educational research comes from a perspective that it is important for children to maintain strong beliefs in their abilities, whatever their relative levels of ability. Researchers in this area have thus tended to see lower self-evaluations of ability as intrinsically unfortunate, regardless of actual levels of performance. For example, much has been made of observations of lower academic self-concepts among children attending schools with ability-selective entry standards than among children attending open-enrolment schools (e.g., Marsh & Hau, 2003). These observations raise some thorny questions about the kinds of goals for fostering children's individual agency that educators should be seeking to achieve. In open-enrolment classrooms, the level of instruction is generally such that children of very high academic ability are often bored, which can lead to disruptive behaviour. More to the immediate point, however, the work can come so easily to these children that they do not learn how to put forth effort because they never have to, and their senses of individual agency, at least with respect to academics, can become so strong that they come to believe they *should* not have to exert effort to master academic material. At the same time, social comparisons consistently inform these children that they do better than their classmates who have often worked much harder, which can also easily lead to an inflated sense of self-importance.

One common educational pattern is for primary school programmes to be open-enrolment, with increasing ability stratification as children progress through secondary school, and even more ability stratification at the university level. For children who have developed ideas that academic mastery (and performance superior to others) should come without effort, the realization of reality that comes with the increased difficulty of the material they are expected to master and the presence for the first time of others at least as gifted can be a shock, and can lead these children to forgo previously assumed goals (e.g., Marsh, 1991) simply because they have come to expect them to be easily attainable and do not know what to do if they are not. This points to the importance of children receiving ongoing opportunities to work on skill development at the upper boundaries of their current skills. It also suggests strongly that there is such a thing as one's sense of individual agency becoming too strong for one's own good, and one way to prevent that is to make sure that even extremely academically able children are aware that there are others equally able, and much more difficult material that no one masters without considerable effort. These issues apply to all forms of training in pursuit of skill excellence, such as athletic, music, and chess programmes.

There are analogous challenges in working with children at the other end of the ability dimension, whose motivation can easily be sapped by repeated observations that their progress is slower than that of most others. With such children, it can be necessary to separate them from the open classroom so that they have enough time to put in the effort required to master academic tasks at all. This can also be crucial in helping them to maintain senses of individual agency, but it can also lead them to develop unrealistic expectations for educational and occupational attainment that can in turn preclude their finding occupations that would be more suited to their abilities. This problem is accentuated in many industrialized nations, where many economic and social privileges are associated with high educational and occupational attainment.

Emerging as a person

During the first 10 years or so of life, children go from being almost completely helpless and dependent on those around them for their very sustenance to active agents in their continuing development who also play active and varied roles in the world around them. In discussing the processes through which this takes place, I have focused on the emergence of skills and abilities, particularly in the academic domain. I have done this for three primary reasons. First, children in many if not most parts of the world today spend large proportions of their waking time in school. Their relative success in adapting to that environment and their levels of achievement within it figure strongly in their occupational opportunities and economic prospects in adulthood. Thus adaptation to the academic domain is important. Second, the academic domain is in many ways simply a microcosm of the rest of the world. The issues involved in adapting to it are very similar to those involved in adapting to many other domains encountered in life. That is, the child's own motivation towards and interest in the activities and opportunities in that environment, in short possibly the child's EPDs for those kinds of activities, contribute strongly to that adaptation. But so also do a child's relative success in attempting those activities, the responses the child receives from the environment to that level of success, and the child's emotional and cognitive reactions to those responses. And, while the academic domain is fundamentally focused on individual performance, it is also fundamentally social. For a child, adapting to the social milieu involves adapting to the task performance and behavioural expectations of teachers and parents, but it also involves adapting to and building social relationships with the other children. And third, finally, there are large individual differences in the extent to which and ease with which children master the tasks presented to them in the academic domain. Whether we like it or not, these differences have proven stubbornly persistent in the face of large and well-intentioned efforts to minimize them.

People encounter many opportunities to invest their efforts in building skills in different domains. When interest in a particular opportunity is not high and/ or development of the necessary skills requires more effort than they prefer to expend, people tend to move on to something else. They also tend to downplay the importance, at least to them, of that activity, which helps to maintain self-esteem. The academic domain is no different from any other in this regard, but the life consequences of disregarding it are greater than for most domains. This is not because the academic domain is necessarily intrinsically of any particular importance in any hierarchy of what *should* matter in thinking about personal worth or sources of self-esteem. Rather, it is because, to varying degrees, societies in most industrialized countries have become organized so that the surest path to economic, environmental, and social security is through education, in the forms of both attainment and achievement. Thus (too) much of how children emerge as people in the world depends on both the kinds of schools they attend and their adaptations to those schools. And, because so much of the processes involved in adapting to school mirror those involved in adapting to other environments, the school adaptation processes have much to teach us. Particularly because it is only relatively recently even in western countries that school attendance became essentially mandatory throughout most of childhood, studying school adaptation can teach us not only about species-typical developmental processes more generally, but also about how cultures get under the skin to become second-nature, and how stable individual differences emerge and are maintained. We still have much to learn in this regard.

Further reading

Dawkins, R. (1982). *The Extended Phenotype: The Long Reach of the Gene*. Oxford: Oxford University Press.

Dijkstra, P., Kuyper, H., van der Werf, G., Buunk, A. P., & van der Zee, Y. G. (2008). Social comparison in the classroom: A review. *Review of Educational Research, 78,* 828–878.

Dweck, C. S. (2006). *Mindset: The New Psychology of Success*. New York: Random House, Ballantine Books.

Goethals, G. R., & Darley, J. M. (1977). Social comparison theory: An attributional approach. In J. M. Suls & R. L. Miller, *Social Comparison Processes: Theoretical and Empirical Perspectives* (pp. 259–278). Washington, DC: Hemisphere.

Hayes, K. J. (1962). Genes, drives, and intellect. *Psychological Reports, 10,* 299–342.

Johnson, W. (2010a). Extending and testing Tom Bouchard's Experience Producing Drive Theory. *Personality and Individual Differences, 49,* 296–301.

Scarr, S., & McCartney, K. (1983). How people make their own environments: A theory of genotype-environment effects. *Child Development, 54,* 424–435.

Adolescence: Transition to Physical Adulthood

At some level it is trite to say that adolescence is a period of transition: all developmental periods are periods of transition, and development itself is one long continuous transition. Despite this, the label sticks especially well for adolescence. Some of the reasons for this are very visible practical and legal ones: before adolescence, humans are immature in body, thought, action, and place in society, whether legal, economic or reproductive. At its close, they are physically mature, sexually and reproductively capable, and legally considered psychologically mature and thus responsible for their actions. Historically at least, they have also been expected to fill adult social, reproductive, and economic roles. Other reasons the transition label sticks are less tangible but often nonetheless seem apparent: prominent psychological theorists such as G. Stanley Hall have popularized the idea that the transitions of adolescence are particularly visible because it is a time of biologically driven 'storm and stress' (White, 1992), involving conflict with parents and other authority figures, volatile moods, and risky behaviour.

There is no question about the reality of the physical, sexual, practical and legal transitions from child-to-be-protected to responsible adult, though the specific ages at which various aspects of adulthood are recognized currently vary considerably from culture to culture, and have varied at least as much in the past. This variance in age of recognition suggests that the personal transition is far less sharp than societies find practical, and both scientific evidence and extra-legal social patterns bear this out. Psychologists are becoming increasingly aware that full cognitive maturity is attained considerably later than the most obvious aspects of physical maturity such as full adult height and reproductive capacity, and attainments of full adult economic, social, and reproductive roles are now commonly delayed well beyond adolescence in many industrialized countries. The 'storm and stress' characterization of adolescence, however, and especially its biologically driven origin, appears to be much more questionable than that of transition (Arnett, 1999). Evidence to date suggests that, for many, adolescence passes quietly. Still, there is a tendency for the period to be more stormy and stressful than other life periods for some, after recognizing considerable individual differences and cultural variation.

Perhaps more accurately, adolescence is a time of differentiation. During it, the individual's range of activities, skills, ideas, behaviours, and emotions becomes broader and more varied. At the same time, differences among individuals become more pronounced as adolescents take the first clear steps towards specific and different adult social roles. The greater diversity and complexity of behaviour and the new experiences this brings challenge the adolescent to synthesize it all into some kind of coherent perspective on the world. Those who meet this challenge tend to set themselves on course to cope well with adult responsibilities and roles, while those who do not are more likely to struggle to do this. Meeting the challenge involves becoming able to act autonomously within cultural norms, including appropriately regulating emotions; developing a sense of individual identity and purpose; and being able to form both close and working relationships with both same- and other-sex peers. Though substantial abstract cognitive development takes place during adolescence and contributes importantly to an individual's new skills, the domains in which these new skills are expressed are primarily social, involving peer and family relations, sexual activity, and occupational and economic roles. For this reason, this chapter focuses on social aspects of life to about the same degree as the previous one focused on cognitive aspects. First, however, I address the physical and sexual development associated with adolescence, as all aspects of social development during this period take place within its context.

Biological v. social changes

In Chapter 4, I discussed the fact that human neonates are very immature relative to those of other species, including our closest primate relatives. Associated with this, their brains grow extremely rapidly in the first year after birth, a process that consumes much more energy than purely physical growth. The neonatal extremity of dependence and rapidity of brain growth differ sufficiently in humans from other species that this period has been considered extended gestation by many. In addition to this unique feature of human development, there are two others (Hochberg, 2008). Contemporary chimpanzees, as well as, apparently, prehistoric hominids such as *Homininae Australopithecus afarensis* ('Lucy'), have two postnatal stages prior to adulthood: infancy and juvenility. Infancy transitions to juvenility with weaning from breast-feeding, and juvenility transitions to adulthood with sexual maturation. These stages are characterized by particular patterns of physical and brain growth, levels of sex hormones, and behaviours evidencing increasing cognitive maturity, self-reliance, and species-appropriate social integration. Humans, however, have four such periods. Following infancy, they experience a uniquely human childhood period of 2-4 years, roughly from ages 3 to 6, during which the rates of physical and cognitive growth are relatively slow but the cognitive, physical, and social developments of infancy are consolidated and a modicum of independence from overt parental support is attained. Consistent with its uniquely human status, human dentition during this childhood period is immature relative to other primates, motor coordination is relatively poor, and children are more dependent on their elders for food and protection. Childhood is followed by a 3-4-year juvenile period, roughly from ages 6 to 10 and analogous to that in other primates (though the ages for them are younger), characterized by initially increased physical growth; very low levels of sex hormones; and rapid acquisition of new cognitive capacities at the beginning of the period, followed by consolidation of the associated behaviours through the rest of the period. The period ends with almost-mature dentition, substantial capacity to look out for and feed oneself, and readiness for sexual maturation. It is probably no accident that in most modern societies children first attend formal schooling at the beginning of the juvenile period, and that the systematic process of synaptic pruning and reduction of brain grey matter begins around age 6 (Gogtay, Giedd, Lusk, Hayashi, Greenstein, Vaituzis, et al., 2004). Finally, humans experience a second period unique to our species: adolescence.

In many ways, the primary transition that takes place during adolescence is the emergence of reproductive capacity. Clearly, all other mammals also make this crucial transition. What sets human adolescence apart is the extended length of the transition period and the extensiveness and shape of the physical and brain growth that take place during it. This developmental extension apparently has the result that, relative to our primate relatives and hominid ancestors, modern humans have a lifespan about 50 per cent longer; relative suppression of body growth during the juvenile period followed by much prolonged brain growth in adolescence; lengthened legs and differently shaped pelvic regions; juvenile facial and other anatomical features, apparently resulting from the longer period of slow body development; and retention of juvenile playfulness and behavioural plasticity into adolescence and adulthood (Konner, 2010). From an evolutionary perspective, all of the features of this developmental extension appear to serve the purpose of offering time, neural and metabolic resources, and opportunity for the adolescent individual to master the relational and occupational skills necessary to function and reproduce successfully in the complex human social community. Of course humans also appear to have done a very good job of filling, even over-filling, the biologically available time.

The fact that extended physical development is associated with the complexity of the social environment highlights an often overlooked distinction between puberty and adolescence. Puberty involves activation of the complex of organs and glands in the endocrine system, including the hypothalamus, pineal body, pituitary gland, and gonads, that culminates in maturity of the reproductive system. Adolescence involves maturation of social and cognitive behaviours. They have distinct developmental sequences, but these sequences are orchestrated to result in an individual capable of producing both gametes and the kinds of behaviour that bring male and female gametes together. Their processes are both driven by the brain, but they involve separate neurobiological mechanisms and take place on their own timetables. At the same time, they are closely linked through reciprocal interactions (Sisk & Foster, 2004).

Mechanisms of puberty

In humans and other mammals, *gonadotropin-releasing hormone* (GnRH) is one of the primary hormones involved in maintenance of reproductive function, and its pulsated releases control the release of several other reproductive hormones. It is considered a *neurohormone*, which means that it is produced in specific neural cells for release at their neural terminals, in the case of GnRH primarily in the preoptic area of the hypothalamus. This area is also involved in other fundamental regulatory processes such as thermoregulation, thirst, non-rapid-eye-motion sleep, and male copulatory behaviour. GnRH is actively produced for a short period during late prenatal and/or early postnatal life to facilitate sexual differentiation and some programming of the central nervous system. Its production declines soon afterwards, and remains very low throughout childhood in humans and juvenility in all mammals. Its increase signals the beginning of puberty. Exactly what triggers this increase has been the subject of much research. Originally, of course, it was thought there might be a single such trigger, but it is becoming increasingly clear that this is not the case. Moreover, to date the primary successes have involved identification of signals that permit puberty to begin but do not actually set it in motion (Sisk & Foster, 2004).

Most of these permissive signals involve energy balance and some perception, clearly not conscious, that the individual has reached sufficient bodily size and formed an appropriate environmental niche, both social and physical, to sustain reproduction. Thus, for example, sensors in the hypothalamus monitor levels of metabolic fuel, insulin, glucose, and leptin in females to ascertain whether sufficient body mass has been attained to support pregnancy, and human females do not enter puberty until, in particular, they have accumulated sufficient adipose tissue. In seasonally breeding species, circadian rhythms may indicate day length that signals onset of the appropriate season. And sensory cues from other members of the species can provide permissive signals. It appears that multiple permissive signals are required, and that they are uniquely integrated in each species. This may not completely explain the onset of puberty, however, as these same factors are involved in other transitions in level of GnRH activity, such as the resumption of fertility after birth and lactation, restricted diet, high energy expenditure, or seasonal anestrus. Within species and particularly within humans, there is great individual variation in timing of both initiation and duration of puberty. The 95 per cent confidence intervals span a period of about eight years, but just before age 11 is a

jobs and better schools). Just to show how hard it can be to get all the facts straight even in what is intended as a conceptual demonstration, there were several errors in Robinson's calculations, and the actual correlation at the state level was -0.46 (Grotenhuis, Eisinga, & Subramanian, 2011). The presence of this error is interesting because Robinson's work was taken at face value for so long, effectively demonstrating the extent to which scientists tend to accept each other's work at face value. In his paper Robinson had demonstrated mathematically that the weighted *ecological* (group-level) correlation is the weighted difference between the overall individual correlation and the average of all within-group individual correlations, with the weights based on the full set of individuals in all groups. He then went on to try to show how this worked out in his literacy and immigration data, but it did not, and he spent quite some effort rationalizing that the weighting could only be considered approximate. As Grotenhuis, et al. (2011) demonstrated, all of Robinson's substantive conclusions were sound, despite his calculation errors, and his literacy and immigration illustration of the association between the two forms of correlation would have worked out correctly had he not made those errors.

Robinson's demonstration of the ecological fallacy involved much lower correlation at the individual level than at the group level, but the correlation present was in the same direction at the individual and group levels. Sometimes the correlations within groups are even in the opposite direction to the correlations across groups. Such actual reversal of associations is known as *Simpson's paradox*, in the context of categorical data. It is particularly likely to lead to mistaken inferences when researchers attempt to use ideas about causation at one level, group or individual, to make causal attributions about direction of association at the other. The name comes from a 1972 paper discussing the paradox (Blyth, 1972) that referred to an earlier paper (Simpson, 1951), but others had noted it before that. Again, though the problem is well known to professional statisticians, it is not well known even among consumers and users of statistical methodology, and it should be. An example from a medical study comparing the effectiveness of one kidney stone treatment with all others offers a good opportunity to highlight the complexities involved (Charig, Webb, Payne, & Wickham, 1986). Overall, the featured treatment was better than the others in the aggregate, and the study authors argued on this basis that it should be preferred, contrary to then-current practice. But, when patients with small kidney stones were considered separately from those with large stones, the reverse was true (Julious & Mullee, 1994): the featured treatment was less effective for those with either small or large stones. This paradoxical result occurred because the simpler and cheaper featured treatment had been considered inferior, so doctors had tended to administer it only to patients with small stones considered less severe, where it was 'good enough often enough'. They had tended to administer the other treatments to patients with large stones, creating a substantial bias in treatment by stone size. Overall, all treatments were more effective with small stones than large stones, indicative of the relative severity of large stones. Because the other treatments were more commonly administered to those with large stones, where any treatment was less effective, the overall effect was spurious.

This suggests that, in practice, the results within groups, or at the individual rather than group level, will be more accurate when the goal is to understand an individual-level phenomenon. To refer back to the original topic that motivated this detour, it would be a mistake to think that factors that operate to differentiate reproductive processes across species might also differentiate within species. As has been discussed by Pearl (2009), however, such a blanket conclusion is premature because of the intricacies of causal possibilities in observed associations between variables. If it were not, any division of data into more homogeneous groups, no matter how arbitrary, should generate better information about the association in question than the aggregate data. In this kidney stone example, separation of the data into groups of large and small stones generated more appropriate results, but the appropriateness depended on the fact that the treatment selected could not have any effect on the size of the stone (severity of the disorder) at the time the treatment was selected, but stone size directly did affect decisions on which treatment to select. Where causal directions are reversed with respect to group division, or, more commonly, unclear or absent, the overall combined results can be more appropriate.

For example (Pearl, 2009), consider two beginning baseball players. Adam maintains a batting average of 0.100 with 10 at-bats and Bob an average of 0.200 with 900 at-bats. Both are generally improving with practice, though their rates of progress are somewhat erratic. The next season Adam maintains a batting average of 0.300 with 90 at-bats, and Bob an average of 0.400 with 10 at-bats. Each season, Adam's average is lower than Bob's, but over the two seasons Adam's is higher than Bob's (0.27 v. 0.22). If I were the coach at the bottom on the ninth with the score tied, I would put Adam in the line-up before Bob. The inconsistency between the seasonal and overall comparisons is driven by the big difference in the two players' at-bats each season, the arbitrariness of the seasonal division with respect to their overall averages, and their relative apparent rates of improvement over that arbitrary division of time. The point here is that whether group or overall results are more relevant depends completely on how the causes involved in the grouping are related to the causes involved in the association of interest. When we do not know these relations, we cannot be at all sure of the appropriateness of inferring that associations that apply across groups also apply within those groups.

Actual reversals of association such as the examples just discussed are relatively rare (Marios & Perlman, 2009). Much more common is the situation where the ecological group-level correlations are much stronger than, but in the same direction as, those at the individual level. A classic example of this is a meta-analysis of the correlation(s) between socioeconomic status (SES) and academic achievement (White K. R., 1982). In the meta-analysis, which was motivated by the widespread belief that SES is strongly correlated with achievement, White noted that some studies had estimated correlations using aggregated levels of analysis such as school district, school, or region; others had used individual student as the level of analysis, and still others had mixed aggregate and individual data. The resulting correlations differed systematically, with those based on aggregate data clustering in the neighbourhood of 0.73, while those based on individual data averaged 0.22. Definitions of SES also differed substantially, and gave some indication of the causal mechanisms driving the difference: at the level of individuals, home environmental characteristics that were sometimes inappropriately used as measures of SES were correlated in between, averaging 0.55.

Debate surrounding how SES is involved in academic achievement persists to this day, but there is increasing recognition that both genetically and environmentally influenced parental characteristics drive their own educational attainment and SES, the school districts in which they choose to locate their families, the kinds of home environments they create for their children, and the genetic material associated with the personality and cognitive ability characteristics involved in academic achievement they transmit to their children. All this means that parents of high SES tend to congregate together in neighbourhoods and school districts, and these school districts tend to attract the best teachers as well, so that student achievement at aggregate levels varies substantially with SES. Nonetheless, within any aggregate grouping, the students who do come from other SES backgrounds than the one most predominant tend to be more similar to their classmates than to those of similar SES in other schools. This makes the individual the appropriate level of analysis in assessing the magnitude of correlation between family SES and academic achievement, but it also makes it very difficult to establish any specifically causal role for SES in achievement even at this level, due to the clear confounding of genetic and environmental influences on both.

The core theoretical rationale for the idea that individual age at puberty may be a facultative adaptation is that natural selection operates on reproductive success, so there should be links between environmental conditions and reproductive strategies, with r-K theory providing guidance as to the kinds of links that might be expected within species. Thus, for example, Belsky, Steinberg, and Draper (1991) suggested that a child growing up in a home environment characterized by conditions such as harsh parenting, internal family conflict, father absence, and/or unstable maternal–paternal relationships subconsciously learns that the world is precarious and family relationships cannot be counted on to make it any less so. Given this, the optimal reproductive strategy for a child in this situation, again subconsciously, is to mature early, initiate sexual behaviour as soon as possible, have multiple rather than fewer sexual relationships and many offspring, and invest relatively little in nurturing those offspring. The human genetic blueprint regarding sexual development and timing of puberty, they suggested, is sensitive to these environmental cues, so that, for example, the surge of GnRH that initiates puberty may be directly responsive to them.

The evidence that earlier timing of puberty is associated with familial dysfunction measured in many different ways is quite strong and consistent (as summarized, for example, by Belsky, Steinberg, Houts, Friedman, DeHart, Cauffman, et al., 2007), but this is not enough to establish the flexibility in timing and dependence of that timing on cues in the family environment that would be required if timing of puberty is a facultative adaptation, nor is it sufficient to specify the aspects of the environment that might be involved. As with academic achievement and SES, such an association could arise because of genetic and family environmental influences transmitted from one generation to the next linking early reproduction with harsh and unstable family circumstances in a manner that is fixed and not at all sensitive to any particular environmental cues. This is especially possible because, though we know there are cohort differences in timing of puberty in humans that must be environmental and we know there are individual differences within cohorts, we do not know either how the environment is involved in timing of puberty and reproductive strategy across species or what are the causal drivers of the differences among humans. Prominent variables that have been considered are father presence or absence, father psychopathology, and various definitions of harsh or insensitive parenting from either parent.

Belsky et al.'s (2007) investigation highlights many of the measurement and conceptual problems involved. They identified a large birth cohort of almost 9,000 infants born during selected 24-hour periods during the first 11 months of 1991 in 24 hospitals in 10 metropolitan regions of the United States, applied some rather loose eligibility criteria such as stable residential proximity to the lab examination sites and absence of serious medical problems in the infant and maternal substance abuse, and applied conditional random sampling within this birth group to obtain a participant sample that included at least 10 per cent single-parent households and 10 per cent mothers with less than high school education, thus assuring adequate representation of lower SES groups. Of the 1,042 European-American families recruited at infant birth, they were able to follow 756 into puberty, so their sample was of good size and, as such studies go, quite representative of the population. They put considerable effort into their procedures and the study extended over a period of 13 years. The families were visited at home when the children were 1, 6, 15, 24, 36, and 54 months old, and mothers and children came to the lab examination sites when the children were 15, 24, 36, and 54 months old and then in first and third grades. During these sessions the children were observed during play and interaction with their parents and completed various developmental tasks. Mothers completed demographic questionnaires and provided information about their own pubertal timing as well as ongoing information about family structure. The children then underwent carefully standardized annual physical examinations of pubertal status at the lab sites when they were in fourth through eighth grades.

Despite the mountain of data this generated and the detailed analyses it made possible, there were no significant effects of any of the variables on timing of puberty for boys. For girls, maternal age of menarche was the strongest predictor of child timing of puberty, indicating the likely importance of common genetic and possibly family cultural influences in driving the first-order associations among environmental conditions, age of menarche, and reproductive patterns. Harsh maternal treatment in childhood also predicted earlier menarche, but interacted with infant negative temperament in a counterintuitive way: those who were low in negativity experienced earlier puberty with less maternal harshness and later puberty than those high in negativity, at least when maternal harshness was high. Maternal sensitivity generated analogous results. The study authors thus shifted away from consideration of the involvement of family structure variables to parenting variables as the most likely mechanisms of association, but this is not consistent with many of the theoretical formulations that have been offered (Belsky, Steinberg, & Draper, 1991; Ellis, 2006).

Another extensive and well, but very differently, designed study encountered analogous difficulties. Tither and Ellis (2008) focused on paternal dysfunction and father absence as the triggers for earlier puberty. They reasoned that longer exposure to paternal dysfunction and/or father absence should have greater effect than shorter exposure, and they could control for common genetic and family cultural influences if they could find a group of sisters who were discrepant enough in age so that the difference in exposure should be notable, and whose parents had separated well before the younger sister reached puberty. This meant relying upon retrospective reports, with all the accuracy problems this creates, as information on the same developmental period had to be available for both sisters despite their age difference. Families with the necessary characteristics are also relatively rare. Tither and Ellis distributed 65,000 circulars seeking study participants in mailboxes in urban areas surrounding Christchurch, New Zealand to obtain 93 pairs of sisters from intact families in which the parents had remained together throughout both sisters' childhoods (to age 16) to compare with 68 pairs of sisters from disrupted families in which the parents had separated when the younger sister was on average 5.4 years old and the older sister was on average 11.8 years old. They were fortunate in that these groups of sister pairs were quite representative of the population from which it came.

Participants reported parental education and occupation, dates of parental separation as applicable, and their own ages of menarche, and rated the warmth of their relationships with their fathers and the extents to which their fathers showed symptoms of psychopathology during their childhoods. The latter two ratings were used to divide the sister pairs into three groups based on the extents of dysfunction in their fathers. There were no main effects of sister type (older or younger) or family type, but there was an interaction between the two such that older sisters in intact families tended to have earlier ages of menarche than younger sisters, but younger sisters in disrupted families tended to have earlier ages menarche than older sisters. The effect was tiny (2% of variance), but it is exactly the kind of effect that would occur if puberty were a facultative adaptation, and other theories explaining the association between timing of puberty and stressful environment would not predict this effect.

Things got more complicated with consideration of paternal dysfunction though. This was done only with the sisters from disrupted families, as very few of the sisters from intact families reported much in the way of paternal dysfunction. Again there were no main effects of sister type or level of paternal dysfunction, but there was an interaction between the two. This interaction accounted for more variance (10%), and indicated that younger sisters from families with serious paternal dysfunction tended to have earlier ages of menarche than those from the other two paternal dysfunction groups, and that younger sisters tended to have earlier ages of menarche than older sisters in families with serious paternal dysfunction. Yet in families without paternal dysfunction, this pattern was reversed, and, overall, sisters in families with moderate paternal dysfunction tended to have the latest ages of menarche, whether they were older or younger. There was no evidence that any of the menarche effects resulted from differences in total family birth order in the participating older or younger sisters between intact and disrupted families. Taken at face value, a longer period of father absence was associated with earlier menarche, especially when paternal dysfunction was serious, but father absence did not matter at all in the absence of paternal dysfunction. In fact, in such situations, older sisters tended to have earlier menarche than younger sisters.

The data thus did not tell a consistent story. If father absence mattered, it did so only when the father was seriously dysfunctional. This means that paternal dysfunction mattered too, but it should also mean that older sisters, who would have been exposed to the paternal dysfunction for longer before their fathers left their homes, should have had earlier menarche, which they did not. Of course family disruption situations are rarely as simple as a dysfunctional parent creating problems in the home for a while and then leaving it completely in the care of a fully functional mother. Fathers often remain in their children's lives after separating from their children's mothers, and mothers partnered with dysfunctional fathers often manifest substantial dysfunction themselves. Complicating things further, despite sometimes horrible histories of early abuse and neglect including malnutrition, poor children from developing countries adopted into affluent western families tend to enter puberty earlier than those who remain in the countries from which they came, and earlier than those who were born in the countries into which they were adopted (e.g., Teilmann, Pedersen, Skakkebaek, & Jensen, 2006). The degree of acceleration appears to vary with length of exposure to the original environment, as older adoptees tend to experience earlier puberty than younger adoptees. As noted above, improved nutrition in particular has been implicated as one of the reasons for the overall population trends towards earlier puberty, so these data do not reconcile easily with either the r-K strategy or better general environment theories of how timing of puberty may be regulated. Though the possibility that timing of puberty is a facultative adaptation to some form of early rearing stress is fascinating, empirical tests of the idea have generated far from clear results and have been riddled with methodological problems.

Brain development during adolescence

One area where developmental science has made huge strides over the last decade or so is in recognizing and characterizing the changes that take place in the brain during adolescence. The adolescent brain differs both from the child's brain and from the adult's brain in just about any area of morphology and function that has been studied, from overall grey and white matter volumes and structural connectivity to neurotransmission, electrophysiology, and stress reactivity (Steinberg, 2010). Its differences in humans mirror those between juvenile rodents and non-human primates and their younger and older counterparts, and maintain consistent associations between brain and behaviour

across sex and age groups in both normal and psychopathological development in humans. Though it is clear that there are individual differences within
these overall patterns and that these differences are responsive at least to some
degree to the environment, current understanding of normative overall developmental patterns and of patterns of development that may contribute to
overt psychopathology is much greater than understanding of more typical
individual differences.

Many of the most significant changes during adolescence take place in the
prefrontal areas of the brain. The overall pattern is a decline in grey matter
volume and associated cortical thickness and an increase in white matter
volume, which alters the ratio of grey to white matter and thus grey matter
density considerably. These changes have generally been attributed to synaptic
pruning and to continuing myelination of the synapses that remain, leading
to much greater efficiency of information processing as associations that were
formed but have not been reinforced by subsequent experience are shed and
myelination of those that remain increases speed of transmission across them.
The patterns of grey matter development vary across major brain regions. Grey
matter volumes in the frontal lobes peak around age 11, but volumes in the
temporal lobes do not peak until about age 14, and cerebellum volumes continue
to increase beyond that (Paus, 2005). White matter volumes continue to grow
well into adulthood, until around age 40 (Bartzokis, Lu, Tingus, Mendez,
Richard, Peters, et al., 2008). There are, of course, individual differences in
these patterns, including sex differences consistent with the overall pattern of
physical maturity: that is, females reach peak volumes 1-2 years before males.
In general, the primary sensorimotor cortices and frontal and occipital poles
reach maturity first. Development (increase in volume to a peak, followed by
decrease to some asymptotic point of relative adult stability) of the remainder
of the cortex follows from back to front (Gogtay & Thompson, 2010). The
superior temporal cortex matures last. It contains areas that integrate associations among information coming from different sensory areas, which suggests
that their maturity is dependent on the maturity of the areas that perform the
functions they integrate (Gogtay, et al., 2004). Individual differences within
these patterns have been related to IQ test scores, with brighter children and
adolescents showing greater increases in grey matter volumes, followed by
steeper declines in grey matter density (Shaw, et al., 2008), but the specific
patterns observed require replication.

Box 8.2   Using the normal to understand the abnormal

Articulation of normal brain developmental patterns has helped to identify abnormal
patterns associated with at least severe forms of psychopathology. For example, schizophrenia typically emerges in early adulthood, but in the last 20 years or so it has started

to be diagnosed, at least rarely, in childhood (Gogtay & Thompson, 2010). These childhood cases clinically resemble cases that were diagnosed in adulthood but have shown particularly poor responses to treatment, suggesting that they are all particularly severe and may be the same, as the patterns of grey matter loss that occur with disease onset in adults appear to be similar (Gogtay & Thompson, 2010). Initial brain scans of these childhood cases showed abnormally small grey matter volumes (Gogtay, 2008), and subsequent prospective studies showed that this occurred through the normal pattern of decreases in grey matter volume moving from the back of the brain to the front, but this normal pattern was greatly accelerated. The deviations from normal development appear to be specific to at least this form of childhood-onset schizophrenia. Another group of children manifesting early psychosis for which a diagnosis of schizophrenia was carefully ruled out showed a similarly distinctive but very different pattern of abnormality of grey matter development (Gogtay, Ordonez, Herman, Hayashi, Greenstein, Vaituzis, et al., 2007), and many of them were later diagnosed with bipolar disorder. In addition to these abnormal patterns of grey matter development, the myelination processes that continue throughout adulthood may be disrupted in schizophrenia (Peters & Sethares, 2004). Addressing this is complex, however, as current structural imaging techniques do not allow complete distinction between grey and white matter. Classification as grey matter depends on the overall intensity of the magnetic resonance imaging signal, and more white matter in one area will increase the overall intensity of that area's signal, making it more likely that the image at any particular voxel (particular place in the brain) will be classified as white matter (Gogtay & Thompson, 2010). This means that it is not completely clear whether the abnormality in these severe cases of childhood-onset schizophrenia is unusually steep decreases in grey matter or unusually steep increases in white matter.

Taken at face though, this abnormal grey matter development in these severe cases of early-onset schizophrenia is especially interesting because analogous progression has been observed in less severe cases that have not emerged until adulthood (Thompson, Bartzokis, Hayashi, Klunder, Lu, Edwards, et al., 2009). In these cases the decrease began later, appeared to affect only the regions for which normal decline begins later, and appeared to be less severe than in the childhood-onset cases. It also varied with form of medication treatment administered to stabilize the emerging psychopathology. Many consider the differences between these patterns in adult-onset and childhood-onset cases to reflect this aspect of the disease process involved in schizophrenia in interaction with normal adolescent development (Gogtay & Thompson, 2010). Additional evidence for this was provided by 52 siblings of childhood-onset cases who did not develop schizophrenia (Greenstein, Vaituzis, et al., 2007). These siblings showed early decreases in grey matter volumes in prefrontal and temporal brain areas in childhood similar to those of their siblings who went on to develop the disorder, but, in their cases, the decreases did not accelerate during adolescence and had normalized by age 20. These siblings who remained healthy also did not show the early parietal area decreases experienced by their less fortunate siblings. The normalization of their developmental trajectories was correlated with improvements in scores on a measure of life function as well. Though these data do little to indicate how function and grey matter development may be linked, nor what triggers or halts abnormal progressions, they do suggest rather strongly that abnormal grey matter development may be a genetic/familial marker of vulnerability to schizophrenia.

Both the difficulty of distinguishing clearly between grey and white matter using structural magnetic resonance imaging and increasing recognition that brain volumes cannot tell the full story of brain development during adolescence have led to increasing attention to changes in white matter during this period. Of course, this has been aided by the development of new imaging techniques, in particular diffusion tensor imaging, which most prominently reveals the architecture, organization, and structural integrity of white matter. Though there are still considerable methodological challenges in implementing this technique so that results can be consistently compared across studies, the data have been clear at least in showing that, as synaptic pruning takes place, the connections that remain are substantially reinforced, and, overall, brain regions become more strongly connected. Moreover, the degree of this improved connectivity is associated with increasing information processing ability and working memory capacity (Smithhorst & Yuan, 2010). One interpretation of the maturational process involved is that many task processes become increasingly automatized during this period as adolescents master many basic academic and other life tasks. This means that, as they are called on to perform these tasks, instead of having to reason through how to do them as they did when they were younger, they simply 'plug in' to the known approach, making it possible to carry out many more of these learned tasks much more efficiently. Within the brain, this reduces the need for 'fishing expedition' synapses, leading to synaptic pruning, and reinforces the connections needed for the learned tasks. It also frees up the remaining 'fishing expedition' synapses for new explorations.

Maintenance of goal-directed behaviour in adolescence

Apparently related to the increased efficiency made possible by increased brain connectivity is the improvement of ability to control and maintain direction of cognitive resources that takes place during adolescence. Reasoning and decision-making capacities develop rapidly during this period, and adolescents often manifest these capacities in ways very similar to adults. At the same time, they may do this very inconsistently, and this inconsistency can lead to inappropriate and even dangerous behaviour. Consistent mature decision-making requires the voluntary, conscious ability to guide behaviour in pursuit of a goal. One of the primary ways in which this ability and its development have been studied is through performance on tasks that require inhibition of so-called *pre-potent responses*. Such tasks pit a task-defined goal response against an instinctive or highly automatized response which must be suppressed. For example, in the anti-saccade task, an experiment participant is presented with a target such as a flash of light in one area of a screen and instinctively looks towards the target (pro-saccade). She/he is then told to look to the opposite position on the screen the next time the target is presented in the same place (anti-saccade). The participant must exert conscious control to suppress the instinct to look towards a flash of light and exert further control to direct the eyes in the opposite direction. The task proceeds through many repetitions, with some cued by preliminary signal to request pro-saccade response and others cued to request anti-saccade response. The participant's degree of cognitive control is measured as the difference in mean reaction times in the pro- and anti-saccade conditions, with smaller differences indicating greater control.

Another famous response inhibition task is the Stroop colour-word task. In one standard version of this task, which has spawned many variations, the participant sees a list of words for colours, such as 'red', 'blue', etc. They are each printed in an ink colour different from that indicated by the word itself. First the participant reads the words, and then the participant says the names of the colours of ink in which the words are printed. Because reading of highly familiar words becomes very automatized, the participant must suppress the tendency to focus on the word's content in order to respond correctly with the ink colour in which the word is printed. The participant's degree of cognitive control is measured as the difference in time required to name the ink colours and the time required to read the words. Again, smaller differences indicate greater control. Many nonhuman primates can be taught to perform variants of these tasks with great accuracy.

Though designed to measure ability to maintain cognitive control, these measures tend to be correlated with measures of sensation-seeking that are in turn correlated with engagement in risky behaviours of the kinds common in adolescence (Chambers, Taylor, & Petenza, 2003). They also tend to show impairment in major psychopathology, much of which emerges during adolescence (Luna & Sweeney, 2004). Infants can perform variants of these tasks (Diamond & Goldman-Rakic, 1989), and they recruit the brain's prefrontal cortex in order to do so, despite the substantial immaturity of this region in infancy. But accuracy and speed of task performance improve considerably throughout childhood, consistently across cognitive control tasks (Luna, Padmanabhan, & O'Hearn, 2010). This indicates that what develops is not the ability to inhibit a pre-potent response *per se*, but ability to do so efficiently and consistently.

Box 8.3   Can fMRI tell us what develops in the brain?

Functional magnetic resonance imaging studies (fMRI) have been instrumental in revealing what develops. These studies indicate which parts of the brain are activated when people carry out specific kinds of activities. When brain neurons are activated, blood flow increases to the area of activation, bringing oxygen and glucose to support the neural activity. fMRI can pick up the rate of blood oxygenation in brain *voxels*. A voxel is an arbitrary cube of brain tissue. To carry out an fMRI scan, a map of the participant's brain, or the specific region of interest within the brain, is effectively placed on a grid defined by the scanning process, and this grid determines the voxels, and thus the resolution of the scan. This means that full brain scans tend to have larger voxels and thus lower resolution than scans focused on specific regions, with sizes typically ranging from 1 mm to perhaps 5 mm. A voxel may contain a few million neurons and tens of billions of synapses, varying with voxel size and brain region. Because all parts of the brain are constantly receiving blood flow, what is informative in using fMRI is comparison between what are known as blood oxygen level-dependent (BOLD) responses when the participant carries out some specified mental activity and BOLD responses when the participant is resting quietly, or performing, for example, a version of the target task that is considered to be less demanding. This means that inferences about brain regions involved in particular tasks are completely dependent on the accuracy of the investigator in assessing the specific mental processes involved not just in performance of the target task but also in the activity with which the target task must be compared, as well as on the relevance of the grid used to locate the assessed voxels within the individual brain that has been imaged.

Because it takes the vascular system time to respond to the brain's need for energy and oxygen, the BOLD response lags inception of neuronal activity by 1-2 seconds. The response itself lasts over 10 seconds, rising continuously and exponentially for 4-6 seconds, remaining at that level if activity must be maintained, and then falling at about the same rate, to a level lower than the baseline. BOLD response is typically sampled several times throughout this period. It is generally regular enough that it is not essential to sample more often than every 1-2 seconds. More important is the length of time it takes to perform the task itself, and the proportion of this time in which any particular brain region must be involved. This varies with participant experience with the task and with factors such as boredom or lapses of attention. The signal is also augmented by various sources of noise, including participant head movement, random brain activity, and competing signals from the scanner itself. These sources of noise often contribute as much to the signal received as the neuronal activity of interest, so studies generally repeat any single stimulus of interest several times. As the noise is random, this repetition improves ability to identify the portion of the received signal that is of actual interest. The better resolution possible with smaller voxels and focus on brain regions rather than the whole brain might make it seem better to work with regions of interest, but smaller voxels have fewer neurons and lower blood flow, so they generate smaller signals that are more difficult to distinguish from noise. They also take longer to scan, which can result in participant discomfort and thus loss of the signal completely.

To draw conclusions about people in general, it is necessary to scan more than one individual, and thus to do something to average images across individuals. Because the measure obtained must be a contrast between two images this creates measurement complications in addition to those just described and the potential difficulties created by the task performance assumptions. The averaging is commonly accomplished by adjusting all the participant brains to a common brain reference atlas. Two of these are in common use. The first, known as Talairach for its compiler, is based on the brain of a single elderly woman. The second highlights the problems with this, though it has problems of its own. It is known as the Montreal Neurological Institute index, and is a probabilistic map that was created by combining scans from more than a hundred individuals. The adjustment is accomplished by stretching, squeezing, and warping the individual participant's brain image to minimize the differences between it and the reference. Following this, each voxel is analysed separately, a process requiring further mathematical assumptions about the pattern of the BOLD response over time and multiple statistical tests, with the attendant potential for inflation of falsely positive statistical results.

Despite the many complications involved in analysing fMRI scans (see Textbox), which have undoubtedly generated many spurious results (Vul, Harris, Winkielman, & Pashler, 2009), fMRI studies rather consistently indicate that cognitive control or response inhibition is exerted via activity in the ventrolateral prefrontal cortex (VLPFC). Within this general region, brain activity involved in response inhibition tasks changes with age, with activity in some subregions appearing to increase with age while activity in other subregions appears to decrease with age, though results have not been consistent across studies (Luna et al., 2010). Differences with age in activity in other brain regions have also been observed. In particular, reductions in activity with age in dorsolateral prefrontal cortex (DLPFC) tend to be associated with increased activity in temporal and parietal brain regions. As noted above, the DLPFC undergoes substantial development during adolescence and its connections with the temporal and parietal regions are also strengthened considerably but with some timing lag. As well, adolescent performance on these inhibition tasks reaches adult levels after substantial increases over childhood levels. Researchers have interpreted the overall pattern of observations as indicating that the increasing maturity of the DLPFC makes possible the adult-level task performance, but the remaining relative immaturity of connections with the medial and temporal lobes that can execute the necessary processes more automatically means that exhibition of adult-level performance requires more effort by adolescents than by adults (Luna, et al., 2010).

Emotion and incentive-driven behaviours in adolescence

This maturity imbalance is consistent with current models integrating adolescent emotional experience and incentive-driven behaviours with brain development (Somerville, Jones, & Casey, 2010). There is considerable evidence that adolescents, particularly early adolescent females, are at greater than average population risk of experiencing significant symptoms of depression and anxiety that interfere with everyday functioning for at least two weeks (Eaton, et al., 2007). Adolescent negative emotions appear to be not only more frequent, but also more intense (Larson, Muneta, Richards, & Wilson, 2002). Negative emotional experience during adolescence has been the focus of more exploration than positive emotional experience, likely because of its clinical connections, but positive emotional experience also appears to be exaggerated in adolescence (Wahlstrom, Collins, White, & Luciana, 2010). This suggests that it is emotional lability overall, via heightened sensitivity to environmental stimuli, that is increased during adolescence. At the same time, it is plain that there are considerable individual differences in the extent to which this is true. Many adolescents do not seem to experience much emotional lability at all, compared to their younger selves, while others do so extremely. Possibly this occurs because the overall rapid pace of developmental changes, coupled with differences in the rates of those changes in specific aspects of brain and body, change overall balance among these various aspects, making the whole system subject to environmentally induced perturbations that increase variance in emotional response patterns. These intense emotional experiences may in turn introduce still greater variance into the overall developmental process.

Along with this often-but-not-universal greater emotional lability, adolescents often manifest lack of ability to exert control over behavioural impulses, leading to poor behavioural choices that often have risky and potentially dangerous consequences (Steinberg, 2008). Adolescents appear to be able to comprehend and reason about the outcomes of potential behaviours clearly and appropriately in the abstract. At the same time, when presented with the same situations in real life, in the right (or perhaps 'wrong' is more apt characterization) contexts such as in the presence of peers, adolescents often do not use these abilities and instead make poor judgements and behavioural choices. This form of mismatch between reasoning ability about behaviour and actual behaviour increases between childhood and early adolescence, and then decreases again between late adolescence and early adulthood. Researcher consensus is growing around models that propose that the mismatch arises because the brain regions most involved in emotional and motivational processes mature earlier than those involved in cognitive control, in particular behavioural inhibition. The brain regions involved in emotional and motivational processes are primarily subcortical, including the amygdale and ventral striatum, while the brain regions involved in cognitive control primarily lie in prefrontal cortex, so this fits with the later progression of brain development in the prefrontal regions. In no sense, however, should these models be interpreted as implying that these structural and functional brain developmental processes take place either in lockstep across individuals or in isolation from the environment. Perhaps especially importantly, these subcortical brain regions appear to be centrally involved in the processing of both reward and social cues. Though the posited mismatch models display both consistency with behavioural and brain data and developmental coherence, they remain highly speculative at present (Steinberg, 2008).

Models to understand risk taking in adolescence

One of these models posits that dopamine activity is central to the mismatch. Coincident with puberty, but apparently not directly related to it, dopamine processing within the brain undergoes substantial reorganization. Dopamine is one of the neurotransmitters most heavily involved in processing reward or appetitive stimuli. There is an initial increase in dopamine receptor density shortly after birth in the subcortical brain regions, followed by reductions in the densities of dopamine receptors in subcortical regions that begins around the age of 9 or 10 and is followed by analogous reductions in cortical regions

(Sisk & Zehr, 2005). In rodents, these reductions appear to be more dramatic in males than in females. Persistence of greater dopamine receptor density in prefrontal cortical brain regions after it has fallen off in the subcortical regions means that dopaminergic activity in the prefrontal cortical regions is much higher in early adolescence than in late childhood or later adolescence. There may be several ways to understand the behavioural consequences of this greater dopaminergic activity. One is that the increased activity is similar to that seen in adults with disorders involving low levels of dopamine function (Gardner, 1999), almost as if the presently 'extra' dopamine receptors in the prefrontal cortex were searching frantically for the opportunity to do their job, leading to pursuit of behaviours targeted to bring reward and thus increase release of dopamine. That is, the adolescent would be experiencing the world as relatively not much fun compared with childhood and thus be seeking that old level of fun through greater and greater sensory stimulation.

Another possibility is perhaps more consistent with observations of greater brain activity in subcortical regions in response to reward during adolescence (Galvan, Hare, Parra, Penn, et al., 2006). This is that the increase in reward-seeking behaviour results from greater dopamine levels reaching prefrontal regions of the brain in response to given levels of reward stimulation, due to immature and thus incomplete buffering between subcortical and prefrontal regions. If this is the case, the adolescent would be experiencing the world as much more fun than in childhood, thus increasing the salience of rewarding stimuli (Dumont, Anderson, Thompson, & Teicher, 2004). Despite the apparent contradiction in these two possibilities, it is not yet possible to put together evidence to distinguish between them (Wahlstrom, Collins, White, & Luciana, 2010). It seems likely that, though the idea of imbalance between subcortical relative maturity and prefrontal cortex relative immaturity (Somerville, Jones, & Casey, 2010) may have merit, and dopamine may play a substantial role in this imbalance, dopamine is far from able to tell the whole story. In particular, the relative immaturity of prefrontal compared to subcortical brain regions may mean that the prefrontal regions cannot as efficiently communicate with the subcortical regions involved in behavioural inhibition as they will be able to in adulthood. If adolescents thus require greater exertion of effort or brain energy in order to control behavioural impulses, the necessary energy simply may be more often depleted.

Another model posits that the increases in circulating gonadal hormones are central to the mismatch between relative maturity of sensation-seeking behaviours and cognitive abilities and relative immaturity of abilities to inhibit impulsive behaviours. Of course these models are not mutually exclusive, and dopamine-associated sensation/reward-seeking tendencies may be enhanced by the increased levels of circulating gonadal hormones during adolescence (Sisk & Zehr, 2005). This is not meant to imply that the behavioural and brain changes that take place during adolescence are directly tied to puberty as animal models make clear that many are not (Sisk & Foster, 2004), as discussed above. Rather, it is meant to suggest that the coincidence of timing between these brain and behavioural changes and puberty could make them act to reinforce each other. In particular, neural circuits may be sensitive to the newly circulating gonadal hormones, and primed to receive them in order to allow the emergence and maturation of adult social behaviours associated with mate seeking as well as overtly sexual behaviours (Sisk & Zehr, 2005). This would imply that these hormones exert organizational effects on the brain during adolescence, analogous to those exerted during gestation. This would make sense from an evolutionary perspective, as it would facilitate development of the many very consistently reported sexual dimorphisms in reproductive behaviour. It is also consistent with observations of sex differences in global changes in brain structure and in trajectories of maturation of the amygdale and striatum (Somerville, Jones, & Casey, 2010), as well as with individual differences in these patterns within the sexes. That is, some of these changes appear to be more closely linked to level of pubertal development than to age, though others appear to be linked more closely to age than to level of pubertal development.

Gonadal hormones as links between brain and social development?

Consistent with this difference in linkage, hormonal changes appear to be especially related to social behaviours, again in ways that contribute to both sexual dimorphisms and individual differences within the sexes. Adolescents of both sexes appear to be particularly strongly subject to peer influence, and to enjoy spending time with peers (Larson & Richards, 1991) based on self-reports, and their heightened emotional sensitivity, coupled with increasing cognitive abilities to appreciate the mental states of others (Parker, Rubin, Erath, Wojslawowicz, & Buskirk, 2006), may leave them especially vulnerable to both the potential social rewards associated with peer approval of engagement in risky activities and the potential social pain associated with ostracism for failure to engage in risky behaviours in which others are participating. Gardner and Steinberg (2005) found empirical evidence for this. They had adolescents and adults play a video game simulating car driving either alone or in the presence of two friends. When playing in the presence of friends, adolescents engaged in more than twice as many risky driving manoeuvres as when playing alone, but driving performance of adults did not differ whether they played alone or in the presence of friends.

Several studies in rhesus monkeys provide suggestive evidence of the processes that may be involved in humans. Wallen and Winston (1984) studied reproductive behaviours in four male and five female monkeys. The monkeys were observed while in a single multi-animal mixed-sex group situation and also in pairs, so that each female was paired with each male. When in pairs, males initiated more sexual behaviours with females than when in the group situation, and the frequency of initiation did not vary with female reproductive cycle as it did in the group situation. Female behaviour differed similarly, but not all aspects of reproductive behaviour showed differences. Perhaps most importantly, in the group situation, females were approached and threatened by other females more often around their times of ovulation than at other times. This suggested that the group situation is necessary to bring out the full range of female reproductive-related behaviours, and that the prospect of threat may deter especially less dominant females from approaching males in group (and more 'natural') situations.

Male rhesus reproductive behaviour may be affected by social status as well, and experience during puberty may be important in establishing individual patterns. Coincident with increasing testosterone levels in puberty, male monkeys mount females with increasing frequency. Wallen (2001) observed males living a large mixed-sex group before puberty and then throughout puberty, assaying testosterone levels throughout the observation periods. She observed that there was no direct association between testosterone levels and frequency of female mounting behaviour. Instead, successful sexual experience, defined as ejaculation, was associated with greater sexual initiation, as even males with low testosterone levels frequently mounted females once they had had a single successful sexual experience, but not frequently before. This has been interpreted as indicating that testosterone is important in motivating appetite for sexual experience and making it possible for young males to overcome hesitation to approach older females, but it is learning of the rewarding ejaculations experience that results that reinforces and maintains the behaviour.

This has been corroborated by experimental manipulations that suppress testosterone in male monkeys. For example, with testosterone suppression, males in social groups including other males showed much greater decreases in sexual behaviour than did males in social groups in which they were the only males (Davis-daSilva & Wallen, 1989). And sexual behaviour decreased more rapidly with testosterone suppression in monkeys low in the dominance hierarchy and those with less sexual experience than in those who were higher-ranking or had more sexual experience Wallen (1999). It is well known that testosterone levels both drive expression of aggressive and sexual behaviour and respond to the consequences of aggressive and sexual behaviours. That is, higher levels are associated with greater tendencies towards these forms of behaviour, but how aggressive or sexual interchanges turn out also affect testosterone levels. When, for example, a male wins an aggressive interchange, testosterone levels tend to rise, but the opposite occurs when a male loses an aggressive interchange, in both humans and monkeys. And sexual and other reproductively oriented behaviours in females vary with hormonal levels as well, consistently across the menstrual cycle but also with more specific fluctuations.

This suggests that individual differences in the mismatch between brain development associated with age and that associated with puberty can contribute to individual differences in the probabilities of involvement in situations that are socially and/or physically risky in humans as well. Moreover, once it takes place, this involvement can have long-term consequences that permanently alter developmental trajectories in more general personality, cognitive, and demographic characteristics. For example, a delinquent activity that results in an arrest, or an unintended pregnancy, can change a life forever. These are nice examples also because they make clear that chance, as well as characteristics inherent in the individual and the environmental context, plays a strong role in the developmental process. Many more adolescents are involved in delinquent activities, particularly relatively minor ones, than are actually caught, and many more young girls have sexual intercourse than actually become pregnant. Aside from this random element, however, the idea of adolescent maturational mismatch strongly suggests that individual differences in timing of puberty may contribute to individual differences in the development of many other characteristics.

A tendency for girls who enter puberty earlier than their peers to experience more detrimental outcomes in many areas of life has long been noted (Mendle, Turkheimer, & Emory, 2007). Some studies have also indicated that girls who mature late tend to experience more positive life outcomes, though these data are much more mixed. Data on boys are much more mixed and also more limited, so I will discuss the sexes one at a time, starting with females. In considering these observations, the focus is not so much on actual timing of puberty, as it was in exploring the idea of pubertal timing as facultative adaptation, but on timing of puberty for an individual relative to that of those in the same social group. For example, in a study of girls in ballet schools, where competition for roles and striving for the ideal ballerina body type is often intense and menarche is often later than in the overall population, girls who matured on time by population standards considered themselves to be early and were more likely to display negative personality and behavioural characteristics than their fellow students who matured late by population standards but on time within their immediate student groups (Brooks-Gunn & Warren, 1985). This is not to say, however, that, if timing of puberty is a facultative adaptation, it could not also be calibrated to timing in the surrounding social group. It is instead to consider the simple measure of timing of puberty relative to the relevant social group alone. There are several possible reasons that early puberty may contribute to detrimental developmental trajectories in girls. These reasons should not be considered mutually incompatible; all could be important, to varying degrees in different individuals.

Associations between delinquency and timing of puberty in girls

First, from a psychosocial perspective, when girls become physically mature they become both attractive to and attracted by young males, drawing the girls into social situations that involve at least the preliminaries of sexual encounters and the social accoutrements that tend to go with them, such as parties that involve late nights and alcohol and drug use. Because timings especially of cognitive but also emotional and motivational maturity are more associated with age than pubertal stage, the maturity mismatch that girls who enter puberty early experience may be greater than average, placing greater than average strain on the cognitive resources available to them to make wise behavioural decisions in these exciting but risky situations. If this is an important reason for the association with emergence of behavioural problems, it would be reasonable to expect that there would be considerable variability in the magnitudes of the association in different cultural groups. It might also make sense that the magnitudes would vary with what Arnett (1995) termed *breadth of socialization*. Arnett categorized societies as broad or narrow, but the idea of breadth is likely much more dimensional in nature. It refers to the extent to which cultures, family groups, and/or societies place clear expectations and restrictions on personal behaviour, especially sensation-seeking and sexual behaviour. Arnett suggested that narrowly socialized groups tend to be smaller, so that most people in the group know each other, as well as less technologically advanced and characterized by greater uniformity of behaviour, less independence and creativity, as well as less manifestation of risky behaviours. Broadly socialized groups, most common in western industrialized countries, in contrast, tend to be larger and more diffuse and thus anonymous, to have few expectations for behaviour, to value autonomy, self-expression, and creativity, but to see greater expression of risky behaviour. In narrowly socialized groups, we might expect relatively little association between timing of puberty and detrimental outcomes, with greater association in more broadly socialized groups.

There is some evidence that this is the case. Anthropological studies indicate that the association with problem behaviour is largely confined to the western world. For example, the Kipsegis of Kenya actually consider early menarche to be advantageous (Borgerhoff Mulder, 1989); parents receive greater compensation when they marry off their early-maturing daughters. Moreover, the magnitude of the association can vary with breadth of socialization in the immediate social group. For example, Caspi, Lynam, Moffitt, and Silva (1993) examined the relation between delinquency and timing of puberty in part of the Dunedin Multidisciplinary Health and Development Study sample. The sample for this study was recruited from all births in New Zealand between April 1972, and March 1973, and still living in the area of Otago three years later. It consisted initially of 1,037 individuals (91% of those deemed eligible) who were assessed every two years during childhood and have been assessed at intervals of 3-6 years since age 15, with continuing follow-ups planned. Study retention has been remarkable; at age 32, 96 per cent of all study participants still living were assessed, made possible at least in part no doubt because participants are flown back to New Zealand for follow-up assessment from anywhere in the world.

In considering the association between timing of puberty and delinquency, Caspi, et al. (1993) noted that rates of delinquent behaviour have tended to be higher in mixed-sex than all-girl schools, likely at least partly simply because adolescent boys are more likely to be involved in delinquent activities than are adolescent girls. In New Zealand, same-sex schools were still quite common for this cohort. Caspi, et al. were able to obtain information about the sex composition of the schools attended for 297 female Dunedin participants still living in the Otago area at age 13. From prior assessments, they had data about family environment, ranging from level of family conflict to achievement orientation to moral-religious orientation. They compared the data reported by the parents of the 165 girls who entered same-sex secondary schools with those reported by the parents of the 132 who entered mixed-sex schools. There were no significant differences on these measures, suggesting that any differences in the groups' rates of delinquency should not be attributed to pre-existing family values that led to school choice.

Caspi, et al. (1993) found that, at age 13, rates of delinquency were higher among early- and on-time-maturing girls than among late-maturing girls in both school settings, but that this was especially true of early-maturing girls in mixed-sex schools. Results were similar for participant reports of awareness of delinquent activities among their peers, but on-time-maturing girls, as well as early-maturing girls, in mixed-sex schools also tended to be more aware of peer delinquent activities than their counterparts in same-sex schools. By age 15, rates of illicit (and thus more seriously delinquent) activities of early-maturing girls overall had declined substantially in both kinds of schools, but especially in the mixed-sex schools. Among on-time-maturing girls, however, they had risen overall, but only among girls attending mixed-sex schools, and not to the level shown by the early-maturing girls in mixed-sex schools at age 13. Rates among late-maturing girls were consistently the lowest and did not vary with age. Moreover, the association between ages 13 and 15 delinquency in girls in same-sex schools was significantly higher than that in girls in same-sex schools (0.63 v. 0.33 after adjustment for pubertal timing, early behaviour problems, and social class). Among girls attending mixed-sex schools, the association between early maturity and delinquency appeared to be mediated by awareness of peer delinquency in girls with no history of behaviour problems, but awareness of peer delinquency appeared to accentuate delinquency in girls with such a history regardless of timing of puberty. Thus Caspi, et al. suggested that peer relations played a major role in drawing especially early-maturing girls into delinquent activities. There were, however, indications that these effects were relatively limited to the period of peak pubertal change for each individual, as rates of delinquency had started to drop off in early maturers by age 15, but were still rising among on-time maturers. The study did not pursue this question long enough to ascertain this clearly, however.

This suggests that, however important psychosocial reasons for an association between early puberty and detrimental social outcomes may be, an additional set of biological reasons may also be important. That is, the hormonal, morphological, and brain changes taking place during puberty may themselves place early-maturing girls at greater social risk. As discussed above, pubertal changes are associated with increased emotional lability, sensation seeking, and risk taking, with development of judgement and self-regulatory capacities lagging somewhat behind. This applies to all, no matter the relative timing of puberty, but there is some evidence that degree of emotional lability, sensation seeking, and risk taking varies with hormonal levels, and early-maturing girls both begin the hormonal surges at earlier ages than their peers and secrete more of the hormones, with higher production levels lasting well into adulthood (Apter, Renila, & Vikho, 1989). This may be accentuated by the tendency for early-maturing girls to progress more rapidly through the pubertal developmental stages (Apter & Vikho, 1983), increasing the degree to which they might be likely to feel isolated and different from their childhood friends and thus more likely to seek and respond to new and more risky social overtures. In addition, the biological consequences of puberty itself may simply hit girls rather hard. In particular, menarche is a rather sudden and dramatic indication of physical development and can be shocking even to girls well prepared for it; because they are early by definition, early maturers may be less psychologically prepared when it occurs (Ge, Conger, & Elder, 2001). At least in western nations, menarche is typically experienced and remembered negatively; the oncoming maturity it signals may be welcomed, but it also tends to bring embarrassment and thus self-consciousness and even secretiveness (Koff & Rierdan, 1996), as well as, for some, bloating and painful cramps.

Finally, though it has received far less research attention, it is possible that there may be transgenerational correlations between genetic and environmental influences that place early-maturing girls at greater risk for detrimental social outcomes. These correlations could be driven simply by the social sequelae associated with early sexual activity, but they may also be much more complex than this. From this simple perspective, girls who mature early are more likely to bear children early, which can short-circuit their educational careers, leaving them with few opportunities to obtain jobs that pay well. If they do bear children very young, they are more likely to end up as single parents, simply because their partners are more likely also to have been young and thus rather economically and/or personally immature. Even if their partners remain present, their partners' educational careers may also have been short-circuited, with the result either way that the family group is more likely to have to cope with the chronic stresses of poverty and the greater risk of psychopathology and chronic physical illness that appears to result (Doughty & Rodgers, 2000; Rowe, 2002). Because timing of puberty is genetically influenced, the offspring of early parents who experience these consequences are likely not just to grow up in these relatively difficult circumstances, but to be genetically predisposed to experience early puberty in their own rights. If timing of puberty is in fact a facultative adaptation, this tendency could be exaggerated by the environmental circumstances in which they grow up. The result could be a pattern of increasingly strong links between early maturation and detrimental social outcomes from generation to generation in some families. These tendencies could be enhanced by analogous selection processes involving development of friendships with others with similar life patterns and interests in engaging in risky activities. The behavioural sciences badly need studies and methodologies that can explore this kind of possibility objectively, as any and all of those mentioned could be involved.

Other associations with pubertal timing in girls

Depression is another one of the detrimental outcomes that has been associated with early puberty in girls, and the association has clearly been linked to timing of puberty rather than pubertal status (e.g., Ge, Conger, & Elder, 2001b). Early-maturing girls experience higher rates of depression than do both boys and later-maturing girls. This is consistent with the overall pattern of sex differences in the prevalence of depression: there are few if any sex differences in childhood, but in adulthood rates are generally considerably higher in women than in men, and adolescence marks the transition period. Girls entering puberty early are also more likely to report somatic symptoms such as abdominal pain, headaches, and upset stomachs than their peers (Aro & Taipale, 1987). With perhaps broader roots in modern society, early-maturing girls are also more likely to suffer from eating disorders (e.g., Keel, Fulkerson, & Leon, 1997). As noted above, the onset of menarche requires some increase in proportion of body fat. Modern society, particularly in western, industrialized countries, appears to be very conflicted about body weight, perhaps especially in females, with obesity rates rising sharply yet heavy emphasis on slimness as an aesthetic ideal. Experiencing the development of increased body fat associated with puberty well before peers may be particularly likely to trigger disordered eating patterns, especially in athletes and dancers for whom it can affect ability to perform in an area in which considerable sense of personal identity has been invested.

Importantly, overall timing of puberty (early, on-time, and late) is associated with academic performance in girls, but in a manner that does not appear to be associated with development of cognitive abilities themselves (Mendle, Turkheimer, & Emory, 2007). This is a difficult topic to explore because academic achievement tends to be relatively stable, and also linked to behaviour problems at school. In turn, behaviour problems are linked to lower engagement and interest in school, and smaller likelihood of continuing education beyond the high school level (e.g., Stattin & Magnuson, 1990). This stability means that in many cases the academic problems precede puberty, but early puberty and its sequelae may accentuate them. This is one area where selection effects may be especially likely. Unfortunately, failure to obtain a good education can have lifetime consequences for occupational and financial success in modern western societies, and these consequences can easily extend from one generation to another. There is little research directly examining this, but what data there are indicate that controlling for sociodemographic background such as parental education and income eliminates associations between timing of puberty and achievement (Koivusilta & Rimpela, 2004). One very viable interpretation of this is that selection effects are indeed important. Consistent with the overall pattern associated with disengagement from school in adolescence, rates of substance abuse, unsafe sexual activity, and overall delinquency are also higher in early-maturing girls than in their later-maturing peers (Mendle, Turkheimer, & Emory, 2007), and these kinds of activities can generate long-term consequences.

Associations with timing of puberty in boys

As noted, associations between life outcomes and pubertal timing in boys have not been very consistent. Partly, this is because boys have not been studied as extensively as girls. One reason for the lack of study is that it is more difficult. Testicular volume is generally considered to be the most accurate measure of pubertal status in males, but it requires the expense associated with physical exam, and the exam itself can be considered invasive. Data on age of menarche in girls are much easier to obtain and generally considered quite accurate (though when asked repeatedly over time in longitudinal studies, correlations between reports can be quite low). Even level of breast development can be measured much more straightforwardly in females than can testicular volume in males. Another reason for inconsistency of results for boys may be that there have been cultural changes since, perhaps, World War II, in how puberty is perceived in boys, at least in western nations. The first studies of the question suggested that boys who entered puberty early tended to have better outcomes, and the boys most at risk for detrimental outcomes were those who entered puberty late (e.g., Clausen, 1975; Mussen & Jones, 1957). This appeared to be mediated by greater social poise and self-confidence in the early maturers, perhaps because they tended to be successful and sought after in sports, in direct contrast to their later-maturing classmates. More recent studies, however, have tended to suggest that both early- and late-maturing boys are at increased risk of detrimental outcomes (e.g., Williams & Dunlop, 1999), and some have even indicated that the risk might focus specifically on early maturers (e.g., Ge, Conger, & Elder, 2001a). One possible reason for these changes over time could be increasing breadth of socialization in western countries (Arnett, 1995).

The kinds of reasons offered for timing of puberty effects in boys have been basically the same as those offered for girls: psychosocial dislocation from childhood peers and mismatch between the social expectations associated with maturity of physical appearance and cognitive and emotional development, increased emotional lability and sensation-seeking associated with the surge in gonadal hormones, and selection effects. The surge in hormones hits all adolescents, however, and, unlike for girls, there does not appear to be evidence that it differs systematically with timing of puberty for boys, making this explanation somewhat less likely for boys (Mendle & Ferrero, 2012). As for girls, early maturation has been associated with greater risk of depression in boys, though overall incidence of depression is lower in boys than in girls (Ge, Conger, & Elder, 2001b). This may involve selection effects, as the association has been observed to be stronger when mothers also report depression (Rudolph & Troop-Gordon, 2010). Greater rates of eating disorders have also been reported in very-early maturing boys, but rates overall are so much lower in boys than in girls that little is known about this (Mendle & Ferrero, 2012). The biggest risks appear to involve behaviours associated with risk-taking and sensation-seeking, including delinquency, substance use, and sexual activity, likely for reasons very similar to those offered for girls (e.g., Halpern, Kaestle, & Halfors, 2007; Negriff & Trickett, 2009). Perhaps because of the social situations they encounter in taking these risks, early-maturing boys also appear to be at greater risk of victimization. Though clearly selection effects could be involved in exposure to these risky situations in the first place, one reason for the victimization of these boys may be simply that they are cognitively less mature than most of the others in such situations, and therefore easier marks.

Epigenetic landscape and robustness

Adolescence is a time of great biological and social change. Biological changes are likely greater than at any other time in extra-uterine life except infancy. Unlike the infant, however, the adolescent has considerable and often rapidly increasing autonomy, which means that his/her chosen (whether consciously or unconsciously) behaviour can exert considerable influence on the developmental trajectory experienced. Moreover, social expectations for adolescents change considerably during this period, but the ways in which these expectations are communicated are often unclear and the messages contradictory from moment to moment. At the same time, how these expectations are met, or not met, in the areas of educational attainment, conformity with legal constraints on behaviour, maintenance of physical safety, responsibility for sexual activity, and avoidance of substance abuse can have lifetime consequences. This suggests that, arguably at least, adolescence may be the period during which the individual, within the contexts present at inception of adolescence, is most powerful in setting his/her own developmental course. Perhaps a good way to conclude this chapter, then, is to discuss the relevance of Waddington's (1957) epigenetic landscape and current applications of the systems dynamics ideas of robustness to biological systems.

Waddington (1905-1975) was a developmental biologist. He is credited with laying the foundations for systems biology, or the approach to study based on the idea that organisms and their function must be understood as wholes, that even readily identifiable component parts cannot be understood in isolation from the rest of the organism. Waddington coined the term 'epigenetic' as a portmanteau of the words 'epigenesis' (the process of cell differentiation in embryonic development) and 'genetic' (Waddington, 1942) to characterize a conceptual model of how genes and environment transact to produce a phenotype. The idea of the epigenetic landscape is that the space of possible developmental phenotypes can be conceived as a large hill consisting of undulating smaller hills and valleys, creating various pathways down which marbles might run. A marble 'organism' begins in some genetically and environmentally defined position at the top of this hill and rolls down it the way rivulets flow down mountains, tracing one of many different possible pathways among the hills and valleys along the way. The particular path traced is a function of the prior directions 'chosen' with some element of chance figuring into the 'selections'. The epigenetic landscape model is useful in thinking about the modern concept of *robustness.*

Robustness allows a system (any system in general but biological organisms as systems in particular) to maintain its properties and functions in the face of external and internal perturbations (Kitano, 2004). I will discuss it in more detail in Chapter 11 with respect to ageing, but one implication of robustness, proposed by Carlson and Doyle (2002), seems particularly relevant to the development of individual differences during adolescence. This is that systems that have evolved or been designed to be robust against frequently encountered perturbations are also likely to be particularly sensitive to certain rare perturbations, and especially so when the system's fragilities are exposed. One way to expose all a system's fragilities at once is for all its components to be undergoing changes in structure and function at similar but interlocking times, in ways that also change their relations to each other. This is in many ways a good description of what happens during adolescence. This is not, however, the only trade-off associated with robustness. A system that can tolerate removal of some of its components due to redundancy and decoupling is vulnerable to dysfunction when one of its components is malfunctioning but cannot be removed. Unfortunately, what can happen then is that the dysfunctional state of function can take on its own robustness, and the very system 'design' that serves to support robustness of adaptive function can be co-opted to maintain the robustness of malfunction instead (Kitano, 2004). These properties of robust systems may help to explain the adolescent's increased vulnerability to development of overt psychopathology as well as less severe but still detrimental trajectories such as those that occur with early parenthood or low educational attainment.

Further reading

Arnett, J. (1999). Adolescent storm and stress, reconsidered. *American Psychologist, 54*, 317–326.

Belsky, J., Steinberg, L. D., & Draper, P. (1991). Childhood experience, interpersonal development, and reproductive strategy – An evolutionary theory of socialization. *Child Development, 62*, 647–670.

Chambers, R. A., Taylor, J. R., & Petenza, M. N. (2003). Developmental neurocircuitry of motivation in adolescence: A critical period of addiction vulnerability. *American Journal of Psychiatry, 160*, 1041–1052.

Gardner, M., & Steinberg, L. (2005). Peer infuence on risk taking, risk preference, and risky decision-making in adolescence and adulthood: An experimental study. *Developmental Psychology, 41*, 625–635.

Gogtay, N., & Thompson, P. M. (2010). Mapping gray matter development: Implications for typical development and vulnerability to psychopathology. *Brain and Cognition, 72*, 6–15.

Pianka, A. R. (1970). On 'r' and 'K' selection. *American Naturalist, 10*, 453–464.

Sisk, C., & Zehr, J. (2005). Pubertal hormones organize the adolescent brain and behavior. *Frontiers in Neuroendocrinology, 26*, 163–174.

Somerville, L. H., Jones, R. M., & Casey, B. J. (2010). A time of change: Behavioral and neural correlates of adolescent sensitivity to appetitive and aversive environmental cues. *Brain and Cognition, 72*, 124–133.

Susman, E., & Rogol, A. (2004). Puberty and psychological development. In R. Lerner, & L. Steinberg, *Handbook of Adolescent Psychology* (pp. 157–183). New York: Wiley.

Young Adult Development: Finding a Place in the World

In the last chapter on adolescence, I focused primarily on the patterns and implications of the physiological and neurological changes that mark the transition from childhood to adulthood that takes place during adolescence. I did so because in much of the world today, despite these changes, the social situation of the adolescent remains very similar to that of the child. That is, the adolescent generally lives with one or two parents, is financially dependent upon them, spends a large portion of the waking hours in school and related activities including homework, and is not considered a fully responsible citizen of the broader social order. All of this changes in young adulthood: most young people make the transition to living independently of their parents, become financially self-supporting, and take on the full responsibilities of citizenship, whether they continue with education or not.

This process involves what I have come to think of as finding a place in the world. By 'place in the world' I mean a way of offering and using one's skills and abilities to make a contribution to the broader society that ideally provides some satisfaction to the individual as well as the financial wherewithal for adequate food, shelter, medical care, etc. I also mean a social situation that ideally offers appropriate stimulation, engagement with others, and emotional support. In childhood, this place in the world is provided primarily by parents, both directly through the homes they provide and indirectly through the access to the broader society that their own places in the world grant to their children, in the form of the neighbourhoods in which they live, the schools they have their children attend, the activities in which they encourage participation, and the social milieu in which they themselves travel. Adolescents become increasingly aware that all of this is 'up for grabs' once they are on their own: they get to, or have to, figure much of it out for themselves, but they do not, and in fact often cannot, yet really get going on the project while they remain with their parents. By young adulthood, however, it becomes finally time that it must be done, ready or not. Despite the near-universality of the developmental challenge, the ways and degrees to which it is met create many opportunities for the greater expression of individual differences.

Erik Erikson and the stages of psychosocial development

Erik Erikson's (1902–1994) thoughts about how this transition is managed have been very influential in the field, and remain so today. Born in Germany, he studied with Anna Freud, Sigmund Freud's daughter, but emigrated to the United States with the rise to power of Hitler. In the United States he maintained a clinical practice and worked with and studied diverse groups including Native Americans in the mid-west and California, civil rights workers, and victims of combat fatigue. Like Freud and Piaget, Erikson conceived of development as involving several stages, each one centred on some activity that could be considered to have reached a crisis. Similar to Piaget, he conceived of each stage as being characterized by a tension between opposing ways of understanding the world, and the resolution of the crisis that this caused as coming to realize how to reconcile these understandings using a new and more sophisticated perspective, and development of a new goal or virtue for which to strive. Unlike both Piaget and Freud, however, he saw this cyclical stage-like process extending throughout the lifespan and, like Vygotsky, as being deeply embedded in the society in which the individual lives.

Erikson (1963; 1968; 1982) theorized eight stages from birth to death. Though not directly relevant to a discussion of young adulthood, his stages resonate with themes I have discussed in earlier chapters and illustrate his perspective on the mechanism of transition from one stage to the next, so I review them all briefly. According to Erikson, the infant first faces the crisis of whether and to what degree to trust caregivers during the first year of life. Optimal resolution of this crisis means learning to trust surrounding others to provide appropriate care, but not so completely as to become gullible. That is, some level of awareness that not every whim will be met should also remain, as it is the source of the development of crisis in the next stage. Successful resolution of this crisis, according to Erikson results in development of the capacity to hope, or perhaps more generally, for optimism. The parallels between this conceptualization of *trust v. mistrust* and attachment theory should be clear. Erikson's next crisis stage is termed *autonomy v. shame* and takes place very approximately from ages 1 to 3. Not coincidentally, this is when the child generally becomes self-reliant for toileting, one of the first steps of real autonomy, but one that also tends to have shame associated with lapses of control. In Erikson's conceptualization, the motivation towards autonomy that characterizes this stage develops from the kernel of mistrust left in resolving the first conflict, and results in emergence of capacity for will. This is consistent with the conceptualization of secure attachment as enabling the development of confidence in the ability to master cognitive challenges and manage emotional responses. Again, according to Erikson, optimal resolution of this crisis involves acceptance of a small kernel of shame in addition to mastery of the first rudimentary autonomies, and addressing this small kernel of shame provides the motivation for development of the next crisis.

This is *initiative v. guilt* and runs from ages approximately 3 to 6. During this period, preschoolers learn to use initiative to construct plans and actions that help them to avoid the kinds of lapses in their own behaviour that can bring on shame, but also learn that too-great enthusiasm for carrying out their own impulses to action can cause them to impinge on the rights of others, bringing on guilt. Acceptance of some level of guilt coincides with the emergence of a sense of purpose, or ability to set goals, and again motivates the next crisis, which is *initiative v. inferiority*. Erikson posited that this crisis runs from approximately ages 6 to 12, but I suggest that it extends well beyond age 12, especially given the trend for educational programmes in many places to ease students into receiving their first formal grades that really 'count' around age 12. Again, not coincidentally, this crisis runs concurrently with the primary school years (or with less formal skill-building under adult tutelage in non-industrialized societies). Erikson conceived of this stage as involving the development of a sense of competence in mastering the skills considered important, presented, and taught by the social group through comparison of one's own performance with those of like others, and the tension characterizing the crisis as involving recognition that, almost inevitably, some of those others sometimes appear to perform better to varying degrees. This is very consistent with the discussion of cognitive development in Chapter 7, and results, after successful resolution, in a sense of one's overall competence, complete with awareness of areas of relative strengths and weaknesses.

As with the others, the small sense of what Erikson termed inferiority that inevitably remains also leads naturally to Erikson's next crisis, which he termed *identity v. role confusion*. Erikson posited that this stage runs from ages 12 to 20, but, again, I would extend its upper boundary considerably beyond this in industrialized countries that tend to have educational requirements for many occupations that generally extend well beyond age 20. It is in articulating the psychological questions and processes and the social processes involved in this 'identity crisis' that Erikson probably made his greatest contributions to the field. The way in which he did so is very relevant to the young adult's life task of finding a place in the world, so I will explore his conceptualization in some detail. For now, however, I note merely that Erikson posited that successful resolution of this crisis results in ability to make a commitment to fulfilling some role.

He termed the next crisis, the crisis of adult development, *intimacy v. isolation* and suggested that it runs from about ages 20 to 40. In actuality, however, I think it likely that this crisis largely overlaps with the identity v. role confusion crisis. It is characterized by exploration of intimate relationships, search for mates, development of mating relationships, and negotiation of those relationships so that they both forge couple identity and allow maintenance of a level of individual identity appropriate to the person. Successful resolution of this crisis brings the ability to love another for that other's own sake. For most people, it is during this age range that they make their decisions about reproduction and begin parenting if they are going to, and ability to love in this way is likely very important in parenting well. Following what I will term resolution of these two crises, Erikson posited a crisis of *generativity v. stagnation*, lasting from about ages 40 to 65. During this period, the adult confronts the need to feel that life has offered the opportunity to leave some kind of useful contribution to the world, a sense of purpose. When this does not seem to be the case, there is a sense of stagnation, regret about earlier decisions, or uselessness. Successful resolution of this crisis involves development of ability to undertake efforts to ensure the well-being of future generations. Erikson's final crisis takes place after age 65, and is characterized by *integrity v. despair*. Integrity is achieved when one views life as having been meaningful and as having offered the opportunity to achieve what was intended, so that death can be faced with equanimity. This is difficult when one is plagued with regrets and frustrations over unfulfilled goals. Successful resolution of this crisis results in wisdom and acceptance of what life situation remains.

Thus, for Erikson, life consists of an ongoing series of environmentally presented challenges with which the person must find some way of coping. These challenges have universal overall themes, but the particulars of each individual's own situation are always unique. The resources each individual brings to these challenges have analogous properties: all humans share many of these resources, in the form of general perceptual, physical, emotional, and cognitive capacities, but each individual's mix of degrees of these capacities is unique. People thus differ in the ways they meet these challenges, and in the extents to which the ways they find can be considered constructive adaptations. Importantly, resolution of a challenge that leaves a person completely comfortable within the environment is not optimal for further development, as the source of emergence of the next challenge is a kernel of awareness of incompleteness in having met the last one. At the same time, if this kernel is too large, sufficient resources will not be in place to confront this next challenge effectively.

The crisis of identity v. role confusion

The term *identity* is used in many rather disparate disciplines spanning the social sciences, the humanities, and many different forms of therapy. Each of these disciplines tends to have its own rather specific denotations and, in particular, connotations. In general, however, 'identity' refers to a definition of the self: a clear and coherent sense of who one is, what one's goals are, how one fits into society, what role or roles one has to play in this grand and ongoing social drama. At bottom, all of the disciplines that consider identity seek to understand how people come to occupy the environmental niches they do, which means understanding how choices, both conscious and unconscious, are made in situations where behavioural options are available as well as how people cope with constraints on the ability to choose and the balance they achieve between action and reaction. Importantly for psychology, whether they are made consciously or unconsciously, conscious interpretation of all choices made takes place within a framework of definitions formed through what one has learned in one's own individual experiences. Yet this learning itself and even the experiences that generate it are shaped by the cultural context imposed by interactions with others. The meanings people attribute to themselves and the ways in which they define who they are and what is important to them both contribute to ongoing actions and interactions and are built upon the responses of others to prior actions and interactions.

Erikson posited that the challenge of adolescence, and I extend the period to young adulthood in modern industrialized countries, is to find a suitable one of these identities and set oneself up to live the social role it prescribes. He believed that many are presented with both so many role options and so much pressure to 'grow up' and select among them that they experience considerable difficulty in resolving the crisis. He also noted that, fortunately, industrialized societies do provide some shelter in which to experience the identity crisis, in the form of what he called a *moratorium period*, during which adolescents in particular are relatively free of responsibilities (they tend to live at home with parents, who support them financially, and are relatively free to experiment with different ideas and role identities). This moratorium period overtly extends to young adulthood on many university campuses.

Most of the empirical research that has explored and tested Erikson's ideas has made use of a measurement protocol developed by Marcia (1966). The protocol basically requires acceptance without question that finding one's identity is the challenge during adolescence and young adulthood, so it does not actually test the foundation of Ericson's theory but rather some aspects of the process of meeting this challenge. Its measurement property is based on the concept that identity in occupational choice, religion, and political affiliation emerges through a continuous developmental process along which landmarks on two dimensions can be posted. One dimension is the extent to which exploration of the realm has taken place. The other is the extent to which the individual has made a commitment to some option available in that realm. Along the exploration dimension, the developmental process is presumed to begin with curiosity about the realm, proceeds to realization that options are available and development of questions about these options, and reaches a crisis of intensity in seeking answers to these questions, optimally followed by arrival at enough answers so that the individual is comfortable making at least 'for now' commitment choices appropriate to abilities, temperament, and resources. The process of actual commitment, however, may take place at a different pace, depending on the individual's experience of the exploratory process and/or on external pressures such as economic constraints or parental expectations.

This operationalization of Ericson's theory led Marcia (1966) to structure his measurement protocol around four identity statuses. (1) In the *diffusion status*, an individual has not thought much about identities and roles, has not really thought about his/her position within a realm and has made no commitment within it. (2) In the *foreclosure status*, the individual has also not explored any variety of identities, options, or ideas, but has either latched onto or been required, perhaps by familial or financial obligations, to make a commitment to some option within the realm of interest. (3) In the *moratorium status*, the individual is currently going through an active exploration of possible identities and roles, asking questions and seeking answers, with the awareness that making any kind of commitment while in this state would be premature and potentially unfortunate. Finally, (4) in the *identity achievement status*, the individual has been through an active exploration of this type, has found at least some answers that seem both attainable within available opportunities and resources, and which feel at some level appropriate to the individual's interests, abilities, temperament, ideals, etc.

Of course, in reality the process of seeking and establishing one's identity is likely continuous and ongoing, rather than categorical with a clearly marked beginning and ending. In general, it is not particularly helpful for analytical purposes to break continuous dimensions or processes into categories, but the tendency to do so is common, and it can help to simplify the situation so that patterns of association can be observed more clearly. This is how Marcia's classification system has tended to be used in the many subsequent studies that have explored the developmental transition from adolescence to adulthood. For example, in a recent study, Hirschi (2012) classified Swiss high school students according to Marcia's (1966) taxonomy, assessed their personalities and degrees of life satisfaction at one time point and followed them over time. He found mean differences in personality among the identity status groups, in particular that conscientiousness was associated with achieving or maintaining a sense of identity or foreclosure, while neuroticism was associated with the emergence of identity exploration over time. In addition, those who had made some identity commitment showed increased satisfaction with their lives over time, while those who entered a period of identity exploration showed decreased satisfaction at entrance.

This study was typical of this area of research in the way in which it made use of Marcia's (1966) classification taxonomy and in the general nature of the results obtained: a period of intense identity exploration and uncertainty is often painful for many, and resolution and a feeling of being ready and able to make a commitment often brings relief from this. Moreover, greater conscientiousness almost by definition carries with it a greater sense of responsibility, which in turn implies higher motivation to make the kind of occupational commitment that will lead to financial independence. But the Hirschi (2012) study was also typical of those in psychology in centring analysis around the individual's presumably rather fixed traits and existence or lack of existence of some exploratory process, with little or no consideration of the possibility of social and perceptual constraints on the options available and how those constraints might impact both the result of the exploration and the individual's ability to adapt well to the resulting commitment over time. Within psychology, there has of course been general realization that the individual explores identity possibilities within a framework of social influences. But, until very recently, studies have tended to focus on questions such as how quality of relationships with parents affects identity status (e.g., Marksman-Adams, 1992) and whether experiences outside the home such as university attendance affects progress in achieving identity (e.g., Munro & Adams, 1977) rather than the impact of variation in opportunity to continue education. Moreover, these studies have tended to acknowledge broader social constraints primarily through noting, as Erikson (1968) emphasized, that the very luxury to explore identity in this manner, never mind the idea that it is part of normal development to do so, may be primarily a feature of modern, western, industrialized societies. That is, they have noted their failure to address the implications of this as study limitations rather than attempting to address them. Thus little is known about how these kinds of constraints actually impact people's lives and psychological well-being.

Incorporating a sociological perspective in understanding development of identity

The field of sociology has taken a different approach to studying identity development. Taking their cues from Mead (1934), sociologists such as Stryker (2007) have tended to view one's sense of identity as emerging through human social rather than introspective action, and in particular through communication with others. Personality traits, patterns of behaviours, abilities, outlooks, and attitudes, according to this view, do not exist in any meaningful way outside the context in which they are manifested and experienced, and this context is always social at base. The individual is thus a product of social interaction, and identity takes shape when one can characterize oneself within it. Mead held that individuals are characterised first by other people, and the process of characterizing oneself involves taking the perspectives of these other people and using the experience of doing so to become aware of one's own sense of self, or identity. This can sound like the individual is completely the product of external social forces, and many sociologists have interpreted it as such. Other sociologists, however, have recognized that how people tend to think of themselves is far from limited simply to the roles they fill: the individual configurations of characteristics people believe themselves to possess within these roles are at least as important as the roles they believe themselves to fill (Kuhn & McPartland, 1954). For example, Kohn and Schooler (1969) and Wilk, Desmarais, and Sackett (1995), among others, have provided evidence that, wherever people tend to start in the hierarchy of occupations and however much their social backgrounds contribute to their obtaining these positions rather than others, their individual responses to occupying those roles contribute strongly to the extent to which and directions in which they move in the occupational hierarchy from there.

Occupational identity offers a good opportunity to explore the developmental processes involved. Occupation is one of the major roles people take on in their lives. For many, if not most, people, occupation provides financial support in industrialized economies and the equivalent in the form of food and shelter in the few truly non-industrialized economies that remain. For most of those whose occupation is spouse and/or parent to others, the connection between occupation and financial wherewithal is not direct, but in these situations the spousal and/or parental relationship defines the means of financial support. Occupation also generally consumes the largest share of most people's waking hours, and the processes involved in the development of an occupational identity are analogous to those in many other areas of life. They are, however, perhaps 'stickier' than some, in the sense that most people need to select and maintain some kind of occupation that will provide financial support. Many occupations require specific forms of education, training, or even legal certification before people can practise them, and generally some employer must make a job offer. Self-employment is always a possibility, but financial resources, not to mention experience in the field, are often practically if not legally necessary in order to get started. This makes it difficult to wake up one morning with the realization that one has been living with the 'wrong' occupational identity and simply take on another one the way one could, for example, in theory at any rate, change religious or political affiliations.

Gottfredson's theory of the development of occupational identity

Arguably at least, the most complete outline of how individuals develop their occupational identities has been presented by the sociologist Linda Gottfredson (1981). It is worth considering her presentation in some detail because it offers a good blueprint for thinking about how individual differences are integrated with generally experienced developmental processes as well as with broad social constraints. In particular, unlike most theories of the development of occupational aspirations and identities which have tended to focus on the roles of values and interests and parental expectations, she explicitly considered how sex, social class, and individual cognitive ability shape both perceived constraints on and motivations to pursue occupational options. Moreover, her conceptualization began with early childhood. Though early childhood is not the focus of this chapter, the processes she posited begin then, and it would not be possible to understand her conceptualization of the processes in young adulthood without understanding the processes posited to take place earlier. These earlier processes are also highly consistent with those I explored in discussing learning processes and Experience Producing Drive Theory in Chapter 7.

The idea of identity is central to these processes. Because the term 'identity' is used in somewhat different ways by different theorists and researchers, I will be specific about how I use it here. In her writings, Gottfredson (1981) actually used the term 'self-concept' but I am going to use the term 'identity' because Gottfredson's 'self-concept' is largely consistent with Erikson's 'identity'. It refers to one's view of oneself, one's beliefs about who one is and who one is not, and who one expects to or wants to become in the future. It is a general concept, in the sense that is the totality of different perspectives on the self, some of them more central and important to the person than others. People tend to be aware of and able to articulate these different perspectives on their identities to varying degrees and may or may not be able to articulate them with any clarity. Despite this, they act on them. The different perspectives on identity include social roles as well as individual psychological attributes such as interests, abilities, personality, values, even beliefs about appearance. Identity is personal: it is one's own view of oneself, and may not be consistent with others' views of who one is, regardless of the roles others' characterizations of one may play in its development.

According to Gottfredson (1981), for young adults faced with the actual prospect of making their first forays into establishing an occupational identity, the components of general identity that are most relevant to development of occupational identity are sex, social class (and cultural and ethnic) background, interests, perceived abilities, and values about life, in particular how much effort one is willing to invest in one's occupation. Young adults, however, bring to their immediate task of occupation selection many pre-existing perspectives on their identities in the relevant components. These pre-existing perspectives impose constraints on consideration of some occupational identities and push them towards considering others more actively. The pre-existing perspectives develop in tandem with general cognitive development throughout childhood, becoming more abstract and complex as general cognitive development facilitates more complex perspectives on the world more generally. Importantly for Gottfredson's conceptualization, at least within the western, industrialized nations where it has been studied most, there appears to be substantial agreement and knowledge among people (at least above about the age of 12) in the images they hold of what is involved in available occupational categories in the senses of how much prestige they confer, the characteristics of people who work in those areas including sex, and the kinds of activities the jobs entail. Of course this does change over time, with economic cycles, the introduction of new technologies, and the waxing and waning of prejudices about what people with particular characteristics 'can' or 'should' or 'cannot' or 'should not' do. It changes rather slowly, however, so the generally held 'occupational map' tends to remain quite stable over time.

This generally common set of perceptions about occupations means that, at least within groups holding them, the variance young people express in the occupations to which they aspire, never mind the variance in the occupations they end up filling, depends on how compatible they find the occupations to be with their already-existing ideas about their identities. Gottfredson (1981) outlined four stages through which she envisioned children's impressions of themselves passing as their own identities develop and they observe adults in the working world. To her, a key feature of the developmental process is that, as children's conceptions of their own identities and understanding of what is involved in various occupations become more cognitively sophisticated, their understanding of their own identities also becomes more narrow. In the first stage, young children come to understand, for example, that they cannot grow up to be fairies or giants or even, realistically, princesses. In the second stage, when they are a little older, perhaps ages 5 to 7, they develop perceptions about which kinds of jobs are appropriate to their sex. In the third stage, their understanding of both the relative status and prestige and the relative difficulty (length of training, cognitive ability required) of various jobs develops and they compare this with their emerging understanding of their own relative cognitive competencies. Finally, in the fourth stage, they develop perceptions about how particular job duties relate to their own interests and abilities and temperament. Once alternatives are rejected at one level of understanding, Gottfredson notes that young people rarely reconsider them. Evidence that this is the case comes from studies that ask people to rank and list their most and least preferred occupations. In these studies (e.g., Slocum & Bowles, 1968), people easily rank lists of occupations in order of preference, but if asked to list their least favourite occupations spontaneously, they tend not to mention the ones that appeared at the very bottoms of their ranked lists, suggesting that they consider them beyond the realm of possibility.

Gottfredson's conceptualization of this developmental process offers an explanation for the 'stickiness' of many sex differences in occupational preferences. If children develop effectively permanent perceptions about what occupations are appropriate to their sex as young as early primary school, they do so at least 10 and often 15 years before they actually make any occupational choices. This means that they do not actively benefit, in the form of seriously considering more options, from whatever (generally rather subtle) signals their society may have started to offer during a period of becoming more welcoming of both sexes participating in all occupations. This form of benefit is left to those 10–15 years younger.

According to Gottfredson, the third stage of development is of awareness of social class, and the roles of ability, education, prestige, and occupation in its attainment. This awareness tends to develop in the later elementary school years, though children in this age range may be far from able to define the term 'social class'. What they do recognize is who is relatively rich and who relatively poor, who is respected in society in general and who is not so respected. This is done through signals of dress, area of residence, style of speech, lifestyle, and social connections. During this same period, children develop an awareness of their relative levels of cognitive abilities, as discussed in detail in Chapter 7. They also develop perceptions about how cognitive abilities are involved in various occupations and, because of the associations in many western industrialized nations between occupational prestige and cognitive and educational requirements, about how hard they as individuals would have to work to become qualified to do various jobs. At first, children tend to express interest in the jobs they see people around them doing, especially when they have external markers such as uniforms. This has tended traditionally to orient boys towards jobs such as tradesmen, police officers, and construction workers, and girls towards jobs such as nurse and teacher. As they grow older, however, children become increasingly aware of other, less overtly visible, occupations, at both higher and lower levels of prestige, education, and training, and begin to include these among their options, to the extent they seem to be open and suitable to them.

The role of parental social class in development of occupational aspirations

Emerging sense of identity must be involved in this process, given the consensus about how occupations are regarded by society. Otherwise, everyone would automatically aspire to the occupations that generate the most prestige and income, but this is not what happens – different young people tend to set their aspirational sights on very different levels within the social occupational hierarchy. Gottfredson (1981) posited that this takes place because a young person will tend to take the social group in which she/he lives as the reference group, orienting ideas about relative success around this level. Parental expectations of course contribute to this, through both expressions about expectations for educational attainment and expressions particularly of what would constitute failure, as most parents do not appear to have upper bounds on their hopes for their offspring. Gottfredson, however, placed great stress on the role of individually perceived cognitive ability in the occupational levels to which young people aspire. Noting that lower-income boys commonly commented in interviews about their occupational plans that going to university would be 'too much work' or 'too hard' (Ginzburg, Ginsburg, Axelrad, & Herma, 1951), she suggested that young people rule out some occupational possibilities based on their own assessments of their abilities as well as the kinds of occupations held by adults in their immediate social groups. The result of this, she posited, is that ranges of occupational prestige considered as reasonable aspirations vary among individuals within any one social class grouping based on perceived ability levels because social class also tends to be correlated substantially but far from perfectly with cognitive ability. Two phenomena can thus emerge in some young people, which she termed *foreshortened horizons* and *effort-acceptability squeeze*.

As Gottfredson noted, the far-from-perfect correlation between social class and cognitive ability means that, within any social class group, there will be some young people with plenty of ability to enter any occupation to which they might aspire, and others who would have to work extremely hard to qualify for and perform competently many of the jobs common among those in their social class group. From the perspective of human resource use, the most unfortunate cases of inconsistency are the high-ability young person growing up in a lower social class, and the relatively low-ability young person growing up in a higher social class. The first young person will have more realistic options for attainment than she/he is likely to pursue, either because these options do not occur to the person, or because of limitations in family resources that can be devoted to training or education. Such young people, and society more generally because it can end up doing without the full potential of their services, suffer from foreshortened horizons. In contrast, the second young person is likely to have relatively high expectations for the level of prestige that should be associated with any occupation pursued, yet become aware that there are few occupations that do not require more ability and effort than she/he is willing to expend. Gottfredson (1981) suggested that recognition of this effort-acceptability squeeze may create considerable anxiety for young people caught in this bind, contributing to alienation and/or deviant or self-destructive behaviour.

According to Gottfredson's conceptualization, then, by the time they reach adolescence, people have, largely subconsciously, established considerable identity 'ballast' that they take largely for granted, in the form of the general level of complexity/prestige and general sex-typing involved in any occupations they might pursue. They may remain very vague and unstable in expressing any preferences or goals for any specific occupations, but they have tacitly narrowed their ranges of potential occupational identities considerably. The development remaining to be accomplished in adolescence and young adulthood concerns, within the framework already established, both coming to understand the kinds of tasks involved in actually doing a job and how one is likely to respond to carrying out those tasks – will they be enjoyable? Onerous? Interesting? Dull? Coming to any conclusions about this involves developing a deeper understanding of one's personality and interests above and beyond the kinds of overall cognitive abilities the school environment tends to tap. It also means giving consideration to other long-term life goals, particularly desire for marriage and family, and development of the identity that that will entail.

Identity formation and desire for marriage and family

Desire for marriage and family makes a good example of a long-term life goal distinct from occupational goals and the emergence of occupational identity, yet which often has considerable impact on them. Moreover, like the developmental processes involved in the emergence of occupational identity in young adulthood, whatever conscious consideration is given to the question of marriage and family begins from the perspective of much tacitly held ballast about what is entailed in taking on roles of partner and parent. And, like occupational identity, much of this ballast was formed during the period when the child was very young and being most actively parented. This is also the period during which much of the sense of one's sexual identity develops. It is a period during which cognitive skills are relatively limited, and intuitive rather than linear and clearly articulated. This means that the ballast tends to be heavily sex-typed in the same way and to the same degree as was the parenting experience received when very young: subconsciously, the young adult understands that being a father or mother means acting the way one's own father or mother acted and being a husband or wife involves treating one's partner the way one's parents treated each other. Importantly, this includes sex-typing of ideas about the extent to which one needs to be a 'good provider'. In what has long been the tradition in the western nations, men were socialized to provide their families' financial support, and women were socialized to take care of the home and children. This tended to orient men more strongly towards forming occupational goals focused around money and prestige and women more strongly towards goals focused around jobs that would not interfere with taking care of their children. For women, this tended to mean neither very high-prestige jobs, because of the time and energy involved in doing them, nor very low-prestige jobs, because they tend not to generate sufficient rewards to be worth the diversion from taking care of the children. This sex dichotomy, of course, has loosened considerably in most of the western nations during the last 50–60 years.

It has done so, however, in ways that have had different consequences in different social classes, at least within many western industrialized nations. In well-educated social groups with substantial financial resources, the sorts of social classes in which many young people who go on to professional occupations grow up, loosening of the traditional occupational sex dichotomies has primarily meant the opening of greater diversity of viable options for both men and women, but especially for women. No longer is it unusual to encounter female physicians, attorneys, politicians, scientists, business managers and executives. Few nations have reached complete parity of representation of females in the professional occupations, nor of rank and remuneration within them, but it is clear that women are accepted and even welcomed much more readily in these occupations than was the case in, say, the 1940s and 1950s. There is also considerable evidence (e.g., Ferriman, Lubinski, & Benbow, 2009) that at least some of the disparities of participation and even rank and remuneration that remain may result from sex differences in interests, willingness to work overtime, and persistence after encountering obstacles, differences that might be summarized as differences in motivation, goals, or the very personal choices involved in any definition of identity. For people in these social classes, at least, the loosening has meant an opening of opportunity that many women have rushed to embrace.

Many women with the abilities and resources to become qualified for such occupations may have been so quick to embrace these opportunities because these occupations are in many ways fun. They offer considerable intellectual challenge to those up for meeting it; generally great autonomy in charting specific working conditions; social rewards in the form of status, often power, recognition, and good remuneration; and, increasingly, the opportunity to travel and make social connections with people throughout the world. For women in lower social classes, who tend to face more limitations in training resources and abilities at least as measured, the loosening of occupational sex dichotomies has come about somewhat differently, and the differences may have different psychological consequences for the women involved, as well as for men. In North America and Europe, opening of many skilled and semi-skilled labour jobs to women came with World War II, during which women were pressed into service in industrial and manufacturing jobs due to both increased war production demand and the fact that much of the normally available male workforce was in the military. As economies were rebuilt following the War, population demographics coupled with increasing automation of industry and an increasing need for workers who provide relatively personal services not requiring extensive education, such as shop clerks and insurance claims adjusters, created an increasing gap between the income any one individual, male or female, in these social groups could earn and the cost of the lifestyle people had come to associate with the middle class – a moderate house with some yard, a car, the resources to take an interesting holiday each year, and freedom from concern about putting food on the table and clothes on growing children. This gap brought many women who would otherwise have stayed home with the children into the workforce and kept them there, often in jobs that are not particularly fun or interesting.

The role of salience in understanding the psychological consequences of loosening occupational sex differences, and thus in understanding identity more generally

Salience refers to the extent to which some object, person, or idea is readily perceivable relative to others that compete for the same kind of perceptual attention. For example, in a photo of a group of people, the woman in the red hat with the large black feather might be most salient to most people, especially if no one else in the photo is even wearing a hat. That is, their eyes might be drawn first to her. With respect to identity, salience refers to the relative probability that a person will focus on one aspect of one's identity rather than another in any particular situation. Most people are aware of several different aspects of their identities, and a number of other aspects may often be quite relevant to their behaviour even without their awareness. Some situations bring these various aspects of identity into conflict, and the behaviour that emerges in such a situation entails some resolution of the conflict that involves the relative saliences of the aspects of identity in conflict.

As Gottfredson (1981) and many others have noted, sex is one of the first aspects of identity of which the young child becomes aware. Though this awareness of the basic fact of sex emerges early, one's understanding of the full implications of one's sex continues to develop throughout childhood and adolescence, and even throughout the lifespan. As noted, this development takes place largely through layering new levels of understanding over ones laid down earlier, generally without replacing the older ones, so that the new and old co-exist, often even when they conflict. For many people during the last 50–60 years, this has meant that relatively rigid ideas about what kinds of occupations were appropriate to their sex were laid down early in childhood. But societal changes taking place during their childhoods have meant that, by the time they were forming their conceptions of the social class levels to which they would aspire, the actual occupational options open to women, along with the economic realities of attaining any particular social class level, had changed. This means that both boys and girls have tended to hold rather narrow conceptions of the occupations that suit their sexual identities relative to the economic realities of meeting their aspirations for social class attainment. This has coincided with increasing educational expectations for many occupations. For example, fifty years ago, hotel managers trained for their positions by starting work after high school as porters or dishwashers, and gradually worked their way up the ranks to management. In recent years, however, hotels expect their managers to have university degrees in hotel management.

As noted, for boys, one of the early-established aspects of their sexual occupationally oriented identities has traditionally been that men are the primary family breadwinners in a family. Often, boys are not completely aware of this aspect of their identities, but it still can have powerful effects on their occupational choices. It likely can have even stronger effects on their psychological adaptation to the roles those choices entail, as well as on their psychological adaptation to their roles within their families. The economic changes that have taken place over the last 50–60 years have made it increasingly difficult to maintain the kind of lifestyle considered 'middle-class' without a university education and, for a family, without both parents working, likely full-time. Even those with university degrees now often face these difficulties. This situation has increased the effort-acceptability squeeze on young men considerably, at the same time often making it necessary for them to accept that they cannot realize the tacitly held identity of being the family breadwinner.

This is where identity role salience comes in. By the time they reach young adulthood, most people (though not all) take their sexual status for granted, so that they are constantly aware of it but they have so many habitual patterns of acknowledging it that their awareness is not the focus of much attention. For example, each morning most people open closets full of clothes appropriate to their sex and select some of them to wear without questioning for a moment that their closets do not contain any clothes appropriate only to the other sex – or if a person's closet does contain their heterosexual partner's clothes, that person does not spend even a second considering wearing any of them. That is, sexual identity is not generally salient when choosing clothes for the day, or even for purchase, because it is simply assumed. In contrast, when looking for the appropriate restroom in a strange building, most people are quite actively aware of matching the symbols on the doors to their own sex: their sexual identity is very salient.

For young men considering occupational options, sexual identity has become much less salient in recent years with respect to the aspects of occupational identity that develop last according to Gottfredson (1981): interests in the specific content areas and particular activities that various occupations involve. This has tended to increase the effort-acceptability squeeze for young men even further, however, because the overall loosening of traditional occupational identity sex dichotomies that has taken place has, very generally at least, tended to make women more welcome in high-status and technical occupations. There has been some loosening of stereotypes that occupations such as nursing and teaching in primary school are 'feminine' as well, but it has not been as strong, and these occupations do not carry as much status (and income) as many of the occupations that have become more open to women, such as physicians, scientists, attorneys, and high-level business executives. The net result of this is that young men face more competition in all occupations, and particularly in those that carry the highest social status, than they used to, because they must compete for the jobs in those occupations with many women as well as with other men. At the same time, the more tacitly held, and thus also not very salient, sexual aspects of their occupational identities, which were formed 10–15 years earlier when overall social attitudes about sex dichotomies in occupations were more strict, continue to suggest that they should be the primary family breadwinners. This can easily set young men up to be perennially dissatisfied with the places in the world open to them, and they may not even be able to articulate why, or, perhaps even worse, feel that it would be 'wrong' to do so.

The changing economic dynamics and loosening of sex dichotomies in occupational identities have created many difficulties for young women in establishing satisfying places in the world as well, but they are fundamentally different. As for young men, the sexual aspects of young women's occupational identities tend to have been established 10–15 years before they actually make their occupational choices, so they tend to be more traditional than is the current society in which the choices are being made, as well as relatively tacitly held. Unlike young men, however, for young women this traditional identity is availability to care for their children. Furthermore, particularly for young women who feel ready to accept the educational and cognitive challenges involved and to invest the necessary effort, many attractive professional occupational options have come to be seen as much more open to women, and thus as aspirations concordant with women's sexual identities, than they were to prior generations of women. This tends to be exciting and empowering, and even the prospect of having to compete for jobs in these occupations with young men can often add to the sense of excitement and empowerment. To the extent they take place, the excitement and empowerment, as well as what remains of resistance to their presence in these occupations, may make their sex more salient to young women than it otherwise would have been, and in a very positive way. That is, whether they perceive themselves to be welcomed trailblazers or mavericks constantly overcoming unstated prejudices, they are reminded often that the presence of their sex in many of these jobs remains a little unusual, or was so until very recently, and they are, at some level, 'beating the odds' by being there. Despite the extra satisfaction with occupational and sexual identity this can bring, there remains for these young women the generally more tacitly held sexual identity of caretaker for their children. This often sets them up for aspiring to do both, and to do both very well, possibly without completely conscious awareness of the standards they are setting for themselves. As for young men then, but for different reasons, their occupational aspirations can leave young women with professional aspirations perennially dissatisfied, not so much with the places in the world open to them, but with the quality of life those places in the world bring.

Young women who do not aspire to professional occupations tend to face a challenge that could be considered to lie between that faced by young men and that faced by young women aspiring to professional occupations. Of course the boundaries between professional and other occupations are not anywhere near as clear-cut as I make them appear here. Still, the contrast serves to highlight an important source of variation in psychological consequences of occupational aspirations. Many non-professional occupations both pay less well than professional occupations and are less inherently interesting and potentially fun. They are also more likely to involve relatively rigid schedules of hours and lower levels of autonomy. This makes them less attractive relative to that more tacitly held female sexual identity of caretaker for one's children. Yet economic pressures may make realizing a life built around the child-caring role unrealistic. At the same time, young women not aspiring to professional occupations may be facing the same kind of effort-acceptability squeeze faced by many young men. This squeeze likely tends to reduce the salience of sexual identity. Young women, however, may also be at least subconsciously aware that somehow they are not getting to experience the excitement and empowerment of their more professionally oriented female peers, thus increasing the salience of their sexual identity, but in a negative way. This can leave these young women, like many young men, feeling perennially dissatisfied with the places in the world available to them, again often without really being able to articulate why.

Salience of race in the development of occupational identity

Since the 1980s, most industrialized societies have become increasingly multicultural and multiracial. Of course this has taken place partly because the world has become more mobile: it has become much more common for people to emigrate from their birthplace to some other culture. Understanding how such emigration affects individuals and how and why some people, but not others, come to emigrate and where they go is a fascinating challenge in its own right, but I must leave it aside for purposes of this book. Instead, I focus on the impact of increasingly multicultural societies on individuals born to and growing up within them. This is challenging enough in its own right because, within any geographic area – city, region, or nation – that has become more multicultural, there is often considerable variation in the extent to which this has taken place. In general, there is more cultural diversity among the lower than the higher social classes. There are many reasons for this. Some are structural and rooted in the destination area: the professional occupations that tend to provide membership in the higher socioeconomic groups generally require more education and training, sometimes even including locally specific credentials, as well as fluency in the local language. The appropriate general educational background for the necessary more specific training can be hard to accumulate in the kinds of circumstances that tend to generate motivation to emigrate from one place to another. Other reasons are selective and rooted in the area of origin: under any particular set of environmental circumstances, some individuals will experience those circumstances more negatively than others and thus be more motivated to seek change by relocating to another place, and some who are motivated to seek change will be more able to accomplish this kind of change than others. In terms of the personality and ability characteristics immigrants tend to display in the societies in which they land, these two forces work at cross-purposes, but the overall pattern of greater multicultural diversity in the lower social classes is a result.

As another broad generality, many studies have shown quite clearly that greater exposure to people from diverse cultural backgrounds increases tolerance for cultural diversity. This does not tend to happen right away. Instead, it happens over time, as people in the dominant or 'home' cultural group accumulate positive experiences with incoming groups, or at least do not accumulate negative experiences. This process is more difficult, much slower, and takes on some different patterns when groups of different sizes with clearly visible racial physical or cultural characteristics have long existed within a society in conjunction with perceptions among many in the larger racial group that those in the smaller racial group are in some sense inferior. This situation has unfortunately been rather common across many societies such as for blacks and native Americans in the United States, Jews in many European countries, blacks and East Indians in Britain, Indonesians in the Netherlands, etc. The process of increasing tolerance is also impeded when there are shortages of resources, when people are more generally fearful (as during wartimes), and during economic downturns when job opportunities are restricted.

When one racial or ethnic group is both dominant and much larger than others, the process of increasing tolerance is also impeded by problems related to group differences in the very salience to group members of their racial/ethnic status. People in the larger and more dominant group are relatively unlikely to give their group status much thought. That is, in considering and developing their identities, they tend to take both their status in the large dominant group and the relative privileges it confers for granted, and shape their identities around the individual characteristics that distinguish them from others within their group. Things are somewhat different for people in minority groups that have experienced overt prejudice in the broader society. They are reminded constantly by the dominant society that they are different, and often these reminders have carried with them the strong suggestion that the dominant group considers them inferior and will block them from access to its resources. The reminders keep their racial/ethnic identity highly salient to such minority group members, and this salience and its negative cast present them with a challenge in developing a positive psychological identity that is not faced by members of the dominant majority group.

The challenge is that, in order to break down the social prejudices and barriers facing them as well as to gain access to the social and economic and physical resources concentrated in the majority group (peacefully at least!), members of the minority group need to demonstrate their worth to the dominant group on its terms. This is very difficult to do without taking on the dominant group's values and it is especially difficult to take on some of the dominant group's values but not others – in particular to avoid taking on the dominant group's view of one's minority group. This is especially the case with respect to occupational goals, because so many jobs require specific educational credentials that require considerable effort and time to obtain (never mind sometimes extensive financial resources to pay for the required education). Following the lead of the famous personality psychologist Gordon Allport (1954), a considerable body of psychological research has been carried out essentially under the assumption that this psychological balancing act is effectively impossible. That is, in developing a mature sense of racial identity, black Americans, for example, must inevitably develop poor self-esteem, because in the process of adapting to the racist society in which they live, they must internalize the dominant group's poor view of their group in order to thrive in the society the dominant group effectively controls (Clark, 1965; Horowitz, 1939; Kardiner & Ovesey, 1951; Markus, 1977;Oakes, Haslam, & Turner, 1994). Research from this perspective has intentionally focused on groups beyond black Americans because its proponents view black Americans as just one of many racial/ethnic groups that have faced analogous situations. It has produced important insights into the roles that racial identity can play in people's overall senses of identity (e.g., Crocker & Luhtanen, 1990) and the kinds of situations that tend to make racial identity salient to individuals (e.g., Cota & Dion, 1986).

Perspectives on racial identity beyond racial salience

The assumption that underlies this research, however, that an individual must take on the broader society's view of the racial group to which the individual belongs, appears not to recognize a rather obvious alternative. That is, members of an oppressed minority group may coalesce tightly around each other, consolidating their resources and upholding views of the worth of their group that transcend the negative views of the broader society. This tends to generate two forms of racial identity, membership in a specific racial group within the broader society as well as membership in the broader society. These can, for groups such as African Americans, be in sharp contrast to each other. This was perhaps first articulated by the sociologist W. E. B. DuBois (1903), who wrote about the inherent struggle involved in developing a positive sense of self as both 'Negro' and American. He noted that many Negro communities of his day maintained strong cultural traditions that rivalled yet were distinct from those of the broader American society in richness, complexity, and cohesiveness, and pointed out that these cultural traditions could be important sources of pride in racial identity for Negroes, regardless of what the broader society thought of them. An alternative and less recognized strand of psychological research has been carried out exploring the extent to which this is true of black Americans in particular, and the consequences that it has for their actions in the world. There is considerable variety in the ways that proponents of this view have defined the two forms of racial identity involved, and the manners in which they can be reconciled.

For example, some theorists working within this strand of research have viewed the dichotomy between identification as Black and identification as American more generally as opposite endpoints on a single dimension (e.g., Baldwin, 1984), while others have viewed these two forms of identification as two dimensions that must somehow co-exist (e.g., Boykin, 1983). Research in this strand has tended to focus on development of models that articulate the processes and stages involved in the emergence of a healthy black American identity (e.g., Cross, 1971), and development of measures that can operationalize the progress of individuals in realizing such an ideal racial identity (e.g., Parham & Helms, 1990). These models and measures have then been used to explore the extent to which they can account for behaviours and attitudes, especially those specifically involving life as a black American, such as attitudes towards utilization of counselling services (Helms, 1984) and behaviour and attitudes specifically centred around African-American culture and community (Baldwin & Hopkins, 1990).

These two research traditions have necessarily provided quite different perspectives on racial identity for black Americans. If identity as Black and identity as American are opposite endpoints of a single dimension, acknowledgement of both is possible only if both are no more than of middling strength or salience. In contrast, if they are separate dimensions, both could be strong or weak. The ways in which they have approached their research and its results can help shed light on how identity is involved in the development and maintenance of individual differences more generally, particularly in young adulthood. Perhaps not surprisingly, empirical results from both of these theoretical perspectives tend to be rather mixed on the questions underlying both of them, which are how and to what degree black Americans come to positive senses of identity, given the negative salience of their race in the broader American society (Cross, 1991; Sellers, Smith, Shelton, Rowley, & Chavous, 1998). One reason for this is that the degree of racial segregation in the United States has changed dramatically during the last 65 years, and these changes have taken place within the lifespans of many people still alive today. In 1950, the country was essentially segregated. In the former Confederate states, this segregation was formalized legally, including legally sanctioned segregated public schools. This was not true in states outside this region, but it almost may as well have been, for all white and black races actually mixed. There were very few black Americans in any of the professional occupations, and most blacks who were fortunate enough to attend universities at all did so at essentially completely black institutions. Racial segregation is no longer legal anywhere, blacks have made major inroads at universities and throughout the professional occupations since then, and the races mix much more frequently, but on average the black American population remains sharply disadvantaged relative especially to the white American population and the proportion of black American males who are or have been incarcerated is appallingly high. There are also some regions of the country that remain far more segregated than others, and much black American poverty tends to remain concentrated in those areas. Though far from complete, the massive changes, as well as remaining regional differences in both common social attitudes and the degree to which blacks intermingle with the rest of society, suggest that many of the inconsistencies in study results likely reflect actual differences in the race-related climates in which the participants in these studies grew up.

Box 9.1 Development of racial identity

In this rapidly evolving social environment, some of the issues involved in the development of racial identity and its impact on the development of occupational identity parallel those involved in the association between sexual and occupational identity, but there are differences as well. Where there is parallel, we should expect similar patterns of influences, but this is not the case where there are differences. Age, and thus relative level of cognitive development, at which awareness of one's group membership emerges is one area that can highlight both the differences and similarities. Almost universally, children become aware very early in life of their membership in either the male or female sex, so that this awareness emerges when their cognitive understanding of the implications of their membership is rudimentary, simply because their cognitive understanding of everything is rudimentary. Awareness of racial identity emerges at far less consistent ages, and age of emergence varies with the kinds of inter-racial situations a child encounters. In turn, the kinds of experiences encountered vary with racial identity status and have varied over time and with the interpretations placed upon these experiences by adults surrounding the child. This creates the potential for a hornet's nest of individual differences in racial identity and its associations with other outcomes, including occupational aspirations and, ultimately, occupational status. For example, it was very common and remains quite common for white American children, particularly those growing up in families with higher socioeconomic status, to encounter very few black Americans at all in their day-to-day lives in some communities. For such white children, the few black Americans they do encounter are often similar to them in many ways: well integrated into the broader society and of relatively high socioeconomic status. This means that the question of racial identity in general, and their own racial identity in particular, is likely to become salient to them only very rarely as they are growing up. Because of the infrequency of racial salience, racial identity is unlikely to become very central to their overall identity (Sellers, Smith, Shelton, Rowley, & Chavous, 1998). Moreover, because their own experiences of the salience of race are so rare, whatever understanding they develop of its importance to others is likely to be heavily influenced as they are growing up by the attitudes of the adults around them towards the subject, particularly their parents and teachers, and by their exposure to the subject through the media. Such children, and the adolescents and adults they become, are unlikely to be aware of their relative naiveté in this area.

The experience of black Americans is almost inevitably inherently different and more varied. When American society was heavily segregated, many black children grew up in exclusively black neighbourhoods, attended all-black schools, and had few encounters independently of adults with white Americans. This made the limitedness of their experiences with other races superficially similar to those of many white American children. Even then, however, it would have been difficult to escape awareness that theirs was the minority group and that the majority group blocked their participation in many of the advantages in the society it dominated. This was because their parents and the other adults around them had to negotiate the broader society and did come into contact, often in service-providing roles, with white Americans who lived lives of very different material circumstances from theirs. The extent to and form in which this was, and still is, made salient to them by day-to-day experiences, however, varied, and still does vary, considerably. Where family and neighbourhood situations had some stability, and parents had been able to come to some kind of psychological resolution of their own occupational and racial identities, black American children could grow up in situations relatively similar to those of many white American children – that is, they could go through much of their childhoods with few encounters of their own with white Americans, and could obtain much of their own sense of racial identity largely through exposure to the attitudes and understandings of the subject held by the adults around them. The understandings they received in this manner, however, had inevitably to be different from that received by white American children because it had to involve some kind of understanding of their group's subordinate position in the broader society. Just what that understanding entailed, however, could vary from some kind of acceptance of the situation to a feeling of obligation to use their lives to challenge it to rejection of the values of the greater society in favour of alternatives of their own creation. Whatever understandings they received in this way, by the time they reached adolescence and young adulthood, it would be difficult to call them naïve on the question of racial identity in the same way that many white Americans could be considered naïve.

Where family and neighbourhood situations were unstable, so that, even during periods when some parts of the country were heavily segregated, children were thrown by the instability into contacts of their own, independently of adults, with white Americans, much about the impact for the development of racial identity for these children depended on the qualities of these experiences. Because I am talking about experiences of children at the hands of adults, much about these experiences would not be under the control, or dependent on characteristics, of the children, but there was still no doubt considerable variation in the quality of the experiences. Control of the experience at the hands of the adult would have meant that, for the child, the quality of the encounter was largely random. Especially in areas where racial segregation was *de facto* rather than legally imposed, sometimes black children would have encountered white adults who treated them quite kindly and with helpful intentions (even if sometimes condescendingly) while other times they would have encountered white adults who treated them with overt hostility. This variation in quality of treatment in encounters could be expected to have systematic influences on the black children experiencing them. That is, those experiencing relatively kind treatment could be expected, in general, to respond at some level more positively than those experiencing overt hostility. Over time, those who, again likely mostly randomly, experienced more relatively positive than negative encounters could be expected systematically to develop somewhat different kinds of racial identity from those who experienced more negative than positive encounters.

Exactly what this might mean for racial identity, however, is very difficult to guess because it leaves out the part of the encounter experience over which any child, no matter how young, does exert control. By control here of course I do not necessarily mean conscious control, though sometimes the control I mean *is* conscious. This control is the child's cognitive and emotional response to the encounter, and it can show large individual differences. The extent to which it will show such differences, however, depends to some degree on the intensity of the encounter. Beyond some threshold the more intense the emotional quality of the adult's treatment during the encounter, the more likely it will be that children's responses will be similar. But for the vast majority of encounters, there will be substantial individual differences in children's responses. These differences will derive from the child's genetically influenced temperament, the degree to which the child has had similar kinds of experiences in the past, the meanings the child has made of these prior experiences, and even the emotional and cognitive states of the child at the specific time of the encounter. Over time, responses to such encounters will build up, or not if there are few such occurrences. Even if the child cannot draw any cognitive interpretation from a particular encounter at the time, the accumulation of any pattern in the encounters will gradually become apparent, leading to the emergence of *cognitive schemas* (Beck, 1967) regarding both understanding of how others see the child's racial identity and how the child him/herself sees that identity. Cognitive schemas are organized patterns of thought or behaviour that consist of frameworks of previously developed ideas about how the world works that contribute to systems of processing new information. They influence what we pay attention to and recall. People are more likely to notice things that fit into their schema, and they tend often to interpret contradictions to schemas as exceptions or distort them to fit the schemas. Schemas tend to remain relatively fixed even in the face of contradictory information. They are very useful, even critical, for processing incoming information efficiently, but can also hinder adaptation to new circumstances. Most aspects of identity can be considered schemas.

Though variation in the kinds of transracial encounters and the responses that black American children growing up in segregated communities in the United States 60 years ago experienced was large, it pales in relation to the variation in such experiences that might take place today. There are at least two reasons for this. One is media exposure. The world is simply so much more closely linked today than it was then, especially of course in industrialized nations such as the United States. It would be very difficult for a child of any ethnic/racial background there to grow up without awareness that their society includes others of very different backgrounds and lifestyles, if only because almost everyone is now exposed at least via television and movies. But society has also become much more integrated, so direct personal encounters with people of other races and ethnicities are now much more common. This greater exposure to cultural/racial diversity increases tolerance for it, but it also increases the salience of cultural/racial identity. This greater salience can, in turn, reinforce perceptions that cultural/racial differences are substantial and deeply rooted. To the extent this takes place it can impact the degree to which a society can become truly culturally or racially integrated. I work here from the assumption that such racial and cultural integration is inherently good and a worthy social goal. Children attending schools with racially and ethnically mixed populations are likely to become very used to being around and interacting with people with very different backgrounds from their own, but they are also likely to develop cognitive schemas about how those differences play themselves out in patterns of characteristics in the specific individuals in the various racial and ethnic groups around them. These specific individuals will of course have their own individual characteristics that do not necessarily reflect those typical of their groups in any coherent way, but they may nevertheless be the ones the children around them build into the cognitive schemas they develop about the racial identities of those groups. And the specific qualities of their own interactions with those individuals will be the ones they build into their own emerging racial identities.

Empirical studies of racial identity

Research in the area of racial identity has not been extensive, and findings from the studies that have been conducted have been mixed. Even the inconsistencies among studies, however, can be helpful in illustrating the issues I have discussed. For example, Dutton, Singer, and Devlin (1998) studied racial identity in American fourth-graders. Their study was interesting for the breadth of racial identity measures assessed and because they pulled their sample from four different schools. One school had a predominantly white and relatively well-to-do suburban student population (7% minority enrolment, including several minority groups in addition to black Americans; 18% received free or reduced-cost school lunches); all the study participants were white. Two had well-integrated urban student populations (60% minority enrolment, of which 38% were black; 58% were receiving free or reduced-cost school lunches); half the study participants were black and the other half white. All the fourth-grade students in the final, urban, school were black, and 86 were receiving free or reduced-cost school lunches. The children were asked to draw pictures of themselves, using boxes of crayons including a wide variety of possible skin tones, to identify their own races and those of children in photographs (black, white, Hispanic, of each sex), to state the races they would prefer to be and not to be and to have as friends and not, and to address 'what you are' and 'what you are not' by making lists in response to each. The pictures the children drew of themselves were scored solely according to the extent to which they could be considered clearly black or clearly white, with scores tailored to match the children's own races. The lists of characteristics were scored 0 if there was no mention of race or ethnicity, 1 if there was one mention on the 'are not' list, 2 if there was one mention on the 'are' list, and 3 if there were two or more mentions on either list.

In the study (Dutton, Singer, & Devlin, 1998), the children from the integrated schools and from the predominantly black school made more references to race/ethnicity in describing themselves than did the children from the predominantly white school, by about 0.5 standard deviation, but there was no difference among the integrated and predominantly black schools. Children from the predominantly white and the integrated schools more frequently indicated they would like to be friends with children of races other than their own, but children from the predominantly white school also more frequently indicated that they would not like to be friends with the black child photographed. But then children from the predominantly black school also more frequently indicated that they would not like to be friends with the white child photographed. Over 90 per cent of the children could accurately distinguish the races of the photographed children, and children from all of the schools were significantly more likely to nominate their own races in response to questions about which child's photograph looked most like them and which they would most prefer to be like. Drawings by children from the predominantly white school were significantly more clearly of their own race than those by children from any of the other schools, by over 0.5 standard deviation. Of course the study itself had undoubtedly made race salient to the children.

Dutton, et al.'s (1998) finding that children from the integrated schools made more references to race/ethnicity than did those from the predominantly white school is consistent with the idea that exposure to other races increases the salience of one's own race. And the findings that children from the integrated schools were more likely to consider friendship with children from other races than were the children from the predominantly black school and less likely to reject friendship with them than children from either of the non-integrated schools are consistent with the idea that exposure increases tolerance. The result indicating preference for being of one's own race surprised Dutton, et al. (1998), as prior studies from the 1960s through early 1980s had found that black children tended to express preferences to be of races other than their own. They interpreted it as indicating growing racial pride among black people as racial tensions throughout society have eased. The observation that children from the predominantly white school drew pictures of themselves that were more obviously of the white race also surprised the study's authors. They suggested that it may because white children, particularly when they have little exposure to people from other races, experience so little conflict over racial identity that they, effectively, take it for granted that they should just either not colour the skin in at all in a drawing on a piece of white paper, or reach automatically for the tanny/peach coloured crayon that was once labelled 'flesh'.

The fact that leaving the skin in the drawing uncoloured automatically meant that it would be perceived as indicating white race confounded interpretation of these results. The children drew themselves before completing any of the other tasks, so racial identity was not primed by those tasks. The results from the various tasks were not significantly correlated, indicating that they tapped different aspects of identity development.

Against this backdrop of inconsistency in Dutton, et al.'s (1998) results with those of prior studies, differences in perceptions about racial identity and inter-action among children of the same races in settings affording very different levels of transracial experience, and little coordination among responses to questions that tapped different aspects of children's understanding about race, it is little wonder that there has been little consistency across studies attempting to address how racial identity is involved in the development of occupational identity. For one thing, this rather scant literature has suffered from a limitation common to much of the psychology literature: it has relied too heavily on samples of college students, often just on black college students, so there is no way to evaluate whether whatever is indicated about how racial identity is involved in develop-ment of occupational identity for them might be different from its involvement for young people in other racial groups. This is particularly problematic for studies of the role of racial identity in the development of occupational identity, especially for older studies, because black American college students have often overcome barriers that affect many of their racial and age peers, but not their age peers from other races to nearly the same degree, simply to *become* college students at all. It is very likely that this alone has some impact on their self-es-teem, self-confidence, the degree to which racial identity is central to their more general senses of identity, and the degree to which they perceive racial barriers to occupational attainment, as well as their attitudes towards the existence of the barriers they perceive relative to the attitudes and perceptions about barriers of their racial and age peers. I am not aware, however, of any studies that have addressed these factors. Most studies have not even noted the extent to which the student populations of the colleges from which the samples were drawn were integrated. Studies have also been based on different conceptualizations of racial identity, and even when conceptualizations have been similar, measures have differed, making comparison still difficult.

Some studies have acknowledged the potential sample-specificity of results from samples of college students who are well-educated, have successfully met most of the broader society's expectations for people of their ages (or they would not be college students), and tend to come from relatively affluent backgrounds. Even these studies, however, generally have not solved these problems. For example, in two studies of relations between racial identity and self-esteem, Rowley, Sellers, Chavous, and Smith (1998) made use of a sample of introductory psychology students at 'a medium-sized university in the southeastern part of the United States', who reported median family income well above that of the country as a whole for one study. For a follow-up in high school students, they combined students from two summer programmes.

One was an educational programme for the academically talented in a relatively rural area of the American midwest and the other was for students from a large urban area in the American south. The latter was not academically selective and included no educational component. Both these samples were from relatively economically disadvantaged families, but they likely differed considerably in the extent to which they had been successful so far in meeting the broader society's expectations for people of their age, as well as their experiences with other races, due to the generally much lower proportion of the population that is black in small towns in the Midwest than in large urban areas in the south, and to the generally more overt presence of racism in the south than in the Midwest.

Another study (Carter & Constantine, 2000) recognized the need to compare black university students with those of other ethnic groups, but used completely different measures relying on different models of racial identity development to assess it in the two groups. This study was specifically designed to investigate the role of racial identity in the development of occupational identity, but combined five aspects of that process, from career exploration and planning to access to and knowledge of information about the working world in general and a single preferred occupation in particular in the measure of 'career maturity', making it impossible to do anything to track how racial identity might be involved in anyone in either group's progress through that process. The inconsistencies in results can be illustrated by considering student perceptions of career barriers. Such perceptions might be among the most likely to produce consistent results, but this has not been the case. For example, Ladany, Melincoff, Constantine, and Love (1997) observed that greater perceived barriers were related to lower vocational exploration and commitment to career choices in urban at-risk high school students, but Evans and Herr (1994) could find no association between perceived career barriers and career aspirations in black American college students. This could possibly be because the college students were more likely to have confidence or at least optimism that they would be able to surmount whatever barriers they perceived. But Rollins (2001) found that black American adolescents who perceived that they faced more racial discrimination also reported greater self-efficacy for making career decisions.

Why all this?

I have devoted considerable space to exploring the role of racial identity in the development of occupational identity, particularly for black Americans in relation to white Americans. I have done this because I think it provides an excellent highly visible example of the ways in which individual differences are involved in the association between any other aspect of identity and the development of occupational identity for anyone. Individuals differ in the degree to which any aspect of identity is central to their overall sense of identity; they differ in the kinds of experiences they have had with respect to that aspect of identity; they differ in the ways that they are temperamentally and genetically oriented to respond even to identical experiences, and they differ for the same kinds of reasons in the constellation of surrounding traits and schemas that also contribute to both the kinds of experiences encountered and the responses to them. For some people, racial identity, or any other specific aspect of identity, will be central to their overall conception of identity, while for others that same aspect of identity will be at most an afterthought. Even those for whom the degree of centrality is similar will differ in how they view their particular identity, even when that identity is the same. They will differ because the people around them tend to hold different views of that identity, because that identity is more or less well-represented among those surrounding people, because they have had different encounter experiences with those others, because they have responded to those encounter experiences differently than others would for temperamental and genetic reasons unique to them, because those differences in response have caused them to seek additional encounters to different degrees and in different kinds of circumstances, and because they have encountered barriers in their freedom to make those choices in different ways and responded to the presence of those barriers in different ways. All of these differences mean that any specific aspect of identity will be differentially salient to different individuals in thinking about occupational identity and that whatever salience it carries will be interpreted and acted upon in different ways. For example, some people who perceive substantial social discriminatory barriers to their participation in some occupation will elect to let those barriers stand in their way and will pursue some other goal instead, while others will do everything they can to surmount those barriers.

This does not mean, however, that systematic patterns in the development of occupational identity cannot be observed. Even more to the point for overall psychological health, it does not mean that systematic patterns of individual differences cannot be identified in success in finding a place in the world in which one's skills and abilities can be applied in a way that brings financial stability and some sense that one is accomplishing something socially useful. We tend to think of these patterns as summarizing causal chains, in which one variable has some direct and calculable impact on another, and this impact would be the same on anyone, all else being equal. To a certain extent this may be true for some associations. But all else is never equal, and the variation in the 'all else' can make all the difference in the outcome. Even when it does not, the variation in the 'all else' can make all the difference in the way the person experiencing the outcome perceives it, and this can make all the difference in the meaning it holds for the person, and thus the way in which anything considered an outcome at one point in time contributes to subsequent psychological development and life outcomes.

For example, two individuals may hold identical jobs, considered good by the broader society around them, and be paid the same well-above-average salary. One of them may be very happy in the position, feeling useful, well compensated, and respected, and finding the job challenging and interesting, while the other may be extremely dissatisfied, finding the job dull, not suited to his/her abilities and interests, poorly compensated, and not offering an appropriate level of respect. The search for a place in the world is highly individual, and the degree to which a person considers himself/herself to have been successful in that search at any one point in time is at least as individual. It is impossible to look at the places at which individuals arrive and say, even with the benefit of hindsight, that those places came about through some particular combination of experiences, attitudes, genetic influences, temperamental qualities, cultural background, etcetera, etcetera, etcetera.

Illustrating individuality of outcomes in empirical data

Two recent studies highlight these themes. Both dealt with the experience of major depression. Major depression is, of course, a particular form of psychopathology. What helps us to understand it may not be relevant either to understanding other forms of psychopathology or to understanding psychological states in people without overt psychopathology. But major depression is one of the most common forms of psychopathology: it may be experienced as a diagnosable clinical condition by as much as 30 per cent of the population at least once in their lifetime. It also shares much variance with other forms of psychopathology, and can be measured continuously, so that it is not unreasonable to think of lower-level depression as low satisfaction with life. It can thus serve as a marker of one's satisfaction with one's place in the world, or at least of one's satisfaction with progress in the search for such as place.

In the first of the two studies, Kendler, Myers, and Halberstadt (2011) carried out extensive interviews with people who had experienced episodes of major depression within the past year. The interviews were intended to draw from the participants their ideas about the reasons that they became depressed, as well as their personal circumstances at the times they became depressed. Using this detailed information, Kendler et al. rated the extents to which they considered the reasons offered by participants for their depressions understandable – really, whether they believed that they themselves (and anyone else) would be likely to become depressed under similar circumstances. They also considered ostensibly objective 'causes' of depression, such as number of prior episodes of depression, vulnerable personality (high neuroticism), comorbidity with anxiety disorders, childhood risk factors for depression (parental loss, sexual abuse, low parental warmth), early age of onset, and genetic/familial risk of depression. Controlling for the negative association between number of prior episodes and level of understandability (which to them indicated overall vulnerability to depression), none of the other measures was associated with understandability. That is, variables that have been robustly and objectively associated with tendency to experience depression did not predict the extent to which an outside (clinically trained) observer considered the reasons people offered for their depressions strong enough to have generated the depressions. People have a strong tendency to look for reasons for their situations, and thus to find them. This does not mean, however, that the reasons they find actually *are* the reasons. At the same time, the objective associations in no sense explain all depressions. It is probably at least as likely that individual perceptions of reasons for the depressions were accurate to some degree, at least for them. This is consistent with a literature on situational depression that has indicated that patients whose depressions are diagnosed as arising from some particular situation do not differ from those who are not diagnosed in this way in recovery rates, pre-existing personality, or familial risk (Hirschfeld, 1981; Joffe, Levitt, Bagby, & Regan, 1993; McGuffin, Katz, & Babbington, 1988; Winokur & Pitts, 1964).

The second study (Kendler & Halberstadt, 2013), was essentially a collection of extensive interviews of 14 monozygotic twin pairs highly discordant for experience of depression. The twins came from a much larger sample including more than 1,500 pairs who have been examined and interviewed over an extended time period. Because these twins were genetically identical and had been raised together, this is about as close as we are likely to come to seeing 'what if?': what life would have been like for someone if this, that, or the other thing had been different. The twins also ranged in age from 45 to 65, so all had had considerable time to accumulate adult experience beyond their shared childhoods. To define discordance, Kendler and Halberstadt required one twin to have reported at least one episode of major depression on at least two assessment occasions. The other twin had to deny having experienced depression on all assessment occasions, and at least 10 years had to have elapsed since the age of onset of the first episode of depression in the co-twin. The generally great similarity between co-twins for experience of depression is indicated by the fact that, from the full sample, only 40 pairs were identified as discordant using this definition. Kendler and Halberstadt interviewed all who were willing, with preference for those who lived within a two-hour drive of their lab. The interviews were conducted with both twins together, and the interviewer was blind to which twin had suffered depression. They lasted 90–150 minutes and focused on the twins' life histories and their similarities and differences, so it quickly became clear which twin had suffered depression. Once this took place, the twins were asked for their interpretations of the reasons for their discordance. Of course this asks directly for exactly the kind of search for reasons and understanding that the first study indicated does not explain much variance in depression.

In two pairs, a single dramatic event appeared to have precipitated a chain of events over an extended period of time that contributed to the differences in the twins' experiences with depression. In one of these pairs, one twin had suffered a serious head injury at age 12 when he hit a rock while driving a small motorcycle very fast. The injury required extensive rehabilitation and time out from school, and appeared to have affected his cognitive ability, limiting his educational attainment, and leaving him, he believed, at a disadvantage in meeting his obligations as a husband, provider, and father. Though this was of course a major event, the twins agreed that, before this accident, this twin had been more aggressive and assertive than his brother, raising the question of relative likelihoods of something like this happening to them. In the other pair, one twin had, in her early 20s, driven onto a major highway slipway the wrong way while intoxicated, and killed a young mother in the resulting head-on collision. This had left her racked with guilt. Again, this was a single major and rather understandably traumatic event, but this story only came to light at the very end of the interview. The twins had reported consistently throughout the interview that their personalities had been different from a young age, with this twin having more of a temper, being more assertive, and getting into more trouble. Compared with the broader sample of MZ twins from which these discordant pairs were drawn, as a group the discordant pairs had a higher rate of major depression in their mothers than MZ twins who were concordant for absence of depression, but a similar rate of major depression in their fathers. They had a very similar rate of major depression in their mothers as MZ twins who were concordant for experience of depression, but a lower rate in their fathers. This suggested they may have been of 'middling' genetic vulnerability to depression. This might mean that it would take a rather dramatic experience to trigger depression for them, but such an experience would be more likely to do so for them than for much of the rest of the population.

None of the rest of the pairs could point to the same degree to single events as having contributed to their different experiences of depression, but the same themes seemed to apply. Differences in personality expressed early appeared to contribute to life choices, gambles if you will, that went wrong or right for chance reasons. Often these choices involved romantic relationships, but occupational situations were also common. Sometimes it was the more adventurous twin who gambled right, escaping depression; sometimes it was the more adventurous twin who gambled wrong. For example, in one pair, one twin got his girlfriend pregnant at age 17, and they married. She had experienced the repeated divorces of her mother, and was absolutely determined to make her own marriage work, despite its inauspicious beginnings. The twin reported that his wife was very tolerant of his many faults and the marriage very strong because of this. His brother had not been so lucky and had suffered repeated depressions associated with messy romantic breakups. In another pair, the shyer twin, who followed her sister in everything when they were children, married her first boyfriend, a somewhat older widower with children, directly after college. The marriage did not go well and broke apart. Her sister went through several relationships before marrying, and did so considerably later and much more successfully. In another pair, the more responsible twin had married, considerably later than her sister, a banker she described as a little bit boring, but a great husband, provider, and father, who had 'grown on her' over the years. In contrast, her less responsible and self-directed sister had played around romantically, dropped out of college, married badly and endured subsequent tumultuous relationships that contributed to her depression. In many pairs, difficulties with romantic relationships were paralleled by less tumultuous but otherwise very similar differences in ability to find and maintain satisfactory employment.

These stories highlight several themes of this book that will continue to be addressed in the next chapters devoted to the adult lifespan and ageing. First, the potential for genetic contribution to life outcomes emerges very early in life and plays out throughout its course. These discordant pairs would be considered at moderate familial risk of depression because of their parental histories. Familial risk is not just genetic, of course, but genetic influences are very important aspects of it. Second, small differences in temperament can contribute to selection into situations that can exert very strong effects on outcomes, even swamping individual control. Third, even small differences in situational experiences accumulate, and the accumulation can create major differences in outcomes over time. Fourth, propensity to plan, set goals, and channel behaviour around those goals seems to help avoid the most disastrous chance events. And finally, it's not just what environments an individual chooses or what happens as a result of those choices that matters. How the individual construes and interprets those experiences is also extremely important.

Further reading

Gottfredson, L. S. (1981). Circumscription and compromise: A developmental theory of occupational aspirations. *Journal of Counseling Psychology Monograph, 28,* 545–579.

Kendler, K. S., & Halberstadt, L. J. (2013). The road not taken: Life experiences in monozygotic twin pairs discordant for major depression. *Molecular Psychiatry, 18,* 975–984.

Kendler, K. S., Myers, J., & Halberstadt, L. J. (2011). Do reasons for major depression act as causes? *Molecular Psychiatry, 16,* 626–633.

Kohn, M. L., & Schooler, C. (1969). Class, occupation, and orientation. *American Sociological Review, 34,* 659–678.

Marksman-Adams, C. (1992). A consideration of intervening factors in adolescent identity formation. In G. R. Adams, T. P. Gulotta, & R. Montemayor, *Adolescent Identity Formation (Advances in Adolescent Development, vol. 4)* (pp. 165–187). Newbury Park, CA: Sage.

Stryker, S. (2007). Identity theory and personality theory: Mutual relevance. *Journal of Personality, 75,* 1083–1102.

Wilk, S. L., Desmaris, L. B., & Sackett, P. R. (1995). Gravitation to jobs commensurate with ability – longitudinal and cross-sectional tests. *Journal of Applied Psychology, 80,* 79–85.

Adult Development: Balancing Work and Family

10

In the last chapter I focused primarily on the development of occupational identity. I did so because taking up some occupation has long preceded and continues to precede establishment of partner/spousal relationships intended to be permanent followed by procreation for most people. Without the financial and emotional stability offered by some occupation, raising a family is much more stressful for parents, and, as indicated in the earlier chapters on infancy, childhood, and adolescence, studies have very consistently suggested substantial associations of parental occupational instability with negative outcomes for offspring as well. Establishment of occupation before family is of course a rather arbitrary chronology of the lifespan. Many if not most people acquire some romantic experiences during adolescence. And many, at least in industrialized countries, go through several serially monogamous sexually intimate relationships before establishing a partnership with someone with whom they intend to remain permanently and with whom they may start families. This is of course far from the universal pattern. Ironically and unfortunately, rates of teenage pregnancy and single-parenthood tend to be higher among those of lower socioeconomic status – those who are also more likely to encounter the financial and emotional stresses associated with occupational instability. And of course some people do not establish families at all.

In this chapter I will focus on the development of and individual differences in romantic and sexual relationships, the processes involved in establishing romantic partnerships intended to be permanent and their evolutionary origins and implications, and the psychological changes that take place with parenthood. Many of the topics I cover are as old as the biological class of mammals, but one in particular is very current and unique to humans. This topic is the major challenges couples currently face in industrialized countries to balance both partners' career goals even before they have children, and the much greater challenges these couples face in balancing work and family demands, desires, and needs after children are born. There have been dramatic changes over the past 50–60 years, particularly in women's career aspirations and in the openness of society to women having such aspirations, and these changes continue today. The changes have been crucial in making fuller use of the skills and knowledge – the human capital – of the female half of the population, but they have also created social pressures on both women and men, and their children, and industrialized countries are clearly still wrestling with appropriate means of coping with these pressures. But I begin with the development of early romantic experiences in adolescence.

Early romantic attraction

The classical understanding of the development of romantic and sexual feelings in the individual was that childhood was a period of dormancy. According to this model, which has been propounded since Anna Freud and Erik Erikson, the capacity to experience sexual and romantic attraction develops rather precipitously in concert with and as a result of the hormonal changes that take place during puberty. Within the last 20 years, however, several key studies have indicated that this model required substantial revision (McClintock & Herdt, 1996). Groups of heterosexual and homosexual adults and males and females all consistently report their first experiences of sexual attraction at mean ages of 9.5 to 10.5, well before puberty has been achieved for most, but right about the time of the first surges of adrenal production at the transition to juvenility. Moreover, they report a gradual progression of activity from first awareness of sexual attraction alone, with no sense of actual interaction with the attractive person, through active fantasy of sexual interaction, and finally the first groping actual activity. Moreover, homosexual adults report their first experiences of such attraction as being with others of their sex, and heterosexuals report the opposite. Of course, as the reports in such studies have been retrospective and made by currently self-identified homo- and heterosexuals, the potential particularly for reporting bias on choice of attractive person and age of experience is large. I am aware of no research specifically on the topic, but anecdotal evidence and ethnographic reports from cultures isolated from western society suggest that children are capable at even younger ages of intense personal attractions externally indistinguishable from the behaviour of an adolescent with a 'crush.' All of this suggests that the emergence of sexual identity is not precipitous and tied in lockstep to gonadal puberty at all, but is instead a more gradual process that involves pre-pubertal changes as well. Moreover, it seems likely that it is fuelled, as in other areas, as much by cognitive development, in the form of knowledge of the world, self-awareness, and social and cultural learning, as by hormones.

The possibility that cognitive development is involved opens the possible reasons for individual differences in sexual behaviour and experiences well beyond those associated with the individual differences in hormonal levels and timing of puberty that have been most often credited with creating these differences. Pubertal hormonal development has been the fall-back explanation because researchers have found little evidence that social expectations about sexual understanding and behaviour that are commonly placed on children during the last years of primary school are powerful enough to create the first stirrings of sexual awareness (McClintock & Herdt, 1996).

Researchers have also suggested that, if social learning is a primary explanation, then the age of first awareness should be later in homosexuals than in heterosexuals, as most industrialized societies do not encourage homosexuality even when they tolerate it. As the reported age of awareness is the same in homo- and heterosexuals, this possibility has been rejected. But both of these conclusions rest on the assumption that the relevant question is whether sexual awareness emerges due solely to biological changes or due solely to social learning experiences. As we have seen throughout this book, development in general takes place through linkages among an individual's ability to process the available stimuli, motivation and ability to pursue or avoid additional stimuli, and manner of interpreting stimuli. This means that development is never driven solely by biology or solely by social learning. It is highly unlikely that development of sexual awareness and behaviour is any different. The reasons offered for dismissing the involvement of social learning also rest on the assumption that children learn what adults intend to teach them, even about their own identities and self-awareness. As I discussed in Chapter 7, this is very frequently not the case. Children learn from all stimuli they receive, whether those stimuli are intended for their ears and eyes or not, and the conclusions they draw from those stimuli reflect their own needs and motivations rather than those attributed to them or desired for them by the adults around them. Their conclusions also reflect reward and punishment experiences well beyond those organized by adults. This means that what children actually understand and experience can often be very different from what adults think they understand and experience and have intended to present to them.

Both the hormonal and social explanations also rest on the assumption that adults' recollections of their experiences, and the ages at which they occurred, are accurate. The potential for inaccuracies of many different kinds in episodic memory has been documented extensively, but the implications of this for longitudinal research are often simply relegated to the limitations sections of papers. Some longitudinal studies ask for dates or ages of experience of life events at several different time points, and these studies find that many participants are not consistent over time in the dates or ages they report for the same experiences. The best way to address this problem would be to ask children about their current experiences with and awareness of sexual attraction, but I have not been able to locate any reports of such research. There may be many reasons for this, including the difficulty of avoiding asking leading questions, but one primary one may be ethical concerns over possibly encouraging promiscuous sexuality in underage children.

The existence of such concerns points to the third reason researchers have offered to dismiss the role of social enculturation in the emergence around age 10 of sexual attractions: the wide diversity of cultural practices and attitudes regarding the development and public expression of sexual maturity. Herdt and McClintock (2000), for example, argued that the fact that pre-colonial New Guinean cultures had cultural practices regarding sexual development in childhood and adolescence that appeared to reflect the importance of age 10 for the first stirrings of sexual attraction provided substantial evidence that the vast differences between the practices in these cultures and those in modern western societies were not important in the timing of this emergence. The consistency is certainly suggestive of the importance of some form of 'biological press' possibly associated with adrenarchy, but the very evidence they cite also strongly suggests that enculturation is also of major importance in the forms of early sexual behaviour observed. For example, many anthropologists have reported that, in these New Guinean cultures, it is common for young boys to leave their mothers at the age of around 8 and go to live with groups of men, adolescent males and other male children. In these cultures (Herdt & McClintock, 2000), people believe that young boys must be inseminated by older boys and men in order to grow up strong (and in fact to avoid weakening and even dying). At first the young boys are strictly the targets of the older adolescents and men in their groups, but, as they become accustomed to their new living situation, they increasingly choose who will inseminate them, thus apparently expressing sexual attraction, around the age of 10. This is very different from the behaviour of your average 10-year-old in North America and Europe.

All in all, it seems likely that the ability to experience romantic attraction develops well before gonadal puberty, and rather gradually, in concert with individual pre-pubertal development as well as individual development of cognitive awareness both of one's own experiences and the surrounding culture. This is important because the presence of sexual attraction is often considered the initial step towards the achievement of romantic love, and the presence of romantic love is considered by many in modern societies to be of great importance in establishing stable, secure, and constructive long-term pair-bonded relationships that can ideally foster both happiness for the members of those pair bonds and optimal development of their offspring (Feeney, 2008). Linking romantic love to lifetime pair bonds and procreation in this way is, however, a largely western and modern phenomenon, as throughout much of history in many cultures marriages have not tended to be established based on romantic love, but rather on economic advantage. Still, romantic love seems to have been and to continue to be important in most cultures (Jankowiak, 1995; Lieberman & Hatfield, 2006), though its importance has often been disruptive of the intended social order. That is, it has been and is often involved in resistance to arranged marriages, and in premarital, extra-marital, and post-marital relationships and the conception of illegitimate offspring.

Early romantic experiences

In modern industrialized countries, where most psychological research has been conducted, it has become common for adolescents to experience their first romantic relationships. For example, Carver, Joyner, and Udry (2003) observed that, in a large nationwide American sample of 12–18-year-olds, 55 per cent reported that they had had at least one romantic relationship during the previous 18 months. Such relationships are not necessarily completely sexual of course, in the sense of including sexual intercourse, but a substantial proportion is. At the same time, many adolescents experience purely sexual relationships. The role of romance in sexual activity is suggested by the finding that, among high-school-aged teens who were sexually active between 1993 and 2003 in the United States sample, 70 per cent reported that both their first and most recent sexual relationships had also been romantic (Manlove, Franzetta, Ryan, & Moore, 2006). Sexual activity is now commonly completely separated from reproductive intent throughout the population. This trend began of course with the first availability of effective contraception in the late 1950s and early 1960s, but it has increased as specific forms of contraception have proliferated and become more reliable, and side-effects and costs have been reduced. This has inspired relaxations of cultural attitudes restricting sexual behaviour outside of marriage, but these changes, though widespread, are far from universal.

As in so many other areas, adolescents are often caught between adult and child cultures with respect to sexual behaviour, and the increased freedom they often experience from direct adult supervision, coupled with the sensation-seeking motivations they experience (see Chapter 8), often leads them to develop some of their own cultural practices and mores. In recent years, one of these has been the concept of 'friends with benefits', or intermittent 'hooking up' (sexual activity) between friends who are not romantically involved. Even among teens who engage in this kind of casual sexual activity, however, it is common that at least one of the partners is hoping the relationship will become romantic (Manning, Giordano, & Longmore, 2006). And most teens report having experienced romantic rejection (Fisher, 2006).

Early romantic relationships and attractions occupy considerable portions of energy and time in adolescent life. To both adolescents themselves and the adults around them, it can seem like everything hangs in the balance pending the next potential encounter with the object of an adolescent's romantic attraction. Despite the apparent intensity of these experiences, there have been relatively few empirical studies of the psychosocial outcomes associated with adolescent romantic relationships, possibly because researchers have mistakenly assumed that they are transitory and trivial (Collins, 2003). Those studies that have been conducted indicate that there are both positive and negative psychological consequences of these relationships, though, as might be expected when effects are mixed, the associations have often not been particularly strong. For example, being in a romantic relationship and the quality of that relationship have been associated with positive self-concept and general competence, both cross-sectionally (e.g., Kuttler, LaGreca, & Prinstein, 1999) and longitudinally (e.g., Masten, Coatsworth, Neemann, Gest, & Garmezy, 1995). There is some evidence that one reason for this may be that being in a romantic relationship often confers status in adolescent peer groups (e.g., Connolly, Craig, Goldberg, & Pepler, 1999). The very experience of being in an adolescent romantic relationship, however, may be an outgrowth of possession of a large and warm peer network, which in turn may be an outgrowth of stable and constructive family relationships (e.g., Conger, Cui, Bryant, & Elder, 2000). This in turn harkens back to the discussion of early attachment in Chapter 5.

At the same time, however, adolescents in romantic relationships have reported having experienced greater conflict than others (Laursen, 1995), and Joyner and Udry (2000) observed that adolescents in the large United States population sample Add-Health study who had begun romantic relationships in the past year had more symptoms of depression than those not in romantic relationships, indicating that experiences in romantic relationships can have their own effects on life experiences. To some degree, these particular negative consequences may reflect the common occurrence of breakups of these young relationships, as breakup of a romantic relationship is one of the most common triggers of episodes of major depression at all ages (Kendler & Halberstadt, 2013; Monroe, Rhodes, Seeley, & Lewinsohn, 1999). One study that examined socializing influences of partner characteristics has also suggested that adolescents who date partners with psychological and behavioural problems show more change in the direction of experiencing such problems themselves than do those who date partners without such problems (Simon, Aikins, & Prinstein, 2008). In contrast, however, eighth-graders with greater substance use problems who dated partners with few substance use problems showed greater decreases in their own substance use problems than those with fewer problems (Aikins, Simon, & Prinstein, 2010). Either way, these studies suggest that early romantic relationships can alter developmental trajectories, and it is likely that they do so sometimes for better and sometimes for worse, depending on a whole series of characteristics of the two individuals involved and their circumstances.

Adolescent sexual relationships and delinquency

There has tended to be a prevailing view that, to the extent that adolescent romantic relationships are important, they are often associated with delinquency and negative outcomes (Collins, 2003). It is not unlikely that, based on as little empirical data as it has been, this is a holdover from moralistic views that romantic and sexual relationships prior to marriage are wrong. One interesting interchange of studies illustrates the subtle problems that such pre-existing ideas can create in research study design and interpretation. Armour and Haynie (2007) used a large, population-representative United States sample to demonstrate – the appropriate word in this case – that adolescents who had initiated sexual activity during the past year both showed higher levels of delinquency than their peers who remained sexually inactive and showed greater increases in delinquency later, controlling for previous levels of delinquency. They inferred from this that teenage sexual activity contributes directly – *causes* at some level – delinquent behaviour. Armour and Haynie's analysis was sound, as far as it went, but another research group questioned their causal interpretation. Harden, Mendle, Hill, Turkheimer, and Emery (2008) noted that the large and representative data set Armour and Haynie had used had over-sampled sibling pairs, including twins, resulting in 534 pairs of same-sex twins, with zygosity information based on reliable self-report information commonly used in twin studies. They used these twins to demonstrate – again the appropriate word – first that this subsample of the full sample generated the same kinds of results as the full sample when analysed as Armour and Haynie had. They then went on to demonstrate – once again the appropriate word – that, within twin pairs discordant for initiation of sexual activity, it was the twin who initiated sexual activity later who tended to show the higher rate of delinquency and to increase more in delinquency over time.

Armour and Haynie had done a good job in their regression analysis of statistically adjusting for the possible confounding presence of many named demographic factors commonly considered risk factors for delinquency, but of course it always remains possible that there are unnamed, unmeasured other variables that also exert confounding influences. Twins share both genetic and family backgrounds, and Harden et al.'s (2008) analysis suggested that something about that shared genetic and family background that had not been overtly measured in the study was confounding the association between age of initiation of sexual activity and delinquency so that, overall, there was greater delinquency among those with early sexual activity, but among those with common background, there was actually *less* delinquency among those with earlier sexual activity. One possibility here is that, especially among social groups where delinquency is common, cross-sex relationships that become serious enough to progress to sexual intimacy offer emotional refuge from some of the factors that otherwise contribute to delinquent behaviour. This would be consistent with the observations of Giordano, Manning, and Longmore (2010), who found that young adolescent sexual relationships were largely characterized, while they lasted, by caring, communication, and commitment, the latter not in the common adult sense of a decision to make the partners' lives together, but in the sense that the partners were sharing this aspect of their lives together for now.

Another possibility, of course, is that twins have a built-in comparison peer, and twins who watch their co-twins become sexually involved without experiencing involvement themselves tend to express their frustration and jealousy by engaging in delinquent behaviour. Studies aiming to identify causal factors with certainty are nearly impossible, but this particular combination of studies did rather dramatically make clear that preconceived ideas about the direction effects *should* take can contribute to overlooking alternative possibilities that study design does not make it possible to address. Unfortunately for social scientists, to hypothesize is too often essentially to develop a pre-conceived idea of what is likely to be, and from there it is a very short step to judgemental ideas about what *should* be.

The above suggests that adolescent romantic relationships may have more commonalities with than differences from adult romantic relationships, at least when the members of the romantic partnership are of about the same adolescent age. In such cases, the differences from adult relationships may lie to great degrees in the relative immaturity of adolescent cognitive and emotional development so that they do not have clear goals for their relationships and experience all their nuances more intensely. This would only be reinforced by their lack of experience of and confidence in their own individual sexuality, and the facts that adolescents generally remain economically and personally dependent on their parents and have yet to make most of their decisions about their independent places in the world. This alone would tend to give their relationships a transitory air, pending all those other life decisions about independence from parents. Things can be quite different when one partner is considerably older, and this may be when adolescents are particularly vulnerable to negative experiences that can have long-lasting consequences. Fortunately, however, this appears to be relatively rare (Collins, 2003).

Selection of sexual and romantic partners: evolutionary perspective

Given some commonality between adolescent and adult romantic relationships, it makes sense to move on to consider how people select their romantic partners, at all ages. Here one of the major strands of research over the last 20 years or so has been overtly evolutionary. This research has largely been from the perspective of parental investment theory (Trivers, 1972). Both theory and empirical observations tend to draw strong parallels between humans and other animals, particularly mammals and especially primates. Parental investment theory is the idea that whatever resources parents invest in any one offspring comes at a cost of the parents' own reproductive fitness and the developmental potential for other offspring. Because the minimum investment for a male is fertilization of an egg with his sperm, but the minimum investment for a female in the environment of evolutionary adaptation was nine months of pregnancy, the substantial risks associated with delivery, and some period thereafter of nursing and care, the female investment was (and remains to a large degree) much greater than the male investment. Thus it is expected that females will be much more selective in general about their sexual and romantic partners than males. According to theory, this creates intense pressure in males to compete for dominance that confers access to desirable females. It is also expected that the sexes will have different considerations in making their selections, and that they will have different concerns about possible and apparent violations of mate exclusivity, as well as different motivations for their own violations of mate exclusivity.

The basic idea is that, because females are relatively vulnerable to environmental assaults of all kinds during pregnancy, especially during delivery, and lactation, they will be more interested in selecting mates who will be loyal to them and good providers of resources. In contrast, males will be more interested in selecting mates who will be fertile providers of many offspring. Both sexes, of course, will be interested in mates who are healthy, resistant to infection, and personally and physically attractive. In considering infidelity, females will be more concerned about an established partner's infidelity if it includes emotional involvement, as this potentially jeopardizes her own resource situation. Males, on the other hand, risk wasting their resources, at least with respect to propagating their genes, if they find themselves investing them in some other man's child due to the infidelity of their established partner. Because men can never be certain of their paternity of any child, the evolutionary psychology argument is that they will be more concerned about evidence of sexual infidelity than emotional infidelity on the part of an established partner.

Though enough research has supported these hypotheses to make them standard textbook fare (e.g., Buss, 1999), things are likely not quite this straightforward. Many have noted that female chimpanzees, bonobos, and langur monkeys have indiscriminate sexual relations, as do many women. And infidelity, if not outright promiscuity, can have reproductive benefits for women, including maintenance or maximization of fertility, trading up for better genes, and reduced risk of inbreeding. There is evidence that women are motivated at some biological level to take advantage of such opportunities, in the form of variation in mating preferences across the menstrual cycle. According to evolutionary psychology theory, the hormonal shifts over the menstrual cycle should have become coordinated through natural selection with variations in mate preferences so that, during the ovulatory phase of the cycle when fertilization and conception are most likely, women should be more motivated to seek mates of high genetic quality. As such males would be in high demand among females, any relationship would also likely be relatively short-term, creating pressure to seek longer-term relationships with other males who might be more likely to stick around to provide resource during the non-ovulatory parts of the cycle. There is considerable evidence that women's preferences do vary across the menstrual cycle (e.g., Gangestad, Simpson, Cousins, Garver-Apgar, & Christensen, 2004).

But the underlying assumption that males who provide regular and steady resources tend to be of lower 'genetic quality' than those who are overtly sexy but not steady providers is large, and there is considerable phenotypic evidence against it. For example, men (actually people in general) who are more intelligent and, independently, more responsible and mature, tend to be better providers and they also tend to be healthier (Gottfredson & Deary, 2004; Roberts, Kuncel, Shiner, Caspi, & Goldberg, 2007) and to have greater longevity (Batty, Deary, & Gottfredson, 2007), affording more opportunity to produce healthy offspring. This is based on modern research of course, and things may have been different during the vast amount of human evolutionary history that took place before the advent of systematic medical care and widespread public knowledge of lifestyle factors that contribute to health.

This is one of the more general limitations of evolutionary psychology: we must infer much about the specifics of the environments in which humans evolved from very sketchy evidence, making attributions of human motivations and specific actions highly speculative. It is often just as possible to construct evolutionary explanations that would explain observations opposite to those made empirically as it is to construct explanations that explain the data as observed. And it is easy to overlook contradictory observations. One of these is the very basic observation that organisms have some basic biological motivation to maximize reproduction. Contradicting this, it has been observed repeatedly that as soon as women are able to control their reproduction, they work to limit it. That is, many if not most women desire to have children and have always made large efforts to do so, but they also have tended to put effort into avoiding having more than, say, three or four surviving children, with two being a common ideal today.

Other perspectives on mate selection

Another approach to the question of how people select mates and/or romantic partners has been to posit that people's mate choices relate in some rational way to their own characteristics, and to evaluate various proposals about the nature of those associations. Everyone has an interest in who mates with whom and why, so the most basic hypotheses derive from folk psychology: 'opposites attract' and 'like marries like'. In general, the data tend to support 'like marries like', but only relatively weakly, leaving plenty of room for individual exceptions where opposites attracted. For example, spouses tend to show small (0.10–0.30) positive correlations for anthropometric measures such as height and weight (Plomin, DeFries, & Roberts, 1977), and on average for personality (Buss, 1984). The average for personality, however, hides variability in assortment for specific personality traits that may range from -0.20 to 0.50. Consistent with evolutionary psychology's theories that people seek mates with high genetic quality and that physical attractiveness reflects that quality, spousal correlations for physical attractiveness tend to be higher, in the 0.40–0.50 range (Murstein, 1972; White, 1980), but so do spousal correlations for IQ and educational attainment (Vandenburg, 1972).

To some degree, the reasons for these latter correlations are likely to be quite different from those for correlations of anthropometric and physical attractiveness measures. These correlations have been measured in populations in industrialized countries, which tend to be quite socially stratified by IQ and educational attainment, so one likely reason for them is simple propinquity: people tend to meet and become acquainted with others who travel at the same social levels as they do. There is no reason that propinquity might not be reinforced by overt searches (conscious or unconscious) for mates with high intelligence and/or educational attainment though, whether because these characteristics serve as some indication of actual 'genetic quality' or simply because they provide social benefits. But the strongest spousal correlations (on the order of 0.6) tend to be observed for political attitudes and religious affiliation. There is evidence that these correlations can be dated to initial mate choice rather than to conversion, accommodation, or persuasion (e.g., Alford, Hatemi, Hibbing, Martin, & Eaves, 2011). This speaks to the role of overt selection in mate choice.

Cognitive and intuitive processes of mate selection

But the constraints of quite similar political and religious attitudes, moderately similar IQ and/or educational attainment and physical attractiveness and a-little-bit similar height and/or weight, coupled with some aspects of personality similarity and some aspects of personality difference, still leave many available mating candidates, at least in our modern, densely populated and mobile industrialized world. In the past, many marriages unquestionably took place because, in small and localized communities there often were not many reasonably accessible options, but this is less likely to be the case today. So how do people choose their mates in this day and age?

One possibility is consistent with evolutionary explanations. This is the possibility that people size up their 'values' on the 'mating market' through intra-sex competition and use those results to seek associations with potential partners with mating 'values' just higher than theirs (Stroebe, 1977). The rationale for this would be that aiming too high is a waste of time and resources and aiming too low is counterproductive, but aiming just a little bit higher than one's own perceived value would result in some advantage and might be a realistic gamble, given that the characteristics that males and females tend to seek differ somewhat. For this possibility even to make sense, there would have to be some rather general agreement about what constitutes mating 'value', but there is substantial evidence that such agreement does exist. Across many diverse cultures, people express similar preferences for personal and physical characteristics in potential mates, and, within sex, rank these preferences similarly (e.g., Buss, 1989). From this perspective, adolescence, with its overt intra-sex competition and intensely felt, often short-term relationships, might serve the adaptive purpose of providing valuable experience in establishing an individual's sense of mating 'value' as well as building relationship skills to be used later in seeking and building more permanent partnerships (Weisfield & Woodward, 2004). To the extent this is the case, it reinforces the view of adolescent relationships as essentially immature and experimental, possibly exaggerated, versions of adult romantic relationships.

Another possibility that may co-exist is that each of us has our own idiosyncratic set of criteria for an ideal mate, consisting of some similarities with ourselves in particular areas and differences in other areas. For example, whether consciously or unconsciously, a woman may be looking for someone like her father, but would run for the hills upon meeting someone who reminded her of her mother. This could be directly coupled with the 'mating value' possibility if, for example, people first assessed the physical attractiveness of potential mates in relation to their own (Murstein, 1971), and then went on to apply further, more idiosyncratic criteria. Though physical attractiveness seems a likely candidate for such initial sorting in otherwise relatively homogeneous populations because it can be assessed immediately and instantaneously, it seems unlikely to trump other broad characteristics such as religious or political affiliation or educational or social class level in more heterogeneous populations. For example, Townsend and Wasserman (1989) observed that American university males screened potential mating partners for physical attractiveness first before applying other criteria. Because most of the people they were screening were fellow university students, however, considerable sorting of the whole potentially available population had already been done for them by their university's admissions office and more was probably accomplished by the classes they attended and campus activities in which they participated. Moreover, while abstract judgements of the relative importance of personal and physical characteristics for mate value may share considerable consistency, specific judgements of specific individuals do not seem to be nearly as consistent. For example, Feingold (1992) found that meta-analytic correlations between self- and other-ratings of physical attractiveness were less than 0.25. And in a sample of 98 couples, Murstein (1976) reported that independent judges rated 21–24 per cent of the participants as above average in physical attractiveness, but 85 per cent of the husbands and 67 per cent of the wives rated their spouses as above average. In comparison, 43 per cent of the husbands and 39 per cent of the wives rated themselves as above average. I would simply add that my own experience is that, as affection for someone, whether romantic partner or not, grows, so does my perception that the person is physically attractive, and I have experienced complete about-faces from my perception at initial meeting to later friendship.

This may take care of the initial sorting process, but it does nothing to account for the development of the content of idiosyncratic ideal criteria, and it does nothing to explain the intense feelings of having found their ideal match that people, adolescents and adults alike, experience at the inception of romantic relationships. Nor is it enough to explain the deep attachment bonds that develop in mating partnerships that persist successfully over long periods of time. In industrialized countries, whatever they might say later, most couples claim at the time to have married for love, so the elements involved in the kinds of attraction involved in romantic love have major life consequences. Clearly, choosing a mate may be superficially similar to making other choices in life: we go through some process of sorting through available options. But there are also clear differences. When we, for example, choose a house or a car or a suit of clothes, the object of our choice has nothing to say about it, but unrequited love is an uncomfortably common fact of the search for mates. Choosing a job may be a more relevant comparison, as, the object of our choice does have something to say about it, but even here, at least consciously, we appear to compromise much more readily than we do in love matches, both in making an initial selection and in sustaining that choice over time.

Box 10.1 Hints about mate selection from twin pairs

Lykken and Tellegen (1993) suggested that if people do have rational but idiosyncratic criteria by which they choose their mates, these criteria, like every other psychological characteristic, should show genetic influences. This should mean, all else being equal, that the spouses of monozygotic twins should be more alike than the spouses of dizygotic twins. They tested this in a sample of twin pairs and their spouses who completed measures of personality traits, self-rated talents, occupational and recreational interests and political attitudes by comparing the correlations of twins with their own spouses and the correlations between the spouses of the MZ and DZ twins on the measures. They also compared differences in standardized scores on the individual measures in spouses of MZ and DZ twins, random pairs, and the MZ twin pairs. The spousal correlations were similar to those from prior research: rather substantial for political attitudes and some recreational interests, and small but positive for traits such as height, personality, self-rated talents, and interests. The correlations between the twins' spouses were smaller than the spousal correlations, and the closest they came to showing indications of genetic influences was for height, the personality trait of traditionalism, and interest in recreational nightlife and camping and hiking. Contributing to the impression that even these observations were chance findings, they all indicated substantial nonadditive genetic variance. Comparison of the score differences yielded similar results: the differences between scores of MZ co-twins were noticeably smaller than those of the other comparisons, but the other comparisons were essentially indistinguishable from each other in magnitude. Thus, while there was the kind of moderate spousal similarity generally observed, it appeared very unlikely that that similarity had come about systematically.

Lykken and Tellegen (1993) pursued the idea of twin similarity in rational choice criteria further by asking their sample of twins to evaluate the mate choices of their co-twins, reasoning that twins should tend to find their co-twins' choices attractive, given their similarity in genetic and rearing backgrounds. Moreover, MZ twins should do so to a higher degree than DZ twins. The questionnaire the twins completed was designed cleverly: the twins were asked to evaluate how similar their choices in clothing and in household furnishings were, how they would feel about taking the kinds of holidays their co-twins tended to take, and how they would feel about holding the jobs their co-twins held. Finally, emphasizing the confidentiality of responses, the twins were asked to think back to when their co-twins had married and to describe how they would have felt about marrying their co-twins' choices.

In both sexes, responses indicated that the twins generally considered their co-twins' choices of clothing and household furnishings similar to their own and evaluated their co-twins' choices of holidays and jobs favourably, with MZ twins doing so to higher degrees than DZ twins. In sharp contrast, though, both sexes and both types of twins were about equally likely to have disliked as liked their co-twins' spousal selections. As a check on this, Lykken and Tellegen asked the twins' spouses to rate the similarity of the twins' choices in the same areas of life, as well as the similarity of their choices of friends. Then they also asked the spouses to report their feelings towards the co-twins when they had first met them. The spousal reports of twin similarity were generally consistent with the twin reports: the twins made generally similar choices, with MZs doing so to a greater degree than DZs. And interestingly, despite the obvious similarity of physical appearance in most MZ twin pairs, a quarter of husbands of MZ twins actually reported disliking their wives' co-twins and only 13 per cent endorsed the response 'could have fallen for her myself'. Among wives of male MZ twins, equal proportions liked as disliked their husbands' co-twins.

Box 10.2   Lessons from mate selection in the age of the internet?

Lykken and Tellegen (1993) concluded, based on their study of twins and their spouses (see previous textbox), that much of the mating process is adventitious: within broad constraints, each of us could fall in love with almost anyone who came along at the right time, in the right circumstances. They suggested that, all our rationales and ideals aside, the capacity for infatuation and complete absorption in another that we experience as the initial experience of romantic love evolved to create a bridge across the chasm between the understanding shared by two acquaintances who might spend an afternoon together here or there and the common understanding needed by two *pair-bonded* individuals committed to sharing their lives and resources and raising common offspring. Recent social developments may be corroborating this view. With greatly increased physical mobility among most industrialized countries, increasing proportions of young adults find themselves in new physical surroundings in which they need to make new friends and seek potential mates. The advent of the internet has facilitated this for many, spawning a host of online dating networks and 'speed-dating' programmes in which participants meet many potential partners in a very short time period, spending literally perhaps five minutes with each in rapid succession and reporting whether they would like to see any of them again. Most of the websites offer participants the opportunity to post their own personal attributes and activities and photos, and to describe the attributes they seek. Participants then evaluate the postings of potential partners and initiate correspondence and/or face-to-face meeting with them if they wish. It has become increasingly common for romantic partnerships to begin with such online essentially written evaluations, but it introduces a radical change from the historical norm in which the first experience potential romantic partners had of each other was tangible and physical, including all those ephemerals such as the light in one's eyes, the wickedly wry grin, and that elusive fragrance of spring that seems to blow into the room when the romantic target enters.

A recent line of research has taken advantage of these new dating opportunities to explore the extent to which people's conscious ideal mate preferences are involved in actual real-time choices. For example, though Fletcher, Simpson, Thomas, and Giles (1999) reported associations of partner relationship quality and stability with extent of partner match to ideals, Eastwick and Finkel (2008) and Todd, Penke, Fasolo, and Lenton (2007) observed that people's ideal partner preferences did not predict their interest in further contact with potential partners encountered in speed-dating sessions, either in the sessions themselves or at short-term follow-up after them. Eastwick, Finkel, and Eagly (2011) carried this further in a series of lab manipulations. They observed that, when university students only briefly saw a potential partner and read a profile description they believed to have been prepared by the person, their romantic ideals were significantly associated with their level of romantic interest in the person. But this was no longer the case after they had had some social interaction with the person. Perhaps important for understanding how partner relationships develop and solidify over time, this appeared to be because they reinterpreted what they thought the person had meant in the profile description so that their experience of the interaction tied more closely with their ideal preferences, rather than because they disregarded their ideal preferences. Moreover, Lenton, Fasolo, and Todd (2010) considered how having a greater number of potential partners from which to choose impacted people's satisfaction with their choices. They found that having more choices did not improve satisfaction with the choice process, nor with the choice made. Together, these studies support Lykken and Tellegen's (1993) proposal that, within broad constraints, mating choices are adventitious, and that what makes them 'work' is the success of the transition from intense infatuation to pair-bonding.

Pair-bonding

Pair-bonding exists in many species spread throughout the animal *phylogeny*, or evolutionary taxonomic grouping, but otherwise closely related species such as prairie and meadow voles can vary considerably in the extent to which they tend to be pair-bonded. Many have assumed that pair-bonding evolved 'to' aid fitness in species in which young are born very dependent on parental care (e.g., Weisfield & Woodward, 2004), but it is not easy to understand differences in extent of pair-bonding in closely related species such as prairie and meadow voles in these terms. Regardless of the questions of necessity for offspring survival, evolutionary selection, and genetic determination, however, paternal involvement in nurturance of offspring tends to be greater in pair-bonded species than in others, and it is certainly common, at least serially, in humans. Pair-bonding is far from universal, however, and shows individual differences in extent of manifestation. Because it by definition involves more than one individual, some of these differences depend not on the individuals directly, but on the viability of the new entity, the pair-bonded couple, that forms. For example, if one partner becomes injured or ill, this places stresses on the relationship that may cause it to sever when it might not have otherwise. But the individual differences in manifestation clearly transcend such stresses as well. In humans, pair-bonding is characterized by companionate love, commitment to joint life as a couple, and sexual exclusivity and intimacy. It is manifested in ways that appear overtly very similar in other animals from mammals to birds.

Like most characteristics I have discussed, pair bonding has both physiological and neurological consequences and signatures or causes. These are fascinating in their associations with and differences from both romantic infatuation and sexual arousal and parental love and altruism. For example, while viewing pictures of their beloveds in relation to other friends in an fMRI scanner, young adults who said they were deeply in love showed greater bilateral activation in the anterior cingulate cortex, medial insulate, caudate, and putamen; and less bilateral activation in the posterior cingulate, amygdale, and right prefrontal, parietal, and middle temporal cortex (Bartels & Zeki, 2000).

The regions preferentially activated are involved in reward processing and also carry many *oxytocin* and *vasopressin* receptors. Oxytocin is a mammalian hormone released in large quantities especially during and after childbirth and during lactation. It is not, however, solely a female hormone and is also involved in sexual response in both sexes and in the kinds of feelings of contentment, social warmth, and security more generally involved in social relationships, especially pair-bonding. Vasopressin is a biochemically closely related mammalian hormone that primarily increases water absorption in the collecting ducts of the kidney nephron, but it also appears to be involved in social behaviour and maternal responses to stress. The regions preferentially deactivated are associated with negative emotions, social judgements, and the assessments of others' intentions and emotions (Bartels & Zeki, 2004). Both sets of regions overlapped but did not completely coincide with regions preferentially activated and deactivated when mothers looked at pictures of their children in comparison with pictures of other children they knew and their own best friends and other adult acquaintances. Some of the differences between romantic and maternal love may contribute to the common perception that people in the throes of romance appear to have gone a little bit 'nuts' in their pursuit of the object of their affection: Marazziti, Akiskal, Rossi, and Cassano (1999) observed that participants who had recently fallen in love showed similar densities of platelet serotonin transporters to patients with obsessive-compulsive disorder, and both groups' densities were significantly lower than those of normal controls.

In both sexes, orgasm is accompanied by a surge in oxytocin (Carter, 1992), apparently enhancing the development of pair-bonding. But the process appears to be reciprocal, at least in women, who are more likely to experience orgasm in marital or pair-bonded relationships (Laumann, Gagnon, Michael, & Michaels, 1994). Moreover, female orgasm facilitates conception; without it, more sperm are emitted from the vagina in 'flowback' (Baker & Bellis, 1993). Women commonly experience their most intense loves with their first sex partners (Kallen & Stephenson, 1982), and men appear to experience especially intense bonds with any sex partner whom they initiate sexually (Peplau, Rubin, & Hill, 1977). This has inspired an evolutionary psychological explanation for the hymen and the painful barrier it imposes until broken: the partner who breaks the hymen is the only one who will ever be able to be completely certain that the woman is not already pregnant, so it may make evolutionary sense for him to be especially strongly bonded to her (Weisfield & Woodward, 2004). Men's testosterone levels drop when they enter committed relationships, and rise if they sever those relationships and re-enter the mating market (Weisfeld, 2004). Testosterone levels drop further when men become fathers, and new fathers tend to show smaller increases in testosterone than other men during casual interactions with women (van der Meij, Buunk, van de Sande, & Salvador, 2008).

These biological and neurological manifestations are merely indications of the profound psychological experience of pair bonding. One way of interpreting the fact that the experience of romantic love is so very rewarding is that these rewards help to motivate and 'cushion' the large transition in psychological focus necessary to move from thinking of oneself as an autonomous individual responsible primarily for one's own actions and support to thinking of oneself in partnership with another, whose sometimes very different motivations, goals, and needs must be honoured and respected as much as one's own. This is the kind of transition many people experience today in industrialized countries with essentially individualistic cultures when they marry or establish a romantic partnership. But in other cultures and at other times in human history, the transition has not always been so sharp. Perhaps especially for women, it has been common in many places at many times to go from living with parents and working to support to support and maintain their home to making a new home with a husband, with no period of independent living and self-support in between. In some of these cultures, however, the psychological transition may have been especially sharp in another way. For example, in much of traditional Chinese society, the practice was for newly married couples to join the households of the husbands' parents, and for the new brides to become effectively household assistants to their mothers-in-law. Even more extreme, in some nomadic nonliterate cultures it has been common for young women to be 'drafted' into mated relationships by being kidnapped by raiding males and brought in to spend their lives in these essentially foreign communities that were often directly competitive with and even hostile to those in which the women had been born and spent their childhoods.

Whether entered into freely in an intense state of romantic love, through business transactions about dowries and bride prices, or, for one partner, through allocation of share of the raiding booty and, for the other, by being dragged against her will, establishing a life together requires countless adjustments in personal habits. It also requires coming to understand the mind and emotions of another, acceptance of some personal characteristics and habits of that other that inevitably strike one as arbitrary and even silly, and compromising some of one's own goals and desires. In return, if the pair bond forms maturely, one receives a reliable source of help, emotional and physical support, and companionship, not to mention sexual gratification, more than making up for the sacrifices. The process of building the new entity that constitutes the couple, however, depends on the abilities and willingness of both partners to make the necessary sacrifices and on the degree to which the results conform to the partners' expectations for their partnership. Both of these components rely heavily on the partners' individual experiences of attachment to their parents (Simpson, Collins, & Salvatore, 2011). Where these attachment relationships have been secure, and in particular have contributed to development of the ability to regulate emotions well (Sroufe & Fleeson, 1986), the process of adaptation to joint life is likely to be smoother, and the result more stable and satisfactory to both partners.

The transition to living in partnership

Though there is considerable evidence that these early attachment relationships are crucial, they are not definitive. That is, social experiences with others throughout childhood and adolescence each contribute to building an individual's relationship skills and expectations. As with confidence in abilities and returns on effort, success over time tends to build expectations for success, the confidence to keep trying, and the skills to succeed, and repeated failures become harder and harder to overcome psychologically, contributing to the development of schemas and defensive patterns of behaviour that can themselves undermine satisfaction with any relationship for either partner or for both. But, again as in other areas of life, these patterns are not irreversible. That is, positive relationship experiences of any kind, but particularly the intimacy involved in positive romantic relationships, can counteract negative relationship experiences earlier in life. Moreover, romantic partners with strong skills and securely attached backgrounds can help to buffer individuals with insecure attachment backgrounds from experiencing some of the risk factors often associated with their insecure attachment histories. At the same time, even for adolescents and adults who have had secure relationship experiences in the past, romantic relationships with partners who become abusive or suffer from personality disorders or other psychopathologies including substance abuse can undermine the advantages otherwise conferred by the secure attachment and relationship background.

Perhaps even more importantly, the new experiences involved in beginning to live intimately in partnership with another person challenge day-to-day coping mechanisms that often have not been previously challenged, even by previous house-sharing relationships such as flat-mates or living within a family. These challenges can, and generally do, bring out aspects of personality and patterns of behaviour in each partner that their previous more casual interactions had not revealed. Each partner's reactions to making these discoveries in the co-partner contribute much to the stability of the relationship and the degree to which the partners each experience it as satisfactory. Some of these discoveries are positive of course: one partner learns that the other happens to know just the right trick to fix the leak in the toilet that makes the water run continuously, or is particularly conscientious about keeping the refrigerator stocked with the condiments they each like. But inevitably some of the discoveries are negative as well: one partner has been in the habit of leaving clothes strewn throughout the bedroom, something that irritates the other no end. Small though they are, clashes like this can have large effects on relationship quality, often because they create power struggles. That is, however the 'irritated' expresses the irritation, if the 'clothes-strewer' takes this expression as an intrusion on his/her right to express the personality trait of spontaneity in private life (or something like that!), the stage is set for building this small difference in habits into a major source of conflict as the 'irritated' may be inclined to feel like a 'doormat' if she/he just accepts the situation to avoid further conflict, and the 'clothes-strewer' may have similar feelings at the prospect of altering habits. Of course, how the 'irritated' originally expresses the irritation contributes to the likelihood that the 'clothes-strewer' will take such a narcissistic perspective on the other's irritation, so the situation is inherently reciprocal.

It also may involve many schemas held subconsciously by both partners. Some of these schemas will involve conceptions of how any two people 'should' relate to one another and resolve disagreements. These are probably the most transparent and easiest to make conscious. Others will involve conceptions of male and female roles in the home and in society more generally and may differ considerably from attitudes on these subjects the partners hold and express consciously. The most subtle ones will involve conceptions of how one 'should' be treated by one's romantic partner, that special person who loves one above all others. For example, people often hold quite specific ideas about the kinds of gifts they should receive from their romantic partners, how their birthdays and other holidays should be remembered, how their partners should respond to the gifts and celebrations they offer, what should be made of alterations in appearance such as new hairstyles or clothing, whether the partners wear 'their' rings, and countless other expectations about the ideal expression of romance. People rarely even realize they hold these ideas until their partners fail to meet their expectations. All of these schemas derive from an individual's observations of and experiences with his/her parents in their relationships with each other and with the individual him/herself as a child, but they also derive from experiences with friends, from movies and books, and from idealized imaginings. What happens when a partner does not meet the individual's expectations depends on the severity of the failure, but it also depends crucially on the individual's own levels of self-esteem, security within the relationship (attachment again), feeling of engagement in an interesting and useful place of his/her own in the world, and ability to step outside his/her own assumptions and expectations to understand the partner's perspective.

Consequences of mature pair-bonding

When couples can weather these communication challenges, the pair-bonded relationship can be very powerful in supporting constructive personal growth and maturity in both parties. One aspect of this that has received recent research attention is the possibility that marriage acts directly to 'rein in' anti-social behaviour in husbands. Two of the original studies in this area (Sampson & Laub, 1990; Laub, Nagin, & Sampson, 1998) have been based on Glueck and Glueck's (1950; 1968) classic longitudinal study comparing 500 delinquent boys born between 1924 and 1935 and living in the area of Boston, MA, to a control group of 500 boys who were not delinquent. The delinquent boys were categorized as such because they had been committed to one of two Massachusetts correctional schools. The boys in the control group attended Boston public schools, and their status as not delinquent was verified by criminal record checks and interviews with parents, teachers, other community leaders, and the boys themselves. Despite this verification process, compared with national averages, they were not unusually law-abiding (Sampson & Laub, 1990). On a case-by-case basis, the boys in the two samples were matched by age, general intelligence, race/ethnicity, and neighbourhood socio-economic status. They spanned the ranges of these variables quite well. The Gluecks originally interviewed and collected data on these boys at an average age of 14, then again 11 and 18 years later, with an overall retention rate of 92 per cent after adjustment for mortality (which was relatively high due to military participation by the boys). The Gluecks themselves used this rich base of data primarily cross-sectionally, but coded data and raw interview records were stored in the library at Harvard Law School, making its use by then-future researchers possible. Sampson and Laub (1990) used these data to observe that, despite clear differences between the groups in rates of delinquency in adolescence that persisted over the course of the study, both groups showed declines in delinquency over time at rates that varied with the strength of marital attachment.

Of course, marriage itself is not a completely random event, and the quality of a marriage is even less random. If marriage and/or its quality actually cause desistance from antisocial behaviour, it must do so over and above any tendencies for personal characteristics or environmental circumstances to contribute to both the formation of a good marriage and the desire to desist from antisocial behaviour. Laub, Nagin, and Sampson (1998) recognized this in their study based on the Gluecks' sample of delinquent boys. They noted strong common associations between personality characteristics and family factors and both marriage and desistance and controlled them statistically to conclude that these pre-existing factors were not sufficient to account for the individual differences in rates of desistance and that early good marriages acted increasingly strongly over time to encourage desistance; however, another more recent study offered clearer evidence of this kind.

Burt, et al. (2010) used a sample of young adult twins who had not married to estimate what the antisocial behaviour patterns of their married co-twins would have looked like at age 29 had those co-twins not married. They observed first that, whether assessed at ages 17, 20, 24, or 29, twins who had married by age 29 had lower rates of antisocial behaviour, and that the differences grew with age of assessment. This suggested that those who marry differ in ways associated with antisocial behaviour even before they marry. At the same time, rates of antisocial behaviour increased in both those who married by age 29 and those who did not, to about the same degree between ages 17 and 20. But they dropped much more slowly after age 20 in those who did not marry by age 29 than in those who did, consistent with the possibility that marriage had its own effects on rate of desistance. Moreover, married members of twin pairs had significantly lower rates of antisocial behaviour than their unmarried co-twins, and MZ and DZ twins were similar in this regard, providing more direct evidence that marriage was in fact the causal environmental factor. The differences between co-twins were smaller than those between random pairs, however, supporting the inference that personal characteristics contribute both to the tendency to marry and the tendency to desist from adolescent levels of antisocial behaviour.

Taken together, these studies reinforce a pattern that developmental scientists would likely do well to consider typical. I have discussed many examples of traits at different ages for which small initial differences grow over time to become large and substantial through individual actions to move towards environments that support the already-existing differences and encourage the individual to develop those traits further in the same directions. In this case, the example reinforces the establishment of a pair-bond as a key developmental milestone in the attainment of adult social maturity. This does not, of course, mean that it is essential: it is far from impossible to become mature while remaining persistently single. But for many, establishing a pair-bond offers important motivation and opportunity for growth in maturity when it goes well, and can set in motion or accelerate pre-existing difficulties in achieving stable adult economic and emotional roles when it goes awry.

Current social challenges to the stability of the pair-bond: maintaining work–life balance

As noted in Chapter 9, over the last 50 years or so, women's participation in the workforce has increased dramatically. The increase has come about for both human and economic reasons, and both are important in understanding the stresses on the pair-bond that the increase has brought. From an economic perspective, the rising costs of living, and particularly of housing, in many industrialized countries has made it difficult for many couples to sustain the standard of living they would like unless both partners work full-time. From a human perspective, stereotypes that women 'cannot' do certain jobs well, or that certain jobs are not appropriate for them, have fallen away and women have stepped forward in large numbers to take advantage of expanding educational and occupational opportunities to establish meaningful and even exciting careers. At the same time, society has become much more geographically mobile, and many career opportunities have demanded increasingly specialized forms of knowledge and experience. These changes have placed many new stresses on the pair-bond, but two of them in particular stand out.

First, increased geographical mobility and job specialization have made it ever more difficult for couples to find equally appealing job opportunities in the same location at the same time. This is the case whether the two partners are in the same field or not. Some employers will work to find jobs for the spouses of employee candidates they really want to hire, but many either cannot or do not, and often the 'found' job is simply not as desirable to the spouse as the original job opportunity is to the primary job candidate. This means that partners must somehow sort through whose career development should have priority. There are as many ways to do this successfully, of course, as there are couples, but there are at least as many ways to see it go wrong, creating resentments that damage the relationship over time. Relocation to take a new job impinges on other values that can impact the couple's relationship as well. For example, many relocations mean moving away from family and friends, to another climate or ambient culture, or even another country, and the partners' relative preferences for these aspects of their residence location may vary considerably. Some couples take on the challenge of trying to maintain their relationship while living temporarily or even permanently in different locations. This situation is often difficult to sustain due to the duplication of costs involved in maintaining two residences, and the costs involved in travel to see each other. Moreover, it often introduces emotional stresses because the partners cannot be as physically and emotionally available to each other as they would be living together and because they end up maintaining largely separate social lives that can introduce added temptations to initiate additional romantic relationships.

The second major stress that women's increased career opportunities have placed on the pair-bond is more subtle, but this does not make it less important. Though disparities remain between the compensation received by men and women and generally favour men, it has become increasingly common for women to make more money than do their male partners. Very often this takes place because the woman in a couple has a more responsible job or one that required more education or training than the man's. For some couples, of course, this matters not at all. But for others it can cause considerable tension. Many people of both sexes have been socialized to believe that men should be the primary family breadwinners. This socialization is not always overt, so that people are often not even aware of holding a schema in which the man makes more money and has higher occupational prestige than the woman. Moreover, because in many couples the man is a few years older than the woman, when the woman earns more than the man, it can indicate that the woman is progressing more rapidly in her career. This situation can cause men to feel inadequate, challenge their self-esteem and sense of social potency, and it can undermine the respect for her partner that a woman feels. Especially when either or both members of a couple are unaware of holding schemas of this kind, tension about the situation can build over time, but it can be very difficult for the partners even to identify its source, much less to discuss it constructively and air their emotions about it.

These are not small questions for many couples. Though investigations of the psychological implications are scanty, one series of longitudinal studies has shown some important patterns that deserve further consideration on many levels. The Study of Mathematically Precocious Youth was established by Julian Stanley at Johns Hopkins University in 1971 (Keating & Stanley, 1971), with the purpose of helping highly talented young people find educational opportunities appropriate to their abilities. The study is now resident at Vanderbilt University (Lubinsky & Benbow, 2006), and consists of five cohorts. The members of four of these cohorts were selected when they were 12 or 13 years old, first because they had scored in the top 3 per cent on a standard achievement test taken by all students in their schools. Those that did so were invited to take the Scholastic Aptitude Test while in the seventh or eighth grades, though this test is designed to assess verbal and mathematical reasoning abilities in university-bound secondary-school students in their last two years of secondary school. From there, the five cohorts were formed using different criteria. The first three consisted of the top 1 per cent, the top 0.5 per cent, and the top 0.01 per cent of early SAT scores from different testing years. The only requirement for the fourth cohort was scores in the top 3 per cent on the first test, but many also took the SAT at ages 12 or 13 and scored within the top 0.5 per cent. The fifth cohort consisted at entry in 1992 of first- and second-year graduate students attending math or science programmes at United States universities ranked among the top 15 in the country. All cohorts have been followed over extended periods of time, as long as 35 years for the oldest ones. In particular, Cohort 5 participants completed a series of items relating to work values and the importance they placed on them in 1992 when they were about 24 and then again in 2003 when they were about 35 (Farriman, Lubinski, & Benbow, 2009). The items included, in abbreviated form, working no more than 50 hours per week, flexibility in my work schedule, working no more than 60 hours per week, enjoying my work, meeting people with whom I can develop friendships, travelling for work, opportunity to learn, prestige, above-average salary, ability to take risks, task freedom, opportunity to advance, etc.

The researchers analysed these work value item data in two ways. First, they examined how mean levels of values changed between ages 24 and 35 for men and women separately, and, second, they examined sex differences in means at both ages. Many items, such as good retirement benefits, respecting colleagues, and using higher-level skills, showed little change in importance in either sex. Merit-based pay structure and opportunity to express leadership increased in importance for both sexes, while satisfaction with work, enjoyment of work, and friendships at work decreased for both. It is certainly possible to infer that by age 35, additional financial responsibilities had made work more necessary and thus less important to consider 'fun' than it had been when participants were in graduate school. The most interesting items, however, had mean responses that changed in different ways for men and women. The most prominent of these were flexibility in work schedule and limited work hours, which increased in importance more for women than for men. That is, there was little or no difference in the importance men and women placed on these aspects of work at age 24, but women valued them more highly on average than did men at age 35. Similarly, men and women placed similar levels of importance on many aspects of work, such as having their work make a difference to others, be challenging, and offer opportunities to learn new things. But men placed more importance than did women on taking risks, salary levels, and prestige of the organization. And women placed more importance than did men on satisfaction with their work, respecting colleagues, and clean working conditions. These differences were accentuated in the half of the participants who had become parents by age 35. That is, there were few if any sex differences at age 24, but by age 35 women who had become parents valued work flexibility and satisfaction with work more than they had at age 24, and more than men did at age 35, and both to a greater degree than did women who had not become parents.

Along with participants in SMPY's Cohort 3, the Cohort 5 participants also completed several questionnaires about more general life values and personal views and life satisfaction. The Cohort 3 participants represented the top 0.01 per cent of cognitive abilities when they were recruited to the SMPY at age 13. When surveyed in 2003, they were about 33 years old and about a third of each sex had become parents. The life value items they completed, in abbreviated form, included being politically active in the community, living close to parents, exercising regularly, being successful in work, having a part-time career, not working outside the home, having children, having strong friendships, being recognized for work accomplishments, being a community leader, maintaining family connections, having a meaningful spiritual life, and spending quality time with children daily. They reported on one item assessing satisfaction with their careers and five items assessing more general life satisfaction. Again, there were many similarities between men and women in values, but women placed more importance on part-time work, having strong friendships, giving back to the community, and maintaining family connections, while men placed more importance on having a full-time career, making a lasting impact, and obtaining monetary wealth. There was no difference in the degree of satisfaction men and women expressed about their lives.

The Cohorts 3 and 5 participants also completed items about personal attitudes involved in their approach to work. These included, in abbreviated form, comfort spending long hours alone, capacity for sustained physical activity, ability to multi-task, ability to control emotions, desire to be recognized as best in field, tendency to put one's needs above those of all others, willingness to express thoughts despite risk of criticism, belief that society should invest in responder's ideas because they are more important than those of others, belief that the most important contribution to humanity is scientific, willingness to state facts despite causing others' discomfort, capacity to resist peer pressure, belief that the most important contribution to humanity involves improving people's lives, being a team player, importance that no one in society be left behind, and duty to help others less fortunate. Men expressed more agreement than did women that society should invest in their ideas because they were better than those of others; the prospect of criticism was less likely to deter them from expressing their views; they were more able to control their emotions; they wanted more to be recognized as best in their fields; they had greater capacity for sustained physical activity; and they were more likely to put their own needs before those of others. Women expressed more agreement than did men that it was important that no one be left behind in society, and they expressed more ability to multi-task.

Of course, there is always the perhaps large possibility of response biases of many kinds in the ways people respond to items such as these, and there may be systematic sex differences in these response biases. Moreover, participants in the SMPY were specifically selected as unusually capable, and thus likely to have high-powered careers of the kind that many who hold them value highly. Their careers may thus be more central to their senses of identity and life goals than those of the majority of the population, making generalizations to that population from this study risky. On the other hand, the very relative centrality of their careers to their identities may have brought some patterns common in the more general population into sharper relief, and it is at least unlikely that these participants did not comprehend the items! Though only a minority of SMPY men acknowledged strong agreement that they put their own needs above the needs of others around them, the absence of women who did so, and the sex differences in gentler expressions of this tendency, hint at the subtle difficulties many couples face in balancing career and life aspirations together. It is impossible not to wonder about the lives of the women married to the men who strongly agreed that they put their own needs over the needs of those around them. As their marriages proceed over time, what goals of their own are these women giving up in order to allow their husbands to pursue their priorities? What stresses does this cause for them? How do they cope with them? Why do they put up with the situation? To what degree are they aware of it? Do some other aspects of their lives or their relationships with their husbands compensate for their sacrifices to their husbands' needs? To what degree do other men (and women) strongly put their own needs ahead of those of others without being either aware of doing so or willing to acknowledge it?

Parenthood and parenting

Parenthood is, of course, first and foremost a physiological, reproductive phenomenon, the biological goal of maturation, and the mechanism through which evolution takes place. It thus makes sense to discuss it first in those terms. The specific ways in which humans raise their children are shaped by culture and education, but they are also driven by biological processes, many of which take place below our level of awareness. As with most other biological processes, our understanding of these, the biological processes of parenthood, comes largely from model organisms, especially rodents. Many of the hormones involved are the same as those involved in pair-bonding and in brain circuits involved in the experience of reward more generally. Species-typical maternal behaviour can be initiated in nulliparous (never given birth) ovariectomized female rats exposed to rat pups, given a course of hormone treatments that mimic pregnancy, labour, and delivery (Moltz, Lubin, Leon, & Numan, 1970). But far less than this appears to be required because virgin female rats could be made maternal by transfusion of blood from rats that had recently given birth (Terkel & Rosenblatt, 1972). Moreover, transfusing blood plasma from rats that had recently given birth to juvenile rats just nine days past weaning had similar effects (Brunelli, Shindledecker, & Hofer, 1987), especially in female juveniles. This suggests that some blood-borne factor triggered by pregnancy and parturition is involved, and that females are somehow better primed to be receptive to it than are males.

Oxytocin appears to be the mechanism, as it can induce fully maternal behaviour in virgin rats in 30 minutes when introduced directly into their brains (Pedersen, Ascher, Monroe, & Prange, 1982). Because antagonists that neutralize oxytocin are only effective in preventing maternal behaviour before it begins (Insel, 2000), oxytocin appears to be necessary to initiate maternal behaviour, but not to maintain it. Oxytocin is also involved in many more generally social behaviours, milk let-down, uterine contractions, orgasm, and reward experience in general. There are substantial sex differences in oxytocin receptor distribution throughout the brain. At the same time, sex differences in parental behaviour are related to testosterone, as testosterone administration reduces maternal behaviour in many mammals (Lonstein & De Vries, 2000), and administration to neonatal rat pups reduces their later maternal behaviour (Juarez, del Rio-Portilla, & Corsi-Cabrera, 1998). But there are large differences across species in the specific characteristics of maternal behaviour, the degree to which it can be primed simply by exposure to hormones and neonates, and the extent and nature of individual differences, even among primate species. This, coupled with our inability to manipulate humans experimentally, makes it difficult to draw specific conclusions about biological programming of human maternal behaviour. Vasopressin appears to be the primary hormonal mechanism involved in paternal behaviour, but testosterone appears to function very similarly in both sexes: castration of male rats improves their maternal behaviour (Lonstein & De Vries, 2000).

One way to understand human species-typical patterns of parental behaviour is to study it in hunter-gatherer cultures that have had little exposure to industrialized society. As noted, few such cultures remain, but substantial ethnographic work from the first two-thirds of the 20th century provided a wealth of descriptive information. One of the cultures in which the most extensive observation of parenting practices has been carried out is the !Kung, an African Bushman people who lived in the Kalahari Desert. They lived in semi-nomadic bands of 10–30 people, with men hunting and making tools and women foraging for nuts, roots, and berries. In this culture, infants in the first 80 postnatal weeks were nursed frequently in short bouts, as often as four times per hour throughout the day, for a total of about eight minutes during the hour (Konner & Worthman, 1980). Within the first 80 weeks of age, age was not associated with length of nursing bouts or with total nursing time, though it was correlated 0.71 with average interval between bouts. If this kind of extremely frequent nursing is actually species-typical and developmentally optimal (and other similarly isolated cultures have shown similar patterns), few infants in industrialized countries today are getting optimal nursing! Even mothers who remain home with their young infants often do not do so anywhere near as long as 80 weeks post-birth, and they are often busy with other tasks that make it difficult to break off four times every hour to nurse for an average of two minutes at a time.

Similarly different from practices in industrialized countries, weaning of !Kung infants typically began during their fourth year, once their mothers became pregnant again, and was completed before the new sibling was born. Weaning was generally a traumatic process, associated with considerable sibling jealousy, so when a mother did not become pregnant again, it was often delayed beyond age 5. Infants did receive supplemental food, beginning at about 6 months of age. The food was often pre-chewed by the mother and 'kiss-fed' into the infant's mouth. Infants slept with their mothers and nursed often throughout the night as well, often without waking their mothers. During the day, mothers carried them in slings that held them upright on the mothers' sides, usually skin-to-skin. As infants became more able to move independently, they spent less time in physical contact with their mothers, but still spent about 42 per cent of their time in physical contact at the age of 18 months (Konner, 1976).

This level of attention to nursing and maintenance of physical contact with one infant suggests that !Kung women generally spent most of their lives actively caring for their children, as they generally went from one pregnancy to the next. Moreover, mortality in childbirth was high, so that many women did not live to menopause. Cultures that required more active labour by women tended to allow less ad libitum nursing, especially when women's work required them to be at specific locations, such as specific cultivation areas, away from the living area. Clearly human infants can survive well without such complete dedication to their whims, especially when some of their care is provided by their fathers.

There has tended to be more variation among cultures in the involvement of fathers with their children than in mothers. There are obvious biological reasons for this: children can get by with no involvement from fathers at all, but that was essentially impossible with mothers in traditional cultures, unless some other lactating female was available. In many human cultures, paternal investment in parenting has been limited to defensive and protective activities, and general food provision to the family or larger unit, in the form of hunted meat. Among the !Kung, however, paternal involvement with children was considerably greater (Barry & Paxson, 1971). In this culture, fathers were often present around the living area, and would hold and fondle their infants, but generally returned them to their mothers whenever they fussed or needed routine care (read 'toileting'). Young children readily approached their fathers, talked to and touched them, and requested food from them, with only rare rebuffs. In a study consisting of a series of observation bouts that required maternal presence to begin data tabulation, 90 per cent of randomly distributed 15-minute time samples involved interaction between mother and infant, while 14 per cent involved interaction between father and infant (Konner, 1976). The sampling framework used in this observational study was biased against fathers, so the point here is really that involvement with fathers was not negligible. With 2–6-year-olds, father involvement took place in 30 per cent of the observations, so fathers appeared to interact more readily as children grew older. There were no differences in frequency of paternal interaction with daughters and sons in infancy, but fathers tended to interact more with sons than with daughters in the older age range. Though this seems in many ways like relatively little direct involvement, it is greater than that shown in several observational studies in industrialized countries today (Konner, 2010).

Adapting to parenthood in modern industrialized societies

As I have discussed, in modern industrialized societies many, if not most, partners work outside the home. It is common that a couple relies heavily on both incomes to maintain the lifestyle they have acquired and desire, and it is also common that both partners are strongly psychologically invested in their careers. Juggling this places pressures on the couple relationship, and these pressures are enhanced by other personal needs such as desire to maintain residence close to other family members and responsibilities such as household responsibilities. Parenthood only increases the difficulty of and pressures on the couple relationship from juggling all these disparate factors because infants and young children require large amounts of attention and investment of energy and are often very financially expensive to raise and educate. But the pressures on the couple relationship are not the only pressures involved in parenthood. In modern life, the birth of a first child changes life dramatically for many at the level of their individual lives as well. The degree of subjugation of one's own specific needs and desires necessary to build a strong pair-bond pales in comparison with that necessary to care for an infant. The changes are often especially dramatic for women, of course, who bear the biological responsibility of carrying the gestating child, giving birth and recovering from it, and nursing the infant (when nursed). But men can be dramatically affected as well, depending on how and to what degree the couple has worked out their relative priorities and the partners are able to make the adjustments inevitably necessary as unforeseen responsibilities emerge over time. As with pair-bonding, unexpressed expectations by both parents can be further sources of tension. For example, Biehle and Mickelson (2012) found that both prospective new mothers and prospective new fathers had unrealistic expectations about how much time and energy each would allocate to infant care and play after the baby was born. Depression and dissatisfaction with the partner relationship in new mothers was greater with greater unmet expectations for partner involvement in infant care while new fathers tended to be pleased when their partners took over more of the care responsibilities than they had expected. There was one exception to this, however: fathers tended to express less satisfaction with the partner relationship when mothers played with the babies more than fathers had expected.

Many older people, whose offspring are grown, refer to parenthood as one of the most satisfying aspects of their lives, and many if not most remain very actively interested and involved in the lives of their grown offspring and take great interest in their grandchildren. Clearly, as well, parenthood has some biological imperative. Without it, the species would die out quickly! Together, perhaps, these two facts create the impression among many, before they become parents, that parenthood is a source of happiness and life satisfaction. This is certainly often true at the very beginning, when an infant is first born, but the larger picture is much murkier, especially while children are very young and during their adolescence. On average, married couples report greater happiness and life satisfaction than single individuals, but the reverse is true of parents: they often report *less* happiness than people who are not parents (Ditella, MacCulloch, & Oswald, 2003). Moreover, there is evidence that, the more children they have, the less satisfaction they report (Twenge, Campbell, & Foster, 2003). Much has been written about the possibility that, instead of marriage causing happiness, happier people are more likely to marry, and of course it is possible that both are true. The same kinds of selection effects may be involved in the negative association between parenthood and satisfaction in one very direct and modern way. That is, people who are better educated and thus have greater access to the financial resources often associated with professional-level jobs also tend to express greater life satisfaction, though the association tends to be logarithmic rather than linear: the extent to which an additional increment to income or SES is associated with greater satisfaction gets smaller with greater income or SES. But better education and more financial resources are also associated with greater and more consistently effective use of birth control, so that better educated people and those with more financial resources are more likely to have the numbers of children they actually want (and for which they can plan financially), rather than the numbers their bodies can produce.

The situation is likely more complicated than this, as you might expect, and expectations and competing goals are likely important. Meta-analysis (Twenge, Campbell, & Foster, 2003) indicated that differences in marital satisfaction between parents and non-parents were greater among those of high SES than among those of middle and low SES. Those of high SES are more likely to be seriously involved in their careers and to have enjoyed considerable freedom of movement in the form of holiday trips and evening outings such as concerts, plays, and nice restaurants before the births of their children. Thus they may tend to experience greater constriction of movement and activity from prior levels, both professional and recreational, afterwards, whether they have only one child or five. This tendency seems to have become more pronounced over time, likely due at least partly to the increased participation and active involvement of women in professional careers. The fact that this greater involvement of women is also associated with lower overall birth rates among high SES couples and delayed childbearing among those who do go on to become parents can only accentuate this pattern, as it means that couples have tended to experience the relative freedoms of the 'double income, no kids' lifestyle for longer and thus to have become more accustomed to it.

These are general patterns, but they make clear myriad sources of individual differences. Individuals differ in expectations in many areas, including career involvement, partner engagement, enjoyment of engagement with young children, commitment to other family relationships and friendships, involvement in activities outside of work and family, etc. But they also differ in willingness to be flexible about their expectations and to tolerate unmet expectations, not to mention differences in abilities to meet their own individual goals, willingness to tolerate inabilities to meet individual goals, abilities to manage interpersonal conflicts when one or both partners is suffering from unmet expectations of one sort or another, abilities to handle stress of any and all kinds, and the ability and willingness to use money to ease stresses (for example by hiring nannies). All of these differences stem from differing childhood backgrounds and experiences as well as from genetic differences that contribute to abilities and temperament. They are all interrelated, but in ways that differ among individuals, so that any one of these variables can contribute to any of the others in an essentially infinite number of ways. Is it any wonder no two of our lives are alike?

Further reading

Biehle, S. N., & Mickelson, K. D. (2012). First-time parents' expectations about the division of childcare and play. *Journal of Marriage and Family, 26*, 36–45.

Buss, D. M. (1989). Sex differences in human mate preferences: Evolutionary hypotheses tested in 37 cultures. *Behavioral and Brain Sciences, 12*, 1–49.

Collins, W. A. (2003). More than myth: The developmental significance of romantic relationships during adolescence. *Journal of Research on Adolescence, 13*, 1–24.

Eastwick, P. W., & Finkel, E. J. (2008). Sex differences in mate preferences revisited: Do people know what they actually desire in a relationship partner? *Journal of Personality and Social Psychology, 94*, 245–264.

Gangestad, S. W., Simpson, J. A., Cousins, A. J., Garver-Apgar, C. E., & Christensen, P. N. (2004). Women's preferences for male behavioral displays change across the menstrual cycle. *Psycholiogical Science, 15*, 203–207.

Lykken, D. T., & Tellegen, A. (1993). Is human mating adventitious or the result of lawful choice? A twin study of mate selection. *Journal of Personality and Social Psychology, 65*, 56–68.

McClintock, M. K., & Herdt, G. (1996). Rethinking puberty: The development of sexual attraction. *Current Directions in Psychological Science, 6*, 178–183.

Moltz, H., Lubin, M., Leon, M., & Numan, M. (1970). Hormonal induction of maternal behavior in the ovariectomized nulliparous rat. *Physiology and Behavior, 5*, 1373–1377.

Sampson, R. J., & Laub, J. H. (1990). Crime and deviance over the life course: The salience of adult social bonds. *American Sociological Review, 55*, 609–627.

Townsend, J., & Wasserman, T. (1998). Sexual attractiveness sex differences in assessment and criteria. *Evolution and Human Behavior, 19*, 171–191.

Trivers, R. L. (1972). Parental investment and sexual selection. In B. Campbell, *Sexual Selection and the Descent of Man, 1871–1971* (pp. 136–179). Chicago: Aldine Publishing.

Ageing and Longevity: Managing Decline

11

Ageing is the process of change in an object or organism over time. Technically, it begins at conception for an organism or creation for an object, and continues until death or destruction. In organisms and many objects such as wine and cheese the initial period of ageing involves improvement in capacity for action or quality. After some period of time, however, ageing involves primarily decline in capacity for action and quality – even the wine 'turns' and the cheese rots. In organisms, the initial period of ageing tends to be termed 'development,' and the term 'ageing' is generally reserved for the changes associated with the later years of life, which primarily involve decline in capacity for action and increased susceptibility to disease.

Ageing is a multidimensional process that takes place on physical, psychological, and social levels. Even within these areas, rates of ageing may vary considerably within any given individual. For example, reaction times tend to be fastest when a person is around 20 years old. They begin to increase, reflecting decline, shortly thereafter. Vocabulary and knowledge and understanding of almost any aspect of the world, however, may increase almost indefinitely throughout life. There are also considerable individual differences in developmental trajectories of performance in all areas that have been measured, so that, for example, some people might attain most rapid reaction time at the age of 20 and 4 months, while for others it might be at age 19 and 2 months and still others 22 and 5 months. Together, these individual differences in ageing trajectories in any one area and intra-individual differences in timing of maximal capacity across dimensions of function make it impossible to state an age at which some kind of general maximum capacity for action is achieved and after which general decline in capacity for action begins.

The social importance of understanding ageing

Ageing has become an increasingly important topic of research for two major social reasons. First, longevity has increased dramatically over the past hundred years. Until around 1800, the average life expectancy for humans was around 40 years (Finch, 2007). It began to increase slowly after that, with improvements in public sanitation and nutrition, reaching the late 40s by around 1900. Since then, however, with improvements in medical treatment, especially sanitary medical practices, immunization, and the development of antibiotics, it has skyrocketed to about 80 years in industrialized countries and has shown few signs of slowing down. Much of this does not reflect increases in human capacity for long life though, as even 2,000 years ago it was not uncommon for some people to live well into their 80s. Instead, much of the increase in life expectancy reflects reductions in infant and child mortality, and reductions in mortality during childbirth for women. That is, the average length of life has gone up as dramatically as it has in large part because so many of the very early deaths have been eliminated. This is not, however, the only reason for the increase in longevity: greater proportions of the population are now living well into their 80s. While increasing proportions of people remain vigorous and active at these ages, many do not. The chronic illnesses that become increasingly common in old age often require expensive medical care and involve considerable debilitation, creating considerable social costs associated with the increased longevity.

The second reason that ageing has become an important topic of research is that, in addition to increased longevity, birth rates have declined in many industrialized countries over the same period. Moreover, they have done so in many places sufficiently to offset the decreases in infant and child mortality, so that the young adult population has come to represent decreasing proportions of the total population. This has several kinds of social repercussions that merit, even demand, government policy action. The most obvious is that people in many industrialized countries have looked forward to retiring from economically productive work around age 65 and often even earlier. When they do so, they rely for living expenses on retirement plans, both private and public, and savings. Their own savings are often insufficient to cover their costs of living and medical care, placing burdens on public resources. Public retirement plans are also generally supported through tax payments by the younger working citizenry, which means that, over time, smaller numbers of the working young are supporting greater numbers of the retired old, and pension programmes are going underfunded. More subtly, younger and older people tend to have different interests and activities. Crime rates, particularly rates of violent crimes, tend to be higher among younger people than among older people, and younger people are more likely to agitate for social and political change. They are also quicker to adopt new technologies and to be interested in the development of educational resources, both for themselves and for their children. But older people are more likely to vote, which can result in their having perhaps unwarranted political influence that can generate social tensions. Fuelling research further, as increasing proportions of the population (including researchers) are, say, over 60 years old but still in good health, there is increasing general curiosity about exactly what is happening to them as they age.

Physiological characteristics of ageing

Most species experience ageing, or *senescence*, throughout the organism, with death as its ultimate consequence. It is characterized by reduced ability to respond to stress and increased difficulty maintaining homeostasis in all bodily systems, as well as increased structural fragility and overall slowing of neuronal transmission. This makes the organism increasingly vulnerable to a host of chronic illnesses, which have the general property of accelerating the overall ageing process. Other physical characteristics include decline in reproductive fertility, slowed movement, and increased cardiac and vascular dysfunction, abnormal tissue growth, oxidative damage, and brain neuron loss. There is considerable variation among species in maximum and average lifespan, with a general but by no means universal tendency for species with larger bodies to live longer than smaller species. Rates of ageing are compared across species using rates of mortality acceleration. In mammals, the lowest absolute rates of mortality are generally around puberty (Finch, 2007), and these rates begin to accelerate soon after.

The brain experiences changes with age as well. Cerebral ventricles expand with age, and overall cerebral volume tends to decrease. Both brain grey and white matter volumes tend to decrease as well. Some brain regions experience declines in volume to greater degrees than others, with the hippocampus, the insula, and the superior parietal gyri being particularly vulnerable to shrinkage. This means that, overall, the cranium increasingly houses empty space. But the brain is also subject to increases in deleterious material known as *neurofibrillary tangles* and *amyloid plaques*. These consist of tangled neurological filaments and accumulated deposits of a large amino acid called *amyloid ⊠-peptide* that impede efficient transmission of neuronal signals. Neurotransmitters such as dopamine, serotonin, and glutamate, as well as their receptors, also tend to decrease. All of these decreases in quantity interfere with communication pathways, but, speed of transmission from one brain region to another also decreases due to decreased dendritic branching, slowing of cerebral blood flow, and de-myelinization (loss of brain white matter). Of course, there are substantial individual differences in the rates at which these changes take place, but these differences tend to be small, at least over relatively short periods of time such as five years, compared with the individual differences that exist among people of similar age at any one point in time, making them difficult to measure.

Cognitive ageing

Functionally, the most pronounced and robust psychological changes associated with old age involve declines in cognitive function. Older people tend to experience increasing difficulties in focusing attention and filtering out distracting sensory inputs. This affects their abilities to perform tasks that involve switching from one activity or focus of attention to another, as well as tasks that involve inhibiting responses in some circumstances but not others, and especially performance in situations that require execution of several tasks concurrently (Kramer & Madden, 2008). To some degree these difficulties reflect the decreases in speed of transmission of neural signals that take place, as overall cognitive slowing imposes greater time constraints on directing focus of attention and/or switching attention from one form of stimulus to another. But these difficulties also reflect decreases in memory function. These memory changes might be the ones older people notice most: the term 'senior moment' has become so common as to be cliché. It refers to a sudden inability to call to mind well-known words or names, often in ways that cause considerable amusement to others and embarrassment and even fright in the persons experiencing them. Such moments occur at young ages as well, often when people are tired and/or have been under stress, but they take place with increasing frequency in older age. Though these moments attract attention because they are dramatic, more mundane laboratory tasks robustly show that declines in all aspects of memory performance in older age are very real (McDaniel, Einstein, & Jacoby, 2008). Theories about why these memory declines take place have revolved around decreases both in the strengths of the neurological traces laid down at the time of encoding and in ability to retrieve traces once they have been laid down.

While there is little question that declines in memory abilities in older age are real, some of the declines in performance on laboratory tasks and in everyday life appear to reflect other aspects of ageing. For example, decreases in sensory capacities such as hearing and vision may require many older people to devote more cognitive resources simply to picking up what is going on in some situation, distracting them from carrying out the kinds of memory rehearsals that people with better sensory capacities execute rather automatically (McDaniel, Einstein, & Jacoby, 2008). Moreover, as knowledge of memory declines with age has become more widespread, it is possible that older people's expectations of memory decline reduce their motivation to maintain good memory habits and practices that impact both memory performance at any one point in time and aggravate whatever more general memory capacity declines are already taking place. There is substantial evidence that older people do believe that their memories are not as good as those of younger people (Hertzog & Hultsch, 2000), and that, among individuals, actual memory performance is correlated with perceptions about declines in performance. This could, however, reflect accuracy of perception rather than some causal influence of belief about inevitability of decline.

Research attempting to distinguish these two possibilities has taken two approaches. First, studies have compared memory performance of older and younger adults in cultures with different attitudes towards older people. For example, stereotypes about the elderly tend to be somewhat negative in the United States, but older people are venerated in much of China. Levy & Langer

(1994) confirmed the existence of these basic attitudinal differences and developed a composite score incorporating four aspects of memory. There were no differences between memory performance in younger Chinese and American adults, but older American adults performed worse than older Chinese adults and younger American adults, while older Chinese adults did not differ significantly in performance from younger Chinese adults. A stronger approach is to compare memory performance when participants are made explicitly aware that their memory is being tested or implicitly primed with stereotypes of poor memory performance in older age with performance when no such manipulation is carried out. Studies that have taken this approach have produced some evidence of greater performance decrements in older participants relative to younger ones during such manipulations, but results have not always been consistent (McDaniel, Einstein, & Jacoby, 2008). Regardless of the specific outcome, this research is important, as the possibility that expectations drive outcomes is real but all too often ignored.

Well-being in older age

Another robust observation of psychological ageing is that, despite increasing constraints on activity and health that tend to undermine psychological well-being when they occur at younger ages, well-being remains stable overall in old age, or even increases (Diener & Suh, 1997). Increased well-being is far from universal, particularly near the end of life, but this just emphasizes the strength of the overall pattern that applies to many. One of the clearest and most paradoxical manifestations of this phenomenon is that social interaction tends to reduce with age, yet social interaction is for most, including older, people a consistent and strong source of pleasure and thus well-being. Several theories have been proposed to explain the reduction of social activity. *Activity theory* has proposed that reductions in activity are primarily socially imposed: people customarily retire from active work, and once they leave the mainstream of activity and society it becomes more difficult to maintain social connections with people who remain in that mainstream. For proponents of this theory, helping elderly people to maintain activities and social connections is of paramount importance in maintaining their well-being. In direct contrast, *disengagement theory* has proposed that withdrawal from activity and social connection is a normal response to the increasing awareness that death, the ultimate withdrawal, is approaching. Only one theory has really addressed the fact that reduced social activity in old age apparently does not undermine psychological well-being. *Socio-emotional selectivity theory* (Carstensen, 1993) has proposed that individuals have the same basic socioemotional goals throughout the lifespan: they seek to feel connected to others, to feel needed, to have new experiences, to learn and grow, etc., but the priorities they assign to these goals change as a function of how much future time they perceive they have. In youth, when life stretches in front of one seemingly forever, people tend to give highest priority to activities in pursuit of goals that build their future prospects, activities such as acquiring information and building social networks. In the process, they may tolerate unpleasant conditions such as exercise regimes or diets that may benefit health or appearance or cantankerous supervisors in otherwise advantageous job opportunities simply because they believe that doing so will serve them well in the future. With age, however, the theory goes, people accumulate experience both in regulating their emotions within situations to avoid negative emotions and in placing themselves in the kinds of situations that tend to generate positive emotions for them. In the process, they learn the kinds of social interactions they particularly enjoy. As their perceived time horizons narrow, people increasingly focus on the present, and have less and less need for information that can be valuable in the future and which tends to come with interactions with more peripheral social partners. They thus focus on interactions with more intimate social partners – family and close friends – and often even drop many more casual social contacts.

Research involving socioemotional selectivity theory

As good theories should do, socioemotional selectivity theory has spawned considerable research. There have been perhaps two major strains to this research. In one, consideration has been given to the observation that future time perspective may inherently be associated with age for everyone, but there are other situations in which time perspective may be shortened. If the theory has merit, people's social interactions should tend also to focus in on close social contacts to the exclusion of more peripheral contacts if they encounter these situations, regardless of age. For example, people considering moving to another city or emigrating to another country showed greater preference for spending time with close social contacts and there were no differences between older and younger adults in this preference (e.g., Frederickson & Carstensen, 1990; Fung, Lai, & Ng, 2001), as did HIV-positive individuals showing symptoms of AIDS (Carstensen & Frederickson, 1998).

These studies have produced evidence consistent with the theory, but stronger evidence would be provided if alternative explanations for the same phenomena could be ruled out. Besides foreshortened time horizon, another possible explanation for reduction in social contact in older age may be reduced resources or energy for engaging in it with anyone. Again, consideration of what happens with reduced resources or energy at younger ages may be relevant. Think, for example, about how you feel about socializing when you have a cold or the flu. For many people, the world closes in and they want nothing more than to curl up in bed with a hot drink in front of a TV and not have anyone bother them at all. If someone is going to be around, many people want that person to be someone who knows them so well that they have no need to manage impressions – they can be every bit as crabby as they feel. This particular situation is temporary (and the person is usually counting on this), and has nothing to do with the kind of foreshortening of time horizon that socio-emotional selectivity theory posits drives reduced social contact in old age, but the effect on social contacts is often very similar. For many people, life in old age can be physically like life with a bad cold for younger people, in terms of physical energy levels and general discomfort in the form of aches and pains. Studies attempting to test the theory, however, have not considered this alternative explanation, instead focusing more on developing evidence in support of it.

Another strand of research spawned by socio-emotional selectivity theory has focused on how older people may regulate their behaviour to maintain positive emotions and avoid negative emotions. This has involved development of evidence from attention and memory task performance that older people are motivated selectively to process positively emotionally valenced information over information with negative emotional valence. That is, despite the decreases in ability to control attention and resist distraction and the decreases in memory function described above, older people simply place more (conscious or unconscious) emphasis on and thus devote a greater proportion of their cognitive resources to processing positively than negatively valenced information. Self-reports suggest that this is the case: older people have tended to report lower likelihood than younger people of escalating conflicts by shouting or name-calling (Burditt & Fingerman, 2005) and to rate the extent to which they focus on controlling their emotions higher (Lawton, Kleban, Rajagopal, & Dean, 1992). These were, however, only their perceptions, though they were not comparing themselves with younger people, but simply rating how they perceived themselves.

One prominent study going well beyond subjective perceptions examined response times to a dot-probe task (Mather & Carstensen, 2003). In the task, an emotional face and a neutral face appeared side by side on a computer screen for one second. Then the faces disappeared and a dot appeared where one of the faces had been. Participants were instructed to press a computer key indicating which side the dot was on. Younger participants did not show any differences in response time no matter whether the dots appeared where negatively, positively, or neutrally emotional faces had been. But older participants were slower to respond when the dots appeared where negatively emotional faces had been than where neutral faces had been, and faster to respond when the dots appeared where positively emotional faces had been than where neutral faces had been. This suggested that the older participants, but not the younger ones, had tended to focus on the positively emotional faces over the neutral faces, and on the neutral faces over the negatively emotional ones. An eye-tracking study suggested that this is not because older people do not notice negative stimuli, but rather because they do not dwell on it (Rosler, Ulrich, Billino, Sterzer, Weidauer, Bernhardt, et al., 2005). Again, the task involved pairs of negative and neutral and positive and neutral pictures. Both older and younger participants tended to glance initially at the negative picture in a pair, but older participants looked away more rapidly. There were no differences in looking times when one of the pictures was positive.

These kinds of attentional biases would affect what information gets encoded, but memory performance and, ultimately, maintenance of emotional state, depends on how the information is maintained and later recalled. Studies have provided evidence that older people are more likely than younger people to manage their memories so that they are positive. For example, one way to regulate emotion is to favour the positive features of the chosen option and the negative features of rejected options in memory. In hypothetical choice situations, older participants did this to a greater extent than did younger participants (Mather & Johnson, 2000). Similar observations have been made for autobiographical memories and interpretations of stressful encounters (Mather & Carstensen, 2005). And Mather and Knight (2005) had older and younger people view pictures with positive, neutral, and negative emotional content and then tested their ability to recall the pictures two days later. They reasoned that, whatever age differences there might be in bias towards better memory for positive emotional content, these differences should be accentuated if people were asked to process the material they had seen more formally. Thus, they asked only half the participants to write descriptions of the pictures they had seen from memory 20 minutes after they had seen them. Both after 20 minutes and after 48 hours, a greater proportion of the pictures remembered by older participants had positive emotional content than those remembered by younger participants, and vice versa for pictures with negative emotional content. Moreover, there was a significant interaction such that the differences in recall after 48 hours between older and younger participants were greater in those who had completed the 20-minute recall exercise than in those who had not. Other assessments of specific cognitive strategies used in memory recall produced similar results: older people appear to devote more resources towards processing information with positive emotional content.

This is important work, but effect sizes have generally been small, and meta-analysis, with all its own faults, has not found them to be particularly robust (Murphy & Isaacowitz, 2008). Small effect sizes in limited experimental conditions may not be particularly important objections to the theory, as very small biases in information processing at any one time or in any one situation could accumulate to very substantial impacts on overall function and psychological state if they occur day in and day out. But is something about age and perception of foreshortened time horizon the reason for even motivated devotion of additional resources? Ascertaining the emergence of this over time would appear to be critical to the theory, but most studies have been cross-sectional. This means that they have not been able to distinguish truly age-related differences from cultural cohort differences. The people considered 'older' who have participated in research studies testing socioemotional selectivity theory over perhaps the last 15 years have commonly been aged 65–85, which has meant, very generally, that they were born in 1910–1940 or so, and most grew up during the Great Depression and/or World War II. These were hard times in most of the industrialized world compared with those experienced by the younger participants in these studies, who have commonly been under-graduate students, aged around 20 and thus born very generally in 1965–1980 or so when life was much gentler in most western industrialized countries. Psychologists are just starting to consider empirically how such world histor-ical events may affect the emotional and personality characteristics and coping techniques of whole cohorts of people, but studies doing so have tended to indicate the presence of such effects. For example, several studies have found effects associated with the September 11 terrorist attacks in the United States. And the psychologist Jean Twenge has published several papers comparing psychological characteristics of 'Baby Boomers' with those of younger gener-ations and their effects on workplace and academic climates, values, sexual behaviours, and other aspects of life. One possible alternative explanation for greater devotion of cognitive resources to maintenance of positive emotion among older people is simply that they have seen more hardship than younger people, overall. They may have thus had more reason to teach themselves to find the 'silver linings' when they were young and simply tend now to exercise those skills still in older age. Testing this would require longitudinal studies rather than the cross-sectional studies used so far.

Relative stability of psychological characteristics in older age

In Chapter 5, I discussed how dynamic systems theory has started to be used in embryology to understand how organisms self-organize during development to reach states that can be described as steady, and the ranges of such steady states that are possible. Of course, there is no such thing as a completely steady state within any organism, human or otherwise: the environment continually presents stimuli of one sort or another and the organism continually adapts and responds in accordance with its capacities and needs. Moreover, though it is possible to think of the human lifespan in terms of development towards some form of adult maturity followed by some period during which that matu-rity is enjoyed and then by some period of decline from that maturity, in reality it is difficult to pinpoint any specific point when maturity, however defined, is reached. Acknowledging the pervasiveness of change, however, many if not most people do attain considerable stability in lifestyle, personality, and cognitive ability during adulthood. Many twin studies have demonstrated that genetic influences contribute strongly to maintenance of this stability. Evidence for this can be provided in several ways. One is to show that correlations between genetic influences on variables measured at two or more times points approach 1.00. Other ways involve decomposition of variance in models of patterns of phenotypic stability and change over time into that attributable to genetic and environmental influences, with results indicating that genetic influences contribute strongly to stability, but not to overt change. Few of these studies have recognized that environmental influences also often contribute to maintenance of psychological stability, but environmental influences are likely every bit as important sources of stability as genetic influences, especially in later adulthood.

For example, Johnson, McGue, & Krueger (2005) examined personality in a sample of twins when they were on average 59 years old, and then again five years later when they were on average 64 years old. Across the 11 personality scales assessed, the average correlation of scores at the two time points was 0.76. Measured freely, the genetic correlations ranged from 0.95 to 1.00, and models specifying the same amounts of variance from the same sources and constraining the genetic correlations to 1.00 showed better fit than the models with freely estimated parameters. But the nonshared environmental correlations were also substantial; they ranged from 0.53 to 0.73. Moreover, measurement error in models such as these contributes to nonshared environmental influences, so these measured nonshared environmental correlations were underestimates of the actual extent to which nonshared environmental influences contributed to personality stability. After adjustment for measurement error, nonshared environmental influences contributed as much to personality stability as did genetic influences. Examination of prior studies of genetic influences on personality stability indicated that similar conclusions would have been appropriate in those studies as well, though the authors of those studies had not addressed the point. Sources of nonshared environmental influences that might commonly contribute to personality in later adulthood include residence in the same community and even the same house, co-habitation with the same spouse or unmarried status, employment in the same job at the same workplace, stable relationships with grown children, and maintenance of consistent patterns of dietary, exercise, and recreation patterns.

Robustness

However well environmental influences contribute to psychological stability, psychological stability is greater in some sense than environmental stability. One day may be particularly stressful, the next relaxing; some days we receive bad news and on others we receive good news, yet somehow we retain our personalities, abilities, and identities throughout. I introduced the term *robustness* in Chapter 8 to refer to the ability to retain core properties in the face of environmental perturbations. It is commonly used in design of engineering systems, where relevant principles have been relatively clearly worked out and their implications can be measured relatively precisely. Increasingly, however, it is being used in the study of biological systems, both within organisms and considering them as wholes. It is inherently a systems-level phenomenon that cannot be understood by looking at the individual components of the system

(Kitano, 2004), and a system must be robust in order to function in unpredictable environments using unreliable components. It has several properties of relevance to ageing that have been operationalized in very formal terms in engineering systems, using mathematics developed during the middle of the twentieth century.

This degree of formalism awaits development for biological systems, but the concepts are relevant. For example, if a system has little sensitivity to some kinds of disturbance, it necessarily has greater sensitivity to other kinds of disturbance. This can be demonstrated using a formula known as Bode's sensitivity integral and its necessity can be proven, but exactly how it applies to biological systems remains to be worked out. Relevant common observations might include the tendency for people to tolerate considerable stress when they must, only to fall apart later at something very minor. Similarly, the flux control summation theorem in engineering states that fluctuation in function of a system is a property of the whole system and thus control of the fluctuation is shared by all reactions or components of the system. This means that, when activity of one reaction or component changes, activities of all the other reactions and components change as well. They may change in compensatory ways so that stability of the original systemic properties are maintained, or they may change in ways that bring about a system with qualitatively different organization from the original. A relevant example here might be what happens following brain lesion from a stroke. Sometimes the brain is able to reorganize around the damaged area so that the person recovers full function. Other times the reorganization results in substantial personality changes that may become every bit as stable as were the original.

Robustness refers to maintenance of system functionality rather than to maintenance of the state of the system. It is thus a concept distinct from that of *homeostasis*, which refers to maintenance of a particular state of a system. For example, humans and other mammals require minimum amounts of oxygen to be delivered to the brain through the bloodstream in order to maintain consciousness. When we run or otherwise tax the oxygen-carrying capacity of the system, heart and breathing rates speed up to deliver more oxygen more quickly to meet the increased demand, robustly maintaining consciousness. At the same time, many aspects of homeostasis are disturbed in response to this change: our body temperatures increase, our muscles activate, we begin to sweat to offset the increase in body temperature, etc., so that robustness is maintained but homeostasis is disturbed. Homeostasis and robustness are related, however, in the sense that they merge when the function to be maintained is one that maintains the state of the system. For example, delivery of oxygen to the brain remains homeostatic when we run. They also overlap when robustness of a subsystem contributes to homeostasis of a higher level of system organization. In the running example, all the disruptions of lower-level homeostasis involved in the robust functional system response, such as increases in heart and breathing rates, contribute to the homeostasis of oxygen delivery that maintains consciousness. Importantly, this emphasizes that a system may maintain robustness of function specifically *by* undergoing changes in structure and/or components.

Maintenance of robustness in any system, whether organic or inorganic, inherently involves trade-offs. The greater the robustness, the more resources must be devoted to the features that make it possible. In engineering systems, however, things are considerably simpler than in biological systems. This is because engineering systems can be optimized by re-designing them starting from scratch. In contrast, design in biological systems takes place through evolutionary selection. This means effectively re-using the same component parts in new and better ways, rather than starting over. The mathematics involved in these constraints have not been worked out, but there is no question that the constraints are substantial.

Box 11.1   Four relevant conceptual properties of robustness in engineering systems (Kitano, 2004)

First, *system control* refers to the existence of *negative and positive feedback loops* that maintain system function. Systems may have access to information that some stimulus is creating a difference between the actual state of some aspect of the system and the optimal state of that aspect. Negative feedback loops occur when a system is calibrated to reduce the difference. Negative feedback thus contributes directly to maintenance of state stability. We set up negative feedback loops for ourselves that help to maintain robustness when we arrange to spend time doing something we particularly enjoy after enduring some period of stress in pursuit of a long-term goal. Positive feedback loops occur when a system is calibrated so that it responds to a stimulus that perturbs the system by reinforcing the effect of the stimulus – that is, by exaggerating it. Positive feedback thus tends to contribute to system instability, but it is also the mechanism through which a system can move from one robust state to another. In particular, this includes movement from robust but non-optimal states to other states that may be more optimal. Positive feedback loops help to build or restore healthy robustness when, for example, a woman endures repeated abuse by her husband with increasing outrage, until one such incident gets her so angry that she overcomes her fear of being on her own and leaves him.

Second, robust systems tend to benefit from possession of *alternative or fail-safe mechanisms*. If a system has multiple ways of achieving a particular function, when some component in one of those ways fails, another can take over. Sometimes the redundancy is literal: the system has more than one identical or highly similar component. More often, the system is diverse, and function can be maintained through use of different combinations of components. For example, a young child who falls down and scrapes her knee may run crying to either Mum or Dad. Mum may tend to acknowledge the pain but then distract the child with a joke so that a moment later she is giggling, while Dad may tend to take a wipe from his pocket and make a big show of cleaning the scrape, then cover it with a large and colourful bandage, a process the child watches with fascination, meanwhile forgetting the pain. Despite their different styles, the child very soon feels much better. Alternative mechanisms are linked with system control in the sense that feedback mechanisms are preserved when one mechanism takes over from another one which has failed or is not available. As well, sometimes the control mechanisms orchestrate switching between alternative mechanisms to maintain function.

A third property that maintains robustness is *modularity*. This is the degree to which a system's components can be separated and recombined. We may be most familiar with the term in construction, where it refers to bundles of project components that can be produced in large quantities and then installed as needed in individual units. Related to this, in engineering design it refers to the erection of a larger system by combining smaller subsystems. One very prominent example of a biological module is the cell, which interacts with both the external environment and other cells. Importantly, a cell has component parts of its own such as organelles and a nucleus, but it also serves as the building block of tissues and organs. When studying networks or ecology, modularity refers to the ways in which the overall system is divided into smaller communities or groups that interact more closely among themselves than with others, often in execution of particular functions. Many have considered the brain to consist of modules that have evolved to carry out particular kinds of actions. Evidence supporting this has often come from studies of neurological damage in stroke victims, who often show amazingly specific limitations in function. Other evidence, however, suggests that, to the extent brain modules exist, they are very flexible, with soft boundaries. For example, recovery of function after stroke is very common, as different brain regions take over for the damaged region. And typically auditory processing regions that would be otherwise useless in deaf people who cannot perceive sound usually rapidly become dedicated to processing sign language as soon as it is introduced. At some level, however, the very existence of these recovery mechanisms shows how the modularity that is present helps to maintain robustness.

The fourth property that maintains robustness is *decoupling*. This refers to isolation of variation at one level from function that takes place at another, creating a buffer from environmental perturbations. Many genes offer this kind of buffer. One example is *Hsp90*. This is a *molecular chaperone*, or a protein that is not present in biological component structures (read modules) when these structures have been assembled and are performing their functions normally, but which gravitate towards and repair these structures when they have been mis-assembled and are unable to function normally. Often the abnormal function has come into being through environmental stress, so Hsp90 is characterized as being up-regulated – more greatly expressed – in response to stress. Hsp90 is one of a class of proteins known as *heat shock proteins* that protect cells when they are exposed to elevated temperatures. It helps to refold mis-folded proteins, and to disintegrate mis-folded proteins that cannot be refolded. A number of these proteins, when mis-folded, are involved in tumour growth, so Hsp90 is one of a number of proteins that disarm the steady parade of potentially cancer-causing mutations that normally take place in individual cells within our bodies. This is a very biochemical example of decoupling, but at a much higher, more familiar level, of life, decoupling that contributes to robustness also takes place when, for example, a person develops the skill of closing the door on the office and its stresses when the work day is over and it is time to go home.

Recognition that robustness is ubiquitous is growing. Kitano (2004; 2010) has suggested that, in dynamic biological systems, evolvability and robustness are linked: the mechanisms that confer robustness facilitate evolution, and evolution selects for these mechanisms. Evolvability entails the existence of flexible capacity to generate novel and diverse phenotypes. This can take place through chance mutations, but this is a risky process because 'messing with' a precisely functioning system is far more likely to disrupt function than to enhance it. The features that confer robustness create this flexibility, buffering the detrimental effects of the chance mutations that do occur, and minimizing reliance of the biological system (organism) on the occurrence of mutations to produce novel phenotypes (Kirschner & Gerhardt, 1998). The structure that most naturally accommodates this has been called the *bow-tie architecture* (see Figure 11.1). It occurs commonly in biological systems, at various levels from overall structure to highly specific processes such as gene transcription (Kitano, 2004).

The bow-tie architecture has many inputs to an evolutionarily conserved core set of processes that are weakly and flexibly but crucially linked to the mechanisms that control the system's overall dynamics. These inputs arise from diverse environmental stimuli and conditions. In turn, the conserved core processes generate many outputs, or diverse reactions to the inputs and products. This means that many different kinds of environmental stimuli are handled by the same set of core processes to generate many different kinds of responses. While this allows for much flexibility in the nature of the inputs and responses, it also means that the source of robustness is this set of core processes through which all the inputs pass. Because of the centrality of these core processes, the system tends to be relatively impervious to commonly encountered inputs, but can be extremely fragile when presented with novel inputs, leading either to catastrophic crash due to core process failure, or to transition to a new qualitative state through substantive reorganization that then becomes robustly stable.

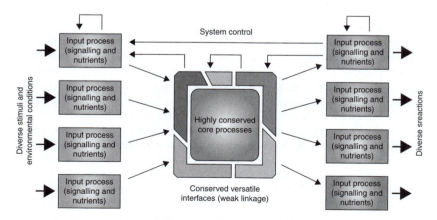

Figure 11.1   The architectural framework of robust evolvable systems

Source: Reprinted by permission from Macmillan Publishers Ltd, on behalf of Cancer Research UK: *Nature Reviews Genetics, 5,* 826–837 doi:10.1038nrg1471 (originally figure 3).

Robustness and ageing

The point of all this is that, by mid-life, many people have developed consider-able robustness at many levels. Their bodies have reached physical maturity, resulting in rather stable physical characteristics that manage variations in most day-to-day conditions almost completely below most people's awareness. They have developed cognitive skills that see them through the day-to-day tasks with which they are typically presented, again almost completely automatically. They have arranged their life circumstances in ways that suit and support their personalities so that they cope with their typical environments in very habitual ways. These ways of coping may or may not be adaptive – most people have some (major or minor) aspect of life that they repeatedly mismanage, creating ongoing sources of stress for themselves. But these ways of coping *are* robust: they allow people to maintain patterns of life and behaviour that show rela-tively little variability over noticeable spans of time. This robustness begins to break down in what we recognize as later life, however, and it constitutes much of what we call ageing. That is, the feedback mechanisms, fail-safe redundan-cies, modular boundaries, and decoupled processes all begin to operate less effectively. Some of this takes place through what we would tend to call 'wear and tear': parts of each component disintegrate over time and through usage, and components lose their precision of function so that combinations of func-tions do not take place in the same time sequences, leading to different outputs. This way of understanding ageing can help us to understand the development of disease, especially the kinds that become increasingly common in old age, and those that are becoming increasingly common in the modern world, such as Type 2 diabetes and cancers.

Type 2 diabetes can be thought of as a natural response in a system that has evolved to be robust to lack of food and a lifestyle that requires great expendi-tures of energy for survival, but is thus fragile to an environmental condition that was rarely experienced in its evolution: regular overfeeding with foods containing large amounts of highly processed sugars and salt, and a sedentary lifestyle. A more serious situation can occur when some components of the system 'misbehave' and the system mechanisms that support the robustness of the core mechanisms are also used to support the misbehaving components. Many forms of cancer provide examples of this: genetic mutations in somatic tissue cells produce pre-cancerous cells in our bodies routinely, and other cells destroy them before they can do any harm. But occasionally both muta-tions that create pre-cancerous cells and increase cellular division rates take place, starting the process of uncontrolled tumour growth within an otherwise supportive system. When this occurs, the cells that destroy such misbehaving cells cannot keep up, and the cancerous disease state becomes robust in its own right, maintained by the genetic heterogeneity that develops within the cluster of diseased tumour cells. This intrinsic robustness of the cancerous cells is supported by mechanisms that maintain normal body functions that act to reduce the effectiveness of the main therapies we use against cancer, which are generally total-body poisons. For example, commonly observed resistance to drugs of all kinds (including those used to treat cancer) develops through up-regulation (increased expression) of genes that produce proteins that act to pump toxic chemicals out of cells, exposing the cancerous cells to semi-processed chemicals that can be used to foster further cancerous growth that offsets whatever direct destructive effects the drugs have on these cells.

Intra-individual variability in old age

Robustness declines in old age even in the absence of overt disease. The primary symptom of this is increasing intra-individual response to essentially all forms of stimuli. Intra-individual variability increases because the precision with which all the system mechanisms and components fit together decreases. It is often difficult to see the increasing variability in response in day-to-day life, or even in the kinds of structured tasks used to measure psychological constructs in research studies because either variability in response is treated as noise, or the task is administered only once in any given study or wave of data collection. Tasks designed to assess very basic cognitive processes, however, show the effects very clearly. These tasks are extremely simple and take very little time to execute. Almost anyone can do them repeatedly and highly accurately without apparent effort at any one execution. Common examples are reaction time tasks, in which the participant pushes a button when she/he sees a symbol flash onto a screen. The time from presentation of the symbol to registry of the button press is the measure taken. Any single execution of this task contains little meaning because it is so quick and simple, but this also means that you can get people to do it over and over without undue fatigue. This makes it possible to obtain very reliable estimates of individual differences in response time by taking the mean time of many executions, but it also reveals that there are individual differences in the variance of response times, and that these individual differences in variability both show stability over time (Hultsch, MacDonald, Hunter, Levy-Benchton, & Strauss, 2000; Rabbitt, Osman, Moore, & Stollery, 2001; Ram, Rabbitt, Stollery, & Nesselroade, 2005) and vary with other variables such as age, other fundamental cognitive tasks, and more complex cognitive tasks (Fuentes, Hunter, Strauss, & Hultsch, 2001; Hultsch, et al., 2000; Li, Aggen, Nesselroade, & Baltes, 2001).

That is, people who tend to perform less well on more complex cognitive tasks also tend to show greater variability in performance on fundamental cognitive tasks (Li, et al., 2001; Li, Lindenberger, & Sikstrom, 2001). They tend to do so when cognitive performance has been low throughout life, but they also tend to do so when low performance on the complex tasks is relatively recent, due for example to dementia (Hultsch, MacDonald, Hunter,

Levy-Benchton, & Strauss, 2000), brain injury (Stuss, Pogue, Buckle, & Bondar, 1994), schizophrenia (Winterer & Weinberger, 2004), or normal ageing (Deary & Der, 2005; West, Murphy, Armilio, Craik, & Stuss, 2002). This association between variability in performance on fundamental cognitive tasks and level of performance on more complex cognitive tasks appears to be independent of the association between overall (mean) level of performance on the fundamental cognitive tasks and performance on more complex cognitive tasks (Li, Lindenberger, Hommel, Aschersleben, Prinz, & Baltes, 2004). It also appears that the increases in variability on fundamental cognitive tasks drive the decreases in level of performance on more complex tasks rather than vice versa, as they predict decline in complex task performance more strongly than decline in more complex cognitive task performance predicts increased variability in fundamental cognitive task performance (Bielak, Hultsch, Strauss, MacDonald, & Hunter, 2010; Lovden, Li, Shing, & Lindenberger, 2007). This suggests that variability in performance on fundamental cognitive tasks may indicate decreasing robustness of many if not all central nervous system processes that impact many levels of cognitive function, and likely physical functions as well. This would be consistent with their being lower-level inputs to higher-level core processes.

Threats to robustness – managing stress

So what might bring on the wear and tear that erodes robustness and increases variability in response? Stress is the most likely candidate. In Chapter 4, I discussed how the body and brain cope with stress in detail, and outlined how individual differences in the ability to do so may develop. Everyone encounters stress throughout their lives, and life would be quite boring without it. In moderate quantities it stimulates personal development and growth, likely helping to maintain robustness. In excessive quantities, however, it disrupts robustness. Even when the stress is relatively temporary and the system can cope with it to maintain function, the outcome after recovery may be increased fragility or vulnerability to future stress – wear and tear. Over the course of a lifetime, this wear and tear accumulates and we see it in the form of ageing. Of course, individuals differ in the extent to which they encounter stressful situations – not everyone is kidnapped or involved in a natural disaster such as a major earthquake, for example. But individuals also differ in the extent of their stress responses to any given source of stress, in their abilities to cope with the stresses they experience, and thus in the extent to which they may experience loss of robustness because of any one experience. This accumulates to extensive individual differences in ageing by late life. We can see it all around us: some 80-year-olds are out running marathons, while others require assistance simply to take care of their own basic hygiene.

Box 11.2 Ageing skin

The skin offers one of the most visible indications of how robustness is undermined through stress and over time, and the changes that take place in it offer a good model of those that take place in many other systems of the body and brain. One kind of stress that affects the skin occurs when it is broken by a wound. The break in the skin heals, but, except in the most minor cases, some *scarring* results. Scarring is a normal part of the healing process, at least in humans and most other mammals who do not experience regeneration, but scar tissue is not identical to the original broken skin it replaces. It consists of essentially the same collagen protein, but its fibre composition is different. Normal unbroken skin has a rather random, loosely structured basket-weave formation, but in scar tissue the fibres are aligned in a single direction. This alignment offers lower responsiveness to environmental conditions such as the ultraviolet radiation in sunlight, and does not permit growth of sweat glands and hair follicles. The alignment of the fibres is a result of the clotting that takes place to halt the bleeding: it makes this clotting process more effective, but also lays down the foundation for the new skin tissue that forms the scar. This foundation is usually exaggerated by over-expression of collagen during the healing process, often making the scar tissue considerably more dense than the surrounding normal tissue.

Of course, wounds can and do occur at any age. Thus the scarring process is not intrinsically associated with ageing in any way. But the skin breaks more easily with age due to the changes that take place with age, and healing takes longer. The reduced ability of scar tissue to respond to environmental conditions and to maintain other forms of normal function is typical of the kinds of loss of robustness that are seen with age. Thus scarring can be considered in some ways a localized acceleration of the ageing process. This has analogies in other aspects of ageing. For example, Type 2 diabetes is considered by many researchers to be a condition that effectively accelerates cardiovascular and even cognitive ageing. Early-onset Alzheimer's disease, which is quite rare, develops when people are in their early 50s, and for which we know specific genetic vulnerabilities, is used as a model of the much more common form of Alzheimer's Disease that generally emerges much later, as well as of normative cognitive ageing.

To understand other changes in the skin with age, it helps to understand how skin is structured. It consists of many layers, but they can roughly be divided into three parts: the *epidermis,* the *dermis*, and the *subcutaneous layer*. The epidermis is the outer part. It consists of skin cells, pigments that provide the colours of skin we see, and proteins. The dermis provides nutrients to the epidermis. It consists of nerves, blood vessels, oil glands, and hair follicles. The subcutaneous layer lies below the dermis and contains fat in addition to the components of the dermis. All the layers include connective tissues consisting of the random, loosely basket-woven collagen fibres that give the skin its firmness of shape, as well as of elastin fibres that give the skin its flexibility and strength. The skin offers a record of many kinds of environmental exposures, but sun exposure has the greatest effects on it. It is easy to see this even in relatively young people by comparing the texture of skin in areas that are rarely exposed to the sun with those that are regularly exposed. The areas rarely exposed look younger and firmer, but what specifically is meant by this?

With age, the epidermis tends to thin. This is not because the number of cell layers decreases, but because pigment-containing cells are sloughed away and not replaced, at a rate of about 6–8 per cent per decade after age 30. Those that remain increase in size to fill the gaps, thinning in the process. This gives the skin of older people a thinner, paler, sometimes almost translucent appearance. With age and especially exposure to sun, skin tends to become more mottled in appearance, with areas of both *hyper-* and *hypopigmentation*. Skin pigmentation, or colour, consists of a genetically mediated composite of reds, blues, yellows, and browns, resulting from red oxygenated and blue de-oxygenated haemoglobin, yellow carotenoids and flavins, and brown melanin. The mottling occurs because the distributions of these various components become increasingly uneven, at least partly because of increased fragility of the blood vessels and arteries in the dermis, leading to somewhat randomly dispersed breakage, but also partly because the decreased number of brown melanin-containing cells spread themselves over the surface of the skin unevenly. Overall, the thinner and less pigmented skin of older people has diminished capacity to cope with exposure to ultraviolet light, which means an acceleration in its ageing process.

Coincident with this, other cells in the epidermis also decline in number and function, leading to reduced immune function that may contribute to increased incidence of skin lesions and tags that can easily become malignant. As well, the dermis experiences considerable change with age. It can decrease in thickness by 20–80 due to decreases in the rates of production of collagen and elastin and changes in protein organization that affect its structure. Ultraviolet light activates the enzymes that break down these proteins. At the same time, the intercellular structures of these proteins weaken, so that the collagen and elastin that remains becomes disorganized and clumped. This is aggravated by decreases in production of the lipids and acids that provide moisture to the skin. Overall, cell turnover rates decrease 30–50 per cent from around ages 30 to 80, contributing to the rather weather-beaten appearance we associate with old age. As should be clear, the changes that take place with age affect all aspects of skin function and involve slowing of the repair and replacement processes that overcome environmental damage in ways that make the repaired skin even more vulnerable to further environmental damage, thus accelerating the ageing process over time.

Changes in appearance with age are very visible: we notice them both in ourselves and in others, and they are not generally associated with beauty. There are considerable individual differences in the extent and rate of these changes: particularly among older groups, in a group of any given age, some will appear much older than others. Some of the impression of age is conveyed by dress and mannerisms and behaviour, of course, but the differences show up in unadorned facial photos too (Christensen, et al., 2004). Thus the differences are not merely behavioural, and skin conditions, especially wrinkles, figure prominently in the judgement of age by appearance (Gunn, et al., 2009). Both relative physical and mental health also contribute to more youthful appearance. At present, understanding these individual differences in rates of ageing in many different characteristics attracts considerable research attention, but results are very mixed. Though the impression that individual differences in rates of ageing must be considerable, many if not most studies, whether of cognitive or physical functions, find very little variance in rates of change with age. Even when variance is perceived, it has rarely been possible to link it consistently to any other factors. Rather, it generally appears that the individual differences have essentially always been present. Some of this difficulty may be statistical: pre-existing individual differences are almost always considerably greater than individual differences in rates of change with age, so that the statistical power of the models used is concentrated there.

The ways in which skin changes with age (see Box 11.2) are normal in the sense that, though they involve gradual loss of function, they do not involve anything we consider to be disease. The skin changes may increase vulnerability to conditions we do consider to be diseased such as skin cancer and eczema, but they are not themselves disease. This is true of many other features or traits that show characteristic changes with age as well. Some of this is arbitrary: we might consider some of the changes to be disease if we had any idea what to do to reverse them, besides the kind of material manipulation involved in cosmetic surgery and application of external moisturizers and other skin care products, but for the most part consideration of ageing changes in the skin as normal reflects the extent to which we consider this wear-and-tear to be inevitable and even 'natural'. Wear-and-tear and mechanical breakdown over time certainly take place in the inorganic world as well, so it makes sense at one level to expect them in the organic world. But at another level, organisms evolve and adapt and have many processes that *do* counteract wear-and-tear quite well over long periods of time. So why do humans and so many other organisms age as they do?

Theories of senescence

In some ways it sounds almost silly to say this, but senescence is the leading cause of death throughout the world; about two-thirds of all deaths can be attributed to it (de Grey, 2007). It sounds almost silly because it is so general: almost anything, or nothing, can be attributed to age. There is always some more proximal cause of death, and senescence, or 'old age' is not even a scientifically recognized cause of death. But the term most typically applies to age-related diseases, the kinds of chronic illnesses that become much more common with age. It is not typically applied to death from accidents, childbirth, or infection – even though deaths from these causes do increase with age too. This is emphasized in the statistic that, in industrialized countries, senescence takes almost 90 per cent of us in the general sense, even if it cannot be listed on our death certificates. Senescence is clearly bad for the individual.

Theories of why senescence takes place have generally fallen into one of two camps. Theories that posit that ageing is programmed propose that it is regulated by biological clocks that turn on and off the expression of particular sets of genes that regulate maintenance, repair, and defence processes. These theories tend to have an evolutionary orientation. In contrast, stochastic theories posit that ageing is essentially no more than the accumulated record of basically stochastic environmental insults. Development of theories integrating evolutionarily driven genetic programming with environmental stress in understanding ageing has, however, become an active area of exploration in recent years. From the evolutionary perspective, one of the early proposals was that senescence is genetically programmed to maximize a population's, rather than the individual's, ability to adapt to changing environmental conditions. In most species, however, including humans for much of their history, senescence is far from the major cause of death; most individuals die from predation, starvation, exposure to cold, infection, or injury, and do so rather young. Realization of this led to the suggestion that senescence results because natural selection is concentrated during early life and gradually weakens with age, to ensure that sufficient numbers reach reproductive maturity. Thus, by some age past which individuals have had several opportunities to reproduce, the force of selection becomes so weak that it does not offset the accumulation of gene mutations that only have deleterious effects thereafter. This theory has been termed 'mutation accumulation' (Charlesworth, 1994), and it implies that there should be considerable variation in the mutations that have such only-late-life effects, because they have experienced little or no selection. *Antagonistic pleiotropy*, or the idea that genes that offer advantages in early life but disadvantages in later life may experience positive selection (Williams, 1957), elaborates on this theory.

The concept of antagonistic pleiotropy led to development of the theoretical construct of *disposable soma* (Kirkwood, 1996). According to theory, an organism requires metabolic resources and system integrity only sufficient to maintain sound physiological condition only as long as it can expect to survive in the environment in which it lives – over evolutionary history, the wild. Thus, for example, because 90 per cent of wild mice die within the first year of life, evolution has had little opportunity to select for characteristics that extend life beyond that. Characteristics that might do this, such as DNA repair mechanisms and antioxidant systems, all require development and maintenance of metabolic resources that often conflict with those that support reproductive capacity directly. The disposable soma theory suggests that evolution will select for those metabolic resources that are most likely to see the organism to reproductive maturity and which drain capacity to devote to reproductive capacity least. Because all resources devoted to longevity do drain reproductive capacity to some degree, however, there should be some trade-off between fertility and survival according to theory (Kirkwood & Austad, 2000). For example, one of the major causes of death in wild mice in the first year of life is cold. According to the disposable soma theory, mice will be naturally selected for a resource that helps to maintain thermogenesis, which can support infants as well, rather than for resources that help the parent mouse to live beyond one year. Thermogenesis requires the same metabolic resources as maintenance of pregnancy – essentially access to nutritive calories – so greater devotion of resources to it may increase risk of starvation during pregnancy, but increase chances of surviving cold for both mother and offspring. Together, the theories of antagonistic pleiotropy and disposable soma converge on the conclusion that, across species, average longevity should vary with sources of extrinsic mortality: when these sources are few, longevity should be greater than when organisms face many sources of mortality (Kirkwood & Austad, 2000).

These theories also converge in suggesting that changes in the patterns of force of selection with age should alter rates of ageing and thus longevity. This has been the focus of manipulation in most experimental tests of the theories, most of which have made use of the fruit fly *Drosophila melanogaster*. In an old joke, a mother-in-law asks her developmental biologist son-in-law to explain the work he does, and he launches into an explanation of his experiments that have resulted in delayed senescence and increased longevity in these flies. She stops him before he can get very far, asking, 'But *why* would anyone want to increase the lifespan of *fruit flies*?' The reason, of course, is that fruit flies make good model organisms because of their rapid breeding times, short natural lifespans and generational turnover, and their large and easily accessible genetic material, and researchers hope that what we can learn from experiments with them applies to humans as well. Experiments restricting breeding to later ages have indicated increased force of selection during the later portions of the lifespan, resulting in extended lifespan for the selected populations (e.g., Rose & Charlesworth, 1980). That is, those capable of breeding healthy offspring at later ages appear to be healthier (more robust) overall. These experiments also have indicated reduced fertility in the later reproducers, particularly early in life, as the disposable soma theory suggests. In fruit flies, however, the particular early-life fitness features depressed when lifespan is extended through artificial selection have varied across studies, ranging from increased body size to longer developmental time in the longer-lived flies (Kirkwood & Austad, 2000).

This kind of response to selection has been interpreted as indicating the involvement of genetic influences on longevity, which would be consistent with the mutation accumulation theory as well. Experiments in model organisms testing for accumulation of mutations that only affect late-life survival, however, have produced very mixed results (Kirkwood & Austad, 2000), and twin studies of genetic influences on longevity in humans have consistently yielded low heritabilities (Le Couteur & Simpson, 2011). Moreover, longevity has been observed to be dramatically longer in many species living in protected environments that provide ready access to shelter (warmth) and sufficient food, such as laboratory environments for model organisms and the modern environment of most industrialized countries today – for humans as well as their pets and other domesticated animals. These differences in longevity have been too dramatic for natural selection alone to account for them. They provide support for the theories that posit that ageing is essentially no more than the accumulated record of basically stochastic environmental insults.

At the same time, apparently stressful environmental conditions appear to be able to induce increases in longevity as well, often with great reduction of fertility during a period of some kind of dormancy – perhaps having evolved to enable the organism to survive an environmental crisis in shape to reproduce when conditions are better. Organisms ranging from nematodes to fruit flies to mice respond to periods in which little food is available by interrupting fertility for some period of time while extending longevity. In the nematode *C. elegans*, for example, under conditions of over-crowding and lack of food, larvae go into a specific dormant state known as 'dauer' in which they do not feed or reproduce. They can survive in this state as long as 60 (compared with a normal lifespan of 17) days – and emerge from it to moult and develop normally and with normal remaining lifespan. In rodents, it is well known that restricting access to food calories slows ageing and interrupts fertility (Finch, 2007). Rodents undergoing such caloric restriction also show greater resistance to many different kinds of stressors (Masoro, 1998). Unlike *C. elegans*, they do not show reduced metabolic rate, but their state does show several biochemical similarities to that of animals in hibernation (Walford & Spindler, 1997).

This has some parallels in humans, though how adaptive they are is questionable, as is any long-term impact on longevity. Young women who restrict caloric intake due to anorexia commonly cease to have menstrual periods, thus interrupting fertility. Whether they live longer is another question completely, one that I do not believe has been investigated. The participants in the Minnesota Starvation Experiment (Tucker, 2006) described in Chapter 7, however, do not appear to have experienced *decreased* longevity, though it is too early to say they experienced increased longevity, and their numbers were too small ever to establish this at all conclusively, no matter what happens to them. The possibility that caloric restriction increases life expectancy in humans is of high research interest at present, despite the lack of appeal to most people of living long but eating little.

The role of menopause in human evolution

The complex evolutionary link between reproduction and longevity raises the question of how human menopause evolved. As described in earlier chapters, human infants are born extremely immature and thus dependent on parents compared with infants of most species, even our nearest evolutionary relatives, and human childhood is unusually long. Yet weaning occurs well before babies are able to acquire enough food on their own to sustain themselves. At one level, this frees the mother to accommodate another pregnancy, but it also places some burden of caring for the already-existing offspring on some broader human community. The human female reproductive lifespan is long, spanning some 30 years (say from ages 15 to 45 in broad generality), but, in women who reach it, menopause tends to take place well before the most debilitating effects of ageing have begun to be experienced; that is, reproduction ceases unusually early in the full human lifespan, even among species that experience some kind of cessation of reproductive capacity without death. During most of human history, of course, reaching the age of menopause was far from usual as many women died during childbirth, but those who did reach menopause often lived for considerable periods after it. Understanding the evolutionary function of this lengthy period of non-reproductive life has been a major challenge. One possible key has been recognition that germline cells – eggs and sperm – differ from those of the rest of the body in a fundamental way (Weismann, 1889). That is, the germline must be able to propagate itself indefinitely, or the species dies out. But this does not mean that reproductive function in any one member of the species needs to be indefinite, and the organs that support reproductive function are subject to the same kinds of wear and tear as the rest of the body. Somehow, however, the germline cells themselves need to remain 'young' within any one member of the species, so that, if fertilization occurs, a healthy offspring is born.

It is not clear at present how this is assured (Kirkwood & Shanley, 2010), but one possible way is through production of more germline cells than can ever be fertilized. Males do this especially as they continually create new sperm cells, in contrast to females who are generally born with all the egg cells they will ever have. This excess production allows natural selection to weed out those that are potentially defective even before conception takes place (Forbes, 1997), though, of course, natural selection operates throughout gestation and afterwards as well, especially right after birth. Egg and sperm cells, as well as stem cells that can become egg or sperm cells, also appear to have greater capacities of damage repair and function maintenance under stress than regular somatic cells (Saretzki, et al., 2008). Despite evidence that germline cells do retain the ability to produce healthy offspring throughout the reproductive lifespan, there is also evidence that this is not complete: they 'age' too. Females lose ovarian follicles containing immature ova at increasing rates after age 35, and male sperm counts begin to decline around age 40 (Kirkwood & Austad, 2000). Rates of chromosomal anomalies such as Down's Syndrome increase particularly with maternal age, but also with paternal age. But at some level links between reproductive system function and ageing may involve ongoing sensitivity of balance between the reproduction and body maintenance to reproductive opportunity. For example, the Pacific salmon is a *semelparous* species that dies after a single reproductive experience, particularly in males. There are many such species; they tend to have evolved to live in conditions under which survival to another opportunity to reproduce is very unlikely. In Pacific salmon, castration before puberty extended lifespan significantly (Robertson, 1961). There is evidence for such effects in *iteroparous* (multiply reproducing) species including humans as well, though they appear to be less dramatic (Brown-Borg, 2007).

Two general hypotheses that are far from mutually exclusive have been suggested to explain the evolution of human menopause. First, as described in Chapter 5, human infants are born as immature and helpless as they are because it was necessary during our evolution to compromise between the size of the evolving infant head and the constraints imposed on its size by the maternal pelvis (Peccei, 1995). Even as it is, the size of the infant head presents considerable mortality risk to the mother, and this risk, in general and specific, increases with maternal age. Maternal death in childbirth places the infant at substantial risk of mortality as well, or at least it did during human evolution. At some maternal age, therefore, the risk associated with additional pregnancies outweighs the benefits, and perhaps menopause evolved at least in part because the costs of maintaining it exceeded the benefits after that point. This might have been especially relevant during human evolution when women commonly went from one pregnancy to another throughout their reproductive lives, and their younger already-existing offspring still required active care when they entered peri-menopause, presuming they reached that age. Second, likely because human infants are so helpless and dependent, our species is almost unique in the extent to which kin in addition to parents provide care and provisioning to the young. The female reproductive lifespan is long enough that a woman's oldest offspring could be expected to reach reproductive age themselves about the time her own reproductive lifespan ended with menopause. The availability of women experienced in childcare and provisioning but not actively involved in their own reproduction would have been very advantageous in enabling even a woman's grandchildren, as well as her own younger offspring, to get the care they needed to reach maturity (Hill & Hurtado, 1991).

This all sounds very reasonable, but it remains only speculation unless it can be demonstrated that overall fitness is enhanced by the presence of female menopause. This must be done using either modern populations in very different material circumstances and health from those of the conditions in which menopause evolved, or through mathematical models. Like all mathematical modelling, taking the modelling approach means making assumptions about human evolutionary conditions, assumptions which may or may not be accurate and which there is no good way to test. Still, several models testing the two theories have been developed (e.g., Hill & Hurtado, 1991; Rogers, 1993; Shanley & Kirkwood, 2001). Results have suggested that menopause only becomes adaptive if the costs of maintaining reproductive capacity for the woman become greater than benefits and she also provides survival benefits to her grandchildren. Thus these evolutionary theories about the origins of human menopause remain mostly attractive speculation.

Managing senescence

However it evolved, humans are stuck with the fact that they age, at least within any foreseeable technological future. It happens to everyone, and industrialized cultures tend to be oriented towards youth, for its energy, vigour, rapid-fire reaction times, quick thinking, smooth skin, and even tendency towards negative emotional response, never mind technological savvy. From this perspective, ageing is mostly about decline in these capacities and characteristics, and accepting this can be psychologically difficult in achievement-oriented societies. The ageing of the 'baby-boom' population born after World War II has brought increasing attention to questions of how to 'age gracefully' (and economically, through maintenance of good health and cognitive function, particularly ability to live independently) and why some people seem to be so much more successful at it than others. Though clearly physical health is very important in this, so apparently are attitudes towards ageing, and especially ways of coping psychologically with decline. It is interesting that two of the most successful techniques for coping psychologically with ageing appear to be either to deny it, or to be escaping it relative to one's peers.

For example, Levy, Slade, Kunkel, and Kasl, 2002) found that positive self-perceptions of how people were ageing assessed as long as 23 years earlier (but after age 50) were associated with 7.5 years of additional life, even after adjustment for age, sex, socioeconomic status, and perceptions of loneliness and functional health. This effect was stronger than those of absence of high blood pressure and/or cholesterol, participation in exercise, maintenance of healthy weight, and non-smoking status. The questions Levy et al. used to assess self-perception of ageing, however, telling. They consisted of items like, 'Things keep getting worse as I get older' (reversed) and 'I have as much pep as I did last year.' If those statements are true (the reverse of the first one, of course) of an older person, it is hardly surprising if she/he lives longer than many peers. If the person believes those statements but they are not true, then living longer than peers may be more surprising, but the group of people endorsing them may consist of some mix of such people, and the result is an average for the whole group of such people. Either way, little insight into constructive coping is offered to the much more common person who is all too aware of decline.

A possibly more constructive perspective is offered by the example of *masters athletes*. Masters athletes are older people who train regularly and compete in sports against their age peers. Most of the formal master's competitions are in individual endurance sports such as running, swimming, and triathlon. They are typically organized in five-year age groups running up to age 100 and above, and running and swimming in particular have kept extensive records of performance that date back to the 1930s. As would be expected, these records show declines in performance with age, but the ages at which declines begin and the steepness of decline varies by activity and distance within activity. There are, however, some surprising observations to be made within these data, and within the experiences of long-term masters athletes. For example, masters records have generally fallen more quickly over time than have open records in the same events, especially for the older age groups, and some long-term masters athletes have posted better times in their 50s than they did as open competitors on the order of 30 years before. There are several reasons for this, including, of course, use of the same continually improving training methods that have enabled steady drops in record times for open competition. Other reasons for the steady and even increasing improvement in masters athletic record performance over time include increasing participation in masters athletic programmes, and increased training among participants.

Sports statisticians have used these record data to compile extensive tables of age-equivalent performances, especially in running. Thus, for example, it is possible for, say, a 65-year-old runner to learn that, on an age-adjusted basis, the world record for 10K is 93 per cent of the time he just ran, so that his time is just about 7 per cent over the world-record time, adjusted for his age. He can also compare his time with time distributions for men in his 65–69 age group, as well as with the time distributions for the 60–64 and 70–74 age groups. He can even compare his time directly with that of others in different age groups by applying a formula that removes age effects from all times, placing them all on a single directly comparable scale. These formulas are not without problems: sometimes they produce results that appear pretty clearly unreasonable, as when an older athlete's time converts to an adjusted time well below the current world record, but in general they work reasonably well. Their availability offers masters athletes a natural way to cast favourable light on their inevitable declines in performance with age. They can use the statistics and formulas and age-graded competitions to see if they are declining less rapidly than their age peers, whether they are improving on an age-graded basis, or gaining on the world record after adjustment for age. The five-year age group competitions too take the sting out of declining performance with age by offering a whole new set of more easily attainable time standards every five years. Many masters athletes thrive on these statistics and look forward with enthusiasm to moving into new age groups so that they can compete again with the advantage of relative youth, maybe even set some records there.

Of course, these athletes are a highly self-selected group, so it is far from clear that what motivates them would motivate people in general. Nevertheless, it is likely that the cognitive decline that takes place in old age has similar features, in that people tend to withdraw from engagement in cognitively taxing activities as they become more difficult with age. Moreover, anyone could make use of statistics of this kind to note relative improvements in skill or capacity even in the face of absolute decline if they are available. There is no requirement for 'expert' performance. It would be interesting to see whether analogous age-graded performance data could be developed reliably for cognitive function and whether people might be motivated to use it similarly to cope psychologically with decline and maintain enthusiasm for engagement in cognitive activity. I suspect the benefits to quality of life of ongoing engagement and enthusiasm apply regardless of whether the ongoing engagement actually retards decline.

Box 11.3   Do masters athletes 'age successfully?'

The steady improvement over time in masters sports records has led participants, their coaches, and many sports scientists and exercise physiologists to hold masters athletes up as prototypical examples of 'successful' ageing (Louis, Nosaka, & Brisswalter, 2012). There is no question that masters athletes, like all seriously training athletes, vastly out-perform the population average performance in their sports for people of their ages, and generally often out-perform such population averages of people as much as 50 years younger. In general, masters athletes express great enthusiasm for the benefits and anti-ageing effects of physical fitness, health, general well-being, and even cognitive function and preservation of youthful appearance and outlook. There is considerable empirical evidence for this as well, at least in the form of better-than-average-for-age physiological statistics in many areas from blood pressure that is measured routinely in everyone to VO2 max, or the body's maximal capacity to transport and use oxygen as intensity of exercise increases, which is typically measured only in serious athletes. This is suggestive that the exercise and training may actually retard the rate of ageing, but it is far from conclusive. Those who choose to be long-term masters athletes in the first place may differ genetically from those who do not in ways that may involve how they age, and, even more likely, the mean differences between masters athletes and the average population at the same age may simply reflect a long-term-stable difference in athletic ability that has distinguished masters athletes from the rest of the population all along. That is, it may be that physical performance capacity of masters athletes is declining at the same rate as that of the rest of the population, but they just continue to have higher capacity as they always have. Masters athletes are receiving increasing research attention, but most studies have focused not on the question of rates of decline in physical capacity compared with the rest of the population, but on quantifying decline in sports performance in athletes and why it might occur.

Identifying why the decline takes place is difficult enough. Some of the reasons for this difficulty involve measurement questions that also complicate comparison of rates of decline in capacity between masters athletes and the rest of the population. Masters athletes notice that they need increasing amounts of time to recover from hard training efforts with age, and that they are increasingly prone not just to exhaustion but also to injury when they over-train. To preserve ability to participate, they very sensibly tend to allow themselves longer recovery periods following hard training efforts and reduce overall training volumes to avoid overtraining. The decreased training resilience they experience which inspires the reduction in training volume results from ageing, but the lower level of training volume in response to it would result in lower performance ability and fitness at *any* age. Quantifying the extents to which overall performance declines with age result from ageing itself and from age-inspired reductions in training volume would require comparing performance declines associated with identical reductions in training volumes in older and younger athletes matched somehow for performance ability, but it is not clear how that matching should be accomplished, and I do not believe that such studies have even been attempted.

Use it or lose it

Whatever the role of decreased training in age-related decline in athletic performance (see Box 11.3), there is no question that decline is sharper when one moves from regular training to no training at all all at any age. This has led to the idea that people retain capacities because they use them, and do not retain them if they do not use them, summarized in the expression 'use it or lose it'. There is no question that there is truth in this idea: almost any skill or ability will deteriorate over time without use, and we all have examples of what happens when we are 'out of practice' at something. The idea is also being discussed widely in both the popular and scientific presses as an antidote to ageing in all its physical and psychological forms. Here the evidence for its truth is much more mixed, especially in the area of cognitive function. All the measurement problems described in the textbox for physical capacities apply to cognitive function as well, but cognitive function involves many additional measurement difficulties that I have not discussed. These measurement difficulties have analogues in physical capacities as well. For example, any assessment of cognitive function relies on performance on some cognitive task or tasks, and performance on any task varies not just with some inherent ability, but also on prior experience with and knowledge of that kind of task. And development of prior experience with and knowledge of tasks depends on opportunity for exposure and motivation to practice. More than this, however, it is clear that it is easier to build many skills when exposure takes place earlier in life rather than later. The world has changed dramatically in the last 100 years or so from technological and information-processing perspectives. This means that older people today experienced a very different kind of education than younger people today experience. We do not know the implications of this for performance on many of the tasks typically used to assess cognitive function, so we do not have good ways to establish how much of the decline in performance on some cognitive tasks is actually a result of biological ageing and how much is limited and later exposure and practice. An analogy in physical capacity is how improvements over time in medical care in infancy and childhood may impact longevity in old age. From the opposite perspective, we do not know to what degree the current childhood obesity epidemic may reduce longevity. If it does, it will be the first time in recorded history that a modern health development has done so.

'Use it or lose it' is an extremely optimistic idea. If it does counteract declines in capacity with age, it is something applicable to everyone. Even if it is only a placebo, it could improve the quality of life for many older people by keeping them engaged in and motivated towards constructive activities.

Further reading

Bielak, A. A., Hultsch, D. F., Strauss, E., MacDonald, S. W., & Hunter, M. A. (2010). Intraindividual variability in reaction time predicts cognitive outcomes 5 years later. *Neuropsychology, 24,* 731–741.

Carstensen, L. I. (1993). Motivation for social contact across the life span: A theory of socioemotional selectivity. In J. E. Jacobs, *Nebraska Symposium on Education, 1992: Developmental Perspectives on Motivation* (pp. 209–254). Lincoln: University of Nebraska Press.

Hertzog, C., & Hultsch, D. F. (2000). Metacognition in adulthood and old age. In F. I. Craik, & T. A. Salthouse, *The Handbook of Aging and Cognition, 2nd Edition* (pp. 417–466). Mahwah, NJ: Lawrence Erlbaum Associates, Inc.

Hill, K., & Hurtado, A. M. (1991). The evolution of premature reproductive senescence and menopause in human females: An evolution of the 'grandmother' hypothesis. *Human Genetics, 2,* 313–350.

Kirkwood, T. B., & Shanley, D. P. (2010). The connections between general and reproductive senescence and the evolutionary basis of menopause. *Annals of the New York Academy of Sciences, 1204,* 21–29.

Kirschner, M., & Gerhardt, J. (1998). Evolvability. *Proceedings of the National Academy of Sciences of the United States of America, 95,* 8420–8427.

Kitano, H. (2010). Violations of robustness trade-offs. *Molecular Systems Biology, 6,* 1–8.

Levy, B. R., Slade, M. D., Kunkel, S. R., & Kasl, S. V. (2002). Longevity increased by positive self-perceptions of aging. *Journal of Personality and Social Psychology, 83,* 261–270.

Louis, J., Nosaka, K., & Brisswalter, J. (2012). The endurance master athlete: A model of successful ageing. *Science & Sports, 27,* 63–76.

McDaniel, M. A., Einstein, G. O., & Jacoby, L. L. (2008). New considerations in aging and memory: The glass may be half full. In F. I. Craik, & T. A. Salthouse, *The Handbook of Aging and Cognition, 3rd Edition* (pp. 251–310). New York: Psychology Press.

Masoro, E. J. (1998). Influence of caloric intake on aging and on the response to stressors. *Journal of Toxicology and Environmental Health – Series B, Critical Review, 1,* 243–257.

Conclusion: Historical Context

12

There is a clear source of influences on both development and individual differences among people at any point in time that I have not discussed. In many ways it is fitting that I have saved it for the concluding chapter because it generally remains unaddressed in research studies. That source is historical context. 'Historical context' is a very broad term. It refers, of course, to the setting in which some event occurs, but 'setting' includes the physical conditions in which people live such as climate, altitude, and agricultural potential; the technological resources available for maintaining secure access to necessities of life such as food, shelter, and medical care, as well as to luxuries including variety of entertainment; access to education and opportunities to improve their circumstances; political climate including freedom from persecution and terrorism as well as freedom of speech, activity, and religion; prevailing cultural attitudes; and economic conditions such as relative stability of prices and employment prospects. Because it is so broad, it is difficult to define how to measure historical context at any one point in time, and this difficulty is compounded because it probably only has meaning if understood in relation to the context of some other point in time. Moreover, because people have always been completely immersed in living their historical contexts, and historical context has tended to change only over rather long spans of years, it has been easy to overlook its implications for psychological development. This may be changing, however, as the pace of 'particularly' technological change has accelerated considerably in the last 100 years, and this may have repercussions for other forms of change in historical context as well.

One example of the influence of historical context is so pervasive that it has become a humourous cliché in recent years: the differences in facility with electronic gadgetry between older adults and very young children, with everyone else ranged all too neatly by age in between. It seems obvious that these differences result because young children are growing up learning to use electronic gadgetry while older adults have been presented with these tools only quite late in life, but this alone raises questions about interpretation of the origins of other skills that young children pick up very quickly compared with older people, such as languages. Theories of canalization and innate language modules have often been invoked to explain children's rapid and apparently automatic language acquisition. These theories have some surface plausibility for a long-established, superficially unique human characteristic such as language but it is very hard to believe that we humans have some kind of innate electronic gadgetry-operating module in our brains, or that our brains have been canalized by evolution to pick up their usage.

Whatever the explanation for age differences in this skill, it makes a good example of the role of historical context in the development of individual differences. At present, the implications of the new reliance on these devices for all forms of social interaction and access to information are generating considerable attention, discussion, and debate, with some pointing to dramatically negative consequences and others extolling the increased potential for human development opening before us. Much of this discussion is based on anecdotal evidence, and such evidence flows in all directions. Unfortunately clear empirical studies have been rare, so we know less about the implications of our 'brave new world' than many would like to think.

There are, however, some areas in which we do have considerable empirical data, and they can be allocated, at least on a first-cut basis, to one of two major conceptual categories: *long-term trends* and *cycles*. Both of these may be discussed most in economics, so some of the most familiar examples come from there, but of course they can take place in any area, and they do. Long-term trends are relatively uniform, often linear, patterns of change that persist over extended periods of time. Examples from economics include the steadily growing trade deficit of the United States and overall growth in gross domestic product in most countries. Eventually most long-term trends level off and even reverse, but they may persist long enough that people begin to rely upon them as permanent, even when they seem to have negative consequences. In contrast to long-term trends, historical cycles take place when particular contexts and situations recur with relatively steady reliability. The most common example from economics is the recurrence of periods of relative economic boom and bust. While there is no question that such cycles take place, they also clearly co-exist with long-term trends.

There are three long-term demographic trends for which substantial and clear-cut empirical evidence has amassed, and these trends all have implications for understanding the development of individual psychological differences so I will discuss each of them in turn.

The Flynn effect

The first has become known as the *Flynn effect*, after James Flynn, who has done the most to document and discuss it (Flynn, 2009). Flynn first compared test scores in situations where the same people had been given IQ tests that were current at the time of administration and IQ tests that had been normed at some previous time. In 17 out of the 18 comparison situations he could locate, the mean scores on the older test norms were higher than those on the current tests, and the one exception involved tests intended for populations of different ages (Flynn, 1984). Flynn went on to examine scores in standardization samples in 14 nations, and found substantial increases in scores over time in all of them (Flynn, 1987). Subsequent studies have shown unequivocally that the rates of gains in nonverbal tests have been greater than those of verbal tests, but even verbal tests have consistently shown gains. The gains have been substantial enough that one of the most commonly used nonverbal intelligence tests, Raven Progressive Matrices (Raven, 1941), is now relegated primarily to use with children and people who have not had much access to education because too many people from industrialized countries now routinely achieve the maximum score. A much more difficult version of the test, the Advanced Progressive Matrices, has been developed for use in these populations. The Flynn effect is generally considered to be a cohort effect, applying to successive generations as they are born. This is likely because IQ is generally considered to be a stable, early-determined characteristic of an individual. But this latter too is an assumption rather than something that has been demonstrated empirically (though, as discussed in Chapter 6, we do not know how to increase IQ in any systematic way). It is actually quite likely that the Flynn effect has been experienced within individuals as well as between cohorts, though it is also likely that the influences of whatever is driving the effect on individuals decrease with age.

Many of the studies documenting the Flynn effect have been conducted in Scandinavian countries that have compulsory military registration for young men. The registration processes include medical exams and intelligence tests. This has made possible the generation of data on score changes from extremely large and highly population-representative samples (at least of males), tested very consistently over extended periods of time. These data have indicated that the effect on average runs on the order of about 5 points, or a third of a standard deviation, per decade. They have also indicated that the rate of increase tends to be slightly greater at the lower-score ranges than at the higher-score ranges, and that, at least in Scandinavia, the overall effect may have begun to level off in the late 1990s (Teasdale & Owen, 2000). This would be consistent with the overall pattern for long-term trends to come to an end at some point. In contrast, however, this particular trend appears to be accelerating in Africa in recent years.

The robust presence of the Flynn effect has generated considerable discussion in legal circles as well as among individual differences researchers. The legal discussion surrounds the use of IQ testing as a criterion for competence to stand trial. It is not uncommon for defence attorneys to argue and courts to accept that defendants who test below, say, an IQ of 70 are not cognitively competent to be considered criminally responsible for their actions. If defendants are tested with tests that have not recently been normed, the defendants may show inappropriately high scores, and be judged cognitively competent when they should not be (Flynn, 2009). The discussion among individual differences researchers is more directly relevant here: it surrounds the reasons for the steady increase in performance on IQ tests. Many suggestions have been offered, including improved nutrition; improved medical care; greater access to, improvements in effectiveness of, and extensions in period of, education (perhaps especially for the greater rates of increase in the lower IQ score ranges); greater exposure to the kinds of questions asked in IQ tests; greater willingness to try cognitively difficult problems; natural selection for high cognitive ability; smaller families, allowing for greater dedication of parental resources to children's development; epigenetic effects of environmental changes on early brain development; gene–environment correlations in conjunction with a general effect of increasing IQ in society at large that impacts the IQs of individuals; and increased *heterosis*. The latter refers to relatively random mating patterns with respect to gene alleles that contribute to better IQ test performance that tend to be dominant over recessive counterparts (Mingroni, 2007).

Of course, these possible explanations are far from mutually exclusive; all of them could even be operative (and likely are), but there has been a tendency to consider each of them in isolation. The strictly environmental explanations have generally been deemed insufficient alone or in aggregate because they cannot explain what Flynn has called the 'IQ paradox' (Dickens & Flynn, 2001). This is the assumption that the rising scores cannot be attributed to population changes in the frequencies of genes involved in IQ test performance because the changes have simply taken place too fast. Given this, it has been thought that environmental changes must predominate, but that they cannot because the heritability of IQ has remained high and steady throughout the period of score increases. As I hope to have made clear in Chapter 3, high heritability does not imply that the *level* of a trait is fixed by the genes, either in the population at large or in individuals. Heritability refers only to genetic variance as a source of population *variance* in observed characteristics. So the 'IQ paradox' is not really a paradox at all, though recognizing this does not help to specify exactly how the genes and environment have transacted in creating the increase in IQ scores.

Most studies that have investigated whether the increases in scores can be attributed to increases in a single general cognitive ability factor have concluded that they cannot; instead the increases must be attributed to measurement properties of individual kinds of test questions that apply differently to people of different ages (e.g., Wicherts, Dolan, Hessen, Osterveld, van Baal, Boomsma, et al., 2004). I suspect this may help to explain the observations that the Flynn effect may be levelling off in industrialized countries with high levels of formal education such as Scandinavia, but accelerating in economically developing regions such as Africa. That is, I suspect that the technological revolution has changed the ways in which people use their brains, and thus the cognitive skills they develop. The skills IQ tests measure were well-coordinated with the technological changes that took place during most of the 20th century, but that has become less true in recent years: perhaps the technological changes and the accompanying brain changes have left the classic intelligence tests behind, at least in industrialized countries. But economically developing regions such as Africa still need to make that transition, and they are, even more rapidly than did the long-industrialized countries.

Analogous trend of increasing height

Sharing many characteristics with the Flynn effect on IQ scores has been the pervasive increase in average height throughout the industrialized world (Johnson, 2010b). First, like most psychological characteristics and in particular intelligence, but unlike some other physical characteristics such as skin colour, height is a developmental trait. That is, both normally increase monotonically throughout childhood, and remain quite stable through adulthood until old age. In saying this, I am distinguishing intelligence from the IQ scores used to measure it, which are generally at least relatively stable even in childhood. Most IQ tests are normed to reflect the average changes in cognitive skills that take place during childhood and even throughout adulthood, so the scores may be very stable even during periods of rapid cognitive development such as very young childhood. But I refer instead to the increases in raw cognitive performance that nicely parallel growth in height. This normal growth means that there are ongoing opportunities for environmental circumstances either to accentuate or interrupt expression of the genes involved. Some of these genes may even be the same ones: the correlation between height and IQ runs about 0.2, and appears to be primarily genetically mediated (Silventoinen, Posthuma, van Beisterveldt, Bartels, & Boomsma, 2006). We know of many gene mutations that are involved in abnormal presentation of either height or intelligence, but, despite the high heritabilities of both, we know of no single genes that have any substantial effect on either: both traits are clearly extremely polygenic. Both also show substantial national mean differences that vary with national income and disparity in national income (Lynn, 2008; Steckel, 2008). These national mean differences could result from national differences in frequencies of relevant genes, or from differences in relevant environmental circumstances, or, of course, from both.

Systematic measurement of intelligence only dates back a little over 100 years at present, while data about height can be obtained going back much further than this, even to prehistoric times in the form of fossilized skeletons. Through the relatively short period of observation of changes in intelligence scores, trends have been monotonically upwards, and this has been true for height during this period as well. Over a longer timespan, however, it is clear that the trend in height has not always been monotonically upward. For example, the increased urbanization, crowding, poorer nutrition and exposure to light and greater exposure to infectious disease associated with the industrial revolution in northern Europe appears to have stunted growth rates, so that 18th-century residents averaged about three inches shorter than their 11th-century ancestors (Johnson, 2010b). As for IQ at present, at least in Scandinavia, height increases in the United States levelled off during most of the 20th century, but they accelerated in the Netherlands, to the point that Americans 100 years ago averaged about three inches taller than the Dutch, but now the Dutch average about three inches taller than Americans (Komlos & Lauderdale, 2007). And South Koreans average about six inches taller than their cousins in North Korea (Schwekendiek, 2009). All of these deviations from some uniform pattern suggest that it is not so much genetic as environmental change that is driving the trends.

Trends in longevity

The third long-term demographic trend for which there is clear evidence is increased human longevity (Vaupel, 2010). I mentioned this trend in Chapter 11, but it is worth discussing in greater detail. The oldest systematic data on this come from Sweden and date back to the 1750s, though, as with height, the trend probably extends back somewhat further but with less regularity. The most straightforward statistic to estimate longevity is *life expectancy*, or the average number of years lived by people within a population. Even a little consideration of this definition, however, will make it apparent that it is too simple. For most of human history life expectancy measured from birth ran about 30 years (Conrad, 2006), but adults in their 50s and even 80s were not at all uncommon. The major reason for this apparent paradox, of course, was that infant and early childhood mortalities were extremely high: as many as two-thirds of all born in medieval England died before age 4 (Buer, 1926), but high rates of mortality for women in childbirth also contributed. In recognition of this, a whole industry of more sophisticated statistics for estimating life expectancy after childhood rapidly grew up as soon as systematic population records began to be kept, fuelled by their use in estimating life insurance premiums. One of the first and most obvious extensions of the basic life expectancy from birth was estimation of remaining life expectancy at each age. Using this measure, even in prehistoric times, life expectancy was in the mid-50s for anyone who made it to adolescence (Caspari & Lee, 2004). This fits much better with intuitive impression of ages in historical populations left by historical records.

It was not until 1994 that Vaupel and Lundstrom introduced the age at which remaining life expectancy declined to five years as a way of tracking changes in the rate of senescence. This measure also rather elegantly but arbitrarily defines a point at which old age can considered to have set in. Swedish records dating back to the 1750s indicated that, in 1861, this age was about 80. It rose perhaps a year or two between 1861 and 1950, but since 1950, its rise has been much sharper, and in 2000 had reached about 88 in Sweden (Vaupel &

Lundstrom, 1994). Japan and the United States have shown very similar trends since 1950 (Vaupel, 2010). This has been interpreted as overturning the idea that there is some fixed maximal human lifespan, and as indicating that the process of senescence has been delayed rather than slowed because the rate of mortality at any given age, which tends to rise with age, increased throughout most of the 20th century and did no better than level off in the second half of the century (Vaupel, 2010).

This suggests that senescence and its associated deterioration is being postponed rather than slowed, presumably by better medical care and nutrition. If that is the case, there is no reason to presume an upper limit on human lifespan. It would be very fortunate for ageing societies if this is the case, as it would indicate that they should be able to count on extending working life, delaying payment of pensions and decreasing medical care costs for people of any given age, while periods of disability remain constant but incept at older and older ages. Data on the reality of this, however, have been mixed (Christensen, Doblhammer, Rau, & Vaupel, 2009). Moreover, it has become clear that the world as a whole is facing an epidemic of obesity, and its implications for life expectancy and later-life health of the currently younger generations, though not completely clear yet, are definitely not positive.

Box 12.1 Evolutionary factors underlying the long-term trends

Intuitively, the long-term trends in these three traits all seem likely to be due at least partly to environments more conducive to maintenance of good physical health, perhaps particularly during gestation, infancy, and young childhood. Offsetting this is the fact that the very improvements in environment that have contributed to better population physical health have also relaxed natural selection for genes that contribute to robust health. This, all else being equal, should suggest that, in addition to all these positive population trends, there should be some negative population trends. And there are: the incidence of myopia (nearsightedness) has increased in many rather diverse parts of the world, including Singapore and Finland (Storfer, 1999). Asthma, other allergic respiratory conditions (e.g., Upton, et al., 2000) and dietary allergies have increased in frequency as well, as have many forms of psychopathology, including autism (e.g., Services. 1999), attention-deficit-hyperactivity syndrome, paranoia, hypomania, depression, and narcissism (Twenge, Freeman, & Campbell, 2012). There is no question that some of these reports of increased psychopathology can be attributed to both greater public awareness of the existence of these conditions and better diagnostic criteria, but some of the studies that have noted increases have adjusted for such trends (e.g., Twenge, Gentile, DeWall, Lacefield, & Schurtz, 2010). This suggests that, however improved our modern environment may be with respect to physical health, it may not be so good for our mental health. Alternatively, perhaps when the physical environment improves, vulnerabilities that might have been manifested physically are instead manifested psychologically.

Another, not mutually exclusive, possibility that has been given some attention is increased *heterosis* (Mingroni, 2007). Heterosis, or *hybrid vigour*, mentioned above as a possible reason for the Flynn effect, is relative genetic diversity due to greater mixing of pre-existing genetic subgroups that have tended to mate among themselves. It exists whenever a population has had a non-random mating pattern that is relaxed towards more random mating, thus increasing the proportions of genetic heterozygotes in the population. There is one more condition, however, that must be met in order for heterosis to account for increasing trends such as those that have been observed. This condition is that the traits experiencing the increases must display *directional dominance*. That is, the genes that influence the trait in the direction experiencing the increases must be relatively genetically dominant and those that influence the trait in the opposite direction must be relatively recessive. There is little question that our world has become much more mobile over the past century and that this has contributed to greater frequency of mating between people who would never even have met each other in the past. Moreover, though it is unquestionably still present, there has been considerable relaxation of social restrictions on transracial, -ethnic, and -religious unions, all of which contribute to genetic diversity and thus could contribute to heterosis. Demonstrating that the last condition of directional dominance has held is, however, much more difficult, and the jury remains out on it.

And some contrasting historical cycles

Some psychological characteristics, however, may change over time in more cyclic form. There is no question that events such as the Great Depression of the 1930s in North America and Europe had profound effects on those who lived through it, as did the privations and combat experiences of World Wars I and II that bracketed it. And the Vietam War of the 1960s in the United States launched a cultural revolution that many believe coloured the generation that came of age during that time. Two American historians have put together a sweeping theory of the cyclical nature of history and how it shapes the lives and psychology of those who live through its events (Strauss & Howe, 1991; Howe & Strauss, 1993; 1997; 2000). They have published their ideas in a series of books rather than in peer-reviewed academic journals, and their books have caught the public imagination, fuelling their careers as public lecturers and consultants. This kind of success can challenge ability to be scientifically objective even in the most rigorous of researchers, but it can also attract sometimes unwarranted criticism from academicians who have been less successful in publicizing their ideas. Strauss' and Howe's books have received mixed reception from academicians, with some calling their sampling methods biased and others praising the scope of their theoretical vision in book review form. Others have conducted their own thorough data analyses, which have not always supported Strauss' and Howe's theses (e.g., Twenge, Freeman, & Campbell, 2012). Still, I think their ideas have enough general merit and empirical support that they bear some detailed consideration here as potential sources of the development of individual psychological differences among cohorts of people born at different times.

The basis of Strauss' and Howe's theory is that American history has consisted of a succession of cycles about as long as a 'full' human lifespan: 80–90 years (Strauss & Howe, 1991). They have focused on American history, which, at least in Euro-American terms, has a beginning in about the early 1500s, well after recorded history was established. This has made things considerably easier for them than a similar project might be in Europe, with its much longer history of still recognizable nations but constantly shifting boundaries. Still, they have extended their ideas to the histories of several other industrialized countries, so they do not apply solely and uniquely to the United States (Howe & Strauss, 1997). Within each of the 80–90-year cycles, they identified four periods of around 20 years, each of which ends with a historical event that tends to serve as a turning point introducing the next phase of the lifespan-length cycle. The four cycles surround two major social events evenly spaced in time. One demands unified social and institutional response, while the other is an outgrowth of something that might almost be thought of as boredom with the lack of crisis: things have become *too* pat.

Because they described cycles, there was, of course, no obvious beginning point for each one. They arbitrarily set the beginning point at what they called the 'High'. This is a period immediately following resolution of some major social crisis, with resolution of the crisis serving as the turning point that initiates it. The crises they identified were the defeat by the English of the Spanish Armada in 1566, the First Indian War in New England that resulted in the death of native American chief Metacom in 1676, the Revolutionary War of the late 1700s, the Civil War that ended in 1865, the Great Depression and World War II, and the current global financial crisis and War on Terror. During periods following resolution of crises, the population as a whole tends to be outward-focused, emphasizing conformity to cultural norms and social stability. There tends to be a collective sense of triumph and satisfaction with ideals.

According to the theory, this is a relatively pleasant period, but it cannot and does not last. People tire of the period's emphasis on social cohesion, institutions, and discipline, and desire to recapture a feeling of spirituality and personal authenticity experienced as lost. This initiates social movements Strauss and Howe characterized as 'awakenings'. They are not alone in identifying such historical movements: several American historians including McLoughlin (1978) and Bellah (1992) have described the same historical periods in very similar terms. The periods Strauss and Howe identified took place in 1512–1540, 1618–1673, 1724–1741, 1822–1842, 1883–1900, and 1961–1981. The first was the Protestant Reformation, followed by the Puritan Movement that began in Europe and Britain and led to much of the colonization of what became the United States, in pursuit of freedom to practise religion in ways contrary to the then-established churches. General scepticism with existing institutions and motivation to go in new directions are two of the primary characteristics of these awakening periods. The third has been termed the 'First Great Awakening' by many American historians. It swept Protestant Europe and the British American colonies, so it was not unique to American history either. It was overtly Christian in focus, and characterized by powerful preaching that was received by congregations as inspiring new awareness of the need for personal salvation by Christ. Prior to this Awakening, Christian practice was largely public, heavily ritualized, and rather emotionally detached and intellectual. With the Awakening came passion and emotional involvement, emphasis on divine outpourings of the Holy Spirit, greater introspection and independent Bible study, commitment to stricter standards of morality, zest for converting others to the faith, and formation of new religious groupings. The next Awakening period was similar in many ways, but with an emphasis on reforms to remediate the many evils of society before the Second Coming of Christ. It was characterized by passionate religious revivals, many of them in frontier areas, soaring church memberships, and the establishment of several new religions including Seventh Day Adventism but also many churches intended to be nondenominational such as the Churches of Christ. The following period was again similar: very oriented towards readying society for the Second Coming of Christ through reform, and inspiring fervent conversions and new religious groupings, including Christian Science.

The most recent awakening was somewhat different, however. It did not focus on religion, though it shared many of the characteristics of the others. Instead it focused on the development in the individual of some form of higher consciousness in general, or the awareness of some kind of ultimate reality beyond immediate experience in general, with no direct connection to Christianity or any other specific religion. Still, people were engaged in ways very similar to the prior Awakenings in pursuit of spiritual knowledge, practical management of self, cultivation of virtues such as 'peace, love, and understanding' (the slogan for the era if anything was), and mass rock concerts that resembled older religious revivals in many ways. And, of course, scepticism of government activities and established materialistic values was rife.

The Awakenings are periods of social unrest and moral and spiritual zeal. Eventually these peter out, leaving society somewhat disorganized, mistrustful of its institutions, weary of striving for something better, but hoping to be able to sit back and relax. Strauss and Howe called the turning point that marks the beginnings of these periods the 'Unraveling'. It is not punctuated so much by a single event, but rather by a mood of retrenchment. The period of intolerance and martyrdom that followed the Protestant Reformation was the first such period they identified, followed by the reaction and restoration after the Puritan Movement in Britain and the American colonies, and then by the French and Indian War before the American Revolution. Strauss and Howe maintained that one Unraveling period, that would have taken place after the American Civil War, was skipped, and they devoted some effort to explaining why. So the last two Unraveling periods were World War I/American Prohibition, and the Culture Wars of the last 20 years of the 20th century. The final turning point is the emergence of the new Crisis whose resolution will kick off the next High period. The crisis destroys what remains of institutional life, but rebuilds it in response to a threat to national survival. Respect for civic authority revives, and people begin to think more collectively, with cultural values directed towards community rather than individual good as they mobilize to meet the looming crisis.

How might these historical cycles relate to development of individual psychological differences?

This articulates the basic cycles of history according to Strauss and Howe, but how does this apply to understanding development of individual psychological differences? Strauss and Howe's answer to this is a key aspect of their theory. They propose that the particular periods of history in which people spend their childhoods and especially their young adulthoods permanently shape their outlooks on the world, and ultimately many of their psychological characteristics, goals, and activities. The result is that some of these factors are shared more strongly by people of similar ages across wide social spectra than they are with people of different ages within those same social spectra. This has been increasingly reinforced in the United States in particular and the industrialized countries more generally by increasing age stratification of activities: children are in school, young adults are in universities or other settings geared towards them, older adults have removed themselves to gated retirement communities. To articulate how phase of life and historical period at time of birth transact, Strauss and Howe divided the lifespan into four groups running parallel in length to the lengths of the historical periods, or about twenty years. They called the first, running from ages 0–20, Youth; the second, running from ages 20–43, Rising Adulthood; the third, running from ages 44–65, Midlife; and the final one Elder.

As evidence for their theory, Strauss and Howe noted that at many points in American history commentators have pointed out that generational cohort groups seemed to share characteristics among themselves, and to differ from previous and subsequent generational cohorts. For example, in 1920, at the end of the Unraveling that built towards the crises of the Great Depression and World War II, Youth were considered overly protected, Rising Adults were called alienated, the Midlife generation was thought of as moralistic, and the Elders as sensitive. In contrast, in 1942, during World War II, Youth were thought of as suffocated (choked off from the world to keep the war from them), Rising Adults were termed heroic (as they marched off to their wartime duties), the Midlife generation was considered pragmatic (in making the necessary sacrifices at home), and the Elders (who led the United States and its allies to victory) were termed inspiring. Moving to 1964, Youth were considered indulged, Rising Adults were termed conformist, the Midlife generation was thought of as powerful, and the Elders as reclusive. By 1986, the Youth were criticized, Rising Adults were considered narcissistic, the Midlife generation was termed indecisive, and Elders were thought of as busy.

This implies not just that different birth cohorts have been perceived differently at the same time in history, but that different birth cohorts have been perceived differently at the same points in their respective lives. For example, those who grew up 'protected' as Youth apparently outgrew any limitations this might have created because they were 'heroic' as Rising Adults fighting in World War II, 'powerful' in Midlife, and still very busy running the country as Elders. This was apparently necessary because the generation to come after them, who had been Youths during the war, grew up to be 'conformist' as Rising Adults, and 'indecisive' in Midlife. Who wants to follow the lead of someone who is indecisive? And the social unrest of the 1960s and 1970s was in many ways a clash between the Baby Boomers who were 'indulged' Youth in the economic boom that followed World War II and grew up to be 'narcissistic' as Rising Adults, and those still very busy Elders who had been 'heroic' back when they were Rising Adults. In other words, the historical period in which one is born helps to set in motion a psychological developmental trajectory, according to the theory.

Also according to the theory, there are patterns to these trajectories that vary with the time in life at which the dramatic social moments of Crisis and Awakening hit people. These two alternating kinds of social moments create relatively 'dominant' and 'recessive' generations, with dominant generations entering Rising Adulthood and Elderhood and recessive generations being born (entering Youth) and entering Midlife at the turning points associated with these social moments. A dominant generation focused on introspection and spiritual development, that Strauss and Howe termed 'Idealist', grows up relatively indulged in the triumphant period following resolution of a crisis (the Baby Boomer generation born after World War II); they inspire a spiritual Awakening (the Viet Nam War protests and hippie, civil rights, and women's liberation movements that followed) as they come of age; fragment into narcissism, then wax moralistic in Midlife; and as Elders provide the visionary leadership necessary to resolve the next crisis (the War on Terror and current global financial crisis?) Because they are so busy with their Awakening, these Idealists raise a rather under-protected, criticized generation of Reactive Youth who grow up taking risks and rather alienated, but mellow out to make pragmatic middle managers during the next crisis in their Midlife, and retire to a rather reclusive but not disrespected Elderhood. They were rather silent as they aged following the culture class Awakening between Baby Boomers and the World War II leaders of the 1960s and 1970s. The Civic generation born after an Awakening is protected to prevent the risk-taking of their elders and grows up practical and externally focused. Good thing too, as the next crisis hits as they come of age. Almost as one, they rise heroically to this occasion (read 'the finest generation': a term often used for the young soldiers of World War II), and return following its resolution to solidify existing institutions and values. As they reach Elderhood, the institutions and values they have espoused become targets to overturn by Rising

Adults in the next Awakening. The Youth following them, who are born and spend their childhoods during the Crisis, grow up even more overprotected than they were, and the crisis leaves its scars in the form of risk aversion and social conformity in Rising Adulthood. They mature to be rather indecisive middle managers who attempt to arbitrate in the cultural battle between the generations surrounding them during the next Awakening in their Midlife, and retire to a position of some influence but less respect as Elders. So birth cohorts share broad general characteristics that of course gloss over large individual differences within cohort, and they interact with each other to push and pull at those broad characteristics on which they differ.

Trends or cycles?

How does this elaborate theory of generational cycles with psychological impact stack up empirically? Evidence is mixed at best, but some of this is undoubtedly related to measurement difficulties. Though Strauss and Howe described the characteristics of generations as if the generations were clearly distinguishable, it is obvious that they are not, even if the patterns Strauss and Howe describe are real. Strauss and Howe knew this too. Moreover, as they noted, even generations at the same points in the cycles have been far from identical in characteristics. Within the theory, some of the differences could certainly be attributed to the natures of the various Crises that have kicked off the cycles and the Awakenings that have punctuated them, but long-term trends in communications and travel, education and commerce, the nature of work life, typical ages of marriage and childbirth, even the nature of warfare, also likely have left their marks on the people who have lived through them. This means that the dichotomy between cycles and trends is too sharp: over time trends tend to peter out and even reverse, and cycles are 'watered down' and left more shallow by long-term trends. This means that differences from generation to generation in personality and values as such constructs are typically measured by psychologists are likely to be observable only at the margins, and may be significant in some samples but not in others depending on the population selectivity of the samples and the exact boundaries used to define the generations. This is generally what empirical data have indicated (e.g., Twenge, et al., 2010. Trzesniewski & Donnellan, 2010).

Thinking about the economy and its impacts on people in different phases of the lifespan helps to clarify this. Economic cycles of relative prosperity and contraction are historical realities that certainly show no signs of disappearing. They are also among the factors contributing to the crises described by Strauss and Howe, though they are probably both more frequent than the 20-year generational patterns they discuss and less regular than they would prefer to suggest. With the most recent economic crisis has come discussion in the mainstream press that people coming of age during periods of economic downturn like this face much more limited job opportunities than those coming of age during more economically robust times. This can delay or even prevent them from entering their careers of choice. It can also have substantial negative impact on their lifetime income earnings, as they accept lower-wage jobs for longer periods of time, even permanently, and employers limit wage increases even when they do hire, especially for newer employees for whom they do not have long-standing obligations.

I devoted considerable attention in Chapter 9 to the importance for healthy psychological development in early adulthood of 'finding a place in the world', and finding such a place is unquestionably harder in industrialized countries when their economies are weak. Leo Tolstoy began his famous novel *Anna Karenina* noting that 'Happy families are all alike; every unhappy family is unhappy in its own way.' People love novels for their ability to bring statements like this, which resonate to us as true, to life, using completely fictional characters and situations. But this statement also carries some truth at the level of the individual: though there are countless individual differences among people all of whom have 'found places in the world' and are 'doing well', the ways people respond to even the same difficulties are at least as variable, and probably more so. Stress responses generally accentuate people's original individual differences, as relatively good copers maintain relative stability despite adversity and relatively poor copers suffer greater effects. So 'happy' individuals are relatively alike but 'unhappy' individuals vary considerably more as they express the effects of the sources of their unhappiness in their own ways.

Coming of age during the most recent economic downturns could be expected to have main effects on incidences of many forms of psychopathology as young adults encounter difficulties in finding appropriate places in the world, and there may be downstream consequences later in their lives as well. Such effects are likely not limited to young adults either. For example, older adults with established careers and families are more likely to face job loss during these downturns. This may not be as common as difficulties in locating a goal job in the first place.

But economic change is not limited to cycles of relative boom and bust. Over the last century, the economies of most of the so-called 'industrialized' countries have gone from domination by manufacturing and agricultural jobs to domination by service jobs. This has increased employer demand for university-educated employees, coincident with massive increases in the proportions of young adults seeking university degrees. This means that the ways in which young adults spend their time have changed considerably. Instead of often beginning an occupation at around age 18 that will see them through to retirement, many, even most, now spend at least a couple of years and sometimes considerably longer studying, with few other obligations, training for very different jobs from those of their parents. These jobs increasingly require high-level verbal and social networking skills as well as analytical skills. And young people are much more likely to change jobs, often several times, throughout their careers, often moving substantial geographical distances, even to different countries, in the process. To whatever extent the activities in which one engages affect psychological characteristics, and we know they do even when we do not know specifically how, these substantial trends in activities will be having impact, whether we can measure it, or have measured it, yet, or not. As it is unlikely these trends will abate any time soon, the effects are unlikely to abate either, and must be considered long-term trends rather than cycles. So the trends and cycles, and the effects they bring about, co-exist and likely sometimes interact.

Individual differences v. developmental change

Individual differences are large and pervasive. So, too, of course, is developmental change: think of the change involved in a helpless newborn growing to be a capable adult. But developmental changes take place over such extended periods of time that interim changes can be very difficult to capture because they are swamped by the sheer volume of individual differences at any point in time in just about any characteristic compared with change in the mean level of that characteristic over easily studied periods such as year to year. This is the case whether the change in mean actually reflects changes in particular individuals (longitudinal study) or differences in one group at one time from an older or younger group at the same time (cross-sectional study). The impact of this contrast between the magnitudes of variance at any one point in time and the differences in mean levels between commonly identified time points has not generally been recognized in psychological studies, whether longitudinal or cross-sectional, due likely to the separation between experimental and correlational psychology I discussed in Chapter 1. This means that its implications for measurement of both difference and change have also been largely overlooked.

The clearest example of the typical situation of which I am aware comes from educational psychology. Educational psychology is a good source of data because children's school achievement is typically tested rather frequently in very standardized forms, with some of the most psychometrically sound tests available. Moreover, educators set clear goals for year-to-year progress in achievement and monitor attainment of those goals closely. And children typically do show substantial absolute achievement progress from year to year: rates of this change are about as large from one year to the next as for any psychological characteristic out there. That is, they run about 0.3 standard deviations on average (William, 2010). This is substantial growth for sure, but it pales in relation to the individual differences within any one age class, which typically run over six standard deviations: usually a little more than three standard deviations below to a little more than three standard deviations above the mean. This presents a real measurement challenge: there is always much more statistical power to detect individual differences at any one point in time than to detect reliable individual differences indevelopmental changes, unless the timespan involved is very long, the measurements extremely accurate, and sample attrition negligible. These are tough standards for psychological studies to meet in practice, and they are confounded by the fact that any measure of change is inherently less reliable than the 'before' and 'after' measures on which it is based because it includes the error in both.

Addressing the challenges ahead

The question of statistical power really comes to a head because interest is growing in quantifying the impacts of individual differences in characteristics such as personality and intelligence on rates of development of other characteristics or outcomes. This means identifying associations between variables with very small variances (the changes) relative to the variances in the variables that must be controlled (the individual differences in level at any one point in time). Despite high interest, considerable methodological effort, and many new methodological developments that make use of the explosion of computer power that has taken place in the last 35 years or so, how to deal with this situation effectively has not been worked out. Doing so will likely require not just new methodological approaches but much more extensive and frequent assessment of study participants. Use of technology such as hand-held mobile recording and transmission devices that make possible daily or even more frequent measurements during real-life situations is increasingly common and probably necessary, but the additional commitment this requires on the parts of participants means that samples will likely become even more selected for dutiful personality characteristics and intelligence than they already tend to be.

If we have learned anything about the development of individual differences, we have learned that it is very idiosyncratic and, at the risk of tautology, unique to the individual. Like the sand in the base of a clown punching-dummy, genetic influences place some constraints on developmental possibilities, and they often help to bring us back to a previously robust point of equilibrium after a particularly strong environmental punch. But the sphere of movement in response to the environment within that range of possibility is large. It is even possible sometimes to pick the clown up and move it wholesale somewhere else, and it may behave somewhat differently there if atmospheric or temperature conditions differ. Twin studies have been invaluable in the understandings we have gleaned about this to date. The most common variety of twins that spend their childhoods together have shown us over and over that even when genetic background is identical in two individuals and they grow up side by side, the result is still two clearly individual adults. Thus their unique experiences, whether systematic to each of them or completely stochastic or some combination, matter. And if they matter to MZ twins, they also matter to the rest of us because twins are just people. It is clear that the experience of being a twin differs in many ways from being a singleton, from conception through gestation and birth, and throughout the rest of the lifespan, but these are differences of quantity not differences in kind. For example, twins growing up together may compete and/or cooperate with each other more than do singletons on many different fronts and for many different resources, but everyone does some competing and cooperating with someone. Our genes may constrain our developmental gyrations, but they do not determine our fates. Yet enough of the rare-as-hens-teeth variety of twins that have been separated and reared apart have been studied to show us that, even when environmental conditions are quite different, those genetic influences will 'out' in noticeable ways. As with unique environmental experiences, if this is true of MZ twins, it is true of the rest of us as well. We all have this genetic sand in our feet. Despite the power of this message, I think we have only begun to make use of the potential of particularly MZ twins to help us understand development in general and the development of individual differences in particular. When they are discordant for something: disease, life outcome, trait measure, whatever, the trajectories involved in the development of their discordance can tell us much about how the rest of us come to be where we are. We need considerable detail about those trajectories to identify the turning points that make the difference, however, and the few in-depth studies to date have been small and heavily dosed with hindsight, as they have tended to be based on extensive personal interviews at a single point in life. The more common and larger studies of discordant twin pairs have tended not to have sufficient assessment detail and, if longitudinal, not to have sufficient frequency of measurement. The other advantage that twin studies allow is some escape from the typical sampling biases encountered in recruiting samples for psychological studies. Because especially MZ twins are rare and stand out for their similarity and for the additional challenges their tandem arrival poses for their parents, it is relatively easy to convince them that they have particular value to science and thus to motivate them to participate. This is far from foolproof of course, but it does have impact.

Qualitative studies of their lives and experiences indicate that, for all their similarities, the lives of MZ twins can take very different paths. The forks in the road that send them on these different paths are often chance encounters. This is the case even when it is clear that particular personality characteristics or abilities contributed to the encounter in the first place. For example, both twins may enjoy taking physical risks in sport and recreation, but only one may have been unlucky enough to have the life-changing serious accident while doing so. When individuals are as closely matched as MZ twins who have grown up together it is easier than for singleton individuals to parse apart the conditions and events that contributed to different outcomes for them and to see the role that chance plays amid the roles played by conscious and unconscious choices emerging from individual characteristics. Aside from the omnipresent possibility of twin effects of various kinds, the general patterns of life for twins have to be the same as for the rest of us. So the chance factors in our histories are major factors in who we all are at any point in time.

Perhaps this means we will never be able to come to a fully integrated understanding of the development of individual differences. And perhaps we would not even want to: if we managed such an understanding, it might be all too tempting to try to organize society so that everyone was slotted into the social niche that society deemed 'most optimal' for that person's characteristics, a *Brave New World* such as Huxley's. This is not a world in which I for one would want to live. But even if complete understanding *is* a pipe dream, we can make progress, and the progress has benefits. I think, for example, of the techniques being used to teach autistic children in very overt ways the social interactive skills that most of us pick up 'out of the air' but which they somehow do not, and the tremendous improvements in quality of life this appears to make possible. Many who have received such instruction have gone on to hold jobs and maintain social relationships, to lead lives out in the mainstream world instead of being warehoused in some institution as they tended to be in the past. Society benefits from this as well: not only do we not have to support them in those institutions, but we gain the benefits of their labours and abilities. These are big things, made possible through improved understanding of the development of individual differences. You could say, 'Yes, but those people are extreme. What about the rest of us in the middle of each distribution?' And you would have a point. It is harder to see that any environmental experience in particular has been of clear benefit when no aspect of development ever appeared abnormal. But that does not mean the benefits are not there. Even if all we get from the study of development of individual differences is better ability to gain insight into our own lives and selves and those immediately around us, this can contribute much to the quality and richness of our experiences.

Further reading

Caspari, R., & Lee, S.-H. (2004). Older age becomes common late in human evolution. *Proceedings of the National Academy of Sciences of the United States of America, 101,* 10895–10900.

Christensen, K., Doblhammer, G., Rau, R., & Vaupel, J. W. (2009). Ageing populations: The challenges ahead. *The Lancet, 37,* 1196–1208.

Flynn, J. R. (1987). Massive IQ gains in 14 nations – what IQ tests really measure. *Psychological Bulletin, 101,* 171–191.

Johnson, W. (2010). Understandiong the genetics of intelligence: Can height help? Can corn oil? *Current Directions in Psychological Science, 19,* 177–182.

Komlos, J., & Lauderdale, B. E. (2007). The mysterious trend in human heights in the 20th century. *American Journal of Human Biology, 34,* 206–215.

Strauss, W., & Howe, N. (1991). *Generations: The History of America's Future 1584– 2069.* New York: William Morrow and Company.

Twenge, J. M., Freeman, E. C., & Campbell, W. K. (2012). Generational differences in young adults' life goals, concern for others, and civic orientation, 1996–2009. *Journal of Personality and Social Psychology, 102,* 1045–1062.

Vaupel, J. W. (2010). Biodemography of human ageing. *Nature, 464,* 536–542.

References

Adams, K. F., Sueta, C. F., Gheorghiade, M., Schwartz, T. A., Koch, G. G., & Uretsky, B. (1999). Gender differences in survival to advanced heart failure: Insights from FIRST Study. *Circulation, 99,* 1816–1821.

Aguiar, A., & Baillargon, R. (2000). Perseveration and problem solving in infancy. In H. W. Reese, *Advances in Child Development and Behavior, Vol. 27* (pp. 135–180). New York: Academic Press.

Aiello, L. C., & Wheeler, P. (1995). The expensive tissue hypothesis – The brain and the digestive system in human and primate evolution. *Current Anthropology, 36,* 199–221.

Aikins, J. W., Simon, V. A., & Prinstein, M. J. (2010). Romantic partner selection and socialization of young adolescents' substance use and behavior problems. *Journal of Adolescence, 33,* 813–826.

Alexander, G. M., Wilcox, T., & Woods, R. (2009). Sex differences in infants' visual interest in toys. *Archives of Sexual Behaviour, 38, 3,* 427–433, DOI: 10.1007/s10508–008–9430–1.

Alford, J. R., Hatemi, P. K., Hibbing, J. R., Martin, N. G., & Eaves, L. J. (2011). The politics of mate choice. *Journal of Politics, 73,* 362–379.

Allman, J. (2000). *Evolving Brains.* New York: Scientific American Library.

Allport, G. (1954). *The Nature of Prejudice.* Cambridge, MA: Addison-Wesley.

Allport, G. W. (1937). *Personality: A Psychological Interpretation.* New York: Holt.

Als, H. (1977). The newborn communicates. *Journal of Communication, 27,* 66–67.

Andrews, M. W., & Rosenblum, L. A. (1991). Security of attachment in infants raised in variable- or low-demand environments. *Child Development, 62,* 686–693.

Andersson, M. (1994). *Sexual Selection.* Princeton, NJ: Princeton University Press.

Apter, D., & Vihko, R. (1983). Early menarche, a risk factor for breast cancer, indicates early onset of ovulatory cycles. *Journal of Clinical endocrinology and Metabolism, 57,* 82–86.

Apter, D., Renila, M., & Vikho, R. (1989). Some endocrine characteristics of early menarche, a risk factor for breast cancer, are preserved into adulthood. *International Journal of cencer, 44,* 783–787.

Armour, S., & Haynie, D. L. (2007). Adolescent sexual debut and later delinquency. *Journal of Youth and Adolescence, 36,* 141–152.

Arnett, J. (1999). Adolescent storm and stress, reconsidered. *American Psychologist, 54,* 317–326.

Arnett, J. (1995). Broad and narrow socialization: The family in the context of a cultural theory. *Journal of Marriage and the Family, 57,* 617–628.

Aro, H., & Taipale, V. (1987). The impact of timing of puberty on psychosomatic symptoms among fourteen- to sixteen-year-old Finnish girls. *Child Development, 58,* 261–268.

Aron, E., Aron, A., & Davies, K. M. (2005). Adult shyness: The interaction of temperamental sensitivity and an adverse childhood environment. *Personality and Social Psychology Bulletin, 31*, 181–197.

Bakalar, J. L., Greenstein, D., Chavez, A., Miller, R., Tossell, J. W., Clasen, L., et al. (2010). Camparative analysis of cortical thickness differentiates children with atypical psychosis from childhood-onset schizophrenia. *Biological Psychiatry, 67*, 249S.

Baker, R., & Bellis, M. (1993). Human sperm competition: Ejaculate manipulation by females and a function for the female orgasm. *Animal Behavior, 46*, 887–909.

Bakermans-Kranenburg, M. J., & van Ijzendoorn, M. H. (2008). Evidence for differential susceptibility: Dopamine D4 receptorpolymorphism (D4 VNTR) moderates intervention effects on toddlers' externalizing behavior in a randomized trial. *Developmental Psychology, 44*, 293–300.

Baldwin, D. A. (1993). Early referential understanding: Infants' ability to recognize referential acts for what they are. *Developmental Psychology, 29*, 832–843.

Baldwin, J. A. (1984). African self-consciousness and the mental health of African-Americans. *Journal of Black Studies, 15*, 177–194.

Baldwin, J. A., & Hopkins, R. (1990). African American and European-American cultural differences as assessed by the worldviews paradigm: An empirical analysis. *Western Journal of Black Studies, 14*, 38–52.

Bandura, A. (1986). *Social Foundations of Thought and Action: A Social Cognitive Theory*. Englewood Cliffs, NJ: Prentice Hall.

Barker, D. J., & Osmond, C. (1986). Infant mortality, childhood nutrition, and ischaemic heart disease in England and Wales. *Lancet, 1*, 1077–1081.

Barker, E. D., & Maughan, B. (2009). Differentiating early-onset persistent versus childhood-limited conduct problem youth. *American Journal of Psychiatry, 166*, 900–908.

Barr, R. G., & Chen, S. (1996). Crying patterns in pre-term infants. *Developmental Medicine and Child Neurology, 38*, 345–355.

Barr, R. G., Trent, R. B., & Cross, J. (2006). Age-related incidence curve of hospitalized Shaken Baby Syndrome cases: Current evidence of crying as a trigger to shaking. *Child Abuse and Neglect, 30*, 7–16.

Barrett, K. S., & Campos, J. J. (1987). Perspectives on development II: A functionalist approach to emotions. In J. D. Osofsky, *Handbook of Infant Development, 2nd ed.* (pp. 555–578). New York: John Wiley and Sons.

Barry, H. I., & Paxson, L. M. (1971). Infancy and early childhood: Cross-cultural codes 2. *Ethnology, 10*, 466–508.

Bartels, A., & Zeki, S. (2000). The neural basis of romantic love. *Neuroreport, 11*, 3829–3834.

Bartels, A., & Zeki, S. (2004). The neural correlates of maternal and romantic love. *Neuroimage, 21*, 1155–1166.

Bartzokis, G., Lu, P. H., Tingus, K., Mendez, M. F., Richard, A., Peters, D. G., et al. (2008). Lifespan trajectory of myelin integrity and maximum motor speed. *Neurobiology of Aging, 31*, 1554–1562.

Bates, J. E., & Pettit, G. S. (2007). Temperament, parenting, and socialization. In J. Grusec, & P. Hastings, *Handbook of Socialization* (pp. 153–177). New York: Guilford.

Bateson, W. (1894). *Materials for the Study of Variation Treated with Especial Regard for Discontinuity in the Origin of Species*. New York: Macmillan and Company.

Batty, G. D., Deary, I. J., & Gottfredson, L. S. (2007). Premorbid (early life) IQ and later mortality risk: Systematic review. *Annals of Epidemiology, 17,* 278–288.

Beck, A. T. (1967). *Depression: Causes and Treatment.* Philadelphia: University of Pennsylvania Press.

Bellah, R. (1992). *The Broken Covenant: American Civil Religion in Time of Trial.* Chicago: University of Chicago Press.

Belsky, J., Fish, M., & Isabella, R. (1991). Continuity and discontinuity in infant negative and positive emotionality: Family antecedents and attachment consequences. *Developmental Psychology, 27,* 421–431.

Belsky, J., Jonassaint, C., Pluess, M., Stanton, M., Brummert, B., & Williams, R. (2009). Vulnerability genes or plasticity genes? *Molecular Psychiatry, 14,* 746–754.

Belsky, J., Steinberg, L. D., & Draper, P. (1991). Childhood experience, interpersonal devleopment, and reproductive strategy – an evolutionary theory of socialization. *Child Development, 62,* 647–670.

Belsky, J., Steinberg, L. D., Houts, R. M., Friedman, S. L., DeHart, G., Cauffman, E., et al. (2007). Family rearing antecedents of pubertal timing. *Child Development, 78,* 1302–1321.

Benedict, R. (1934). *Patterns of Culture.* Boston: Houghton Mifflin.

Benenson, J. F., Tennyson, R., and Wrangham, R. W. (2011). Male more than female infants imitate propulsive motion. *Cognition, 121, 2,* 262–267, DOI:10.1016/j.cognition.2011.07.006.

Berenbaum, S. A. (1999). Effects of early androgens on sex-typed activities and interests in adolescents with congenical adrenal hyperplasia. *Hormones and Behavior, 35,* 102–110.

Berenbaum, S. A., & Hines, M. (1992). Early androgens are related to sex-typed toy preferences. *Psychological Science, 3,* 203–206.

Berge, C. (1998). Heterochronic processes in human evolution: An ontogentic analysis of the hominid pelvis. *American Journal of Physical Anthropology, 105,* 441–459.

Bergman, K., Sarkar, P., O'Connor, T. G., Modi, N., & Glover, V. (2007). Maternal stress during pregnancy predicts cognitive ability and fearfulness in infancy. *Journal of the American Academy of Child and Adolescent Psychiatry, 46,* 1454–1463.

Bersaglieri, T., Sabeti, P. C., Patterson, N., Vanderploeg, T., Schaffner, S. F., Drake, J. A., et al. (2004). Genetic signatures of strong recent positive selection at the lactase gene. *American Journal of Human Genetics, 74,* 1111–20.

Bertram, L., McQueen, M. B., Mullin, K., Blacker, D., & Tanzi, R. E. (2007). Systematic meta-analyses of Alzheimer disease genetic studies: The AlzGene database. Nature Genetics, 39, 17–23.

Biehle, S. N., & Mickelson, K. D. (2012). First-time parents' expectations about the division of childcare and play. *Journal of Marriage and Family, 26,* 36–45.

Bielak, A. A., Hultsch, D. F., Strauss, E., MacDonald, S. W., & Hunter, M. A. (2010). Intraindividual variability in reaction time predicts cognitive outcomes 5 years later. *Neuropsychology, 24,* 731–741.

Birney, E. E. (2007). Identification and analysis of functional elelments in 1% of the human genome by the ENCODE pilot project. Nature, 447, 799–816.

Bishop, K. M., & Wahlsten, D. (1997). Sex differences in the human corpus callosum: Myth or reality? Neuroscience Biobehavioral Review, 21, 581–601.

Borgia, G. (1985). Bower destruction and sexual competition in the satin bower bird (Ptilonorhynchus violaceus). *Behavioral Ecology and Sociobiology, 18,* 91–100.

Blair, C., Granger, D., Willoughby, M., Kivlighan, K., & Investigators, F. L. (2006). Maternal sensitivity is related to hypotholamic-pituitary-adrenal axis stress reactivity and regulation in response to emotion challenge in 6-month-old infants. *Annals of the New York Academy of Sciences, 1094,* 263–267.

Blyth, C. R. (1972). On Simpson's paradox and the sure-thing principle. *Journal of the American Statistical Association, 67,* 364–366.

Borgerhoff Mulder, M. (1989). Early maturing Kisegi women have higher reproductive success than later maturing women and cost more to marry. *Behavioral Ecology and Social Biology, 24,* 145–153.

Borgia, G. (1985). Bower quality, number of decorations and mating success of male satin bower birds (Ptilonorhynchus violaceus): An experimental analysis. *Animal Behavior, 33,* 266–271.

Borgia, G., & Wingfield, J. C. (1991). Hormonal correlates of bower decoration and sexual display in the satin bowerbird (Ptilonorhynchus violaceus). *Condor, 93,* 935–942.

Bouchard, T. J. (1997). Experience Producing Drive Theory: How genes drive experience and shape personality. *Acta Paediatrica Supplement, 422,* 60–64.

Bouchard, T. J., Lykken, D. T., McGue, M., Segal, N. L., & Tellegen, A. (1990). Sources of human psychological differences: the Minnesota Study of Twins Reared Apart. *Science, 25,* 223–228.

Bowlby, J. (1969). *Attachment and Loss, Vol. 1: Attachment.* New York: Basic Books.

Bowlby, J. (1973). *Attachment and Loss, Vol. 2: Separation: Anger and Anxiety.* London: Hogarth.

Bowlby, J. (1980). *Attachment and Loss, Vol. 3: Loss, Sadness, and Depression.* New York: Basic Books.

Boyce, W. T., Chesney, M., Alkon, A., Tschann, J. M., Adams, S., Chesterman, B., et al. (1995). Psychobiologic reactivity to stress and childhood respiratory illnesses: Results of two prospective studies. *Psychosomatic Medicine, 57,* 411–422.

Boykin, A. W. (1983). The academic performance of African-American children. In J. Spence, *Achievement and Achievement Motives* (pp. 321–371). San Francisco, CA: Freeman.

Bramble, D., & Lieberman, D. E. (2004). Endurance running and the evolution of homo. *Nature, 432,* 345–352.

Brewster, A. L., & Nelson, J. P. (1998). Victim, Perpetrator, family, and incident characteristics of 32 infant maltreatment deaths in the United States Air Force. *Child Abuse and Neglect, 22,* 91–101.

Brooks-Gunn, J., & Warren, M. P. (1985). The effects of delayed menarche in different contexts: Dance and non-dance students. *Journal of Youth and Adolescence, 14,* 285–300.

Brown-Borg, H. M. (2007). Hormonal regulation of longevity in mammals. *Ageing Research Review, 6,* 28–45.

Brunelli, S. A., Shindledecker, R. D., & Hofer, M. A. (1987). Behavioral responses of juvenile rats (rattus-norvegicus) to neonates after infusion of blood plasma. *Journal of Comparative Psychology, 101,* 47–59.

Bryden, M. P., McManus, I. C., & Bulman-Fleming, M. B. (1994). Evaluating the empirical support for the Geschwind-Behan-Galaburda model of cerebral lateralization. *Brain and Cognition, 26,* 103–167.

Buer, M. C. (1926). *Health, Wealth, and Population in the Early Days of the Industrial Revolution.* London: George Routledge & Sons.

Burditt, K. S., & Fingerman, K. L. (2005). Do we get better at picking our battles? Age group differences in descriptions of behavioural reactions to interpersonal tensions. *Journals of Gerontology Series B – Psychological and Social Sciences, 60*, P121–P128.

Burger, J., Kirchner, M., Bramanti, B., Haak, W., & Thomas, M. G. (2007). Absence of the lactase-persistence-associated allele in early Neolithic Europeans. *Proceedings of the National Academy of Sciences of the United States of America, 104*, 3736–3741.

Burks, B. S. (1928). The relative influence of nature and nurture upon mental development: A comparative study of foster parent-foster child resemblance and true parent–true child resemblance. In *Twenty-seventh Yearbook of the National Society for the Study of Education, Part 1*. Bloomington, IL: Public School Publishing Company.

Burt, S. A., Donnellan, M. B., Humbad, M. A., Hicks, B. M., McGue, M., & Iacono, W. G. (2010). Does marriage inhibit antisocial behavior? *Archives of General Psychiatry, 67*, 1309–1315.

Buss, A., & Plomin, R. (1984). *Temperament: Early Developing Personality Traits*. Hillsdale, NJ: Erlbaum.

Buss, C., Davis, E. P., Muftuler, L. T., Head, K., & Sandman, C. A. (2009). High pregnancy anxiety during mid-gestation is associated with decreased gray matter density in 6–9-year-old children. *Psychoneuroendocrinology, 35*, 141–153.

Buss, D. M. (1999). *Evolutionary Psychology: The New Science of the Mind*. Boston, MA: Allyn and Bacon.

Buss, D. M. (1984). Marital assortment for personality dispositions: Assessment with three different data systems. *Behavior Genetics, 14*, 111–123.

Buss, D. M. (1989). Sex differences in human mate preferences: Evolutionary hypotheses tested in 37 cultures. *Behavioral and Brain Sciences, 12*, 1–49.

Butler, R., & Ruzany, N. (1993). Age and socialization effects on the development of social comparison motives and normative ability asesssment in kibbutz and urban children. *Child Development, 64*, 532–543.

Butterworth, G. E. (1977). Object disappearance and error in Piaget's stage IV task. *Journal of Experimental Child Psychology, 23*, 391–401.

Calhoun, J. B. (1962). *The Ecology and Sociology of the Norway Rat*. Bethesda, MD: Health, Education, Welfare, Public Health Services.

Caminiti, R., Ghaziri, H., Galuske, R., Hof, P. R., & Innocenti, G. M. (2009). Evolution amplified processing with temporally dispersed slow neuronal connectivity in primates. *Proceedings of the National Academy of Sciences of the United States of America, 106*, 19551–19556.

Campos, J. J., Witherington, D., Anderson, D. L., Frankel, C. I., Uchiyama, I., & Barbu-Roth, M. (2008). Rediscovering development in infancy. *Child Development, 79*, 1625–1632.

Camras, L. A., & Witherington, D. C. (2005). Dynamical systems approaches to emotional development. *Developmental Review, 25*, 328–350.

Carlson, J. M., & Doyle, J. (2002). Complexity and robustness. *Proceedings of the National Academy of Sciences of the United States of America, 99 (Supp. 1)*, 2538–2545.

Carr, P. B., & Dweck, C. S. (2011). Intelligence and motivation. In R. J. Sternberg, & S. B. Kaufman, *The Cambridge Handbook of Intelligence* (pp. 748–770). New York: Cambridge University Press.

Carrel, L., & Willard, H. F. (2005). X-inactivation profile reveals extensive variability in X-linked gene expression in females. *Nature, 434*, 400–404.

Carstensen, L. l. (1993). Motivation for social contact across the life span: A theory of socioemotional selectivity. In J. E. Jacobs, *Nebraska Symposium on Education, 1992: Developmental Perspectives on Motivation* (pp. 209–254). Lincoln: University of Nebraska Press.

Carstensen, L. L., & Frederickson, B. L. (1998). Influence of HIV status and age on cognitive representations of others. *Health Psychology, 17*, 494–503.

Carter, C. (1992). Oxytocin and sexual behavior. *Neuroscience and Biobehavioral Reviews, 16*, 131–144.

Carter, R. T., & Constantine, M. G. (2000). Career maturity, life role salience, and racial/ethnic identity in black and Asian American college students. *Journal of Career Assessment, 8*, 173–180.

Carver, C., Johnson, S. L., Joormann, J., Kim, Y., & Nam, J. Y. (2011). Serotonin transporter polymorphism interacts with childhood adversity to predict aspects of impulsivity. *Psychological Science, 22*, 589–595.

Carver, K. K., Joyner, K., & Udry, J. R. (2003). National estimates of adolescent romantic relationships. In P. Florsheim, *Adolescent Romantic Relationships and Sexual Behavior: Theory, Research, Practical Implications* (pp. 23–56). Mahwah, NJ: Lawrence Erlbaum Associates.

Caspari, R., & Lee, S.-H. (2004). Older age becomes common late in human evolution. *Proceedings of the National Academy of Sciences of the United States of America, 101*, 10895–10900.

Caspi, A., Lynam, D., Moffitt, T. E., & Silva, P. A. (1993). Unravelling girls' delinquency: Biological, dispositional and contextual contributions to adolescent misbehaviour. *Developmental Psychology, 29*, 19–30.

Caspi, A., Sugden, K., Moffitt, T. E., Taylor, A., Craig, I. W., et al. (2003). Influence of life stress on depression: Moderation by a polymorphism in the 5-HTT gene. *Science, 301*, 386–389.

Catmur, C., Gillmeister, H., Bird, G., Liepelt, R., Brass, M., & Heyes, C. (2008). Through the looking glass: Counter-mirror activation following incompatible sensorimotor learning. *European Journal of Neuroscience, 28*, 1208–1215.

Cavalli-Sforza, L. L., & Feldman, M. W. (1981). *Cultural Transmission and Evolution: A Quantitative Approach*. Princeton, NJ: Princeton University Press.

Chambers, R. A., Taylor, J. R., & Petenza, M. N. (2003). Developmental neurocircuitry of motivation in adolescence: A critical period of addiction vulnerability. *American Journal of Psychiatry, 160*, 1041–1052.

Charig, C. R., Webb, D. R., Payne, S. R., & Wickham, O. E. (1986). Comparison of treatment of renal calculi by open surgery, percutaneous nephrolithotomy, and extracorporeal shockwave lithotripsy. *British Medical Journal (Clinical Research Edition), 292*, 879–882.

Charlesworth, B. (1994). *Evolution in Age-Structured Populations*. Cambridge: Cambridge University Press.

Chomsky, N. (1965). *Aspects of the Theory of Syntax*. Cambridge, MA: MIT Press.

Christensen, K., Doblhammer, G., Rau, R., & Vaupel, J. W. (2009). Ageing populations: The challenges ahead. *The Lancet, 37*, 1196–1208.

Christensen, K., Iachina, M., Rexbye, H., Tomassini, C., Frederiksen, H., McGue, M., et al. (2004). 'Looking old for your age': Genetics and mortality. *Epidemiology, 15*, 251–252.

Clark, K. B. (1965). *Dark Ghetto*. New York: Harper & Row.

Clausen, J. A. (1975). The social meaning of differential physical and sexual maturation. In S. E. Dragastin, & G. H. Elder, *Adolescence in the Life Cycle: Psychological
Change and Social Context* (pp. 25–47). Washington, DC: Hemisphere.

Clearfield, M. W., Diedrich, F. J., Smith, L. B., & Thelen, E. (2006). Young infants
reach correctly in A-not-B tasks: On the development of stability and perseveration.
Infant Behavior and Development, 29, 435–444.

Coelho, M., Luiselli, D., Bertorelle, G., Lopes, A. I., Seixas, S., Destro-Bisol, G., et al.
(2002). Microsatellite variation and evolution of human's lactase persistence.
Human genetics, 117, 329–339.

Cohen, L. B., & Marks, K. S. (2002). How infants process addition and subtraction
events. *Developmental Science, 5,* 186–201.

Collins, W. A. (2003). More than myth: The developmental significance of romantic
relationships during adolescence. *Journal of Research on Adolescence, 13,* 1–24.

Conel, J. L. (1963). *The Postnatal Development of the Human Cerebral Cortex.*
Cambridge, MA: Harvard University Press.

Conger, R. D., Cui, M. K., Bryant, C. M., & Elder, G. H. (2000). Competence in early
adult relationships: A developmental perspective on family relationships. *Journal of
Personality and Social Psychology, 79,* 224–237.

Connellan, J., Baron-Cohen, S., Wheelwright, S., Batki, A., and Ahluwalia, J. (2000).
Sex differences in neonatal social perception. *Infant Behavior and Development, 23,*
1, 113–118.

Connolly, J. A., Craig, W., Goldberg, A., & Pepler, D. (1999). Conceptions of cross-sex
friendships and romantic relationships in early adolescence. *Journal of Youth and
Adolescence, 28,* 481–494.

Conrad, l. (2006). *The Western Medical Tradition.* Cambridge: Cambridge University
Press.

Coplan, J. H., Smith, E. L., Trost, R. E., Scharf, B. A., Altemus, M., & Bjornson, J.
(2000). Growth hormone response to clonidine in adversely reared young adult primates: Relationship to serial cerebrospinal fluid corticotropin-releasing factor concentrations. *Psychiatry Research, 95,* 93–102.

Corder, E. H., Saunders, A. M., Strittmatter, W. J., Schmechel, D. E., Gaskell, P. C.,
Small, G. W., et al. (1993). Gene dose of apolipoprotwin E type 4 allele and the risk
of Alzheimer's Disease in late onset families. *Science, 261,* 921–923.

Coren, S. (1990). *Left-Handedness: Behavioral Implications and Anomalies.* New
York: Elsevier.

Cosgrove, K. P., Mazure, C. M., & Staley, J. K. (2007). Evolving knowledge of sex differences in brain structure, function, and chemistry. *Biological Psychiatry, 62,* 847–855.

Cota, A. A., & Dion, K. L. (1986). Salience of gender and sex composition of of ad hoc
groups: An experimental test of distinctiveness theory. *Journal of Personality and
Social Psychology, 50,* 770–776.

Coulon, M., Guellai, B., & Streri, A. (2011). Recognition of unfamiliar talking faces
at birth. *International Journal of Behavioral Development, 35,* 282–287.Crocker,
J., & Luhtanen, R. (1990). Collective self-esteem and in-group bias. *Journal of
Personality and Social Psychology, 58,* 60–67.

Cronbach, L. J. (1957). The two disciplines of scientific psychology. *American
Psychologist, 12,* 671–684.

Cronin, H. (1991). *The Ant and the Peacock.* New York: Cambridge University Press.

Cross, W. E. (1971). Negro-to-Black conversion experience. *Black World, 20,* 13–27.

Cross, W. E. (1991). Rethinking nigrescence. In W. E. Cross, *Shades of Black: Diversity in African-American Identity* (pp. 189–217). Philadelphia: Temple University Press.

Csikszentmihalyi, M. (1996). *Creativity: Flow and the Psychology of Discovery and Invention.* New York: Harper Perennial.

Cunnane, S. C., & Crawford, M. A. (2003). Survival of the fattest: Fat babies were the key to the evolution of the modern human brain. *Comparative Biochemistry and Physiology Part A: Molecular and Integrative Physiology, 136,* 17–26.

Darwin, C. R. (1871). *The Descent of Man, and Selection in Relation to Sex (Vols. 1 and 2).* London: John Murray.

Darwin, C. (1859). *The Origin of Species.* London: John Morris.

Davies, W., & Wilkinson, L. S. (2006). It's not all hormones: Alternative explanations for sexual differentiation of the brain. *Brain Research, 1126,* 36–45.

Davis-daSilva, M., & Wallen, K. (1989). Suppression of male rhesus testicular function and sexual behavior by a gonadotropin-releasing hormone agonist. *Physiology and Behavior, 45,* 963–968.

Dawkins, R. (1982). *The Extended Phenotype: The Long Reach of the Gene.* Oxford: Oxford University Press.

Day, L. B., Westcott, D. A., & Olster, D. H. (2005). Evolution of bower complexity and cerebellum size in bowerbirds. *Brain, Behavior, and Evolution, 66,* 62–72.

Deary, I. J., & Der, G. (2005). Reaction time, age, and cognitive ability: Longitudinal findings from age 16 to 63 years in representative population samples. *Aging, Neuropsychology, and Cognition, 12,* 187–215.

Deary, I. J., Whiteman, M. C., Starr, J. M., Whalley, L. J., & Fox, H. C. (2004). The impact of childhood intelligence on later life: Following up the Scottish Mental Surveys of 1932 and 1947. *Journal of Personality and Social Psychology, 86,* 130–147.

de Grey, A. D. (2007). Life span extension research and public debate: Societal considerations. *Studies in Ethics, Law, and Technology, 1,* 1–10.

de Regnier, R. A., Nelson, C. A., Thomas, K. M., Wawerka, S., & Georgieff, M. K. (2000). Neurophysiological evaluation of auditory recognition memory in healthy newborn infants and infants of diabetic mothers. *Journal of Pediatrics, 137,* 777–784.

de Regnier, R. A., Wawerka, S., Georgieff, M. K., Mattia, P., & Nelson, C. A. (2002). Influences of postconceptional age and postnatal experience on the development of auditory recognition memory in the newborn infant. *Developmental Psychobiology, 41,* 2162–2225.

DeCasper, A. J., & Fifer, W. P. (1980). Of human bonding: Newborns prefer their mothers' voices. *Science, 208,* 11741–11776.

DeCasper, A. J., & Spence, M. J. (1986). Prenatal maternal speech influences newborns' perception of speech sounds. *Infant Behavior and Development, 9,* 1331–1150.

Del Giudice, M. (2009). Sex, attachment, and the development of reproductive strategies. *Behavioral and Brain Sciences, 32,* 1–67.

Deminiere, J. M., Piazza, P. V., Guegan, V., Abrous, N., Maccari, S., & Le Moal, M. (1992). Increased locomotor response to novelty and propensity to intravenous self-administration in adult offspring of stressed mothers. *Brain Research, 586,* 135–139.

Detterman, D. K. (1978). The effect of heartbeat sounds on neonatal crying. *Infant Behavior and Development, 1,* 364–368.

Dewing, P., Chiang, C. W., Sinchak, K., Sim, H., Fernagut, P. O., Kelly, S., et al. (2006). Direct regulation of adult brain function by the male-specific factor Sry. *Current Biology, 16,* 415–420.

Dewing, P., Shi, T., Horvath, S., & Vilain, E. (2003). Sexually dimorphic gene expression in mouse brain precedes gonadal differentiation. *Brain Research and Molecular Brain Research, 118*, 82–90.

Diamond, A., & Goldman-Rakic, P. S. (1989). Comparison of human infants and rhesus monkeys on Piaget's AB task: Evidence for dependence of dorsolateral prefrontal cortex. *Experimental Braqin Research, 74*, 24–40.

Dickens, W. T., & Flynn, J. R. (2001). Heritability estimates versus large environmental effects: The IQ paradox resolved. *Psychological Review, 108*, 346–369.

Diener, C., & Suh, E. (1997). Subjective wellbeing and age, an international analysis. In K. W. Schaie, & M. P. Lawton, *Annual Review of Gerontology and Geriatrics, vol. 8* (pp. 302–324). New York: Springer.

Dijkstra, P., Kuyper, H., van der Werf, G., Buunk, A. P., & van der Zee, Y. G. (2008). Social comparison in the classroom: A review. *Review of Educational Research, 78*, 828–878.

DiPietro, J. A., Novak, M. F., Costigan, K. A., Atella, L. D., & Reusing, S. P. (2006). Maternal psychological distress during pregnancy in relation to child development at age 2. *Child Development, 77*, 573–587.

Ditella, R., MacCulloch, R. J., & Oswald, A. J. (2003). The macroeconomics of happiness. *Review of Economics and Statistics, 85*, 809–827.

Doughty, D., & Rodgers, J. L. (2000). Behavior genetic modeling of menarche in U.S. females. In J. L. Rodgers, D. C. Rowe, & W. B. Miller, *Genetic Influences on Human Fertility and Sexuality: Theoretical and Empirical Contributions from the Biological and Behavioral Sciences*. Boston, MA: Kluwer.

Draper, P., & Harpending, H. (1982). Father absence and reproductive strategy: An evolutionary perspective. *Journal of Antrhopoligical Research, 38*, 255–273.

Dubb, A., Gur, R., Avants, B., & Gee, J. (2003). Characterization of sexual dimorphism in the human corpus callosum. *Neuroimage, 20*, 512–519.

DuBois, W. E. (1903). *Souls of Black Folk*. Chicago: A. C. McClurg.

Dudley, J. T., Yuseob, K., Liu, L., Markov, G. J., Gerold, K., Chen, R., et al. (2012). Human genomic disease variants: A neutral evolutionary explanation. *Genome Research, 22*, 1383–1394.

Dumont, N., Anderson, S., Thompson, A., & Teicher, M. (2004). Transient dopamine synthesis modulation in prefrontal cortex: in vitro studies. *Developmental Brain Research, 150*, 163–166.

Duncan, J. (2010). *How Intelligence Happens*. London: Yale University Press.

Durham, W. H. (1979). Toward a coevolutionary theory of biology and culture. In N. A. Chagnon, & W. Irons, *Evolutionary Biology and Human Social Behavior: An Anthropological Perspective* (pp. 149–174). North Scituate, MA: Duxbury Press.

Dutton, S. E., Singer, J. A., & Devlin, A. S. (1998). Racial identity of children in integrated, predominantly white, and black schools. *Journal of Social Psychology, 138*, 41–53.

Dweck, C. S. (2006). *Mindset: The New Psychology of Success*. New York: Random House, Ballantine Books.

Eastwick, P. W., & Finkel, E. J. (2008). Sex differences in mate preferences revisited: Do people know what they actually desire in a relationship partner? *Journal of Personality and Social Psychology, 94*, 245–264.

Eastwick, P. W., Finkel, E. J., & Eagly, A. H. (2011). When and why do ideal partner preferences affect the process of initiating and maintaining romantic relationships? *Journal of Personality and Social Psychology, 101*, 1012–1032.

Eaton, L. K., Kann, L., Kinchen, S., Shanklin, S., Ross, J., Hawkins, J., et al. (2007). Youth risk behavior surveillance – United States, 2007, surveillance summaries. *Morbidity and Mortality Report, 57*, 1–131.

Eisenberg, N., Fabes, R. A., Guthrie, I. K., & Reiser, M. (2000). Dispositional emotionality and regulation: Their role in predicting quality of social functioning. *Journal of Personality and Social Psychology, 78*, 136–157.

Ekman, P. (1972). Universals and cultural differences in facial experssion of emotion. In J. Cole, *Nebraska Symposium on Motivation: Vol. 19 Current Theory and Research in Motivation* (pp. 207–283). Lincoln, NE: University of Nebraska Press.

Ellis, B. J. (2006). Determinants of pubertal timing: An evolutionary developmental approach. In B. J. Ellis, & D. F. Bjorklund, *Origins of the Social Mind: Evolutionary Psychology and Child Development* (pp. 164–188). New York: Guilford.

Ellis, B. J. (2004). Timing of pubertal maturation in girls: An integrated life history approach. *Psychological Bulletin, 130*, 920–958.

Ellis, B. J., Boyce, W. T., Belsky, J., Bakermans-Kranenburg, M. J., & van Ijzendoorn, M. H. (2011). Differential susceptibility to the environment: An evolutionary-neurodevelopmental theory. *Development and Psychopathology, 23*, 7–28.

Enattah, N. S., Sahi, T., Savilahti, E., Terwilliger, J. D., Peltonen, L., & Jarvela, I. (2002). Identification of a variant associated with adult-type hypolactasia. *Nature Genetics, 30*, 233–237.

Erikson, E. H. (1963). *Childhood and Society (2nd Ed.)*. New York: Norton.

Erikson, E. H. (1968). *Identity: Youth and Crisis*. New York: Norton.

Erikson, E. H. (1982). *The Life Cycle Completed*. New York: Norton.

Evans, K. M., & Herr, E. L. (1994). The influence of racial identity and the perceptions of discrimination on the career aspirations of African-American men and women. *Journal of Vocational Behavior, 44*, 173–184.

Fallucca, E., MacMaster, F. P., Haddad, J., Easter, P., Dick, R., May, G., et al. (2011). Distinguishing between major depressive disorder and obsessive-compulsive disorder in children by measuring regional cortical thickness. *Archives of General Psychiatry, 68*, 527–533.

Fagan, J. F., Holland, C. R., & Wheeler, K. (2007). The prediction, from infancy, of adult IQ and achievement. *Intelligence, 35*, 225–231.

Farriman, K., Lubinski, D., & Benbow, C. P. (2009). Work preferences, life values, and personal views of top math/science graduate students and the profoundly gifted: Developmental changes and gender differences during emerging adulthood and parenthood. *Journal of Personality and Social Psychology, 97*, 517–532.

Feeney, J. A. (2008). Adult romantic attachment: Developments in the study of couple relationships. In J. Cassidy, & P. R. Shaver, *Handbook of Attachement, 2nd Edition* (pp. 456–481). New York: Guilford.

Feingold, A. (1992). Good-looking people are not what we think. *Psychological Bulletin, 111*, 304–341.

Ferrari, P. E., Visalberghi, E., Pauknet, A., Fogassi, L., Ruggiero, A., & Suomi, S. J. (2006). Neonatal imitation in infant macaques. *PLoS Biology, 4*, 1501–1508.

Ferrari, P. F., Rozzi, S., & Fogassi, L. (2005). Mirror neuron responding to observation of actions made with tools in monkey ventral premotor cortex. *Journal of Cognitive Neuroscience, 17*, 212–226.

Ferreira, A. J. (1965). Emotional factors in prenatal environment. *Journal of Nervous and Mental Disease, 141*, 108–118.

Ferriman, K., Lubinski, D., & Benbow, C. P. (2009). Work preferences, life values, and personal views of top math/science graduate students and the profoundly gifted: Developmental changes and gender differences during emerging adulthood and parenthood. *Journal of Personality and Social Psychoogy, 97*, 517–532.

Festinger, L. (1954). A theory of social comparison processes. *Human Relations, 7*, 117–140.

Fifer, W. P., & Moon, C. (1989). Psychobiology of newborn auditory preferences. *Seminars in Perinatology, 13*, 4304–4333.

Finch, C. E. (2007). *The Biology of Human Longevity: Inflammation, Nutrition, and Aging in the Evolution of Lifespans.* Amsterdam: Elsevier.

Fischer, K. W., & Silvern, L. (1985). Stages and individual differences in cognitive development. *Annual Review of Psychology, 36*, 613–648.

Fisher, H. E. (2006). Broken hearts: The nature and risks of romantic rejection. In A. C. Crouter, & A. Booth, *Romance and Sex in Adolescence and emerging Adulthood: Risks and Opportunities* (pp. 3–28). Mahwah, NJ: Lawrence Erlbaum Associates.

Fisher, R. A. (1930). *The Genetical Theory of Natural Selection.* Oxford: Clarendon.

Fisher, R. A. (1918). The correlation between relatives on the supposition of Mendelian inheritance. *Transactions of the Royal Society of Edinburgh, 52*, 399–433.

Fitch, R. H., & Denenberg, V. H. (1998). A role for ovarian hormones in sexual differentiation of the brain. *Behavioral and Brain Sciences, 21*, 311–352.

Fletcher, G. J., Simpson, J. A., Thomas, G., & Giles, L. (1999). Ideals in intermediate relationships. *Journal of Personality and Social Psychology, 76*, 72–89.

Flynn, J. R. (1987). Massive IQ gains in 14 nations – what IQ tests really measure. *Psychological Bulletin, 101*, 171–191.

Flynn, J. R. (1984). The mean IQ of Americans: Massive gains 1932–1978. *Psychological Bulletin, 95*, 29–51.

Flynn, J. R. (2009). *What is Intelligence?* Cambridge: Cambridge University Press.

Foerster, K., Coulson, T., Sheldon, B. C., Pemberton, J. M., Clutton-Brock, T. H., & Kruuk, L. E. (2007). Sexually antagonistic genetic variation for fitness in red deer. *Nature, 447*, 1107–1110.

Fogel, A., Nwokah, E., Dedo, J. Y., Messinger, D., Dickson, K. L., Matusov, E., et al. (1992). Social process theory of emotion: A dynamic systems approach. *Social Development, 1*, 122–142.

Folstad, I., & Karter, A. J. (1992). Parasites, bright males, and the immunocompetence handicap. *American Naturalist, 139*, 603–622.

Forbes, L. S. (1997). The evolutionary biology of spontaneous abortion in humans. *Trends in Ecology and Evolution, 12*, 446–450.

Foster, D. L., Padmanabhan, V., Wood, R. I., & Robinson, J. E. (2002). Sexual differentiation of the neuroendocrine control of gonadotropin secretion: Concepts derived from sheep models. *Reproduction Supplement, 59*, 83–99.

Fox, N., Kagan, J., & Weiskopf, S. (1979). The growth of memory during infancy. *Genetic Psychology Monographs, 99*, 91–130.

Fraley, R. C., & Spieker, S. J. (2003). Are infant attachment patterns continuously or categorically distributed? A taxometric analysis of strange situation behavior. *Developmental Psychology, 39*, 387–404.

Francis, D. D., Diorio, J., Liu, D., & Meaney, M. J. (1999). Nongenomic transmission across generations in maternal behavior and stress responses in the rat. *Science, 286*, 1155–1158.

Frankenhuis, W. E., & Panchanathan, K. (2011). Individual differences in developmental plasticity may result from stochastic sampling. *Perspectives on Psychological Science, 6,* 336–347.

Frederickson, B. L., & Carstensen, L. L. (1990). Choosing social partners: How old age and anticipated endings make people more selective. *Psychology and Aging, 5,* 335–347.

Freed-Brown, G., & White, D. J. (2009). Acoustic mate copying: Female cowbirds attend to other females' vocalizations to modify their song preferences. *Proceedings of the Royal Society B: Biological Sciences, 276,* 3319–3325.

Frisch, R. E., Wyshak, G., & Vincent, L. (1980). Delayed menarche and amenorrhea in ballet dancers. *New England Journal of Medicine, 303,* 17–19.ss

Fuentes, K., Hunter, M. A., Strauss, E., & Hultsch, D. F. (2001). Intraindividual variability in cognitive performance in persons with chronic fatigue syndrome. *Clinical Neuropsycholgist, 15,* 210–227.

Fung, H. H., Lai, P., & Ng, R. (2001). Age differences in social preferences among Taiwanese and mainland Chinese: The role of perceived time. *Psychology & Aging, 16,* 351–356.

Fuster, J. M., & Alexander, G. E. (1971). Neuron activity related to short-term memory. *Science, 173,* 652–654.

Galton, F. (1869). *Hereditary Genius: An Inquiry into its Laws and Consequences.* London: Macmillan.

Galvan, A., Hare, T., Parra, C., Penn, J., Voss, H., Glover, G., et al. (2006). Earlier development of the accumbens relative to orbitofrontal cortex might underlie risk-taking behavior in adolescents. *Journal of Neuroscience, 26,* 6885–6892.

Gangestad, S. W., Simpson, J. A., Cousins, A. J., Garver-Apgar, C. E., & Christensen, P. N. (2004). Women's preferences for male behavioral displays change across the menstrual cycle. *Psychological Science, 15,* 203–207.

Gardner, E. L. (1999). The neurobiology and genetics of addiction: Implications of the reward deficiency syndrome for therapeutic strategies in chemical dependency. In J. Elster, *Addiction: Entries and Exits* (pp. 57–119). New York: Russell Sage Foundation.

Gardner, M., & Steinberg, L. (2005). Peer infuence on risk taking, risk preference, and risky decision-making in adolescence and adulthood: An experimental study. *Developmental Psychology, 41,* 625–635.

Gaultney, J. F., & Gingras, J. L. (2005). Fetal rate of behavioral inhibition and preference for novelty in infancy. *Early Human Development, 81,* 379–386.

Ge, X., Conger, R. D., & Elder, G. H. (2001a). The relation between puberty and psychological distress in adolescent boys. *Journal of Research on Adolescence, 11,* 49–70.

Ge, X., Conger, R. D., & Elder, G. H. (2001b). Pubertal transition, stressful life events, and the emergence of gender differences in adolescent depressive symptoms. *Developmental Psychology, 37,* 404–417.

Geary, D. C. (2010). *Male, Female: the Evolution of Human Sex Differences, 2nd Ed.* Washington, DC: American Psychological Association.

Gelman, R. (1978). Cognitive development. *Annual Review of Psychology, 29,* 297–332.

Geschwind, N., & Behan, P. (1982). Left-handedness: Associations with immune disease, migraine, and developmental learning disorders. *Proceedings of the National Academy of Sciences, 79,* 5097–5100.

Geschwind, N., & Galaburda, A. M. (1987). *Cerebral Lateralization: Biological Mechanisms, Associations, and Pathologies.* Cambridge, MA: MIT Press.

Ghent, L. (1957). Some effects of deprivation on eating and drinking behavior. *Journal of Comparative Physiological Psychology, 50*, 172–176.

Gilliard, E. T. (1969). *Birds of Paradise and Bowerbirds*. London: Weidenfeld and Nicolson.

Ginzburg, E., Ginsburg, S. W., Axelrad, S., & Herma, J. L. (1951). *Occupational Choice: An Approach to a General Theory*. New York: Columbia University Press.

Giordano, P. C., Manning, W. D., & Longmore, M. A. (2010). Affairs of the heart: Qualities of adolescent romantic relationships and sexual behavior. *Journal of Research on Adolescence, 20*, 983–1013.

Glover, V., O'Connor, T. G., & O'Donnell, K. (2009). Prenatal stress and the programming of the HPA axis. *Neuroscience and Biobehavioural Reviews, 35*, 17–22.

Gluckman, P. D., Hanson, M. A., & Spencer, H. G. (2005). Predictive adaptive responses and human evolution. *Trends in Ecology and Evolution, 20*, 527–533.

Glueck, S., & Glueck, E. (1950). *Unraveling Jevenile Delinquency*. New York: Commonwealth Fund.

Glueck, S., & Glueck, E. (1968). *Delinquents and Nondelinquents in Perspective*. Cambridge, MA: Harvard University Press.

Goethals, G. R., & Darley, J. M. (1977). Social comparison theory: An attributional approach. In J. M. Suls, & R. L. Miller, *Social Comparison Processes: Theoretical and Empirical Perspectives* (pp. 259–278). Washington, DC: Hemisphere.

Gogtay, N. (2008). Cortical brain development in schizophrenia: Insights from neuroimaging studies in childhood-onset schizophrenia. *Schizophrenia Bulletin, 34*, 30–36.

Gogtay, N., & Thompson, P. M. (2010). Mapping gray matter development: Implications for typical devleopment and vulnerability to psychopathology. *Brain and Cognition, 72*, 6–15.

Gogtay, N., Giedd, J. N., Lusk, L., Hayashi, K. M., Greenstein, D., Vaituzis, A. C., et al. (2004). Dynamic mapping of human cortical development during childhood through early adulthood. *Proceedings of the National Academy of Sciences of the United States of America, 101*, 8174–8179.

Gogtay, N., Ordonez, A., Herman, D. H., Hayashi, K. M., Greenstein, D., Vaituzis, C., et al. (2007). Dynamic mapping of cortical development before and after the onset of pediatric bipolar illness. *Journal of Child Psychology and Psychiatry, 48*, 852–862.

Goldsmith, H. H. (1993). Temperament: Variability in developing emotion systems. In M. Lewis, & J. M. Haviland (Eds.), *Handbook of Emotion* (pp. 353–364). New York: Guildford Press.

Goldsmith, H. H. (2000). *The Toddler Behavior Assessment Questionnaire Revised*. Madison, WI: University of Wisconsin Department of Psychology.

Goldsmith, H. H., & Campos, J. (1982). Toward a theory of infant temperament. In R. Emde, & R. Harmon, *Attachment and Affiliative Systems* (pp. 161–193). New York: Plenum Press.

Goldsmith, H. H., & Rothbart, M. K. (1996). *Prelocomotor and Locomotor Laboratory Temperament Assessment Battery (version 0.5, Technical Report)*. Madison, WI: University of Wisconsin Department of Psychology.

Golub, H. L., & Gorwin, M. J. (1985). A psychoacoustic model of the infant cry. In B. M. Lester, & C. F. Boukydis, *Infant Crying: Theoretical and Research Perspectives* (pp. 59–82). New York: Plomin.

Goodwin, B. (1993). Development as a robust natural process. In W. D. Stein, & F. D. Varela, *Thinking About Biology: an Invitation to Current Theoretical Biology* (pp. Lecture Notes, vol. 3, 323–346). Reading, MA: Addison-Wesley.

Gottfredson, L. S. (1981). Circumscription and compromise: A developmental theory of occupational aspirations. *Journal of Counseling Psychology Monograph, 28,* 545–579.

Gottfredson, L. S., & Deary, I. J. (2004). Intelligence predicts health and longevity, but why? *Current Directions in Psycholoigical Science, 13,* 1–4.

Granier-Defferre, C., Bassereau, S., Ribeiro, A., Jacquet, A. Y., & DeCasper, A. J. (2011). A melodic contour repeatedly experienced by near-term fetuses elicits a profound cardiac response one month after birth. *PLoS One, 6,* e17304.

Greenstein, D., Vaituzis, C., et al. (2007). Dynamic mapping of cortical devleopment before and after the onset of pediatric bipolar illness. *Journal of Child Psychology and Psychiatry, 48,* 852–862.

Grotenhuis, M. T., Eisinga, R., & Subramanian, S. V. (2011). Robinson's ecological correlations and the behavior of individuals: Methodological corrections. *International Journal of Epidemiology, 40,* 1123–1125.

Guellai, B., & Streri, A. (2011). Cues for early social skills: Direct gaze modulates newborns' recognition of talking faces. *PLoS One, 6,* e18610.

Gunn, D. A., Rexbye, H., Griffiths, C. E., Murray, P. G., Fereday, A., Catt, S. D., et al. (2009). Why some women look young for their age. *PLoS One, 4,* e8021.

Gur, R. C., Mozley, L. H., Mosley, P. D., Resnick, S. M., Karp, J. S., Alavi, A., et al. (1995). Sex differences in regional cerebral glucose metabolism during a resting state. *Science, 267,* 428–531.

Gutman, D. A., & Nemeroff, C. B. (2002). Neurobiology of early life stress: Rodent studies. *Seminars in Clinical Neuropsychiatry, 7,* 89–95.

Haith, M. M. (1973). Visual scanning in infants. In L. G. Stone, H. T. Smith, & L. B. Murphy, *The Competent Infant: Research and Commentary* (pp. 320–323). New York: Basic.

Halpern, C. T., Kaestle, C. E., & Halfors, D. D. (2007). Perceived physical maturity, age of romantic partner, and adolescent risk behavior. *Prevention Science, 8,* 1–10.

Halpern, D. F. (2000). *Sex Differences in Cognitive Abilities, 3rd Edition.* Mahwah, NJ: Lawrence Erlbaum.

Hamilton, W. D. (1964). The genetical evolution of social behaviour I and II. *Journal of Theoretical Biology, 7,* 1–52.

Hane, A. A., & Fox, N. A. (2006). Ordinary variations in maternal caregiving influence human infants' stress reactivity. *Psychological Science, 17,* 550–556.

Harden, K. P., Mendle, J., Hill, J. E., Turkheimer, E., & Emery, R. E. (2008). Rethinking timing of first sex and delinquency. *Journal of Youth and Adolescence, 37,* 373–385.

Harlow, H. F., Harlow, M. K., & Hansen, E. W. (1963). The maternal affectional system of rhesus monkeys. In H. R. Rheingold, *Maternal Behavior in Mammals* (pp. 254–281). New York: Wiley.

Harman, C., Rothbart, M. K., & Posner, M. I. (2007). Distress and attention in early infancy. *Motivation and Emotion, 21,* 27–43.

Harris, G. W., & Naftolin, F. (1970). Hypothalamus and control of ovulation. *British Medical Bulletin, 26,* 3–97.

Harvison, K. W., Molfese, D. L., Woodruff-Borden, J., & Weigel, R. A. (2009). Neonatal auditory evoked responses are related to perinatal maternal anxiety. *Brain and Cognition, 71,* 369–374.

Haslinger, B. (2005). Transmodal sensorimotor networks during action observation in professional pianists. *Journal of Cognitive Neuroscience, 17,* 282–293.

Hayes, K. J. (1962). Genes, drives, and intellect. *Psychological Reports, 10*, 299–342.

Hazlett, H. C., Poe, M. D., Gerig, G., Styner, M., Chappell, C., Smith, R. G., et al. (2011). Early brain overgrowth in autism associated with an increase in cortical surface area before age 2 years. *Archives of General Psychiatry, 68*, 467–476.

Heils, A., Teufel, A., Petri, S., Stober, G., Riederer, P., Bengel, D., et al. (1996). Allelic variation of human serotonin transporter gene expression. *Journal of Neurochemistry, 66*, 2621–2624.

Helleday, J., Bartifai, A., Ritzen, E. M., & Forsman, M. (1994). General intelligence and cognitive profile in women with congenital adrenal hyperplasia (CAH). *Psychoneuroendocrinology, 19*, 343–356.

Helms, J. E. (1984). Toward a theoretical explanation of the effects of race on counseling: A black and a white model. *Counseling Psychologist, 12*, 153–165.

Henderson, H. H., & Wachs, T. D. (2007). Temperament theory and the study of cognition-emotion interactions across development. *Developmental Review, 27*, 396–407.

Henrich, J., & Boyd, R. (2002). On modeling cognition and culture: Why cultural evolution does not require replication of representations. *Journal of Cognitive Culture, 2*, 87–112.

Herdt, G., & McClintock, M. (2000). The magical age of 10. *Archives of Sexual Behavior, 29*, 587–608.

Herrmann, H., Stewart, D. E., Diaz-Granados, N., Berger, E. L., Jackson, B., & Yuen, T. (2011). What is resilience? *La Revue Canadienne de Psychiatrie, 56*, 258–265.

Hertzog, C., & Hultsch, D. F. (2000). Metacognition in adulthood and old age. In F. I. Craik, & T. A. Salthouse, *The Handbook of Aging and Cognition, 2nd Edition* (pp. 417–466). Mahwah, NJ: Lawrence Erlbaum Associates, Inc.

Heyes, C. (2001). Causes and consequences of imitation. *Trends in Cognitive Sciences, 5*, 245–261.

Heyes, C. (2010). Where do mirror neurons come from? *Neuroscience and Biobehavioral Reviews, 34*, 575–583.

Higley, J. D., & Suomi, S. J. (1996). Reactivity and social competence affect individual differences in reaction to severe stress in children: Investigations using nonhuman primates. In C. R. Pfeffer, *Intense Stress and Mental Disturbance in Children* (pp. 3–58). Washington, DC: American Psychiatric Press.

Hill, K., & Hurtado, A. M. (1991). The evolution of premature reproductive senescence and menopause in human females: An evolution of the 'grandmother' hypothesis. *Human Genetics, 2*, 313–350.

Hill, W. G. (2005). A century of corn selection. *Science, 30*, 683–684.

Hirschfeld, R. M. (1981). Situational depression: Validity of the concept. *British Journal of Psychiatry, 139*, 297–305.

Hirschi, A. (2012). Vocational identity trajectories: Differences in personality and development of well-being. *European Journal of Personality, 26*, 2–12.

Hochberg, Z. (2008). Juvenility in the context of life history theory. *Archives of Disease in Childhood, 93*, 534–539.

Hodgkinson, C. A., Goldman, D., Jaeger, J., Persaud, S., Kane, J. M., Lipsky, R. H., et al. (2004). Disrupted in schizophrenia (DISC1): Association with schizophrenia, schizoaffective disorder, and bipolar disorder. *American Journal of Human Genetics, 75*, 862–872.

Holbourn, A. H. (1943). Mechanics of head injuries. *The Lancet, 242*, 438–441.

Horowitz, R. (1939). Racial aspects of self-identification in nursery school children. *Journal of Psychology*, 91–99.

Howe, N., & Strauss, W. (1993). *13th Gen: Abort, Retry, Ignore, Fail?* New York: Vintage Print.

Howe, N., & Strauss, W. (1997). *The Fourth Turning.* New York: Broadway Books.

Howe, N., & Strauss, W. (2000). *Millenials Rising.* New York: Vintage Books.

Huizink, A. C. (2008). Prenatal exposure and temperament: A review. *European Journal of Developmental Science, 2,* 77–99.

Huizink, A. C., Dick, D. M., Sihvola, E., Pulkkinen, L., Rose, R. J., & Kaprio, J. (2007). Chernobyl exposure as stressor during pregnancy and behaviour in adolescent offspring. *Acta Psychiatrica Scandinavica, 116,* 438–446.

Hultsch, D. F., MacDonald, S. W., Hunter, M. A., Levy-Benchton, J., & Strauss, E. (2000). Intraindividual variability in cognitive performance in older adults: Comparison of adults with mild dementia, adults with arthritis, and healthy adults. *Neuropsychology, 14,* 588–598.

Huxley, R. R., Shiell, A. W., & Law, C. M. (2000). The role of size at birth and post-natal catch-up growth in determining systolic blood pressure: A systematic review. *Journal of Hypertension, 18,* 815–831.

Insel, T. R. (2000). Toward a neurobiology of attachment. *Review of General Psychology, 4,* 176–185.

Iocoboni, M. (2005). Neural mechanisms of imitation. *Current Opinion in Neurobiology, 15,* 632–637.

Irwin, D. E., Irwin, J. H., & Price, T. D. (2001). Ring species as bridges between micro-evolution and speciation. *Genetica, 112–113,* 223–243.

Izard, C. E. (1971). *The Face of Emotion.* New York: Appleton-Century-Crofts.

Jahromi, L. B., Putnam, S. P., & Stifter, C. A. (2004). Maternal regulation of infant reactivity from 2 to 6 months. *Developmental Psychology, 40,* 477–487.

Jankowiak, W. (1995). *Romantic Passion: A Universal Experience?* New York: Columbia University Press.

Jensen, A. R. (1998). *The g Factor.* Westport, CN: Praeger.

Joffe, R. T., Levitt, A. J., Bagby, R. M., & Regan, J. J. (1993). Clinical features of situational and non-situational major depression. *Psychopathology, 26,* 138–144.

Johnson, W. (2007). Genetic and environmental influences on behavior: Capturing all the interplay. *Psychological Review, 114,* 423–440.

Johnson, W. (2010a). Extending and testing Tom Bouchard's Experience Producing Drive Theory. *Personality and Individual Differences, 49,* 296–301.

Johnson, W. (2010b). Understanding the genetics of intelligence: Can height help? Can corn oil? *Current Directions in Psychological Science, 19,* 177–82.

Johnson, W., Krueger, R. F., Bouchard, T. J., & McGue, M. (2002). The personalities of twins: Just ordinary folks. *Twin Research, 5,* 125–131.

Johnson, W., McGue, M., & Krueger, R. F. (2005). Personality stability in late adulthood: A behavioral genetic analysis. *Journal of Personality, 73,* 523–551.

Johnson, W., McGue, M., & Iacono, W. G. (2007). How parents influence school grades: Hints from a sample of adoptive and biological families. *Learning and Individual Differences, 17,* 201–219.

Joyner, K., & Udry, J. R. (2000). You don't bring me anything but down: Adolescent romance and depression. *Journal of Health and Social Behavior, 41,* 369–391.

Juarez, J., del Rio-Portilla, I., & Corsi-Cabrera, M. (1998). Effects of prenatal testosterone on sex and age differences in behavior elicited by stimulus pups in the rat. *Developmental Psychobiology, 32,* 121–129.

Julious, S. A., & Mullee, M. A. (1994). Confounding and Simpson's paradox. *British Medical Journal, 309*, 1480–1481.

Kagan, J. (2008). In defense of qualitative changes in development. *Child Development, 79*, 1606–1624.

Kagan, J. (2002). *Surprise, Uncertainty, and Mental Structures*. Cambridge, MA: Harvard University Press.

Kagan, J., & Snidman, N. (2004). *The Long Shadow of Temperament*. Cambridge, MA: Harvard University Press.

Kagan, J., Snidman, N., Kahn, V., & Towsley, S. (2007). The preservation of two infant temperaments through adolescence. *Monographs of the Society for Research in Child Development, 72(2)*, Serial No. 287.

Kallen, D., & Stephenson, J. (1982). Talking about sex revisited. *Journal of Youth and Adolescence, 11*, 11–24.

Kardiner, A., & Ovesey, L. (1951). *The Mark of Oppression*. New York: Norton.

Karlberg, J. (2002). Secular trends in pubertal development. *Hormone Research, 57 (Supplement)*, 19–30.

Kauffman, S. A. (1993). *The Origins of Order: Self-Organization and Selection in Evolution*. New York: Oxford University Press.

Keating, D. P., & Stanley, J. C. (1971). Extreme measures for the exceptionally gifted in mathematics and science. *Educational Researcher, 1*, 3–7.

Keel, P. K., Fulkerson, J. A., & Leon, G. R. (1997). Disordered eating precursors in pre- and early-adolescent girls and boys. *Journal of Youth and Adolescence, 26*, 203–216.

Kendler, K. S., & Halberstadt, L. J. (2013). The road not taken: Life experiences in monozygotic twin pairs discordant for major depression. *Molecular Psychiatry, 18*, 975–984.

Kendler, K. S., Myers, J., & Halberstadt, L. J. (2011). Do reasons for major depression act as causes? *Molecular Psychiatry, 16*, 626–633.

Kermack, W. O., McKendrick, A. G., & McKinlay, P. L. (2001 (reprinted from 1934)). Death-rates in Great Britain and Sweden. Some general regularities and their significance. *International Journal of Epidemiology, 30*, 678–683.

Kim-Cohen, J., Caspi, A., Taylor, A., Williams, B., Newcombe, R., Craig, I. W., et al. (2006). MAOA, maltreatmnet, and gene-environment interaction predicting children's mental health: New evidence and a meta-analysis. *Molecular Psychiatry, 11*, 903–913.

King, A. P., & West, M. J. (1983). Female perception of cowbird song: A closed developmental program. *Developmental Psychobiology, 16*, 335–342.

King, A. P., West, M. J., & White, D. J. (2003). Female cowbird song perception: Evidence for plasticity of preference. *Ethology, 109*, 335–352.

King, S., Mancini-Marie, A., Brunet, A., Walker, E., Meaney, M. J., & Laplante, D. P. (2009). Prenatal maternal stress from a natural disaster predicts dermatoglyphic asymmetry in humans. *Development and Psychopathology, 21*, 343–353.

Kirkwood, B. L., & Austad, S. N. (2000). Why do we age? *Nature, 409*, 233–238.

Kirkwood, T. B. (1996). Human senescence. *Bioessays, 18*, 1009–1016.

Kirkwood, T. B. (2005). Understanding the odd science of aging. *Cell, 120*, 437–443.

Kirkwood, T. B., & Shanley, D. P. (2010). The connections between general and reproductive senescence and the evolutionary basis of menopause. *Annals of the New York Academy of Sciences, 1204*, 21–29.

Kirschner, M., & Gerhardt, J. (1998). Evolvability. *Proceedings of the National Academy of Sciences of the United States of America, 95*, 8420–8427.

Kisilevsky, B. S., Hains, S. M., Brown, C. A., Lee, C. T., Cowperthwaite, B., Stutzman, S. S., et al. (2009). Fetal sensitivity to properties of maternal speech and language. *Infant Behavior and Development, 32*, 59–71.

Kitano, H. (2004). Biological robustness. *Nature Reviews Genetics, 5*, 826–837.

Kitano, H. (2010). Violations of robustness trade-offs. *Molecular Systems Biology, 6*, 1–8.

Koff, E., & Rierdan, J. (1996). Premenarcheal expectation and postmenarcheal experiences of positive and negative menstrual related changes. *Journal of Adolescent Health, 18*, 286–291.

Kohn, M. L., & Schooler, C. (1969). Class, occupation, and orientation. *American Sociological Review, 34*, 659–678.

Koivusilta, L., & Rimpela, A. (2004). Pubertal timing and adolescent careers: A longitudinal study. *Annals of Human Biology, 31*, 446–465.

Komlos, J., & Lauderdale, B. E. (2007). The mysterious trend in human heights in the 20th century. *American Journal of Human Biology, 34*, 206–215.

Konner, M. J. (1976). Maternal care, infant behavior and development among the !Kung. In R. B. Lee, & I. DeVore, *Kalahari Hunter-Gatherers* (pp. 218–245). Cambridge, MA: Harvard University Press.

Konner, M. J., & Worthman, C. (1980). Nursing frequency, gonadal function, and birth spacing among !Kung hunter-gatherers. *Science, 207*, 788–791.

Konner, M. (2010). *The Evolution of Childhood: Relationships, Emotions, Mind.* Cambridge, MA: The Belknap Press of Harvard University Press.

Kramer, A. F., & Madden, D. J. (2008). Attention. In F. I. Braik, & T. A. Salthouse, *The Handbook of Aging and Cognition, 3rd Edition* (pp. 189–249). New York: Psychology Press.

Kruglyak, L., & Nickerson, D. A. (2001). Variation is the spice of life. *Nature, 27*, 234–236.

Kuhn, M. H., & McPartland, T. (1954). An empirical investigation of self-attitudes. *American Sociological Review, 19*, 68–76.

Kuttler, A. F., LaGreca, A. M., & Prinstein, M. J. (1999). Friendship qualities and social-emotional functioning of adolescents with close, cross-sex relationships. *Journal of Research on Adolescence, 9*, 339–366.

Laban, O., Dimitrijevic, M., van Hoersten, S., Markovic, B. M., & Jancovic, B. D. (1995). Experimental allergic encephalomyelitus in the rat. *Brain, Behavior, and Immunity, 9*, 9–19.

Lacanuet, J.-P., Granier-Deferre, C., & Busnel, M.-C. (1995). Human fetal auditory perception. In J.-P. Lacanuet, W. P. Fifer, N. A. Krasnegor, & W. P. Smotherman, *Fetal Development: A Psychobiological Perspective* (pp. 233–268). Hillsdale, NJ: Erlbaum.

Ladany, N., Melincoff, D. S., Constantine, M. C., & Love, R. (1997). At-risk urban high school students' commitment to career choices. *Jorunal of Counseling and Development, 76*, 45–52.

Larson, G. E., Haier, R. J., LaCasse, L., & Hazen, K. (1995). Evaluation of a 'mental effort' hypothesis for correlations between cortical metabolism and intelligence. *Intelligence, 21*, 267–278.

Larson, R. W., Muneta, C., Richards, M. H., & Wilson, S. (2002). Continuity, stability, and change in daily emotional experience across adolescence. *Child Development, 73*, 1151–1165.

Larson, R., & Richards, M. H. (1991). Daily companionship in late childhood and early adolescence: Changing developmental contexts. *Child Development, 62,* 284–300.

Laub, J. H., Nagin, D. S., & Sampson, R. J. (1998). Trajectories of change in criminal offending: Good marriages and the desistance process. *American Sociological Review, 63,* 225–238.

Laumann, E., Gagnon, J., Michael, R., & Michaels, S. (1994). *The Social Organization of Sexuality: Sexual Practices in the United States.* Chicago: University of Chicago Press.

Laursen, B. (1995). Conflict and social interaction in adolescent relationships. *Journal of Research on Adolescence, 5,* 56–70.

Lawton, M. P., Kleban, M. H., Rajagopal, D., & Dean, J. (1992). Dimensions of affective experience in 3 age groups. *Psychology and Aging, 7,* 171–184.

Lazarus, R. S. (1991). Progress on a cognitive-motivational-relational theory of emotion. *American Psychologist, 46,* 819–834.

Le Couteur, D. G., & Simpson, S. J. (2011). Adaptive senectitude: The prolongevity effects of aging. *Journal of Gerontology Series A – Biological and Medical Sciences, 66A,* 179–182.

Leggio, M. B., Molinari, M., Neri, P., Graziano, A., Mandolesi, L., & Petrosini, L. (2000). Representation of action in rats: The role of cerebellum in learning spatial information by observation. *Proceedings of the National Academy of Sciences of the USA, 97,* 2320–2325.

Lengua, L. J. (2008). Anxiousness, frustration, and effortful control as moderators of the relation between parenting and adjustment in middle-childhood. *Social Development, 17,* 554–577.

Lenton, A. P., Fasolo, B., & Todd, P. M. (2010). Who is in your shopping cart? Expected and experienced effects of choice abundance in the online dating context. In N. Kock, *Evolutionary Psychology and Information Systems Research: A New Approach to Studying the Effects of Modern Technologies on Human Behavior* (pp. 149–167). New York: Springer.

Leppanen, J. M., Molson, M. C., Vogel-Farley, V. K., & Nelson, C. A. (2007). An ERP study of emotional face processing in the adult and infant brain. *Child Development, 78,* 232–245.

Levy, B. R., Slade, M. D., Kunkel, S. R., & Kasl, S. V. (2002). Longevity increased by positive self-perceptions of aging. *Journal of Personality and Social Psychology, 83,* 261–270.

Levy, B., & Langer, E. (1994). Aging free from negative stereotypes: Successful memory in China and among the American deaf. *Journal of Personality and Social Psychology, 66,* 989–997.

Levy, J. (1976). Cerebral organization and spatial ability. *Behavior Genetics, 6,* 171–188.

Lew, A. R., Hopkins, B., Owen, L. H., & Green, M. (2007). Postural change effects on infants' AB task performance: Visual, postural, or spatial? *Journal of Experimental Child Psychology, 97,* 1–13.

Lewis, M. (1967). The meaning of a response, or why researchers in infant behavior should be oriental meta-physicians. *Merrill-Palmer Quarterly, 13,* 7–18.

Li, S.-C., Aggen, S. H., Nesselroade, J. R., & Baltes, P. B. (2001). Short-term fluctuations in elderly people's sensorimotor functioning predict text and spatial memory performance: The Macarthur successful aging studies. *Gerontology, 47,* 100–116.

Li, S.-C., Lindenberger, U., & Sikstrom, S. (2001). Aging cognition: From neuromodulation to representation. *Trends in Cognitive Sciences, 5,* 479–486.

Li, S.-C., Lindenberger, U., Hommel, B., Aschersleben, G., Prinz, W., & Baltes, P. B. (2004). Transformations in the couplings among intellectual abiliities and constituent cognitive processes across the life span. *Psychological Science, 15*, 155–163.

Lieberman, D., & Hatfield, E. (2006). Passionate love: Cross-cultural and evolutionary perspectives. In R. J. Sternberg, & K. Weis, *The New Psychology of Love* (pp. 274–297). New Haven, CT: Yale University Press.

Lonstein, J. S., & De Vries, G. J. (2000). Sex differences in the parental behavior of rodents. *Neuroscience and Biobehavioral Reviews, 24*, 669–686.

Lorenz, K. Z. (1965). *Evolution and the Modification of Behavior.* Chicago: University of Chicago Press.

Louis, J., Nosaka, K., & Brisswalter, J. (2012). The endurance master athlete: A model of successful ageing. *Science & Sports, 27*, 63–76.

Lovden, M., Li, S.-C., Shing, Y. L., & Lindenberger, U. (2007). Winthin-person trial-to-trial variability precedes and predicts cognitive decline in old and very old age: Longitudinal data from the Berlin Aging Study. *Neuropsychologia, 45*, 2827–2838.

Lubinsky, D., & Benbow, C. P. (2006). Study of Mathematically Precocious Youth After 35 Years. *Perspectives on Psychological Science, 1*, 316–345.

Luders, E., Narr, K. L., Zaidel, E., Thompson, P. M., & Toga, A. W. (2006). Gender effects on callosal thickness in scaled and unscaled space. *NeuroReport, 17*, 1103–1106.

Luna, B., & Sweeney, J. A. (2004). Cognitive development: fMRI studies. In M. S. Keshaven, J. L. Kennedy, & R. M. Murray, *Neurodevelopment and Schizophrenia* (pp. 45–68). New York: Cambridge University Press.

Luna, B., Padmanabhan, A., & O'Hearn, K. (2010). What has fMRI told us about the development of cognitive control through adolescence? *Brain and Cognition, 72*, 101–113.

Lykken, D. T., & Tellegen, A. (1993). Is human mating adventitious or the result of lawful choice? A twin study of mate selection. *Journal of Personality and Social Psychology, 65*, 56–68.

Lynn, R. (2008). *The Global Bell Curve: Race, IQ, and Inequality Worldwide.* Atlanta, GA: Washington Summit Publishers.

Maccari, S., Piazza, P. V., Kabbaj, M., Barbazanges, A., Simon, H., & Le Moal, M. (1995). Adoption reverses the long-term impairments in glucocorticoid feedback induced by prenatal stress. *Journal of Neuroscience, 15*, 110–116.

Madden, J. (2001). Sex, bowers, and brains. *Proceedings of the Royal Society of London Series B, 268*, 833–838.

Maguire, E. A., Burgess, N., Donnett, J. G., Frackowiak, R. S., Firth, C. D., & O'Keefe, J. (1998). Knowing where and getting there: A human activation network. *Science, 280*, 921–924.

Maguire, E. A., Gadian, D. G., Johnsrude, I. S., Good, C. D., Ashburner, J., Frackowiak, R. S., et al. (2000). Navigation-related structural change in the hippocampi of taxi drivers. *Proceedings of the National Academy of Sciences of the United States of America, 97*, 4398–4403.

Maher, B. (2008). The case of the missing heritability. *Nature, 456*, 18–21.

Malmstrom, H., Linderholm, A., Liden, K., Stora, J., Molnar, P., Holmlund, G., et al. (2010). High frequency of lactose intolerance in a prehistoric hunter-gatherer population in northern Europe. *BMC Evolutionary Biology, 10*, 89.

Mampe, B., Friederici, A. D., Christophe, A., & Wermke, K. (2009). Newborns' cry melody is shaped by their native language. *Current Biology, 19*, 1994–1997.

Manlove, J., Franzetta, K., Ryan, S., & Moore, K. (2006). Adolescent sexual relationships, contraceptive consistency, and pregnancy prevention approaches. In A. C. Crouter, & A. Booth, *Romance and Sex in Adolescence and Emerging Adulthood: Risks and Opportunities* (pp. 181–212). Mahwah, NJ: Lawrence Erlbaum Associates.

Manning, W. D., Giordano, P. C., & Longmore, M. A. (2006). Hooking up: The relationship context of 'nonrelationship' sex. *Journal of Adolescent Research, 21,* 459–483.

Marazziti, D., Akiskal, H. S., Rossi, A., & Cassano, G. B. (1999). Alteration of the platelet serotonin transporter in romantic love. *Psychological Medicine, 29,* 741–745.

Marcia, J. (1966). Development and validation of ego-identity status. *Journal of Personality and Social Psychology, 3,* 551–558.

Marcus, G. (2008). *Kluge.* Boston, MA: Houghton Mifflin Company.

Marios, P. G., & Perlman, M. D. (2009). How likely is Simpson's paradox? *The American Statistician, 63,* 226–233.

Marksman-Adams, C. (1992). A consideration of intervening factors in adolescent identity formation. In G. R. Adams, T. P. Gulotta, & R. Montemayor, *Adolescent Identity Formation (Advances in Adolescent Development, vol. 4)* (pp. 165–187). Newbury Park, CA: Sage.

Markus, H. (1977). Self-schemata and processing information about the self. *Journal of Personality and Social Psychology, 35,* 63–78.

Marsh, H. W. (1991). Failure of high-ability high schools to deliver academic benefits commensurate with their students' ability levels. *American Educational Research Journal, 28,* 445–480.

Marsh, H. W., & Hau, K. T. (2003). Big-fish-little-pond effect on academic self-concept: A cross-cultural (26-country) test of the negative effects of academically self-selective schools. *American Psychologist, 58,* 364–376.

Maslow, A. H. (1970). *Motivation and Personality, 2nd Ed.* New York: Harper & Row.

Maslow, Abraham H. (1943). A Theory of Human Motivation, *Psychological Review,* 1943, vol. 50, pp. 374–396.

Masoro, E. J. (1998). Influence of caloric intake on aging and on the response to stressors. *Journal of Toxicology and Environmental Health – Series B, Critical Review, 1,* 243–257.

Masten, A. S., Coatsworth, J. D., Neemann, J. L., S. D., Tellegen, A., & Garmezy, N. (1995). The structure and coherence of competence from childhood through adolescence. *Child Development, 66,* 1635–1659.

Mather, M., & Carstensen, L. L. (2003). Aging and attentional biases for emotional faces. *Psychological Science, 14,* 409–415.

Mather, M., & Carstensen, L. L. (2005). Aging and motivated cognition: The positivity effect in attention and memory. *Trends in Cognitive Sciences, 9,* 496–502.

Mather, M., & Johnson, M. K. (2000). Choice-supportive source monitoring: Do our decisions seem better as we age? *Psychology and Aging, 15,* 596–606.

Mather, M., & Knight, M. (2005). Goal-directed memory: The role of cognitive control in older adults' emotional memory. *Psychology and Aging, 20,* 554–570.

Mattick, J. S. (2009). The genetic signatures of noncoding RNAs. *Public Library of Science Genetics, 5,* e10000459.

Mayer, A., Lahr, G., Swab, D. F., Pilgrim, C., & Reisert, I. (1998). The Y-chromosomal genes Sry and Zfy are transcribed in adult human brain. *Neurogenetics, 1,* 281–288.

Mayr, E. (1963). *Animal Species and Evolution*. Cambridge, MA: Harvard University Press.

Mayr, E. (1942, 1999). *Systematics and the Origin of Species, from the Viewpoint of a Zoologist*. Cambridge, MA: First Harvard University Press.

McCall, R. B., Eichorn, D. H., & Hogarty, P. S. (1977). Transitions in early mental development. *Monographs of the Society for Research in Child Development, 171, 42*, 1–94.

McClintock, M. K., & Herdt, G. (1996). Rethinking puberty: The development of sexual attraction. *Current Directions in Psychological Science, 6*, 178–183.

McCormack, K. M., Sanchez, M. M., Bardi, M., & Maestripieri, D. (2006). Maternal care patterns and behavioural development of rhesus macaque abused infants in the first 6 months of life. *Developmental Psychology, 48*, 537–550.

McDaniel, M. A., Einstein, G. O., & Jacoby, L. L. (2008). New considerations in aging and memory: The glass may be half full. In F. I. Craik, & T. A. Salthouse, *The Handbook of Aging and Cognition, 3rd Edition* (pp. 251–310). New York: Psychology Press.

McEwen, B. S. (1991). Non-genomic and genomic effects of steroids on neural activity. *Trends in Pharmacological Science, 12*, 141–147.

McEwen, B. S., & Wingfield, J. C. (2003). The concept of allostasis in biology and biomedicine. *Hormones and Behavior, 43*, 2–15.

McGuffin, P., Katz, R., & Babbington, P. (1988). The Camberswell Collaborative Depression Study III: Depression and adversity in the relatives of depressed probands. *British Journal of Psychiatry, 152*, 775–782.

McLoughlin, W. G. (1978). *Revivals, Awakenings, and Reform: an Essay on Religion and Social Change in America, 1607–1977*. Chicago: University of Chicago Press.

Mead, G. H. (1934). *Mind, Self, and Society*. Chicago: University of Chicago Press.

Meaney, M. J. (2010). Epigenetics and the biological definition of gene x environment interactions. *Child Development, 81*, 41–79.

Meaney, M. (2001). Maternal care, gene expression, and the transmission of individual differences in stress reactivity across generations. *Annual Review of Neuroscience, 24*, 1161–1192.

Meaney, M., Aitken, D. H., & Sapolsky, R. M. (1991). Environmental regulation of the adrenocortical stress response in female rats and its implications for individual differences in aging. *Neurobiology of Aging, 21*, 323–331.

Mehler, J., Jusczyk, P., Lambertz, G., Halsted, N., Bertoncini, J., & Amiel-Tison, C. (1988). A precursor of language acquisition in young infants. *Cognition, 29*, 1431–1478.

Meltzoff, A. N., & Moore, M. K. (1977). Imitation of facial and manual gestures by human neonates. *Science, 198, 4312*, 75–78.

Meltzoff, A. N., & Moore, M. (1994). Imitation, memory, and the imitation of persons. *Infant Behavior and Development, 17*, 83–99.

Mendle, J., & Ferrero, J. (2012). Detrimental psychological outcomes associated with pubertal timing in adolescent boys. *Developmental Review, 32*, 49–66.

Mendle, J., Turkheimer, E., & Emory, R. E. (2007). Detrimental psychological outcomes associated with early pubertal timing in adolescent girls. *Developmental Review, 27*, 151–171.

Mendel, J. G. (1901). Translated as Experiments in plant hybridization. In C. T. Druery, *Journal of the Royal Horticultural Society, 26* (pp. 1–32).

Miller, G. (2000). *The Mating Mind: How Sexual Choice Shaped the Evolution of Human Nature*. London: Heinemann.

Mingroni, M. A. (2007). Resolving the IQ paradox: Heterosis as a cause of the Flynn efect and other trends. *Psychological Review, 114*, 806–829.

Moffitt, T. E., Caspi, A., Harkness, A. R., & Silva, P. A. (1993). The natural history of change in intellectual performance: Who changes? How much? Is it meaningful? *Journal of Child Psychology and Psychiatry and Allied Disciplines, 34*, 455–506.

Moltz, H., Lubin, M., Leon, M., & Numan, M. (1970). Hormonal induction of maternal behavior in the ovariectomized nulliparous rat. *Physiology and Behavior, 5*, 1373–1377.

Monroe, S. M., Rhodes, P., Seeley, J. R., & Lewinsohn, P. M. (1999). Life events and depression in adolescence: Relationship loss as a prospective risk factor for first onset of major depressive disorder. *Journal of Abnormal Psychology, 108*, 606–614.

Montague, D. P., & Walker-Andrews, A. S. (2001). Peekaboo: A new look at infants' perception of emotion. *Developmental Psychology, 37*, 826–836.

Moon, C., & Fifer, W. P. (2000). Evidence of transnatal auditory learning. *Journal of Perinatology, 20*, S37–S44.

Moon, C., Panneton Cooper, R. P., & Fifer, W. P. (1993). Two-day-olds prefer their native language. *Infant Behavior and Development, 16*, 495–500.

Morokuma, S., Doria, V., Ierrullo, A., Kinukawa, N., Fukishima, K., & Arulkumaran, S. (2008). Developmental change in fetal response to repeated low-intensity sound. *Developmental Science, 11*, 47–52.

Morokuma, S., Fukushima, K., Kawai, N., Tumonaga, M., Satoh, S., & Nakano, H. (2004). Fetal habituation correlates with functional brain development. *Behavioural and Brain Research, 153*, 459–463.

Morris, R. G., Garrud, P., Rawlins, J. N., & O'Keefe, J. (1982). Place navigation impaired in rats with hippocampal lesions. *Nature, 297*, 681–683.

Moss, H. A. (1967). Sex, age, and state as determinants of mother–infant interaction. *Merrill-Palmer Quarterly Journal of Developmental Psychology, 13*, 19–36.

Muller, J. (1826). *Zur Vergleichenden Physiologie des Gesichtssinnes des Menschen und der Tiere.* Leipzig: C. Knobloch.

Munafo, M. R., Durrant, C., Lewis, G., & Flint, J. (2009). Gene x environment interactions at the serotonin transporter locus. *Biological Psychiatry, 65*, 211–219.

Munakata, Y. (1997). Perseverative reaching in infancy: The role of hidden toys and motor reaching in the AB task. *Infant Behavior and Development, 20*, 405–416.

Munro, G., & Adams, G. R. (1977). Ego-identity formation in college students and working youth. *Developmental Psychology, 13*, 523–524.

Murphy, N. A., & Isaacowitz, D. M. (2008). Preferences for emotional information in older and younger adults: A meta-analysis of memory and attention tasks. *Psychology and Aging, 23*, 263–286.

Murstein, B. (1971). A theory of marital choice and its applicability to marital adjustment. In B. Murstein, *Theories of Attraction and Love* (pp. 100–151). New York: Springer.

Murstein, B. I. (1972). Physical attractiveness and marital choice. *Journal of Personality and Social Psychology, 22*, 8–12.

Murstein, B. I. (1976). *Who Will Marry Whom? Theories and Research in Marital Choice.* New York: Springer.

Mussen, P. H., & Jones, M. C. (1957). Self-conceptions, motivations, and interpersonal attitudes on late and early maturing boys. *Child Development, 28*, 243–256.

Nagy, E., Kompagne, H., Orvos, H., & Pal, A. (2007). Gender-related differences in neonatal imitation. *Infant and Child Development, 16*, 267–276.

Negriff, S., & Trickett, P. K. (2009). The relationship between pubertal timing and delinquent behavior in maltreated male and female adolescents. *Journal of Early Adolescence, 30,* 528–542.

Oakes, P. J., Haslam, S. A., & Turner, J. C. (1994). *Stereotyping and Social Reality.* Cambridge, MA: Basil Blackwell.

Obel, C., Hedegaard, M., Henriksen, T. B., Secher, N. J., & Olson, J. (2003). Psychological factors in pregnancy and mixed-handedness in the offspring. *Developmental Medicine and Child Neurology, 45,* 557–561.

Obel, C., Henriksen, T. B., Secher, N. J., Eskenazi, B., & Hedegaard, M. (2007). Psychological distress during early gestation and offspring sex ratio. *Human Reproduction, 22,* 3009–3012.

O'Brien, D. P., & Overton, W. F. (1982). Conditional reasoning and the competence-performance issue: A developmental analysis of a training task. *Journal of Experimental Child Psychology, 34,* 274–290.

O'Connor, T. G., Heron, J., Golding, J., & Glover, V. (2003). Maternal antenatal anxiety and behavioural/emotional problems in children: A test of a programming hypothesis. *Journal of Child Child Psychology and Psychiatry, 44,* 1025–1036.

Olendorf, R., Rodd, F. H., Punzalan, D., Houde, A. E., Hurt, C., Reznick, D. N., et al. (2006). Frequency-dependent selection in natural guppy populations. *Nature, 441,* 633–636.

Olry, G., & Haines, D. E. (2005). Interthalamic adhesion: Scruples about calling a spade a spade? *Journal of the History of the Neurosciences, 14,* 116–118.

Panksepp, J. (1998). *Affective Neuroscience: The Foundations of Human and Animal Emotions.* New York: Oxford University Press.

Papousek, M., & von Hofacker, N. (1998). Persistent crying in early infancy: A nontrivial condition of risk for the developing mother-infant relationship. *Child Care, Health, and Development, 24,* 395–424.

Parham, T. A., & Helms, J. E. (1990). Black racial identity scale. In J. E. Helms, *Black and White Racial Identity: Theory, Research, and Practice* (pp. 245–247). Westport, CT: Greenwood.

Parker, J. G., Rubin, K. H., Erath, S. A., Wojslawowicz, J. C., & Buskirk, A. A. (2006). A developmental psychopathology perspective. In D. Cicchetti, & D. J. Cohen, *Developmental Psychopathology (2nd Ed.): Theory and Methods* (pp. 96–161). New York: Wiley.

Paton, J. J., Belova, M. A., Morrison, S. E., & Salzman, C. D. (2006). the primate amygdala represents the positive and negative value of visual stimuli during learning. *Nature, 439,* 865–870.

Paus, T. (2005). Mapping brain maturation and cognitive devleopment during adolescence. *Trends in Cognitive Sciences, 9,* 60–68.

Pavlov, I. P. (1927). *Conditional Reflexes.* New York: Dover Publications.

Pearce, J. W., & Pezzot-Pearce, T. D. (2007). *Psychotherapy of Abused and Neglected Children (2nd ed.).* London: Guilford Press.

Pearl, J. (2009). *Causality: Models, Reasoning, and Inference (2nd Ed.).* New York: Cambridge University Press.

Peccei, J. S. (1995). The origin and evolution of menopause: The altriciality-lifespan hypothesis. *Ethology and Social Biology, 16,* 425–449.

Pedersen, C. A., Ascher, J. A., Monroe, Y. L., & Prange, A. J. (1982). Oxytocin indudes maternal behavior in virgin female rats. *Science, 216,* 648–650.

Penke, L., Denissen, J. J., & Miller, G. F. (2007). The evolutionary genetics of personality. *European Journal of Personality, 21*, 549–587.

Peplau, L., Rubin, Z., & Hill, C. (1977). Sexual intimacy in dating relationships. *Journal of Social Issues, 33*, 86–109.

Peters, A., & Sethares, C. (2004). Oligodendrocytes, their progentiors and other neuroglial cells in the aging primate cerebral cortex. *Cerebral Cortex, 14*, 995–1007.

Pfeiffer, C. A. (1934). Functional capacities of ovaries of new-born after transplantation into adult ovariotornized rats. *Proceedings of the Society for Experimental Biology and Medicine, 31*, 479–481.

Phoenix, C. H., Goy, R. W., Gerall, A. A., & Young, W. C. (1959). Organizing action of prenatally administered testosterone propionate on the tissues mediating mating behavior in the female guinea pig. *Endocrinology, 65*, 369–382.

Piaget, J. (1936/1954). *The Construction of Reality in the Child (translated by M. Cook from French)*. New York: Basic Books.

Pianka, A. R. (1970). On 'r' and 'K' selection. *American Naturalist, 10*, 453–464.

Plomin, R., DeFries, J. C., & Roberts, M. K. (1977). Assortative mating by unwed biological parents of adopted children. *Science, 196*, 449–450.

Plotsky, P. M., & Meaney, M. J. (1993). Early postnatal experience alters hypothalamic corticotropin-releasing factor (CRF) mRNA, median eminence CRF content and stress-induced release in adult rats. *Molecular Brain Research, 18*, 195–200.

Posner, M. I., & Rothbart, M. K. (2007). *Educating the Human Brain*. Washington, DC: American Psychological Association.

Preschtl, H. F. (1965). Problems of behavioral studies in the newborn infant. *Advances in the Study of Behavior, 1*, 75–98.

Prior, V., & Glaser, D. (2006). *Understanding Attachment and Attachment Disorders: Theory, Evidence, and Practice*. London: Jessica Kingsley Publishers.

Rabbitt, P. M., Osman, P., Moore, B., & Stollery, B. (2001). There are stable individual differences in performance variability, both from moment to moment and from day to day. *Quarterly Journal of Experimental Psychology A: Human Experimental Psychology, 4*, 981–1003.

Raikkonen, K., Pesonen, A.-K., Heinonen, K., Lahti, J., Komsi, N., Eriksson, J. G., et al. (2009). Maternal licorice consumption and detrimental cognitive and psychiatric outcomes in children. *American Journal of Epidemiology,170*, 1137–1146.

Raikkonen, K., Seckl, J. R., Heinonen, K., Pyhala, R., Feldt, K., Jones, A., et al. (2010). Maternal prenatal licorice consumption alters hypothalamic-pituitary-adrenocoritcal axis function in children. *Psychoneuroendocrinology, 35*, 1587–1593.

Ram, N., Rabbitt, P., Stollery, B., & Nesselroade, J. R. (2005). Cognitive performance inconsistency: Intraindividual change and variability. *Psychology and Aging, 20*, 981–1003.

Rao, S. C., Rainer, G., & Miller, E. K. (1997). Integration of what and where in the primate prefrontal cortex. *Science, 276*, 821–824.

Raven, J. C. (1941). Standardization of progressive matrices, 1938. *British Journal of Medical Psychology, 19*, 137–150.

Reinisch, J. (1981). Prenatal exposure to synthetic progestins increases potential for aggression in humans. *Science, 211*, 1171–1173.

Reiter, E. O. (1987). Normal and abnormal sexual development and puberty. In G. M. Besser, & A. G. Cudworth, *Clinical Endocrinology: an Illustrated Text* (pp. 12.1–12.28). Philadelphia: Lippincott.

Resnick, S. M., Berenbaum, S. A., Gottesman, I. I., & Bouchard, T. J. (1986). Early hormonal influences of cognitive function in congenital adrenal hyperplasia. *Developmental Psychology, 22,* 191–198.

Reynolds, J. D. (1987). Mating system and nesting biology of the Rednecked phalorope Phaloropus lobatus: What constrains polyandry? *Isis, 129,* 225–242.

Reynolds, S. M., Dryer, K., Bollback, J., Uy, J. A., Patricelli, G. L., Robson, T., et al. (2007). Behavioral paternity predicts genetic paternity in satin bowerbirds (Ptilorhynchus violaceus), a species with a non-resource-based mating system. *Auk, 124,* 857–867.

Richerson, P. J., Boyd, R., & Henrich, J. (2010). Gene-culture coevolution in the age of genomics. *Proceedings of the National Academy of Sciences of the United States of America, 107,* 8985–8992.

Rimoin, D. L. (2007). A half century of medical genetics: Where do we go from here? *American Journal of Human Genetics, 81,* 670–672.

Risch, N., Herrell, R., Lehner, T., Liang, K. Y., Eaves, L., Hoh, J., et al. (2009). Interaction between the serotonin transporter gene (5-HTTLPR), stressful life events, and risk of depression: A meta-analysis. *Journal of the American Medical Association, 301,* 2462–2471.

Roberts, B. W., & Caspi, A. (2003). The cumulative continuity model of personality development: Striking a balance between continuity and change in personality traits across the life course. In U. Staudinger, & L. Ulman, *Understanding Human Development: Lifespan Psychology in Exchange with Other Disciplines.* Dordrecht, The Netherlands: Kluwer Academic.

Roberts, B. W., & DelVecchio, W. F. (2000). The rank-order consistency of personality traits from childhood to old age: A quantitative review of longitudinal studies. *Psychological Bulletin, 126,* 3–25.

Roberts, B. W., Kuncel, N. R., Shiner, R., Caspi, A., & Goldberg, L. R. (2007). The power of personality: The comparative validity of personality traits, socioeconomic status and cognitive ability for predicting important life outcomes. *Perspectives on Psychlogical Science, 2,* 313–345.

Robinson, W. S. (1950). Ecological correlations and the behavior of individuals. *American Sociological Review, 15,* 351–357.

Robertson, O. H. (1961). Prolongation of the life span of kokanee salmon (Oncorhynchus nerka kennerlyi) by castration before beginning of pubertal development. *Proceedings of the Natrional Academy of Sciences of the United States of America, 47,* 609–621.

Rogers, A. R. (1993). Why menopause? *Evolution and Ecology, 7,* 406–420.

Rogoff, B. (1990). *Apprenticeship in Thinking: Cognitive Development in Social Context.* New York: Oxford University Press.

Rollins, V. B. (2001). Perceived racism and career self-efficacy in African American adolescents. *Dissertation Abstracts International, 59(3-B),* 5059.

Rose, M. H., & Charlesworth, B. (1980). A test of evolutionary theories of senescence. *Nature, 287,* 141–142.

Rose, S. A., Feldman, J. F., & Jankowski, J. J. (2001). Visual short-term memory in the first year of life: Capacity and recency effects. *Developmental Psychology, 37,* 539–549.

Rosenblum, L. A., & Pauley, G. S. (1984). The effects of varying demands on maternal and infant behavior. *Child Development, 45,* 305–314.

Rosler, A., Ulrich, C., Billino, J., Sterzer, P., Weidauer, S., Bernhardt, T., et al. (2005). Effects of arousing emotional scenes on the distribution of visuospatial attention: Changes with aging and early subcortical vascular dementia. *Journal of the Neurological Social Sciences, 229,* 109–116.

Rosner, B. S., & Doherty, N. E. (1979). The response of neonates to intra-uterine sounds. *Developmental Medicine and Child Neurology, 21,* 723–729.

Ross, S. M., & Dannemiller, J. L. (1999). Color contrast, luminance contrast, and competition in exogenous orienting in 3.5-month-old infants. *Infant Behavior and Development, 22,* 383–404.

Rothbart, M. K., & Bates, J. E. (2006). Temperament. In W. Damon, R. Lerner, & N. Eisenberg, (. Eds), *Handbook of Child Psychology, Vol. 3: Social, Emotional, and Personality Development, 6th Ed.* (pp. 99–166). New York: Wiley.

Rowe, D. C. (2002). On genetic variation and age at frist sexual intercourse: A critique of the Belsky-Draper hypothesis. *Evolution and Human Behavior, 23,* 365–372.

Rowley, S. J., Sellers, R. M., Chavous, T. M., & Smith, M. A. (1998). The relationship between racial identity and self-esteem in African American college and high school students. *Journal of Personality and Social Psychology, 74,* 715–724.

Rudolph, K. D., & Troop-Gordon, W. (2010). Personal accentuation and contextual amplification of pubertal timing: Predicting youth depression. *Development and Psychopathology, 22,* 433–451.

Rutter, M. (2006). *Genes and Behavior: Nature-Nurture Interplay Explained.* Oxford: Blackwell.

Rutter, M., Thapar, A., & Pickles, A. (2009). Gene–environment interactions: Biologically valid pathways or artifacts? *Archives of General Psychiatry, 66,* 1287–1289.

Sachser, N., & Kaiser, S. (1997). The social environment, behaviour, and stress – a case study in guinea pigs. *Acta Physiologica Scandinavica Supplementum, 640,* 83–87.

Salk, L. (1962). Mother's heartbeat as an imprinting stimulus. *Transactions of the New York Academy of Sciences, 24,* 7537–7563.

Sampson, R. J., & Laub, J. H. (1990). Crime and deviance over the life course: The salience of adult social bonds. *American Sociological Review, 55,* 609–627.

Sapolsky, R. M., Uno, H., Rebert, C. S., & Finch, C. E. (1990). Hippocampal damage associated with prolonged glucocorticoid exposure in primates. *Journal of Neuroscience, 10,* 2897–2902.

Sapolsky, R. M., Romero, L. M., & Munck, A. U. (2000). How do corticosteroids influence stress responses? Integrating permissive, suppressive, stimulatory, and preparatory actions. *Endocrine Reviews, 21,* 55–89.

Saretzki, G., Walker, T., Atkinson, S., Passos, J. F., Bareth, B., Keith, W. N., et al. (2008). Down regulation of multiple stress defense mechanisms during differentiation of human embryonic stem cells. *Stem Cells, 26,* 455–464.

Scarr, S. (1996). How people make their own environments: Implications for parents and policy makers. *Psychology of Public Policy and the Law, 2,* 204–228.

Scarr, S., & McCartney, K. (1983). How people make their own environments: A theory of genotype–environment effects. *Child Development, 54,* 424–435.

Schneider, M. L., & Coe, C. L. (1993). Repeated social stress during pregnancy impairs neuromotor development of the primate infant. *Journal of Developmental and Behavioural Pediatrics, 14,* 81–87.

Scholz, B., Kultima, K., Mattsson, A., Axelsson, J., Brunstrom, B., Halldin, K., et al. (2006). Sex-dependent gene expression in early brain development of chicken embryos. *BMC Neuroscience, 7,* 12.

Schwartz, C. E., Wright, C. I., Shin, L. M., Kagan, J., & Rauch, S. L. (2003). Inhibited and uninhibited infants 'grown up': Adult amygdalar response to novelty. *Science, 300*, 1952–1953.

Schwekendiek, D. (2009). Height and weight differences between North and South Korea. *Journal of Biosocial Science, 41*, 446–454.

Scrimshaw, N. S., & Guzman, N. (1995). A comparison of supplemental feeding and medical care of preschool children in Guatemala: 1959–1964. In N. S. Scrimshaw, *Community-Based Longitudinal Nutrition and Health Studies: Classical Examples from Guatemala, Haiti, and Mexico* (pp. 1–28). Boston, MA: International Foundation for Developing Countries.

Segal, N. L. (2000). *Entwined Lives: Twins and What They Tell US About Human Behavior.* New York: Plume.

Seidner, L. B., Stipek, D. J., & Feshbach, N. D. (1988). A developmental analysis of elementary-school aged children's concepts of pride and embarrassment. *Child Development, 59*, 367–377.

Sellers, R. M., Smith, M. A., Shelton, J. N., Rowley, S. A., & Chavous, T. M. (1998). Multidimensional model of racial identity: A reconceptualization of African American racial identity. *Personality and Social Psychology Review, 2*, 18–39.

Services, C. D. (1999). *Changes in the population of persons with autism and pervasive developmental disorders in Calfironia's Developmental Services System: 1987–1999.* Sacramento, CA: A report to the legislature.

Shanley, D. P., & Kirkwood, T. B. (2001). Evolution of the human menopause. *BioEssays, 23*, 282–287.

Shaw, P., Eckstrand, K., Sharp, W., Blumenthal, J., Lerch, J. P., Greenstein, D., et al. (2007). Attention-deficit/hyperactivity disorder is characterized by a delay in cortical maturation. *Proceedings of the National Academy of Sciences of the United States of America, 104*, 19649–19654.

Shaw, P., Kabani, N. J., Lerch, J. P., Eckstrand, K., Lenroot, R., Gogtay, N., et al. (2008). Neurodevelopmental trajectories of the human cerebral cortex. *Journal of Neuroscience, 28*, 3586–3594.

Sibly, R. M., & Brown, J. H. (2007). Effects of body size and lifestyle on evolution of mammal life histories. *Proceedings of the Natrional Academy of Sciences of the United States of America, 104*, 17707–17712.

Silventoinen, K., Posthuma, D., van Beisterveldt, T., Bartels, M., & Boomsma, D. I. (2006). Genetic contributions to the association between height and intelligence: Evidence from Dutch twin data from childhood to old age. *Genes, Brain & Behavior, 5*, 585–595.

Simon, V. A., Aikins, J. W., & Prinstein, M. J. (2008). Romantic partner selection and socialization during early adolescence. *Child Development, 79*, 1676–1692.

Simpson, E. H. (1951). The interpretation of interaction in contingency tables. *Journal of the Royal Statistical Society, Seres B, 13*, 238–241.

Simpson, J. A., Collins, W. A., & Salvatore, J. E. (2011). The impact of early interpersonal experience on adult romantic relationship functioning: Recent findings from the Minnesota Longitudinal Study of Risk and Adaptation. *Current Directions in Psychological Science, 20*, 355–359.

Sisk, C. L., & Foster, D. L. (2004). The neural basis of puberty and adolescence. *Nature Neuroscience, 7*, 1040–1047.

Sisk, C., & Zehr, J. (2005). Pubertal hormones organize the adolescent brain and behavior. *Frontiers in Neuroendocrinology, 26*, 163–174.

Slater, A. (2000). Visual perception in the young infant: Early organization and rapid learning. In D. Muir, & S. A., *Infant Development: the Essential Readings* (pp. 95–116). Malden, MA: Blackwell.

Slater, A., & Morison, V. (1985). Shape constancy and slant perception at birth. *Perception, 14*, 337–344.

Slater, A., Earle, D. C., Morison, V., & Rose, D. (1985). Pattern preferences at birth and their interaction with habituation-induced novelty preferences. *Journal of Experimental Child Psychology, 39*, 37–54.

Slijper, E. J. (1942). Biologic-anatomical investigations on the bipedal gait and upright posture in mammals, with special reference to a little goat, born without forelegs. *Proceedings Koninklijke Nederlandse Akademie Van Wetenschappen, 5*, 407–415.

Slocum, W. L., & Bowles, R. T. (1968). Attractiveness of occupations in high school students. *Personnel and Guildance Journal, 46*, 754–761.

Smith, L. B. (2009). Dynamic systems, sensorimotor processes, and the origins of stability and flexibility. In J. P. Spencer, M. S. Thomas, & J. L. McClelland, *Toward a Unified Theory of Development* (pp. 67–85). Oxford: Oxford University Press.

Smith, L. B., Thelen, E., Titzer, R., & McLin, D. (1999). Knowing in the context of acting: The task dynamics of the A-not-B error. *Psychological Review, 106*, 235–260.

Smithhorst, V. J., & Yuan, W. (2010). White matter development during adolescence as shown by diffusion MRI. *Brain and Cognition, 72*, 16–25.

Somerville, L. H., Jones, R. M., & Casey, B. J. (2010). A time of change: Behavioral and neural correlates of adolescent sensitivity to appetitive and aversive environmental cues. *Brain and Cognition, 72*, 124–133.

Spence, M. J., & Freeman, M. S. (1996). Newborn infants prefer the maternal low-pass filtered voice but not the maternal whispered voice. *Infant Behavior and Development, 19*, 199–212.

Sroufe, L. A., & Fleeson, J. (1986). Attachment and the constrcution of relationships. In W. W. Hartup, & Z. Rubin, *Relationships in Development* (pp. 51–71). Hillsdale, NJ: Lawrence Erlbaum.

Stattin, H., & Magnuson, D. (1990). *Pubertal Maturation in Female Development: Paths Through Life.* Hillboro, NJ: Erlbaum.

Steckel, R. H. (2008). Biological measures of the standard of living. *Journal of Economic Perspectives, 22*, 129–152.

Steinberg, L. (2010). A behavioral scientist looks at the science of adolescent brain development. *Brain and cognition, 72*, 160–164.

Steinberg, L. (2008). A social neuroscience perspective on adolescent risk taking. *Developmental Review, 28*, 78–106.

Steinmetz, H., Staiger, J. F., Schlaug, G., Huang, Y., & Jancke, L. (1995). Corpus callosum and brain volume in women and men. *Neuroreport: An International Journal for Rapid Communication of Research in Neuroscience, 6*, 1002–1004.

Stellman, S. D., Wynder, E. L., DeRose, D. J., & Muscat, J. E. (1997). The epidemiology of left-handedness in a hospital population. *Annals of Epidemiology, 3*, 156–164.

Sten, J. M. (1997). Offspring-induced nurturance: animal-human parallels. *Developmental Psychobiology, 31*, 19–37.

Sterling, P., & Eyer, J. (1988). Allostasis: A new paradigm to explain arousal pathology. In S. Fisher, & J. Reason (Eds.), *Handbook of Life Stress, Cognition, and Health* (pp. 629–650). New York: John Wiley & Sons.

Stetefeld, J., & Ruegg, M. A. (2005). Structural and functional diversity generated by alternative mRNA splicing. *Trends in Biochemical Sciences, 30*, 515–521.

St James-Roberts, I., & Menon-Johansson, P. (1999). Predicting infant crying from fetal movement data: An exploratory study. *Early Human Development, 54*, 55–62.

Stohr, T., Schulte Wermeling, D., Szuran, T., Pliska, V., Domeney, A., & Welzl, H. (1998). Differential effects of prenatal stress in two inbred strains of rats. *Pharmacology, Biochemistry, and Behavior, 59*, 799–805.

Storfer, M. (1999). Myopia, intelligence, and the expanding human neocortex: Behavioral influences and evolutionary implications. *International Journal of Neuroscience, 98*, 153–276.

Strauss, W., & Howe, N. (1991). *Generations: The History of America's Future 1584–2069*. New York: William Morrow and Company.

Stroebe, W. (1977). Self-esteem and interpersonal attraction. In S. Duck, *Theory and Practice in Interpersonal Attraction* (pp. 79–104). London: Academic Press.

Stryker, S. (2007). Identity theory and personality theory: Mutual relevance. *Journal of Personality, 75*, 1083–1102.

Stuss, D. T., Pogue, J., Buckle, L., & Bondar, J. (1994). Characterization of stability of performance in patients with traumatic brain injury: Variability and consistency on reaction time tests. *Neuropsychology, 8*, 316–324.

Suomi, S. J. (2008). Attachment in rhesus monkeys. In J. Cassidy, & P. R. Shaver (Eds.). *Handbook of Attachment: Theory, Research, and Clinical Applications, 2nd Ed.* (pp. 173–191). London: The Guilford Press.

Suomi, S. J. (2006). Risk, resilience, and gene x environment interactions in rhesus monkeys. *Annals of the New York Academy of Sciences, 1094*, 52–62.

Suomi, S. J. (1991). Up-tight and laid-back monkeys: Individual differences in the response to social challenges. In S. Brauth, W. Hall, & R. Dooling (Eds.). *Plasticity of Development* (pp. 27–56). Cambridge, MA: MIT Press.

Susman, E., & Rogol, A. (2004). Puberty and psychological development. In R. Lerner, & L. Steinberg, *Handbook of Adolescent Psychology* (pp. 157–183). New York: Wiley.

Szewczyk-Sokolowski, M., Bost, K., & Wainwright, A. B. (2005). Attachment, temperament, and preschool children's peer acceptance. *Social Development, 14*, 379–397.

Tanner, J. M. (1990). *Foetus into Man: Physical Growth from Conception to Maturity*. Cambridge, MA: Harvard University Press.

Tanner, J. M. (1975). Trend toward earlier menarche in London, Oslo, Copenhagen, the Netherlands, and Hungary. *Nature, 24*, 95–96.

Teasdale, T. W., & Owen, D. R. (2000). Forty-year secular trends in cognitive abilities. *Intelligence, 28*, 115–120.

Teilmann, G., Pedersen, C. B., Skakkebaek, N. E., & Jensen, T. K. (2006). Increased risk of precocious puberty in internationally adopted children in Denmark. *Pediatrics, 118*, 391–199.

Tennes, K. H., & Lampl, E. E. (1964). Stranger and separation anxieity in infancy. *Journal of Nervous and Mental Distress, 139*, 247–254.

Terasawa, E., & Fernandez, D. L. (2001). Neurological mechanisms of the onset of puberty in primates. *Endocrine Review, 22*, 111–151.

Terkel, J., & Rosenblatt, J. S. (1972). Humoral factors underlying maternal behavior at parturition: Cross transfusion between freely moving rats. *Journal of Comparative and Physiological Psychology, 80*, 365–371.

Thelen, E. (1985). Developmental origins of motor coordination: Leg movements in human infants. *Developmental Psychobiology, 18*, 1–22.

Thelen, E., & Smith, L. B. (1994). *A Dynamic Systems Approach to the Development of Cognition and Action*. Cambridge, MA: MIT Press.

Thomas, A., & Chess, S. (1977). *Temperament and Development*. New York: Brunner/Mazel.

Thomas, A., Chess, S., & Birch, H. G. (1968). *Temperament and Behavior Disorders in Children*. New York: New York University Press.

Thompson, P. M., Bartzokis, G., Hayashi, K. M., Klunder, A. D., Lu, P. H., Edwards, N., et al. (2009). Time-lapse mapping of cortical changes in schizophrenia with different treatments. *Cerebral Cortex, 19*, 1107–1123.

Thorndike, E. L. (1901). Animal intelligence: an experimental study of the associative processes in animals. *Psychological Review Monograph Supplement, 2*, 1–109.

Tinbergen, N. (1951). *The study of instinct*. New York: Oxford University Press.

Tither, J., & Ellis, B. J. (2008). Impact of fathers on daughters' age at menarche: A genetically and environmentally controlled sibling study. *Developmental Psychology, 44*, 1409–1420.

Todd, P. M., Penke, L., Fasolo, B., & Lenton, A. (2007). Different cognitive processes underlie human mate choices and mate preferences. *Proceedings of the National Academy of Sciences of the United States of America, 104*, 15011–15016.

Tooby, J., & Cosmides, L. (1990). On the universality of human nature and the uniqueness of the individual: The role of genetics and adaptation. *Journal of Personality, 58*, 17–68.

Townsend, J., & Wasserman, T. (1998). Sexual attractiveness sex differences in assessment and criteria. *Evolution and Human Behavior, 19*, 171–191.

Trenerry, M. R., Jack, C. R., Cascino, G. D., Sharbrough, F. W., & Ivnik, R. J. (1996). Sex differences in the relationship between visual memory and MRI hippocampal volumes. *Neuropsychology, 10*, 343–351.

Trivers, R. L. (1972). Parental investment and sexual selection. In B. Campbell, *Sexual Selection and the Descent of Man, 1871–1971* (pp. 136–179). Chicago: Aldine Publishing.

Trzesniewski, K. H., & Donnellan, M. B. (2010). Rethinking 'Generation Me': A study of cohort effects from 1976–2006. *Perspectives on Psychological Science, 5*, 58–75.

Tsuchiya, N., Moradi, F., Felsen, C., Yamazaki, M., & Adolphs, R. (2009). Intact rapid detection of fearful faces in the absence of the amygdala. *Nature Neuroscience, 12*, 1224–1225.

Tucker, T. (2006). *The Great Starvation Experiment: The Heroic Men Who Starved So that Millions Could Live*. New York: Free Press.

Turkheimer, E. (2000). Three laws of behavior genetics and what they mean. *Current Directions in Psychological Science, 9*, 160–164.

Twenge, J. M., Campbell, W. K., & Foster, C. A. (2003). Parenthood and marital satisfaction: A meta-analytic review. *Journal of Marriage and Family, 65*, 574–583.

Twenge, J. M., Freeman, E. C., & Campbell, W. K. (2012). Generational differences in young adults' life goals, concern for others, and civic orientation, 1996–2009. *Journal of Personality and Social Psychology, 102*, 1045–1062.

Twenge, J. M., Gentile, B., DeWall, C. N., Ma, D., Lacefield, K., & Schurtz, D. R. (2010). Birth cohort increases in psychopathology among young Americans, 1938–2007: A cross-sectional meta-analysis of the MMPI. *Clinical Psychology Review, 10*, 145–154.

Uher, R., & McGuffin, P. (2009). The moderation by the serotonin transporter gene of environmental adversity in the aetiology of mental illness. *Molecular Psychiatry, 15*, 18–22.

Upton, M. N., McConnachie, A., McSharry, C., Hart, C. L., Smith, G. D., Gillis, C. R., et al. (2000). International 20-year trends in the prevalence of asthma and hay fever in adults: The Midspan family study surveys of parents and offspring. *British Medical Journal, 321*, 88–92.

Urbanski, H. F., & Ojeda, F. R. (1987). Gonadal-independent activation of enhanced afternoon luteinizing hormone release during pubertal development in the female rat. *Endocrinology, 121*, 907–913.

van Bakel, H. J., & Riksen-Walraven, J. M. (2004). Stress reactivity in 15-month-old infants: Links with infant temperament, cognitive compentence, and attachment security. *Developmental Psychology, 44*, 157–167.

van der Meij, L., Buunk, A. P., van de Sande, J. P., & Salvador, A. (2008). The presence of a woman increases testosterone in aggressive, dominant men. *Hormones and Behavior, 54*, 640–644.

Vandenburg, S. G. (1972). Assortative mating, or who marries whom? *Behavior Genetics, 2*, 127–157.

van Heteren, C. F., Boekkooi, P. F., Jongsma, H. W., & Nijhuis, J. G. (2000). Fetal learning and memory. *The Lancet, 336*, 1169–1170.

Vaughn, B. E., Bost, K. K., & van Ijzendoorn, M. H. (2008). Attachment and temperament: Additive and interactive influences on behavior, affect, and cognition during infancy and childhood. In J. Cassidy, & P. R. Shaver (Eds.). *Handbook of Attachment: Theory, Research, and Clinical Applications, 2nd Ed.* (pp. 192–216). London: The Guilford Press.

Vaupel, J. W. (2010). Biodemography of human ageing. *Nature, 464*, 536–542.

Vaupel, J. W., & Lundstrom, H. (1994). Longer life expectancy? Evidence from Sweden of reductions in mortality rates at advanced ages. In D. A. Wise, *Studies in the Economics of Aging* (pp. 79–104). Chicago: University of Chicago Press.

Vogt, G., Huber, M., Thiemann, M., van den Boogaart, G., Schmitz, O. J., & Schubart, C. D. (2008). Production of different phenotypes from the same genotype in the same environment by developmental variation. *Journal of Exprimental Biology, 211*, 510–523.

von Hofsten, C. (1984). Developmental changes in the organization of prereaching movements. *Developmental Psychology, 20*, 378–388.

Voubumanos, A., Hauser, M. D., Werker, J. F., & Martin, A. (2010). The tuning of neonates' preference for speech. *Child Development, 81*, 517–527.

Vul, E., Harris, C., Winkielman, P., & Pashler, H. (2009). Puzzlingly high correlations in fMRI studies of emotion, personality, and social cognition. *Perspectives on Psychological Science, 4*, 274–290.

Vygotsky, L. S. (1978). *Mind in Society*. Cambridge, MA: Harvard University Press.

Vygotsky, L. S. (1981). The genesis of higher mental functions. In J. V. Wertsch, *The Concept of Activity in Soviet Psychology* (pp. 144–188). New York: Sharpe.

Waddington, C. H. (1942). The epigenotype. *Endeavor, 1*, 18–20.

Waddington, C. H. (1957). *The Strategy of the Genes: A Discussion of Some Aspects of Theoretical Biology*. London: Allen and Unwin.

Wahba, M. A., & Bridwell, L. G. (1976). Maslow reconsidered: A review of research on the need hierarchy theory. *Organizational Behavior and Human Performance, 15*, 212–240.

Wahlstrom, D., Collins, P., White, T., & Luciana, M. (2010). Developmental changes in dopamine neurotransmission in adolescence: Behavioral implications and issues in assessment. *Brain and Cognition, 72*, 146–159.

Walford, R. L., & Spindler, S. R. (1997). The response to caloric restriction in mammals shows features also common to hibernation: A cross-adaptation hypothesis.

Journals of Gerontology – Series B – Psychological and Social Sciences, 52, B179–B183.

Wallace, A. R. (1892). Note on sexual selection. *Natural Science, 1*, 749–750.

Wallen, K. (1999). Risky business: Social context and hormonal modulation of primate sexual drive. In K. Wallen, & J. Schneider, *Reproduction in Context* (pp. 289–323). Cambridge, MA: MIT Press.

Wallen, K. (2001). Sex and context: Hormones and primate sexual motivation. *Hormones and Behavior, 40*, 339–357.

Wallen, K., & Winston, L. A. (1984). Social complexity and hormonal influences on sexual behavior in rhesus monkeys (Macaca mulatta). *Physiological Behavior, 32*, 629–637.

Walsh, R. A. (1994). Effects of maternal smoking on adverse pregnancy outcomes: Examination of the criteria of causation. *Human Biology, 66*, 1059–1092.

Weinstock, M., Matlina, E., Maor, G. I., Rosen, H., & McEwen, B. S. (1992). Prenatal stress selectively alters the reactivity of the hypothalamic-pituitary adrenal system in the female rat. *Brain Research, 595*, 195–200.

Weisfeld, G. E. (2004). Adolescence. In C. R. Ember, & M. Ember, *Men and Women in the World's Cultures* (p. New York). Kluwer Academic/Plenum Publishers: 42–56.

Weisfield, G. F., & Woodward, L. (2004). Current evolutionary perspectives on adolescent romantic relations and sexuality. *Journal of Child and Adolescent Psychiatry, 13*, 11–19.

Weismann, A. (1889). *Essays Upon Heredity and Kindred Biological Problems*. Oxford: Clarendon Press.

West, M. J., King, A. P., White, D. J., Gros-Louis, J., & Freed-Brown, G. (2006). The development of local song preferences in female cowbirds (Molothrus ater): flock living stimulates learning. *Ethology, 112*, 1095–1107.

West, R., Murphy, K. J., Armilio, M. L., Craik, F. I., & Stuss, D. T. (2002). Lapses of intention and performance variability reveal age-related increases in fluctuations of executive control. *Brain and Cognition, 49*, 402–419.

West-Eberhard, M. J. (2005). Developmental plasticity and the origin of individual differences. *Proceedings of the National Academy of Sciences, 102, Supp. 1*, 6543–6549.

West-Eberhard, M. J. (1983). Sexual selection, social competition, and speciation. *Quarterly Review of Biology, 58*, 155–183.

Westerhausen, R., Kreuder, F., Sequeira, S., Walter, C., Woerner, W., Wittling, R. A., et al. (2004). Effects of handedness and gender on macro- and microstructure of the corpus callosum and its subregions: A combined high-resolution and diffusion-tensor MRI study. *Brain Research on Cognitive Brain Reserves, 21*, 418–426.

White, D. J. (2010). The form and function of social development: Insights from a parasite. *Current Directions in Psychological Science, 19*, 314–318.

White, D. J., Gros-Louis, J., King, A. P., & West, M. J. (2006). A method to measure the development of song preferences in female cowbirds, Molothrus ater. *Animal Behavior, 72*, 181–188.

White, D. J., Gros-Louis, J., West, M. J., King, A. P., & Tuttle, E. M. (2010). Effects of singing on copulation success and egg production in brown-headed cowbirds (Molothrus ater). *Behavioral Ecology, 13*, 487–496.

White, D. J., King, A. P., & West, M. J. (2002). Facultative development of courtship and communication in juvenile male cowbirds (Molothrus ater). *Behavioral Ecology, 13*, 487–496.

White, D. J., King, A. P., West, M. J., Gros-Louis, L., & Paphakian, M. A. (2007). Constructing culture in cowbirds (Molothrus ater). *Journal of Comparative Psychology, 121,* 113–122.

White, K. R. (1982). The relation between socioeconomic status and academic achievement. *Psychological Bulletin, 91,* 461–481.

White, S. H. (1992). G. Stanley Hall: From philosophy to developmental psychology. *Developmental Psychology, 28,* 25–34.

Whiting, J. W. (1965). Menarcheal age and infant stress in humans. In F. A. Beach, *Sex and Behavior.* New York: John Wiley.

Wicherts, J. M., Dolan, C. V., Hessen, D. J., Osterveld, P., van Baal, O. C., Boomsma, D. I., et al. (2004). Are intelligence tests measurement invariant over time? Investigating the nature of the Flynn Effect. *Intelligence, 32,* 509–537.

Widdowson, E. M., & McCance, R. A. (1959). The effect of food and growth on the metabolism of the newly born. *Acta Paediatrica, 48,* 383–387.

Widdowson, E. M., Mavor, W. O., & McCance, R. A. (1964). The effect of undernutrition and rehabilitation on the development of the reproductive organs: Rats. *Journal of Endocrinology, 29,* 129–126.

Wilk, S. L., Desmarais, L. B., & Sackett, P. R. (1995). Gravitation to jobs commensurate with ability – longitudinal and cross-sectional tests. *Journal of Applied Psychology, 80,* 79–85.

William, D. (2010). Standardized testing and school accountability. *Educational Psychologist, 45,* 107–122.

Williams, G. C. (1957). Pleiotropy, natural selection, and the evolution of senescence. *Evolution, 11,* 398–411.

Williams, G. C. (1966). *Adaptation and Natural Selection: A Critique of Some Evolutionary Thought.* Princeton, NJ: Princeton University Press.

Williams, G. C. (1975). *Sex and Evolution.* Princeton, NJ: Princeton University Press.

Williams, J. M., & Dunlop, L. C. (1999). Pubertal timing and self-reported delinquency among male adolescents. *Journal of Adolescence, 22,* 157–171.

Williams, L. M., Liddell, B. J., Kemp, A. H., Bryant, R. A., Meares, R. A., Peduto, A. S., et al. (2006). Amygdala-prefrontal dissociation of subliminal and supraliminal fear. *Human Brain Mapping, 27,* 652–661.

Wills, T. A. (1981). Downward comparison processes in social psychology. *Psychological Bulletin, 90,* 245–271.

Wilson, A. B., Ahnesjo, L., Vincent, A. C., & Meyer, A. (2003). The dynamics of male brooding, mating patterns, and sex roles in pipefish and seahorses (family signathidae). *Evolution, 57,* 1374–1386.

Wilson, J. G. (1973). *Environment and Birth Defects.* London: Academic Press.

Winokur, G., & Pitts, F. N. (1964). Is reactive depression an entity? *Journal of Nervous Mental Disorders, 138,* 541–547.

Winter, J. S., & Faiman, C. (1972). Serum gonadotropin concentrations in agonadal children and adults. *Journal of Clinical Endocrinological Metabolism, 35,* 561–564.

Winterer, G., & Weinberger, D. R. (2004). Genes, dopamine, and cortical signal-to-noise ratio in schizophrenia. *Trends in Neuroscience, 2,* 683–690.

Wood, D. (1986). Aspects of teaching and learning. In M. Richards, & P. Light, *Children of Social Worlds* (pp. 191–212). Cambridge: Polity.

Wood, D. J., Bruner, J. S., & Ross, G. (1976). The role of tutoring in problem solving. *Journal of Child Psychology and Psychiatry, 27,* 89–100.

Worhtman, C. M. (1986). Developmental dyssynchrony as normative experience: Kikuyu adolescents. In J. B. Lancaster, & B. A. Hamburg, *School-Age Pregnancy and Childbearing: Biosocial Dimensions* (pp. 95–112). New York: Aldine.

Wynn, K. (1992). Addition and subtraction by human infants. *Nature, 358,* 749–750.

Xu, J., Burgoyne, P. S., & Arnold, A. P. (2002). Sex differences in sex chromosome gene expression in mouse brain. *Human Molecular Genetics, 11,* 1409–1419.

Yang, X., Schadt, E. E., Wang, S., Wang, H., Arnold, A. P., Ingram-Drake, L., et al. (2006). Tissue-specific expression and regulation of sexually dimorphic genes in mice. *Genome Research, 16,* 995–1004.

Zuk, M., Johnsen, T. S., & Maclarty, T. (1995). Endocrine-immune interactions, ornaments and mate choice in red jungle fowl. *Proceedings of the Royal Society of London Series B, 265,* 205–210.

Index

Printed and bound in Great Britain by
CPI Group (UK) Ltd, Croydon, CR0 4YY